THE HISTORICAL INSCRIPTIONS OF SOUTHERN INDIA

THE HISTORICAL INSCRIPTIONS OF SOUTHERN INDIA

(COLLECTED TILL 1923)

AND OUTLINES OF POLITICAL HISTORY

BY

ROBERT (SEWELL)

PUBLISHED, UNDER ORDERS OF GOVERNMENT, BY THE UNIVERSITY OF MADRAS

EDITED FOR THE UNIVERSITY

BY

S. KRISHNASWAMI AIYANGAR, M.A. HONY. PH.D.

Honorary Correspondent, Archaeological Survey of India,
Fellow of the Asiatic Society of Bengal,
Professor of Indian History and Archaeology,
University of Madras
(1914-1919)

GYAN

Published by

GYAN

Gyan Publishing House
5, Ansari Road
Daryaganj, New Delhi-110002
Phone: 011-47034999, 9811692060
E-mail: books@gyanbooks.com

Distribution Network
gyanbooks.com
India, USA, Canada, UK, Australia, France

ISBN : 978-81-212-2273-0 (PB)
First Published, 1932

2nd Impression 2021

Printed at: Gyan Press, Delhi.

The Historical Inscriptions of Southern India
Author: Robert (Sewell)

THE HISTORICAL INSCRIPTIONS OF SOUTHERN INDIA

(COLLECTED TILL 1923)

AND OUTLINES OF POLITICAL HISTORY

BY

ROBERT SEWELL

PUBLISHED, UNDER ORDERS OF GOVERNMENT, BY THE UNIVERSITY OF MADRAS

EDITED FOR THE UNIVERSITY

BY

S. KRISHNASWAMI AIYANGAR, M.A., HONY. PH.D.
Honorary Correspondent, Archæological Survey of India,
Fellow of the Asiatic Society of Bengal.
Professor of Indian History and Archæology,
University of Madras
(1914–1929.)

MADRAS
PRINTED AT THE DIOCESAN PRESS, VEPERY
1932

EDITOR'S PREFACE

It is almost fifty years since the late Mr. Sewell published the first volume of the 'Lists of Antiquarian Remains' in the Madras Presidency under the orders of the Government of Madras issued in the January of the year 1881. He had already published two works, 'A Report on the Amaravati Stupa', and 'A Chronological History of South India', in the years 1880–81 on the subject to justify the Government's choice of him for this first work on the Archæological Survey of Southern India. Two years later, he published the second volume of the 'Lists of Antiquarian Remains,' as a mere extension of the work he was asked to undertake by the G. O. under reference. He lived for 43 years after this, and had been more or less constantly engaged in the study of subjects relating to archæology and chronology, contributing a number of papers and issuing a number of works on the subject. The most popular and perhaps best known of his works is the history of 'A Forgotten Empire—Vijayanagar,' published in the last year of the last century. It is this work with which his name is closely associated. The late Mr. Sewell had to read all published literature on Indian archæology and antiquities for the purpose of the Lists referred to above, and was one of a few scholars who had kept themselves in close touch with work that was going on in this particular branch ever since. As such he was among the select few, fully qualified to carry recent research work one step forward in the production of a digest of all that work in the 'Chronological History of South India' which is now published. He was at work on this during the last years of his life, and was at work on the manuscript almost up to the time of his death at the ripe age of 82. The work needs no commendation and will speak for itself.

At his request the Government of Madras undertook the financial responsibility for the publication, and provided the funds. They wished, however, that the work should be published by the Madras University. Mr. Sewell himself accepted the suggestion to include it in the Madras University Historical Series and expressed his assent by stating that he would regard it an honour that it should be so included in the Series.

In deference to his expressed wishes, I agreed to see the work through the press for him, and I was appointed Editor by the University. In the meanwhile, Mr. Sewell passed away, and the responsibility of editing consequently became more heavy, and even delicate in some respects. In regard to the editing of it, I have left it entirely as it emerged from the hands of the late Mr. Sewell, except for the correction of a few obvious errors and the adoption of the international system of transliteration consistently. The errors were few indeed, but the author had to adopt a partial transliteration system with a view to lowering the cost of printing, which would have been heavy had it been published in England. When the decision was taken to publish it in India, I adopted with his approval, which I had previously obtained of him, a uniform system of transliteration.

In regard to the matter of the work itself, the text is as the author wrote it. Wherever it required modification, (it would have been modified after discussion with him had he lived) since he did not live to make the modification himself, I have indicated the position in foot notes. I have verified every statement that seemed to call for it, and have restudied positions where the author himself felt that a re-study, or a reference to the original, was necessary ; and even in respect of these

I have left the text as it is, and have indicated the results of my verification only in foot notes. It was impossible I could have adopted any other method in the regrettable condition that I could not obtain his approval for any modification. This applies with more force to the expression of his views. Such as it is, the work is issued to the public in the form in which the author had it written without the benefit, however, of a possible modification, which might have been made had he lived to see it through the press.

Apart from the changes indicated above, I have added a map and an index, for both of which I am alone responsible. I acknowledge with pleasure the assistance rendered by my friend, Professor C. S. Srinivasachariyar, till recently of the Pachaiyappa's College, Madras, and now of the Annamalai University.

Having been acquainted with the author ever since the publication of his work, 'A Forgotten Empire', it is matter for gratification to me that I should have been enabled to render him this assistance, and I am grateful to the Syndicate of the University of Madras for having given me the chance of doing him this good service, posthumous as it has unfortunately become. My gratification is all the greater, seeing that he has actually referred to, and cited with expression of genuine appreciation, several of my works published during my tenancy of the Chair of Indian History and Archæology at the Madras University, even in respect of certain matters of controversy between us, about which he did not show himself in complete agreement in the correspondence that passed between us at the time. It is with genuine pleasure therefore that I record my gratitude to him for his goodwill and esteem. Now that the work, which has been occupying my spare time during the last three years particularly, has reached its completion, it is with a sense of relief that I bid goodbye to it, though it might for a time leave a void in my daily occupations.

S. KRISHNASWAMI AIYANGAR.

MYLAPORE, MADRAS,
24th January, 1932.

ABBREVIATIONS

References given in the form '355 of 1912' = the number of the inscription noted in the Annual Reports of the Epigraphical Department of the Archæological Survey, Southern Circle.

A. A. R. = The annual reports of the Archæological Survey of India, issued in book-form.

B. and V. C. = Alan Butterworth and V. Venugopal Chetty's '*Collection of the Inscriptions on Copper-plates and stones in the Nellore district.*'

C. P. = Copper-plate inscription.

D. K. D. = Fleet's '*Dynasties of the Kanarese districts.*'

E. C. = 'Epigraphia Carnatica.'

E. I. = 'Epigraphia Indica.'

E. H. D. = R. G. Bhandarkar's '*Early History of the Dekhan.*'

E. R. = Epigraphical Annual Reports made to the Government of Madras.

Forg. Emp. = '*A Forgotten Empire*' by Robert Sewell.

I. A. = 'Indian Antiquary.'

J. R. A. S. = Journal of the Royal Asiatic Society.

J. B. B. R. A. S. = Journal of the Bombay Branch of the Royal Asiatic Society.

K. Ā. = Kollam Āṇḍu, or Malayālam Era.

K. Y. = Kaliyuga Era.

Lists of Antiquities = '*Lists of Antiquities in the Madras Presidency*' by Robert Sewell, 1886.

Mys. A. A. R. = Mysore Annual Archæological Reports.

R. S. A. Nayaks = R. Sathyanatha Aiyar's '*History of the Nayaks of Madura.*'

T. and S. I. = '*Tamil aud Sanskrit Inscriptions,*' by Burgess and Natesa Sastri, 1886.

T. A. S. = Travancore Archæological Survey Series.

S. I. I. = 'South Indian Inscriptions.'

V. R. = V. Rangāchāri's 'Lists of Inscriptions, topographically arranged, in 3 vols.'

NOTES

(i) Inscriptions which are undated and those which mention only the regnal year of the ruler are generally omitted in this work unless they possess some independent historical value, in which case they are gone into. Records of the former class may prove misleading in cases where the ruler named belongs to a dynasty in which there was more than one member who bore the same name. Students who wish to examine all known records of a particular prince can refer to the voluminous Index attached to vol. III of V. Rangachārya's valuable work, 'Inscriptions of the Madras Presidency' (1919), and, for years since the publication of those volumes, to the annual reports of the Epigraphical Department of the Archæological Survey of South India.

(ii) I have chosen to use the A. D. reckoning of years in preference to that of Śaka years or those of the Kaliyuga or other systems for two reasons. One reason concerns brevity and economy of space, and saving of expense in printing. It is preferable to record a date as '3 Jan: A.D. 1552' rather than to state it as it stands in the original, viz., 'Śaka 1473 expired, Virōdhakrit, Pushya Śukla 7.' The second reason concerns the common habit in India of using the current as well as the expired year of the era. An inscription bearing date merely 'Śaka 1525' may refer to the current year which by solar reckoning, began on March 28 A.D. 1602, or to the expired year which ended on March 27 A.D. 1604; or to the current year which by luni-solar reckoning, began on March 14 A.D. 1602 or to the expired year which ended on March 19 A.D. 1604—in the latter case the description covering a period or more than two years.

R. S.

ADDITIONS AND ALTERATIONS

(Owing to a slight misunderstanding of instructions, the press struck off the first ten or twelve formes leaving some few printing blemishes uncorrected, and with typographical arrangements slightly different from the rest. Hence the errata slip which has become necessary.)

PAGE

1. Last para first line for *write* read *writes*.

5. ,, last line for *hraldom* read *thraldom*.

,, f. n. 2. line 2 for, the author *is* read *was*.

7. ,, f. n. 1. line 11, for *or* read *of*.

11. ,, line 2 for *six years* read *one year*.

13. Under B. C. 27 last line for and *their* read *the*.

24. ,, last line for *650* read *660*.

41 ,, [A. D. 907, 2nd para add at the end, *S. I. i. III. iii 1402. Ep. Rep. 1907. p. 71.*]

46. ,, ,, 940, 2nd para for thirty-*four* year read *fourth*.

47. C. 950 ,, for (E xv, 50) read (E. I. xv. 50)

66. line 2. for Lord Kedah read Lord *of* Kedah.

86. last line for *Rajamall* read *Rājamalla*.

87. line 2. for Mallikhārjnna read *Mallikārjuna*. This misspelling occurs again and again.

91. ,, A. D. 1098 para 2. *Cri* read *Cri*.

92. ,, A. D. 1102. l. 2. for Vīra-*ganga* read Vīra-Ganga.

94. ,, A. D. 1113 para 3. for Vikrama-*ganga* read *Ganga*.

99. ,, ,, 1125 ,, 1. put bracket before 728.

,, ,, 1126 ,, 2. line 4. omit the second *been*.

102. ,, ,, 1137 ,, line 3. for E read W.

103. ,, ,, 1139 para 5. line 1. omit , after Godavari.

107. f. n. line 4. for Kanni read Nanni.

112. under A. D. 1160 l. 4 third para from the end, for *Lachahala* read *Lachchala*.

118. para 2. last word for *death* read *deaths*.

125. under A. D. 1192 2nd para line 4 for *Telugul* read *Telugu*.

126. para 2. line 1. for *Pathappi* read *Pottappi*.

131. para 3. line 2. for *Sahāsa* read *Sāhasa*.

134. under A. D 1217 2nd para line 2. omit ⊙ before Yadava.

137. para 3. line 2. for *the* soldier read *a*.

141. under A. D. 1233 para 2. omit brackets before *which* and *597*.

144. ,, ,, 1243 line 3. change ⊙ after 1919 into a (;).

146. f. n. line 3. insert *of* before *Kukula*.

150. under A. D. 1253 last but one line for *Iadia* read *India*.

159. ,, 1270 para 5 for E. c. viii read E. C. viii.

160. ,, 1273 para 5 for *Geneol* read *Geneal*.

167. ,, 1290 para 5 last line for *1920* read *1290*.

180. ,, 1316 last line for *Śinghana* read *Śankara*.

183. ,, 1328 after insert a (;).

206. ,, 1398 para 2. for x. *mb.* read x. *Mb.*

215. ,, 1414 para 3 for *l.* N. read *i.* N.

ibid ,, 1426 para 2 for iv. ch read iv. Ch.

220. f. n. last line for *see the* omit *the*.

232. f. n. line 3 for *son Sāluva* read son *of Sāluva*.

244. f. n. line 1 for *Harsan* read *Hassan*.

259. under A. D. 1570 para 2 put in a (,) between 409 and 495.

279. f. n. line 1 for *Record* read *Records*.

305. under A. D. 1775 line 1, for *Bengal* read *Oudh*.

HISTORICAL INSCRIPTIONS OF SOUTHERN INDIA

INTRODUCTION

A FEW traces of palæolithic man, consisting of chipped stone implements, have been found in Southern India; but they are not numerous, and they belong to an age whose distance from the present is so remote that to attempt to fix it is a matter of pure conjecture.

After apparently a great gap in time we come to the neolithic age, and, following it with no such gap, to the iron age. Bruce Foote, the geologist of Southern India, came to the conclusion that the people of the iron age were direct descendants of the neolithic folk. All these three are combined in the term 'pre-historic' civilizations.

In the neolithic age weapons and tools were made of the hardest procurable stones, skilfully flaked, chipped and polished. Axeheads were indented at the sides and bound to wooden shafts by withes cut from the forest. Hand-made pottery was used. Numerous remains of neolithic burials have been found in the Southern Dekhan and in the Districts of the Madras Presidency.

In the iron age weapons were constructed of that metal; swords, spears, arrow heads and useful tools have been found in great numbers. Pottery was decorative, and many fragments of figurines have been discovered representing men, women and animals. Burials were in dolmens and cromlechs, and early Tamil literature abounds in allusions to the dead having been placed in great pottery urns before interment, many of which have been found in the South. Rude stone circles marked the burial place in many instances.

The iron age gradually merged into the very early historic period. Originally, it cannot be doubted, the unit of mankind was the family. Then, as population increased, families living side by side, owing to the existence of common interests found themselves almost insensibly forced into obedience to a tribal chief whose rule met the general needs of the community. And after a lapse of time this union of families developed into a union of tribes, and this last union grew into the formation of nations; the whole process being primarily due to the disagreement of the units. Firstly family against family, then tribe against tribe, and finally nation against nation; each unit being formed for defence against other units. At the last stage the historic period begins.

'The earliest invaders or settlers about whom anything at all definite is known,' write Vincent Smith in his *Oxford History of India*, 'were the people of the *Rigveda* hymns, who called themselves Āryans, and are conveniently designated as Indo-Āryans. . . . They were akin to Iranians or Persians, who also called themselves Āryans.' But Southern India remained for a long time free of their influence, their appearance in the South being the result of peaceful penetration by missionaries or small colonies. These introduced a new religion into that country; the ancient Dravidian rites were gradually abandoned, and their place was taken by Vẹdic Brahmanism.

During the later period there appears to have been a marked increase in mining and trading, and the inhabitants of Southern India were now introduced to the markets of central Asia and greatly profited thereby. A large quantity of the world's stock of gold, then becoming very popular amongst the rich, came from the territories now known as the Presidency of Madras and the Nizam's Dominions.[1]

It is impossible to assign any definite date to the spread of Āryan influence in South India, partly because that spread, as has been stated, was gradual, but Vincent Smith has suggested about 2000 B.C. as a mean date.

The latest theory seems to be that there were two Āryan irruptions, one about 2500 B.C. and one about 1500 B.C. (Barnett, '*Antiquities of India*, pp. 7, 8.)

As far back as the time of the *Purānas* the people of South India were known as belonging to three nations, Pāṇdyas, the Chōḷas and the Kēralas. The *Rāmayāna* adds a fourth, namely, the Telugu country of the Āndhras. Their languages, and when they acquired the art of writing, their alphabets, were quite distinct. The Tamil alphabet is Semitic in character. This division of nations lasted down to comparatively modern times. But there were many sub-divisions.

With regard to the trade of these times it must be noted that early Chaldæan inscriptions speak of ships of Ur, the capital city; and that from at least the fourteenth century B.C. gold, silks, spices, pearls, etc. . . . had been passing from India to the Assyrian monarchy, carried on both by caravans on land, and by the coasting trade by sea. There was also active trade with China.

Indian products were known to the Syrians of King Solomon's Day, 1000 B.C. by their Indian names, as we know from the ancient Jewish records. On an obelisk of Shalmanezer III at Babylon are represented Indian elephants and apes.

From about the year 700 B.C. events can be treated more historically. By this time Āryanism had flooded all north India. The remains of the aboriginal tribes had either been absorbed, reduced to servitude, or driven into the hills and forests. But the South remained principally Dravidian. The ancient Vedic theology had been expounded in the *Brahmanas*, the philosophic *Upanishads* and the educational *Vēdāngas*. The various Indian communities resulting from the fusion of Āryan and Dravidian races are known to have been very numerous. The *Mahābhārata* mentions six different kingdoms as existing on the Ganges River, Hastināpura, Mattra, Panchāla, Benares, Magadha and Bengal. There was another kingdom in Gujarat, another in the Indus Valley, another in the Kalinga country. But there must have been many more in the Dekhan and Peninsula and other parts. The *Rāmāyana* names numbers of states in northern India, and fourteen kingdoms south of the Tungabhadra river. About 300 B.C. Megasthenes enumerates 118 nations as existing in India. Even after the greater number of north Indian states had been absorbed in the Empire of Magadha, King Asōka (*circ.* 250 B.C.) makes mention of numerous states outside his own territory and bordering thereon.

[1] On the subject of ancient trade and commerce between India and the West Professor V. Ball's article '*A Geologist's Contribution to the History of Ancient India*', published in the *Indian Antiquary* for 1884 (pp. 228 ff.) affords most valuable information. He believes that the Egyptians traded with India, though at present there is not much proof of this. Arabia certainly did, and so did the Phœnicians.

Judging from the known history of later years it is practically certain that all these small states lived in a condition of perpetual warfare with one another. Certainly the early literature, the *Rāmāyana*, the *Mahābhārata* and the ancient Tamil poems testify that such was the case.

About the seventh century B.C., therefore, we must assume that 'India' consisted of a large number of distinct states, constantly striving to destroy and absorb one another or struggling for existence. Foreigners, especially merchants from Persia, were no doubt settled in many of the coast towns and frontier cities. Somewhat later we have the evidence to this effect of the Greek writer Hekataius of Miletus (549–486 B.C.) who mentions places in India known to him. Trade in gold, spices, etc., was carried on by sea from the Malabar Coast, while the silk trade was confined to the Coromandel Coast. Maritime trade along the coasts had to contend with the dangers of piracy which appear to have been always prevalent.

At last, during the seventh century, sixteen of the kingdoms of northern India were, after constant fighting, swallowed up in the supremacy of Magadha, and by the year 600 B.C. or thereabouts the King of Magadha, Śiśunāga, became practically an Emperor; being in possession of great territories in the north from the Hindukūsh to the Narmadā river, and from the Indus to Gayā, where Rājagriha became his capital.

Four sovereigns in succession ruled over Magadha after the death of Śiśunāga. The fifth was Bimbiśāra who came to the throne in 543 or 528 B.C.[1] The birth of Buddha had taken place about 563 B.C.

Bimbiśāra enlarged his dominions by conquest, and became very powerful. His principal queens were a princess of the great Lichchavi clan, and a daughter of the King of Kōsala. He had only been three years on the throne when he was threatened from the north-west;[2] for Cyrus the great King of Persia conquered Bactria, Kābul and Gandhāra and practically all the country to the west of the Indus. Bimbiśāra, however, was not actually attacked by Cyrus, but the danger became greater with the advent to the Persian throne in 522 B.C. of Darius son of Hystaspes, whose general, Skylax, sailed down the Indus to the sea, thus allowing his master to annex the Indus valley about the year 512 B.C. Bimbiśāra was murdered by his own son Ajātaśatru who seized the throne of Magadha (about 500 B.C.).[3]

This crime roused the country against Ajātaśatru and he was compelled to fight the Lichchavi and Kōsala clans. He defeated them, annexed Vaisāli, the Lichchavi capital, and constructed a frontier fortress at Pātaliputra (Patna) on the bank of the Ganges.

In 483 B.C., according to general present estimate, the Buddha died and attained *nirvāṇa.* The occasion of his death was also the occasion, according to the Siṇghalese *Mahāwaṁśa* for the arrival in Ceylon of Vijaya, a prince exiled from Bengal, who became the first recognized king of the island, reigning thirty-eight years. He is said to have landed in Ceylon on the day of Buddha's death. The chronicle states that he sent an embassy to the Pāṇḍya king of the Tamil country.

[1] For these early dates I rely principally on the publications of Dr. L. D. Barnett, *Antiquities of India* (1913), and the *Cambridge History of India* (1922). The late historian Vincent Smith, in his *Oxford History of India* (1919) makes the dates about forty years earlier in each case. All however agree that the Maurya Chandragupta seized the throne in 322 or 321 B.C.

[2] The underlying assumption that Bimbiśāra's authority extended to the N.-W. Frontier has no evidence to support it. Such evidence as is available is of a contrary tendency and would make Bimbiśāra ruler of an extended Magadha and no more.—*Editor.*

[3] Such is the story as told in Buddhist literature. But Vincent Smith disbelieves the accusation made against Ajātaśatru (*Oxford History of India*, pp. 47, 48).

In Persia at this time the reigning king was Xerxes, who succeeded Darius Hystaspes in 486 B.C. In his war against the Greeks he made use of a body of Indian bowmen. This was in 479. A little later Darius Codomanus of Persia had in his army fifteen war-elephants from India.

Ajātaśatru of Magadha died about 475 B.C. and was succeeded by Darśaka and the latter by Udayin (*circ.* 450 to 417 B.C.). Udayin, also called Udāsin or Udaya, founded the city of Kusumapura close to the fortress of Pātaliputra. In 417 B.C. or thereabouts Nandivardhana came to the throne, and after him Mahānandin, the last of the dynasty.

About 371 B.C. this last king's illegitimate son Mahāpadma Nanda usurped the throne of Magadha, and established a short dynasty that reigned for half a century. During their supremacy the country was greatly disturbed by internal dissension and by the epoch-making invasion of Alexander of Macedon and his armies of Greeks.

Alexander had by the year 331 B.C. conquered the King of Persia and destroyed his dynasty, and had seized Egypt and founded the city of Alexandria. In 330 he was in Persia and in the next year made preparations for the conquest of Northern India. In 327 he advanced through the passes of the Hindukush, subduing the frontier tribes, and in 326 arrived at the Indus river. Crossing the river he was joined by a local ruler Āmbhi, King of Taxila, who was at feud with his neighbouring chiefs, with a force of 5,000 men, and the allies then marched to the Hydaspes or Jhelum river, where he was resolutely opposed by king 'Poros' or Puru on the eastern bank. Alexander made a détour, effected a crossing and attacked his opponent. The battle is known to European historians as the battle of the Hydaspes. Alexander won a great victory, slaughtered 12,000 men and captured or destroyed 200 elephants. Puru was wounded and submitted to the invader, who treated him with kindness and consideration. Alexander proceeded on his eastward march till he reached the Biās river, or Hyphasis, beyond which his soldiers refused to venture. Faced with open mutiny Alexander was compelled to retreat, and did so, leaving Puru, now his friend, as sovereign over twelve distinct nations that occupied the territory between the Jhelum and Biās rivers. In October 326 B.C. he sailed down the Jhelum, guarded on the banks by his army of 120,000 men. Great slaughter followed when any opposition was met with, and the journey to the sea lasted for ten months. In October 325 B.C. he started from the neighbourhood of Karāchi and marched back to Persia, suffering terrible hardships on the way. Eventually he arrived at Susa, with a mere remnant of his troops, in May 324 B.C.

Alexander died in Babylon in June 323 B.C.

Before passing on, one or two notes may be found useful. About the year 444 B.C., as we learn from the *Mahāwamsa* the King of Ceylon was called Pāṇḍu Vāsudeva; and in 377 Pāṇḍuka-Abhaya, was king. Both these rulers were probably connected with the royal family of Pāṇḍyas of Madura.

About 420 B.C. was the date of the Greek writer Herodotus. Ktesias lived about 400 B.C.

After Alexander's expedition Europe learned much more about India than had ever been previously known, and the Indians of the north were brought into more intimate relations with the peoples of the west. A great increase of trade took place, welcome to both sides, and fostered by protection of caravans travelling by land and by the establishment of Alexandria as a mart for commercial activity. This led to the settlement in Indian cities of Greek merchants and the presence there of foreign travellers. Greek philosophy, religion and science were studied in India and the Buddhist and Jaina philosophies were discussed in Athens.

For a time however these amenities were checked by the coming to great power of Chandragupta, the Maurya king, who overthrew the Nanda dynasty of Magadha and usurped the throne in 322 or 321 B.C. His first endeavour was to drive out the Macedonian garrisons left behind by Alexander, whose generals he succeeded in defeating. Then he seized the throne of Magadha and became the practical Emperor of the whole of northern India.

In 305 B.C. Chandragupta was attacked by Seleukos Nikator, who then ruled over Western Asia, but the attack failed and peace was made, Chandragupta receiving large cessions of districts west of the Indus, and giving 500 elephants in exchange.

In 302 B.C. Seleukos sent Megasthenes as ambassador to the Court of Chandragupta. Megasthenes has left behind him a most valuable record, the *Indika*, in which he describes all that he saw and heard while at Pātaliputra and on his journeys. Chandragupta's capital was a great walled city and Megasthenes said the walls were furnished with 570 towers and 64 gates.

If the *Kauṭilya Arthaśastra*, as we have it, was really, as alleged, the work of Chandragupta's Brahman Minister Chāṇakya, *alias* Kauṭilya *alias* Vishṇugupta, we should learn a great deal from it concerning the condition in his day of the mass of the king's subjects, and of the mode of government of the country; but there seems to be some doubt as to its genuineness, and an opinion has been growing up that it may be, in part at least, a composition of later years.[1] This being so I refrain from quoting from it passages which, if genuinely the production of a minister of the crown, would prove that the people of the time must have led most miserable lives owing to State persecution.[2] The late Dr. Vincent Smith's remarks in his *Oxford History of India*, p. 92, are very much to the point if the *Śastra* was actually written by Kauṭilya, as the author believed. 'The dark spots on the picture', he writes, 'are the appalling wickedness of the statecraft taught in the *Arthaśastra* and the hateful espionage which tainted the whole administration'. The work has been translated by R. Shamasastri in the *Indian Antiquary* for 1905 (pp. 5, 47, 110), and I would especially call attention to the section in Book V, *The Conduct of Government Officers*, sub-section 'Replenishment of the Treasury.' *(p. 301 Ed. of 1915)*.

Apart from the statements made in the *Arthaśastra* we gather some notion as to the sort of lives led by the people under the rule of Chandragupta and his successors from independent sources. Justin, a Roman writer (*Epitoma Pompei Trogi*, 15, 4,) dealing with the period when Chandragupta was reigning triumphantly after his campaign against Seleukos, says that the Hindu monarch after his victory 'had forfeited by his tyranny all title to the name of liberator, for, having ascended the throne, he oppressed with servitude the very people whom he had emancipated from foreign thraldom.' Three centuries later Strabo (xv. 1, 40) asserts that Chandragupta forced all farmers,

[1] See *I.A.*, vol. liv for September 1925, p. 171, and the opinions of scholars referred to therein.

[2] In regard to this opinion of the late Mr. Sewell, attention may be invited to the chapters on the Arthaśāstra in the late Mr. F. J. Monahan's work, *The Early History of Bengal*. The author is one who had made a special study of the work in comparison with the other sources, and the following sentences are taken from a summary at the end of the chapters, in which a detailed examination of the work had been undertaken by him :—

'The picture which the work presents is that of a paternal government, tempered by respect for religion and custom, and, probably, limited also by the power and privileges of guilds and corporations. Though the government was not democratic, it is likely that the life of the guilds and various other associations may have afforded occasion for such democratic processes as elections, debates, and decisions by majority vote.'

'On the whole, it may be claimed for the *Arthaśāstra* that its general spirit is enlightened and humane, and though in some places it advocates methods and expedients flagrantly repugnant to our ideas of public morality, the general objects held in view are the maintenance of law and order, the punishment of the wicked, and the protection of the peaceable citizen' (pp. 137, 138).—*Editor*.

great and small, to hand over to the Government Treasury three-quarters of the produce of the land, keeping only one-quarter for the maintenance of themselves and their families ; and that Chandragupta assumed, as a general principle that he was the absolute owner of the soil of all the lands that came under his rule.

That the subjects of the Maurya Kings were liable to torture for non-payment of Government demands is proved by the words of King Aśōka, who, after his conversion to Buddhism, recorded in his Kalinga edicts his regret that individuals had been subjected to undeserved imprisonment and torture.

About the year 296 B.C. Chandragupta, warned by the Jain teacher Bhadrabāhu of the near approach of a terrible famine which it was prophesied would last twelve years, is said to have abdicated, devoted himself to an ascetic life and journeyed with Bhadrabāhu to Śrāvana-Beḷgola in Mysore, where shortly afterwards the latter died. Chandragupta survived him for twelve years and then, after the custom of the Jains, starved himself to death. His followers in large members are said to have travelled southwards to Punnāḍ.

He was succeeded about 296 B.C. by his son Bindusāra, surnamed Amitra-khada, known to the Greeks as Amitrochates, who was on friendly terms with Antiochus Soter of Western Asia. He is believed to have enlarged his dominions towards the South and, at any rate, to have ruled North Mysore. Deimachos was the ambassador of Antiochus at the Court of Bindusāra.

On the latter's death, at a date variously estimated as 273 or 268 B.C., (I accept the latter) there followed a period of confusion, for a struggle ensued between Bimbisāra's sons for the monarchy. It ended in a decisive triumph for Aśōka, a younger son ; who, it has been stated was guilty of terrible atrocities before he finally crushed his elder brother.

Aśōka was not actually crowned till 264 B.C., four years after his father's death.

Eight years after his coronation, viz. in 256 B.C. Aśōka made war on the King of Kalinga. It was conducted in savage fashion. Later on in life the king, in his edicts, admits that he was responsible for the deaths of 100,000 of his enemy's people, and the carrying away into captivity of 150,000 more, while a still greater number died of want and starvation. These horrors made a deep impression on Aśōka's mind. Two years later he became a convert to Buddhism and governed for the rest of his life with kindness and moderation. His rock-cut edicts amply testify to his love of justice and mercy, and to his desire that all his subjects should act up to those principles. That being so it may be assumed that to the best of his ability he abolished such parts of former codes as encouraged cruel treatment of the people. In his Kalinga edicts he specially laments that some of his officials had inflicted unjust imprisonment and torture on individuals.

Aśōka's territories comprised all northern India, and the Kalinga country, Dekhan, and part at least of the South as far as the North of Mysore. He had friendly relations with neighbouring states, and even with others so far away as Syria, Egypt, Macedonia, Cyrene, Epirus and Corinth. He recognized as sovereigns in their own lands the Āndhra Kings of the Telugu country, the Chōla and Pāṇḍya rulers of the Tamils, the King of the Kērala coast, and the King of Ceylon. A number of other nationalities are mentioned in the edicts and placed in the same class as the Āndhras. He sent members of his family to spread Buddhism in Ceylon.

As regards the southern limit of Aśōka's territories we must be guided by the commencement of the Jatinga-Rāmēśvara, Brahmagiri and Siddhāpura Edicts, all of which are engraved on rocks near the village of Siḍḍhāpura in the Chitaldrug district of northern Mysore, 'From these we learn,' writes Dr. Hultzsch in his new and comprehensive work on the Edicts of Aśōka (*Introd., p. xxxviii*), 'that the head-quarters of Aśōka's southernmost province was a place of the name Suvarṇagiri, and that his representative there, just as at Ujjayini, was a royal prince (*Āryaputra*).' Brahmagiri and Siddāpura belonged to a district called Isila, which was subordinate to the Viceroy at Suvarṇagiri. Dr. Hultzsch suggests that Suvarṇagiri may have been the same as the modern Kanakagiri in the Nizām's State, south of Maski.[1]

Aśōka died about 226 B.C.,[2] and after him the Maurya Empire gradually broke up. The Eastern Provinces were ruled by his grandson Daśaratha, and the Western by another grandson Samprati, but very little is known about them. The last known Maurya King Brihadratha was assassinated by his commander-in-chief Pushyamitra about 184 B.C., who established a new and short-lived dynasty, that of the Sungas. From 184 B.C., therefore, though we hear of Maurya princes for several centuries more as ruling fragments of the country, especially in the South, the Maurya Empire ceased to exist. As an instance of these small principalities it may be noted that as late as the seventh century A.D. one of them in the Konkan, ruled by Maurya chiefs, was subdued by the Chāḷukya sovereign Pulakēśin II.

About the time when Aśōka's power was strongest two important provinces, Baktria and Parthia, broke away from the Seleukid sovereignty, and became independent. The former was ruled by Greek kings, who were formally recognized by the King of Syria, Antiochos, about 208 B.C. After this the Greeks settled down firmly in Baktria, and largely influenced the history of the north-west of India and beyond the frontier. That history, however, belonging to the north, I pass it by. But before doing so I append a note which serves to shew the intercourse which existed about this period between India, Western Asia and Europe.

After the Greek Kings of Baktria had firmly established themselves in independence the Indians adopted many words from their western neighbours. A large number of terms used in astronomy, astrology and coinage in India are derived from the Greek. The art of the time shews strong Greek influence especially in Gandhāra and the north-west.

In the wars between Rome and Carthage which took place at this time Indian elephants trained to war were used by the Carthaginians. About 170 B.C. the Persian army included 120 elephants, as we learn from the Jewish chronicle of the time (*1 Maccabees, viii. 6*). In 163 B.C. there were thirty-two war elephants carrying Indian drivers (mahouts) and howdahs in the army of

[1] The discovery of the Aśōka Edicts at Maski, otherwise Māsangi and even Piriya Māsangi, Kan. for bigger Māsangi, raises the possibility that Aśōka had a viceroyalty corresponding to the land of Kuntala, the Southern Mahrata country, so called. Maski is in a gold producing district and the edicts were actually discovered in prospecting for gold. The probability of a viceroyalty in this region becomes the more since the Tamils, in their classical literature, locate the northern (Vaḍuga) frontier (Vaḍugar-Munai) somewhere about this region. The existence of a place called Kanakagiri, about twenty miles across Hampi, the site of the old Vijayanagar, makes it probably enough the seat of the viceroyalty; the more so, as some of the Aśōka Edicts were found further south in Mysore, and more recently to the eastwards at Gooty. The Mysore edicts happen to be addressed to the Governor of a division named Iśila. Iśila seems to be the Prakrit equivalent of Riṣyaka, and in the region of Hampi there is a Riṣyamukha Parvata, and the division might well have gone by that name. Iśila being almost the exact equivalent in Prakrit, or Pāḷi, or the Sanskrit Riṣyaka. In later epigraphs, almost in the same region, some chieftains claim to have belonged to Vāli Vaṁśa, which seems to indicate that the tradition that Hampi was the kingdom of Kishkinda was kept alive in the tenth and eleventh centuries A.D. (*Ep. Ind.* xiii, 186–87). So the location of Svarṇagiri either at Kanakagiri or somewhere near seems quite probable.—*Editor.*

[2] This is Dr. Barnett's date. Vincent Smith placed the event in 232 B.C. and the *Cambridge History of India* in 237 or 236 B.C.

Antiochos Eupator of Syria (*1 Maccabees, vi. 30–37*). On a frieze in a tomb in Marissa in Palestine believed to date from about 100 B.C., painted in fresco on the wall is a figure of a fully caparizoned elephant certainly Indian. A fresco at Pompeii, lately discovered by Professor Spinazzola represents the Goddess Venus in a chariot drawn by four elephants.

To return to the history proper—it has been shewn that Aśōka's Empire broke up after his death; and amongst other ruling dynasties that then come to the front were the Chētas of Kalinga, with whom South India had little to do, and the Āndhras of the Telugu country to their South. The Āndhras were Buddhists. They are known to have ruled from at least 250 B.C., but they came to great power about the year 220, and remained in a dominant position till the third century A.D.

The position of the new Sunga King Pushyamitra was very precarious. There began in his time a great tribal movement in Mongolia and Turkestan. One of these tribes, the Śakas, driven out of their own country north of the Jaxartes, or Syr Daryā river, by the incursions of hordes from Western China known as the Yueh-chi, were forced over the mountain borderland southwards and began to settle in India in large and increasing numbers. About 170 B.C. war broke out between Pushyamitra and the Āndhra king Yajña Śrī Śātakarṇi in which the former's son Agnimitra was victorious.[1] At that time the Āndhra monarch was ruling over a large extent of country including Berar, part of the Central Provinces and Hyderabad, as well as over his own Telugu tracts; which fact accounts for the Kālinga Khāravēla's inscription of about 159 B.C. calling the Āndhra ruler 'Lord of the West.' Pushyamitra also had to contend with the Hellenistic king of Baktria, Menander, about 155 B.C., who was victorious in several campaigns and eventually forced his way into parts of Oudh and Rajputana. About 153 B.C. Khāravēla, who has just been mentioned allied himself with the Āndhra king Pūrnōtsanga and attacked the Sunga king. Khāravēla stormed Rājagriha, penetrated into Magadha, and compelled Pushyamitra to make peace.

It is interesting to note, as regards the great antiquity of the city of Kānchī (Conjeveram), that Patanjali notices its existence as early as 150 B.C.

Pushyamitra's successor, his son Agnimitra, when he came to the throne in 148 B.C. was heavily burdened with political difficulties; and as these increased in later years, partly owing to the numerous incursions of hordes of Śakas and Pahlavas into his country, the supremacy of Magadha rapidly declined, and finally disappeared. The invaders triumphed and themselves became rulers of northern India from about 50 B.C. or later.

About 27 B.C. the last king of the Kāṇva dynasty, which had succeeded that of the Sungas, was killed by an Āndhra king whose name is not known; and from that time forward till about A.D. 300 Northern and Western India were practically under the foreign rule of the Śakas, firstly that of the Kushan dynasty, and from about A.D. 100 that of the Satraps or Kshatrapas.

With the decay of the kingdom of Magadha the Āndhras had been growing in strength. Their coins have been found in many places, on the West as far as Nasik; and an inscription bearing the name of the family proves that in Eastern Mālwa, Āndhra rule had succeeded that of the Sungas about 50 B.C. In later years they made Vengi near the Godavari river their capital. Their kings bear the family name Śātakarni or Sātavāhana. They were enthusiastic followers of the religion

[1] Opinions differ as to the real result of the war. [Sewell is apparently mixing up two separate persons. Dr. Barnett gives under this date reference to the war between Agnimitra and Yajña Sēna, King of Vidarbha and *Āndhra*. This king was ruling over Vidarbha according to the drama Mālavikāgnimitra. The Āndhra King later on was Pūrnōtsanga as Sewell says. There is no Āndhra King Yagña Śrī Śātakarṇi about this time in any of the Āndhra lists.—*Editor*.]

of Buddha, and erected, in the neighbourhood of the Krishna river a number of great *stupas* built to enshrine the relics of their honoured teacher. The most elaborate of these was the well-known *stūpa* at Amarāvati, a huge dome encrusted with sculptured marbles, and having round it marble rails and gateways. The art of this period shews certain traces of Greek and Persian influence.

By the beginning of the Christian era the great Republic of Rome had given way to a still greater empire, and we learn from the writings of Strabo (A.D. 20) and Pliny (A.D. 77) that there existed in Rome an inordinate love of importation of luxuries from the East. Trade with India, therefore, enormously increased and there is reason to suppose that numbers of Roman merchants made their centres of trade, if not their homes, in such places as Madura and in the sea-port towns of the west coast, sending Indian products to Rome and receiving in return Roman goods. Large numbers of Roman coins have been found in South India. The Peutingerian Tables place a temple of Augustus, the Roman Emperor, on the Malabar coast. Strabo mentions an embassy which the Pāṇḍya king of Madura sent to Augustus Cæsar, probably in 22 B.C. Pliny recommends to the Romans a geographical study of the route to India, which he says is a very important subject because 'in no year does India drain our Empire of less than 550 millions of sestertices, giving back her own wares in exchange.' He mentions the Kalinga, Āndhra and Pāṇḍya kings. (*History Natural xii. 18, 41 ; vi. Caps 22, 24, 26 : Bostock and Riley's translation*). He mentions an embassy which was sent to Claudius Cæsar in Rome in A.D. 41, following on the adventure of a certain freedman, Annius Plocamus, who farmed the Red Sea customs, and who in a gale was carried to Ceylon where he was treated kindly and brought to the notice of the king. He tells us of the port of Muziris in Malabar (Muyirikoḍu); of the Kēralaputra, king of that country; of the Chēras; of how the seas were infested by pirates; of Cochin; of the Pāṇḍya king and his capital Madura. He describes the Indian banyan-tree and the many products of the country.

The author of the *Periplus* (A.D. 80) and the geographer Ptolemy (A.D. 130) mention the articles of trade brought from India, and especially from South-India in their days: beryls, spices, muslins, precious stones, cottons, etc. They tell us of the Godavari and Bhīma rivers; of Masulipatam (*Masolia, Mesolus*); of Gūḍūr near Masulipatam and Kanchikacharla on the Krishna river (*Koddura, Konṭakossyla Emporium*); of the port of Korkai (*Kolchoi*); of the Vindhya mountain range (*Vindius*); of Travancore, known by its ancient name Purali (*Paralia*); of Karuvūr on the Kāvērī river; of the beryl mines at Paḍiyūr in the Chēra kingdom, which were called by the name of the old tract in which they were situated, viz., the Padināḍu (*Pounnaṭa*); of Pālūr in Ganjam (Pālūra); and of many other places.

In A.D. 71 the city of Jerusalem was sacked by the Romans, and a number of Jewish refugees are said to have fled to the Malabar coast. There is no definite proof of the fact, though it is certain that a Jewish colony existed there from a very ancient date.

An Indian embassy was received by the Emperor Trajan in Rome in A.D. 107; another by Antoninus Pius in A.D. 138; in A.D. 336, another was sent to Constantine; and in A.D. 361 an embassy from Ceylon was sent to the Emperor Julian.

There being no known inscription in Southern India earlier than 250 B.C. or thereabouts of the reign of Aśōka, the lists which follow begin from that date, with appended historical notes where requisite.

LIST OF INSCRIPTIONS IN SOUTHERN INDIA, WITH HISTORICAL NOTES

Remarks enclosed in square brackets [ ] are historical notes, additional to the Text which deals with the contents of inscriptions.

B.C. 250–237. [This is roughly the period of the inscriptions of Aśōka, the Maurya king of Magadha. They have been found engraved on rocks, in caves, and on pillars, in several places in India. Those that exist in the south are at Jaugada, 18 miles north of Ganjam, at Maski in Raichur District of the Nizam's Dominions, and in the neighbourhood of Siddhāpura in the Chitaldrug District of Mysore.[1] Aśōka's edicts were promulgated, and engraved on rocks and pillars after his complete conversion to the gentle teachings of Buddha in order that the principles therein inculcated might be instilled into the minds of generations yet to come. He revolted from the horrors of war and from the abominable system of government hitherto adopted and he fully recognized the duty of a sovereign to his people. Want of space prevents any insertion here of long extracts from his edicts, but a few may be given. In Rock Edict XIII he mentions the slaughter and captivity of the people of Kalinga caused by his war with that country and states that now this was 'a matter of profound sorrow and regret to his sacred majesty . . . if now a thousandth part were to suffer the same fate it would be a matter of regret to [him].' . . . 'Even upon the forest folk in his dominions his majesty looks kindly.' . . . 'He desires that all persons should have security, and peace of mind.' . . . 'He exhorts his successors to take pleasure in patience and gentleness. He asserts, as a principle of good government by a sovereign that "all men are my children." He declares himself "ready to do the people's business in all places", the welfare of all folk is what I must work for' and so on.

The Jaugada Edict is addressed to his subordinate officials in that region. Here again he declares that every man in the country [conquered by him] is his child, and he wishes them all to enjoy prosperity and happiness. Hence he enjoins on his officers to act justly, to see that the king's orders in the matter of the welfare of his subjects are obeyed, to release any man who has been unjustly imprisoned or tortured, and generally to work hard in the interests of the population over whom they are placed.

In the Siddhāpura Edicts the king states that more than two and a half years had elapsed since he became a lay-hearer of the Buddhist preachers, and more than six years since he entered the community of ascetics. He commands all men to obey their parents, to respect all living creatures, to be truthful, to follow the teachings of Buddha, to honour their teachers, and to give every man his due.

[1] Early this year (1929) a complete set of edicts of Aśōka has come to light at or near Gooty in the Anantapur District of the Madras Presidency. The Archaeological Department is at work on this new find.—*Editor*.

The Maski inscription is specially important in that it specifies the king's personal name Aśōka, while the rest only give him his royal titles.

Aśōka recognized as independent sovereigns in his day the Chōla, Pāṇḍya, Chēra and Āndhra Kings in Southern India.

(*For further information see the introduction above*).]

[About this time the Āndhras of the Telugu country began to acquire power, consequent on Aśōka's conquest of their northern neighbours, the kings of Kalinga.]

B.C. 220. [From about this date the Āndhras became dominant on the East Coast, and over large tracts in the interior.]

B.C. 200. [Foundation about this time of the Buddhist stupa or tope at Amarāvati on the site of the ancient city of Dharaṇikōta on the Krishna river—renowned for the extreme beauty of its marble sculptures.]

B.C. 180. [Northern India began to suffer seriously from the settlement in their midst of Śaka tribes, driven over the frontier down into India from the north by Mongolian hordes. The Mauryan Empire came to an end in B.C. 184, and Pushyamitra established the Sunga dynasty which with difficutly held its own for about a hundred years.]

B.C. 179. [Accession of the Āndhra King Yajñaśrī Sātakarani.[1] He is said to have been defeated by Prince Agnimitra, son of Pushyamitra of the Sunga dynasty of Magadha about B.C. 170, but Dr. Barnett holds that the Sātakarṇi got the best of it in the end.]

B.C. 163. [The King of Kalinga, Khārāvela, about this time in alliance with the Āndhra King, Pūrṇōtsanga reduced the 'Rāshṭrikas and Bhōjakas,' and stormed the city of Rājagriha, whose king fled.]

B.C. 155. [The Greko-Baktrian Menander invaded northern India and after 25 years of fighting, in which he forced his way temporarily into parts of Oudh, Rajputana and Kathiāwār, eventually retired.]

B.C. 153. [Khāravēla compelled the Sunga King Pushyamitra to make peace.]

B.C. 150. [The effect of the Śaka inroads into northern India became more and more serious from now onwards. But it is believed that in general theirs was a peaceful penetration and that they mingled amicably with the people, gradually acquiring power over them.]

[1] This entry of the late Mr. Sewell, under 179 B.C., makes his position clear as to the authority upon which he makes the note. This is probably from Professor Barnett's *Indian Antiquities*, page 41 (entries under 170 and 153 B.C) where the name is set down correctly as Yagñasena. But he is made an Āndhra and a Śātakarṇi, on what authority is not clearly stated. Kāļidāsa's drama, Māļvika-Agnimitra is the authority for the data regarding Agnimitra's war against the Vidarbha king Yagñasena. Between him and a paternal first cousin of his, there was a war of succession. Agnimitra espoused the cause of the latter though he was the son of a younger brother, and ultimately made the country of Vidarbha into two states divided by the river Varada. The northern of these two parts, and therefore, that on the immediate neighbourhood, was given over to Yagñasena, and over the southern part he placed Mādhavasena, his own brother-in-law, as against the *prakritiyamitra*, a neighbour, whose interests naturally clashed with those of his own. The drama always uses the term 'Vidarbha' for the state and 'Vaidarbha' for the king, and leaves us in little doubt as to what is actually meant. This is made much more clear by the people being spoken of as '*Krathakaiśikas*, the people who inhabited Berar, even according to the sixth book of the Raghuvaṁśa, where the *svayamvara* of Indumati is described in detail. The state of Vidarbha thus indicated is a comparatively narrow one and can hardly be regarded as synonymous with that of either the Āndhras or of a Śātakarṇi at any time of the history of that dynasty. Vidarbha is to be regarded as a distinct geographico-political entity. Whether the dynasty that ruled over the territory was Āndhra or no by blood relationship, it was distinctly Vaidarbha in point of political character. It would be too much to argue, in the circumstances, that the Vidarbha rulers figuring in these transactions were in any sense Āndhras and for the name actually given, there is no warrant whatsoever in the Paurāṇic lists of the Āndhras anywhere.—*Editor*.

B.C. 145. [A Chola Tamil, by name Elāra, succeeded in making himself King of Ceylon, though he was not a Buddhist. He ruled for 44 years when he was killed by a Singhalese prince. Duṭṭhagāmaṇi. *Mahāvaṁśa*. ch. xxi.]

B.C. 101. [Duṭṭhagāmaṇi became King of Ceylon, and reigned for 24 years. During his reign there was much fighting between Singhalese and Tamils.]

B.C. 100. [Approximate date of the arrival in North India of the Kushan tribe of the Yueh-chi, who were driven over the border. They gained great power in Baktria, and after a time their King, Kadphises I conquered Hermaios, the last Greek king of Baktria and made himself sovereign over that country, as also of Gandhāra; the date of Kadphises is placed by Vincent Smith as late as A.D. 40.]

B.C. 72. [The Sunga dynasty of Magadha came to an end, King Dēvabūmi being murdered by his minister the Brahman Vāsudēva, who seized the throne and founded the short lived Kāṇva dynasty.]

B.C. 58. [This date has been accepted by some authorities as marking the beginning of the reign of the Kushan King Kanishka; but there has been much controversy on the point. Vincent Smith makes his accession as late as A.D. 120. At any rate the year 58 B.C. is remarkable as that of the establishment of the 'Vikrama' era in chronology. Kanishka's kingdom in the end included the north-west of India as far east as Benares, and the country southwards to Sindh. His capital was Peshawar.]

B.C. 43. [The King of Ceylon Vaṭṭagāmaṇi Abhaya was attacked in the fifth month of his reign by an army of Pāṇḍya Tamils, and was defeated. For fourteen years Ceylon was ruled over by five Tamils in succession who usurped the throne. The last of them was killed in 29 B.C. when Vaṭṭagāmaṇi-Abhaya regained the throne.]

B.C. 27. [One of the Āndhra kings, either (12) Kuntala, (13) Śāta Śātakarṇi, or (14) Pulumayi I, slew Suśarman the last king of the northern Kāṇva dynasty. After this the Śaka rulers gained the upper hand and their Kushan dynasty governed the country till about A.D. 125.]

B.C. 22. [A Pāṇḍya king sent an embassy to Augustus Cæsar in Rome. He received it at Samos.] (*Strabo, xv. 2, 4*).

A.D. 1. [The following was the political condition of Southern India at this time. The Ganjam and Vizagapatam country was probably governed by the King of Kalinga. The Āndhra king ruled the Godavari and Krishna tracts, with parts of Nellore, Cuddapah and Kurnool. North of what is now the Madras Presidency they had greatly extended their power so as to govern the whole of the Dekhan and even far to the north of it. The Chōla king held the territories lying between Pulikat and Rāmnād on the eastern side of the peninsula, with capital at Puhār on the Kāvērī river (Kānchi or Conjeveram was a Viceroyalty). The Pāṇḍyas held Madura, Tinnevelly, Travancore, part of Coimbatore, Cochin and the Palni Hills. The Chēras ruled the country to the north and west of the Pāṇḍya dominions.

The country between the mouths of the Krishna and the Pālār river was the 'Toṇḍaimaṇḍalam.' (See *Prof. Krishnaswami Aiyangar's 'South Indian Culture', p. 63.*)]

A.D. 20. [For a note as to the flourishing condition of trade between South India and Rome at this time see *Introduction* above.]

A.D. 47. [This trade received an impetus by the discovery made by Hippalos of the regularity of the north-east and south-west monsoons in the Indian Ocean; but it declined after the death of Nero at Rome as his successors discountenanced the love of luxury prevalent in his day.

The Indo-Parthian king Gondophares was now reigning in the Panjab and Sindh.

A.D. 70–80. (Approximately). [The author of the '*Periplus*' mentions the Kēraḷa and Pāṇḍya kings and another called 'Saraganes', which probably stands for Sātakarṇi, the family name of the Āndhra king.

Pliny tells us that the Āndhra king was stronger than the King of Kalinga. The former had an army of 100,000 foot, 2,000 horse, and 1,000 elephants. Both he and Arrian write about the Pāṇḍyas and their capital city Madura. (*For further remarks on the* **Periplus** *see the Introduction.*)]

A.D. 78. [Epoch of the Śaka era in India, which Fleet believed to be the year of accession of the Śaka king Nahapāna, one of the western Kshatrapas, ruling about Nasik.]

A.D. 99, 107. [Indian embassies were sent to Rome in these years, the earlier by Wīma Kadphises of the Kushan dynasty in the north.]

A.D. 113. [Approximate date for the accession of the Āndhra king Vilivāyakura II, or Gautamiputra Śātakarṇi. He is believed to have resided at Dhānyakaṭaka (Amarāvati), while the heir-apparent ruled the Western territories from Paithān. Dr. Barnett's date for this is A.D. 106.]

A.D. 124–25. [Vilivāyakura II sought to crush the rule of the Śaka Satrap Nahapāna and made war on him. He was very successful and wrested from the foreigners the territories of Gujarāt, Mālwa, Kāthiāwār, parts of Central India, Berar, Nasik, Poona and the Northern Konkan. Nahapāna seems to have met his death in the war. He was succeeded by his co-regent Chāshṭhana, son of Ghsamōṭika, who recovered most of the territories north of the Narbada and established a Śaka dynasty which lasted for about 250 years. He made Ujjain his capital. He was known to Ptolemy as 'Tiasthenes'.]

A.D. 138. [Approximate date for the accession of the Āndhra king Pulumāyi II, Vāśishṭhīputra, who married a daughter of the Śaka Satrap Rudradāman I, grandson of Chashṭhana.]

A.D. 145. [Rudradāman made war on his son-in-law, Pulumāyi II the Āndhra king, and inflicted on him a severe defeat. The Āndhras lost all the territory that had remained to them in the west after Chāshṭhana's victory, retaining, beyond their own territory proper, only Nasik and Poona. This loss was a severe blow to them and the family never recovered from it. Nasik and Poona were after this governed by an off-shoot of the Āndhra royal family, the members of which were known as the Chūṭu-Śātakarṇi's. They were eventually crushed by the Kadambas about A.D. 350.]

A.D. 145–46. Inscription at Jangli-guṇḍu, Adoni Taluk, Bellary, of the Āndhra 'king of the Śatāvāhana family', Pulumāyi II, in his eighth regnal year. He is the 'Siro Polemaios' of Ptolemy. (*Ep. Ind. xiv, 153*). The record proves Āndhra rule in that tract and at that time.

A.D. 150. Approximate date for the accession of the Chōḷa king Karikāla Chōḷa. The earliest Chōḷa king known by name was Perunarkiḷḷi I. He had a son Ilanjēṭ-Śenni,[1] who was father of Karikāla. The grand-father and grand-son together fought against the Chera king, Kuḍakkō-Neḍumśēral-Ādan I with the result that both Perunarkiḷḷi and Ādan I lost their lives in the same battle, and the Choḷa throne fell to Karikāla Chōla, his father having probably died earlier. His capital was Puhār, or Pugār or Kāvēripaṭṭanam on the bank of the Kāvērī river.

[1] The prefix Iḷam (= 'young') seems to imply that Karikāla's father did not come to the throne.

He was a very powerful monarch. He is said to have made an expedition to the north. He is also said to have dammed the Kāvērī and constructed irrigation channels—a great work of which we find an echo in the Singhalese *Rājāvaḷiya*, which says that, in the reign in Ceylon of Vankanāsika Tissa, father of Gajabāhu I, 12,000 Singhalese had been carried off to the mainland by the Chōḷa King—possibly as labourers. It states that prince Gajabāhu, accompanied by only one man, who however was a giant went to the Chōla king and by threats induced him to send these men back to the island. At the same time Gajabāhu carried back to Ceylon a number of treasures including the begging-bowl of Buddha which had been carried off from the island 200 years earlier in the time of Vattagāmini Abhaya.

The wealth of Karikāla Chola is described in the old Tamil poems as fabulous. The old Tamil poems relate of him that he gave 160,000 gold pieces to the author of the *Paṭṭinappālai*. (*S.I.I. ii. 375 ; Ep. Ind. xv, 46.*) His daughter married the Chēra King Perum-Śēral-Ādan II.

Arrian, the Greek geographer flourished about this time. About this time also, the Pāṇḍya King Neḍunjeḷian Pāṇḍya I came to the throne in Madura. He was contemporary with Karikāla Chōla and the Chēra King Ādan II. He is said to have defeated an 'Āryan' army in the Dekhan. He is also called 'Ugra Pāṇḍya' or 'Ugra Peruvaḷudi.' His capital was Korkhai on the Tāmraparṇi river, but it was afterwards removed to Madura. The Vēḷvikuḍi grant of about A.D. 770 says that after the reign of Neḍunjeḷian I (*cir.* A.D. 190) the Pāṇḍya country was occupied by the Kaḷabhras who, V. Venkayya thought, might be the Karnāṭas.[1]

A.D. 173. [Probable date of accession of Gajabāhu I, King of Ceylon, determined by its distance in time from the date of Buddha's death which is taken, as in modern computation to have occurred in 483 B.C. It is important to fix this date because Gajabāhu is known to have been a contemporary of the Chēra King Śen-guṭṭuvan who invited him to visit him at his capital city Vanji.

(*Mahāwaṁśa ch. xxxv*).]

A.D. 175. [About this time there was war in South India. Karikāla Chōḷa quarrelled with his son-in-law the Chera Ādan II and fought against him. The Pāṇḍya Neḍunjeḷian allied himself with Ādan II. The allies were badly beaten at the battle of Veṇṇil and Ādan II was so ashamed at his ill-success that he starved himself to death. He was succeeded by his son Śenguṭṭuvan on the Chēra throne.]

A. D. 180. [Conjectural date for the death of Karikāla Chōla and accession of his elder son Neḍumuḍi-Kiḷḷi who was also called by many other names in the Tamil Epics, such as 'Vaḍivēr-Kiḷḷi,' 'Velvēr-Kiḷḷi' and 'Māvaṇ-Kiḷḷi.' He also fought with the allied Chēras and Pāṇḍyas and won a battle against them at Kāriyāṛu. Neḍumuḍi-kiḷḷi had a younger-brother Śeṭ-Śenni-Nalam Kiḷḷi who revolted and besieged his King at Uraiyūr and Āmūr, near Trichinopoly. The Chēra King Śenguṭṭuvan, however, took the field against Nalam-kiḷḷi and rescued Neḍumuḍi-kiḷḷi after fighting a battle at Nērivāyil when, so say Chēra records, he defeated nine 'Kiḷḷis' or Chōla royal princes.

Śenguṭṭuvan has other successes laid to his credit by his admirers, namely that he vanquished certain Āryan princes in the north, Kanaka and Vijaya; and captured the town of Viyalūr from local Kongu chiefs.

A great misfortune befel the Chōla king Neḍumuḍi-Kiḷḷi about this time. His capital Puhār was completely destroyed by a great storm, when the sea broke in and ruined the city. It was

[1] This grant states that the Kaḷabhras came some considerable time after one Mudukuḍumi 'of many sacrifices' —The Kaḷabhras could not be Karnāṭakas as the two are mentioned together.—*Editor*.

apparently after this, when he had taken refuge in Uraiyur, that he was besieged there by his brother, as above mentioned.[1]

Neḍumuḍi-Kiḷḷi was father of the Tonḍamān prince Iḷandiraiyan by an illicit amour with, so says tradition, a Nāga princess.

Professor Krishnaswami Aiyangar believes this age of Śenguṭṭuvan Chēra to have been the age of the *Śangam* at Madura.]

A.D. 200. [Conjectural date for the accession of the Chōla King Perunarkiḷḷi II, whose relationship to his predecessors is not known; and also for that of the Chēra King Śey or Yānaikkaṭ-Śey. There was war between these kings. And King Śey also fought against the Pānḍya King Neḍunjeḷian II who, at the battle of Talai-Ālangānan, captured King Śey and held him prisoner. Opinions differ as to the date of this battle and of these kings' reigns. Dr. Barnett places it in A.D. 125. Prof. Krishnaswami Aiyangar, I understand, in about A.D. 300. I claim no superior knowledge.

After this history is almost a blank in the extreme south till about the sixth century A.D. We know no name of any Chēra King after King Śey till the reign of Perum-Śēral Irumporai. No Chōla ruler's name is known till the date of Kō-Chchengaṇ except a possible Śubha-dēva. And with the exception of two names, with no guide as to relationship, no Pānḍya kings' names are known till the reign of Kaḍungōn. The two names are Ugra-Peru-Vaḷudi (a title), and Nan-Māran. Perum-Śēral-Irumporai (Chēra), Kōchchengaṇ (Chōla) and Kaḍungōn (Pānḍya) all belong to the sixth century A.D. On the other hand we have full information of the flourishing Pallava dynasty of Kānchi during the whole of this interval.

It should be noted that, since the middle of the second century A.D., the provinces of Nasik and Poona had been governed by the Chūṭu-Śatakārṇi's, a branch of the Āndhras. Hāritīputra-Chūṭu-Kadānanda-Śātakarṇi established himself as independent at Baṇavāśi. The family was defeated by Bappa, the first prominent Pallava King about A.D. 225.]

A.D. *c.* 225. [Bappa had been Governor of large tracts under the last Śātavāhana (Āndhra) King, Pulumāyi III. The Āndhra kingdom had now shrunk to small size, consisting practically of nothing but the Telugu provinces, and Bappa finally put an end to the Āndhra dynasty and, ruling himself from Kānchi, seized their dominions. Following him his descendants became a first-class power. Pallava rule lasted for over 600 years. The old Āndhra capital at Amarāvati became the seat of a Pallava Viceroyalty, and we find Bappa's son Śivaskanda I issuing orders about A.D. 234 (Bappa's 10th year) to his Viceroy at Dhannakaḍa (= Amarāvati). The Pallavas then ruled the whole Coromandel coast; and the power of the Chōlas proportionally declined.

(The origin of the name 'Pallava' is a subject greatly debated, and it need not here be considered.)]

A.D. *c.* 234. Copper-plate inscription found at Mayidavōlu in the Kistna District. It was issued by Śiva-Skandavarman, heir-apparent to the new Pallava throne, in the 10th year of the reign of his father Bappa, who established the Pallava dynasty. The order was given to the Pallava Viceroy at 'Dhannakaḍa' or Amarāvati; and consisted of a grant of villages in the 'Āndhra country' (*Āndhrapatha*). (*Ep. Ind. vi. 84*).

[1] He is also said to have attacked Madura fruitlessly, having been driven back by the Pānḍya King Neḍunjeḷian II. and he is credited with having attacked Vānji, the Chera King's capital, but with little effect.

Another copper-plate record was found at Koṇḍamūḍi, on the north-bank of the Krishna near its mouth which is reported to be in characters closely resembling those of the Mayidavōlu plates. It purports to have been issued in the tenth regnal year of Jayavarman Mahārāja, who was in his 'Camp of Victory' at Gūḍur, near by, at the time. It is not known who this Jayavarman was, but it is just *possible* that it may have been a name adopted by Bappa.[1]

(*Ep. Ind. vi. 315 ; V. R. ii. Guntūr, 838.*)

A.D. 250, or thereabouts. [Accession (according to Professor Jouveau-Dubreuil's date) of the second king of the Pallava Dynasty, Śivaskandavarman.]

A.D. *c.* 257. Hīrahadagali plates (Bellary District). Grant by Śivaskandavarman, Pallava king, in his eighth year of reign. Sacrifices offered by him are mentioned. He gave away a village in the 'Śātāhaniraṭṭha.' This was in the country which had been ruled by the Chūṭu-Sātakarṇi branch of the Āndhras. (*Ep. Ind. i, 2.*)

About the same time another set of plates, now in the British Museum, mention the Yuvarāja (crown prince) Buddhavarman and his wife Charu-dēvī. Buddhavarman was son of Śivaskanda.

(*Ep. Ind. viii. 143.*)

A.D. 275. [In Ceylon Vohāraka Tissa came to the throne in succession to his father Śirināga I. Tissa's brother Abhaya Nāga revolted, and fled to the main land. There he collected an army of Tamils. With these he returned to the island, defeated Tissa, and caused him to fly for refuge to the Malaya country, whither he was pursued and killed, Abhaya carrying off Tissa's queen.

(*Mahawaṁśa ch. xxxvi.*)

A.D. 319–20. [Chandragupta I, chief of a small principality near Pātaliputra, who had been very energetic and had made himself independent about A.D. 308, was crowned in 319–20. He married a princess of the Lichchavi family. His descendants came to great power, their empire, that of the 'Guptas', embracing the valley of the Ganges, Allahabad, Tirhut, Bihar and Oudh.]

A.D. 336. [He was succeeded in this year by his son, Samudragupta, who raised large forces and waged many wars. After defeating, according to his panegyrist (e.g. the Allahabad pillar inscription—*Ep. Ind. xv*, 246) nine local kings he warred successfully against eleven kings of the Gangetic plain. Then he seized southern Kōsala and the valley of the Mahānadi; defeated the King of Kalinga; took Mahēndragiri in Ganjam, the Kolēr Lake country and Piṭhāpur north of the Godāvari; crossed that river and seized Vengi, now a Pallava centre governed by a Viceroy named Hastivarma. Then he defeated the Pallava king himself, Vishnugōpa I of Kānchi, captured him and his city and restored him to his throne. Shortly after this his attention was called to the west and about A.D. 340 he reduced a chief on the Malabar coast. Samudragupta reigned till about A.D. 380.

Between A.D. 364 and 380 he received an embassy from King Kīrtti-Śrī-Mēghavaṇṇa of Ceylon, whose reign began, according to the revised chronology, in A.D. 354. The *Mahāwaṁśa* (ch. xxxvii) relates that during that reign a Brahman princess 'from Kalinga' brought the tooth-relic to Ceylon. (*See Ep. Ind. xv. 246.*)

About A.D. 375 the Gupta king, after a period of fighting succeeded in getting the better of the Śaka Satraps, and he and his successors finally crushed Śaka power before the end of the century.

[1] The word 'Bappa' merely means 'father.' It would not be surprising if on his acquisition of real power this ruler adopted a more high-sounding name.

After the departure from Kanchi of Samudragupta, the Pallava king induced the Kadamba chief of Banavāsi to form a defensive alliance with him against attacks from the north. Although actnally the power of the Pallava lost strength after the Gupta raid and the Kadamba family became proportionally stronger, the latter acknowledged the Pallava sovereign as their political superior. Banavāsi had been captured from the Āndhra Chūṭu-Sātakarṇis. The Pallava king Vishṇugopa I crowned the Kadamba Mayūraśarma about A.D. 340.]

A. D. 340. A record at Talgund, Shimoga District, Mysore, gives an account of the foundation of the long-lived Kadamba dynasty of Banavāsi. It belongs to the reign of Kākusthavarman (A.D. 425-450), and presents the history of the times from a Kadamba standpoint. A Brahman named Mayūraśarma went to Kānchi as a theological student, rebelled against the life, became a freebooter, raised a force, fought against Pallava troops, seized lands in the Dekhan and as far east as Śrīśailam, levied tribute from the Bana chiefs of North Arcot, whose residence was at Tiruvallam, and finally became so troublesome that the Pallava king came to terms with him, and about A.D. 340 recognized him as legitimate lord of Banavāsi, Hāngal, and other larger tracts. Mayūraśarma finally put an end to the Chūtu-Sātakarṇi rule in that country.

(*Ep. Carn. iv. Introd. 1 ; Ep. Ind. vii. 105 ; viii. App. ii. 19.*)

About the fourth century A.D. A set of plates from Komarti in Ganjam, dated in the sixth year of the Sālankāyana chief Chandavarman. We hear also of his son Vijaya-Nandivarman, and of an earlier ruler Dēvavarman who issued an order to the villagers of Ellore in his thirteenth year. This is in Prakrit, the others are in Sanskrit. These chiefs were descendants, probably, of the Āndhras, and still retained some local power in Vengi and the neighbourhood.

(*E.R. iv. 142 ; Ep. Ind. ix. 56.*)

[The Pallavas, though secure at Kānchi at the time could not extend their power as much as they wished because of the constant opposition of the Bana chiefs of North Arcot and the neighbourhood, who were also known as 'Mahvali' chiefs. The two families were therefore very hostile to one another. But Professor Jouveau-Dubreuil holds that Pallava power extended as far south as Pudukotta. And this led to the Pallava king procuring the assistance of a Ganga chief of the Mysore country towards the conquest of the Baṇas, who ruled the tracts 'West of the Telugu road ']

A.D. 436. Date of accession, according to Fleet, of the Pallava king Simhavarman I. He consecrated, perhaps about A.D. 450, the Ganga King Harivarman, or Ayyavarman, 'to conquer the Bāna dominions.'

(*Ep. Carn. ii, Introd. App. A ; Ep. Ind. vii. 110.*) *J.R.A.S. 1915, pp. 476, 485.*]

A.D. 425–450. Period of the Talgunḍ record of Kadamba Kakusthavarma referred to above, *s.v.* A.D. 340.

A.D. c. 426(?). [According to Professor Jouveau-Dubreuil the Pallava Kumāra-Vishṇu II, came to the throne about A.D. 425. A record of his second year witnesses the gift of the village of Chandalūr in Nellore District by him (*Ep. Ind. viii. 233*). Relying on date of the Penukonda plates of A.D. 458 (*see below*), this inscription would seem to belong to a year considerably earlier. For three reigns intervened between Kumāra-Vishṇu II and Simhavarman I, and the latter came to the throne in the year ending August 25, A.D. 436.]

A.D. 446. This Uruvupalle copper-plate grant of this date was issued in the eleventh year of Pallava Simhavarman I. It shews that his predecessor Vijava Skandavarman died and he came to the throne ten years earlier. (See *s.v., A.D. 458 below.*) He made a grant to a rock-cut temple, the *Mūlasthāna*, at Tirukkaḷukuṉṟam in Chingleput District.

(*Ep. Ind. iii. 277; Dubreuil 'Antiquities', p. 43.*)

A.D. 420. Approximately (but about 450 according to Dubreuil). Grant of a village in the neighbourhood of Vengi by the Pallava Vīrakūrchavarman, son of Skandavarman III.

(*Ep. Ind. i. 397; Ind. Ant. v. 50, 154; viii. 168.*)

A.D. 450, roughly. The Kadamba Śāntivarma ruling at Baṇavāśi. An inscription gives him Āndhra titles, probably derived from the Chuṭu-Sātakarṇi chiefs of Āndhra stock ejected by the Kadambas, and it calls him 'Master of the entire Karnāṭa region.' Grant by one of his family in his third year. (*E. C. vi. Kd. 162.*)

About the same time. Record on copper-plates from Rāgōlu in Ganjam. Vaśishṭhīputra Śaktivarman ruling Piṭhāpūr. He is called 'Lord of Kalinga.' (*Ep. Ind. xii. p. 1.*) The prefix to his name is evidently derived from the Āndhras.

Rice places at this time an interesting stone inscription of Dēvavarman-Śivanandavarman, prince of the dynasty of Kadambas of Baṇavāśi and son of king Krishnavarman I by a princess, 'daughter of Kaikeya.' It is at Anaji in North Mysore. It states that Krishnavarman having been completely defeated and ruined by the Pallava Rāja Nanakkāsa, Śivananda retired into a life of seclusion and penance. (*E. C. xi. Dg. 161.*)

A.D. 458, August 25. Notice of the early Ganga king Mādhava II, from Penukoṇḍa. The date is as stated, and, as it is given as the twenty-second year of the Pallava king Simhavarman I, it makes the latter's accession in the year ending 25th August A.D. 436. It says that Mādhava II had been crowned by Pallava Skandavarman. Skandavarman was son of Simhavarman I and therefore it would seem that he, being Yuvarāja, had been appointed by his father to conduct the ceremony in question. (*J. R. A. S. 1915, p. 471. f. 485.*)

A.D. 466. Mercara (Coorg) Treasury plates. Grant by the Ganga king Avinīta, son of Mādhava II. The date is defective in two respects and cannot be safely trusted.

(*E. C. i. Coorg Inscriptions, No. 1.*)

A.D. 471–72. Date of accession of the Kadamba king of Banavāśi, Mrigēśavarman, according to a record of his third year = A.D. 473–74. (See *Fleet, Sans. and Old Kan. Inscriptions No. xxxvi, Ind. Ant. 1878, p. 35.*) He claims to have defeated the Western Gangas. (*Ep. Ind. v. 157.*)

A.D. 477–78. Record of the Kadamba Mrigēśavarman in his eighth year. (*Ind. Ant. 1877, 24.*)

A.D. c. 490. An undated record at Siraguṇḍa in Mysore of the Ganga king Durvinīta; stating that when he received the Konguṇi crown from the 'Kāḍuveṭṭi' (i.e. the Pallava) king, his younger brother was roused to anger, and to pacify him 'the people of Nandyāl granted him a share in a village.' (*E. C. vi. Cm. 50; E. C. xii, Mi. 110.*)

The *Mahāwaṁśa* relates that at this time about A.D. 496, a Tamilian named Pāṇḍu probably a Pāṇḍya prince, landed in Ceylon with an armed force, slew king Mittasēna who had, in the previous year, usurped the throne of the island, and himself seized it. Pāṇḍu surrounded himself with Tamils, and he and several successors ruled Ceylon for over twenty years.

(*Mahawaṁśa ch. xxxviii.*)

A.D. 500. [Professor Dubreuil fixes this as the date of accession of the Kadamba king Ravivarman. He slew Vishṇuvarman I, and defeated the Pallava Skandavarman V, and established himself at Halsi.]

A.D. 500. [Vincent Smith (*J. R. A. S. 1914, p. 137*) places about this time a Vishṇukuṇḍin chief, Mādhavavarma, who married the daughter of the Vākāṭaka chief Harishēna, and by the latter's influence succeeded in getting possession of the Vengi country, south of the Godavari river. Harishēna claimed to have conquered the Āndhra country and Kalinga. It is believed, however, that by the term 'Āndhra' may be meant the country that had been ruled by the Śālankāyana chiefs further west than Vengi. Nevertheless Mādhavavarma settled himself at Denḍalūr close to Vengi. Since the Pallavas undoubtedly ruled that tract, these Vishṇukuṇḍins must have been only minor chiefs.]

A.D. *c.* 500. The Pikira grant of a village in the 'Munḍarāshṭra' province by the Pallava prince Simhavarman II, son of the Yuvarāja Viśhṇugōpa. It was issued from his camp at Mēnmātūra. (*Madras Museum, V. R. ii. Madras 183* ; *Ep. Ind. viii. 159.*) He also gave a village in the Vengi country. (*Ind. Ant. viii. 154.*)

An inscription in the Punganūr Taluk, Chittoor District, and therefore in the ancient 'Pulināḍu,' of Prithivipati, brother of the Ganga king Durvinīta. (*V. R. i. Chittoor 215 ; 326 of 1912.*)

About this time, according to Jouveau-Dubreuil's chronology the Kadamba Ravivarma came to the throne. The date cannot be far wrong for his father's accession has been fairly proved to have taken place in A.D. 471. Ravivarman claims to have conquered the Pallava Chanḍadanḍa of Kānchi, i.e. Skandavarman V ; also he claims to have conquered the Western Ganga king, and that at least he had some temporary success is shewn by his grant of two villages near Talakāḍ, the Ganga capital in Mysore. (*Ep. Ind. viii. 146.*)

[The beginning of the sixth century A.D., then, found the whole country disturbed. The Pallavas and Gangas had united against the turbulent Bāṇa chiefs, but the Kadambas had warred against both the allies. Kadamba Mrigēśavarma claims a victory over the Gangas, while somewhat earlier the Pallavas had 'ruined' the Kadamba country for the time being. (See above *s. v.* A.D. 450.)]

A.D. 517–18. Mallōhalli plates, No. 2, in Mysore. Grant by the Western Ganga king Durvinīta in his thirty-fifth year. A pedigree of five generations is given. It makes his accession as in A.D. 483–84 (*E. C. ix, D—B 68*). The Kuḍlūr grant (*Mysore Arch. Sur. 1921, p. 1920*) states that he fought many battles, some of which are mentioned, viz., those at Andāri, Alattūr, Puruḷare and Pernagara ; that he captured the 'Kāḍuveṭṭi' (i.e. the Pallava king, and if so the friendships existing between their families did not last long) ; and that he ruled over the 'Pānāḍu and Punnāḍu' countries. The Punnāḍu country was in South Mysore.

[About this year A.D. 517, or 523 according to another computation, Dhatusēna seized the throne of Ceylon from the Pānḍya usurpers who had ruled since A.D. 496. He extirpated the Tamils in the island. (*Mahawamśa ch. xxxviii.*)]

A.D. 545. **September** 21. Sangoli C. P. grant, made from Banavāśi. The Kadamba king Harivarman reigning there. (*Ep. Ind. xiv. 163.*) [The date may be September 22, A.D. 526, but is probably as given. Granted this, his accession was in A.D. 537–38.]

A.D. 541–42. Halsi C. P. grant. This record shews that Uchchangi, on the extreme northern border of Mysore, was then a Kadamba possession, being ruled by Śivaratha, uncle of the reigning king Harivarman. (*Ind. Ant. vi., p. 30.*)

[A.D. *c.* 550. Approximate date for accession of the early Chāḷukya king in the Dekhan, Pulakeśin I. His grandfather Jayasimha, a chief of the Mānavya-gōtra claiming descent from Hāritī, had acquired great power half a century earlier in the country about Bijapūr. His success was mainly due to the fact that the persistent inroads of Huns and Śakas into the Dekhan had broken up the Gupta Empire. The last Gupta king Bhānugupta became, in the early sixth century A. D. a tributary of the Hun leaders. Pulakēśin's original capital was Paithān. He afterwards seized Bādāmi, or Vātāpi, and the surrounding country from the Kadamba king. Harivarma (A.D. 537 to 550). Pulakēśin married Durlabha-dēvī. He was also called 'Raṇavikrama'.]

A.D. c. 556. Bannahaḷḷi C. P. grant. The seventh regnal year of Kadamba Krishnavarma II whose accession M. Jouveau-Dubreuil places in A.D. 550. It gives a pedigree of his forefathers for four generations. *(E. C. v. Bl. 121.)*

A.D. 565. [The Chāḷukya Kīrttivarmā I came to the throne in succession to his father Pulakēśin I. He fought a number of battles and before the year A.D. 570 defeated a confederation of Kadamba princes, headed by Krishnavarman II. The Kadambas are little heard of after this. They succumbed to the Chāḷukyas. Kīrttivarma is said in inscriptions to have conquered seventeen southern nations. He began the construction of the cave-temples at Bādāmi. He also claims to have defeated the kings of Kalinga.]

A.D. 575. Conjectural date, according to Dubreuil, for the accession of the Pāṇḍya king Kaḍungōn at Madura, who founded a dynasty that lasted about 300 years. Prior to Kaḍungōn the Pāṇḍya country had lain under a long interregnum of Kaḷabhra rulers. The Vēḷvikuḍi grant and the two Sinnāmānūr grants are one authority for this. (Since published *Ep. Ind. xvii, 291 ; S.I.I. iii, pt. iv, 441 ff.*) *(Ep. Rep. 1908, p. 62 ; Ep. Ind. viii, 318 ; Ind. Ant. 1908, p. 193 ; 1922, p. 221.)*

About this time the 'Rēnāṇḍu 7000' country (i.e., the districts of Cuddapah and Kurnool) was ruled by a family of Telugu Chōḍa chiefs (See *General : Tables s. v. Chola*). They claimed descent from Karikāla Chōla, and used the tiger-seal of that house. The date rests on the assumption that a chief of the third known generation, Mahēndra, was named after the Pallava king Mahēndravarman I. The late V. Venkayya held that this family may represent the 'Chu-li-ye' chiefs described in A.D. 639 by the Chinese traveller Hiuen-Thsang.

(Ep. Rep. 1904–5, p. 48.)

A.D. 594, February 10. Polamūr, Godavari District. Grant, in his forty-eighth regnal year by the Vishṇukuṇḍin king Mādhava III, fixing his accession as in the year following February 10, 546. He states that he had 'crossed the river (Godavari) in order to attack in the East.' His capital being at Deṇḍalūr, south of that river, he was probably marching to attack the kingdom of Kalinga. *(Ep. Rep. C. P. No. 7 of 1913–14 ; Journal of Department of Letters, Univ. of Calcutta. XI. (31, A. D. 192.)*

The fourth Vishṇukuṇḍin chief Vikramēndravarman gave a grant of villages on the Krishna river bank at Ṛavirēva (modern Ravirēla). *(Ep. Ind. iv, 193.)*

[The Vishṇukuṇḍins were descendants of Mādhava II who had married a Vākāṭaka princess, and had been installed as ruler of the Vengi country in place of the Sālankāyanas, by the Vākāṭaka king.]

A.D. c. 600. The Pallava kings Simhavishṇu-Pōtarāja *alias* 'Avanisimha' and Mahēndra-Pōtarāja I are mentioned in several inscriptions of about this date at the rock-cut temples at Mahābalipuram (*Ep. Rep. 1923, p. 24 ; 661–665 of 1922*); and in many other places in what was afterwards the territory of the Chōḷas. Simhavishṇu is said to have won many victories.

A record in the cave-temple at Vallam (*V. R. i. Chingleput 242 ; 185 of 1892*) shews that the poet Appar lived in the reign of Mahēndra I. Appar was one of the composers of the *Tēvāram* hymns. Mahēndra is here called by his *biruda* 'Guṇabhara.'

At Trichinopoly, at the cave temple on the hill, are two inscriptions on pillars. Here Mahēndra is said to have gazed 'on the power of the Chōla' while the rock is called the 'diadem of the Chōla province', and the Kāvērī river is named the 'beloved of the Pallava'. It would seem therefore that Pallava power had by this time spread to the south; that the country near to and east of Trichinopoly belonged to the Chōla; that the Kāvērī river had been crossed by the Pallava king; and that he had ejected the Chola chief from Trichinopoly.

(*V. R. iii. Trichin. 777, 778 ; 63, 64 of 1888 ; S.I.I., i, 28.*)

That Mahēndra I was actually dominating large tracts at this time is shown by his having excavated many cave temples at Trichinopoly, Vallam, Śīyamangalam, Daḷāvānūr; Mahēndravāḍi, Manḍagapaṭṭu . . . [1] etc. (*Ep. Rep. 1904–5.*)

One of his inscriptions is at the Mahēndravāḍi temple near Sholinghar. (*Ep. Ind. iv, 152.*) Another is at Śīyamangalam in North Arcot. (*Ep. Ind. vi, 319.*) M. Jouveau-Dubreuil has written at length about these rock-cut temples in several recent works—'Pallava Antiquities', etc. . . . . He holds that though the Pallavas were driven out of their northern possessions by the conquering Chāḷukyas, they ruled as far south as Pudukota.

[In A. D. 597 the Chāḷukya king Kīrttivarmā I was succeeded by his brother Mangalēṣa. A Mātanga tribe was destroyed by Mangalēśa; and he defeated in 609 Buddharāja, the Kaṭachuri ruler of Chēdi, in the Mahākōsala country of Central India (*Vaḍner plates, Ep. Ind. vi, 294 ; xii, 30.*) He slew a 'Chāḷukya' chief in the Konkan, perhaps a rebel, called 'Svāmiraja'. Mangalēśa is said to have lost his own life in an endeavour to secure the throne for his own son Dhruvarāja *alias* Indravarman, in opposition to the claims of the rightful heir, Pulakēśin II, son of Kīrttivarma I. Pulakēśin II succeeded in gaining the throne in A.D. 609. (*Ind. Ant. 1881, p. 57 ; 1891, p. 3.*)

Pulakēśin (A.D. 609–642) was very successful. He drove the Mauryas from the Konkan, completely crushed the Kadambas of Baṇavāśi, defeated king Harsha of Kanauj about A. D. 620 when the latter tried a campaign to his south; defeated the Pallava Mahēndra I and drove him out from the northern Telugu country, taking the city of Pithāpūr; and defeated also the kings of Kōsala and Kalinga (*Ep. Ind. ix, 200*). He established his brother Kubja Vishṇuvardhana at Vengī, and the latter became the founder of the very important Eastern Chāḷukya dynasty.

(*Ear. Hist. Dekh., p. 2 ; Ep. Ind. iii, 2.*)

The Kaśākuḍi plates of A. D. 738–39 say that Mahēndra I defeated Pulakēśin II at Puḷḷalūra near Kānchi. W. Chāḷukya records say that Pulakēśin II 'made the leader of the Pallavas take refuge behind the ramparts of Kānchi.' But this is not a claim to have actually captured Kānchi, which he would have done if victorious, and this leads to the supposition that he was really beaten back from Puḷḷalūra, after having advanced as far as that place.

Kubja Vishṇuvardhana became ruler of the Vengi country in A.D. 615, and henceforth the Chāḷukya families have to be treated separately as Western and Eastern Chāḷukyas. He was practically king in the year following July 8, A.D. 614.

(*Ind. Ant. xx, 1891, pp. 1, 93, 266.*)]

[1] The Manḍagapaṭṭu inscription says that Mahēndra 'abandoned the use of bricks, timber, metals or mortar' in constructing his shrines, thereby implying that previously temples had been raised by the use of those materials.

A.D. 619. A C. P. grant now in the Madras Museum of this year's date shews that part of Ganjam District including the Aska Taluk was ruled by members of the Śailōdbhava family, of whom at the time Mādhavavarman II 'Mahāsāmanta Sainyabhīta', grandson of Mādhava I, was feudatory to King Harsha of Thanēsar. *(V. R. i. Ganjam 12 ; E. I. vi, p. 143.)*

A.D. 630. [The Pallava king Narasimhavarman I came to the throne probably in this year in succession to Mahēndra I. His territory was shrunk in the north by the Chāḷukya conquest, but somewhat expanded in the south. In his reign lived Gñāna Sambandar *(Ep. Ind. iii, 278)*. The reign is remarkable for the construction by him of the great rock-cut group of temples at Mahābalipuram, on the coast south of Madras, the original name of which was 'Māmallapuram' after Māmalla, a *biruda* of Narasimha.

He fought several battles and inflicted in A.D. 642 a crushing defeat on the Chāḷukya king, as will be seen from the notes below.]

A.D. 631. The Chinese pilgrim Hiuen-Thsang visited India, and travelled in various parts for about twelve years. He left behind him a most valuable book of notes and observations on his journeys and what he saw. He states that Buddhism was declining and Brahmanism on the increase.

A.D. 632. July 7. Chipurapalle C. P. grant, Vizagapatam District. It shews Kubja-Vishṇuvardhana as sovereign at that time and place. He is called 'Vishama Siddhi', and was then in his eighteenth regnal year. It fixes his accession as in the year following July 8, A.D. 614. *(V. R. iii Vizag. 16 ; Ind. Ant. xx, 1891, p. 15.)*

A.D. 633. [Death of the Eastern Chāḷukya king Kubja-Vishṇuvardhana, and accession of his son Jayasimha I.]

A.D. 635. October 31. Two grants of land on the same day by the E. Chaḷukya Vishṇuvardhana II, son according to one and nephew according to the other, of Jayasimha I, the occasion being a lunar eclipse in Kārttika in the third regnal year. It appears to me that this third year must be that of Jayasimha. No hint as to the year, either the cyclic year or that of any era, is given. But there was a lunar eclipse in Kārttika on October 31, A.D. 635, and this was Jayasimha's third year. Vishṇuvardhana's own third regnal year would be A.D. 665–66 and there was no eclipse in Kārttika in that year. The Epigraphist suggests that Vishṇuvardhana had been adopted as his son by Jayasimha.

(Ep. Rep. 1917. App. A., C. P. 14, 15 and Report §20.)

A.D. 634–35. Aihoḷē inscription of the W. Chāḷukya Pulakēśin II. He is said to have, before this date, subdued the kings of Kalinga and Kosala, taken Piṭhāpur, occupied the Kolēr Lake country near Ellore, defeated the Pallavas near Kānchi, and crossed the Kāvērī.

(Ep. Ind. vi, 1.)

[Thus it appears that the Chāḷukyas swept the whole Pallava country from north to south. The latter however recovered themselves a little later.]

Pallava Narasimha I was able to keep his court in Kānchi. About A.D. 640 he received as a guest Prince Mānavamma of Ceylon, son of Kassapa II, who had left the island on account of internal plots and disturbances, and the two became great friends. Narasimha I reorganized his forces, attacked the Chāḷukya intruders, fought several battles and gradually drove them back into their own country. In this he was assisted by Mānavamma. . . . His success was such that he was able to advance his armies to the

Chāḷukya capital, Bādāmi, finally capturing and destroying the city. This was in A.D. 642. Ever since then he was known by his having assumed the title 'Vātāpikoṇḍa' or capturer of Vātāpi (Bādāmi).

Many distinguished religious leaders and poets flourished at this time. Appar, already mentioned, and Tirugñāna Sambandar, two of the 63 Śaiva devotees, composed the *Tēvāram* collection of Śaiva hymns. One of these devotees Śiruttoṇḍa Nāyanār assisted in the destruction of Bādāmi, and he was visited by Tirugñāna Sambandar—a fact which fixes the date of these authors. Śiruttoṇḍa Nāyanār appears to have been one of Narasimha Pallava's generals.

Three of Narasimha's battles against the Chāḷukyas are mentioned, viz., at Pariyaḷa, Maṇimangalam and Śūramāra (*S.I.I., vol. i, 144 f, the Kūram,* C. P. grant). Another record credits him with a victory over the Kaḷabhras.

That this complete defeat of Pulakēśin II really occurred is supported by admissions in their own records which state that, after the destruction of Bādāmi, the city 'was left without a sovereign for thirteen years.' It is a fact that there is no known record of Pulakēśin II after A.D. 642, and that his successor only began to reign in 655. Pulākēśin is said to have been killed in the war.

[Narasimha is said in some records to have 'conquered Ceylon', but this is a poetic exaggeration. He only sent troops to Ceylon to assist Mānavamma to recover his throne, about A.D. 668. (Cf. the *Mahāwaṁśa, ch. xlvii.*)]

About this time, according to the Malepāḍu C. P. grant, a family of 'Chōla-Mahārājas', claiming descent from Karikāla Chōla, were ruling the 'Rēnāṇḍu 7000' country—parts of Cuddapah, Kurnool and Nellore Districts. The grant mentions Puṇya-kumāra *alias* Pormukha-Rāma as ruling, and gives his pedigree for four generations. The late V. Venkayya believed these chiefs to be the 'Chuliye' alluded to by the Chinese visitor Hiuen Thsang in A.D. 639 (*V. R. i. Cudd. 435, 455. E. R. 1904-5, p. 48*). Puṇya-kumāra is mentioned on a *vīrakal* at Chippili, near Madanapalli in Cuddapah District.

(*E. I. xi, 337, see below, s. v. End of the eighth century A.D.*)

A.D. c. 650. Niḍamarru, Guntur District. C. P. grant of the village, insufficiently dated, by E. Chāḷukya king Jayasimha I. (*Ep. Rep. 1917, App. A. No. 7.*)

[In the Pāṇḍya country about this time was reigning King Māravarman-Arikēśari-Asamasaman. His principal achievements were victories at Pāḷi and at Nelvēli (Tinnevelly), the latter over an army of *Vilvēli*, or bowmen. He conquered the Kērala king. (*See the Vēḷvikuḍi and two Śinnamanūr grants. Ep. Rep. 1907, 1908, p. 62 ; Ind. Ant. 1908, p. 193 ; 1922, p. 211 ; Ep. Ind. viii, 318 ; also Ep. Ind. xvii, 291 ff. & S.I.I. iii, pt. iv, 441 ff.*)]

A.D. 654. After September 24 this year and before July 655, according to the Talamanchi, plates in the Nellore District and the Nērūr grant, began to reign the W. Chāḷukya king Vikramāditya I. He collected forces after the thirteen years' interregnum alluded to above and attacked his Pallava enemy. A long war followed, during which it is claimed for Vikramāditya that he defeated three Pallava kings. These must have been Narasimha I, Mahēndra II and Paramēśvara-Pōtavarman I (*V. R. ii, Nellore 483 ; B. and V. C. i, 189 ; Ind. Ant. vii, 163. See below s. v., A.D. 674 ; also Ep. Ind. ix, 200*). The date of the Talamanchi grant is July 13, 650. It was issued in the sixth year of Vikramāditya I.

A.D. 654–55. C. P. grant, Collector's office, Kurnool. Two villages granted in fourth year of W. Chāḷukya Vikramāditya I (*V. R. ii, Kurnool i, Ind. Ant. xi, 67, J. B. B. R. A. S. xvi, 238*). It shews that Kurnool was then ruled by the Western, not Eastern, Chāḷukya king.

A.D. 657–58. Grant of land in Kurnool by the same (*V. R. ii, Kurnool 5 ; J.B.B.R.A.S. xvi, 235*). Vikramāditya's third regnal year.

A.D. 663. Another grant in Kurnool by the same king in his tenth year.

(*V. R. ii. Kur.* 6 ; *J. B. B. R. A. S. xvi, 238.*)

Grant of a village in Godavari District by the Eastern Chālukya prince, or king, Indravarmā, son of Kubja-Vishṇuvardhana. This is Indra-Bhaṭṭāraka whose actual reign only lasted for seven days. He probably ruled the Godāvāri tract for his father.

(*Ep. Rep. 1922, App. A*, C.P. *2.*)

[He was defeated by Indravarman, king of Kalinga, and a combination of chiefs.]

A.D. 664. March 13. Nellore District Indra-Bhaṭṭāraka's son Vishṇuvardhana II was now Eastern Chāḷukya king. A C. P. grant of this date shews him on the throne (*V.R. iii B.M. p.* 1721, *C. P. 2 ; Ind. Ant. VII, 186 ; VIII, 320*). The grant is one of his second year.

A.D. 668. Feb. 17. Grant by the same in his fifth year. This and the last one shew that he came to the throne between 18 February and 13 March A.D. 663 (*V.R. iii. Bm. C.P. 3 ; Ind. Ant. vii, 191 ; xx, 9 ; E.I. vii App. 93 ; E.R. 1917, App. A, 14–15*).

[The Pallava king Paramēśvara-Pōtavarman *alias* Iśvara-Potarāja came to the throne in A.D. 670. He and his predecessors Narasimha Varman, whose reign ended in 668, and Mahēndravarman II (668–70), had been at war, as above stated, with the Western Chāḷukya Vikramāditya I, another of whose names was 'Raṇarasika'. Western Chāḷukya records claim for Vikramāditya that (in or after A.D. 670) he defeated 'Īśvara-Pōtarāja', and took Kānchi, the Pallava capital, 'but did not destroy it.'

Pallava records also tell us that Paramēśvara-Pōtavarman seized 'the city of Raṇarasika', i.e., a city of Vikramāditya Chāḷukya's, but we are not told its name.

It is impossible to fix exact times and places, but it seems clear that the Pallavas were beaten and that the Chāḷukya king entered Kānchi, about A.D. 670, or it may be about 674.

Vikramāditya seems to have pushed on to the south, where he was opposed by the Pāṇḍya king Kōchchaḍaiyan, and near Trichinopoly a battle was fought at Peruvaḷanallūr as well as at Mangaḷāpuram and Marudūr. Pallava and Pāṇḍya records equally claim that in this battle the Chāḷukya was defeated. Vikramāditya evidently had now against him a combination of Pallavas, Pāṇḍyas and Chōlas—though about the last nothing is known. He was at Uragapura on the south bank of the Kāvēri river on April 25 A.D. 674 (*see below*).

(*See the Kūram grant, near Kanchi, S.I.I. i,* 144 ; *Ind. Ant. viii, 275 ; xxii, 57 ; the Kaśakuḍi grant S.I.I. ii, 342 ; the Gadval plates, Ep. Ind. x, 100 ; Ep. Rep. 1907, p. 62 ; 1908, p. 63.*)]

Mānavamma, king of Ceylon, who had been driven out of his country a second time and had lived at the Pallava King Narasimha's court at Cōnjeveram, returned to Ceylon in 668 (a date conclusively established by Dr. Hultzsch). He seized the usurping Singhalese king Hatthadātha II, decapitated him, and obtained the throne for himself.

A.D. 671. The Nausāri grant of this year, made by one of the Gujarāt branch of the Chāḷukya family, mentions the Chāḷukya victory over the Pallava king. (*Ep. Ind. viii, 229.*)

A.D. 673. May 6, Chandalūr (Guntur District, Ongole Taluk) C. P. grant, shews the Eastern Chāḷukya Vijaya-Siddhi, otherwise Mangiyuvarāja, son of Vishṇuvardhana II ruling that country. (*V. R. ii Guntur, 346 ; Ep. Ind. viii, 292.*) He succeeded his father in A.D. 672.

A.D. 674, April 25. The W. Chāḷukya king Vikramāditya I was on this day at Uragapura, south of the Kāvēri river, to which place he had penetrated in his southward raid after the capture of Kānchi (*Gadwal plates, Ep. Ind. x, 100*). The Kēndūr plates of a later date (A.D. 749) say that Vikramāditya in his southern campaign was opposed by a confederacy of Pallavas, Chōḷas, Pāṇḍyas and four other nations. (Kēndūr is in the Poona District.) (*See E. I. vii, 230 ; ix, 102.*)

A.D. 680. Grants by the W. Chāḷukya Vikramāditya I in Anantapur and Bellary Districts, shewing that he ruled those tracts. (*Ep. Rep. 1903, p. 8.*)

[This, however, was his last year. He was succeeded in the year following October 10, A.D. 680 by his son Vinayāditya-Yuddhamalla. The Kēndūr plates say that Vinayāditya broke up the South Indian confederacy just mentioned. In the course of the war his son Vijayāditya was captured but effected his escape. (*Ep. Ind. ix, 200*).]

A line of princes of the Āḷupa or Āḷuva family established themselves about this time as rulers of a tract in Shimoga District, N. Mysore, with residence at Humcha, the ancient Pombuchcha. They were vassals to the Chāḷukya kings, and as such were allowed to extend their power to the north in the Baṇavāśi province of the former Kadamba-Maṇḍala. The first known chief was Guṇasāgara (680–692). (*Ep. Ind. ix, 15 ; Ind. Ant. xix, 147 ; E. C. vi. Kp. 38 ; ix. Dg. 66.*)

[The Āḷupas were ejected from Baṇavāśi in A.D. 753 when the Rāshṭrakūṭa Dantidurga overcame the Chāḷukya Kīrttivarma II.]

A.D. 689–90. Nandyal, Kurnool District. Grant by the W. Chāḷukya Vinayāditya, then in possession of that country, in his tenth regnal year. He is called 'Yuddhamalla' and 'Satyāśraya.' (*V. R. ii. Kurnool 546, 564-A ; Ind. Ant. vi, 86 ; J. B. B. R. A. S. xvi, 242.*)

A.D. c. 690–91. Grant in Kurnool District by the same in his eleventh regnal year. (*V. R. ii. Kurnool, 12-A ; Ind. Ant. vi, 88.*)

[**A.D. 690.** The Pallava king Narasimhavarman II came to the throne. His family were now in little power, and the king seems to have devoted himself to pious works. He built the 'Shore Temple' at Māvalivaram and Kailāsanātha Temple at Kānchi. He was also known as 'Rājasimha.' For a list of his ancestors see inscription on a pillar at Vāyalūr in Chingleput District. (*V. R. i. Chingleput 1235 ; 368 of 1908.*)]

A.D. 692, June 22. Vinayāditya of the W. Chāḷukyas reigning in N. W. Mysore. (*E. C. viii. Sb. 571.*)

A.D. 694, October 9. Grant by the same in his fourteenth year, shewing him reigning in Kaḍūr District in N. Mysore. The village given was in the Baṇavāśi District. The date makes this king's accession as in the year following October 9, 680. (*E. C. xi. Dg. 66.*) The Āḷupa chief is here said to be governing the 'Kadamba' country.

In another grant of his year the W. Chāḷukya king states that the Western Ganga chiefs were the 'hereditary servants' of his family. (*Ep. Ind. v. 157.*)

A.D. c. 695. Mention of the Āḷupa chief Chitravāhana as ruling at Humcha. Inscription in Kadūr District, W. Mysore. (*E. C. vi, Kp. 37.*)

[**A.D. 696.** In this year the W. Chāḷukya king Vijayāditya, son of Vinayāditya, came to the throne; and also the Eastern Chāḷukya Jayasimha II. The former cultivated friendly relations with the Rāshṭrakūṭa king Indra II, to whom he gave in marriage a Chāḷukya princess. The issue of this marriage was the Rāshṭrakūṭa Dantidurga who became so powerful that he destroyed for a time the W. Chāḷukya monarchy.]

A.D. c. 700. Accession of the Pāṇḍya king Arikēśari-Parākrama *alias* Rājasimha I. The alliance between the Pallavas and Pāṇḍyas in opposition to the Chāḷukyas was of short duration, and in this reign they were at open war again. They met in battle at Śankaramangai, or, as it is otherwise called, Śankaragrāma. Each side claims the victory. Arikēśari is also renowned in an old Tamil poem for having won a victory at Tiru-Nelvēli (Tinnevelly); also at Viḷiñam, Koṭṭāru, Śēvūr, Pūlandai, Nāraiyāru and Kaḍaiyal against the Chēra king; and at many other places against unnamed enemies (*I.A. 1922, p. 211 ; T.A.S., i, 153 ; E I. xvii, 291.*) He is said to have 'renewed the walls of Kūḍal, i.e., of Madura and of Vanji and Kōḷi (Uraiyūr).'

(*Arch. Rep. 1907, §§ 12–20 ; 1908, § 18 ; Ind. Ant. viii, 198, 273 ; S. I I., ii, 361.*)

In A.D. 715. The Pallava king Paramēśvara-Pōtavarman came to the throne. He is stated to have been at war with the Chēra or Kēraḷa king and to have won two battles at Maṇṇai and Nenmeli; also to have fought against the Pāṇḍya king, perhaps Arikēśari, and to have defeated him at Karūr. He only reigned two years.

A.D. 717–779. Reign of the Pallava Nandivarman II. The elder line came to an end with the king last mentioned. Nandivarman belonged to the junior branch. There seems to have been much confusion and disturbance in the matter of succession. He was opposed by, perhaps amongst others, a prince named Chitramāya. This prince was supported by the Pāṇḍya king Arikēśarin, otherwise called 'Māran' and 'Parānkusa' ('*History of the Śrī Vaishnavas' by T. A. Gopinātha Rao, pp. 18–25*). Nandivarman was supported by his general Udayachandra, by a subordinate chief Perumbiḍugu-Muttaraiyan (*see below*), and by the Adigaimān chief. Then were fought some at least of the battles mentioned above, viz., Śankaramangai, Maṇṇai or Maṇṇaikuḍi, Nēlvēli and others. The Pāṇḍya defeated Adigaimān at Pugaliyūr, near Trichinopoly; but Nandivarman, so say the Pallava eulogists, after that inflicted a severe defeat on the Pāṇḍya king at Karuvūr. The Kāśākuḍi grant mentions these events and says that the Pallava general Udayachandra himself slew the Pallava pretender Chitramāya. The grant states explicitly that Nandivarman was 'chosen by the subjects', thereby implying that he was not undisputed heir to the throne. He was descended from Bhīma, brother of Simhavishṇu, and was the son of Hiraṇya by Rohinī.

(See '*The Pallavas' by Jouveau-Dubreuil, p. 18 ; V.R. i. Chingleput 1235 ; 368 of 1908.*)

A.D. 717. Perumbiḍugu-Muttaraiyan is mentioned above as having assisted Nandivarman II, the Pallava king to gain his throne. He was therefore living in 717. He belonged to a family of Tanjore chiefs, who are mentioned in three inscriptions at Śendalai near Tanjore, which give the names—

i. Perumbiḍugu-Muttaraiyan I *alias* Kuvāvan-Māran,

ii. Iḷangōvaḍiyaraiyan *alias* Māran-Paramēśvara,

iii. Perumbiḍugu-Muttaraiyan II *alias* Śuvāvan-Māran.

A later member of the family is noted below, *s. v. A.D. 830* (*V.R. ii, Tanjore, 1287, 1288, 1290 ; 65 to 68 of 1897 ; Ep. Rep. 1907, § 22 ; Ep. Ind. xi, 154 ; xiii, 136*). Perumbiḍugu-Muttaraiyan II travelled from Tanjore to Kānchi to meet the Pallava Nandivarman II, and to offer his services.

(*Anbil plates, Ep. Ind. xv, 49.*)

A.D. c. 730. Record at Paṭṭadakal, anciently Kiśuvoḷal, undated, speaks of the W. Chāḷukya Vijayāditya, whose reign ended in 733, and of his son Vikramāditya II as reigning together. It mentions their names together and calls them 'the great kings', 'the supreme kings', in the plural. *(Ind. Ant. 1881, p. 164.)*

A.D. 733–747. Reign of W. Chāḷukya Vikramāditya II. An inscription on a pillar in a temple at Kānchi commemorates the generosity of this king in that, having conquered and entered the city, he did not confiscate the property of the temple, but actually returned it *(V.R. i. Chingleput 256 ; 8 of 1888 ; Ep. Ind. iii, 359)*. The Vakkalēri grant of A.D. 757–58 (see below) says. that Vikramāditya II's raid on Kānchi was made 'immediately after the time of his anointment', made a rapid descent on the Toṇḍaimaṇḍalam which he 'reached with great speed', attacked Pallava Nandivarman II, defeated him, seized much spoil, and entered Kānchi, but spared the city and gave much gold to the Rājasimhēśvara temple there. Note that the Paṭṭadakal record last mentioned (*s.v. A.D. 730*) which is an inscription of Vikramāditya's queen Lokamahādēvi says that the king 'conquered Kānchi three times.' The Pallavas, therefore, it would be reasonable to infer, put up a good fight before their final defeat. After this Pallava power began to decline.

(Cf. *the Vakkalēri grant, E.C. x. Kl. 63, Ind. Ant. viii, 23 ; Ep. Ind. v, 200 ; S I.I., i, 146.*)

A.D. 738–39. Kāśākuḍi plates of the twenty-second year of Pallava-Nandivarman II. Much information is given in them regarding the Pallava kings from Simhavishṇu downwards. This has been duly noted above. *(S.I.I. ii. 342 ; see also ibid i, 144.)*

[**A.D. 740–41.** About this time we learn that the Pāṇḍya king Arikēśari-Parākarma *alias* Rājasimha I, fought against the W. Chāḷukya Vikramāditya II, at the battle of Vēṇbai.

(Ind. Ant. 1922, 211.)

A.D. 743-44. The accession of the W. Chāḷukya Kīrttivarmā II took place in the year following April 7, 743, as is shewn by a correct date noted next below.]

A.D. 749, April 7. Kēndūr plates, Poona District, an inscription in the sixth year of W. Chāḷukya, Kīrttivarma II. The date is a sound one, and proves his accession as after April 7, 743. It is stated that he entered Kānchi but spared it, whence it must be assumed that he accompanied his father when he entered that city. *(Ep. Ind. ix, 200.)*

A.D. c. 750. About this date or later, two records in East Mysore speak of a battle that took place when the Western Ganga king Śrīpurusha-Muttarasa fought against the 'Kāḍuveṭṭi', i.e., the Pallava king of Kānchi. Both are epitaphs of soldiers who fell in the fight. One of them was a grant by Śrīpurusha's son, Duggamāra Ereyappa, to the family of the deceased ; and it mentions that the death occurred 'when the army went to Kampli.' Neither of these grants is dated.

(E. C. ix, Ht., 21 ; x, Mb., 255.)

[The W. Gangas having been, up to about this time, dependents of the W. Chāḷukyas, it may be that Śrīpurusha assisted Chāḷukya Vikramāditya II in his raid on Kānchi, and, by sending a force to Kampli, protected the Chāḷukya line of communications.]

A.D. 750, April 21. Jāvaḷi C. P. grant of the village of Beḷḷūr in Western Mysore to Brahmans by the W. Ganga king Śrīpurusha, in his twenty-fifth year. The date is correct as to the Nakshatra, but the week day, Tuesday, is given as Monday. This may be held not to invalidate the date, and if so it fixes this king's accession as in the year following April 21, 725. If so, the dates fixed by Fleet and Dubreuil and given in the genealogical tables in this volume are too late. (See *s.v.*, A.D. 776–77 below.)

Another inscription, undated but of about the same time, at Āsandi in the same taluk, says that Śrīpurusha's son, Vijayāditya, was ruling that tract. *(E. C vi. Mg. 36; Kd. 145.)*

A.D. 753. In this year the Western Chāḷukya ascendancy completely collapsed. Dantidurga, prince of the Rāshṭrakūṭa dynasty, son of Indra II and of a Chaḷukya princess, raised armies, swarmed over Chāḷukya territories, seized their capital, and afterwards proceeded to conquer the Pallavās. He was actually in occupation of Kānchi some time after A.D. 754.

(Ind. Ant. 1906, 228.)

The Rāshṭrakūṭas were a powerful line of chiefs who had ruled in the Dekhan since the fourth and fifth centuries A.D. *(Ibid. 1879, p. 10; the Miraj plates.)*

Dantidurga after this success assumed royal titles.

As to his actual occupation of Kānchi it is attested by Tirumangai-Āḷvār who, speaking of Dantidurga under his other name 'Vairamēgha', says that he 'was bowed down to by the people of the Tonḍa country' and that his army 'surrounded Kānchi'. *(Ind. Ant. 1906, pp. 228-32.)*

He seems, at the height of his power, to have ruled the north of the peninsula from sea to sea. *(Sāmangad C. P. grant; Ind. Ant. 1882, p. 108; Ep. Ind. v, 157.)*

[The Jain teacher Akaḷanka flourished at this time at Kānchi.

(Ep. Ind. iii, 186; Ep. Rep. 1904-5, p. 57.)]

A.D. 754-55. Reign of the W. Ganga king Śrīpurusha; record in East Mysore near Kōlār in his twenty-eighth year, the year Vikrama. Given that his accession was in A.D. 725-26 (see above) the year intended was evidently Vikrama of A.D. 754-55, though that would be his thirtieth year. *(E. C. x. Kl. 6.)*

A.D. 757-58. Vakkalēri plates. A very important record with pedigree of the Western Chāḷukya kings down to the reigning sovereign Kīrttivarma II. At the date of the grant he was in camp at a place in the Sholapur District, Bombay, a long way north of Bādāmi, his capital. It looks as if he had fled after Dantidurga's seizure of the W. Chāḷukya dominions.

(E. C. x, Kl. 63; S.I.I. i. 145.)

A.D. 766-67. An inscription of the fiftieth year of the Pallava king Nandipōttarasa or Nandivarman II (no details of date are given, but his accession is known to have been in A.D. 717), at Panchapānḍavamalai, close to Arcot, on a rock. *(Ep. Ind. iv, 136; V. R. i. N. Arcot, 631; 10 of 1895. For the 47th year of reign, see V. R. i. N. Arcot, 608; 55 of 1887.)*

A.D. 766-67. Near Kōlār in E. Mysore, inscription dated only in the forty-second regnal year of the W. Ganga Śrīpurusha, which year—his reign began in A.D. 725-26—*(see above, s.v. A.D. 750)*, was A.D. 766-67. It states that Śrīpurusha's Queen was ruling Āgali, while his son Duggamāra-Ereyappa governed the Ganga tract, and especially Kōlār, for the king. *(E. C. x. Mb. 80.)*

[**A.D. 767-68** was the year of accession of the Pānḍya king Jaṭila-Parāntaka, according to the Vēḷvikuḍi C. P. grant of his third year, which the Epigraphist to Government has fixed as A.D. 769-70. *(See below.)*]

A.D. 768, March 23. Talagaon C. P. grant of this date. Rāshṭrakuṭa Krishna I reigning. His son Gōvinda is mentioned. This record shews that his nephew and predecessor (as sovereign). Dantidurga must have died before this date; and, as the latter left no heir, his uncle Krishna I succeeded to his dignities,—dignities which Dantidurga had increased to a kingdom. Krishna I is the king mentioned in the Alās grant and other records. He constructed the rock-cut temple of Ellora, and he patronized the religious teacher Akaḷanka. *(Ep. Ind. xiii, 276; vi, 171; ix, 194; xiv, 123.)*

A.D. 769–70. The Vēlvikuḍi grant, decided by the Epigraphist V. Venkayya to belong to this date, is important for the history of the Pāṇḍya kingdom. It was issued in the third regnal year of Pāṇḍya Jaṭila-Parāntaka *alias* 'Tennan-Vānavan.' Before this year he is stated to have defeated the 'Kāḍava', i. e., the Pallava king Nandivarman II at Pennāgaḍam (on the south bank of the Kāvēri river). He had also defeated the Āyavēḷ chiefs of Vēṇāḍ (Travancore), and the Kuṛumbas at Nāṭṭukuṛumbu. His later battles are said to have been at Viṇṇam, Vēlūr, Śeḷiyakudi, Āyiravēli, Āyirūr and Pugaliyūr; and it is claimed for him that he destroyed Viḷiñam, and fortified Karavandapuram. (*See below, s.v., A.D. 783.*)

The grant contains a long account of the king's ancestors, all of which need not be assumed to be authentic history, but part of which is undoubtedly reliable. (*Ind. Ant. xxii, 57–75 ; and 1922, p. 211 ; Ep. Rep. 1908, §§ 15 ff. ; Trav. Arch. Ser. i, p. 188.*)

A.D. 770–71. A village near Madura granted by the minister of the Pāṇḍya king Jatila Parāntaka. The given date is K. Y. 3871, with no other details.

(*V. R. ii. Madura, 21 ; E. I. viii, 317.*)

A.D. 770–71. In the same year the Alās plates inscription, which records the grant of a village in the Kolhāpūr country, tells us that the grant was made when Gōvinda II (son of the Rāshṭrakūṭa king Krishna I and himself then a prince, cousin of Dantidurga) was in camp on the borders of the Palnāḍ Taluk, south of the Krishna river, at the confluence of the Krishna with the Mūsi 'after he had humbled the lord of Vengi,' and had taken from him his treasury, his forces and his country. (*E.I. vi*, 208.)

[We learn from this that the Rāshṭrakūṭas really humbled the Eastern Chāḷukyas at this time, whose king was Vishṇuvardhana IV, though it need not be assumed that the former actually annexed the Vengi country. At a later date, A.D. 794, the Paithān plates state that Gōvinda II was opposed to the Vengi ruler; and it is a boast of the Eastern Chāḷukya Vijayāditya II that he 'fought 108 battles in 12½ years against Gangas and Raṭṭas,' i.e., Rāshṭrakūṭas. Though his reign was 30 years later than A.D. 770, it shews that the two powers were hostile to one another.

Fleet expresses a doubt whether the Alās plates are genuine (*E.I. vii, 198*), but were not perhaps based on some other genuine document; but he does not deny that the information contained in them may be correct. A later record of A.D. 794 (*q.v. below*) states that Gōvinda II fought against the ruler of Mālwa.]

A.D. 772. June 23. Bhandak C. P. grant of Rāshṭrakūṭa Krishna I. (*E.I. xiv, 121.*)

A.D. c. 774. The Taṇḍantōṭṭam plates grant of a village in Tanjore, in his fifty-eighth regnal year, by the Pallava king Nandivarman II, son of Hiraṇyavarman. It shews that at that time he reigned over the Tanjore country.

(*V.R. ii, Tanjore 65 ; C.P. No. 7 of 1912 ; Dubreuil 'Pallavas,' p. 62.*)

A.D. 776–77. Dēvarahalli stone inscription in central Mysore, of the fiftieth year of the Western Ganga king Śrīpurusha. This confirms the date given above for his accession, (*See s.v. A.D. 750*), viz., after April 21, 725. The only date given in the record is Ś. 698, which began on March 20, 776 if taken as an expired Śaka year. In that case, coupling this document with the Jāvali grant (*above*), we should have his accession fixed as in the interval between March 20, and April 21, 726. But, if taken as a current Śaka year, it would be in the interval between April 21, 725 and March 20, 726. In any case it confirms my accession date as after April 21, 725. The record mentions the battle fought by Bhūvikrama at Viḷanda. (*E.C. iv, Ng. 85.*)

A.D. 778–79. Inscription at Tiruvallam, North Arcot District, on a boulder in the river of the sixty-second year of the Pallava Nandivarman II. It shews that his vassal the Bāṇa chief (name not given) whose residence was at this place, was governing the country called 'Vaḍugavaḻi' or the 'Telugu road', or as in some records 'west of the Āndhra road.'[1]

(S. I.I. iii, p. 88, No. 42 ; V.R. i. N. Arcot, 330 ; 76 of 1889.)

A.D. 779. December 22. Dhulia plates of Rāshṭrakūṭa prince 'Karka,' son of Dhruva who was younger brother of Gōvinda II *alias* 'Prabhūtavarsha.' The record distinctly states that the reigning king was Gōvinda II. This settles the doubt that existed as to whether Gōvinda II actually came to the throne or not. *(E. I. viii, 182.)*

A.D. c. 783–814. Reign of Rāshṭrakūṭa Gōvinda III at Uḍipi to N. W. of Mysore. Some inscriptions on *vīrakals* record the deaths of men in a fierce battle that took place during this reign. The Āḷupa chief Chitravāhana was ruling the country about Humcha in Mysore. Baṇavāsi was ruled by a certain Rājāditya. Quarrels arose. 'The Kolli-Pallava Nolamba became angry.' There was a great fight and much slaughter. The Āḷupa chief Raṇasāgara attempted to oust Chitravāhana and the latter seized the town of Udiyavāra. Another Āḷupa chief Śvētavāhana fought against Raṇasāgara and defeated him. Then Prithivisāgara entered Udiyavāra and apparently became the principal Āḷupa chief. He is also known by the names 'Udayāditya' and 'Uttama Pāṇḍya.' The accounts given are confusing and it is unwise to attempt to say exactly who 'Prithivisāgara' was. Was that perhaps another name of Chitravāhana ?

(E.C. viii, Sb. 10 ; Ep. Rep. 1901, p. 5.)

A.D. 783. A record at Naregal shews that cattle-raiding, with tribal fighting as a result, was prevalent at this time. *(E. I. vi, 160.)*

A.D. 783. The Rāshṭrakuta king, or prince, Dhruva is represented in the Rādhanpūr plates to have captured and imprisoned the W. Ganga chief Śivamāra II *alias* Śaigoṭṭa, to have released him and again captured him. (This chief was finally reinstated by the Rāshṭrakūṭa king Gōvinda III.) Dhruva is said also to have gone to the Tungabhadra river and fought against the Pallavas (*E. I. vi, 239*). [The Ganga chiefs now owned the Rāshṭrākuṭas as their overlords.]

A.D. 783–84. Madras Museum plates of the seventeenth year of the Pāṇḍya king Jaṭila-Parākrama. The events of his reign up to date are enumerated. He fought battles at Viṇṇam, Śeḻiyakkudi and Veḷḷūr. He warred with the 'Adiyan' (Adigaiman) chief of Tanjore and the kings of the Pallava and Kerala families (the Pallava was possibly a Nolamba-Pallava chief of Uchchangi). He defeated the Adiyan of Tanjore at Ayirūr, Pugaliyūr, and at Āyiravēli on the north bank of the Kāvēri. He went to the Kongu country, captured its ruler, subdued the country and advanced as far as Pērūr in Coimbatore District. He fought the king of Vēṇāḍ (Travāncore), and destroyed the Chēra stronghold Viliñam.[2] He fortified Karavandapuram.[3]

(I. A. 1893, p. 57 ; Trav. Arch. Ser. i, 153, 188.)

[1] The original is 'Vaḍugavaḻi mērku' meaning Telugu Road West as opposed to Telugu Road East. In those early days both Kannaḍa and Telugu countries were alike Vaḍugu. Hence there must have been two roads Eastern and Western leading into the Telugu and Kannaḍa Country answering to the two now existing.—*Editor.*

[2] As to Viḻiñam, see below *s.v.* A.D. 793.

[3] The late Mr. Sewell is somewhat confused here, the confusion having arisen from the imperfect summarising of the originals. The war actually described is really one between the Pāṇḍya Jaṭila Parākrama, for the time being allied with the Gangas, the Pallavas under Nandi Varman Pallavamalla, the Adigaiman chief of Tagaḍūr (Dharmapuri, Salem District), and the Chera king for the time being. The Adigaiman chief had advanced southwards in a

[A.D. 788–820. This period is assigned as that of the active life of the great teacher Śankarāchārya.]

A.D. 793–94. Trivandrum Museum plates of the twenty-seventh year of the Pāṇḍya king Jaṭila-Parāntaka, whose accession was in A.D. 767–68. He had before his seventeenth year (*see above*) destroyed the Chēra or Kērala Town of Viḻiñam. This record shews that, some time during the next ten years, he had had to abandon Viḻiñam and retire to Karaikkōṭṭai. He was followed thither by the Chēra army, and seemingly suffered a reverse. (*Trav. Arch. Ser. i, 154.*)

A.D. 794. May 4. Paithan plates. Reign of Rāshṭrakūṭa Gōvinda III. His uncle Gōvinda II is said to have fought against the ruler of Mālwa, the Pallava lord of Kānchi (Dantivarman), the Ganga king (Śripurusha), and 'him of Vengi' (the E. Chāḷukya Vishṇuvardhana IV). It also mentions that Gōvinda II had been deposed, and his throne seized by his brother Dhruva. (*E. I. iii, 103.*)

A.D. 797–805. Maṇṇe plates, East Mysore. Date irregular, but of this period (*see below s.v. A. D. 805*). Pedigree of the W. Gangas given from Mādhava II down to the reigning Sivamāra II. Of him it is stated that he was 'anointed to the kindgdom by the crowned kings', the Rāshṭrakūṭa Gōvinda III and the Pallava Nandivarman ; 'they with their own hands binding the crown on his brow.' The dates do not well agree, for while we have Gōvinda III reigning at this time, the reign of Nandivarman of Kānchi had come to an end in A.D. 769.[1] (*E. C. ix. Nl. 50.*)

A.D. 798. According to the *Guruparamparais* the Vaishṇava sage Nammāḻvār was alive in this year. He is believed by some to have been the son of the Minister to the Pāṇḍya king of Madura. Tirumangaiaḻvār flourished at the same time.

(*T. A. Gopinatha Rao's 'History of the Śrīvaishṇavas', pp. 18-21, 26.*)

A.D. 799. Accession of the E. Chāḷuyka king Vijayāditya II Narēndra-Mrigarāja who is declared in inscriptions to have fought 108 battles in twelve and half a years against the 'Gangās and Raṭṭas (i.e. Rāshṭrakuṭas)'. Rāshṭrakūṭa records say that the Chāḷukya was completely defeated and abjectly humbled by Gōvinda III.

About the end of the eighth century A.D. Dr. Hultzsch has published a Tamil inscription on a rock at Takōpa, Wat Nāmuang, in the Malay Peninsula at Maṇigrāmam[2] (the old name of the place), which speaks of a temple of Vishṇu there ; also of a body of men, probably Hindu colonists, and of bow-men 'men of the vanguard,' who were evidently soldiers of a force placed there for protection of trade. (*J. R. A. S. 1913, p. 337 ; 1914, p. 397.*)

Belonging to the same period are a number of undated inscriptions, whose age is judged by the characters of the script, giving the names of a series of Telugu-Chōḍa Mahārājas governing the Rēnāṇḍu country, i.e., a 7,000 village tract in Cuddapah and Nellore Districts. They claim descent

campaign as far as Tanjore, perhaps even farther south, from where he was driven back fighting all the way. The battles mentioned are all of them battles fought by the Pāṇḍya against the combined enemies. The Adigaiman Chief was only chief of Dharmapuri (Tagaḍūr). The Pāṇḍya advanced to very near Dharmapuri, fought the Pallavās on the one side and defeated them ; and fought the Chēras on the other side, pursued the defeated Chēra army, went into the Coimbatore District, built a temple to Vishṇu at Kanjivāy Pērūr, then advanced through the Chēra country, defeated and destroyed the Chēra stronghold of Viḻigñam marching across to the Pāṇḍyan frontiers, fortified Karavandapuram. This is the account as it appears actually in the Museum plates studied in the light of Pāṇḍya Charters known as the Vēḷvikuḍi and Śinnamanūr Plates.—*Editor.*

[1] The latest year of Nandivarman's reign is his sixty-fifth year as noted in an epigraph in the Varāha cave at Mahābalipuram. This would correspond to A.D. 782–3.—*Editor.*

[2] Maṇigrāmam figures as one of the three communities under whose protection the charitable work was placed.—*Editor.*

from Karikāla Chōla. Four generations are mentioned, ending with Puṇyakumāra. (*V. R. i. Cuddapah, 309, 318, 350, 405, 409, 435, 550, 560 ; 380, 384, 393, 396, 400, 405, 408 of 1904 ; 350, 352 of 1905 ; 466 of 1906. See above, s.v., A. D. 634–35.*)

A.D. 802, November 13. Maṇṇe plates, E. Mysore (*See above s.v., A. D. 797*). These plates have a sound date, naming the eclipse of the moon on the day stated. Reign of Rāshṭrakūṭa Gōvinda III. His father Dhruva is called 'Dhora.' Gōvinda humbled the Pallavas, and reduced the Eastern Chāḷukyas of Vengi, so says the record, to such a condition that their king came and built the walls of a fortress for Gōvinda. (*E. C. ix. Nl. 61.*)

[This king of Vengi would be Vijayāditya II who claims to have fought 108 battles against the Rāshṭrakūṭa king and his Ganga ally. The inscription calls Gōvinda's elder brother 'Śaucha Kamba *alias* Raṇāvalōka.']

[**A.D. 805.** Date of accession, according to Fleet, of the Western Ganga king Śivamāra II. He is said to have been anointed by the Rāshṭrakūṭa Gōvinda III, then reigning, and by the Pallava Nandivarman (*see note above s.v. 797*). The reign of Nandivarman II had come to an end in or about A.D. 779. I suggest that this Nandivarman who anointed 'with his own hands' Śivamāra II may have been the prince Nandivarman who afterwards reigned as Nandivarman III, deputed for the purpose by his father Dantivarman then on the throne.[1]

(*E. I. vi, 59 ; v, 157 ; S. I. I. ii, Part v.*)]

A.D. 808, July 27. Rādhanpūr plates of Rāshṭrakūṭa Gōvinda III. He was then at Mayūrakhaṇḍī, a hill-fort near Nasik. The inscription relates, amongst other previous events of his reign, that he had transferred his capital to Malkhēd, and then sent an insolent message to the Vengi king, i.e., Vijayāditya *alias* Narēndra-Mrigarāja, commanding him to come and build the fortifications round the city. This must have been before A.D. 802 (*see above*). (*E. I. vi, 239.*)

A.D. 809, perhaps January 28. Record in E. Mysore of the W. Ganga king Śivamāra II *alias* Narasimha. The year 'Sarvajit' named=A.D. 808–9, but the details of the date are irregular. (*E. C. ix. Dv. 44.*)

A.D. c. 810. Inscription (*vīrakal*) in Chitaldrūg District, N. Mysore. Undated. It commemorates the death of a chief who was a vassal of the W. Ganga king. The chief was governing the Noḷamba country and was named 'Singapōta.' His lord's name is not stated but only his title 'Permmānaḍi' is given; but it is mentioned that 'Duggamāra rose up suddenly and established himself by force.' Duggamāra was younger brother of the Ganga king Śivamāra II, and it may be that the fight in which Singapōta lost his life was between the supporters of Śivamāra, who was continually in trouble with the Rāshṭrakūṭa Gōvinda III, and those of Duggamāra.

(*E. C. xi. Cl. 8.*)

A.D. 812–13. C. P. grant in a village near Uppinangāḍi, S. Kanara. It shews that Rāshṭrakūṭa Gōvinda III, 'Prabhūtavarsha' was reigning there at the time.

(*V. R. ii. S. Kanara 300–A ; I. A. xii, 13 ; xxiv, 9 ; E. I. iv, 340.*)

A.D. 812, December 14. Torkheḍe plates of Gōvinda III Rāshṭrakūṭa. The inscription states that he made his younger brother Indra II king of Gujarāt (*Lāṭa*).

[Indra founded a dynasty there.] (*E. I. iii, 53.*)

A.D. 813. The Kaḍaba C. P. grant of Rāshṭrakūṭa Gōvinda III shews him ruling in Central Mysore. It is lengthy and poetical, but of no historical interest. (*E. C. xii Gb., 61.*)

[1] See note above.—*Editor*

A.D. 814-15. Accession of the Rāshṭrakūṭa king Amōghavarsha or Śarva. The date is ascertained by an inscription at Śirūr, Dhārwār District, of June 16, 866 (*Ep. Ind. vii, 198; ix, 24; I.A. xii, 252; E.I. iv, 278*). He was incessantly at war with the E. Chāḷukyas throughout his long reign.

[King Sēna I, or Śilāmēgha Sēna, became king of Ceylon in this year. The *Mahāwaṁśa* (*Ch. L. v, 19*) tells us that in his reign the Pāṇḍya king, probably Śrīmāra, who boasts of having conquered Ceylon, attacked the island with an army. King Sēna was defeated and fled. The Pāṇḍya victor seized the city of Anurādhāpura, sacked it and destroyed the palaces and after 'spreading destruction over the land', returned to India. This may have taken place about A.D. 830. The larger Śinnamānūr grant (*V.R. ii. Madura, 367; C.P. 14 of 1907*) mentions the victories of Śrīmāra Pāṇḍya; saying that he defeated Māya Pāṇḍya, gained victories at Viḷiñam (a Chēra town) and at Kunnūr in Ceylon; also that he fought a great battle at Kuḍamūkku (believed to be Kumbhakōnam) against Gangas, Pallavas and Chōla chiefs. The Chōla family was, then, gaining a little influence at this time.]

(?) A.D. 827-28. Inscription at Guḍimallam in the Chittoor District, dated only in the forty-ninth year of the Pallava Dantivarman or Dantivikrama, whose accession according to Dubreuil was in A.D. 779. [According to T. A. Gopinātha Rao the accession was in A.D. 808-9.][1] It mentions his feudatory the Bāṇa chief Vijayāditya, possibly Vijayāditya I, as ruling the country.

(*V.R. i. Chittoor 60; 226 of 1903; E.I. xi, 222; I.A. 1911, p. 104.*)

[The country governed by the Bāṇas had amongst its chief town Punganūr and Kāḷahasti, and was known as the tract 'west of the Telugu (or Āndhra) road.' It seems to have been a rough country, subject to constant strife on account of raids and cattle robberies.]

A.D. c. 830-54. Reign of Pallava Nandivarman III. Two inscriptions in Tanjore District. One of them calls the King 'Viḍēlviḍugu.' Undated.

(*V.R. ii. Tanjore, 1253, 1296; 283 of 1901; 10 of 1899; I.A. 1908, p. 170.*)

[An old Tamil poem says that this king fought battles at Ṭeḷḷār (in South Arcot), whence was derived his title 'Teḷḷāṟṟerinda'; at Naḷḷār, and Paḷaiyāṟu in the Tanjore country; at Kuṟugōḍu, perhaps the town so named on the Tungabhadra river, or the one in Kōlār District, Mysore; and at Veḷḷār.]

A.D. 830-854. Inscription of the third regnal year of the same king in the neighbourhood of Kānchi. (*E.I. vi, 319.*)

[**A.D. 843.** Probable date of accession of Sēna II, king of Ceylon. The *Mahāwaṁśa* narrates that, in revenge for the wanton attack of the Pāṇḍya king on Ceylon (*above s.v. A.D. 814-15*), Sēna II sent an army to the mainland with the object of dethroning the Pāṇḍya king, and substituting for him a Pāṇḍya prince who had rebelled against his lord and begged aid from the Singhalese. Madura was besieged[2] and the king was dethroned. The prince being placed on the throne of Madura, the Singhalese retired. The *Mahāwaṁśa's* story goes that when the Singhalese arrived in India, the Pāṇḍya king was absent on one of his campaigns. This points to the king having been Varaguṇa II who waged war in the north, for Śrīmara's wars were in the south; and if so this destruction of Madura must have taken place after Varaguṇa's accession, i.e., after A.D. 862.

[1] It ought really to be after A.D. 782-3.—*Editor.*

[2] The *Mahāwaṁśa* says that the battlements and towers of Madura were burnt, which seems to shew that the fortifications had been constructed of wood.

When he hurriedly marched back to Madura, the Pāṇḍya king's army was depleted, the king fought, was wounded and fled, only to die of his injury. This would fix the date as about A.D. 878, Varaguṇa II's last year, and if so the rebel prince may have been his own brother Parāntaka-Vīra-nārāyaṇa. But this fixture is only supposition as the Singhalese chronology is not quite finally settled.
(Mahāwamśa, ch. li.)]

A.D. 844–888. C. P. grant, undated, of a village in 'Gudravāra-Vishaya', near the Gōdāvari, by the E. Chāḷukya king Guṇaka-Vijayāditya III. His principal achievement, mentioned in several records, was that he 'cut off the head of Mangi in battle', also that he 'frightened the (Rāshṭrakūṭa) Krishna II and Śankila and burned their city Kīraṇapura.' Hence we gather that the incessant wars between Eastern Chāḷukya and Rāshṭrakūṭa kings continued to devastate the country.
(V.R. ii, Kistna 7 ; Masulipatam plates ; I.A. xx, 103 ; xiii, 53 ; E.I. v, 122.)

A long account of the deeds of Guṇaka-Vijayāditya is given in the Piṭhāpuram grant, and the Maliyapūndi grant of Amma Rāja II of a later date (*E. I. ix, 47 ; I. A. vii, 16*). Mangi is described as ruling the 'Nōḍamba' (for Noḷamba) country. Śankila is called 'Lord of Dāhala', and Hultzsch identifies him with Śamkaragaṇa or Śankuka, son of Kokkala I of the Kalachūri chiefs of Chēdi, whose sister married Rāshṭrakūṭa Krishna II (877–913 A.D.) [1]

Another achievement of Gunaka-Vijayāditya's was that he 'burned Chakrakūṭa.'[2] The identity of this place has been much questioned, and I am not in a position positively to decide the point.
(See I. A. 1884, p. 50, Ep. Rep. for 1923, p. 97.)

Another record says that he seized Mānyakhēṭa (or Malkhēḍ), the capital city of the Rāshṭrakūṭas and after burning it, retired. This was during the reign of Rāshṭrakūṭa Krishna II and therefore after A.D. 877–78 (*E. I. vii, 26*). See below *s.v. A.D.* 930.

Three inscriptions near Ongole in Guntur District of the same period mention the E. Chāḷukya general Panḍaranga, and one of them states that he 'conquered the Venginādu,' which was the home-territory of his own sovereign, Guṇaka. Light is thrown on this otherwise curious assertion by an inscription (*Ind. Ant. 1884, p. 50*) which says that the Vengi country was at this time 'pervaded by the army of the Rāshṭrakūṭas.' It must be understood therefore that Panḍaranga drove the Rāshṭrakūṭa forces out of the Venginādu.
(838–840 of 1923 ; and Report, p. 97.)

[A.D. *c.* 846–880. Estimated period of reign (or rule ?) of the Chōla leader Vijayālaya, who seized Tanjore and laid the foundation for the great fortunes of his descendant kings. His grandson changed the political condition of South India, and established a kingdom that eventually became an empire.]

Ninth century A.D. About this time the Vaiḍumba chief Irigayya, or Erega, was at war. A *vīrakal* at Ālētipalli, in Chittoor District, commemorates the death of a soldier in a battle when he was 'supporting the throne of Erega,' or Irigayya. Another *vīrakal* in the same neighbourhood, in honour of a man who lost his life in a cattle-raid, mentions the Vaiḍumba Rāja, Manuja-Trinētra, probably the same as Ganḍa-Trinētra.
(V. R. i. Chittoor 148, 153, 162, 167, 168, 170 ; 295, 296, 298, 290 of 1905 ; 439 of 1914 ; 533 of 1906 ; E. R. 1907, p. 78.)

[1] The Government Epigraphist believes that this Śankila was a Vaiḍumba chief, who is mentioned in another inscription as having been an enemy of the Chōla chiefs of his day. *(E. R. 1923, p. 98, § 10.)*

[2] Chakrakūṭa has been identified satisfactorily with Chakrakōta or Chitrakōt near Jagdalpur, the capital of the State of Bastar. (Vide *Ep. Ind.* ix, 178–79.)—*Editor.*

A.D. c. 850. Two inscriptions at Tiruvallam, N. Arcot District, are copies made about A.D. 991 when the temple there was restored by Rājarāja Chōla I, of older ones of about this date. One of them refers, under the title of 'Bāṇa-Mahādēvi', to Kundavvai, wife of the Bāṇa chief Bāṇa-Vidyādhara *alias* Vikramāditya I, who was ruling the country 'west of the Telugu Road' in the twenty-third year of the Pallava king (his suzerain) Nandivarman III.

(*V. R. i. N. Arcot, 331, 332 ; Chittoor, 63 ; 77, 78 of 1889 ; 229 of 1903 ; E. R. xi, 224.*)

[Sometime in the ninth century there was a colony of Tamil traders at Takua-pā (Takōpa) in Wat-Nāmuang, Malay Peninsula. A Tamil inscription has been found there belonging to this period. It shews that there was a temple of Vishṇu at that place, which was the 'refuge of the members of Maṇigrāman (a trading guild on the west coast) and of the bowman.' Dr. Hultzsch published the record. He concludes that there was a colony of Tamils in the Malay Peninsula, guarded by soldiers. (*J. R. A. S., April, 1913.*)][1]

A.D. 855. Inscription in a temple near Tanjore records a gift made to a temple there by the Queen of the Pallava Nṛipatunga, in his second year. (Chronology according to Jouveau-Dubreuil). It shews Pallava influence at this period in Tanjore.

(*V. R. ii. Tanjore, 1270 ; 300 of 1901.*)

A.D. 858. June 23. Accession of Aḍakkan *alias* Śrīvallabha, Āy chief of the Malaināḍu (Vēnād) country of Travancore (*see Genealogical Tables, s.v. Kērala Kings*). He was son of Karunandan, son of Śaḍaiyan. Date fixed by an inscription (*Trav. Arch. Ser. i. No. 1 ; V.R. iii. Trav., 215*). His fourteenth and twenty-second years are mentioned in other inscriptions.

(*V. R. iii. Trav., 196, 197 ; Trav. Arch. Ser. ii, 1–15.*)

A.D. 861–62. Bāhūr in French territory, north of Tanjore. An inscription shews that the Pallava Nṛipatunga gave three villages to a college at that place in his eighth year, which was about the date stated. It proves that he was actually sovereign of the country at the time. (*V. R. iii. French Terr., 18 ; E. I. iv, 180*)

A.D. 862. Between March 22 and November 22. Accession of the Pāṇḍya king Varaguṇa II. A great deal of fighting in his reign. By his fourth year he had carried his arms north-eastward towards Tanjore, and from thence he gained ground gradually across territory then ruled by the Pallavas, and under them by Chōla and Bāṇa chiefs, till he reached Araiśūr on the southern Pennār river where he encamped in his sixteenth year 877-8. In this campaign he reduced those chiefs temporarily, the former at Iḍavai; and he destroyed the fortifications of Vēmbil (modern Vēmbaṟṟūr). In 877–78 he was attacked by the Ganga king Prithivipati I and the Pallava Aparājita in alliance, and during his enforced retreat he fought a battle at Śrīpurambiyam, or Tirupurambiyam, close to Kumbhakōnam where he was defeated, Prithivipati I being killed in the action. The important inscriptions regarding events of his reign are the following—105, 414, 690, 705 of 1905 ; 51 of 1895 ; 84 of 1910 ; *E. I. ix, 84 ; xi. 253 ; E. R. 1906, § 25 ; 1910, § 31.* An officer of his, who had accompanied Varaguṇa when he captured the town of Iḍavai on the north bank of the Kāvērī, constructed a tank near Dindigul (*V. R. ii. Madura, 8 ; S. I. I. ii, 53*).

A.D. 864–65. Inscription in Chittoor District in the eleventh year of the Pallava king, Nṛipatunga. (*V. R. i. Chittoor, 331 ; 459 of 1905.*)

[1] For a corrected reading and rendering of the Inscriptions, see *J. R. A. S.* for 1914, pp. 397–8.—*Editor.*

A.D. 868. December 30. Grant of land in Cochin by the Āy king of Vēṇāḍ (*See Kērala Kings in Genealogical Tables*), Vikramāditya-Varaguṇa. Vēṇāḍ was now dependent on Madura and the Āy king was named 'Varaguṇa' after the Pāṇḍya king Varaguṇa II.

(*Trav. Arch. Ser. i. 187 ; V. R. iii. Travancore 2.*)

A.D. 870–71. South Mysore. Inscriptions shewing the western Ganga king Rāchamalla II on throne, with his younger brother Būtarasa, i. e., Būtuga, as Yuvarāja. (*E. C. iii, Nj. 75.*)

A.D. c. 870. An inscription at Vaḷḷimalai in North Arcot District shews that a cave temple was excavated by the Ganga Rāchamalla. Another shews that he founded a Jaina shrine. These are undated and it seems doubtful which Rāchamalla is referred to. The relationship mentioned is also confusing. (*V. R. i. N. Arcot 710 A, 710 B ; 6 of 1895 ; 91 of 1889.*)

A.D. 870–71. Record at Aivarmalai, Madura District, of the eighth regnal year of Varaguṇa Pāṇḍya II, proving accession in A.D. 862–63. (*V. R. ii. Madura 242 ; 705 of 1905.*)

A.D. 872–73. Trichinopoly cave-inscription of the eleventh year of the Pāṇḍya king Varaguṇa II. It shews that he had been at Niyamam near Tanjore, after he had fought at Iḍavai and destroyed the fortifications of Vēmbil, both of which places are on the north side of the Kāvērī river, and therefore in territory belonging to the Ganga chief.

(*Ann. Rep. on Arch. 194–30, p. 270.*)

A.D. 874. November 22. Gift to a temple near Trichinopoly by Varaguṇa Pāṇḍya II in his thirteenth year. It makes his accession as in the year ending with November 22, A.D. 862.

(*V. R. iii. Trich. 683 ; 84 of 1910 ; E. I. xi, 253.*)

A.D. 876–77. The Rāshṭrakūṭa king Śarva Amōghavarsha reigning in N. W. Mysore. Under him 'Indra' governing the Baṇavāśi 12,000 country (? the Noḷamba chief Mahēndra I).

(*E. C. viii. Sb. 865.*)

A.D. 877–78. Inscription at Ambāsamudram, Tinnevelly District, of the sixteenth year of Varaguṇa Pāṇḍya II, who made a grant when encamped at Araiśūr on the southern Pennār river on his way to an attack on the Pallava king. (*V. R. iii, Tinnevelly 29 ; 105 of 1905 ; E. I. ix, 84.*)

Another record of about the same date at Rāmanāthapuram, near Dindigul, mentions Varaguṇa's expedition to Iḍavai. (*V. R. ii. Madura 8 ; 690 of 1905.*)

[Vēmbil=Vēmbaṟṟūr=Tiruviśalur near Kumbhakōnam. Varaguṇa's successes there and at Iḍavai in the neighbourhood took place when he was on the march northwards and before he reached Araiśūr. The history of what happened afterwards seems to be made clear by several records and by a passage in the *Mahawaṁśa* (ch. li), which has already been quoted (*above, s.v. A.D. 843*). While Varaguṇa was absent at Araiśūr, king Sēna II of Ceylon sent over an army to the mainland with the object of deposing Varaguṇa and placing another on the throne of the Pāṇḍyas. About the same time, i.e., about A.D. 877–78, which was the last year of Sēna II, the Ganga king Prithivīpati I effected an alliance with the Pallava king Nṛipatunga, whose country was in danger from the Pāṇḍya's advance, and together, the Ganga and Pallava forces—the latter led by the crown prince Aparājita—attacked Varaguṇa. A great battle was fought at Śrīpurambiyam or Tirupurambiyam, which ended in the defeat of the Pāṇḍya leader, but in the course of which Prithivīpati I lost his life. Varaguṇa perforce retired towards Madura ; and, if we are to believe the Singhalese story, he died there of wounds received in battle. His successor Parāntaka-Vīranārāyaṇa, his own brother who had rebelled and had received the support of king Sēna, was then placed on the throne. (Cf. record at Ambūr, *E. I. iv, 182.*)]

A.D. 877–78. An inscription at Guḍimallam near Kāḷahasti shews that in this year, which was the twenty-fourth year of the Pallava king Nṛipatunga, the 'country west of the Telugu road,' i.e., the country of the Bāṇas was ruled by the Bāṇa chief Vāṇavidyādhara *alias* Vikramāditya Prabhumēru I. *(V. R. Chittoor 62; 228 of 1903; S. I. I. iii, No. 42; E. I. xi, 226.)*

A.D. 877–78. Inscription of the W. Ganga Prithivīpati I. It mentions the Chōla Rāja as now a prominent political person. This may have been Vijayālaya or his son Āditya I who restored the Chōla monarchy. (*V. R. Chittoor 226, 33 of 1912.*)

[In some year between A.D. 877, the first year of the Rāshṭrakūta king Krishna II, and 888, the last year of the Eastern Chāḷukya king Guṇaka-Vijayāditya III, the latter, in the course of his war with the former, captured Krishna's capital city Malkhēd (Mānyakhēṭa), sacked and burned it. Vijayāditya held the place for a time and then retired. That this really took place is proved by the Cambay plates (*below s.v., A.D. 930*), which, from a Rāshtrakūṭa point of view, mention that during their king Krishna's reign 'his enemies abandoned Mānyakhēṭa.' It is possible however that this retreat did not take place till somewhat later than A.D. 888 though it must have taken place before A.D. 913 when Krishna's reign ended.]

A.D. *c.* 877-78. Several inscriptions of this period refer to a great battle at Sorēmati which followed a raid made on the Pulināḍu country of the Chittoor District by an allied force of soldiers sent by the Western Ganga and Noḷamba-Pallava chiefs. Apparently after this raid and in consequence of it these allies were attacked by a combined army of the Vaiḍumba and Bāṇa chiefs. Action was joined at Sorēmati, and the Ganga and Noḷamba forces were beaten and compelled to retire. Many of the records are epitaphs of soldiers who were killed (*V. R. i. Chittoor 167, 168, 170, 175, 180, 196, 243, 255, 256; 295, 296 of 1905; 542, 556, 571 of 1906; 306, 318 of 1912, etc.*). One record of the Noḷamba-Pallava chief Mahēndra I (whose mother Jayabbe, the daughter of Ganga Rāchamalla I is mentioned) says that he 'destroyed the Chōla and other rivals' and 'succeeded in sowing dissensions among those outside his frontiers.' (*E. C. xii Si. 38.*)

From these inscriptions we learn that the Noḷamba chief Mahēndra I, called also 'Mayindādi,' had, under the orders of his suzerain the Ganga 'Daḍige' Rāchamalla, 'marched against Talakāḍu' apparently before he invaded the Pulināḍu. [Though why the Ganga chief should have wanted his subordinate to attack one of the principal Ganga towns is a puzzle.] The Government Epigraphist thought perhaps in consequence of some internal dissensions in the Ganga kingdom Talakaḍ had fallen into the hands of some rival Ganga chief (*E. R. 1913, pp. 90, 91*). Acting under the same orders Mahēndra sent his two generals, 'Kaḍuveṭṭi' Muttarasa and Madura, to invade the Bāṇa country of the Pulināḍu; and they did so and burned the town of Permāvi, and destroyed Kōyaṟṟūr. The Bāṇa chief 'Vīra-Chūḷāmaṇi', i.e., Vijayāditya II 'Prabhumēru,' assisted by the Vaiḍumba chief Gaṇḍa-Trinētra, attacked the invaders. There was a sanguinary battle at Sorēmati, and the Noḷamba-Ganga allies were beaten back.

As to the date of these events we are aided by the inscription at Dharmapuri, anciently Tagaḍūr, in Salem District (*348 of 1901; V. R. ii. Salem 81*) which shews Mahēndra Noḷamba at that place in the year A.D. 878–79, Ś. 800. This place was far from his own country, and as it is about fifty miles only from Talakāḍ it is reasonable to suppose he was there only because he had gained temporary possession of Talakāḍ; we therefore date the battle of Sorēmati at about A.D. 877–78. As additional support it may be noticed that a few years later, viz., in A.D. 892 the Ganga and Noḷamba chiefs had quarrelled and were openly fighting one another. (*See E. R. 1913, Rep. § 13.*)

The Bāṇa Vīra-Chūḷāmaṇi who fought in the battle was then a prince, probably, and represented his father.

[If my date for this battle is accurate, it will be noticed that South India was convulsed with fighting at this time, for nearly all the nations of that country were up in arms and at war. This state of things gave the Chōla family a chance to redeem their fallen fortunes.]

A.D. 878–79. Ś. 800. The Noḷamba chief Mahēndra I. Gift to a Jaina temple at Dharmapuri (ancient Tagaḍūr) in Salem District (*V. R. ii. Salem, 81 ; 348 of 1901*). He is mentioned about this time in a village record in Central Mysore, which states his parentage. (*E. C. xii. Si. 24.*)

A.D. 879–80. Ambūr in N. Arcot. Inscription of the twenty-sixth year of the Pallava chief Nṛipatunga, commemorating the death of a servant of the W. Ganga chief Prithivīpati I (now deceased—killed in battle) during a cattle raid. These raids, accompanied by constant violence and outrage, appear to have been of common occurrence, judging by the number of memorial *Vīrakals* which have been found. Women as well as cattle were carried off. No one's property was safe, nor could they tell from day to day when a descent would be made on their village, and their daughters outraged. Deaths in fighting were very numerous. The robber bands were sometimes the males of a village, sometimes of a group of villages, sometimes of a whole district (nāḍu). In these pages no note is made of individual epitaphs unless they contain some date or historical allusion. V. Rangachāri's lists may be consulted, especially in the districts of North Arcot, Chittoor and the neighbourhood. (*V. R. i. N. Arcot, 536, 537 ; E. R. 7, 8 of 1896 ; E. I. iv, 182.*)

A.D. c. 880. Accession of the Chōla king Āditya I, who restored the fortunes of his family after they had been in an inferior position for a long period. Also accession of the Pallava king Aparājita (*E. I. ix, p. 84*). [Āditya completely crushed Aparājita, and brought Pallava ascendancy to an end.]

A.D. 880–900. Tiruvorriyūr, Chingleput District. Two inscriptions shew that the Bāṇa chief of the day was a feudatory of the Pallavas. (*V. R. i. Chin. 1027, 1030 ; 158, 161 of 1912.*)

[About this time, i. e., the fourth quarter of the ninth century, the Pāṇḍya king Parāntaka-Vīranārāyaṇa is said in the larger Śinnamanūr grant to have fought at Kharagiri, seized Ugra, and destroyed Pennāgaḍam—situated on the Kāvērī.]

A.D. 888. Early in the year. Inscription in Coorg of the eighteenth regnal year of the W. Ganga king Rāchamalla II, who came to the throne about 870. His titles only are given. (*E. C. i. Coorg, 2.*)

A.D. 888–918. Masulipatam plates. Record in the reign of the Eastern Chāḷukya king Chāḷukya-Bhīma who gave to Brahmans a village near the Krishna river in memory of his son who, at the age of sixteen, was killed in battle. The king is said to have defeated the armies of the Rāshṭrakuṭa king Krishna II and his allies the kings of Gujarāt and Karṇāṭa. Battles were fought at Niravadyapura and Peruvangūr, and the young prince fell after having killed from his elephant the Rāshṭrakūṭa general Gunḍayya. (*V. R. ii. Kistna, 9 ; E. R. 1914, p. 84.*)

A.D. c. 890. A Mysore inscription of the Noḷamba-Pallava Mahēndra I, named 'Maindam Noḷamban,' represents him as ruling the whole Gangavāḍi country. It commemorates a death during a cattle-stealing raid. (*E. C. ix. Ht. 9.*)

A.D. 892–93. (Ś. 815, Paridhāvi). Gift to a temple at Dharmapuri, Salem District, by Mahēndra I of the Noḷamba-Pallavas. Below the inscription is one of his son Ayyappa-dēvā. (*V. R. ii. Salem, 74 ; 304 of 1901.*)

A.D. 892. April 17. Copper-plate inscription which gives the date of coronation as stated, of the Eastern Chāḷukya king Chāḷukya-Bhīma. Unfortunately the details do not work out satisfactorily and I have not thought it advisable to alter Fleet's date for that king's accession, viz., A.D. 888. *(E. R. 1918. C. P. 14 of App. A.)*

A.D. 892. Two inscriptions from Dharmapuri, Salem District, shew the Noḷamba-Pallava chief Mahēndra I called 'Mahendrādhirāja' ruling as far south as that place in the year stated. He claims to have destroyed the Bāṇa race. An inscription at Iggali states that the Western Ganga king Rāchamalla died in the course of a battle which he was fighting against the Noḷamba. These statements would seem to shew that after the battle of Sorēmati, whether it was a Noḷamba victory or defeat, the Noḷamba chief eventually got the upper hand. Then, for some reason, a quarrel broke out between Mahēndra I and his suzerain the Ganga ruler. Both sides took up arms and a battle was fought which ended in a victory for Mahēndra. The Noḷamba chief was then enabled to rule over the Gangavāḍi territory—for a time at least. *(E. I. x, 54–70 ; V. R. ii, Salem 74 ; 304 of 1901 ; E. R. 1913, p. 90 f; see below s.v. A.D. 897–98.)*

A.D. c. 895. Inscription in Travancore State of the twenty-eighth year of Vikramāditya Varaguṇa, the Āy king, or chief, of Vēṇāḍ. My only reason for assigning the date 895 is because this same king had given a grant in A.D. 868 (*see above*, and A.D. 895 is about twenty-eight years later.) T. A. Gōpinātha Rao stated his belief that Vikramāditya was called 'Varaguṇa' after the Pāṇḍya Varaguṇa II. *(V.R. iii. Trav. 2 ; T.A. S. i, pp. 1, 17, 187.)*

A.D. 896. The country about Hassan in West Mysore was ruled over by a Ganga chief whose titles only are given. *(E. C. v. Hn. 28.)*

A.D. 897. The Noḷamba chief Noḷipayya ruling in Central Mysore. *(E. C. xii. Mi. 52.)*

A.D. 898. Record at Guḍimallam, Chittoor District, dated in Ś. 820, of the Bāṇa chief Vijayāditya II. He and his parents are named but only the titles are given. *(V. R. i. Chittoor, 57 ; 223 of 1903 ; E. I. xi, 227 ; xvii, 1 ; I.A., 1911, p. 104.)*

A.D. 899. Inscription of a Ganga chief in the Āsandināḍu tract, Kāḍūr District, Mysore. The date is somewhat doubtful, but apparently belongs to this year. It mentions a local chief who was supported by the Noḷamba ruler. At this time the Ganga and Noḷamba families were at enmity with one another, and a little later Noḷamba Mahēndra was killed by Eṛeyappa, son of the Ganga Būtuga I who was now governing the Gangavāḍi country. *(E. C. vi. Kd. 141.)*

A.D. c. 900. The date is quite uncertain, but has been so estimated. The Syrian Christian plates shew Sthāṇu Ravi reigning as king in Travancore. *(V.R. Trav. 89, 90 ; T.A.S. ii, 60, 70.)*

A.D. 903. Early in the year. Grant by the W. Ganga king Rāchamalla II, Satyavākya. Pedigree given in which the following points are noticeable. (5) Durvinīta is said to have fought at Andāri, Ālattūr, Poraḷarē, Pelnagara and other places; (8) Bhūvikrama conquered the Pallavas at Viḷanda, he being also named 'Srīvallabha'; (9) Śivamāra I is called 'Navakāma'; (12) Śivamara II defeated the 'Army of Vallabha,' i. e., the Chāḷukya king. *(E. C. x. Kl. 90.)*

A.D. 904. November 25. A long copper-plate grant at Gaṭṭavāḍi, Nanjangūd Taluk, Mysore, gives a pedigree of the Ganga chiefs. In addition to the information obtained from the last record noted above, we are told that Eṛeyappa III defeated the Chāḷukyas at Rājarāmaḍi ; that Rāchamalla II fought a battle at 'Rēmiya' [Is this a misreading for 'Sāmiya'?] ; that Būtuga I conquered Mahēndra Noḷamba in three fights, the last being at Sāmiya ; and that Eṛeyappa IV captured the fortresses of Tippēru, Sūrūr and Penjēru or Henjēru and slew Mahēndra. (*E.C. xii. Supplement, Nanjangūd Taluk, No. 269.*)

[The history of these few years in Mysore and the neighbourhood may now be summed up. Mahēndra I, the Noḷamba chief, had fallen out with the reigning Ganga, and had been temporarily victorious in a battle fought against him, so that he ruled part of Salem District in A.D. 892. Then the Ganga Būtuga I took the field, fought three battles against Mahēndra, and in the end defeated him at Sāmiya, Būtuga's son Ereyappa having distinguished himself in the capture of these fortresses. Mahēndra was thus finally beaten before A.D. 904. Shortly afterwards Mahēndra was killed by Eṛeyappa, the Ganga prince.]

A.D. 905. Record of the Bāṇa chief Vijayāditya II. (*V. R. i. Chittoor, 58 ; 224 of 1903 ; E.I. xi. 228 ; see above s.v. 898–99.*)

[An inscription of this period shews that the Kērala king Sthāṇu-Ravi, or Ravi II, was on friendly terms with Āditya Chōla. The two kings jointly conferred a title on a chief in Tanjore. (*V.R ii. Tanjore, 1403 ; 286 of 1911.*)]

A.D. 905. Ś. 827. The Bāṇa king Vijayāditya, identified by Dr. Hultzsch as Vijayāditya II, Prabhumēru, ruling in Chittoor District.

(*V.R. i. Chittoor, 58 ; 224 of 1903 ; E.I. xvii, 1.*)

A.D. 907. The war between the Ganga and Noḷamba chiefs is mentioned in an inscription in North Mysore, where at the date of the record the Rāshṭrakūṭa king Krishna II was ruling, which seems to shew that he occupied Noḷamba territory, probably after the death of Mahēndra I, the Noḷamba chief. (*E.C. xi. Jb. 19.*)

[**A.D. 907.** Accession of the afterwards powerful Chōla king, Parāntaka I, between January 15 and July 25. These dates are derived from the Grāmam and Kūram inscriptions.

(*V.R. i. S. Arcot, 559 ; Chingleput, 394 ; E.I. vii, 1 ; viii, 261 ; 735 of 1905 ; 34 of 1900.*)

(*See below s.v. A.D. 943, 946.*)

An inscription of a later date at Tirumālpuram in North Arcot District refers to Parantaka's father Āditya I, calling him by a name which signifies that he died at Toṇḍaimān-Āṛṛūr, near Kāḷahasti.

The Anbil C. P. grant, issued in the reign of Parāntaka II, gives many details about the latter's ancestors. Amongst other things it mentions that Parāntaka I married the daughter of the Kērala king Paluvēṭṭaraiyar. Paḷuvēṭṭa is alluded to in three inscriptions at Tiruvaiyyāṛu, and in one of them his daughter is said to have been the queen of 'Vikrama-Chōla Iḷangōvēḷār.' Since the last title means *Yuvarāja* or heir-apparent, it seems likely that before Parāntaka I came to the throne he had been known as 'Vikrama-Chōla.' (*E. I, xv. 44.*)]

A.D. 908. South Mysore. The Ganga king Eṛeyappa IV *alias* Nītimārga ruling that country. He is called 'Lord of Kuvalāla and Nandagiri.' (*E. C. iii. Ml. 30.*)

A.D. 909. An inscription of the Chōla king Parāntaka I's third year. His father Āditya I having conquered the Pallavas (as above shewn), and the W. Gangas having defeated the Noḷamba-Pallava chief, Parāntaka, shortly after his accession, made war on the Pāṇḍyas. He captured their capital city Madura, and assumed the name by which he is known in the record under notice, viz., 'Madurai-koṇḍa.' By this victory he regained possession of the territory of the earlier Chōlas, which for many years had fallen into the hands of the Pāṇḍya kings, and also became lord over the old Pāṇḍya kingdom.

This was the result of his first war against Rājasimha Pāṇḍya III. This inscription proves that his seizure of Madura took place before A.D. 909–10.

(*J.R.A.S. 1913, 526 ; E. R. 1907, §§ 32–35 ; V. R. ii. Tanjore, 399 ; 29 of 1907.*)

[At this time Kassapa V of Ceylon had been on the throne, according to Hultzsch's revised chronology, since A.D. 1906.]

A.D. 909. An inscription in E. Mysore of Ś. 831, represents as reigning there the Bāṇa chief 'Bejeyitta' who, according to the most recent chronology, must be Vijayāditya Bāṇa II, called 'Pugalvippavar-Gaṇḍa.' It records local fighting and slaughter. (*E. C. x. Mb. 229.*)

A.D. 909. At Allūr near Trichinopoly, in third year of Parāntaka Chōla I. Gift of land by the queen of the Ganga Prithivīpati II, here called 'Vīrachōla-Iḷangōvēḷār.' (*See note above s. v., A. D. 907.*). It recognizes that the Chōla king was now suzerain. (*V. R. iii. Trich., 343 ; 376 of 1903.*) This is emphasized by another inscription at the same place in which the same Ganga chief bears the name 'Parāntaka-Kuñjaramallar' (*Ibid., No. 347 ; 380 of 1903*). He was now vassal to the Chōla king and was protected by him.

A.D. 911. Rāshṭrakūṭa 'Akālavarsha' Krishna II reigning in N. W. Mysore. Baṇavāsi was ruled by a subordinate, Kaliviṭṭa. (*E. C. vii. Sk., 219 ; viii. Sb., 88.*)

A.D. 913. The Western Ganga prince Eṛeyanga, or Eṛeyappa IV, called by the title 'Nītimarga-Perumānaḍigaḷ,' ruling in S. E. Mysore, under Prithivīpati II. (*E. C. ix. Cp. 161.*)

A.D. 915. Record of the ninth year of Parāntaka Chōla I, who is recognized as supreme in the former Ganga territory of North Arcot. The Chōla king had, in or before this year, conferred the conquered Bāṇa country on the Ganga chief Prithivīpati II, giving him the title 'Śembiyan-Māvalivāṇar-aiyan.' In this record this Prithivīpati II is called 'Lord of the Bāṇas;' also he is said to have won a battle at Vallāḷa, but against whom is not stated.

(*V.R. i. N. Arcot, 633 ; 9 of 1896 ; S.I.I. ii, 376.*)

By this time Parāntaka Chōla had also conquered and reduced the Vaiḍumba chief Śandaiyan. (*E. I. xv, 50 ; E. R. 1904–5, p. 57.*)

An inscription without date in a village near Punganūr in the ancient Pulināḍu country, now Chittoor District, tells of a son of this Ganga Prithivipati II, the lord of the Bāṇas, named 'Vikkiyaṇṇa' (probably = Vikramāditya) who had a quarrel with a member of the Pallava family, Pallava-Dhavaḷa, and in a fight was killed.

(*V.R. i. Chittoor, 221, 222 ; 332, 333 of 1912 ; E.I. xi, 238.*)

[**A.D. *c.* 916–17.** The reign of Kassapa V, king of Ceylon, came to an end, according to Hultzsch's revised chronology, in A.D. 916, or perhaps 917. His successors reigned only seven months, and then Dappula V obtained the throne in 917. Shortly before the death of Kassapa V, we are told in the *Mahāwaṁsa* (ch. lii), the Pāṇḍya king, Rājasimha III, sent many presents to, and begged aid from Kassapa against the Chōlas who had seized his country in or before A.D. 909. Kassapa sent over to the mainland an army to his assistance. Rājasimha led both armies against Parāntaka's troops but was defeated and retired leaving the Singhalese to carry on the war alone. But their army was attacked by disease and their general died from it, and they returned to Ceylon.

Dappula V having become king of the island, Rājasimha, driven to desperation, crossed over to Ceylon, and the two kings prepared for a fresh war against the Chōlas. But owing to grave internal disturbances Dappula had to abandon the enterprise. And the Pāṇḍya king fled to the

Kērala country, leaving his crown 'and other apparel' in Ceylon. This event may have taken place in A.D. 917–18. Amongst the apparel was 'the necklace of Indra', as we learn from the story of what took place later. (*Mahāwaṁśa, ch. liii ; see S.I.I. ii. 375 ff, 387.*)

This was the second war with Ceylon of Parāntaka I, who then assumed the title '*Saṁgrāma Rāghava.*']

A.D. 918. Record at Tiruppārkaḍal, N. Arcot, of the twelfth year of Chōla Parāntaka I. It mentions the above invasion by the Pāṇḍya and the king of Ceylon, which therefore took place in or before that twelfth year. (*V.R. i. North Arcot, 653 ; 693 of 1904.*) This receives support from the Udayēndiram plates of the fifteenth year of Parāntaka, the genuineness of which has however been disputed. A battle had, it appears, been fought at Vēlūr, probably that in which the Pāṇḍyas and Singhalese had been defeated.

A.D. 918. The Masulipatam plates shew that in this year the East Chāḷukya king Amma Rāja I *alias* Vishṇuvardhana, or Rāja Mahēndra was reigning at Drujjūru (modern Dzuzzūr) on the Krishna River. He came to the throne in this year.

(*V.R. ii. Kistna 4 ; I.A. viii, 77 : xx. 266 ; E.I. v, 131.*)

[About this time, in the Noḷamba-Pallava chief's family Ayyappa-dēva-Nanniga, son of Mahēndra I, began to rule his country. He made friends with the Ganga chief Ereyappa.]

(*E.I. x, 54.*)

A.D. 920. July 18 (?) Central Mysore. An inscription alludes to a grant of land made by Noḷamba Ayyappa-dēva and mentions eclipse of sun on that day. But the date given in the record fell about three months later (*E.C. xii. Si. 39*). Another of about the same date in Mysore mentions the same chief and says that he 'surrounded Ganga' and fought a battle. If this be a fact he made friends with the Ganga chief later on. (*E.C. xii. Mi. 71.*)

A.D. 920. Grant of land in West Mysore made by the Ganga chief 'Satyavākya-Vīra', son of Eṛeyappa IV, i.e., his eldest son Narasiṁha. (*E.C. v. Ag. 61.*)

A.D. 921. C.P. grant at Udayēndiram of Parāntaka Chōla I's fifteenth year. The West Ganga chief Prithivīpati II joined together two villages, one of which was Udayēndiram (*V.R. i. North Arcot, 367-A ; S.I.I. ii, p. 375*). The document gives a long account of the events up to date of Parāntaka's reign, and of the Ganga chiefs' exploits.

A.D. 922. Two records in the Bellary District, of date Ś. 844 Chitrabhānu, shew that the Rāshṭrakūṭa king Indra III was then ruling that country (*E.R. 271, 272 of 1918*). He is called 'Nityavarsha.'

[About this time the Kēraḷa king Kanṭha II *alias* Kōkkanḍan-Vīranārāyaṇa, was reigning on the west coast. He was apparently a feudatory of Parāntaka Chōla I. He reigned at least twenty-four years. (*V. R. i. Coimbatore, 106, 107, 141, 144 ; E. R. 147, 148 of 1910 ; 12, 15 of 1891.*) He seems also to have been called 'Ravikōdai'. Parāntaka married a Kēraḷa princess.]

The Udayēndiram C. P. grant says that Parāntaka's capital was Koḷi, which = Uraiyūr near Trichinopoly. (*S.I.I. ii, 375.*)

In the Vengi country there was great confusion for two years about this time. The reign of the Eastern Chāḷukya Amma I of Vengi came to an end in A.D. 925. He was succeeded by his son 'Bēta'-Vijayāditya V who only reigned for fifteen days, when the throne was seized by a member of the junior branch, Tādapa or Tārapa, who was himself assassinated after a month by Vikramāditya II, uncle of Amma I. This Vikramāditya II reigned for eleven months. A civil war followed and the king was defeated and dispossessed by his grand-nephew Bhīma II who, in the absence of Bēta Vijayāditya, had a sound title to the throne. Eight months later Bhima II was killed by Yuddhamalla, son of Tādapa, who succeeded in retaining the throne for seven years, from about A.D. 927–934. Bēta Vijayāditya retired apparently into private life and became the ancestor of the later Piṭhāpūr chiefs. The Maliyapūṇḍi grant says that he was banished by Chāḷukya Bhīma III.

The Maliyapūṇḍi grant mentions another member of the family Rāja-Mārtāṇḍa as having lost his life during the fighting (*B. and V.C. i, 170 ; E.I. ix, 47*). The grant states that the rival princes harassed their subjects at this time.

A.D. 928. C. P. grant by the Kalinga-Ganga king Dēvēndravarma, son of Anantavarma, concerning the village of Tāmaracheruvu. The date is the fifty-first year of the Ganga Era, which = A.D. 928–29 with the epoch taken, as appears correct, as A.D. 878–79. Another grant of the same year mentions Dēvēndra's son Satya. (*V.R. i. Ganjam, 4, 5 ; I.A. x, 243 ; xiii, 273.*)

A.D. 929. Ś. 853, Virōdhi. Inscription at Dharmapuri (ancient Tagaḍūr) Salem District, of the Nōḷamba-Pallava Iṛuga, son of Aṇṇiga. It shews that this country was ruled by a Noḷamba chief even though it lay in Ganga territory and the Noḷambas had been defeated by the W. Ganga chiefs Būtuga I and Eṛeyappa. (*V.R. ii, Salem 82 ; E.R. 198 of 1910.*)

A.D. 930. January 17. Inscription at Kalas shews Rāshṭrakūṭa Gōvinda IV reigning (*E.I. xiii, 326*). Also (same year) reigning in North Mysore. (*E.C. xi. Dg. 119.*)

A.D. *c.* 930. The Noḷamba chief, Ayyappa-dēva's son Aṇṇiga, gave a village in East Mysore to a member of the Ganga family who had assisted him in driving away a raid made by the Sāntara chief of Humcha, and had distinguished himself by bravery in a battle.

(*E.C. x. Gd. 4.*)

A.D. 930, May 10. The Cambay copper-plate grant relates that on this day the Rāshṭrakūṭa king Gōvinda IV weighed himself against gold at Kapitthaka on the Godavari river and gave away 600 villages as Brahman *Agrahārams*, and 800 villages to various temples. The pedigree of the family is given. About king Krishna II, Akālavarsha, the record states that in his day 'his enemies abandoned Mānyakhēṭa.' This confirms the E. Chāḷukya story which runs to the effect that their king Guṇaka-Vijayāditya had burnt Mānyakhēṭa (for Malkhēḍ). The date of this 'burning' must have been between A.D. 878 and 888, which last year was the last of the reign of Guṇaka-Vijayāditya. The 'abandonment' must have taken place before A.D. 913, which was Krishna II's last year. (*E. I. vii, 26.* See above *s.v. A.D. 846–47.*)

[There is strong evidence to the effect that Gōvinda IV was a bad king and a bad man. The inscription specifically declares that he was not guilty of cruelty to his elder brother Amōghavarsha II, but that only proves that accusations to that effect were rife, and it is a fact that Amōghavarsha was deprived of the throne, which was his by right of birth, by Gōvinda.]

A.D. 933–942. Some inscriptions at Tiruvoṟṟiyūr, near Madras, in Saidapet Taluk of this period are dated between the twenty-seventh and thirty-fifth years of the Chōla king Parāntaka I. One of his twenty-ninth year (A.D. 935–36) shews that he was then on good terms with the Chēra, or Kēraḷa, king Vijayarāghava, for the latter's daughter Iravi-Nīli gave a lamp to the temple at that place. Parāntaka's son Arinjaya is alluded to, being called 'Arindagai'. (*V.R. i. Chingleput, 1036–39 ; 168–170 of 1912.*) The Kēraḷa family was then tributary to Parāntaka.

(*Above s.v. A.D. 922–23.*)

A.D. 934. The temple at Tirunāmanallūr, in South Arcot, was founded, according to an inscription there of the twenty-eighth year of Parāntaka Chōla I, by his son Rājāditya, whose mother was Kokkiḷānaḍi ; another record mentions Rājāditya's wife as daughter of the chief of 'Lāṭa.' This lady had an elder brother, also named Rajāditya, who bore the title 'Pugaḷvippavagaṇḍa,' (a title similar to that of the Bāṇa king Vijayāditya III), and this latter Rājāditya had a son Vīra Chōla Lāṭa-rāja,[1] who was feudatory to the Chōla king Rājarāja I.

(*V.R. i. S. Arcot 903; Chittoor 256 ; 363 of 1902 ; 375 of 1911 ; E. I. iv, 137 ; VII i. 133.*)

A.D. 934. In the Vengi country the E. Chāḷukya Bhīma III began to reign, having ousted his predecessor Yuddhamalla. He granted some land in the Gudravāra-vishaya. One of his *birudas* was '*Karayilladāta.*' (*Brit. Mus. plates, V.R. ii. Kistna 8 ; E.I. v, 135 ; I.A. xx, 270.*)

A.D. 934–945. Reign of the E. Chāḷukya, Chāḷukya-Bhima III. He lived in disturbed times, being opposed on all sides. He had to deal with the supporters, in his own kingdom, of Yuddhamalla II whom he had driven from the throne. He fought with and claimed to have defeated the Rāshṭrakūṭa king Gōvinda IV ruling the country to his west. The Noḷamba-Pallava chief Ayyappa-Nanniga, assisted by a force sent by the Western Ganga chief Ereyappa, jointly fought against him, and these enemies of his were joined by the Baṇavāśi chief Bijja *alias* Dantivarman, and several other local rulers.

(*See the Kalachumbaṟṟu grant of Bhīma's successor Amma II ; and E.I. vi, 47 ; ix, 47; vii, 177.*)

A record of Ganga Eṛeyappa's at Bēgūr near Bangalore refers to his war with the E. Chāḷukya king, calling Bhīma II by the name 'Vīra Mahēndra and Gaṇḍamahēndra'. It makes out that Bhīma attacked the Noḷamba country, and that Ereyappa assisted Noḷamba Ayyappa's defence against aggression. This must have taken place before A.D. 938 which was Ereyappa's last year. There was a battle at Tumbēpāḍi, and a Nāgattara chief, feudatory to Eṛeyappa, lost his life. (*E.C. ix. Bn. 83 ; E.I. i, 346 ; vi, 47, vii, 77 ; x, 54.*)

A.D. 935. An inscription at Kīḷ Muttugur in North Arcot shews that there was a serious raid on that country by people from Mysore, the Ganga country, driving off cattle and committing outrages in the villages. It is dated in the twenty-ninth year of the Chola Parantaka I then ruling over the old Bāṇa territory.

(*E.I. iv, 177 ; V.R. i. N. Arcot, 322; 1 of 1896. For another note of this year see above, s.v. A.D. 933–942.*)

A.D. 936, June 25. Inscription shewing the Noḷamba chief Annayya then ruling in Anantapur District. (*759 of 1916.*)

A.D. 937. In north Mysore the Rāshṭrakūṭa king 'Amōghavarsha' Baḍḍiga was now reigning. (*E.C. xi. Cd. 76.*)

A.D. 938. In this year in the month of March in north-west Mysore Rāshṭrakūṭa Krishna III *alias* Kannara, is named as supreme over that country and the Baṇavāśi 12000 tract. Māchiyarasa was governing in Baṇavāśi. (*E.C. viii. Sb. 70, 71.*)

[There is, however, an inscription bearing date A.D. 939–40 and giving the name of Amōghavarsha as king in North Mysore (*E.C. xi. Cd. 77.*). The date is Ś. 861, 'Vikāri' and = the end of the year A.D. 939.]

[1] This reference and its bearing are discussed in my article Rājēndra, the Gangaikoṇḍa Chola in the *Journal of Indian History II, 330.* (Reprint, p. 14.)—*Editor.*

A.D. 938. Death of the Western Ganga king Ereyappa IV and accession of his son Rāchamalla III; but the latter was in 939 murdered by his brother Būtuga II who seized the throne with the support of Rāshṭrakūṭa Krishna III. *(See Fleet in E. I. vi, 40.)*

A.D. 939. N.-W. Mysore. Krishna III, Rāshṭrakūṭa, sovereign. *(E. C. viii. Sb. 471, 476.)*

A.D. 940. N.-W. Mysore. The same. The ruler of Baṇavāsi under him, was Manchiga *(See s. v. A.D. 938) alias* Māchiyarasa. *(E. C. viii. Sb. 75, 77.)*

A.D. 940. Inscription at Tiruvoṟṟiyūr, Chingleput District, of the thirty-four year of Parāntaka Chōla I. It refers to an expedition made by him to the north and to the destruction of Nellore by his forces. *(V. R. i. Chingleput 1029; 150 of 1912.)*

A.D. 941. Two inscriptions in N. and N.-W. Mysore. Krishna III, *alias* 'Kannara,' reigning. *(E. C. viii. Sb. 83; xi. Cd. 75.)*

A.D. 941. An inscription at Siddhalingamaḍam in South Arcot of the fifth year of Krishna III, Rāshṭrakūṭa, shews that by that time, in conjunction with the feudatory W. Ganga chief he had captured Kānchī and Tanjore from Parāntaka Chōla I. *(V. R. i. S. Arcot, 778; 375 of 1905.)*

[Other inscriptions of Krishna III's reign shew that he was considered supreme lord in parts at least of the Chingleput and South Arcot Districts from about this time up to the date of his death. He must therefore have inflicted a severe defeat on Parāntaka Chōla. *(V. R. i. S. Arcot 633; 232 of 1902.)*]

A.D. 941–943. During this period Parāntaka Chōla I invaded Ceylon, then under king Udaya III, whose accession took place in 941. After A.D. 943 records of Parāntaka state that he 'took Ceylon.'

[Parāntaka's third war with Ceylon is described in the *Mahāwaṁśa (ch. liii, 39–51; liv, 48)*. King Udaya was a drunkard, and Parāntaka, hearing of his incapacity and desiring at the same time to become absolute lord of the whole Pāṇḍya kingdom, demanded from him the crown jewels and apparel which Rājasimha III, the Pāṇḍya king, had left in Ceylon about A.D. 918 at the close of the second war. On Udaya's refusal to surrender them Parāntaka sent an army to take them by force. His general was successful. Udaya was defeated, and the Pāṇḍya jewels, etc., were taken to the mainland. The chronicle adds that Udaya sent over an army to the Chōla country in retaliation, and that the expedition was successful, the regalia in question being recaptured and taken to Udaya's capital. This recapture may have taken place at any time between A.D. 943 and 949, when Udaya's reign terminated. It is possible that the reason why Parāntaka gave way in this matter was because of the danger he was in from an attack by the Rashṭrakūṭas. Udaya died while repairing his palace, which the Chōla army had destroyed.]

A.D. 942, December 22. Grant of a village in Central Mysore by the Noḷamba-Pallava chief Dilīpaya, *alias* Iriva-Noḷamba. *(E. C. xii. Si. 28.)*

A.D. 943, January 14. Inscription at Grāmam in S. Arcot, of the thirty-fifth year of Parāntaka Chōla I. It makes his accession in the year following January 14, 907. *(V. R. i. S. Arcot 559; 735 of 1905.)*

A.D. 944. Record shewing that the tracts called the 'Kogali 500' and the 'Māsavāḍi 40,' were ruled by a chief connected with the Chāḷukya family, named Kaṭyēra; subordinate to the Rāshṭrakūṭa king. These tracts were parts of Hadagali and Harpanhalli taluks. *(V. R. i. Bellary 267; 75 of 1904.)*

A.D. 945, December 5. Coronation-day of the E. Chāḷukya king, Amma Rāja I, as stated in the British museum plates (*V. R. iii. B. M. 9; cf. the Masulipatam plates; V. R. ii. Kistna 3;*

and the Maliyapūṇḍi plates B. & V. C. i. 164 ; I. A. vii, 5 ; viii, 74 ; xx, 271 ; xxiii, 123 ; E. I. v, 131 ; ix, 47). The grants were of villages in the Kistna and Nellore Districts. Family pedigree and events of former reigns are given. (*See also I. A. 1890, p. 102.*)

A.D. 946. Kūram record of fortieth regnal year of Parāntaka Chōla I. It states that he had 'entered Īḻam' (Ceylon) (*V. R. i. Chin. i, 394 ; S. Arcot, 559 ; 34 of 1900; 735 of 1905 ; E. I. vii, 1; viii, 261*). The details of the date are sufficient to prove it to have been July 25, A.D. 946 ; and shews that his accession was not later than that day in A.D. 907. (*See above s. v. A. D. 907, 943.*)

Central Mysore was being governed by Iriva *alias* Dilīpayya, the Noḷamba chief (*E. C. xii. Si. 14*). There was fighting in that country between local chiefs (*Ibid. Si. 35*), two years later.

• [**A.D. 947-949,** Parāntaka Chōla I died in A.D. 947 and was succeeded by his son Rājāditya I. About this time, and possibly on account of the change in the Chōla kingdom, the Rāshṭrakūta king Krishna III, aided by his Western Ganga feudatory Būtuga II, made an organized attack on the Chōla kingdom. Advancing as far as Takkōla, close to the present railway station at Arconum, he was confronted by his enemy's army led by king Rājāditya in person. A battle took place and Būtuga killed Rājāditya. This is believed to have taken place in A. D. 949, and it was certainly not later, though it may have been a little earlier. That Būtuga killed Rājāditya with his own hand seems certain, but the exact details are not well known. The Āṭakūr inscription says that Būtuga acted 'treacherously', or 'stealthily', but explicitly states that he stabbed Rājāditya with a dagger and killed him. The result of the battle was a victory for the Rāshṭrakuṭas and Krishna III rewarded Būtuga by giving him the lordship of the Baṇavāsi 12000 country. As Būtuga already held the fiefs of Beḷvola, Purigeri, Kisukāḍ and Bāgenāḍ by grant from Amōghavarsha III, king Krishna's father, he became a strong power for the time, being confirmed in those grants by his sovereign.

The Āṭakūr inscription which belongs to the year A.D. 949–50 relates that while the Rāshṭrakūṭa army was making a state progress through his dominions after the battle, Būtuga gave a certain person a hound, and that when this hound attacked a wild boar, both the hound and the boar lost their lives.

We may therefore take, with some reservation, the year A.D. 949 for Rājāditya's death, and consequently for the accession of his successor Gaṇḍarāditya.]

A.D. 949. The Āṭakūr inscription alluded to in the above note (*E. C. iii. Md. 41; E .I. ii, 168 ; vi, 40; vii, 192 ; xii, 123 ; see also V. R. i. N. Arcot, 44, 579; S. Arcot, 778, 622, 633, etc. ; 2 of 1897 ; 428 of 1902 ; 375 of 1909 ; 119 of 1906 ; 232 of 1902*).

A.D. 950. The Anantapūr country was ruled by the Noḷamba chief Irivi, or Dilīpayya. Some records, one of which is of A. D. 948, tell the customary story of village raids, cattle-lifting, slaughter, destruction of a village, and outrage of women. (*Mysore Arch. Rep. for 1923 ; Nos. 32, 33, 34, 54 ; 726, 728 of 1916 ; and E. C. x. Ct. 49.*)

A.D. c. 950. The Anbil plates (*E xv, 50*) mention the Chōla prince Ariñjaya, son of Parāntaka Chōḷa I. saying that he married a Vaiḍumba princess. Their son was Parāntaka Chōla II.

A.D. 951. The Rāshṭrakūṭa king 'Kannara', i.e., Krishna III reigning in N.-W. Mysore. (*E. C. viii. Sb. 570.*)

A.D. 952. Record at Ukkal in North Arcot District of the sixteenth year of the same king, proving his occupation of that country. It mentions the Noḷamba-Pallava chief Dilīpayya under the title 'Noḷamba-Tribhuvanadhīra *alias* Pallava-Murāri' (See below, *s. v. A. D. 962*

V. R. i, N. Arcot, 304 ; 25 of 1893). The inscription, which is on a temple, seems to disclose an act of high-handed injustice[1] on the part of the village authorities. They state that they are prepared to sell certain lands surrounding the village which have hitherto been held as communal property, and they add this remarkable declaration, viz., 'No persons shall be allowed to produce deeds of gift or deeds of sale in order to shew that the land thus sold belongs to themselves. We, the assembly, shall levy a fine . . . of gold . . . from the inhabitants who produce such deeds.' (*S. I. I. iii, p. 11.*)

[A.D. 952. King Mahindu IV of Ceylon came to the throne in this year according to Dr. Hultzsch's Singhalese chronology. He was attacked by an army sent from the Tamil country by a king whom the *Mahawamśa* calls the 'Chōla-Vallabha'.[2] It is not known to whom this refers. 'Vallabha' is a Chāḷukya title. The Chōla kings of the time of Mahindu IV (A.D. 952–968) were Gaṇḍarāditya and Ariñjaya. (*Mahawamśa, ch. liv.*)]

A.D. 952. The Western Ganga Nanniya-Ganga Būtuga II ruling in West Mysore (*E. C. v. Bl. 123*); and in North Arcot where he is called 'Prithvi-Ganga', and is shewn to be a vassal of Rāshṭrakūṭa Krishna III. (*V. R. i. N. Arcot, 586 ; 346 of 1901.*)

A.D. 953. Inscription at Tirukkaḻukuṉṟam, Chingleput District, of the seventeenth year of Rāshṭrakūṭa Krishna III, entitled 'He who captured Kānchī and Tanjore.' He had seized the principal cities of the Chōla kingdom after the battle of Takkola (*E. I. iii. 282*). There is another of the nineteenth year (A.D. 955–56) at the same place.

A.D. 954. North-West Mysore under the rule of Rāshṭrakūṭa Krishna III, cattle raids and deaths (*E. C. viii. Sb. 240, 474*). And in A.D. 955–56 (*ibid. Sb. 202*).

A.D. 955 (?) According to the author of an article (*E. I. xii. 121*), this was the first year of Parāntaka Chōla II, *alias* Sundara Chōla, Rājakēśarivarman. Two of his queens are named, one being a Chēra princess who lived till 1012. He had a general named Śiriya-Vēḷār, who was killed in Ceylon in the king's ninth year (*see 116 of 1895*). This would be in A.D. 963–64, during the reign of Mahindu IV, king of Ceylon, and the war in which he lost his life would be the same as is referred to above (*s. v., A. D. 952*).

[1] The inscription referred to here (No. 7 *S.I.I.* iii, pt. I, page 11) is unfortunately in an imperfect state of preservation. Enough of it is however left to catch the purport of the inscription sufficiently clearly to see that it is of the contrary import to what is stated here, and contains in it nothing that smacks of any 'high-handed injustice'. The village assembly met and apparently distributed the unoccupied lands of the village under certain conditions among those who were willing to take them up for cultivation. For one reason or another several of these lots that were thus allotted remained uncultivated. On a subsequent occasion the same village assembly met and resolved to make a fresh distribution of these lands and arranged accordingly. They were bound to see that the new occupants of these lands were not disturbed in their possession by those to whom they were formerly distributed, as having a previous title. The resolution of the committee therefore threatens very severe penalties upon those who would take it upon themselves to obstruct the new occupants in their peaceful possession of the lands for purposes of cultivation. The heavy fines which are prescribed are also prescribed against the members of the committee who had undertaken the general supervision of the village itself. This is the usual procedure that is adopted and the position could be made clear by reference to a number of other inscriptions of a similar import, not exactly all of them of the same kind in all detail. For a mere corroboration, reference may be made to the following inscriptions taken at random from *South Indian Inscriptions*, vol. vi, only recently published, relating to localities very near Ukkal itself. Nos. 344, 351, 369, 370, 434, corresponding to the Annual Report of the Epigraphist 1898, Nos. 61, 68, 84 and 149. —*Editor*.

[2] The reference leans clearly to the Chōḷa, in which case the title is Vaḷabha. Tam. Vaḷavan, one of the many generic names for the Chōlas.—*Editor*.

A.D. 955. Rock inscription on the Bāvāji Hill at Vellore, N. Arcot, shewing that in this year the Nolamba-Pallava chief Tribhuvanadhīra (*see above s. v. 952*) bought the village of Ukkal from 'Vīra Chola', i.e., the Western Ganga chief Prithivīpati II, who bore that title. The reigning suzerain was the Rāshṭrakūṭa king Krishna III (*V. R. i. N. Arcot 592 ; 10 of 1887 ; E. I. iv. 81*). The inscription is dated in the twenty-sixth year of his reign (i.e., 962–63).

A.D. 956. At Tiruvorriyūr, Chingleput District, an inscription of the twentieth year of Rāshṭrakūṭa Krishna III witnesses a gift to the temple by a certain *Sanyāsin*, who became an ascetic out of grief for the death at the battle of Takkōla (in 949) of the Chōla king Rājāditya (*above, s. v. 947–49*). (*V. R. i. Chingleput 1050 ; 181 of 1912.*)

A.D. 958. Gift of villages to the Umāmahēśvara temple at Bezwada, on the Krishna river by the Eastern Chāḷukya king Amma-Rāja II; which temple, the inscription states, had been built by king Vijayāditya-Narēndra-Mrigarāja of the same dynasty (about a century or more earlier). (*V. R. ii. Guntūr 813 ; C.-P. No. 11 of 1915.*)

A.D. 958. North-West Mysore ruled over by Rāshṭrakūṭa Krishna III. (*E. C. viii. Sb. 501.*)

A.D. 959. West Mysore ruled by the W. Ganga chief. His personal name is omitted and only the usual Ganga titles are given. Although not so stated it is fairly certain that he was a vassal of Rāshṭrakūṭa Krishna III. (*E. C. vi. Cm. 42.*)

A.D. 959. Record of a 'Noḷambādhirāja', i.e., Irivi-Dilīpayya, ruling in Anantapūr District. (*731 of 1917.*)

A.D. 960. Record of the twenty-fourth year of Rāshṭrakūṭa Krishna III shewing that the Vaiḍumba chief of the Tsandavōlu country south of the Krishna river was subject to him. (*V.R. i. S. Arcot 668; 267 of 1902; E.R. 1904-5, p. 57.*) Nevertheless a Vaiḍumba chief (possibly the same) had given his daughter in marriage to the Choḷa prince Ariñjaya, son of Parāntaka I. And thirty years later the Vaiḍumba family was again subject to the Chōla monarch.

(*E.I. vii. 138 ; V.R. ii. Nellore 239 ; B. and V.C., Gūḍūr Taluk, 88.*)

A.D. 961. In East Mysore an inscription shewing Irivi-Noḷamba II ruling that tract (*E.C. x. Mb. 126*). He was a vassal of the Rāshṭrakūṭas. Two years later he is found ruling in Anantapur District. (*55 of 1917.*)

A.D. 962. Rāshṭrakūṭa Krishna III supreme in North Arcot, with the Noḷamba-Pallava Dilīpayya, ruling that country under him, called in the rock-cut Bāvāji inscription 'Tribhuvanadhīra.'

(*See above s.v. A.D. 955, where this record is noted. See also S.I.I. i, p. 75.*)

A.D. 962. Two inscriptions in South Arcot shew the Vaiḍumba chief, Śandaya-Tiruvayya-Śrīkaṇṭha, making gifts to temples in that region. One is dated in the twenty-fifth year of Krishna III and both mention him, proving Rāshṭrakūṭa overlordship and the temporary collapse of the Chōlas. (*V.R. i., S.A. 567, 721 ; 743, 16 of 1905.*)

A.D. 963. Rāshṭrakūṭa Krishna III reigning in North Arcot in his twenty-seventh year. Inscription at Takkōla near Arconum railway station, where the great battle took place in which the Chōla king Rājāditya was, in A.D. 949, defeated and killed.

(*V.R. i. North Arcot 44, 579 ; 2 of 1897 ; 428 of 1902.*)

In the same year a record of cattle-robberies and deaths of villagers in Shimōga taluk, Mysore, shews Krishna III reigning. (*Mysore A.A.R. 1923, No. 115, p. 116.*)

[About this time in the Mysore country Satyavākya-Mārasimha III became Western-Ganga chief. An inscription at Kārya in Mysore (*E.C. iii. Nj. 192*), which bears date A.D. 968 and is one of his fifth year, would make his accession in 964–65; but another of his tenth year is dated October 25, A.D. 971 and this would fix it as having occurred in the year following October 25, 961 (*E.C. iv. Ng. 51*). His principal exploit was that for some reason not very clear, he quarrelled with Poralchora II, now the ruler of the Noḷambavāḍi country under Rāshṭrakūṭa domination, called himself 'Noḷamba-kulāntaka' (death to the Noḷamba family), and about A.D. 970, made war on him. Fleet's theory as to the origin of the war was that the Noḷamba chief had become restive under the Rāshṭrakūṭa yoke, and that Mārasimha, loyal to the latter, determined to assist his overlord by crushing down any opposition to him. In any case the war took place, the Noḷamba chief was completely defeated, and his province fell under Ganga rule. Mārasimha advanced and 'despoiled the ruler of Baṇavāsi'—possibly because the said ruler had also become disaffected towards the Rāshṭrakūṭa king.] (*E.I. v. 151.*)

A.D. 964. Inscription in North Mysore relating to the tract called the 'Kadambaḷige 1000,' which was ruled by a Rāshṭrakūṭa official, and was said to contain 'treasures, hidden stores, and 1,000 soldiers.' (*E.C. xi. Hk. 30, 33.*)

A.D. 965. The Pulināḍu country, Chittoor District, was ruled in this year by a chief Vijjaladēva, who is not otherwise heard of. He was a vassal of the Rāshṭrakūṭa king. An inscription at Embādi near Punganūr, and several *vīrakals*, attest that a town near by, Uppunelli, was attacked and captured with much loss of life, by whom is not stated.

(*V.R. i. Chittoor 201–207 ; 578–584 of 1906.*)

A.D. 965. An inscription in East Mysore mentions the plunder of a town in the reign of Rāshṭrakūṭa Krishna III. (*E.C. ix. Ma. 75.*)

[A.D. 965–66 is the probable date of accession of the Chōla Āditya II. He could hardly be called a king, as the fortunes of his family were at a very low ebb. Almost the only thing for which he is renowned is that in many inscriptions he is said to have 'taken the head of the Pāṇḍya king', his enemy. He reigned about five years (See *E.R. 1921, p. 109*). About the same time, i.e., between 965 and 969 we hear, from the other side of a Vīra Pāṇḍya 'who took the head of the Chola', and called himself 'Chōlāntaka' (*474 of 1909 ; 101 of 1905 ; E.I. ix, 84.*)]

A.D. 965. The Western Ganga Mārasimha III ruling in South Mysore. (*E.C. iv. ch. 48.*)

A.D. 965, March 6. Gift of land in Anantapūr District by Poralchōra II of the Noḷamba-Pallava family, grandson (so-stated) of Iriva-Noḷamba. (*V.R. i. Anant. 127 ; 93 of 1913.*)

A.D. 965 (?) An inscription in Ganjam District of the Kalinga-Ganga or Eastern Ganga king or prince Indravarman *alias* Rājasimha, is dated in the eighty-seventh year of the dynasty. Another of his is dated in the ninety-first year, and a third in the 149th year, shewing that he lived to a good old age. He was son of Dānārṇava. The eighty-seventh year of the dynasty, if my interpretation is accurate fell in about A.D. 964–65 (See *Genealogical Tables ; Kalinga-Ganga Kings ; notes*). Unfortunately the name Indravarman, or Dēvēndravarman, does not occur in the list on which my Table is founded till A.D. 1070, and that Indravarman's father was not named Dānārṇava. The Indravarman and Dānārṇava of the inscription may have been princes of the royal house. (*V.R. i. Ganjam 13, 290 ; I.A. xiv. 131 ; E.I. iii. 127.*)

A.D. 966, February 17. An inscription at Koḷagallu in Bellary District of the date given states that the Rāshṭrakūta king Krishna III had died in this year and had been succeeded by Khoṭṭiga. Krishna III's death, therefore, must have taken place between February 23, 965 and February 17, 966. (*V.R. i. Bellary 84 ; 236 of 1913 ; see E.H.D., p. 54.*)

A.D. 966. The Noḷamba-Pallava chief Irivi-Noḷamba *alias* Dilīpayya, ruling in East Mysore (*E.C. x. Kl. 245*). Mention of his son Ayyapa-dēva (*17 of 1917*).

A.D. 967, March 29. Rāshṭrakūṭa Khoṭṭiga reigning supreme, with imperial titles in North Mysore. [The date is given according to the lunar *tithi* quoted, but the week-day given in the inscription is incorrect for that *tithi*.] (*E.C. viii. Sb. 531.*) It commemorates deaths during cattle-stealing affrays. (*See also E.C. xi. Hk. 23, 931.*)

[In A.D 968, according to the revised chronology, king Sēna V came to the throne in Ceylon. The *Mahāwaṁśa* tells us inroads of Tamils caused great trouble to the islanders during his reign. The invaders 'oppressed the people and took by force what belonged to them'. (*Mahāwaṁśa, ch. 54.*)]

A.D. 968, May 10 (?) (The given week-day does not suit the given *tithi*). Record in North Mysore of the Rāshṭrakūṭa Khoṭṭiga, *alias* 'Nityavarsha'. (*E.C. xi. Cd. 50, 74.*)

[Sometime between A.D. 966 and 972, apparently, a Pāṇḍya king Śaḍaiyan-Māran came to the throne. An inscription at Śinnamānūr of the reign of Rājēndra Chōla I mentions Śaḍaiyan-Māran's forty-sixth regnal year. (*440 of 1907. E.R., 1908, § 39.*)

[About the year A.D. 969 the Chōla king Āditya II was ousted from the throne by his cousin Madurāntaka Uttama Chōla (*See E.R., 1921, p. 109*). The name shews the antagonism existing between the Chōlas and Pāṇḍyas.

About A.D. 970 the Western Ganga Mārasimha III (*See note above s.v., 963*) made war on the Noḷamba-Pallava chiefs, and his general Chāmuṇḍa-Rāya succeeded in storming and capturing the principal Noḷamba stronghold, Uchchangi. He appears to have annexed the Noḷambavāḍi country and to have crushed the power of the ruling family (*E.I. v. 157; iv, 350*). His success, however, was not long-lived for the Chōlas got the upper hand a few years later.

In this year also came to the throne of the Eastern Chāḷukyas of Vengi, king Dānārṇava, who reigned for three years. After him there is an unexplained interval of twenty-seven years of 'anarchy' in the Vengi country till Śaktivarman came to the throne in A.D. 999.]

A.D. 970. An inscription in N. Mysore represents the Western Chāḷukyas as ruling over that country in this year in the person of Vikramāditya IV; but there is reason to believe it spurious. The date is very much elaborated and burdened with details very uncommon at this period; and the country concerned was at this time certainly ruled by the Western Gangas and their Rāshṭrakūṭa overlords. (*E. C. xi. Cd. 25.*)

A.D. 971. The Western Ganga Mārasimha III, 'Satyavākya-Noḷamba-Kulāntaka' ruling over central Mysore. (*E. C. v. Cn. 262, 267.*)

Another inscription, of the tenth year of the same ruler, who is also called 'Guttiya-Ganga,' is dated October 25 of this year. Its wording is interesting. It represents him as governing the Gangavāḍi 96,000 country after 'having extracted the thorns from it', i.e., after having crushed all opposition. The date being in his tenth year, it makes his accession as in the year following October 25, A.D. 961. (*E. C. iv. Ch. 9; Ng. 51.*)

An inscription near Sorab in N.-W. Mysore mentions a certain Śāntivarmma as ruling over the Baṇavāsi 12,000 territory. He was perhaps one of the Kadamba family. (*E. C. viii. Sc. 44.*)

In this year died the princess Pāmbabbe, a sister of the Western-Ganga Būtuga II. She devoted herself to a life of penance for thirty years. (*E.C. vi. Kd. 1.*)

A.D. 972. An inscription in Cuddapah District says that a Vaiḍumba chief, whose title alone is given—' Bhuvana-Trinētra '—was crowned in this year. It is uncertain who this was. (*V. R. i. Cudd. 583; 325 of 1905.*)

In the same year a record at Bāgali in Bellary District shews ' Nityavarsha ' Khoṭṭiga, the Rāshṭrakūṭa king, as reigning there. (*V. R. i. Bell. 271; 79 of 1904; E.R. 1903, p. 78.*)

An inscription, whose date is at the end of this year, in Sōrāb Taluk, N.-West Mysore, mentions as sovereign the Rāshṭrakūṭa Kakka (or Karka or Kakkala) who had by now succeeded Khoṭṭiga. (*E.C. viii. Sb. 455.*)

A somewhat doubtful date, but between May 22 and June 19 of this year in an inscription in Kāḍūr District, Western Mysore, shews the Western Ganga Mārasimha III ruling there in his eleventh year (*E. C. vi. Kd. 147*). Another in Central Mysore of Mārasimha III, called ' Noḷamba Kulāntaka.' (*E.C. viii, p. 103.*)

A.D. 973. The Rāshṭrakūta power which had subdued and ruled over large parts of Southern India succumbed in this year. King Khoṭṭiga had been defeated by Sīyaka II *alias* Harsha, the Paramāra king of Malwa about two years earlier (so Dr. Barnett's chronology), and this greatly weakened him. In 973 the representative of the old Western-Chāḷukya dynasty which had been sunk in oblivion for over two hundred years, Tailapa or Taila II, afterwards called ' Āhavamalla,' ruling apparently some tract under the Rāshṭrakūṭas, revolted against the new king Kakkala and completely defeated him. Tailapa, no doubt by long preparation, had made himself powerful enough to accomplish this great design, and by his success he reestablished the fortunes of the Western Chāḷukya family. He held Bellary and parts at least of Mysore for a few years till the coming of Rājarāja Chola I. (*I. A. viii. 15.*)

A.D. 974, November 9. In Travancore (Vēṇāḍ) a grant of land was made by Śrī Vallabhan-Kōdai, who seems to have borne several names; viz., ' Indu-Kōdai,' ' Ravi-Kōdai,' ' Kallimukkan.' (*V. R. iii. Trav. 93; E I. ix, 234; Trav. A.A.S. iv, Part I, p. 1; i, 176; Mamballi copper-plates.*)

Month Āshāḍha, day of month illegible. Record in Kōlār District, E. Mysore, stating that the Noḷamba-Pallava leaders had heard of the death of the Western-Ganga Mārasimha III. One of them is called the son of ' Chōrayya,' probably Poralchōra II. This shews that Mārasimha's death had occurred before July 974. (*E. C. x. Mb. 84.*)

[Mārasimha was a follower of the Jain religion, and he starved himself to death at Bankāpūr in Dharwar District, having probably abdicated during his life-time.]

A.D. 975. On the base of a pillar on the Chandragiri hill at Śrāvana-Beḷgoḷa is a record of Mārasimha's death by starvation. (*E. C. ii. Sb. 38; E. I. v. 151.*)

Inscription at Muḷgunḍ, Gadag District, of the W. Ganga prince Pañchaladēva, successor of Mārasimha III. ' Pañchala,' therefore, may be another name for Rāchamalla IV (*E. I. vi.* 257.). On the other hand this year (A.D. 975) is the date allotted by Fleet to a Pañchaladēva who was defeated and killed by the W. Chāḷukya king Tailapa II. (*E. I. vi. 40.*)

In this year a dispute regarding an endowment which had been made by the Noḷamba chief Nanni-Noḷamba, son of Irivi-Noḷamba II, at an earlier date, was settled. Inscription in Chitaldroog District, N. Mysore. (*E. C. xi. Hr. 1.*)

A.D. 977. A force of marauders from the Noḷambavāḍi tract raided into the Manḍya Taluk of Mysore District and destroyed the village of Maliḍūru. *Virakal* in memory of a favourite soldier of the W. Ganga Rāchamalla who lost his life in the fighting. (*E. C. iii. Md. 107.*)

In this year a grant for construction of a tank in E. Mysore was made by the 'Noḷambādhirāja,' no other name being given. (*E. C. x. Cb. 45.*)

[Rāchamalla IV, Ganga chief, had as minister Chāmuṇḍa-Raja who erected the colossal Jain image of Gummaṭa-Bhujabalin at Śrāvaṇa-Beḷgoḷa.]

A.D. 978. Early in the year. The Ganga prince Rakkasa-Ganga was ruling a tract in Coorg for his father Rāchamalla IV. (*E. C. i. 4.*)

A number of inscriptions in the Kēraḷa country, dated only in regnal years but believed to belong to the period (roughly) A.D. 991 to 1036, go to shew that the Kēraḷa king Bhāskara-Ravivarman-Tiruvaḍi was in A.D. 978 ruling Malabar, Cochin and part of Travancore for his predecessor Indu-Kōdai, who had probably retired into private life. Bhāskara-Ravivarman came actually to the throne about A.D. 982 (*See below*). (*T. A. S., ii. 31. No. 7.*)

[Mahinda V, king of Ceylon, came to the throne in this year according to the revised chronology. The island, however, lay under the heel of invaders from the Kéraḷa country of the Malabar Coast and the 'Karṇāṭaka'—perhaps Tamils—and following an insurrection Mahinda fled to Rohana after a nominal rule of twelve years. (*Mahāwaṁśa, ch. 55.*)]

A.D. 979. An inscription in West Mysore witnesses a local raid and its accompanying casualties, carried out by a certain Śāntivarma, who has been thought to belong to the Kadamba family of Baṇavāśi. The W. Chāḷukya Nurmaḍi-Tailapa II was reigning at the time in that country, having driven out the Rāshṭrakūṭas. (*E. C. viii. Sb. 530.*)

In this year a record in the Trichinopoly District shews that the Chōla king Uttama-Chōla gave a grant of land to a temple. (*V. R. iii. Trich. 692 ; 454 of 1908.*)

A.D. 980, April 22. A record of this date shews 'Āhavamalla' Tailapa II, the restorer of the W. Chāḷukya monarchy, reigning in Bellary District. (*710 of 1919.*)

[About this time, as two *Vīrakals* in Eastern Mysore assert, the Noḷamba chief (no name is given) was fighting against the Chōla king. No date is mentioned. The fixture of 'A.D. 980' is according to Rice. The Noḷamba leader was himself killed in the battle. (*E. C. ix, Ht. 47, 48.*)]

June 8, 980. In a village near Belgaum is an inscription of the W. Chāḷukya king Tailapa II. It states that he conquered the 'Chōlas and Laṭas,' and 'cut off the heads' of Raṇasthamba (unidentified) and Kakkala (Rāshṭrakūṭa) (*E. I. xvi. 1*). (This story of decapitation appears to be mere poetry.)

[Tailapa married Kakkala's daughter Jākabbe, or Jākkalādēvī.]

A.D. 982, March 20. Date of the death of the last of the Rāshṭrakūṭas: viz. the king, or prince, Indra IV, also called 'Raṭṭa Kandarppa' grandson of Krishna III and son-in-law of Rāja Chūḍāmaṇi, who is called a Ganga-rāja. The latter has not been identified. The date of the Śravaṇa Beḷgoḷa inscription No. 57 is a perfectly sound one. (*E. C. ii. Śr. Bel. 57, 58; xii. Si. 27.*)

September 20. Grant by a feudatory chief, in the Gadag District, of the Western Chāḷukya king Tailapa II, shewing his complete triumph over the Rāshṭrakūṭas. (*E. I. iv. 204.*)

Probable year of accession of the Kēraḷa king Bhāskara-Ravivarman on the demise or abdication of Indu-Kodai (see above, *s. v.* 978). Ravivarma reigned at least fifty-eight years. Eleven records of his reign have been examined by Dewan Bahadur L. D. Swamikannu Pillai. (*T. A. S. ii. 31.*)

A record dated (only) in 'K. Y. 4083' of the thirteenth year of Maduıāntaka-Uttama-chōla tends to shew that the accession of that king took place in A.D. 969–70.

(*V. R. ii. Tanjore 292; 265 of 1907; I. A. 1925, p. 61.*)

A.D. 985. **Between June 25 and July 12.** Date of accession of the great Chōla king Rājarāja I as determined by Prof. Kielhorn. (*E. I. viii, App.*)

[When Rājarāja came to the throne the political condition of Southern India was favourable for his prospects. The Rāshṭrakūṭa domination of the country to his North-West and West had been crushed by the successes of the W. Chāḷukyas, and the hold of the latter on that territory was not yet secure. North of him the Eastern Chāḷukyas maintained their own, but were not threatening any invasion of Chōla lands. To his South and South-West the dominions of the Paṇḍyas lay under his own rule, or were governed by local families of no great power. The power of the Gangas in Mysore and the neighbourhood had been largely diminished, as had that of the Noḷamba chiefs whose fortunes fell with those of their Rāshṭrakūṭa overlords. Early in his reign, as we know from the Tiruvālangāḍu plates (*see below s. v., A.D. 1017–18*) the Pāṇḍya Amarabhujanga submitted to him; and so also did the Vaiḍumba chiefs who ruled over the country south of the Krishna river (*below, s. v. A.D. 992–93*). These last were threatened with danger from the W. Chāḷukyas and protected themselves by submitting to the Chōla king.]

A.D. 986. Inscription in N.-W. Mysore, near Sorab, of king 'Tehılaha', i. e., the W. Chāḷukya Tailapa II, then reigning over the country after his explusion of the Rāshṭrakūṭas.

(*E. C. vii. Sb. 413.*)

A.D. 987. Record in Bellary District shewing the same king, 'called Āhavamalla', ruling there. (*V. R. i, Bell. 273; 81 of 1904.*)

Parts of Bellary and Anantapur were locally ruled by a Kadamba chief, called 'Āryavarman', Lord of Baṇavāsi. (*E. R. 1903–4, p. 8.*)

He was a feudatory of the W. Chāḷukyas.

A.D. 989, December 1. Rājarāja Chōla I reigning in Tanjore in his fifth year.

(*V. R. ii. Tanjore 389 ; 19 of 1907 ; E. I. ix. 207.*)

A.D. 990. A Kadamba chief of the Baṇavāsi family, Ādityavarma, was ruling the Kōgali 500 tract, Bellary District under the W. Chāḷukya Tailapa II. He is also mentioned in a record of two years later. (*V. R. i. Bell. 293 195; 101, 36, of 1904.*)

A.D. 991. (?) Two records of the fourteenth and fifteenth years of the Keraḷa king Bhāskara-Ravivarman, also called 'Gōvardhana-Mārttāṇḍa.' The date is not certain.

(*V. R. iii. Travancore 180, 181 ; T. A. S. ii. 32, 34.*)

A.D. 991. Extensive tribal fighting in North-West Mysore, in the reign (so stated) of the W. Chāḷukya Tailapa II. The population of fifty *nāḍus* rose and fought against a chief of Sāntaḷige.

(*E. C. viii. Sb. 477.*)

A.D. 992. Tailapa II ('Āhavamalla') reigning over North Mysore. (*E.C. xi. Dg. 114.*)

A.D. 992. In the same year an inscription in Nellore District, Gūḍūr Taluk, mentions as sovereign Rājarāja Chōla in his eighth year, and as local ruler the Vaiḍumba chief Vishṇudēva *alias* 'Durai-araśan' (*sic*, as title). Three generations of Vaiḍumba chiefs are known by name in this century, viz., Śandaiyan Tiruvaiyan I, his son Śaṁkara, and the latter's son Sōmanātha. Śaṁkara's elder brother was Śandaiyan Tiruvaiyan II. (*V. R. ii. Nellore 239 ; B. & V. C. Gūḍūr Taluk 88.*)

A.D. 992. The Kogali and Saundatti tracts, Bellary District and Belgaum were now locally ruled by Ādityavarman of the Kadamba family, under the W. Chāḷukya Tailapa II. An inscription mentions a victory gained by Tailapa over the Chōḷa king. Such a victory is not otherwise recorded; but there may have been a local clash of arms. (*V. R. i. Bellary 195 ; 36 of 1904.*)

A.D. 992. An inscription of this year at Darśanankoppam in South Travancore states that Rājarā I, recognized there as overlord, had before that time 'destroyed the ships at Kāndaḷūr-Śālai'. A later record (*below, s.v.* A.D. *998–99*) says that this event took place 'in his (Rājarāja's) tender youth.' This shews two things—(i) the exploit recorded was performed probably before Rājarāja came to the throne; (ii) The king was reigning over the old Pāṇḍya dominions.

(*T. A. S. xiv. 237, C, E.*)

Dr. Hultzsch (*S. I. I. ii, p. 241, note*) gives as the correct rendering of the passage—'He caused to be destroyed the ships of Śēralan (the Chēra king) at Kāndaḷūr, which is situated on the sea.' It was a sea-port on the Malabar coast.[1]

A.D. 992. A record of Rājarāja Chōla I's eighth year engraved on a rock at Pañchapāṇḍavamalai, close to Arcot, mentions a tributary ruler, the Lāṭarāja, Vira Chōla, son of Pugaḷvippavarganḍa. The latter is a title borne by one of the Bāṇa chiefs; and the name 'Vira Chōla' would imply that the Bāṇa family had submitted to Rājarāja. (*E. I. iv. 137.*)

A.D. 994. Rājarāja Chōla I's occupation of the Pāṇḍya country seems to have been complete by now, seeing that records of his tenth and eleventh year (994-996) have been found at Ambāsamudram and at Suchīndram near Cape Comorin in A D. 999 (*E. I. v. 48, 119, 123, 124 of 1905*). He was called 'Mummaḍi Chōla,'[2] implying that he had brought three kingdoms under his crown.

(*S. I. I, ii. Part V. Introd;. E. R. 1905, § 11.*)

[Before the year A.D. 995, i. e. within the first ten years of his reign, Rājarāja Chōla I had consolidated the hold of his family over the whole Pāṇḍya country, had conquered the Kēraḷa lords, and reduced the Bāṇas and Vaiḍumbas, but apparently had not yet succeeded in forcing submission from the Gangas and Noḷamba-Pallava chiefs of the Mysore country.]

A.D. 995. An inscription at Tennēri in the Chingleput District mentions the former Chōla king Madurāntaka Uttama in the eleventh year of his successor and supplanter Rājarāja I; but I do not gather that Uttama is declared to be still living. (*V. R. i. Chingleput 446; 199 of 1901.*)

A.D. 996, June 14. Gift by Rājarāja Chōla I for repairs to a tank at Bāhūr now in French territory. The Rāshṭrakūṭas had held this country up to about A.D. 968, as is proved by a number of Krishna III's inscriptions found there. The Chōla dynasty was now in full possession.

(*V. R. iii. French Terr. 8; 178 of 1902, E. I. vii. 169.*)

A.D. 996, December 1 and 28. Two dated inscriptions of the twelfth year of the reign of Rājarāja Chōla I in South Arcot. They help to confirm the accession date fixed above.

(*362 of 1917; 553 of 1921.*)

A.D. 997. In E. Mysore, Rājarāja Chōla reigning there. (*E. C. ix. Ht. 111.*)

[In A.D. 997 the Western Chāḷukya king Satyāśraya II, Rājarāja's enemy, came to the throne in succession to Tailapa II. Satyāśraya held the north of the Madras Presidency and part of Mysore while Rājārāja dominated all the south. Rājarāja's records claim for him that about this time or earlier he reduced to submission the Western Ganga chiefs and the Pallava chiefs of the Noḷamba territory.]

[1] Mr. T. A. Gopinatha Rao has identified this port with Trivandram, the modern town of which this port must have formed a part. His explanation of the achievement is hardly acceptable. T.A.R. II. A. 5.—*Editor.*

[2] In this sense the form of the word is Mummuḍi – three Crowns. This title was assumed in his fourteenth year by Rājaraja I. The form Mummadi occurs in records of earlier years and means *thrice* Chola or Choḷa three times over. Vide. *S.I.I. iii.* p. 5 n.—*Editor.*

A.D. 997, May 24. Rājarāja Chōla I reigning in S. Arcot in his twelfth year. The date agrees with the accession-date mentioned above, viz., June–July 985. *(557 of 1921.)*

A.D. 998. Inscription at Mēlpāḍi, near Vellore in N. Arcot of Rājarāja Chōla I's fourteenth year, in which he is called 'Mummaḍi[1] Chōla', is important. It mentions his conquests up to date. 'In his tender youth' he destroyed the ships at Kāndaḷūr-Śālai. The conquests of his reign were (i) the Pāṇḍya (kingdom, the Tiruvālangāḍu plates add the name of Amarabhujanga as that of the conquered Pāṇḍya king); (ii) the Ganga country; (iii) the Noḷamba country; (iv) the Vengi country (this is an exaggeration, apparently); (v) Coorg; (vi) Taḍiyapāḍi, otherwise called Taḍigaipāḍi. In this year 998–99 a vassal chief (who bore the name of his sovereign) Mummaḍi[2]-Chōla-Pōśan, lord of Araiśūr, also called Īrāyiravan-Pallavaraiyan, made a gift to the village assembly.

(S. I. I. iii. p. 29, No. 19.)

[Later inscriptions seem to shew that there were no further conquests between this year and A.D. 1004. Another record, also of this year explains the above reference to the Vengi kingdom. It does not say that Rājarāja conquered that country, but that he 'restored order in it after it had been twenty-seven years without a ruler.' In other words he assisted the Eastern Chāḷukya prince Śaktivarman to regain for himself the throne of Vengi after many years of anarchy. Śaktivarman's reign began in A.D. 999 or thereabouts. *(S. I. I. ii. Part V, Introd.)*]

A.D. 999. The Ganga chief Nītimārga was ruling in S. Mysore. *(E. C. iv. Ch. 10.)*

A.D. 999, June 5. Rājakēsarivarman Rājarāja Chōla I reigning in Travancore in his fifteenth year. It agrees with the accession date fixed above (489 of 1918).

A.D. 999, August 29. An inscription at Suchīndram, near Cape Comorin, shews that Rajarāja Chōla I was at that place on that day (*above, s. v., A.D. 994*). (*V. R. iii. Travancore, 169; E. I. v. 48; T. A. S. ii. p. 1*). The list of his conquests given is the same as in the Mēlpāḍi record of this year, mentioned above. *(s. v., A.D. 998.)*

A.D. 999. Inscription shewing the Western Chāḷukya Satyāśraya II reigning in N. W. Mysore, and, under him, Kēśari-Bhīma ruling the Baṇavāśi country. *(E. C. viii. Sb. 234.)*

[About the end of the tenth century A.D. is believed to be the date of the grant of a village near Cochin, at Muyirikōḍu (ancient Muziris) or Cranganore by the Kēraḷa king Bhāskara Ravivarman to the local colony of Jews headed by Joseph Rabban.

(V. R. iii. Cochin 3, I. A. xiii. 334.)]

A.D. 1000. Date in the sixteenth year of Rājarāja Chōla I. Grant in Muḷbāgal Taluk, E. Mysore, made by a 'Noḷambādhirāja', not otherwise named. It proves a Chōla conquest over the Noḷamba-Pallava chief. *(E. C. x. Mb. 208.)*

A.D. 1000, September 23. Inscription of the fifteenth year of Rājarāja Chōla I in Tanjore District. *(V. R. ii. Tanjore 638; 27 of 1906; E. I. ix. 208.)*

[About this time Rājarāja I sent his son Rājēndra to the north on an expedition against Kaḷinga. *(S. I. I. ii. Introd., Part V.)*]

A.D. 1001. Mahmud of Ghazni's first expedition into North-Western India. He advanced as far as Peshawar. This year, probably or at least between 1001 and 1004 Rājarāja I waged war against Ceylon, then under king Mahindu V. He was so successful that he was able to grant Singhalese

[1] The reading of the text in both cases is *Mummuḍi*.—See note above.—*Editor*.

[2] *Ibid.*

villages to the Tanjore temple and to rename the Island 'Mummuḍi-Chōla-Manḍalam' (*S. I. I. ii. 424–28*). The Tamils seem to have flooded Ceylon at this period (*Mahāwaṁśa, ch. 55*). Mahindu had fled from his capital in or about A.D. 978 (*q. v. above*.)]

A.D. 1001. Records near Madura of Rājarāja's seventeenth year prove that his conquest of the Pāṇḍya kingdom was complete. (*132, 134 of 1910.*)

A.D. 1003. Inscription in East Mysore of the nineteenth year of Rājarāja Chōla I. It adds to the list of conquests mentioned up to his fourteenth year and noted in the Mēlpāḍi inscription (*above s. v. 998–99*), stating that he had (presumably since his fourteenth year) conquered (viii)Kollam, or Quilon, and (ix) Kalinga. (*E. C. x. Mb. 123.*)

A.D. 1004. An inscription in a village near Mysore states that a Chōla general Aprамēya fought with and defeated a Hoyśala chief, whose minister was named Nāgama.

(*E. C. iii, T. N. 44.*)

[This is the first we hear of the Hoyśala chiefs, afterwards to become very famous in the history of South India. They were a family of hill chiefs residing in the extreme west of Mysore near the ghāts, at Angaḍi in the Muḍgere Taluk. The battle took place at Kaleyūr near Talakāḍ on the south side of the Kāvērī river.]

A.D. 1004 (?). Accession year of the Kongu-Chōla chief Kōnāṭṭān-Vikrama-Chōla, who lived till at least his fortieth year of rule. Many records of his in the Coimbatore District. (*V. R. i. Coim. 77–121, 190, 470 : 549–551 of 1893 : 614 of 1905 ; 222 of 1909 ; 142–155 of 1910.*) He ruled the country about Erode and to the south of it, evidently under the Chōla king. His accession-date depends on a record at Tingaḷūr of his fortieth year in 'Ś. 9 [67] ' (*sic*). So it is not certain.

In the twentieth year of Rājarāja Chōla I (1004–05) his vassal, the Vaiḍumba chief Nannamārāyar gave a gift to a temple (*S. I. I. iii. No. 52*). The chief is not otherwise known.

A.D. 1004, July 20. An inscription in the Bijapur District shews the W. Chāḷukya king Irivibēḍanga Satyāśraya II reigning there (*E. I. xvii. 7*). The date, which mentions an eclipse of the sun is a sound one.

A.D. 1004, September 20. Record near Trichinopoly. Rājarāja Chōla I reigning there in his twentieth year and again in his twenty-second year on December 2, 1006.

(*V. R. iii. Trich. 821, 828 ; 62, 69 of 1914.*)

A.D. 1005. This was Rājarāja Chōla's twenty-first regnal year. An inscription at Hoṭṭūr in Dhārwār District states that the Chōla king with an army of 900,000 men invaded the Raṭṭa country, sacking the towns. They 'pillaged the whole country [about Dhārwār], slaughtered women, children and Brahmans, and taking the girls destroyed their caste'. Rājarāja's inscriptions claim a complete victory for him, saying that he conquered the 'Raṭṭa 7½-lakh country'. The Chāḷukya records however assert that the attack was a mere raid and that the Chōla forces were driven away to their own territory. It appears from the records of Rājendra I, son of Rajarāja, that it was he who commanded the invading army (*E. I. xvi. 73 ; S.I.I. ii, Part V, Introd.; Fleet, D.K.D. p. 433; § S.I.I. i. 31. See below s. v., A.D. 1010, and E. R. 1904, § 17.*)

In this year took place Mahmud of Ghazni's second expedition into North India.

A.D. 1005. The large Leyden grant mentions that in this the twenty-first year of Rājarāja's reign he permitted the 'Lord of Kaṭāha and Śrīvishaya' (i. e. Kēḍah in the Malay Peninsula, and Palembang) to present a village near Negapatam for the support of the Buddhist temple at that place, which had been constructed by the former lord of Kaṭāha, Chuḍāmaṇi of the Śailēndra family, father of the present donor; the latter's name being Śrīmāra Vijayōttunga.

(*V. R. ii. Tanjore 890-A; I. A. xxii. 45; vii. 224; T. & S. I., p. 204.*)

A.D. 1006. C. P. grant witnessing the gift of the village of Tāmaracheruvu by Indravarma, the Ganga king of Kalinga. The village is said to be situated in the Varāhavartani District. It is dated in the 128th year of the dynasty, the epoch of which era I have stated above to be, in my opinion, A.D. 877–78. That this view is correct is supported by the record in question, for the details given of the date mention an eclipse of the moon in the month of Mārgaśira, which took place on December 7, 1006. (*V. R. i. Ganjam 2; I. A. x. 243; xiii. 122.*)

[Mahmud of Ghazni's third invasion of Northern India took place in this year, when he attacked Multan.]

Inscription of the Western Chāḷukya 'Āhavamalla-Sattiga', i. e. Satyāśraya II at Chēbrōlu in Guntur District, dated in Ś. 928, Parābhava (*V. R. ii. Guntur 84; 145 of 1897*). This sufficiently disposes of the Chōla claim to having conquered the whole Raṭṭapāḍi 7½-lakh territory. Evidently Rājarāja Chōla made a bold bid for conquest, but failed in this attempt.

In the same year an inscription at Hoṭṭūr in Dharwar District describes an important victory as having been gained by the Western Chāḷukya king Satyāśraya II over Rājaraja Chōla I. It states that Rājarāja had invaded the Kánarese country and devastated it 'killing women and children and Brahmans and carrying off girls', but that he was finally defeated and driven out, and his conqueror Satyāśraya made a triumphant progress through the South of his dominions. (Chōla records, however, claim a victory for Rājarāja; whichever way it was there was manifestly much slaughter of the people, and cruel treatment of them). (*E. I. xvi. 73; E. R. 1904, § 75.*)

A.D. 1007. An inscription, in S.-E. Mysore of Rājarāja Chōla I's twenty-third year, no other date being stated—mentions his victories as noted above up to his twenty-first year (*s.v., A.D. 1005*), and adds to them that he took 'the 1200, ancient Islands'. (*E. C. ix. Cp. 128, 130–132.*)

[The last statement shews that trade with the East, the islands in the Bay of Bengal, Sumatra, Malaya, etc.—had begun in Rājarāja's reign; or at least, if it had begun earlier, became now of greater importance. It continued into the reign of Rājēndra who also claims to have taken 'many ancient islands.' In all probability, the Chōla kings at this time sent over troops to defend Indian settlers and merchants trading in those regions.]

[In this year Mahmud of Ghazni attacked Northern India for the fourth time.]

A.D. 1008, June 14. Rājarāja Chōla I reigning in South Arcot (*387 of 1922*).

[Mahmud of Ghazni invaded N. India for the fifth time, and fought a great battle against a coalition of Hindu rulers near Ohind on the Indus. He captured Nāgarkōt or Kāngra, and carried off immense booty. (*Barnett, 'Antiquities,' p. 75.*)

The Western Chāḷukya king Vikramāditya V, succeeded Satyāśraya II in this year.

A.D. 1008, October-November. An inscription at Ukkal, dated on the '124th day of the 24th year' of Rājarāja Chōla I. It mentions his conquests as in the 23rd year (*above*), but does not allude to the 'ancient islands.' His complete conquest of the Pāṇḍya kingdom is proved by his issue of orders to the people of that country, now re-named the 'Rājarāja-Vaḷanāḍu'. The villagers had held lands and cultivated them in certain villages, which villages had afterwards been bestowed by the Crown on 'Brahmans and Jains', evidently as *agrahārams*. The villagers refused to pay their taxes on these lands to the new landlords. The king commands that all lands on which the taxes have not been paid, for the third year between the sixteenth and twenty-third years, shall be confiscated and shall become the common property of the village, and as such may be sold by the village councils. (*S. I. I. iii. 14, No. 9; 15, No. 10; 24, No 15.*)

A.D. 1009. Inscription at Māmallapuram, Chingleput District, of Rājarāja Chōla I. It mentions his conquest of Ceylon as well as those noted in earlier records. It shews that the Nolamba country was then ruled by a Pāṇḍya prince, subject to the Chōla monarchy. Rājarāja gave his daughter in marriage to the Eastern Chālukya Prince Vimalāditya, who afterwards came to the throne at Vengi (*S. I. I. i. 63; ii. 241, note; T. A. S. ii. 1*). The Toṇḍamaṇḍalam country was renamed by Rājarāja the 'Jayaṁkoṇḍa-Chōla-Maṇḍalam.'

A.D. 1010, May 1. Inscription at Ālūr in Gadag Taluk, Dharwār District. It mentions the Noḷamba chief Irivi-Noḷamba as having married a daughter of the Western Chāḷukya king Satyāśraya II. This Irivi may have been a grandson of Irivi-Noḷamba II. He is called 'Ghaṭeya-ankakāra' and is given his Pallava title 'Lord of Kānchi, best of cities.' He is not stated to have been ruling the Noḷamba country; and he may have given way before the power of the Chōla king and retired to the Chāḷukya territories north of the Tungabhadra river. Nevertheless, the record noted below (*s. v. A.D. 1011–12*) claims Noḷamba allegiance to the Chāḷukya Crown.

(*E.I. xvi. 27; E.R. 1914, 86; Fleet. D.K.D. 434; S. I. I. ii. 139.*)

[The truth apparently is that the Noḷamba family was in a difficult position, owing loyalty to its former Chāḷukya overlords while overawed by the strength of the Chōla king. Rājarāja asserted his suzerainty over the Nōḷamba country by renaming it the 'Nigarili-Chōla-*paḍi*.']

July 12. Inscription of the twenty-sixth year of Rājarāja Chōla I in Tanjore District. The date is a sound one, and makes July 12, A.D. 985, the last possible day for the king's accession (*V. R. ii. Tanjore 1201; 624 of 1909; E.I. xi. 241*). There is another of September 26 at Tiruvallam.

(*E. R. March, 1890, p. 2.*)

A.D. 1010, November 8. The Sūḍi (Dhārwār District) plates shew that the Princess Akka-dēvī, sister of the W. Chāḷukya king Vikramāditya V, was then ruling the 'Kiśukād-70' division. Other records shew that this rule was apparently continuous up to A.D. 1054. (*E.I. xv. 73, C.D., etc.*)

[Rājarāja proclaimed his sovereignty over the Ganga country of Mysore and the neighbourhood by giving new names to its tracts. One was called by him the 'Rājarāja-vaḷanāḍu'; another, the 'Vikrama-Chōla-Vaḷanāḍu'.]

A.D. 1010. An inscription in E. Mysore shews that its local ruler was the Noḷamba chief Chōrayya. (*E.C. x. Ct. 118; E.I., xvi. 27.*)

[Bhōjadeva, the Paramāra king of Mālwa, came to the throne about this time. He made war on the Western Chāḷukyas at a later date.]

A.D. 1010, May. Coronation-day of the Eastern Chāḷukya king, Vimalāditya, according to the Raṇastipūṇḍi grant of his eighth year. (*E. I. vi. 347; see below s.v., A.D 1018–19; V.R. ii. Godavari 8.*)

Rājarāja Chōla I recognized as king in Eastern Mysore (*E. C. iv. Kr. 16*); and in 1012 in a village near Seringapatam, where an inscription states that he had conquered the Ganga and Noḷamba territories. His general 'Panchavan' is mentioned. (*E.C. iii. S.R. 140.*)

[Fleet held that in this year the Noḷamba country was ruled by a Noḷamba-Pallava chief, feudatory to the W. Chāḷukya king (*But see note above, s.v. 1010, May 1*). (*Bombay Gazetteer I, Part II, p. 433; E.R. 1903–04, p. 8.*)]

A.D. 1012, May. A long inscription at the Tanjore temple of the twenty-sixth year of Rājarāja Chōla I enumerates his exploits as above given, but adds nothing as done of importance since A.D. 1006. The date of the record is the 319th day of the 26th year, i.e., about May, A.D. 1012. It expressly states that Rājarāja founded the Tanjore temple, calling it 'Rājarājēśvara' and literally endowing it from treasures seized from his enemies. Great gifts were given by his sister Kundavvai and others. (*S.I.I. ii. 1, 236.*)

A.D. 1012, May 30. Accession of Rājēndra Chōla I, in succession to his father, Rājarāja I. This date is settled by an inscription at Eṇṇāyiram in South Arcot, which, with correct details, shews that the twenty-seventh day of the thirtieth year of this Rājēndra = 25th June A.D. 1041 (*341 of 1917*). Other records support this fixture (*Kielhorn, E.R. viii. 260, and App. 291*). Rājarāja seems to have abdicated, and to have lived a little longer. (*See below, s.v. A.D. 1013–14.*)

The extent to which the Tanjore temple was benefited at the cost of the villages is shewn by certain records found there. The king commanded the villagers to supply servants to the temple *and to pay for their support therein*, and these servants were no less than 750 in number, 400 were women, 128 were watchmen, 199 were Brahmachāris. All these were supported, not by the temple treasury-officers, but by the villages (in addition to their ordinary taxation) from which they came.[1] This payment was made compulsory. Each watchman was given 100 *kalams* of paddy for his maintenance.

A record in N.-W. Mysore makes the Western Chāḷukya Vikramāditya V supreme in that territory, with Chaṭṭaya ruling Baṇavāśi under him. (*E.C. viii. Sb. 471.*)

[It looks therefore as if Rājarāja had not quite succeeded in reducing the Noḷamba chiefs. (*above, s.v. A.D. 1010.*)]

A.D. 1012. In the first year of Rājendra Chōla's reign, the Tinnevelly country had passed away from the rule of its own princes and was governed by a 'Chōla-Pāṇḍya' viceroy. Several inscriptions of this period mention one of these viceroys, who from his name would appear to be a Pāṇḍya prince, vassal to the Chōla. He is called Jaṭāvarman-Sundara-Chōla-Pāṇḍya.[2]

(*V. R. ii. Tinn. 2–20; 70–88 of 1907.*)

A.D. 1013. There are several inscriptions dated in the twenty-ninth year of Rājarāja Chōla I, which began June–July 1013, Rājēndra I having come to the throne in May 1012. They seem to prove Rājarāja's abdication in favour of his son, and his devotion of his waning life to religious matters (*S. I. I. ii, pp. 121–134: iii. 88–123*). About this time he assumed the title 'Jayaṁkoṇḍa.'

[1] The Inscriptions to which reference is made here are Nos. 57, 69, and 70 of Vol. II of the Tanjore Inscriptions. All these are records in the Great Śiva temple at Tanjore, built and endowed by Rāja Rāja. Of these three records the first is a continuation of the third. They certainly refer to numbers of villages in the three great divisions of Chōla-Maṇḍalam, Pāṇḍya-Maṇḍalam, and Toṇḍai-Maṇḍalam, from which the number of servants given above were drawn for service in the temple. According to the text of the inscription, of which there is a more or less correct translation given (see paragraph 1 of the translation) on page 320 of Vol. II of the South Indian Inscriptions. Rāja Rāja lays it down clearly that the lower servants were to be paid from the head-quarters temple treasury at Tanjore, while the upper servants were to be paid in the up-country treasuries of the temple. The purpose of this division was apparently that these temple servants were to be men of respectable character, possessed of property and relations and therefore reliable from the point of view of the temple. The distinction is very carefully stated, and there can be no mistake about it. The villages themselves had to be villages given over to Brahmans (*Brahmadēya*) and all the servants had to come from such villages. They therefore had no manner of a connection with the villages of the public, nor with the general administration as such. It will thus be seen that the statement in the text is almost about the reverse of the truth.—*Editor*.

[2] This was a Chōla prince and was in fact a son of Rājēndra I E.R. 1906. Section 17.—*Editor*.

That the Pallava chiefs were now subject to the Chōla king, at any rate professedly, is shewn by two inscriptions at Tanjore of this year. One of these chiefs, a vassal of Rājarāja's, bore that king's name and was called 'Īrāyiravan-Pallavaraiyan *alias* Mummuḍi Chōla Pōśan.' He was chief of Araiśūr. Another, later, bore the name of king Rājēndra I, being called 'Uttama-Chōla Pōśan' (or Bhōja), 'Uttama-Chōla' being a name of Rājēndra (*S.I.I. ii. 141, 222 ; Nos. 33, 55 ; iii, p. 109, No. 54*). This last is at Tiruvallam in North Arcot, and belongs to the fourth year of Rājēndra I, A.D. 1015–16.

In A.D. 1013–14, the rwenty-ninth year of Rājarāja I, as an inscription at Tiruvaiyār, Tanjore District, tells us, the Eastern Chāḷukya king Vimalāditya gave a gift to the temple there. Vimalāditya married Kundavvai, Rājarāja's daughter, and was on friendly terms with his father-in law. V. Venkayya accounted for the fact that Vimalāditya's reign is sometimes stated to have lasted for seven years and sometimes for eleven years is due to the fact that although his accession was in A.D. 1011 he was for four years a prisoner of the Chōla king, and was not really independent till 1015.

(*215 of 1894.*)

[Vimalāditya's marriage was very important, as it was the first which united the Eastern Chāḷukya and Chōla crowns.]

An undated record at Mahēndragiri, Ganjam, says that Rājēndra Chōla had actually conquered Vimalāditya and had erected a pillar of victory on the hill there. Below the inscription are two emblems, the Chōla tiger and the Pāṇḍya fish, implying that the two kingdoms fought in alliance against the Chāḷukya monarch (*V. R. i. Ganjam, 425 ; 396 of 1896 ; E. I. vi. 347*). There is no clue to the actual date of this campaign, which may have taken place in Rājarāja's reign, when Rājēndra commanded his father's army.

An inscription of date 1013–14 shews the W. Chāḷukya king Vikramāditya V reigning in Bellary District. (*722 of 1922.*)

[It has been suggested that about this time Rājēndra I introduced the Tamil script into the conquered Pāṇḍya territory where previously the people wrote in Vaṭṭeḷuttu. (*E.R. 1905, § 13.*)]

A.D. 1014. Record of the third year of Rājēndra Chōla I, shewing him reigning in S. E. Mysore (*E. C. ix, cp. 127*). Another of date November 7, 1014, in Trichinopoly (*29 of 1920*). Another of the third regnal year but without details, in Trichinopoly District witnesses a gift to a temple made in memory of a gallant officer of the Chōla Rāja's elephant-corps who lost his life in the war between Rājēndra, then crown prince, and the Western Chāḷukya Irivibeḍanga-Satyāśraya (which took place in A.D. 1005–6.) (*V. R. iii. Trich. 283 ; 515 of 1912.*)

A.D. 1015. Inscription in N.-W. Mysore of the Western Chāḷukya king Jayasimha III, whose accession seems to have taken place in this year (*E. C. viii. Sb. 16*). Another at Bandaḷike in the same province in the same year of the same king (*E. C. vii. Sk. 220*). (See note to A.D. 1160 below on the subject of W. Chāḷukya succession at this time.)

[These inscriptions testify that N.-W. Mysore still lay under W. Chāḷukya influence at this date in spite of Chōla assertions of the defeat of the northern power.]

A.D. 1016. Another record in N.-W. Mysore of the W. Chāḷukya Jayasimha III.

(*E.C. vii. Sk. 307.*)

A.D. 1017. March 26. Rājēndra Chōla I reigning in his fifth year in Trichinopoly. It helps to confirm the date given above for his accession.

(*V. R. iii. Trich. 595 ; 275 of 1905 ; E. I. viii. 261.*)

A.D. 1017. Inscription in Bellary District shewing that the W. Chāḷukya Jayasimha I was reigning there in this year (*V. R. i. Bellary 471*). The king is called by his *biruda* 'Jagadēkamalla'.

The Tanjore inscription of Rājēndra I's sixth year gives a list of his achievements up to date, and the list is confirmed by other records. (i) He captured the Iḍaitturaināḍu (generally taken as Eḍetorē in Mysore, but by Fleet identified with the Raichūr *doab* between the Krishna and Tungabhadra rivers); (ii) Vanavāśi (Baṇavāśi); (iii) Koḷḷippākkai[1] (on the Krishna river ?). [These two places were taken from the W. Chāḷukya king.]; (iv) Maṇṇaikkaḍagam, or Maṇṇai (Maṇṇe near Bangalore, then ruled by the Noḷamba chief); (v) after close fighting in Ceylon he captured the 'crown of Īḷam', (Ceylon), and (vi) the 'beautiful crown of the queen of Īḷam'; and (vii) 'the crown of Sundara and the pearl necklace of Indra which the Pāṇḍya king had given up to the king of Īḷam'; (viii) the crown of Kēraḷa; (ix) 'many ancient islands.' (*S. I. I. ii. 92*). [It seems probable that most, if not all, of these expeditions were carried out by Rājēndra's son Rājādhirāja I; for the latter's inscriptions mention them as successes gained by him also—it must be noted that many of these so-called conquests were only temporary ones. It is certain for instance, that the W. Chāḷukya king was not driven out of the territories mentioned, but retained his hold of them.]

[Ceylon had been overrun by Tamils in the reign of Rājarāja I, but Rājēndra organized a regular campaign and carried it to complete success. He captured the king of Ceylon Mahindu V, and kept him prisoner at the Chōla capital till Mahindu's death twelve years later. He carried off Mahindu's queen and seized the crown-jewels of Ceylon, and the crown-jewels of the Pāṇḍya monarchy which had been left in Ceylon (*see above s.v., A.D. 917*), and which included 'the priceless diamond bracelet that was the gift of the gods' (otherwise called the 'necklace of Indra').

The *Mahāwaṁśa* (*ch. 55*) adds that the country people of the island saved from capture or death their young prince Kassapa, and had him brought up in secret till he was twelve years old.]

Rājēndra is said, in inscriptions of his seventh year, to have seized the Kēraḷa crown 'which Paraśu-Rāma had deposited in Śāndimat [or Śāndima, or Sāndimattīvu] which is believed to be one of the islands on the west coast. His seventh year began May 30, 1018.

(*S.I.I. i, 95 ; ii, 92, 220, 333, 402 ; J.R.A.S., 1913, 222, etc.*)

The Tiruvālangāḍu C. P. grant of Rajēndra's sixth year (A.D. 1017–18) gives details of his achievements, but it is somewhat confusing as the Sanskrit portion of it is a later addition to the Tamil portion of the year in question. The Sanskrit portion alludes to his conquest of Kaḍāram which did not take place till at least the king's fifteenth regnal year (A.D. 1026–27).

(*V.R. i. Chittoor 370 ; E.R. 1906, p. 66.*)

A.D. 1018. An inscription in Channapaṭna Taluk, Bangalore District, Mysore, gives a list of Rājēndra Chōla's achievements up to his seventh regnal year, but adds nothing new to the list given in the previous year (*above*). (*E.C. ix, cp. 42.*)

A record at Bāgali, Bellary District, shews that in this year that province was ruled by the Western Chāḷukya king Jayasimha III, and that under him the Noḷamba chief

[1] Has since been identified with Kulpak between Ḥaidarabad and Warangal in the Nizam's Dominions.—*Editor*.

Udayāditya, *alias* Jagadēkamalla-Noḷamba, governed very extensive tracts. He is alleged to be then ruling the whole Gangavāḍi, Kadambaḷigē and several other provinces besides the Noḷambavāḍi country. Whether this is all true or part of it exaggerated is not certain, but the record certainly shews that the people of that tract still held firm to W. Chāḷukya supremacy, in spite of the Chōla attacks on it. (*V. R. i. Bellary, 279; 87 of 1904.*)

Between May 10 and December 3 of this year the Chōla king Rājēndra I associated with himself as joint sovereign his son Rājādhirāja I, and the latter's reign is always held to have begun at this time though his father lived and ruled till 1043.

(*See E. I. iv. 216 ; V. 205 ; vii, 169 ; SII. iii, 52 ; E. C. ix, Ht. 142 ; 75 of 1895.*)

A record of this year at Raṇastipūṇḍi, near Guḍivāḍa, N. of the Krishna river, shews that the Eastern Chāḷukya king of Vengi, Vimalāditya, was crowned on May 10 A.D. 1011. (*E. I. vi. 347.*)

A.D. 1019, October 9. Record in Trichinopoly District of the eighth year of Rājēndra Chōla I. It helps to confirm the accession date, May 30, 1012 given above.

(*V.R. iii. Trich. 831 ; 72 of 1914.*)

In this year, May 30, 1019–May 30, 1020, an inscription in Kolar District, Mysore, shews Rājēndra I reigning there in his eighth year. No other date is given. It gives the same list of his conquests as was given in A.D. 1017–18 (*see above*) with no addition. (*E. C. X. Kl, 106 a.*)

December 1019 or January 1020. A record at Baḷḷigāmve (Beḷagāmi, Shimōga District) Mysore, gives the name, as ruler of the Baṇavāśi 12,000 country under his cousin Jayasimha III of the W. Chāḷukyas, of prince Kundamarasa, otherwise called Kunda or Kundiga, son of Satyāśraya II. (*E. C. vii. Sk. 125.*)

A.D. 1020, July 7. 'Muḍigoṇḍa' Rājēndra Chōla I reigning in South Mysore. The date agrees with his accession-date stated above (*E. C. iv. Hg. 16*). The record belongs to his ninth year.

Another record of the ninth year, which began May 30, 1020, gives a list, of his successes as above, up to (x = 10) the crown of Kēraḷa which Paraśurāma left in Śāndimattivu ; and adds to it a later success which must have come to him about A.D. 1019. This was during a war between him and the W. Chāḷukya king Jayasimha III, who held the west and north-west of Mysore as well as the country on the north and west of the Tungabhadra river. Rājēndra's inscriptions declare that he (xi) 'made Jayasimha turn his back at Musangi' and imply that he drove him out of Mysore and Bellary and Anantapur into the Dekhan. They assert boldly (probably because of this) that he 'conquered the Raṭṭa 7½ lakh territories' having captured them at Musangi [This last is certainly not the case]. The inscription referred to is at Mēlpāḍi, near Vellore (*S.I.I. iii. 27*). Musangi is believed to be the same as Uchchangi-droog.[1]

[At Mēlpāḍi at this time lived the celebrated Śaiva pandit Lakuḷīśvara. (*E. I. v. 228.*)

About this time Rājēndra Chōḷa I gave his son Mummaḍi Chōla a viceroyalty over the conquered Pāṇḍya and Kēraḷa kingdoms, a territory which had been administered by the prince since about A.D. 1017. His new title was 'Jaṭāvarman Sundara-Chōla-Pāṇḍya' (*A. R. iv, 1904-5, p. 129. E.I. xi. 292*). *See also the Tiruvālangāḍu grant* (*E.R. 1906, p. 66*). The date of creation is obtained from the Mannārkōvil inscription of Rājēndra's twenty-fourth and his son's fifteenth year.]

[1] For another identification with Maśangi or Maski see Rājēndra, the Gangaikoṇḍa Chōla. *J. I. Hist.*, vol. ii, p. 817.—*Editor.*

July 22. Rājēndra Chōla I reigning. S. Arcot District (386 of 1922).

A.D. 1021. Early in the year. Inscription at Nandigunḍa in South Mysore of king Rājēndra Chōla I. It mentions all his former triumphs, and includes (No. xi) the victory of Musangi but nothing later. (*E. C. iii. N. 134.*)

A.D. 1021, 1023. Inscription in Bellary District. The W. Chāḷukya 'Jagadēkamalla' Jayasimha III reigning in both years. (*294 of 1918.*)

[From this it would seem that Jayasimha III was not driven quite out of this tract in 1020, as the Chōlas declared.]

A.D. 1022. Fighting in Mysore between rival chiefs, viz., the Kongāḷva chief Rājēndra-Chōla-Prithivi and the Hoyśala chief Nripakāma (*See also below s. v. A.D. 1026*). An account of a battle is given. (*E. C. v. Mj. 43.*)

In the Mysore District a Ganga chief, whose name is not stated was ruling (*E. C. iii. Md. 78*), by consent, it must be presumed, of Rājēndra Chōla—or else in defiance of him.

North Mysore 'Jagadēkamalla' (note the Chāḷukya name), a Noḷamba-Pallava chief, was ruling, having his residence in 'Kapili' (? Kampli on the Tungabhadra river). (*E. C. xi, Mk. 10. See below s. v. A.D. 1027.*)

On August 16 of this year the E. Chāḷukya king Rājarāja-Narēndra I came to the throne, in commemoration of which the grant was made of the village of Korunelli near the Godāvari river. (*Brit. Mus. C. P. V. R. B. M. 9 ; I. A. xiv. 50; xxiii, 131.*)

[The *Mahabharata* was translated into Telugu by Nannaya-Bhaṭṭa under this king's patronage (*E. I. vi. 31*).]

[A good proof of the assertion made in a foregoing note that Rājēndra I did not succeed in completely reducing the Western Chāḷukya king is afforded by the fact that the Noḷamba chiefs acknowledged themselves vassals of the Chāḷukyas at least up to A.D. 1052. Witness records of A.D. 1010, 1018, 1022, 1027, 1030, 1044, 1052. Nevertheless Rājēndra had by now assumed the title 'Gangaikonḍa' implying that he had completely conquered and annexed the Gangavāḍi country,[1] and that the Ganga chiefs were now Chōla vassals.]

A.D. 1023. Rājēndra Chōla I ruling in E. Mysore. (*E.C. ix, Ht. 10.*)

This was Rājēndra's twelfth year, and an inscription at the Tirumalai Hill in North Arcot mentions his victories and successes up to date. The earlier ones have been already noted, ending in A.D. 1020 with (No. xi) the defeat of Jayasimha. The list gives in addition, those between his ninth and twelfth year, as follows—(xii) capture of 'Śakkarakoṭṭam belonging to Vikrama Vīra,' or Chakrakōṭa ; believed to be an event in a northern expedition against Kalinga, and the place to be a fortress in the Bastar State, Ganjam. (xiii) Madura-Manḍalam the Pānḍya capital, or another place of similar name ? (xiv) Navanidhikula, Nāmanaikkōṇam, Pañchapalli belonging to Veñjilai-Vīra, Māśuṇidēśa—all as yet unidentified places. (xv) a raid to the north when king Indraratha, or Dhīratara was captured at a battle at Ādinagar—locality not known (Indraratha is said to belong to the Chandra-kula). (xvi) Orissa. (xvii) The Kōsala kingdom and defeat of king Dharmapāla at Danḍabutti, (which has not been identified). (xviii) Takkaṇa-Lāṭa, or Southern *Gujarat* and defeat of its king Rāṇaśura. (xix) Bengal, 'where Gōvindachandra was put to flight and Mahīpāla terrified,'

[1] This is not the meaning of the title. The title was assumed from his having brought the Ganges to his new capital Gangaikonḍa Śoḷapuram. See *J. I. Hist.*, article above referred to.—*Editor.*

in a battle at Śangukoṭṭam on the Sea (not identified), where elephants were captured. (xx) Uttira Lāṭa, or Northern *Gujarat*. (xxi) The River Ganges. (*S.I.I. i. 95, ii. 139 ; E. I. ix. 229.*)

[These extensive claims must not be accepted as proofs of actual conquest, and at present there is no evidence forthcoming in support of them all. All that can be definitely asserted is that between 1020 and 1023 the Chōla king had been very active in many different directions.]

A.D. 1024. Inscription at Mālūr near Bangalore of the thirteenth year of Rajēndra I (*E. C. ix. Cp. 24*). Since inscriptions of the twenty-third and twenty-seventh years of this king contain similar statements of victories but add nothing to the statements made in the present record it has to be presumed that all the conquests claimed belong to the period before the close of his thirteenth year, i.e. before May 30, 1025 (*See E. C. ix. Cp. 82, 83 : Nl, 7a.*). These successes are as follows, in addition to those named in the last noted record, and therefore give us details of an oversea expedition sent to Malaya in about A.D. 1024–25. [With the exception of the case of 'Kaḍāram,' the mention of other places 'captured' may merely refer to some military occupations by detachments of Tamil troops sent as garrisons in support of trad.]. (xxii) Kaṭāha or Kaḍāram.

[Kaḍāram is almost certainly a South-Indian perversion of the name Kēḍah, a state on the west coast of the Malay Peninsula. Another inscription calls it 'Kiḍāram'. The large Leiden grant of the twenty-first year of Rājarāja Chōla I, A.D. 1005–6, tells us that in that year a village was granted for the support of the Buddhist temple at Negapatam on the east coast of Tanjore District. The donor, owner presumably by purchase, was the 'Lord of Kaṭaha' also called 'Lord of the Śrīvishaya 'country', Śrīmāra Vijayōttunga, son of Chuḍāmani of the Śailēndra family. Srīvishaya was the kingdom of Palembang and is so-called in an inscription of A.D. 775 found at Vieng-Sa in the south of the Bay of Bandon, which also says that the then king belonged to the Śailēndra family. In Chinese annals Palembang is called San-fo-Ts'i, and the annals of Song mention in A.D. 1003 and 1008 two embassies sent by Chulāmaṇi and Śrimāra VI [Jayottunga] to China.[1]

(*Madras Review, 1902, and Arch. Sur. of Burma Report 1911–22, p. 6 ; Bulletin de'lécole Francaise d'Extrême Orient. Tome xviii, No. 6.*)

[1] In regard to the whole of this item, reference may be made to my article 'Rajendra the Gangaikonda Chola' in the *Journal of Indian History*, vol. ii., pt. iii., pp. 317–70 and 'Researches in the Geography of Ptolemy' by Col. Gerini (*Asiatic Society Monographs.*)

Śakkara-Kōṭṭam has been identified with a place near Jagdalpur, the capital of the state of Bastar.

Madhura Mandalam is not the Pāndya capital but is a place like the following four :

Navanidhi Kula,
Nāmanaikkōṇam,
Panchapaḷḷi, and
Māśuṇidēśa,

all places which must be looked for in the tributary states of Orissa, between the Central Provinces and the Nizam's Dominions on the one side, and the coast region of Kalinga on the other.

There is a place Panchapaḷḷi in this region.

Māśuṇidēśa must be merely a translation of the territory of Bastar under the Naga-Vaṁśi rulers.

There is also a Madhura Manḍalam in the locality on the maps.

For Ādinagar a suggestion has been made, and it may possibly be Jajnagar in Orissa. Indraratha referred to along with it may be Indravarman of Kalinga reigning at the time.

Dakkina Lāṭa and Uttara Lāṭa have no reference to Gujarat. Both of them refer to the division of Bengal Rāḍha, in the region near Burdwan.

Mahīpala referred to there is a reference to 'Oṭṭa-Mahī-Pala' in Tamil meaning simply the Oḍra or Orissa king. *Śangu-Kōṭṭam* : There is no warrant for a battle of Śangu-Kōṭṭam. The correct reading of the text is the defeat of the Orissa king at the Sangama (junction) of the Ganges with the sea. The actual expression being 'Sangama-Oṭṭa-Mahī-pālanai.'

The present grant shews that for some reason Rājēndra had, about 1024–25 quarrelled with the Ruler of Kēḍah and sent over an expedition which ended with the latter's defeat. The Lord Kēḍah at the time was Samgrāma-Vijayottunga, successor and perhaps son of Srīmāra Vijayōttunga; he was captured and his city was seized; his treasures, the (*Vidyādhara*) *tōraṇam* at the gate of the city, and two doors set with jewels were carried off. (xxiii) Mā-damalingam (said to be Jaya in the Malay Peninsula); (xxiv) Mā-ppapālam 'defended by water' (? on west-coast of Isthmus of Krā); (xxv) Talai-Takkōlam (on the Isthmus of Krā); (xxvi) Pannai 'watered by the River' (East coast of Sumatra); (xxvii) Mā-yiruḍingam 'by the sea', (a state dependent on Palembang); (xxviii) Ilangāśōkam (Lengasuka; a Malay state tributary to Kēḍah); (xxix) Ilāmuridēśam (Lāmurī, called by Marco Polo 'Lambri', in the far north of Sumatra, where there are many places whose names begin with 'Lam', *e.g.*, Lam Djamoe, Lam Baroe, etc.) (xxx) Mānakkavāram (the Nicobar Islands); and one or two other places.

[After this year the king seems to have ceased from warfare till the end of his reign.]

Jayasimha III of the Western Chāḷukyas grant at Yēwūr (*I.A. 1879, p. 10.*)[1]

Indravarman of Kalinga, in the 146th year of the dynasty, reigning at Kalinganagara (*V.R. i. Ganjam 3 ; I.A. x p. xii. 243 ; 122 ; T. and A.S. 164.*)

He was reigning also in Bellary District on November 23, 1025. (*V.R. i. Bell. 185 ; 489 of 1914.*)

A.D. 1025. The lengthy C.P. grant in 31 plates of the grant of a village to the temple at Tiruvālangāḍu. The Sanskrit portion is about this date. The Tamil portion belongs to Rājēndra Chōla I's sixth year (A.D. 1017–18). It contains a list of his conquests up to the last mentioned date. The Sanskrit portion adds his conquest of Kaṭāha. (*V.R. i. Chittoor 370 ; E.R. 1906, p. 66.*)

[Rājēndra I established his capital at Gangaikonḍa-Chōlapuram, near Chidambaram about this time.]

Another inscription shews Jayasimha Chāḷukya reigning in this year in North-West Mysore, with Kundamarasa ruling the Baṇavāsi 12,000 country. (*E.C. viii. Sa, 7.*)

A.D. 1026. Kassapa of Ceylon became king in this year at the age of twelve. Before he came to the throne (the *Mahāwaṁśa* relates) the Chōla king Rājēndra sent to the island an army of 95,000 men in order to seize the prince, but the expedition was unsuccessful. Because of this, no doubt, it is not mentioned in Chōla records. Kassapa, on mounting the throne, was called 'Vikrama-Bāhu'. (*J.R.A.S. 1913, p. 523 ; S.I.I. ii. 92.*)

Early in A.D. 1026 the Kongāḷva chief ruling on the western border of Mysore 'marched against the base Poyśala' *i.e.*, attacked the Hoyśala chief, probably Nripakāma, and was victorious at the battle of Maṇṇi, (so says the inscription which is on a *vīrakal* erected in honour of a soldier who fell). [*E.C. v. Ag. 76 ; cf. Mj. 43 of the year 1022–23.*]

The Kalinga-Ganga king Indravarman gave a grant (C.P.) in the 149th year of his dynasty. (*V.R. i. Ganjam 13 ; C.P. No. 4 of 1914.*)

A.D. 1027. N.-W. Mysore. Nanni-Sāntara of Humcha, ruling part of the country. (*E. C. vii. Sk. 53.*)

Kāḍaram or Kiḍāram or in another form Kāḷagam, all meant the same place and a suggestion has been made to identify them with Katra of Katraea in the east coast of Sumatra not far from the powerful kingdom of Śrī Vijaya at Palambang. The Chinese knew of it at the time by two names San-fo-Tsi, equivalent of Śrī Bhoja, and San-fu-Tsai, the equivalent of Śrī Vijaya, the kingdom of Palambang being known by two names viz., Śrī Bhoja or Śrī Vijaya.—*Editor*.

[1] Since republished in Ep. Ind. XII, 269 *ff.*—*Editor*.

An inscription in Kādūr District, Mysore, mentions the earliest known Hoyśala chief as ruling in his seventh year, namely, Nṛipa-Kāma. He is called 'Kāma-Poyśala, *alias* Rāchamalla-Permmāḍi.' *(E. C. vi. Mg. 19 ; See above s. v., A. D. 1022.)*

East Mysore was now under Rājēndra Chōla I. *(E. C. x. C. 13.)*

Part of Bellary District was being ruled by the Noḷamba-Pāllava chief Jagadēkamalla Udayāditya. His wife's name was Sigā-dēvī. Other records of his are found in 1030 and 1033, and (above) in 1022. *(V. R. i. Bell. 16, 42, 75, 76 ; 64, 65 of 1904 ; 199, 208 of 1913.)*

The northern part of Bellary District was under the direct rule of the W. Chālukya king Jayasimha III. Inscriptions of his of this date are found in Kurugōḍu *(E. R. 1903-4, p. 8)*, also in 1028-29 in N. W. Mysore. *(E. C. vii. Sk. 177.)*

An inscription of the end of this year alludes to severe fighting at Baṇavāsi which was attacked by someone. In the fighting 'Māraja, son of Kaleyabbe' was killed. This Mahārāja was possibly a son of the Hoyśala Vinayaditya whose wife was Kaleyabbe, and if so was grandson of Nṛipa-Kāmā. Whoever he was, he died in obedience to his duty to Nṛipa-Kāmā, so says the record *(E. C. v. Mj. 44)*. The Sāntara chief at this time also had a wife named Kaleyabbe.

A.D. 1028, December 24. Grant at Kulenūr (published by Dr. Barnett) of the W. Chāḷukya queen Kundala, wife of Kunda son of Satyāśraya II, who was ruling Baṇavāsi *(E. I. xv. 329.)* Kunda was also ruling that country in A.D. 1031. *(E. C. vii. Sk. 30.)*

A.D. 1030. Rājēndra Chōla I's inscription at Tanjore of his nineteenth year only repeats the list of achievements as given in his thirteenth year *(above s. v., A. D. 1024–25)* ; shewing that he had not been active since that year. *(S. I. I. ii. 105.)*

A.D. 1032, December 6. Jagadēkamalla-Udayāditya, the Noḷamba chief ruling the Noḷamba-vāḍi 32,000 tract under the W. Chāḷukya Jayasimha III *(253 of 1918)*. Record in Bellary District.

Five *Virakals* in Sorāb Taluk, Shimōga District, Mysore, record deaths which occurred during a raid carried out by a chief named Śāntayya, who ruled the Eḍēnāḍ country, for the purpose of cattle-stealing. *(E. C. viii. Sb. 60-64.)*

Jayasimha III of the W. Chāḷukyas continued to reign in N.-W. Mysore. *(E. C. vii. Sk. 20a ; viii. Sb. 191.)*

A.D. 1033. An inscription in Kolar District of the twenty-second year of Rājēndra Chōla I gives a list of his achievements, noting nothing new since his thirteenth year. *(E. C. x. Kl. 109 a.)*

A record of November 4, 1033, in S. Mysore and some mutilated ones in E. Mysore of his twenty-second year shew that this king was reigning in that country. *(E. C. iv. Hg. 17 ; x. Bg. 6, 7.)*

Rājēndra I sent an embassy to China in this year which is noted in the Chinese annals, where his name is rendered 'Lo-cha-into-lo chu-lo.'

Another record of his bears date November 25, 1033. *(E. I. iv. 69 ; vi. 20.)*

A.D. 1034. Long inscription at Mālūr of the twenty-third year of Rājēndra Chōla I. It adds no achievements of his to those mentioned above as having taken place before 1024. *(E. C. ix. Cp. 82, 83.)*

A.D. 1035. Rājēndra Chōla I reigning, in his twenty-fourth year in E. Mysore. *(E. C. x. Kl. 14.)*

Jayasimha III of the W. Chāḷukyas reigning in Bellary District *(V. R. i. Bell. 285 ; 93 of 1904)* ; and in N. Mysore, where the Noḷamba chief Jagadēkamalla-Udayāditya ruled under him. *(E. C. xi. Dg. 71.)*

A.D. 1036, April 8. A record of Rājēndra Chōla I's twenty-fourth year, which agrees with his accession as on May 30, 1012. But, to the date is added that the day was the '230th' day of that twenty-fourth year; and here there is some mistake, for April 8, 1036 was 313 days later than May 30, 1035, the first day of the twenty-fourth year. *(188 of 1918.)*

September 16, another record of the same king in his twenty-fifth year (335 of 1917).

October 22 and December 22 or 23. The W. Chāḷukya Jayasimha III reigning in Bellary District. *(V. R. i. Bell. 120 ; 200 of 1913 ; 258 of 1918.)*

Inscription in Tinnevelly District of Jaṭāvarman-Sundara-Chōla-Pāṇḍya, son of Rājēndra Chōla I in the former's sixteenth year. (*See above s. v., A.D. 1020–21.*) This proves conclusively, that the Chōla king had completely reduced the whole Pāṇḍya dominions.

(V. R. iii. Tinnevelly 82 ; 111 of 1905 ; E. R. 1905, p. 56.)

A.D. 1037, November 21. Inscription at Hoṭṭūr in Dharwar District shewing Akka-dēvi, sister of the W. Chāḷukya kings Vikramāditya V and Jayasimha III, ruling the Baṇavāsi 12000 province. *(E. I. xvi. 75.)*

Two later inscriptions in the same year shew Jayasimha III ruling still in Bellary and N. Mysore, with ' Jagadēkamalla-Immaḍi-Noḷamba-Pallava ruling locally.

(228 of 1918 ; E. C. xi. Dg. 126.)

Another shewing Rājēndra Chōḷa I reigning in South Mysore. *(E. C. iv. Hg. 104.)*

A.D. 1038. Record of the twenty-seventh year of Rājēndra-Chōla I, with a full list of all his achievements as given up to the end of A.D. 1024 (*cf. v. above*) and containing no reference to any later success (*E. C. ix. Nl. 4.*). This is a Tamil inscription at Ālūr.

A.D. 1038. On April 9, or May 3 was crowned the Kalinga-Ganga king Vajrahasta V, son of Kāmārṇava VI and the Vaiḍumba princess Vinaya-Mahādēvī. He was also called Anantavarman.

(E. I. iv. 183 ; where the date is given as May 3 ; v. App. 50, No. 355, where it = April 9. See also E. I. xi, p. 148 ; V. R. i. Ganjam 143 A.)

[Vikrama-Bāhu, king of Ceylon, who was earlier known as prince Kassapa, died of disease this year. A general named Kitti or Kīrti usurped the throne but was killed after seven days by Mahālāna Kīrti. Vikrama Bāhu had made a new set of crown jewels and a new throne to replace those carried off by Rājēndra Chola I. *(Mahāwaṁśa 56.)*]

Jayasimha III, W. Chaḷukya, continued to reign in N.-W. Mysore. *(E. C. vii. Sk. 153.)*
And also in A.D. 1040. *(E. C. viii. Sb. 557.)*

A.D. 1039, November 22. Inscription in Trichinopoly District of the twenty-second year of Rājādhirāja Chola I. It proves that his creation as joint-king with his father Rājēndra must have taken place before November 22, 1018.

(V. R. iii. Trich. 890 ; 81 of 1895 ; E. I. iv. 218.)

At Kanyā-Kumāri (Cape Comorin) are inscriptions of the twenty-eighth to the thirty-first years of Rājēndra Chōla I, shewing him as sovereign over the farthest corner of the old Pāṇḍya realm, now completely absorbed and in Chōla possession (*T. A. S. i. 237, Nos. F to J*). The twenty-eighth year began May 30, 1039.

A.D. 1040, June 22. Rājēndra Chōla I reigning in the Pondicherry country, now French territory. *(187 of 1919.)*

August 27. Śirūr (Dharwar District). Inscription shewing the Noḷamba-Pallava chief

Jagadēkamalla-Nurmaḍi, 'Lord of Kānchī', ruling in that country under Jayasimha III of the W. Chāḷukyas. 'Nurmaḍi' is another form of 'Immaḍi[1]' (*above s. v., A.D. 1037.*). (*E. I. xv. 334*).

[*N.B.*—These Kanarese inscriptions speak of the 'Pērdorē' river, the 'Kirudorē' river, and the 'Eḍedorē' country. Fleet informs us that the Pērdorē is the Krishna and the Kirudorē the Tungabhadra river, while the Eḍedorē is the country between the two rivers, generally known as the Raichūr Dōāb.]

About this time or later (the date is not exactly determined by the inscriptions) the W. Chāḷukya king Sōmēśvara I, either acting for his father or himself ruling, made an expedition to the north against King Bhōja of Dhārā in Malwa, whom he defeated so severely that Bhōja fled. Dhārā was sacked and burnt. Among Somēśvara's lieutenants in this war was prince Eṛeyanga, son of the Hoyśala chief Vinayāditya.]

A.D. 1041, May 6. Rājēndra Chōla I reigning in Trichinopoly District in his twenty-ninth year. (*V. R. iii. Trich. 824 ; 65 of 1914.*)

He was also reigning in E. Mysore, where in this year serious cattle-raids took place (*E. C. ix. Ht. 11*). And in his thirtieth year (1041–42) in E. Mysore, when an inscription names him as the king who 'took the east country, Gangai, and Kaḍāram'. (*E. C. x. Kl. 149 b.*)

June 25. A sound date in an inscription shewing Rājēndra Chōla I reigning in S. Arcot on the 27th day of his thirtieth year. It fixes his accession-date as May 30, 1012. (*341 of 1917*).

[About this time, that is to say in the third year of the usurper-king of Ceylon Mahālāna Kitti, according to the *Mahāwaṁśa* (ch. lvi), the Singhalese under him fought against the Chōlas and by them were defeated. 'The Tamils seized again the crown and all the treasure and sent them to the king of Chōla.' The *Mahāwaṁśa* says that Kitti cut off his own head. Rājādhirāja's inscriptions say that he defeated four Singhalese kings, and killed one of them. (*Below s. v. 1046 A. D.*)].

The W. Chāḷukya king Jayasimha III still reigning in Bellary District. (*V. R. i. Bell. 229 ; 501 of 1914*).

A.D. 1042, January 18. An inscription of the Kalachūri king Karṇa-dēva, or Kannama dated from his camp on the Wain-Ganga river in the Central Provinces, helps to fix his date. (*E. I. ii. 297*).

A.D. 1042. Rājēndra-Chōla I reigning on July 23 this year in Tanjore (*V. R. ii. 700 ; 403 of 1902 ; E. I. vii. 169*).

The W. Chāḷukya Jayasimha III was still supreme this year in N.-W. Mysore, but he must have died very shortly afterwards, as this is the year of his son and successor Sōmēśvara I's accession (*E. C. viii, Sa, 108 bis, and 109 bis*). There is a grant by him dated early in A.D. 1043 in N. Mysore, but he may have died before the date given, or he may have retired shortly before his death from the burden of rule. (*E. C. xi. Dg. 19*).

A.D. 1043. Inscription shewing Rājēndra Chōla I reigning in E. Mysore in his thirty-second year which began on May 30, 1043. This is his last known record (*E. C. ix. Ht. 142*). He must have died shortly afterwards.

[Rājādhirāja now became sole occupant of the Chola throne. He tried to assist in the consolidation of his empire by associating his younger brother and his sons with different portions

[1] Nurmaḍi means a hundred-fold and Immaḍi two-fold in Kannaḍa. In the compound it means simply many fold or many times over.—*Editor.*

of the conquered territories. He gave them the titles 'Vānavan[1]' (for the Bāṇa country); 'Mīnavan' (for the old Pāṇḍya kingdom); 'Vallavan,' (for Chāḷukya territory, after, probably, his defeat of Somēśvara I); 'Tennavan' (for Southern Pāṇḍya dominions); 'Gangan' (for the Gangavāḍi province); 'King of Lanka' (for Ceylon); 'Pallavan' (for the former Pallava kingdom); and 'Protector of the people of Kānyakubja' (probably after his defeat of the Singhalese king, or prince, Vīra Salamēgha, who was said to have come to the island from Kanauj).

Mr. S. Krishnaswami Aiyangar justly remarks ('*Ancient India*', *p. 110*) that at this time Rājēndra I being dead 'there seems to have been a tendency to throw off the yoke on the part of all the subordinate allies of the Chōla.'

It is difficult to give an exact order to Rājādhirāja's campaigns. My impression is that his war with Ceylon was the earliest and took place in about 1041–42. A list is given below (*s. v.*, ***A. D.*** *1046.*)].

A.D. 1044, April 5. Date of installation of the Noḷamba-Pallava chief Trailōkyamalla-Nanni-Noḷamba by the W. Chāḷukya king Sōmēśvara (alias 'Trailōkyamalla-Āhavamalla') (*V. R. i. Bellary 130 : 232 of 1913*). At the end of this year he was ruling some districts in North Mysore and Dhārwār. (*E. C. xi. Dg. 20*).

On December 23 Sōmēśvara I was supreme in Bellary District. (*235 of 1918*).

There is an inscription of Rājādhirāja Chola I in Trichinopoly District of his twenty-sixth year, corresponding to March 14 of this year. (*V. R. iii. Trich. 884 ; 75 of 1895 ; E. I. iv. 216*).

[Probably in this year or the next began the Chōla war against the Western Chāḷukya king arising from disputes as to the overlordship of the Noḷambavāḍi and Gangavāḍi countries in Mysore and south of the Tungabhadra river. Rājādhirāja claims to have defeated Āhavamalla-Sōmēśvara I, and to have 'caused to fly' his sons 'Vikki,' (Vikramāditya VI) and Vijayāditya. He pursued the enemy and drove him over the Tungabhadra northwards as far as Koḷḷipākkai, which is believed to be a town on the south bank of the Krishna[2]. This town he burned.

(*Fleet, D. K. D. 437, 438 ; S. I. I. iii. 51*).

[Nevertheless we find, that the people of Bellary and northern Mysore tenaciously held to their subjection, for some years after this, to the Chāḷukya throne, and declined to accept Chōla over lordship.]

A.D. 1045, May 9. Record in Tanjore of the twenty-seventh year of Rājādhirāja.

(*V. R. ii. Tanjore 666 ; 3 of 1914.*)

August 5. The W. Chāḷukya Āhavamalla-Sōmēśvara I recognized as supreme in Bellary, with, as local governor, the Noḷamba chief, subordinate to whom was a certain Udayāditya Sinda.

(*V. R. i. Bellary 142 ; 193 of 1913.*)

October 28. Sōmēśvara I was encamped at Huvina-Hadagalli in Bellary District. Nanni-Noḷamba, his vassal was the local Pallava ruler. (*V. R. i. Bellary 215, 217 : 441, 443 of 1914.*)

[A rather puzzling record; for, since Hadagalli is in the south of Bellary bordering on Mysore, either the war had not yet taken place, or, after their defeat, the Chāḷukya king had found himself strong enough to return to the country from which he had been ejected. One of the records says that the grant, of which it is a witness, was made when the king had 'returned from a raid,' (*and see below, note to record of December 3, 1046*).]

[1] Vanavan in the sense of Bana does occur in compounds like Vānavan-Mahādēvi, sometimes, but the general significance of the term is *Chēra*. This seems the intended meaning in this context.—*Editor*.

[2] See note above p. 62 and p. 81 following and note under A.D. 1067.—*Editor*.

An inscription at Kāḷahasti, Chittoor District, of the twenty-eighth regnal year of Rājādhirāja Chōla I mentions three of his conquests, *viz* : (i) He captured Mānābharaṇan-Vīra-Pāṇḍya—probably a member of the old Pāṇḍya royal family who attempted to throw off the yoke of the Chōla,—and decapitated him; (ii) He conquered the Chēra king or king of Kēraḷa; (iii) He conquered Ceylon. All these events therefore took place in or before A.D. 1045. (*V. R. i. Chittoor 79 ; 283 of 1904.*)

In this year the Kalinga-Ganga king Vajrahasta V from his capital Dantapura granted 35 villages to a local chief. (*V. R. iii, Vizagapatam 213–A ; C. P. 16 of 1908.*)

A.D. 1046, December 3. A very important inscription at Maṇimangalam, Chingleput District, of twenty-ninth year of Rājādhirāja Chōla I counting from the beginning of his co-regency with Rājendra I. His achievements up to date are mentioned as follows—(i) He defeated the Pāṇḍya prince Mānābharaṇan and cut off his head (Dr. Hultzsch gives good reason for believing the prince to have been of the Pāṇḍya stock ; (ii) War with the Kēraḷas, when he seized Vīra Kēraḷa and caused him to be trampled to death by an elephant; (iii) Drove Sundara-Pāṇḍya (not identified) to Mullaiyūr; (iv) killed the king of Vēṇāḍ (Travancore); (v) Put to flight the Chēra (Kēraḷa) king and destroyed his ships at Kāndalūr-Śālai (as did his grandfather Rajarāja I, to which event it may possibly be that this is an allusion); (vi) Fought the W. Chāḷukyas and caused Vikramāditya and Vijayāditya to flee and burned the town of Koḷḷipākkai (*see above, s. v., A. D. 1044, note*); (vii) War with Ceylon in which he took the crowns of four kings, *viz*: Vikrama-Bāhu, Vikrama Pāṇḍya[1] (who had usurped the throne of Ceylon in A.D. 1041 according to Hultzsch's chronology), Vīra Salāmēgha of Kanauj (another Singhalese usurper who according to the *Mahawaṁśa* was named Jagatipāla and was an ' Aryan of the race of Rāma ') and Śrīvallavan-Madana (who had come to India and taken up his abode with ' Kannara '); (viii) A renewed war with the W. Chāḷukyas when he made an expedition to the Tungabhadra river and destroyed the town of Kampli, on its bank and a royal palace ; (ix) He performed the horse sacrifice. (*S. I. I. iii. 51, No. 27, 28 ; Mahwaṁśa ch. 55.*)

[While we cannot exactly fix the order of date of these events, it seems reasonable to suppose that the expedition to Kampli took place later than the war when, according to this account, the W. Chāḷukya princes were put to flight ; and this justifies the belief that after that flight, if it really occurred, the Chāḷukyas had returned and again taken possession of their territories south of the Tungabhadra (*see note above s.v., A.D. 1045*), and that this return caused Rājādhirāja to send a second expedition against them, in the course of which Kámpli was destroyed. But even so, we find the Chāḷukyas back in those territories and ruling over them for some years later (*V.R. i. Chingleput 791*). If these inscriptions are to be believed, Rājādhirāja was guilty of barbarous cruelty towards his enemies. Besides the slaughters mentioned, he is said to have captured the queen-mother of Ceylon and cut off her nose. This may however be meant as a mere metaphor. (*E.C. ix. Dv. 75.*)]

A.D. 1047, March 29. Sōmēśvara I of the W. Chāḷukyas recognized as king in Bellary District (*see note above*). (*711 of 1919 ; V.R. Bell. 200–211 ; 41 of 1904 ; 484 of 1914.*)

An inscription in E. Mysore in the same year shews Rājādhirāja Chōḷa reigning there (*E.C. x. Ct. 30*). Also at Cape Comorin—Kanyā-Kumāri. (*T.A.S. i. 161*).

In N.-W. Mysore Sōmēśvara was sovereign. (*E.C. vii. Sk. 151*).

The Vengi country was ruled over in this year by the Eastern Chāḷukya king Rājarāja Narēndra, alias Vishṇuvardhana VIII, who began to reign in 1022 A.D. (*V. R. ii. Godavari 88 ; 183 of 1893*).

[1] The *Mahawaṁśa* says that Vikrama Pāṇḍya was killed by Jagatipāla.

On March 29, 1047 Akkadēvī, aunt of Sōmēśvara I and ruling the Kiśukāḍ division, made a grant of a village to a Jain temple. (*E.I. xvii, 121.*)

A.D. 1048. Sōmēśvara I ruling in Bellary District. Inscription at Kalkambha. Under him ruled the Noḷamba-Pallava chief Trailōkyamalla-Nanni-Noḷamba. (*V.R. i, Bell. 78 ; 67 of 1904.*)

Sōmēśvara I continued to reign over N.-W. Mysore (*E. C. vii. Hl. 107*). In the Ganjam District the Kalinga-Ganga king Vajrahasta V (1038–1070) was supreme. (*E.R. C.P. No. 3, App. A. 1918–19.*)

[It is however doubtful whether the date, is July 10, 1048, or July 30, 1049.]

Rājādhirāja was reigning in South Arcot and Pondicherry. Records of date : February 26 and March 2. (*330 of 1917 ; 176 of 1919*).

A.D. 1049–51. Record of Rājādhirāja Chola I's 32nd year in Kolar District, Mysore. It enumerates his successes (*E. C. x. C.B. 21*) ; and one of his thirty-third year in South Mysore (*ibid. iv. Gu. 93*). Another, similar, of the same regnal year, is in Bangalore District (*ibid. ix. Dv. 76*), and another in Kolar District (*Ibid. x. Mb. 105, C.*) Another also of the thirty-third year, in E. Mysore, mentioning his exploits shews incidentally that the landlord's share of the field produce (*Mēlvāram*)[1] in the time of this king was a three-fifth part of all the wet crops grown and a quarter of the dry crops. This, at least, was the case in the Maṇṇai-nāḍu division. (*E.C. ix., Nl. 25*).

[Mr. S. Krishnaswami Aiyangar (*Ancient India, p. 181*) thinks that the Government under this sovereign took one-sixth of the produce. This is not the place for a discussion, but I quote what the inscription of the time states. The commander of the king's army declares that he accepts the proportion I have mentioned as the correct amount of the landlord's share of the crop.]

A.D. 1051. W. Chāḷukya king Sōmēśvara I, ' Trailōkyamalla,' in N. Mysore. (*E.C. xi., Hk. 65.*)

A.D. 1052, May 28. Date of the death of Rājādhirāja Chōla I, in battle at Koppam when fighting against the W. Chāḷukyas, and of the accession of his brother Rājēndradēva, who was crowned on the battle-field. [The date is derived from that of the Maṇimangalam inscription (*S.I.I. iii, 58 ; 3 of 1892*) of the eighty-second day of Rājēndradēva's fourth year which corresponds to August 17, 1055 (*See below*). He reigned till 1053. (*See also ibid. i. 31, etc.*)

The war which broke out between the Chōlas and the W. Chāḷukyas was evidently caused by the Chōla king Rājāditya's attempts to crush the power of the Chāḷukyas and their vassals, the Ganga and Noḷamba chiefs, and the refusal of these to give way. The Chōla forces advanced Westwards and North-Westwards, and finally a great and decisive battle took place at Koppam. Now Koppam has been variously declared to be the place of that name on the upper Tunga river in West Mysore—which would mean that the Chōla's enemies had been driven backwards for a long distance towards the edge of the Western Ghāts before the decisive battle was fought and (by Dr. Fleet) to be a place far to the North of this, close to Khidrāpūr and standing in a loop of the river Krishna in Belgaum District, at the confluence of that river with the Panch-ganga where there is a temple of Koppēśvara. This latter identification would seem the most probable

[1]The question in this record is the sharing of the produce between the owner of the land and the cultivator. The owner's share for wet lands is two-fifths and for dry land a quarter. The term *Mēlvāram* makes this clear, and this has nothing to do with the state demand, which alone is under reference in Ancient India *locus citi* and which is confirmed in clear terms in 641 of vol. V. S.I.I. (A. 281 of 1895).—*Editor.*

inasmuch as one of Rājēndradēva's boasts is that he planted a pillar of victory at Kollāpuram, believed to be the same as Kolhāpur, which is 30 miles West of Khidrāpūr.

The Yēwūr Inscription B (*E. I. xii. 296*) says that at Koppam—the site of the battle was a 'proper great *tīrtha*', or holy place on the bank of a *pēr-ār*', or great river; and this description suits the place near Khidrāpūr where there still is a temple of Koppēśvara, or Īśvara of Koppam. The *pēr-ār* may mean the Krishna, which was known by that name equally with the river in Cochin known as the 'Perar'. A record of A.D. 1071 at Aṇṇigere in Dharwar District states that the Chōlas in their advance had burned some Jain temples in the Beḷvola province into which they had penetrated,—temples which had been erected by Ganga princes—and that at the end of the War Rājādhirāja Chōla was killed. It may be therefore that the Chōla armies had first devastated the Ganga country, and then, crossing the Tunga and Bhadra rivers high up in their course had moved northwards into the 'Raṭṭa' country proper, where the battle of Koppam took place.

(*E. I. xii. 296 ; E. C. xi, Bn. 108, D. K. D. Bombay Gazetteer, p. 241.*)

Be this as it may the battle of Koppam was an important and bloody engagement. The Chāḷukya forces were led by the royal princes and the Chōla king Rājādhirāja and his brother Rājēndradēva were present in person. When the opposing armies met Rājēndradēva seems to have been on an elephant in the first line, having in second line behind him the force under the immediate command of the king himself. The Tanjore inscription (*S. I. I. ii. 303*) says of Rājēndradēva that he had the army of his elder brother at his back. A record at Tiruvallam (*S. I. I. iii. p. 111.*) tells us that prince Rājēndradēva's elephant was charged by enemy elephants and apparently turned tail and carried his rider towards the second line where Rājādhirāja 'stopped it'. Then, as I read the story, the Chōla second line came into action ; the archers of the enemy concentrated their aim on the Chōla king's elephant ; the animal was wounded in the forehead, and several arrows pierced the king himself and killed some of the men who were on the elephant with him ; Rājādhirāja was killed ; Rājēndradēva ordered up several fresh regiments and made so determined an advance that he bore down all opposition and in the end won a complete victory.

So say Chōla records which state that Rājēndradēva captured 'enormous booty' after the battle and made prisoners of two queens. Chāḷukya records on the contrary claim the issue of the fight as a Chāḷukya victory and say that the Chāḷukyas even followed it up by seizing the Chōla capitāl, Kanchi.

On the Chālukya side, fighting for Ahavamalla Sōmēśvara I (who does not appear to have been present), were some Chāḷukya princes, amongst them certainly Jayasimha the king's youngest son. The Maṇīmangalam record avers that he was killed, but this was not the case. Other accounts say that he fled the field. Several chiefs, named lost their lives, amongst them the Noḷamba chief Nanni-Noḷamba.

It is difficult to say what happened after the battle, for the tales told by the inscriptions and by court-poets are absolutely at variance. Chōḷa accounts say that the Chōla armies pressed on and that Rājēndradēva, now king, erected a pillar of victory at Kollāpuram (Kohlāpūr). Bilhaṇa, in his *Vikramānkadēvacharita*, declares that the Chaḷukya armies pressed forward and captured the Chōla capital Kāñchī driving the Chōla king into the jungles. Judging from the fact that W. Chāḷukya power grew in strength for some years after this and that the Noḷamba province remained a possession of the Chāḷukyas, it would seem most probable that Rājēndradēva retired shortly after the battle to his own country. He certainly did not succeed in conquering the Chāḷukyas.]

Mailāḷā-dēvī, senior queen of Sōmēśvara I, was now (1052–53) administering the Baṇavāsi 12000 province. *(E.I. xvi. 338.)*

Trailōkyamalla Noḷamba-Pallava was ruling in the Harpanhalli and Huvina-Hadagali Taluks of Bellary District, viz. the Kōgali 500 and other tracts. *(V.R. i, Bell. 245 ; 523 of 1914.)*

A.D. 1053, November 28. Grant at Nandanapūṇḍi, in the Vengi country 'between the two rivers', by the E. Chāḷukya Rājarāja-Narēndra in his thirty-second year. The date agrees with the date given for his accession—August 16, 1022. *(V.R. ii. Godavari 7 ; E.I. iv. 300 ; v. 31).*

December 24. A grant of the W. Chāḷukya Sōmēśvara I. His son Sōmēśvara ruling parts of Dhārwār District. He is given the E. Chāḷukya title—' Lord of Vengi, best of cities'. *(E.I. xvi. 53).*

Early in this year we have an inscription at Nirālgi, Dharwar District, of which the date, though not very regular, appears to be as stated, which makes the Kadamba chief Arikēśari making arrangements for the upkeep of a tank. *(E.I. xvi. 66).*

December 29. In Tanjore an inscription of Rājēndradēva calls this year the thirty-sixth of his reign. This could only be correct if his reign is reckoned as having begun in the same year as that of his elder brother, i.e. in A.D. 1018. But it does not appear from other records that he was ever considered as reigning jointly with Rājādhirāja. *(V.R. ii. Tanjore 23 ; 14 of 1908 ; E.I. x. 121. See also V.R. i, Chittoor 210 ; 321 of 1912, where possibly a mistake has been made in the king's name which is given as ' Rajadhiraja', now dead.)*

Two records shew the W. Chāḷukya Sōmēśvara I still reigning, one in N. and one in N.-W. Mysore, in this year. *(E.C. xi, Jl. 10 ; viii. Sb. 87).*

In this year the E. Chāḷukya king Rājarāja I gave a village to the poet Nannaya Bhaṭṭa, who translated the *Mahābhārata* into Telugu. *(E.I. v. 31).*

A.D. 1054, May 10. An inscription at Honwāḍ, Beḷgaum District, shews that the *W. Chāḷukya king* Somēśvara I was reigning there then *(I.A. 1890, p. 270)*. And so does one in N.-W. Mysore. *(E.C. vii. Sk. 118).*

An inscription at Tiruvallam of Rājēndradēva-Chola's third year, and another in Mysore mention the battle of Koppam and chronicle the king's success. The contents of both are noted above, *s.v.* 1052, May 28. *(S.I.I. iii. 111 ; E.C. x. Kl, 107).*

A.D. 1055. In the Bellary District the Chāḷukya Sōmēśvara I was reigning. *(V.R. i. Bell. 196 ; 37 of 1904).*

An inscription, believed to be of this year (the date is rather doubtful) at Bankāpūr, Dhārwār District, shews that, in spite of the Chōla attack of A.D. 1052 the Baṇavāsi 12000 and the Gangavāḍi 96000 provinces continued to acknowledge as their sovereign the Chāḷukya king Āhavamalla-Sōmēśvara *(E.I. xiii. 168)*. Under him Kadamba Arikēśaridēva ruled at Baṇavāsi.

A 'terrible famine' took place this year, according to an inscription at Ālanguḍi in Tanjore District. It is commented on by Mr. P. N. Ramaswami in *I.A. 1923, pp. 193–94.*

This was the fourth year of Rājēndradēva-Chola. The Maṇimangalam inscription alluded to above *(s.v., A.D. 1052, May 28)* relates many details about the events of his reign up to date. This one *(S.I.I. iii. 58 ; 3 of 1892)* adds details about his war in Ceylon. The record mentions honours conferred on the king's near relatives. His uncle Gangaikoṇḍa Chōla was created 'Irumaḍi-Chōla'. He gave titles to his four younger brothers. Mummaḍi Chōla was named 'Chōla-Pāṇḍya'. Vīra Chōla, 'Lord of Uraiyūr' or 'Koḷi', was named 'Karikāla Chōla'.

Madurāntaka was named 'Chola-Ganga' (in assertion of sovereignty over the Gangapāḍi country).

Parāntakadēva was named 'Chōla-Ayōdhya-Rāja'.

Titles were also given to his six sons, viz., 'Uttama-Chōla,' 'Vijayālayan,' 'Chōla-Kēraḷa', 'Chōla-Janakarāja', 'Sundara-Chōla' (whom we hear of later), and 'Chōla-Kānyakubja.'

Two grandsons were named 'Chōla-Vallabha' and 'Nṛipēndra Chōla.'

The king's war against Ceylon is described shortly. He despatched an army thither, captured Vīra Salāmēgha who was 'King of the Kalingas, and cut off his head, and seized the two sons of Mānābharaṇan' king of the people of Lanka. This exploit is mentioned in an inscription of October 27, 1057 at Belaṭūru (*E I. vi. 213*). Dr. Hultzsch points out that these princes, Vīra Salāmēgha and Mānābharaṇan, must be different from the two princes of the same name mentioned as having been killed by Rājādhirāja (*See above, s. v., A. D. 1046*). The earlier Mānābharaṇan was a Pāṇḍya prince. This one is distinctly stated to have been king of Ceylon.

[The date of this inscription is August 17 A.D. 1055, and the war must have been waged and finished before that date. The *Mahāwaṁśa* (ch. lvii) confirms this. Vijaya-Bāhu became king of Ceylon in A.D. 1054, according to Hultzsh's revised chronology, and we are told that there was war between him and the Chōla king after the death of his predecessor, or a continuation of a war. On his accession Vijaya-Bāhu made preparations for driving the invaders out of the island, which was 'forcibly held' by them; But the Singhalese were defeated and Vijaya Bāhu fled for refuge to a hill-fortress, while the Tamils devastated the country.]

An inscription of this year at Cape Comorin shews that Rājēndradēva was paramount there at the time. (*T. A. S. viii. 161, No. iii*).

The E. and W. Chāḷukyas seem to have been on good terms as there is an inscription at Drākshārāma, which is in E. Chāḷukya territory, stating that in this year A.D. 1055–56 the daughter of the minister of the W. Chāḷukya Āhavamalla-Sōmēśvara I made a gift to the temple there. (*V. R. ii. Godavari 90; 185 of 1893*).

A.D. 1057, November 25. Rājēndradēva supreme in Pondicherry territory, in his sixth year. (*180 of 1919*). Also in South Mysore on October 27, 1057. (*E. C. iv. Hg. 18*).

An inscription of the Kalinga-Ganga king Vajrahasta V is dated in Ś. 979, which is A.D. 1057–58 and one, a. C. P. grant in the Collector's office Ganjam, of the Kalinga-Ganga Queen Daṇḍi-Mahādēvi is dated in the year 180 of the dynasty, which year, with the epoch A.D 877–78, was also A.D. 1057–58. (*See Genealogical Tables, Kalinga-Ganga dynasty, Notes.*) (*V. R. i. Ganjam 10; E. I. vi. 133*).

A.D. 1058. An inscription at Tirukkōyilūr in South Arcot of the sixth year of Rājēndra-dēva Chōla refers to the battle of Koppam and to the pillar of victory set up at Kollāpuram. Others shew him at Pondicherry on April 9 and September 27, 1058. (*181, 183 of 1919*).

(*V. R. I. S. Arcot 851; 1239 of 1900; E. I. vii. 145.*)

Early in the year the W. Chāḷukya king Āhavamalla-Sōmēśvara I was reigning in N. Mysore, (*E. C. vii. Sk. 83*); and as an inscription of December 24, 1058 proves, reigning also in Bellary District (*201 of 1918*).

In Ganjam District the Kalinga-Ganga king Vajrahasta V was reigning—inscription of February 8, A.D. 1058, witnessing a gift by his general Samaya (*R. C. i. Ganjam 143 A; E. I. iv. 183; the Nadagam plates, the date of which is February 8 not March 4 as sometimes stated*).

Late in the year an inscription in Coorg shews the reigning chief to have been Rājēndra-Kongāḷva. (*Coorg Ins. 35*).

A record of this year at Ālūr near Mysore city names as reigning sovereign Rājēndradēva-Chōla in his seventh regnal year. It mentions his war with the Chāḷukya and the battle of Koppam, but no historical event since then. (*E.C. iv. 69*).

[It would seem then that the Chōlas held South Mysore at this period, while the Ganga chief, ruling under the W. Chāḷukya, held the north and west of the present Mysore State.]

In Guntūr District the reigning sovereign was the E. Chāḷukya Rājarāja-Narēndra. (*663, 671 of 1920*).

A.D. 1059, June 3. Rājēndradēva Chōla reigning in Pondicherry in his seventh year. It was, however, his eighth really, as his eighth year began on May 28, of this year—an error in the original, probably. (*179 of 1919*).

On July 27 Sōmēśvara I, W. Chāḷukya, was reigning in Bellary (*292 of 1918*); and at the end of the year in N. Mysore (*E.C. xi. Cd. 78*); and in Anantapur District. (*392 of 1920*).

A.D. 1060. The same king ruling in N.-W. Mysore. (*E.C. vii. Sk. 152*),

The ninth year of Rājēndradēva began on May 28, 1060. An inscription in Trichinopoly is dated in the 9th year of Rājēndradēva and the 3rd year of his brother Vīra Rājēndra which seems to shew that the latter had been made co-regent with the king in Rājēndradēva's sixth year. (*V.R. iii. Trichinopoly 896; 87 of 1895*).

Another record at Karuvūr in Coimbatore District belongs to this year. It mentions the battle of Koppam and shews Rājēndradēva Chōla as king. (*S.I.I. iii. 39*).

The W. Chāḷūkya Sōmēśvara I was reigning in N. Mysore, and a record of this year in that tract states that the Ganga chief Nanniyaganga Vikramāditya was then his vassal. (*E.C. xi. Dg. 140*).

[The southern part of the Gangavāḍi province had become subject to the Chōla throne.] (*Above s.v., A.D. 1058*).

A.D. 1061, June 20. Date of a C.P. grant of the village of 'Tāmaracheruvu', Godavari District, by the Kalinga-Ganga king Anantavarman-Vajrahasta V then reigning. (*V.R. ii. Madras 188; E.I. ix. 94*).

On the same day, in Bellary District, the W. Chāḷukya, Sōmēśvara I was reigning (*293 of 1918*), and in N.-W. Mysore (*E.C. vii. Sk. 5*); and, two years later in the same country. (*Ibid. Sk. 11*).

In 1061–62 the Hoyśala chiefs began to come into prominence in Mysore. A record shews Hoyśala Vinayāditya as ruling in West Mysore. [He must have been under the Ganga chief]. (*E.C. vi. Cm. 7*).

Mention of Dēvēndravarman-Rājarāja, son of the Kalinga-Ganga king Vajrahasta V in a record of this year which is dated in the 183rd year of the dynasty—[the epoch being A.D. 877–78.] (*E.I. iii. 130; V.R. i. Ganjam 6—the Chicacole plates*). He protected the E. Chāḷukya prince Vijayāditya, Viceroy of Vengi, against the Chōlas (*I.A. xviii. 161, 171; E.I. iv. 183*). There is another record of his, in the 184th year of the dynasty, A.D. 1062–63,—a C.P. grant from Parlakimeḍi in Ganjam District. (*E.R. 1921, App. A. Nr. 1*).

A.D. 1062. Sōmēśvara I 'Ahavamalla' W. Chāḷukya king was still reigning in N.-W. Mysore (*E.C. vii. Ci. 18*). Another inscription in the same locality confirms this and adds a passage about the Sāntaḷigē 1000 tract, saying that Vīradēva Sāntara (of Humcha), whose queen was named Chāgalā had 'freed the Sāntaḷige 1000 from those who had no claim to it, making them powerless.' He was vassal to the Chāḷukya (*E.C. viii. Nr. 47*). [The significance of this at present not apparent.]

A.D. 1063. March 13. This is the earliest possible date for the accession of the Chōla king Vīra Rājēndra, brother and successor of Rājēndradēva. The circumstances surrounding the latter's death are not at all clear. An inscription at Ālangudi, quoted by Dr. Hultzsch (*S.I.I. iii. 191*), dated in Rājēndradēva's third year says, or implies that he 'died on an elephant.' But we know that this cannot be the case because, as we have seen, inscriptions of his reign are extant up to his ninth year. Moreover there is an inscription of his twelfth year, the date of which, though doubtful, may be taken with reservation as February 15, 1063. This is in S. Mysore (*E.C. iv. Hg. 115*). Another record, but this time of Vīra Rājēndra, shows that the latter's reign began before September 10, 1063, and therefore we must place the limits of his accession as from March 13 to September 10 of that year, within which period Rājēndradēva died. (*See 113 of 1896*).

Then arises the question of whether a short reign intervened between these two in the person of Rājēndradēva's son Rajamahēndra, an inscription of whose third year is extant. Dr. Hultzsch has shewn cogent reasons for believing that he did not reign; one being based on the fact that the title 'Rājakēsari' was assumed by Vīra Rājēndra, Rājēndradēva having borne the title 'Parakēsari,'—these titles, according to Chōla law, being used alternately in regular succession. If there had been an intervening reign Vīra Rājēndra must have been a 'Parakēsari' king. It may be taken therefore that Rājamahēndra either did not reign at all, or that he was for a year or two joint ruler with his father.

The inscription of the third year of Rājamahēndra mentioned above is at Tiruppāppuliyūr in S. Arcot (*119 of 1902*). It states that 'his war-elephant frightened Āhavamalla [i.e. Sōmēśvara I] on the bank of a river and caused him to flee in terror.' This may be held to indicate that prince Rajamahēndra had been present at the battle of Koppam in A. D. 1052.

In the Vengi country in this year the E. Chāḷukya king Rājēndra II came, or should have come, to the throne in succession to his father Rājarāja-Narēndra. The new king was three-quarters Chōla by blood, his grandfather and his father both having married Chōla princesses. He himself married Madhurāntakı, daughter of the Chōla king Rājēndradēva. Seven years later he succeeded in uniting the two crowns. (*S.I.I. i. 31 f.; E. I. vi. 334*).

Two records of about this time (*V. R. i. Chittoor 174, 246; 537, 573 of 1906*) mention the Chōla prince Adhi-Rājēndra, son of Vīra-Rājēndra in his third year. [He came to the throne for a very short time about A. D. 1070, and his third year must refer to his holding of some local government].

An inscription in 1063–64 of 'Tribhuvanamalla' Hoyśala, i.e. Vinayāditya, with his son Ereyanga. He is represented as 'protecting the hill-country and others of the Gangavāḍi 96000.' [He was therefore becoming a prominent leader under the Ganga chief. The family of the latter was seriously weakening]. (*E. C. vi. Kd. 161*).

In this year we have the first mention of the Kōnamaṇḍala chiefs of the Haihaya family, who claimed descent from Kārtavīrya and who ruled over the Delta country of the Gōdāvari. They are mentioned at intervals in inscriptions from now till about A. D. 1318. They were never of great political importance. (*E. I. iv. 83.*)

A.D. 1064. An inscription at Tiruvālangāḍu, Chittoor District (*14 of 1896 ; S. I. I. iii. 134*) of the E. Chāḷukya king Rājēndra II in his 2nd year states of him that he had (i) captured herds of elephants at Vairāgaram and (ii) 'raised the eastern region' probably meaning that he was strengthening the Vengi kingdom ; or, perhaps, as suggested by Dr. Hultzsch, that he took Vengi from his uncle Vijayāditya VII, who appears to have received it from the Chōla king Vīra Rājēndra (*S. I. I. iii. 132 ; the Tiruvoṟṟiyūr inscription, 106 of 1892*). If the latter was the case we shall have to assume that Vijayāditya VII was attempting to oust his nephew Rājēndra II from his throne, and in the attempt was supported by the Chola king, but that the designs of the Chōla and of his E. Chāḷukya friend were frustrated by Rājēndra II. The latter appears afterwards to have forgiven his uncle and to have allowed him to hold office as viceroy under him. This is the theory supported by Fleet. (*Ind. Ant. xx, 276.*)

Dr. Hultzsch has suggested another theory, *viz.* that Rājēndra II did not succeed in securing his father's throne till after his seizure of the Chōla throne in A.D. 1070, and that Vijayāditya VII actually was E. Chāḷukya king from 1063 to 1070, being supported by Vīra Rājēndra Chōla. (*S.I.I. iii. 128.*)

The Tiruvoṟṟiyūr inscription referred to (*V. R. i Chingleput 1000 ; 106 of 1892 ; 131 of 1912*) appears to belong to the year A.D. 1071–72, the 2nd year of Kulōttunga Chōla I as *Chola* king. It calls him 'Rājakēśari-Rājēndra-*Chola*.'

[Vairāgaram has now been shewn to have been Wairāgarh, otherwise Vajra in the Bastar State.]

Rājēndra II (E. Chāḷukya) also claims (iii) to have taken Chakrakōṭṭa, or Chakrakūṭa, the old capital of Bastar. (*E. I. ix. 178, x. 26 ; E. C. x, Kl. 108.*)

There appears to have been an attempt on the part of the Pāṇḍya prince Vīra Pāṇḍya to gain the Pāṇḍya throne in defiance of Vīra Rājēndra, but he was defeated by the Chōla forces, and the Chōla king created his son Gangaikoṇḍa-Chōla 'Chōla-Pāṇḍya' in token of Chōla supremacy over the Pāṇḍya country. (*Karuvūr inscription S. I. I. iii, 36 ; etc.*)

In this year Vishnuvaradhana-Vijayāditya of the Western Chaḷukyas, younger brother of Vikramāditya I was ruling the Noḷambavāḍi province under Sōmēśvara I. Record of date May 3, 1064 (*E. I. iv. 212. See also E. C. xi. Mk. 29*) His residence was Kampli. And on April 4 Sōmēśvara himself was reigning in Bellary (*286 of 1918*) ; and in N. Mysore. (*E. C. xi. Dg. 141.*)

December 26. An inscription of this date in the Bellary District seems to afford additional proof that the E. Chāḷukya Vijayāditya VII was attempting to cultivate friendly relations with the W. Chāḷukya branch—having already done so with the Chōla king—as it shews him giving a grant to a temple in what was certainly territory ruled by Sōmēśvara I. (*V. R. Bell. 216 ; 442 of 1914.*)

Three memorial stones at Honnāḷi in N.-W. Mysore of this year shew the continuance of wholesale cattle-raids by villagers. (*E. C. vii, Hl. 2, 3, 4.*)

The Baṇavāśi 12000 country was now being ruled by Toyimadēva, son of Akkādēvī of the W. Chāḷukya family, aunt of the reigning king. (*Above s.v., A.D. 1010.*) (*E. I. xvi. 81.*)

[It is very difficult to fix exact dates for the events of the next two or three years, and to follow precisely the course of events. We can only go by assertions made in inscriptions, which are often very vague, and only mention glorious victories without saying how and why the wars arose in which those victories were gained. I recommend here a study of Prof. S. Krishnaswami Aiyangar's '*Ancient India*' ch. vi.

A.D. 1064–65 was the second regnal year of the Chōla king Vīra Rājēndra, and a record of that year at Tiruveṇgāḍu (*S. I. I. iii. 193 ; 113 of 1896.*) alludes to a great war, in or previous to that year, fought by the Chōla forces against those of the W. Chāḷukya king Sōmēśvara I. Vīra Rājēndra was immediately opposed by Vikramāditya VI and Jayasimha IV, sons of Sōmēśvara. Sōmēśvara had, it appears, sent an army into the Vengi country. It was defeated, and the two Chāḷukya princes were driven altogether out of the Gangavāḍi province (in western and north-western Mysore), and compelled to retire across the Tungabhadra river. The Chōla forces pursued them and a battle was fought at Kūḍalsangamam in which the Chāḷukya princes were completely beaten. So say Chōla inscriptions.

[This Kūḍalsangamam Fleet holds to have been a place close to Khidrāpūr in Belgaum, near to which place there are two confluences of the Krishna river (called the 'Kūḍala'-Krishna); with other rivers. Near to it is Koppam where the great battle had been fought in A.D. 1052. (*E. I. xii. 296*). Another theory would make Kūdalsangamam, a confluence of the Tunga and Bhadra rivers,[1] and the battle there to have preceded the Chāḷukya retreat northwards over that river. This theory is supported by an inscription at Karuvūr (*58 of 1890*), the rendering of which would have that meaning.]

Later inscriptions of the reign of the E. Chāḷukya Rājēndra II, when he had become Kulottunga Chōla I, say that he 'drove Vikkaḷan (Vikramāditya) VI from Nangili (in Kolar District) by way of Maṇaḷūr to the Tungabhadra river, and conquered the Ganga country and Jayasimha IV.' [This looks like a description of Vīra Rājēndra's campaign, and it is perhaps possible that, being now a Chōla king, Kulōttunga's records ascribe to him victories won by an earlier Chōla king. But it is useless to speculate and we do not even know why Sōmēśvara I should have sent an expedition to Vengi.]

The Karuvūr inscription of Vīra Rājēndra's 4th year, 1066–67 (*S. I. I. iii. 31*) says that when the Chōla forces attacked and destroyed the army of the W. Chāḷukyas which had been sent to the Vengi country, the king cut off the head of a dead chief, Chāmuṇḍa-Rāja (probably of Baṇavāśi), seized his daughter, wife of Irugayan, and cut off her nose. It describes the battle in poetic style. (For events after this battle see below and note generally Dr. Hultzsch's remarks in *S. I. I. Vol. III, 33–39*, etc.)

An inscription at Perumbēr in Chingleput District, belonging to Vīra Rājēndra's seventh year (1069–70), is the only one which credits him with any success in Ceylon, and it states very shortly that he 'subdued the Śingaḷa country.' The fact appears to be, if we may believe the *Mahāwaṁsa* (Ch. lviii), that Chōla power in the island met with a severe reverse; which probably accounts for the absence of boasting in other Chōla records. Vijaya-Bāhu of Ceylon had come to the throne in A.D. 1054. Ten years passed, years of great confusion, when the Tamils were very strong. At one time the islanders refused to pay taxes to the Chōla officials and that led to a fresh invasion and much slaughter. In Vijaya-Bāhu's eleventh year (1064–65) the army of the Chōla king suffered a severe defeat. Vijaya-Bāhu took the field in person and advanced northward to drive the Tamils out of the island, and a battle was fought near Anurādhāpura (V. 57). The Singhalese were defeated and Vijaya-Bāhu retired to a hill fortress. Desultory warfare followed

[1] Or, as suggested by Prof. S. Krishnaswami Aiyangar (*Anc. India, p. 121*) the junction of the Krishna and Tungabhadra rivers in Kurnool District. In this work the learned author has discussed the difficult historical problems of the time.

for two or three years and gradually his position became stronger. Then he attacked Pulatthi, the Chōla stronghold in the island, and at last took it. He followed up this success by driving the Tamils out of the island. Then he entered his capital in triumph in his fifteenth year (A.D. 1068–69) Kulōttunga Chōla I's record at Tirukaḷukkuṉṟam of his fourteenth year only states that he 'attempted' to conquer Ceylon (*S. I. I. iii. 143.*). We may therefore take the Singhalese account of what happened as correct.

A.D. 1065. An inscription in the Kolar District, Mysore, of the E. Chāḷukya Rājēndra II's third year mentions as his triumphs up to date only his capture of elephants, his victory at Chakrakōṭa, and that he took 'the country towards the East,' i.e., the Kalinga country. (*E.C. x. Mb. 49 a*). The same is the case with another record of the third year at Sōmamangalam, Chingleput District. (*S. I. I. iii. 139*).

A.D. 1066. The Karuvūr inscription (*S. I. I. iii. 36*) of Vira-Rājēndra Chōla's fourth year gives us some more information as to events of his reign. (i) He gave the government of the Pāṇḍya country to his son Gangaikoṇḍa Chōla with the title of 'Chōla Pāṇḍya', and he made Muḍikonda Chōla, 'Sundara Chōla'. He cut off the head of the chief of Pottappi, of the Kerala king or prince Vāran, and of a prince of Dhára. (ii) He caused to be trampled to death by an elephant Vīrakèśarin Pāṇḍya, probably son of the Pāṇḍya Śrivallabha. (*V. R. i. Trich. 2 ; 58 of 1890*).

[The Pottapi-nāḍu is the country about Kāḷahasti in Chittoor District. The chiefs came to the front under the Chōla kings (See pedigree of the Gaṇḍa-Gōpāla chiefs.)]

The battle of Kūḍalsangamam is mentioned in an inscription of this year at Mālūr in S.-E. Mysore, its date being the fourth year of Vīra-Rājēndra Chola. (*E. C. ix. Cp. 85.*)

An inscription of the 4th year of 'Rājakēśarin, *alias* Uḍaiyār-Rājēndra Chōla' in the Trichinopoly District, mentioning him as sovereign, has been interpreted as belonging to the E. Chāḷukya Rājēndra II, afterwards Kulōttunga I. But it seems hardly probable that this can be a correct identification. It is fairly certain that in A.D. 1066-67 the people of that country would not have acknowledged the E. Chāḷukya prince as their overlord, whatever they may have done later. Moreover the title awarded to him proves that he was then reigning as a *Chōla* king. The record probably belongs to the year A.D. 1073–74.

(*V. R. iii. Trich. 34 ; 386 of 1903; E. R. '904, p. 12.*)

In Western Mysore in this year the local chief was Rājēndra-Prithvi-Kongāḷva. (*E. C. v. Ag. 93.*)

In N.-W. Mysore Sōmēsvara I, W. Chāḷukya, was king. (*E. C. vii. Sk. 19.*)

In N. Mysore two records mention as ruling in that country the 'Vengi-Mahāmaṇḍalēśvara Vishṇuvardhana-Vijayāditya,' under, apparently, Jayasimha IV, the W. Chāḷukya prince. This might be taken as Jayasimha's younger brother so-called, but for the appellation 'Vengi-lord'. It could hardly have been the E. Chāḷukya Vijayāditya VII, as he is not known to have governed territory under the W. Chāḷukyas, nor was he called 'Vishṇuvardhana.' Probably the allusion to Vengi was a name assumed after the W. Chāḷukya raid into that territory (*E. C. xi. Cd. 47 ; Dg. 11*). One of these is dated September 22nd.

A Sāntara family inscription, N.-W. Mysore, of this year says that the Humcha chief Vīra-Sāntara was ruling there having 'freed the Sāntaḷige 1000 from claimants and troubles.' (*See above s.v., A.D. 1062*).

A.D. 1067. At Maṇimangalam, Chingleput District, is an important inscription of the 5th year of Vīra-Rājēndra Chōla, of which the latest possible date is September 10, 1068. After mentioning the events of his reign summarized above it states that, burning with rage at his defeat at Kūḍalsangamam, the W. Chāḷukya king sent a letter to Vīra Rājēndra challenging him to meet him once more at the same place. Vīra Rājēndra proceeded to Kāndai (or Karandai ?)—probably a village near Kūḍal, and was there on the appointed day ; but though he waited there a full month the enemy never appeared. Wherefore the Chōla king burned many places in the Raṭṭapāḍi (Sōmēsvara's dominions) and set up a pillar of victory on the Tungabhadra river bank. [Another inscription says that he burnt Kampli].

Then he summoned to his court Sōmēśvara's son, Vikramāditya VI, and appointed him W. Chāḷukya king (claiming thereby that he had dethroned Sōmēśvara.) In doing so he, while at the same time branding him as a 'liar', decorated him with a rich necklace. [As I read this account and compare it with others the truth seems to be somewhat as follows—we know from other sources that Sōmēśvara I of the W. Chāḷukyas drowned himself in the Tungabhadra river on March 30, 1068. It was probably Vikramāditya VI who had challenged Vīra-Rājēndra, and, equally probably, he was prevented from meeting the Chōla forces at Kūḍaḷsangamam owing to his having heard of his father's suicide. The father being dead prince Vikramāditya, being only the second son and his elder brother Sōmēśvara II succeeding to the throne, was induced to enter into friendly relations with the Chōla king, perhaps with an eye to some subsequent political assistance to suit his own ends, and journeyed to the Chōla camp or capital. There he was received sympathetically, and Vīra Rājēndra proclaimed Vikramāditya king, with the object of first ousting Sōmēśvara II and next of strengthening his own position by becoming an ally of Vikramāditya's. He decorated the latter and, so says the *Vikramānkadēva charita*, gave him his daughter in marriage].

(V. R. i. Chingleput 787 ; 2 of 1892 ; S. I.I. iii, p. 64, No. 30).

The inscription mentions a number of chiefs who opposed Vīra-Rājēndra and states that he cut off their heads ; amongst these we note the names of a Ganga, a Noḷamba, a Pallava (' Kāḍava ') and a Vaiḍumba chief. It continues the story by saying that after his investiture of Vikramāditya VI, Vīra-Rājēndra marched to the Vengi country, fought a battle at Bezwada, advanced to the Godāvari river, entered Kalinga and attacked Chakrakōṭṭa. He conquered Vengi and bestowed it on the East Chāḷukya Vijayāditya VII. Then he returned hastily to his country, where, says the inscription, there had been trouble—'the goddess of victory had shewn hostility in the interval.' This trouble was probably caused by the intrigues of the East Chāḷukya king Rājēndra II. [The capture of Vengi is unlikely]. *(S. I. I. ii, 234 ; E. I. x. 26).*

A record of this year shews the W. Chāḷukya Sōmēśvara I reigning in N. W. Mysore.

(E. C. vii. Sk. 169).

An inscription at Kulpak, anciently Koḷḷipāka, 45 miles N. E. of Hyderabad of date October 22, 1067 shews that the sovereign over that country was the W. Chāḷukya Sōmēśvara I.

(Hyderabad Archæol. Soc., January 1916, p. 28).

A.D. 1068. Two records of Vīra Rājēndra Chōla at Tinḍivanam in South Arcot and at Tiruvallam in North Arcot imply that Sōmēśvara II., now W. Chāḷukya king, was furious when he heard that Vīra-Rājēndra Chōla had attempted to oust him from the throne in favour of Vikramāditya VI, but before he could take any action Vīra Rājēndra burnt the city of Kampli and set up a pillar of victory, the site of which is named as Karaḍikal. *(S. I. I. iii. 200 ; 16 of 1890 : 207 of 1902).*

On March 30, 1068, the W. Chāḷukya king, suffering greatly from an attack of malignant fever, drowned himself in the Tungabhadra river at Kuruvaṭṭi. His son 'Bhuvanēkamalla' Sōmēśvara II succeeded and was crowned on April 11. His younger brother Jayasimha IV, had been made viceroy over the Noḷambavāḍi province with, apparently, the latter's own younger brother Vijayāditya associated with him as co-viceroy, in A.D. 1064–65, as both names are mentioned as ruling there in that year (*V. R. i. Bellary ii. 295; E. I. iv. 212; xv. 94 Cj ; 103 of 1904 ; E. C. xi, Mk, 29*). Vijayāditya's residence was at Kampli, Jayasimha also ruled the Kōgali tract (*For the date April 11 see E. C. vii. Sk. 136*). From this latter record it would appear that these Chāḷukya princes were overlords in the Noḷamba country, while the actual governor of it was Vikrama-Noḷamba.

Another grant of this year in Bellary District mentions Jayasimha, Sōmēśvara II's brother, as ruling there (*V. R. i. Bellary 11*). But another seems to show that in N.-W. Mysore the Hoyśalas were gaining strength, as it makes Hoyśala Ereyanga ruling in Shimōga District in the same year. (*E. C. vii. Sk. 64*).

In Ganjam District the Kalinga-Ganga king Vajrahasta V was reigning. His queen, daughter of a Haihāya chief, gave a gift to a temple. (*V. R. i. Ganjam 399 ; 248 of 1896*).

A.D. 1069, March 12. Vīra Rājēndra Chōla supreme in Tanjore in his 6th year. This inscription fixes his accession-date as on or after March 13, 1063. An inscription in Chittoor District of his 7th year is dated in Ś. 991, or A.D. 1069–70. The 7th year began with March 13, 1069. (*V.R. i. Chittoor 288; 273 of 1904*)

From an inscription at Tiruvallam in North Arcot, we learn that prince Adhi-Rājēndra son of the Chōla king Vira Rājēndra had either been made co-regent with his father in 1067–68, or had been given a local government, for it quotes him as ruling on the 200th day of his 3rd year. (*S. I.I. iii. 114, 129.*). [Adhi-Rājēndra was brother-in-law to the W. Chāḷukya Vikramāditya VI. Vīra-Rājēndra appears to have died in this year, and Bilhaṇa relates that Vikramāditya VI heard of the death and was informed that the Chōla kingdom was in a state of anarchy. He proceeded to Kānchī, assisted Adhi-Rājēndra to put down a rebellion, and, taking him to Gangaikoṇḍa-Chōlapuram placed him on the Chōla throne. Then he marched back to the Tungabhadra. After a short time he heard that Adhi Rājēndra had been killed in a fresh rebellion and that the E. Chaḷukya king Rājēndra II 'lord of Vengi' had seized the throne of the Chōlas.

(*Fleet, D. K. D. Bombay Gazetteer, 445*).

Vīra Rājendra's official title had been 'Rajakēsari'. Adhi-Rājēndra, in accordance with custom had the alternate title 'Parakēśari'. Since the E. Chāḷukya Rājēndra II, when he became Chōla king and was named Kulōttunga I, took the title 'Rājakēśari' that in itself proves that there must have been a short reign between Vīra-Rājēndra and Kulōttunga I. It proves therefore Vīra-Rājēndra's death and Adhi-Rājēndra's having been, for a short time, king.

This same inscription mentions a settlement of temple accounts which had been made in the 8th year of king Vīra-Rājēndran. Now that year began, at the earliest on March 13, 1070. Hence Adhi-Rājēndra's reign must have been confined to the months between March 13 and June 9, 1070, which last was the date of Kulōttunga I's seizure of the throne.]

A.D. 1070, June 9. [It has been already pointed out the E. Chāḷukya Rājēndra II was by blood three-quarters Chōḷa. He seems to have resolutely set himself the task of seizing the Chōḷa throne since the date of his own father's death. He got the better of his uncle Vijayāditya VII who was aided by the Chōḷa and Kalinga kings, and on the death of Vīra-Rājēndra Chōḷa, finding himself now strong enough, he made a bold stroke, marched to the south, overcame all opposition, apparently put the young king Adhi-Rājēndra to death, and seized the Chōḷa throne. He thus united in his own person the Chōḷa and Eastern Chāḷukya thrones and, commanding the services of both nations, became overwhelmingly powerful over all south India.]

The date of his accession is fixed by two records at Drākshārāma, Godavari District (*V. R. ii. Godavari, 292, 295 ; 386, 389 of 1893 ; E. I. vi, 221 ; vii, 7, n. 5*), and is quite clearly June 9, 1070.

The new emperor does not seem to have been called by his Chōḷa name Kulōttunga quite at the beginning of his reign, judging from the inscriptions. He had other names or *birudas* given such as 'Jayadhara', 'Rājanārāyaṇa', 'Karikāla', 'Virudarāja-bhayamkara' etc. (*S. I. I. i 69 ; E. R. 1901, p. 9 ; S. I. I. iii. 129, 140*).

It is not necessary to quote all the dated inscriptions of his reign which are very numerous but only those of historical interest. When he seized the Chōḷa throne he became sovereign over all of what is now the Madras Presidency and Mysore, except parts of Ganjam, which were under the Kalinga-Ganga rulers, the Kērala country below the western Ghats, and the northern and north-western parts of Mysore which still owned the domination of the Western Chāḷukya family. The Ganga and Noḷamba chiefs of the latter tracts seem to have hesitated for some time as to their political conduct—they being loyal to the Chāḷukyas but overawed by the new strength of the Chōḷas.]

Coorg was being ruled by the Kongāḷva chief Rājēndra-Prithvi (*See above s. v., A.D. 1058*). (*E. C. i. Coorg, 49, 50*).

May 20, 1070. This day, calculation shews, was the day of accession to the throne of the Kalinga-Ganga kings of Dēvēndravarman I (*E. R. 1919 ; C. P. No. 4 of 1918–19. See also E. R. 1921, p. 93, and C. P. Nos. 1 and 2 of App. A for 1920–21*). [Dēvēndravarman assisted the E. Chāḷukya Vijayāditya VII in his struggles with his nephew Rājēndra II, afterwards Kulōttunga Chōla I].

A.D. 1071, February 25. An inscription in Hūvina-Hadagali Taluk, Bellary District, shews that on this day the W. Chaḷukya prince Vikramāditya VI had his camp at Gōvindavāḍi, after defeating in battle a certain general named Biddayya. Who this was is not known (*V. R. i. Bell. 182 ; 127 of 1913*). Vikramāditya VI was in Anantapūr also, late in this year. (*455 of 1920*).

Early in the year, and again in December, Sōmēśvara II, Vikramāditya's elder brother is shewn as reigning in N.-W. Mysore (*E. C. vii. Hl. 81 ; Sk. 129 ; viii, Sb. 317*). Kīrttivarma II of the Kadambas of Hāngal was locally ruling as his vassal.

Allusion has already been made (*s. v., A.D. 1064–65*) to the Tiruvoṟṟiyūr inscription of the 2nd year of Kulōttunga-Chōla I, which has I think wrongly been assumed to belong to that period. It is probably a record of that king dating from his assumption of the Chōla throne on June 9, A.D. 1070. Though it certainly calls him 'Rājēndra', his E. Chāḷukya title, it also gives him the purely Chōla title 'Rājakēśari', and the family name of 'Chōla'. It gives a list of taxes. (*V. R. i. Chingleput 1000 ; 131 of 1912*).

Another inscription of the 2nd year of Kulōttunga Chōla I at Kolār in Mysore proves that he was already recognized as king in the eastern Gangavāḍi territory (*S. I. I. iii. 136 ; 131 of 1892*). That tract had been re-named 'Vijaya-Rājēndra-Mandalam', after this king's Chāḷukya name.

A.D. 1072. Early in this year a grant of a village in N. Mysore was made by 'Trailōkyamalla-Noḷamba-Pallava-Jayasimha', i.e. the W. Chāḷukya prince Jayasimha IV, brother of the king. It proves that he was ruling the Noḷambavāḍi province (*E.C. xi. Mk, 28, also E.I. iv. 214; Fleet in Bombay Gazetteer, xv. 443; and E.C. xi. Cd. 82*). The last mentioned inscription names Vikramāditya VI, as overlord in N. Mysore in A.D. 1073.

On December 24, Kulōttunga Chōla I was reigning in Tanjore in his 3rd year.

(*55 of 1911; E.R. for 1922, p. 91*).

A.D. 1073, July 27. King Dēvēndravarman of the Eastern Gangas of Kalinga reigning in Vizagapatam District. The date if accepted—the '*dakshiṇāyana* Samkrānti' is quoted, but the given tithi corresponded with the *Simha* Samkrānti—confirms the fixture of A.D. 877–78 for the epoch of the Kalinga-Ganga royal era. The wrong quotation may have been due to carelessness in the framing of the original record. (*V.R. iii. Vizag. 68. A; E.I. iii. 130*).

November 7. Inscription at Kāvantandalam, near Conjeeveram, of the 4th year of Kulōttunga Chōla I. The given date is perfectly correct; and it proves that the Tamils considered the king's reign to have begun in 1070 when he mounted the throne of the Chōlas, and not from any accession to the East Chāḷukya throne in succession to his father who died in 1063.

(*S.I.I. iii. 172; 206 of 1901*).

In N.-W. Mysore Sōmēśvara II, of the W. Chāḷukyas was king.

(*E.C. viii. Nr. 30*).

A.D. 1074. Several inscriptions prove that the same king, also called 'Bhuvanēkamalla,' was reigning N. and N.-W. Mysore. The Sorab taluk was then included for political purposes in the 'Baṇavāsi 12000' District, and both were locally governed by Sōmēśvara II's minister Udayāditya of the Ganga family. He also ruled over the 'Sāntaḷigi 1000' (*E.C. viii. Sb. 299; vii. Sk. 295, 221*). The last noted one shews that Udayāditya was also called 'Vikrama-Ganga.' On October 7, a record in Dharwar shews Sōmēśvara reigning there, and tells us that the princes Vikramāditya VI, and his younger brother Vishṇuvardhana-Vijayāditya were then at Bankāpūr, where they made a gift to a temple. Vijayāditya is also given Pallava titles, perhaps implying that he ruled the Noḷamba country. (*E.I. xvi. 68*).

In W. Mysore the local ruler was Hoyśala Vinayāditya. (*E.C. vi. Cm. 15*).

On December 24, 1074, an inscription of Sōmēśvara II in Bellary District.

(*V.R. i. Bell. 173; 475 of 1914*).

An inscription of this year, or of the year A.D. 1075–76 ('Ś. 997'), in Ganjam District shews Dēvēndravarman-Rājarāja I, as the reigning Kalinga king. He claims to have defeated, amongst other rulers, the kings of Vengi and the Chōḷas. This must allude to the expeditions of Kulōttunga-Chōla I as an E. Chāḷukya prince, and of the Chōla king Vīra-Rājēndra, both of whom are asserted in their inscriptions to have marched to the north but do not claim an actual conquest of Kalinga.

(*V.R. i. Ganjam 142; 271 of 1896*).

At Conjeeveram is an inscription of Kulōttunga Chōla I's 5th year which began June 9, 1074. After referring to his early triumphs at Vayirāgaram and Śakkarakōṭṭam (or Chakrakoṭṭa), it states that he vanquished the king of Kuntaḷa (i.e. drove back the W. Chāḷukya forces); crowned himself on the banks of the Kāvēri (i.e. at Gangaikonda-Śōḷapuram); and decapitated an unknown

Pāṇḍya king. It represents the head of the latter as lying outside the city 'pecked by kites' during his coronation-ceremony. This is often repeated in his inscriptions.

(*S.I.I. iii. 125, 139, 143, Nos. 64, 68 ; I.A. 1892, p. 281*).

[Bilhaṇa in his *Vikramānkadēva-Charita* narrates the events that occurred after the seizure of the Chōla throne by Kulōttunga Chōla I, and his account requires notice. When Vikramāditya VI (then only a prince of the W. Chāḷukya house) heard of the untimely death of his brother-in-law the young Chōla king Adhirājēndra, and of Kulōttunga's seizure of the throne he marched towards the Chōla capital bent on vengeance ; but Kulōttunga had made a secret alliance with Vikramāditya's elder brother, king Sōmēśvara, between whom and Vikramāditya there had been long-standing antagonism and Sōmēśvara, pretending that he was supporting Vikramāditya in a second line of battle, suddenly placed his brother in a very awkward position. Vikramāditya attacked his Chōla enemy in front, and then learned that he was hemmed in by two opposing armies, his king having betrayed him. However he was completely successful in the fight that ensued, beating off the Chōla troops and taking Sōmēśvara prisoner. But he could do no more and retired to the Tungabhadra. This is Bilhaṇa's account of the affair, which the Chōla king's inscriptions allude to when they say that Kulōttunga won a great victory over Vikramāditya and drove him out of the Ganga country from Maṇalūr, by way of the Nangili ghāt, as far as the Tungabhadra.

Vikramāditya followed up his success by deposing his brother Sōmēśvara and himself mounting the throne of the W. Chaḷukyas in A.D. 1076].

That the Ganga country had been under rulers of different dynasties about this time is emphasized by an inscription at Kittūr, in South Mysore of the year 1079, which typifies that country as an adulteress with a succession of lovers. (*E.C. iv, Hg. No. 56*).

A.D. 1075. Between December 25 this year and June 30, 1076, came, to the throne of the W. Chāḷukyas, Vikramāditya VI, who deposed his elder brother Sōmēśvara II, and mounted the throne in his stead (*See E. C. xv. 348*). The Ālūr inscription of Vikramāditya's 16th year of date December 25, 1091, proves that he came to the throne on or after December 26, A.D. 1075.

(*I.A. 1879, 21*).

On September 8, Kulōttunga-Chōla I was reigning in Pondicherry territory.

(*177 of 1919*).

An inscription of the month of December this year in N.-W. Mysore quotes the W. Chāḷukya Sōmēśvara II as still on throne with Bhuvanēka-Udayāditya-Ganga ruling locally.

(*E.C. vii, Sk. 130*).

Cattle-raids on a large scale took place in N.-W. Mysore in this year. Several local chiefs combined, swooped on the villagers, robbed them of their cattle, slaughtered the men and carried off the women. (*E.C. viii, Sb. 314*).

A.D. 1076, March 13. An inscription of the first year of Vikramāditya's new 'Chāḷukya-Vikrama' era, which was introduced apparently by him, and which by luni-solar reckoning began on March 8, 1076, the day on which the tithi Chaitra-Śukla 1 ended. It shews as local ruler in N.-W. Mysore, at Kuruva, the Ganga chief Nanniya-Ganga-Rakkasa-Ganga. (*E.C. vii. Hl. 14*).

On July 27 of this year Kulōttunga-Chōla I's second son Rājarāja was installed as Viceroy of Vengi. A grant of villages was given to a leader Mummaḍi-Bhīma for valuable services rendered, in the wars against the 'Ganga, Kalinga, and Kuntala' (W. Chāḷukya) kings, to Kulōttunga.

(*E.I. vi. 334 ; E.R. 1922, p. 97*).

[It is advisable here to enter a note about the viceroyalty of Vengi. The E. Chāḷukya prince Vijayāditya VII had been appointed viceroy there, so say Chōla records, by the Chola king Vīrarājēndra; but it still remains open to question whether in reality he was not himself actually E. Chāḷukya king till his nephew Rājēndra II made himself king of both nations in 1070. At any rate Rājēndra allowed Vijayāditya to remain in his post as viceroy of Vengi, but under himself as king. There Vijayāditya remained till 1078. It has been suggested that the reason for his recall was that he had been intriguing with the Rāja of Kalinga; that he fled to Kalinga and ended his days in the western part of that country. As evidence of this we have a passage in an inscription to depend upon—'when Vijayāditya, beginning to grow old, left Vengi . . . and was about to sink into the ocean of the Chōlas (Dēvēndravarman) Rājarāja (of Kalinga) caused him to enjoy prosperity for a long time in the western region'. (*I.A. xviii. 171; xx. 276*)].

A C. P. grant from Rājāpura in the Bastar State gives a list of achievements of Vikramāditya VI (W. Chāḷukya) and these appear to refer to events that happened before he came to the throne as it mentions in the end that, as he was on his way home, after accomplishing all these great deeds, he heard of his father's death by suicide in the Tungabhadra river. Many of the triumphs related are manifestly apocryphal. He is said (i) to have repeatedly defeated the Cholas, and to have plundered Kānchī while yet Yuva-raja; (ii) to have helped the king of Mālwa to gain his throne; (iii) to have attacked Ceylon; (iv) to have slain the 'lord of Kēraḷa'; (v) to have conquered the Ganga and Vengi kingdoms and Chakrakōṭa. (*E.I. ix. 108*).

A.D. 1077, February 10. Inscription in Guntur District of the 7th year of Kulōttunga Chōla I as Chōla king, but here called by his E. Chāḷukya name 'Saptama Vishṇuvardhana.' Gifts by Gonka II of Velanāṇḍu, before he came to the throne, son of Guṇāmbikā wife of Nanna.

(*V. R. ii. Guntur 90; 151 of 1897; E. I. vi. 278*).

June 25. Record at Hulgūr, Bankāpūr division of Dharwar District, shewing the Beḷvola and Purigere tracts ruled by Jayasimha IV of the W. Chāḷukyas. (*E. I. xvi. 329*).

August 6. Inscription at Yēwūr of Vikramāditya VI ('B' of Dr. Barnett's paper).

(*E. I. xii, 268*).

December 25. Vikramāditya VI reigning at Beḷagāmi (Baḷḷigāmvē in N.-W. Mysore).

(*E. C. vii. Sk. 124*).

The Kongāḷva princess Padmalā-dēvī, wife of Rājēndra-Chōla-Kongāḷva ruling in Coorg.

(*Coorg: Inscriptions 43; Rice*).

Some inscriptions at Humcha in N.-W. Mysore throw light on the pedigree of the Sāntara chiefs of that place. They belong to this year. We learn from one that the Ganga chief 'Arumuḷidēva had a daughter Chattalā who was married to the Pallava chief (i.e.), probably, the Noḷamba-Pallava chief, and that her sister, the Ganga princess Kanchalā was married to the Sāntara chief Vīra or Bīra-Dēva. These last had four sons, Taila, Goggiga or Govinda *alias* Nanni-Sāntara, Oḍḍuga or Oḍḍamarasa *alias* Vikrama Sāntara, and Barmmadēva. The record No. 36 confuses us by calling the mother of these four sons in one place Chattalā and in another Bīrala (The last however may be a title derived from 'Vīra'). No. 39 calls Chattalā the daughter of the Ganga chief Rakkasa-ganga[1]. (*E. C. viii, Nr. 35, 36, 39, 40*).

[1] Mr. Sewell's confusion seems to have little foundation in the records. The second daughter had two names Kanchala and Virala according to No. 35. No. 36 mentions only the latter. The Ganga chief, the younger brother of Rājamall, had the alternative name according to No. 36.—*Editor*.

In. N.-W. Mysore an inscription of Vikramāditya VI. 2nd year states that the Hāngal province was governed by Mallikhārjuna. [According to Fleet this name does not occur among the Kādamba rulers of Hāngal till about A.D. 1132. *Bombay Gazetteer I., Pt. II, p. 559*].

(E. C. viii, Sb. 172).

A.D. 1078. In Central Mysore the E. Chaḷukya king Vikramāditya VI was reigning. Under him Hoyśala Vinayāditya ruled the whole 'Gangavāḍi 96,000' province.

(E. C. xii, Tp, 105).

On February 17,1078 Anantavarman-Chōḍaganga, son of Dēvēndravarman Rājarāja became king of Kalinga. His mother was Rājasundarī, daughter of Kulōttunga Chōla I. He had a very long reign. Two records of his mention his 72nd year (*I.A. xviii. 161 ; E.I. iv, 183 ; vi. 198 ; V.R. i. Ganjam 147, 148 ; III Vizag. 212 ; 392 of 1896*).

In this year Vira-Chōla, third son of Kulōttunga Chōla was appointed viceroy of Vengi in succession to Rājarāja the second son who had held the post since July 27,1076. He is said to have been installed at Jagannāthapuram (modern Cocanada), an inscription commemorating an order issued by him is dated August 23, 1078. (*V. R. ii, Godavari 48-A ; E. R. 1888, July. p. 2 ; S.I.I. i. p. 49 ; ii. 231 ; I. A. xix, 423 ; xxi. 282, 286 ; E. I. vi. 334*).

A.D. 1079, January 21 and December 26. Vikramāditya VI reigning in N.-W. Mysore and Anantapur. (*E. C. vi. Sk. 135 ;* 439 of 1920 *;* 697 of 1919).

In. W. Mysore Rājēndra-Prithvi-Kongāḷva was the local chief. An earlier ruler named Adaṭarāditya is mentioned. *(E. C. v. Ag. 99)*.

May 9 and July 25. Two inscriptions shewing Kulōttunga Chōla I reigning in Pondicherry territory. *(178, 184, of 1919)*.

Other records of this year shew Vikramāditya VI reigning in N.-W. Mysore and Bellary, having his residence at Kalyāṇa. Jayasimha IV, his brother, was ruling Baṇavāśi province; Tambarasa governing the Sántaḷige tract; and Nigalankamalla Pāṇḍya, one of the Pāṇḍyas of Uchchangi, governing the Noḷamba province. (*E. C. viii. Sa. 109 ; vii Sk : 293 ; V. R. i. Bellary 278 ; 86 of 1904 ; E. R. 1903–04, p. 8*).

[From now onwards for more than a century the Noḷamba province was locally governed by Pāṇḍya chiefs of Uchchangidrūg, always hostile to the Chōla monarchy].

A.D. 1080. Inscription at Perumbēr, Chingleput District, dated in the 11th regnal year of Kulōttunga Chōla. It mentions the events of his reign as they had been given in his 5th year (*above s. v., A. D. 1064–75*), but nothing new. *(S.I.I. iii. 173)*.

A gift was made to the temple at Drākshārāma, Godavari District, in this year by the wife of the minister of the late Chōla Viceroy, Rajarāja, son of Kulottunga I.

(V. R. ii. Godavari 86, 181 of 1893).

The W. Chāḷukya Yuvarāja Jayasimha IV ruling N.-W. Mysore early in the year, as well as Baṇavāsi and other tracts. *(E. C. vii, Sk. 293, 297)*.

An inscription of December 24, 1081, at Lakshmēśvar names, as then reigning the W. Chāḷukya Vikramāditya VI, and states that his brother Jayasimha (IV) was his *Yuvarāja*. It gives the latter the titles usually applied to the Pallava family which had ruled the Noḷambavaḍi tract for a long time. *(E. I. xvi. 58)*.

A.D. 1081. There were more cattle-raids and resulting deaths in N.-W. Mysore in this year. Vikramāditya VI reigning. *(E. C. vii. Sb., 336)*.

An inscription commemorating the grant of a village in Vizagapatam District by the Kalinga-Ganga king Anantavarma-Chōḍaganga, then residing at Kalinganagara, gives a pedigree of his family. It omits Vajrahasta III altogether, declaring the four brothers (*see Table*) to be sons of Guṇārṇava II. (*V. R. iii. Vizag. 211*).

A.D. 1082. The Eastern-Ganga, or Kalinga-Ganga king Anantavarma-Choḍaganga reigning in Ganjam. Date, Mārgaśira Śuk. 13, in the 204th year of the dynasty (*E. R. 1920-21, App. A, C. P. 2*). The date = December 7, 1082.

August 22. Kulottunga Chōla I reigning in Pondicherry territory. (*212 of 1919*).

A.D. 1083, January 11. Vikramāditya VI reigning in Anantapur (414 of 1920). There was more cattle-raiding and robbery in South Mysore. (*E. C. iv, Hg. 80*).

The two inscriptions of Kulōttunga Chōla I at Tirukkaḷukkuṅṛam (Chingleput district) and Tanjore, which give an account of the doings of that king up to his 14th and 15th years (A.D. 1083–85), must now be noticed. They recount his early adventures at Vayirāgaram, and Chakrakoṭṭa, his defeat of the W. Chāḷukya forces, his seizure of the Chōla throne, and his attempt to conquer Ceylon. Then comes the following list of successes—(i) He seized the Gangapāḍi country and the Baṇavāsi tract which latter was governed by prince Jayasimha IV of the W. Chāḷukyas; and took 1,000 elephants at Navilai; (ii) He fought against the Pāṇḍyas of Madura, (perhaps some rebel princes) defeated them, and assumed the title 'Maduraikoṇḍa; (iii) He seized the hill-country on the west, took the Podiyil mountain and the pearl fisheries in the gulf of Manaar, marched to Cape Comorin and captured Koṭṭāru, a town near the Cape. In this expedition he slew all the fighting men'; (iv) He planted settlements of Chōla troops along the roads for protection. (v) He massacred the inhabitants of Coorg.

(*S. I.I., ii, 230 ; iii. 130, 143 ; I. A. 1892, 281 ; 37 of 1891 ; 30, 32 of 1909*);

[The year A.D. 1083–84 was the 30th year of king Vijaya-Bāhu of Ceylon (*above s. v. A.D. 1064-65*). We learn from the ***Mahāwaṁsa*** (ch. LX) that he had received embassies from both Kulōttunga Chōla and the W. Chāḷukya king Vikramāditya VI, and that he sent messengers from Ceylon to the Chōla monarch. Kulōttunga cut off the noses of these messengers, and on their return to Vijaya Bāhu he declared war against the ferocious Chōla king, and made preparations for a campaign; but a rebellion broke out in the Island and he was compelled to desist].

A.D. 1084. In this year Kulōttunga Chōla I's son Vira Chōla was recalled by his father from his post as Viceroy of Vengi, and his eldest brother Rājarāja-Chōlaganga *alias* Vishṇuvardhana VIII, was appointed Viceroy in his place (*E. I. vi, 334 ; V. R. ii, Godavari, 364 ; S. I.I. i, 49 ; E. I. v, 70*). The most important record of this event is the Tēki grant of May 22, 1084.[1] According to that document the Vengi territory included the country from Mahēndragiri in the north to Mannēru, Nellore District, in the south. This would mean that Southern Kalinga was then in the hands of the Chōlas (*Krishnaswami Aiyangar, 'Ancient India', p. 145*). Vira Chōla married a Ganga princess. (*S I.I. iii, 120*).

Part of the Gangavādi province was now ruled by the Hoysala chief Vinayāditya. (*E. C. v. Ak. 6*).

Vikramāditya VI of the W. Chāḷukyas reigned in N.-W. Mysore. (*E. C. viii. Sb. 235, 236*).

[1] The date as stated in the Tēki record is not quite a sound one.

[This contradicts the assertion made that Kulōttunga Chōla I had conquered the 'Gangavāḍi 96000'. The latter of these inscriptions mentions continual cattle-robberies].

The Eastern-Kalinga king Anantavarma-Chōḍaganga was reigning near Chicacole. (*E. R. 1919, App. A., C. P. No. 6*).

A.D. 1085. Jayasimha IV (W. Chāḷukya) ruling Bellary district. (*233 of 1918*).

A.D. 1086, March 12, 1086. An inscription in Tanjore district of Kulōttunga Chola I's 16th year. (*V. R. ii, Tanjore 696 ; 399 of 1902 ; E. I. vii. 170*).

Another of his 17th year near Bangalore gives a list of his achievements similar to that of 1083 (*above*), and mentions nothing new since then. (*E. C. ix. Cp, 77*).

A.D. 1087, December 25. Nilgunḍa plates of Vikramāditya VI, W. Chāḷukya king. On this day he was at Kalyāṇa. (*E. I. xii. 142*).

An inscription of the year 1087–88, Kulōttunga Chōla's 18th year, at Śrīrangam, gives a similar list of events of the reign as in 1083 (above), adding nothing new. (*S.I.I. iii, 148*).

A.D. 1088. Vīra Chōla, Kulōttunga's son, was again sent as Viceroy to Vengi, superseding his brother Rājarāja. (*E. I. vi. 334*).

An inscription belonging to this year, Ś. 1010, in Tamil characters has been found at Loboe Toewa, Baros, in the Island of Sumatra. It records a gift to a temple by a body of persons who are called the 'fifteen-hundred'—probably a military garrison of Chōla-Tamils stationed there for protection of trade (*E.R. August 1892, p. 11 ; J.R.A.S. 1913, April*). [The rise and progress of Hindu Emigration to an influence in the far East will form a fascinating subject for future research. It is certain that Java was completely Hinduized by the 7th century of our era, all the older temples there being built in South Indian style. Hindu influence was strong in Burma and Siam from the 7th to the 12th century. The 11th and 12th centuries were the great building age in Burma, and amongst the numerous Buddhist structures at Pagan is a temple of Viśhnu, permitted, as we may suppose, to be constructed for the use of Hindu worshippers,—artisans perhaps employed in the buildings, and others].

Vikramāditya VI reigning in N.-W. Mysore (*E.C. viii. Sb. 388 ; Sa. 103 ; vii, Sk. 14*). The Sāntara chief Tailapa was ruling the Sāntaḷigē 1000.

A.D. 1089. End of the year. Vikramāditya VI reigning in W. Mysore, with Hoyśala Vinayāditya as local ruler. (*E.C. vi. Kd. 22*).

Kulōttunga Chōla I reigning in Trichinopoly in his 20th year. His triumphs related, but no addition made to the list given in 1083 (*above*). (*S. I.I. iii, 152*).

A.D. 1090. Early in the year. Record at Arkalgūḍ, Hassan district, W. Mysore, shewing, as locally ruling, Mādeyarasa-Changāḷva. (*E.C. v. Ag. 65*).

The Kalinga-Ganga king Anantavarma-Chōḍaganga was ruling in this year in Vizagapatam District. (*V. R. iii. Vizag. 63 ; 99 of 1909*).

About this time, so it would appear, Kulōttunga Chōla I made an expedition against Kalinga. His son Vīra-Chōla, now Viceroy of Vengi, is expressly stated in the Pithāpuram plates to have been appointed for the purpose of 'conquering the north', and as his appointment was in A.D. 1088 and he relinquished it in 1092 we may take 1090 as about the date of the war which ensued. The campaign is mentioned in the Tiruviḍai-Marudūr inscription of Kulōttunga's 26th year (1095–96) and in other records, but in none earlier than 1090. Several vassal chiefs joined in the war on the Chōla side, as also did Kulōttunga's son Vikrama Chōla, then 'quite a youth' (*so stated in S. I. I. ii, 307*). The Velanāṇḍu chief Rājēndra-Chōḍa I, then a prince, son of Gonka I was one of them. And, if we judge aright the Amarāvati pillar inscription of about A.D. 1100, discovered by me during the excavations of the Buddhist Stupa there in 1877, so also was a Pallava chief by name Simhavarman.

In the course of this campaign Rājēndra-Chōḍa of Velanāṇḍu, cousin of Vedura II, who was minister to Vīra Chōla, Viceroy of Vengi, defeated a chief often called 'Telugu-Bhīma', a vassal of the king of Kalinga, and drove him to take refuge in the Colair (Kōlēru) lake near Ellore (Koḷanu). Thither he was pursued and killed. The incident is alluded to in several inscriptions. One, at Tanjore, calls the unfortunate leader 'Telugu Bhīma of Koḷanu' (*S.I.I. ii. 307*). [This Bhīma may well have been the Kōta chief of Amarāvati, Bhīma I, to whom in my genealogical Tables I have assigned the date 'circ. 1100'].

Velanāṇḍu Rājēndra-Chōḍa was richly rewarded by Kulōttunga Chōḷa. The king adopted him as his son and made over to him, as Governor, large tracts in the Telugu country. (*E.R. 1903, p. 52; 1905, p. 53; S.I.I. iii, 178; E.I. vi, 146, 334; iv, 32; v. 95; V.R. ii, Tanjore, 983*).

An inscription at Cape Comorin, dated in the 9th year of Parāntaka-Pāṇḍya, and which belongs from palæographic evidence to about this period, credits him with having 'taken Kuḷam (Koḷanu) from Telugu Bhīma and subjugated the Kalinga country. Parāntaka therefore may have been another chief who joined Vīra Chōla in this northern campaign.

(*T. A. S. iii. 19*).

A.D. 1091. The W. Chāḷukya Vikramāditya VI reigning in Bellary District. (*V. R. i. Bell. 8, 10, 83; 255 of 1913; 672 of 1922*).

A.D. 1092. Three dates are given in an inscription of the reign, in Bellary District of the same king Vikramāditya VI. The first is incorrectly stated. The second (correct) is 1092–93. Under him the Noḷamba province was ruled by Tribhuvanamalla Pāṇḍya of Uchchangi, his vassal. (*V. R. i. Bell, 183; 128 of 1913*).

On March 2 an inscription in N.-W. Mysore shews Vikramāditya VI reigning, and mentions another instance of serious tribal fighting and slaughter. (*E. C. viii, Sb. 392*).

Vikramāditya VI gave a gift to the temple at Drākshārāma, Godavari District, in this year. (*V. R. ii, Godavari 160; 255 of 1893*).

Hoyśala Vinayāditya was now locally ruling in Central Mysore (*E. C. xii. Tp. 57*) under the W. Chāḷukya king.

In E. Mysore Kulōttunga Chōla I held sway. (*E. C. x, C. B., 24*).

[Vīra Chōla's Viceroyalty of Vengi seems to have come to an end in this year].

A.D. 1093. An inscription of June 26, 1093 shews Vikramāditya VI reigning. It is on a slab now at the Madras Museum. (*V. R. ii, Madras, 308*).

Hoyśala Vinayāditya was ruling in W. Mysore. (*E. C. vi, Tk. 76*).

Other inscriptions of his are in Central and N. Mysore. His vassal Ereyanga, son of Hoyśala Vinayāditya, was governing the former country. (*E. C. v, Cn, 148; xi, Hk, 3*).

A.D. 1095. A record of this year alludes to the conquest of Kalinga by Kulōttunga Chōla I. It mentions, as his favorite wife Tyāgavallī. (*S. I. I. iii. 155, V. R. ii. Tanjore 983*).

The Hoyśala chief Vinayāditya was ruling over the Hassan District of S.-W. Mysore in this year. His inscription of this year states that his power was 'extending on all sides', which may mean that he had received an extension of the territory under his rule. (*E. C. v, Hn. 107*).

A.D. 1096. Late in the year, Vikramāditya VI reigning in N.-W. Mysore (*E, C. vii. Sk. 114*). Another record of his in 1096–97 in the same country gives the name of his vassal there, the Sāntara Rāja Tailapa, who received rewards for valour in war. (*E. C. viii. Sa. 80*).

A.D. 1097. In this year the Bastar State in Ganjam was ruled by Sōmēśvara of the Nāgavaṁśi family. His father was Dhārāvarsha, his son Kanhara or Krishna. Sōmēśvara drove out of Chakrakūṭa in that State a certain Madurāntaka who had seized it, and slew him. (*E. I. x, 26, 37*).

An inscription of this year shews Kulōttunga Chōla I reigning, under his Chāḷukya titles, at Drakshārāma, Godāvari District. (*V. R. ii, Godavari, 35 ; 476 of 1893*).

A.D. 1098. April. 2. Kulōttunga Chōla I reigning in Pondicherry, (*201 of 1919*).

In 1098–99 Vikramāditya VI (W. Chāḷukya) reigning in Bellary; and again in 1099–1100. (*V. R. i, Bell. 89, 92 ; 42, 45 of 1904*). Also in N. W. Mysore (*E. C. vii, Sk. 13, 106*). In Central Mysore the Hoyśala Vinayāditya was ruling, so that certainly his power was spreading (*See above s. v. A. D. 1095. (E. C. v. cn. 207*).

For Vikramāditya's inscription of May 17, 1098 See *E. I. xv, 348*. This is at Gadag.

The *Mahāwaṁśa* relates that in this year Vijaya Bāhu of Ceylon sent a naval expedition to the coast of the mainland and despatched messengers to Kulōttunga Chōla, but that the latter simply ignored them. This was in Vijaya Bāhu's 45th year. The Singhalese commander was not strong enough to attack and therefore retired. [From this date till A.D. 1168–69 the *Mahāwaṁśa* says very little about affairs in India].

An inscription of the 29th year of Kulōttunga Chōla I merely repeats the achievements mentioned already in his 15th year (*above s. v., A. D. 1084 ; E. C. x. Mb. 42, b*). [*42 f.* belongs to his 27th year, and 42 *c.* to his 35th year, A.D. 1104–5. Both contain similar lists].

A.D. 1099, June 5. Another record in Bellary of king Vikramāditya VI then reigning there. (*213 of 1918*).

1099–1100. Inscription of Kulōttunga's 30th year shewing him reigning close to Cape Comorin. It adds nothing new to his successes in 1084–85. (*S.I.I. iii. 159*).

An interesting record of Kulōttunga at Simhāchalam in Vizagapatam District. It is in Tamil characters and has been much damaged, but it is said certainly to be an inscription of the reign of Kulōttunga. The date, however, is uncertain (*V. R. iii. Vizag. 191 ; 363 of 1899*). [It has been stated in the Epigraphist's Report for 1900 that this conclusively proves an actual *conquest* by the Chōla king of the Kalinga country. I think that such an assumption goes a little too far].

A.D. 1100. Three records shew the country about Erode in Coimbatore District ruled by a Kongu-Chōla governor Abhimāna-Rājādhirāja-Chōla, under Kulōttunga Chōla I. (*V. R. i. Coim. 225, 226, 244 ; 573, 574, 592 of 1905*).

Hoyśala Vināyaditya is now said to be ruling the whole Gangavāḍi province under the W. Chālukya king. (*E. C. vi. Kd. 164*).

The Noḷambavāḍi province was ruled by Tribhuvanamalla Pāṇḍya, (*E. C. xi. Dg. 151*), under the W. Chālukya king.

Record at Drākshārāma of the 31st year of Kulōttunga Chōla I (*V. R. ii. Godavary, 271 ; 365 of 1893*). He is given his E. Chaḷukya titles.

An inscription in W. Mysore mentions the queen of the Hoyśala chief Eṛeyanga, by name Mahādēvī, daughter of Irukkapāla, who was son of Tēja Rāja. Tēja Rāja is called a member of the Chōla family, and one of his sons, brother of Irukkapāla is called 'Pāndya' a curious combination (*E. C. v. Ak. 102a*). This Pāndya assisted in the deposition of Sōmēśvara II and the enthronement of Vikramāditya VI.

Another record of Kulōttunga, of this year, is in Tinnevelly District—additional proof of his conquest of the Pāndya realm. (*V. R. iv. Tinn : 305*).

A.D. 1101. Vinayāditya Hoyśala's reign ended, and that of his grandson Baḷḷaḷa I began A. D. 1100–01. The former's son Eṛeyanga did not reign. Baḷḷāḷa I continued to rule as vassal to the Chāḷukya king. An inscription of his dated in 1101–02 is in Hassan District, West Mysore (*E. C. v. Bl. 199*). The record defines his territories as bounded by the Konka-nāḍi, Āḷvakeḍa (S. Kanara) Bayalnād (the Wainād), Talakāḍ, and Sāvimale (unidentified)].

A. D. 1102. Record in Tumkūr District, Central Mysore (*E. C. xii. Tp. 30*) of the Hoyśala prince Vira-ganga *alias* Vishṇuvardhana, shewing him ruling there for his brother Baḷḷāla I.

June 22, 1102. Vikramāditya VI, W. Chāḷukya, reigning at Lakshmēśvar, the ancient Puligerē. His minister, Bhīma, is mentioned. (*E. I. xvi. 31. A*).

Aug. 14. Rāmar-Tiruvadi, Raja of Vēnāḍ (Travancore) ruling at Quilon. (*T. A. S. v. 40*).

December 17. Vikramāditya reigning in Bellary. (*673 of 1922*).

In this year two inscriptions of the 33rd year of Kulōttunga Chōla I, mentioning his triumphs ; but none later than those recorded up to 1090. (*E. C. x. Mb. 54 ; Sd. 9*).

A. D. 1103. Vikramāditya, W. Chāḷukya, reigning in N.-W. Mysore (*E. C. vii. Sk. 98, 131*). Another inscription in Shimoga District of the same king and year gives a pedigree of the Sāntara chiefs of Humcha (*E. C. viii. Tl. 192*). Another, in the same country, mentions an extensive raid into it, cattle-stealing and slaughter on a large scale, by a Kadamba chief Rēchidēva, son of Tailapadēva. (*E. C. viii. Sc. 563 ; See also E. C. vii. Hl. 66*).

In this year Hoyśala Baḷḷāla I married at the same time and in the same pavilion three sisters, daughters of the lord of 'Sindagerē in Āsandinād'. The boundaries of his territory are given as above, *s. v., A.D. 1102–03*, and he is said to have ruled the Gangavāḍi, Noḷambavāḍi and Baṇavāsi provinces under the W. Chāḷukya king (*E. C. vi. Cm. 160*). The inscription is in Kādūr District, W. Mysore.

A. D. 1104, March 3, 1104. Hoyśala Baḷḷāla I ruling the Gangavāḍi province under his sovereign Vikramāditya VI after whom he is called 'Tribhuvanamalla'. (*E. C. v. Hn. 161*).

April 10, 1104. Vikramāditya VI reigning in Bellary District. (*214 of 1918*).

May 5, 1104. Kulōttunga Chōla I reigning in Trichinopoly and also in his 39th year on Jan. 31, 1109; and in his 40th year on Dec. 10, A. D. 1109 (*V. R. iii. Trichi. 109, 112, 111; 177, 180, 179 of 1914*). Another of his on July 19, 1104 in Tanjore. (*521 of 1922*).

A.D. 1106. [Apparently in this year the Hoyśala Chief Baḷḷaḷa I died and was succeeded by his brother Vishṇuvardhana, who reigned till 1141, under the W. Chaḷukya king of Kalyāṇa].

In this year in Kurnool District, at Tripurāntakam the Chōla king Kulōttunga I was reigning. The local ruler was the Konidena (Telugu-Chōḍa) chief Pottapi-Kāmadēva.

(*V. R. ii. Kurn ; 357 A, 359 ; 265, 267 of 1905*).

In S.-W. Mysore Vikramāditya VI, Chāḷukya was supreme. (*E. C. v. Cn. 169*).

A.D. 1107, February. Inscription at Niḍuguṇḍi, Vikramāditya reigning, with, as his vassal, the Kādamba chief Tailapa II ruling over the Hāngal (Pānungal) 500 village tract. (*E. I. xiii. 12*).

December 29. The Kadamba chief Tailapa II ruling locally at Lakshmēśvar.

(*E. I. xvi. 31 B*).

Vikramāditya reigning in N.-W. and N. Mysore in 1107–08 (*E. C. vii, Sk. 192 ; xi. Dg. 128*) ; and in Bellary. (*V. R. i. Bell. 10*).

A great cattle-stealing raid took place this year in S. Mysore. A band of men, numbering as many as 100 horse and 1600 foot, attacked the villages and looted the peasantry (*E. C. iv. Hg. 79*).

The Velanāḍu Chief 'Gonka Raja', probably Gonka I, gave a village on the Gunḍlakama river in Kammanāḍu to the ṭemple at Tripurāntakam. (*V. R. ii. Kurnool 369 ; 277 of 1905*).

A. D. 1108. Vikramāditya VI reigning in N. Mysore (*E. C. xi. Jl. 12 ; Dg. 12*) ; and in N.-W. Mysore (*E. C. vii. Sk. 294*). Also in the Noḷamba province where the local Governor was Tribhuvanamalla Pānḍya (*V. R. i. Bellary 286 ; 94 of 1904*). This chief continued to rule there for some years (*V. R. Bellary 183, 234, and several records 289–297 ; 94-105 of 1904 ; 128 of 1913 ; 450 of 1914*). (*E. C. xi Dg. 99*).

At Gooty (Gutti) in this year a local chief Bommarasa collected the taxes for the W. Chāḷukya king's Treasury (*Bombay Gazetteer, vol. I, 452—Fleet*).

A. D. 1109. Kulōttunga Chōla I reigning at Katnagiri in Trichinopoly District. The date is apparently July 13 ; but if so the regnal year was the 39th, and not, as stated in the record, the 38th. (*V. R. iii Trich. 113 ; 181 of 1914*).

Vikramāditya VI reigning in W. Mysore, with Tribhuvanamalla Pānḍya governing the Noḷambavāḍi country (*E. C. xi. Dg. 135*). The same king reigning in Anantapur District, where an inscription mentions the chief called 'Ghaṭeyanka,' giving him Chōla titles. This is probably the Niḍugal chief Mangi, who is given the same name in another inscription thirty years earlier. (*410, 439 of 1920*).

A. D. 1110, October 29. Kalachūri Billama ruling locally at Mutgi. [The name is not given by Fleet or Kielhorn in their dynastic lists. It may be a *biruda* of Permāḍi, or perhaps that chief's own family name. Billama was contemporary with the W. Chāḷukya Sōmēśvara III].

(*E. I. xv. 26*).

December 25. Record in the Kōgali 500 District (part of Bellary) of Vikramāditya VI (*V. R. i. Bell. 235, 2434 ; 451, 459 of 1914*). An inscription of his reign in N. Mysore bears date late in A.D. 1011. (*E. C. xi. Jl. 9*).

Several inscriptions in South Travancore prove that the Chōla king was ruling that country. Amongst others there is a record of Kulōttunga Chōla I at Variyūr of date A.D. 1110-11. (*T. A. S. i. 237, B. to Q*, One, 'R', gives Pānḍya titles to Vikrama-Chōla, calling him 'Māravarman' as well as 'Chōla-Panḍya.')

East Mysore remained under Kulōttunga Chōla I. (*E. C. ix, Nl. 3*).

A. D. 1111. An inscription of Kulōttunga Chōla I in South Arcot is dated on the 294th day of his 41st regnal year, or March 31, A.D. 1111. (*158 of 1918 ; S. I. I. iii. 192*).

Records of Vikramāditya VI in Bellary and N.-W. Mysore (*V. R. i. Bell. 15 ; 277 of 1918 ; E. C. vii, Sh. 89*) ; and of Kulōttunga Chōla in Chittoor and Chingleput, in the former case on March 15 of this year (*129 of 1922 ; S.I.I.* iii. 164). In the latter he is said to have 'conquered the Gangavāḍi country'.

The second, and this time successful, expedition to Kalinga of armies of Kulōttunga Chola appears to have taken place in this year or early in the next, the hero of which was his general Karuṇākara Tonḍamān of Vanḍalūr. The Kalinga-Ganga king Anantavarma-Chōḍaganga was a grandson of Kulōttunga, his father having married the Chōla king's daughter Rājyasundarī.

The late V. Venkayya believed that the expedition was sent in order to assist the king of Kalinga in his endeavour to crush some rebellions in the north of his dominions. Whether this is so, or whether the object was simply one of conquest, or of punishment of the Kalinga ruler for failure of payment of tribute, Prof. Krishnaswami Aiyangar thinks (*Ancient India, p. 145*) it is as yet not clearly determined. An inscription of Kulōttunga's 42nd year (1111-12) in Trichinopoly District mentions the War (*V. R. iii*). (*Trich. 162 ; 608 of 1904*).

A.D. 1112. Vikramāditya VI reigning in September and on December 30, 1112 (*E.I. xiii. 36 ; 279 of 1918*). And during the year 1112-13 in N.-W. Mysore where an inscription referring to local tribal fighting and death-casualties mentions Govindarasa as the ruler of the Baṇavāsi tract and part of Mysore. (*E.C. viii. sb, 327, also V.R.i. Bellary 266, 74 of 1904*).

In the same year Kulōttunga Chōla was reigning over Kurnool in his 43rd year, the local ruler being Kāma, or Kāmadēva Chōda, of the Konidena branch of Telugu-Chōḍa chiefs (*V.R. ii. Kurnool 355, 356 ; 262, 263 of 1905*).

In. N.-W. Mysore one of the local rulers was the Kadamba (?) chief Kīrttidēva. (*E. C. viii Sb. 468*).

Another of Kulōttunga's records of his 43rd year, in the Mālūr taluk of Kolar District, E. Mysore, does not mention his Kalinga campaign, but refers briefly to some of his early successes (*E. C. x., Mr. 101*). He was reigning in Tanjore on November 15. (*323 of 1910*).

A.D. 1113. In this year we have records shewing Vikramāditya (W. Chāḷukya) reigning in Anantapur (on October 20, 1113); and in N. Mysore, where Tribhuvanamalla Pāṇḍya continued to govern the Noḷambavādi province. (*605 of 1920*; *E. C. xi. Dg. 149*).

Kulōttunga was reigning over E. Mysore. (*E. C. ix. Nl. 38 r ; E. C. x, Sd, 66 ; C. B. 25*).

In West Mysore the local Governor was Hoyśala Vishṇuvardhana also called 'Vikrama-ganga-Poyśala'. (*E. C. v. Hn. 149.*)

In S. Kanara the Āḷupa chief Kavi-Āḷupēndra ruled. (*V. R. ii. S. Kanara 293 ; 106 of 1901*).

Anantavarma-Chōḍaganga continued to reign over Kalinga in spite of (or in consequence of) Kulōttunga Chola's expedition thither. An inscription of Ś. 1035 (A. D. 1113-14) is dated in his 38th year (*V. R. i. Ganjam, 258 ; 380 of 1896*). [I have accepted Fleet's decision that his accession date was Feb. 17,1078; and yet I am bound to state that out of about forty inscriptions of his reign, found in Ganjam District, many of them would, like the present one, make his reign begin in A. D. 1076-77]. (*See E. I. iv. 183 ; I. A. xviii. 161*).

A. D. 1114. Inscriptions of Kulōttunga I. One at Chidambaram in his 44th year on March 3, 1114, mentions that a stone had been sent over to him by the king of Kamboja and that it had been inserted in the temple building (*E. I. v. 105 ; V. R. i. S. Arcot 5*). It mentions his sister Kundavvai. Another of the 45th year, Ś. 1037, is at Bhīmāvaram, Godavari district. In this as is natural, he is given his E. Chālukya name 'Vishṇuvardhana' (*V. R. ii, Godav. 32 ; E. I. vi. 219*). His minister was a chief of Pallava stock. Another, of date December 9, 1114, is at Drākshārāma in the same district (*V. R. ii ; Godav. 280 ; 374 of 1893. E. I. vi. 279*). And another in Mysore (*E. C. iv. Kr. 34, 31.*). As to the last which is at Kannambāḍi, a record of four years later shews the town recognizing as their ruler Hoyśala Vishṇuvardhana (*below, s. v., A. D. 1118-19*). Another of his 45th year in Tanjore alludes to his expedition to N. Kalinga. (*V. R. ii. Tanjore 983; E. R. 1905, p. 53*).

In Central Mysore, Hoyśala Vishṇuvardhana was ruling in this year under the W. Chāḷukyas. (*E. C. xii. Tp. 81*).

A.D. 1115. Vikramāditya VI reigning in Guntur District (700 of 1920). At Srāvaṇa-Beḷgoḷa an inscription shews that Hoyśala Vishṇuvardhana, now in great power, had a Ganga-Rāja for his minister. (*E. C. ii. Sr. Bel. 47*).

In Guntur District at Chēbrōlu an inscription of this year shews that the country was locally ruled by the Velaṇāṇḍu chief Chōḍa (*alias* Rājēndra-Choḍa) Kulōttunga Chōla's protégé and adopted son. (*V. R. ii. Guntur, 89 ; 150 of 1897*).

A.D. 1116. Kulōttunga Chōla I's 47th year. Record in Tinnevelly District at Māramangalam (the ancient Korkai). (*V. R. iii. Tinn. 310, 312, 313 ; 161, 163, 164 of 1903*). This record shews that he was ruling the Pāṇḍya kingdom. Another at Śrīrangam (*S.I.I. iii. 168*). Another in Tanjore on February 21 (518 of 1920).

A record in the Mysore District states that now Hoyśala Vishṇuvarḍhana, *alias* 'Biṭṭiga' ruled over the whole of the Gangavāḍi province as far south as the Kongu country (*E. C. iv. ch. 83*). In this year, for some reason, he marched against 'the Pāṇḍya' i.e. Tribhuvanamalla Pāṇḍya who was Governor of the Noḷambavāḍi pro.ince, and a battle was fought at Dummē, a village being destroyed (*E. C. vi. Cm. 99, 100*). He was also ruling in South Mysore, where two years earlier Chōla rule prevailed. In an inscription of this year in Mysore District, Yeḷandūr Taluk, he is credited with having captured Talakāḍ. (*E. C. iv. Yd, 6*).

[This last appears to be quite correct. The Hoyśala chief, acting of course under his Chāḷukya overlord, succeeded in driving the Chōla king out of South Mysore, probably in this year. Mr. Krishnaswami Aiyangar states that now the Chāḷukya boundary was along a line drawn through the Kongu border, Nangili and Koyāttur. (*Ancient India, p. 146*)].

The Baṇavāsi province was now ruled by Gopanarasa. An inscription mentions cattle-raids and deaths of villagers. (*E. C. viii. Sb. 337*).

A. D. 1117. An inscription in W. Mysore of this year shews Hoyśala Vishṇuvardhana still acknowledging the Chāḷukya king as his sovereign. But this subservience did not last long (*E. C. v. Bl. 116*). Another, in the Hassan District, refers to more cattle raids and deaths in this year. (*E. C. v. Hn. 4*).

In January, 1117 and on November 26 Kulōttunga Chōla was reigning in Tanjore. (*515 of 1920 ; V. R. ii. Tan., 1230 ; 653 of 1909 ; E. I. xi. 242*).

In March an inscription shews Vikramāditya VI reigning in N. Mysore, with Tribhuvanamalla-Pāṇḍya, his vassal, ruling the Noḷambavaḍi province. (*E. C. xi. Dg. 166*).

A record of date March 10, 1117 at Bēlūr in Mysore makes it plain that now the Hoyśala chief Vishṇuvardhana was acquiring greater importance. He is said (i) to have captured Dorásamudrá [This in earlier days in conjunction with his brother Baḷḷāla] ; (ii) to have seized the Gangavāḍi province and burnt the Ganga chief's town Talakāḍ ; (iii) to have spread his rule over the Mysore country. It is added that he defeated the Pāṇḍya and 'protected' the Noḷamba province (*E. C. v. Bl. 58, 71*). At the end of the year an inscription in the Mysore District also mentions his capture of Talakāḍ which means that he had been successful in a revolt against Chōḷa domination in South Mysore. (*E. C. iii. Ml. 31*).

[The Hoyśala family now it is clear, began to be actively aggressive, taking advantage, perhaps of the old age of both the Chāḷukya and Chōla kings. Vishṇuvardhana, having been successful in the South and West marched to the North, passed through the Noḷamba and Baṇavāsi provinces and penetrated as far as the Krishna River. The Kadambas of Goa and Silāhāras of the Konkan also seem to have taken up arms against the aged W. Chāḷukya king at the same time. To his aid came the Sinda chief Achugi II and gave battle. He defeated the Hoyśala general Ganga Raja in a night attack at Kannēgāla and pursued him to Bēlūr. Then he turned to the West, drove away the Kadamba and Silāhāra forces and took Goa. *(Ancient India, p. 142)*].

Now, also, there were great disturbances on the East. The territory of Anumakoṇḍa (Warangal) had been conferred on a chief of the Kākatiya family 'Tribhuvanamalla' Bēta or Betma by the W. Chāḷukya king Vikramāditya VI, to whom he was feudatory. Beta's son Prōla II was now ruling that territory with Warangal as his capital. On December 24, 1117, an inscription at his capital shews him ruling. He had only lately succeeded his father. Later on he engaged in warfare with his neighbours and greatly increased his power. *(E. I. ix. 256)*.

A.D. 1118. On January 7, 1118, an inscription at Mannarguḍi near Tanjore shews Kulōttunga Chōla I still living *(E. I. v. 48.)*; also one of January 1925.
(S.I.I. iii. 71 ; and V. R. i. Chinglepul 797, 1069).

[He died or retired on or before June 29, on which date his son Vikrama Chōla came to the throne. Vikrama was the fourth son of Kulōttunga I, and it must therefore be assumed that his three elder brothers had died before this date,—also that Vikrama was well advanced in years at the time of his accession, his father having reigned for 50 years.

Vikrama was Viceroy of Vengi and was there when he heard of the vacancy of the throne. He at once went to Kānchi and was crowned. An inscription at Piṭhāpuram says that then the Province of Vengi 'became devoid of a ruler' *(S.I.I. iii. 180)*. He had the *birudas* 'Tyāgasamudra' and 'Akaḷanka'. It seems that Kulōttunga Chōlā's adopted son Rajendra-Chōḍa wavered in his allegiance to the Chōla crown on Kulōttunga's death. He had locally governed in part at least of the Vengi territory; but records in this year and in A.D. 1120–21 show him as a feudatory of the W. Chaḷukya monarch. Hence the lament of the Pithāpuram inscription. By 1127 he had again accepted the suzerainty of the Chōla. An 11th century inscription whose exact date is not known has been published by Dr. Hultzsch in *S.I.I. ii. p. 117*. It belongs to the reign of a Chōla king, possibly Kulōttunga I, and it is worth studying for the sake of the very long list of taxes enforced on the villagers of the time].

June 29, 1118. Date of accession to the Chōla throne of Vikrama Chōla.
(E. I. viii. 260).

An inscription at Tanjore relates some of the events of his earlier life, *e. g.*: He put to flight 'Telugu Bhima of Koḷanu' and destroyed the Kalinga country. *(See above)*.
(S.I.I. ii. 307 ; also iii. p. 75 of his 4th year).

That he ruled over part at least of Coimbatore is shewn by an inscription there.
(V. R. i. Coimb. 135–137 ; 558–560 of 1908).

December 18, 1118. Proof of the statement made above that Vikrama Chōla lost his hold on the Vengi country for a time immediately on his departure thence for Kānchī is given by an inscription of this date which shows the W. Chāḷukya Vikramāditya VI ruling over 'the Vengi 14000 country.' *(819 of 1922)*.

Early in the year the Hassan District of Mysore is shewn as ruled over by Hoyśala Vishṇuvardhana. *(E. C. ii. Sr. Bel. 45, 59)*.

On May 4 the same chief was resident at, and ruling from, Talakāḍ *(E. C. iv. Kr. 31)*. He is now called the 'Capturer of Talakāḍ Kongu, Nangali, Uchchangi, Baṇavāsi and Hāngal.'

An inscription of Kulōttunga Chola's 49th year (which began on June 9, 1118) is at Drākshārāma, Godavari District, and in the Vengi country.

(*V. R. ii. Godav. 99, 268 ; 194, 362 of 1893. See also V. R. i. S. Arcot, 784, 785, 792 ; 381, 382, 389 of 1909*).

The country about Erode was ruled locally, under the Chōla crown, by a Kongu-Chōla Viceroy Rājādhirāja Vīra Chōla. A record of his 5th year is at Vijayamangalam.

(*V. R. i. Coimb. 245 ; 593 of 1905*).

At the end of the year 1118, a 'Chōḍa-dēva Mahārāja' was ruling over the Kommanāḍu tract. Inscriptions in Ongole Taluk. This was perhaps Chōḍa Ballaya of the Konidēna branch of the Telugu-Chōḷa chiefs. (*V. R. ii. Guntur 253 ; B. & V. C. 1113*).

A.D. 1119. Inscription in Tanjore of date = March 26, 1119, naming the 49th year of Kulōttunga Chōla I. (*V. R. ii. Tanjore, 1224 ; 647 of 1909 ; E. I. xi. 241*).

June 28. Record of his 50th year. (*V. R. ii. Tanjore, 496 ; 459 of 1912*).

October 13 of the same year. The record calls it his 49th year in error. (*519 of 1920*).

[This is the last mention of him as king and since Vikrama's date of accession is certainly June 29, 1118, it may be presumed that possibly Kulōttunga I had abdicated on that date but lived a little longer in retirement.]

In A.D. 1119–20. The W. Chaḷukya King Vikramaditya VI was reigning in Bellary.

(*V. R. i. Bell. 97 ; 50 of 1894*).

In this year an inscription in Vizagapatam District, of a grant of a village by the Kalinga-Ganga king Anantavarman-Chōḍa Ganga shews that he was then reigning over that country. It gives a full pedigree of the reigning family.

(*See above s.v., A.D. 1081 ; V. R. iii. Vizag. 213*).

A. D. 1120. Vikrama Chōla reigning in Kolar District, E. Mysore (*E. C. x. Sd. 9*) and in Tanjore on June 4 and December 24, 1120. (*V. R. ii. Tanjore 155; 164 of 1908 ; 502 of 1920*).

A Drākshārāma inscription of this year shews the W. Chāḷukya Vikramāditya VI as reigning over the Vengi country about the Godavari river. This confirms the remark made above that in 1118–19, the local ruler of the Vengi province, Rājendra-Choḍa of Velanānḍu, left his allegiance to the Chōla crown and went over to the W. Chāḷukyas (*V. R. ii. Godavari 112, 237, 238, 251 ; 207, 331, 332, 345 of 1893*). This state of things continued in the next year, A. D. 1121–22.

(*V. R. ibid. 241, 262, 293, 299, 340; 335, 356, 387, 393, of 1893; etc.; E. I. iv. 37, 38*).

In 1120–21 a Telugu-Chōḍa chief Beṭṭa, who has not been identified, was ruling the Pottapināḍu (Kāḷahasti tract). (*V. R. i. Cuddapah, 797; 583 of 1907*).

A. D. 1121. The W. Chāḷukya king Vikramāditya VI reigning in Anantapur and Bellary districts ; the Noḷamba country still ruled by Tribhuvanamalla Pānḍya.

(*V. R. i. Anant. 26, 27; Bell. 234; 89, 90 of 1913; 450 of 1914; 341 of 1920*).

Early in the year Hoyśala Narasimha II was governing in W. Mysore. (*E. C. v. Hassan, 106*).

A. D. 1122. On May 10 and July 19, Vikrama Chōla reigned in Tanjore. Another inscription of this year shews him reigning in Coimbatore District, then part of Chōla territory.

(*V. R. ii. Tanjore 943 ; i. Coim. 135 ; 564 of 1904 ; 438 of 1918 ; 558 of 1908 E. I. viii. 262*).

Tribhuvanamalla Pānḍya ruling the Noḷamba province. (*E.C. xi. Cd. 34; 341 of 1920*).

Hoyśala Vishṇuvardhana ruled in W. Mysore as vassal of the W. Chāḷukya.

(*E. C. vi. Cm. 151*).

On August 14 the Western Ganga chief Nanniya-Ganga died. (*E. C. vii. Sh. 13*).

Mention in an inscription of this year in Anantapur District of a local chief, Chittarasa, perhaps of the Bāṇa family. (*356 of 1920*).

The Kongu Chōla chief, Rājādhirāja Vīra Chōla was ruling locally in Coimbatore District in his 5th year. There are many records of his up to his 21st year (*V. R. i. Coim. 245, 441. . . . 477; 593 of 1905 ; 141...156, 229 of 1909*). In 150 of 1909 he is said to be ruling 'the two Kongus together'.

A very long inscription at Dāvaṇigere of king Vikramāditya VI (date the end of 1122 A. D.) gives a complete pedigree of the W. Chāḷukya royal family, differing in some respects from those of other records. It deserves careful examination. (*E. C. xi. Dg. 1*).

At the end of A. D. 1122 two inscriptions in W. Mysore mention as then ruler of that country Hoyśala Vishṇuvardhana. His territory is here said to be included by Nangali on the East (the Nangali ghat leads down from the Mysore plateau towards N. Arcot); Kongu, Chēra and Ānaimalai on the south ; the Barakanūr ghāt on the west ; and the 'great river' (*Peddore*, which may here stand for the Tungabhadra, but is generally the Krishna river). He thus is said to be ruling the whole of Mysore. It records the death of the Hoyśala prince Udayāditya, brother of Vishṇuvardhana. The Hoyśalas had now subjugated the Gangavāḍi and Noḷambavāḍi territories and the Niḷagiris. (*E. C. v. Hn. 102, 116 ; vi. Cm. 151*).

Vikramāditya VI reigning in Kurnool, and on the Godavari at Drākshārāma. (*V. R. ii. Kurnool 252 ; Godav. 333, 334 ; 259 of 1905 ; 427, 428 of 1893*).

A. D. 1123. On January 6, 1123, Vikramāditya VI was reigning in Bellary (*245 of 1918*). About the same time he is shewn reigning in N. Mysore (*E. C. xi. Dg. 127*). On September 3 is an inscription of his, shewing him encamped at Baṇavāsi (*Nilgunda plates E. I. xii. 142*) ; and there is another Bellary record of his, dated December 25, 1123 (*287 of 1918*). During the year 1123–24, we have another of his inscriptions at Drākshārāma. (*V. R. ii. Godavari, 265; 359 of 1893*).

Vikrama Chōla was reigning at Tanjore on February 7, 1123. (*V. R. ii. Tan. 667 ; 4 of 1914 ; 245 of 1918*). And on August 19 (*V. R. ii. Tanjore 602 ; 489 of 1907 ; E. I. x. 123*) and on November 7. (*V. R. ii. Tan. 641 ; 30 of 1906 ; E. I. ix. 209*).

Inscription of Hoyśala Vishṇuvardhana in this year in W. Mysore. (*E. C. vi. Kd. 119*).

A. D. 1124. Early in 1124, inscription of Vikramāditya VI in N. Mysore, mentioning as ruler of the Noḷambavāḍi territory Tribhuvanamalla Pāṇḍya, younger brother of Tribhuvana-Vīra-Noḷamba-Pallava (*E. C. xi. Dg. 155*). In April the local ruler of the Noḷamba tract is said to be 'Rāya-Pandya', no other name, (*ibid* 122.) Another inscription of 1124–25 gives as the name of the Noḷamba ruler 'Vijaya-Pāṇḍya' (*E. C. xi. Cd. 13*). [All these are probably names of one chief].

In the Dhārwar District in this year Vikramāditya VI was reigning, having under him his son-in-law Jayakēśi II of the Kadambas of Goa (*E. I. xvii. 117; see also E. I. xiii. 298*). In the Cuddapah District one of his subordinate rulers was a certain Atyana-Chōla Mahārāja, governing the Rēnāṇḍu tract. He perhaps belonged to the farmily of Chōlā Mahārajas, some of whose names are given in the genealogical tables below (*V. R. i. Cuddapah, 348 ; 350 of 1905*). A number of their records are found in Cuddapah.

Hoyśala Vishṇuvardhana was ruling over Central and West Mysore in this year. (*E. C. v. Cn. 149 ; Bl. 228*).

There was a very serious famine this year in the Chōla territories. (*I. A. 1923, p. 193*).

A. D. 1125. On January 2, 1125 (if Mr. Swamikannu Pillai's fixture of date is accepted), some country south of the Krishna river was ruled by the Kolanu Rāja Okkeṭṭugaṇḍa. Inscription in Tanuku Taluk, Kistna District. *728 of 1890*).

On August 18 an inscription shews Vikrama Chōla reigning in Tanjore. (*V. R. ii. Tanjore 935 ; 556 of 1904 E.I. viii. 263*).

Vikramāditya VI, W. Chāḷukya king, reigning at Koḷḷipāka (Kulpak, N. E. of Hyderabad), and in N.-W. Mysore (*J. Hydr. A. S. 1916, p. 31 ; E. C. vii. Ci. 61*).

The great sage Rāmānujāchārya completed his *Srī Bhāshyam* in this year (*Hist. of the Srī Vaishṇavas by T. A. Gopinatha Rao, p. 34.*)

Cattle raids and accompanying slaughter and outrage in N.-W. Mysore in this year. (*E. C. vii. Hl. 65*).

Vikrama Chōla was reigning in his 8th year in Cuddapah District, an inscription mentions the gift of a village by his vassal the Telugu Chōḍa chief Vimalāditya-Madhurāntaka-Pottapi-Chōla, son of Siddha. (*V. R. i. Cudd. 793 ; 579 of 1907*).

At Rajahmundry the local ruler was Vishṇuvardhana, probably he who was uncle to Vijayāditya III of the Piṭhāpur chiefs who claimed descent from the E. Chāḷukya royal family. (See genealogical table below). (*V. R. ii. Godavari, 79 ; 41 of 1912 ; E. I. iv, 229*).

A. D. 1126. An inscription in N.-W. Mysore shews the W. Chāḷukya king Vikramāditya VI as still living on January 10, 1126 (*E. C. viii. sb., 170 ; similarly E. C. vii. Sh. 56.*). He was reigning in N. Mysore later in the year, as is shewn by a record which mentions as ruler of Noḷambavāḍi 'Tribhuvanamalla Pāṇḍya, defeater of the designs of Rājigā Chōla.' This Pāṇḍya chief may perhaps be Rāya Pāṇḍya. (*Above s. v. A. D. 1124-25 ; E. C. xi. Hk. 68*).

Another of his inscriptions, this time in N.-E. Kurnool at Tripurāntakam, discloses the extent of his dominions on the east. A vassal chief of his, Govinda, nephew of Anantapāla, was ruling over the 'Koṇḍapalli 300 Districts,' and Koṇḍapalli is close to Bezwada on the Krishna river. This confirms what has been said above that the Chōla crown had by this time been lost to the W. Chāḷukya the Vengi and neighbouring territories. (*V. R. ii. Kurnool, 351, 368 ; 258, 276 of 1905*).

A record at Bāgali, Bellary District, dated in the 51st year of the Chāḷukya-Vikrama era (which = Parābhava as stated) also shews Vikramāditya as reigning. That year began in March 1126. He died shortly after March 1126, having reigned 51 years. (*V. R. i. Bell. 289 ; 97 of 1904*).

[Vikramāditya's successor as W. Chāḷukya king was Somēśvara III, his son, also called Bhūlōkamalla, who reigned 12 years. He came to the throne on a day between July 24 and October 5, 1126.]

There is a record of Vikrāma Chōla's 9th year at Conjeveram (*S.I.I. iii. 186*), containing no new information.

In the Vēṇāḍ country (Travancore) two records shew Vīrakēraḷa reigning. (*V. R. iii. Trav : 8 ; T. A. S. iv, 17 ; I. A. xxiv, 253*).

In South Mysore the Hoyśala Vishṇuvardhana now reigned as an independent sovereign. (*E. C. iv. Yd, 8. iii. Sr. 34*).

A. D. 1127. Inscription, early in 1127, in N.-W. Mysore of W. Chālukya Bhūlōkamalla-Somēśvara III, and another of the same on July 10 in Bellary. The Banavāśi and Sāntara provinces were governed by the Kādamba chief Tailapa II under the W. Chāḷukya throne. The first of these inscriptions commemorates the death of Barmma Sānta, an enemy of the Sāntara chief, who lost his life in a battle when a force of Tailapa's was besieged in Īśāpura by one of the Sāntara leaders.

(*E. C. viii. Sb. 141 ; 234 of 1918*).

Vīra-Kēraḷavarman was reigning in Vēṇād (Travancore). (*T. A. S. iv, Pt. I, 17*).

In Central Mysore Hoyśala Vishṇuvardhana was reigning. (*E. C. v, Cn, 260*).

In East Mysore and at Chēbrolu, south of the Krishna river in Bapatla taluk, Guntur District, Vikrama Chōla was supreme. From this it may be argued that by now he had recovered the territory south of the river from the possession of Rājēndra-Chōḍa of Velanāṇḍu and his new suzerain, the W. Chālukya king. (*E. C. x. Sp. 61 ; V. R. ii. Guntur* 92, 93, 112; 153, 163 of 1897).

A. D. 1128. Inscriptions of date April 15, August 25 and September 23, 1128, in Trichinopoly and Tanjore Districts shew that Vikrama Chōla was reigning there then.

(*S. I. I. iii. 178 ; 502, 509 of 1922*).

More savage cattle robberies and slaughter of peasants took place in N.-W. Mysore this year.

(*E. C. vii. Sk. 238*).

A record at Drākshārāma, Godavari District, refers to gifts bestowed by a certain Kōnamaṇḍala chief, by name Vikrama Rudra. This is probably a *biruda* of Kōna Rajēndra Chōḍa I, son of Rājāparēndu, as stated in the inscription, or of his elder brother Mummaḍi-Bhima II.

(*V. R. ii.Godav : 188 ; 283 of 1893.*)

Another inscription at the same place witnesses a gift made by Līlāvati, queen of the Kalinga-Ganga king Anantavarma-Chōḍaganga. Another mentions his queen Rājalā, and a third yet another named Padmalā. In one of these the local ruler is said to be Vishṇuvaradhana Māhārāja ruling in his second year. (*V. R. ii. Godav : 217, 219, 220, 221 ; 312, 314–16 of 1893 ; I. A. xviii. 161*).

From now onwards for more than 60 years we often hear of a Niḍugal family of Chōlas, resident in North Mysore (*E. C. xii. Introd. pp. 7, 8, 10*). One of these was in this year 1128–29 ruling that tract from his capital Penjēru (Hemāvati in the North of Śira Taluk[1], Tumkur District). His name was Irungōḷa-Chōḷa, and he ruled over the Roḍḍa, Śire, Haravē and Sindavāḍ tracts as well as over Niḍugal. About this time Hoyśala Vishṇuvardhana captured a fort belonging to Irungōḷa-Chōla. (*E. C. iv. Ng. 70*).

In Central Mysore the Noḷamba chief Udayāditya is said in an inscription to be "extending his kingdom on all sides". (*E. C. xii. Si.* 9).

A. D. 1129. The Digambara Jaina preceptor Mallishēna starved himself to death at the Dhavaḷasarasa *tīrtha*. He died on March 10, 1129. His epitaph is at Śrāvaṇa-Beḷgoḷa. (*E. I. iii, 184*).

The W. Chālukya King Sōmēśvara III was ruling in the Palnāḍ Taluk of Guntur District, south of the Krishna river. (*V. R. ii. Guntur, 509 ; 596 of 1909*).

Hoyśala Vishṇuvardhana ruled in W. Mysore, where an inscription of his mentions as his vassal the Ganga chief Barmma-bhūpa of Āsandi (*E. C. vi. Tk. 66*). At the end of the year 1129 Vishṇuvardhana was in residence at Dorasamudra. (*Ibid. Mg. 22*).

A. D. 1130. Records of Hoyśala Vishṇuvardhana ('Biṭṭi') at Dorasamudra and in W. Mysore (*E.C.v. Ak.41 ; vi. Cm. 137*). The latter of these mentions his son Narasimha and his grandson Baḷḷāḷa.

Sōmēśvara III, W. Chāḷukya, was reigning at Bellary and in Central Mysore (*V.R. i. Bell. 126 ; 230 of 1913 ; E.C. xii. Tp, 104*). The date of the Bellary inscription is October 5, 1130, and it

[1] Hemāvati is in the Madakasira taluk of the Anantapur District. It is to the north of the Sira taluk. Undoubtedly. *Editor.*

was in the 5th year of the king's reign. This fixes his accession as on or before October 5, 1126. (*See above*). In the latter record Hoysala Vishnuvardhana is mentioned as ruling over the whole Gangavāḍi 96000, but as the W. Chāḷukya king's vassal.

In Tanjore Vikrama Chōla reigned. Inscription thereof, dated May 15, 1130.

(*V. R. ii. Tanjore 158; 167 of 1908; E.I. xi. 122*).

At Bāpatla, South of the Krishna river, the local ruler was the Velanāṇḍu chief Sunāmbā. wife of Velanāṭi Rājēndra-Choḍa, gave a gift to the temple there. (*V. R. ii. Guntur 67; 230 of 1897*).

A. D. 1131. In N.-W. Mysore the W. Chāḷukya king Bhūlōkamalla Sōmēśvara III reigned with, under him, Mayūravarma as chief of Baṇavāsi, in which province, it appears, was then included the Sorab tract. (*E. C. vii. Sk, 133 ; viii, Sb. 80*).

The Hoysala king Vishṇuvardhana, often called 'Biṭṭi' or 'Vīraganga', held South Mysore. On March 7, 1131, his senior queen Sāntala-dēvī died, as an inscription at Śrāvaṇa-Beḷgoḷa records.

(*E. C. iii. Md. 50 ; ii. Sr. Bel. 53*).

Vikrama Chōla was reigning in Tanjore in his 13th year on June 25, 1131.

(*V. R. ii. Tanj. 780 ; 97 of 1910 ; E. I. xi, 243*).

In Vizagapatam the Kalinga-Ganga king Anantavarman-Chōdaganga reigned in his (so-called) 57th year [This number seems to be in error for 54th year]. (*V. R. iii, Vizag. 221 ; 367 of 1905*).

A. D. 1132. An inscription of date = May 23, 1132 mentions this as the 15th (?) year of Vikrama Chōla. (*193 of 1917*).

In Hassan District, S.-W. Mysore, a record names Hoysala Vishṇuvardhana as reigning.

(*E.C. v. Cn. 271*).

In Guntur District we find Velanāḍu Rājēndra-Chōḍa, otherwise called 'Gonka-Rāja', ruling on November 6 (*631, 645 of 1920*). In the same year a certain 'Velanāṭi Gonka, son of Chētana (?) and grandson of Rājēndra-Chōḍa made a gift to a temple in the Kistna District (*V. R. ii. Kist. 92-K*). In the Narasaraopet taluk, Guntur District, 'Chōḍa-nripati' ruled at Nādēndla. The names as given of his immediate ancestors shew that he was one of the Koṇḍapadmaṭi chiefs.

(*V. R. ii. Guntur, 276 ; 214 of 1892 ; Godavari, 179 ; 274 of 1893*).

A. D. 1133. Vikrama Chōla reigning in S. Arcot on March 9, 1133, in his 15th year.

(*349 of 1921*).

Early in 1133 Hoysala Vishṇuvardhana reigning in South Mysore (*E. C. iii. Md. 29*). An inscription at Dorasamudra of this year mentions in exaggerated terms some of his successes, e.g. 'He brought Kānchī under his command', 'He shook the pride of the Chōla.' [The latter claim may, with reservation, be allowed, but the former is certainly not true.]

(*E. C. v. Bl. 124*).

Between May 10 and July 14, 1133, Vikrama Chōla died and was succeeded by his son Kulōttunga Chōla II. [It will be well to note here how the condition of South India, in the matter of its ruling families, was changing at this period. The Hoysalas were gradually capturing Mysore from the W. Chāḷukyas, and holding the Chōlas back. The Chōlas were by no means so strong as before, and several great families in their dominions were beginning to be restive. The Kalachūri family was rising to power, and that of the W. Chāḷukyas was diminishing.]

At Drākshārāma, Godavari District, the Velanāṇḍu chief Gonka II was ruling.

(*V. R. ii. Godavari 179 ; 274 of 1893*).

A. D. 1134. An inscription in Bellary District shews the W. Chāḷukya Sōmēśvara III reigning there in his 8th year. The date, which mentions a solar eclipse, is a sound one. It makes his accession as on or after July 24, 1126. *(695 of 1919).*

An inscription of Hoyśala Vīraganga Vishṇuvardhana states that he was ruling over the whole Gangavāḍi province and implies that these included all the country up to the Tungabhadra river; but this must not be taken too literally. *(E. C. v. Ak. 30).*

A. D. 1135. There are several inscriptions of Hoyśala Vishṇuvardhana in this year in Central, West and South Mysore.

(E. C. iv. Ng. 3 ; v, Hn. 89 ; Bl. 170 ; iii. Tn. 129 ; vi. Kd, 35).

An inscription in Trichinopoly District is dated on August 22 and one in Tanjore on August 19, 1135, each during the 3rd year of Kutōttunga-Chōla II, then reigning.

(V. R. iii. Trich. 84, 87 of 1914).

Also in Guntur District and at Bezwada.

(V. R. ii. Guntur 47 ; Kistna 127 ; 210 of 1897; 380 of 1918).

On May 17, 1135, in Anantapur District Sōmēśvara III was king *(337 of 1920).*

During the year two inscriptions at Drākshārāma mention the local Kōnamaṇḍala chiefs Mummaḍi-Bhīma II and Satya I, his half-brother.

(V. R. ii. Godavari 194, 139 ; 289, 234 of 1893).

On August 19, in Tanjore, an inscription of Kulōttunga Chōla II's 3rd year *(380 of 1918).*

A.D. 1136. Some inscriptions naming as king in western Mysore, Hassan District, Hoyśala Vishṇuvardhana. He still holds his W. Chāḷukya title 'Tribhuvanamalla.' He was ruling the Gangavāḍi 96000 province. Mention of his wife Bammalā-Dēvī as herself ruling the 'Āsandi-500' division. He is stated to have defeated the Noḷamba ruler of the Pāṇḍya family and captured Uchchangi; to have made an expedition to the Telugu country; to have seized the Baṇavāsi and Hāngal districts, etc.

(E. C. v. Ak. 32, 144 ; Bl. 17, 117.) [Taila II of Hāngal died in 1135–36, perhaps during the war].

Record in Guntur District of Gonka II of Velanāṇḍu in his 4th year, shewing that his rule began on or after August 5, 1132, the date of the inscription being August 4, 1136. Another mentions his wife Gunḍāmbikā. His sovereign is named as Kulōttunga Chōla II.

(V. R. ii. Guntur 19, 20, 72 ; 182, 183, 255 of 1897).

A.D. 1137. Cattle raids and rape of women in South Mysore. *(E. C. iv. Hg. 50).*

In Central and West Mysore Hoyśala Vishṇuvardhana was ruling, but still acknowledging the E. Chāḷukya Vikramāditya VI as his overlord. He was at Uchchangi, the Noḷamba chief's capital, during the year; but whether as a visitor or as ruler of that place is not clear. One record commemorates the death of one of his fighting men when he plundered Hāngal, so that the claim made for him that he captured that place may be accepted as correct.

(E. C. vi. Cm. 71, 161 ; xii, Tp. 14).

In Guntur District Kulōttunga Chōḷa II reigned, having under him Kāma-Chōḍa-Mahārāja of the Konidēna branch of the Telugu-Chōḍas (See genealogy). His wife was Śrīyā-dēvī.

(V. R. ii. Guntur, 224, 225 ; 164, 165 of 1899 ; 697 of 1920).

A.D. 1138. [In this year the W. Chāḷukya king Sōmēśvara III ceased to reign and was succeeded by his son Jagadēkamalla II, who continued to reside at Kalyāṇa.]

In Bellary District at Kurugōḍu the Sinda chief Rachamalla was ruling on August 11, 1138, subject to the W. Chāḷukya sovereign.

(*V. R. i. Bell. 128 ; 206 of 1913. Cf, ibid : No. 119 ; 69 of 1904*).

In the Godavari District a record at Drākshārāma shewing Kulōttunga-Chōla II reigning there. (*V. R. ii. Godavari 180 ; 275 of 1893*).

In Vizagapatam the king was the Kalinga-Ganga Anantavarman-Chōḍaganga, reigning in his 65th year. (*V. R. iii. Vizag. 228, 231 ; 354, 357 of 1905*).

In Central, South and South-west Mysore Hoysala Vishṇuvardhana ruled, subordinate to the W. Chāḷukya throne. His son Narasimha governed a tract under his father (*E. C. v. Ak. 124; iv. Ng. 28 ; xii. Kg. 3*). Another record of his mentions the death of a soldier at the fighting at Hāngal, as in the last year (*above*), (*E. C. v. Bl. 202*). Another of the same year relates to one of the constant faction fights or tribal fights which devastated Mysore in these times. A chief called Kāmeya-Nāyaka marched against a general called Bāna-Kalyāṇa. On the march a force collected by twelve other Nāyakas 'from the east,' probably sent from the Bāṇa country to support Bāṇa-Kalyāṇa, fell on Kāmeya's army and Kāmeya himself was killed (*E. C. xii. Tp. 63*). Another inscription refers to more village raids on other people's cattle, and deaths resulting (*E. C. viii. Sb. 414*).

A.D. 1139. In South-west Mysore Hoysala Vishṇuvardhana reigned. His son Narasimha is named as local ruler in an inscription (*E. C. v. Ak. 17, 18; J. R. A. S. 1915, p. 529*). Others shew Vishṇuvardhana reigning in Central and Western Mysore, but always as a vassal of the W. Chāḷukya king. (*E. C. v. Ak. 105 ; Hn. 114 ; Cn. 199 ; vi. Cm. 144 ; Kd. 32*).

In Cuddapah District, at Pushpagiri, inscription of the local ruler 'Trailōkyamalla' Mallidēva I, of the Telugu-Chōḍa chiefs (see genealogical table of the 'Gaṇḍa-Gōpālas'). (*V. R. Cud. 85, 86 ; 316, 317 of 1905*).

In Anantapur the local ruler was Irungōḷarasa, subordinate to the W. Chāḷukya king Jagadēkamalla II. He belonged to the Sinda family. (*See Table*) .

(*V. R. i. Anant. 31 ; 78 of 1912*).

In N.-W. Mysore Jagadēkamalla II reigning as king. Under him a Western-Ganga chief Ekkala, son of Mārasimha (*see Table of W. Gangas*). (*E. C. viii. Sb. 140, 233*).

At Drākshārāma Godavari, District, are two inscriptions of this year proving Kulōttungā-Chōla II to have been reigning there. His local feudatory was the Velanāṇḍu chief Kulottunga-Chōḍa-Gonka, (Gonka II). (*V. R. ii. Godav. 170, 290 ; 265, 384, of 1893*).

In Vizagapatam Anantavarma-Chōḍa-Ganga, the Kalinga-Ganga king was still reigning.

(*V. R. iii. Vizag. 218*).

In South Kanara the Ālupa chief Bhujabala Kavi-Āḷupēndra held sway.

(*V. R. ii. S. Kan. 194 ; 176 of 1901*).

A.D. 1140. In Central and West Mysore, Hoysala Vishṇuvardhana ruled. The Sāntara chief Jayakēsi raided the Hāngal tract and drove off the villagers' cattle. A *vīrakal* commemorates a death during the raid (*E. C. vi. Cm. 122 ; Kd. 79, 80*). Mention is made of Vishṇuvardhana's queen Barmmalā-dēvi, daughter of Gōvinda of the Pallava family, who resided at Hāngal. Amongst the triumphs of Vishṇuvardhana it is recorded that he defeated the Chōla king (perhaps earlier in his life) ; that he also defeated Irungōḷa, and that he seized the Nangali Ghāt (the pass which leads down from the Mysore plateau into the N. Arcot country), then Chōla territory. (*E. C. xii. Gb. 13*).

Kulottunga Chōla II reigned in Guntur in his 8th year. Record of date = August 19, 1140. (*705 of 1920*). [This shews that his accession was earlier than August 19, 1133.]

Another Drākshārāma inscription commemorates a gift to the temple there by Kāṭama-Nāyaka of Koḷanu, one of the Chōla king's generals.

(*V. R. ii. Godavari 109 ; 204 of 1893 ; I. A. xiv. 55*).

A.D. 1141. The W. Chāḷukya king Jagadēkamalla continued to reign in Anantapur and Bellary Districts. Inscriptions of dates = May 17 and August 10.

(*V. R. i. Bell. 127 ; 205 of 1913 ; 393 of 1920*).

In W. Mysore Hoyśala-Vishṇuvardhana was ruling. He was residing at the time of inscription at Bankāpur in Dharwar District. The date = September 2, 1141 (*E. C. vi Kd. 96*). Another record shews him ruling over Central Mysore in 1141–42. It records local disturbances, with unruly chiefs fighting one another and devastating the country. (*E. C. xii. Tp. 25*).

At Drākshārāma, Godavari river, are two inscriptions of this year shewing as local ruler Kulōttunga-Choda-Gonka II, chief of Velanāṇḍu (*V. R. ii. Godav. 252, 301 ; 346, 395 of 1893*). Also one in Guntur District. (*V. R. ii. Guntur 36 . 199 of 1897 ; 646 of 1920*).

At Rēpalle, Guntur District, gift made to a temple by the Koṇḍapadmaṭi chief Buddha-Rāja.

(*V. R. ii. Guntur 612 ; 240 of 1897*).

In this year 1141–42 Hoyśala Vishṇuvardhana died at Bankāpur. An inscription in Kaḍūr District, Mysore, relates the fact and states that while the body was being removed in State to the capital, the cortege was attacked (the country was, as has already been noticed, in a very disturbed state, wholesale robberies by bands of armed men being of frequent occurrence). In the fight which took place a certain Binna-gauḍa, probably a village headman, rescued a royal elephant which was carrying treasure, but in doing so lost his own life. He was handsomely honoured after death by a gift made by the new head of the Hoyśala family Narasimha I to the former's son, Būtegauḍa. (*E. C. vi, Cm. 96 ; J. R. A. S., 1915, p. 529*).

This year, then, saw the accession of Hoyśala Narasimha I. The exact date is doubtful.

On December 24, 1141, a record at Tanuku, Kistna district, names as ruler in his 15th year the Piṭhāpur Raja 'Vishṇuvardhana'. See under date August 8, 1142 for another. (*743 of 1920*).

A.D. 1142. An inscription whose date was in the end of the year 1142, in S. Mysore, relates the doings of two local chiefs who fought one another, one of them storming a fort high on the Nīlagiri hills. This is said to have taken place during the reign of Hoyśala Vishṇuvardhana. It does not prove that Vishṇuvardhana was alive at the end of 1142. (*E. C. iv, Ch. 20*).

In April 1142, a record shews Hoyśala Narasimha I as ruling in S. Mysore, near Mysore city. But this, again, does not prove that he was then reigning. He may have been governing during his father's illness. (*E. C. iii, Ml. 56*).

Inscription of Narasimha I as chief in Central Mysore in 1142–43. His mother Lakshmi mentioned. (*E. C. v, Cn. 186.*)

In N. Mysore the W. Chāḷukya Jagadēkamalla II was supreme on August 8, 1142 (*E.C. xi, Dg. 61*). Another record of his 5th year (1142–43) is at Anantapur.

(*V. R. i. Anant. 21 ; 84 of 1903*).

An inscription in N. Mysore, whose stated date is at the end of the year 1142, mentions Sōmēśvara II, W. Chāḷukya king, as still reigning, and Vīra Pāṇḍya ruling the Noḷambavāḍi province. [There is probably a mistake somewhere, possibly in the original.] (*E. C. xi, Dg. 4*).

On August 8, 1142, a record at Tanuku, Kistna District, with a sound date noting a lunar eclipse, names as ruler the Pithāpur Rāja 'Vishṇuvardhana' in his 17th year (*see above December 24, 1141*). (748 of 1920).

An inscription of date November 10, 1142, at Tanjore of Kulōttunga Chōla II, reigning in his 10th year. (*V. R. ii, Tanjore 932 ; 553 of 1904 ; E. I. xi, 289*).

According to Kielhorn (*E. I. v, List of Northern Inscriptions, Nos. 363, 367 ; vi, 198 ; viii. App. i, p. 17*), the Kalinga-Ganga king Kāmārṇava VII came to the throne in this year. Some Ganjam records make his reign begin in A.D. 1146–47. (*See entry below s. v. 1146*).

At Drākshārāma, Godavari District, the Velanāṇḍu chief Kulōttunga-Gonka II was ruling. (*V. R. ii, Godav. 183 ; 278 of 1893*).

At Konidēna in Guntur, the ruling chief was Tribhuvanamalla-Pottapi Chōḍa of the Telugu-Chōḍa family, son of Kāma and Śriyādēvī. (*V. R. ii, Guntur, 239 ; 179 of 1899*).

Irungoḷa Chōla of the Niḍugal family of Chōla-Mahārājas ruling in Anantapur, as a feudatory of the W. Chāḷukya king (*V. R. i. Anant. 122, 123 ; 85, 89 of 1913*). [No. 86 of 1913 is a *vīrakal*, in honour of a man who fell in one of the great cattle-robberies that were so common at the time. In this one a Vaiḍumba family leader boasts of having stolen the cows of his neighbours].

A.D. 1143. On January 11, 1143, and on January 27, Kulōttunga-Chōla II is shewn reigning in Tanjore in his 10th year (*528, 347 of 1918*). Also on March 24 on the Godavari (*The Chellūr plates, V. R. ii, Godav. 48-B ; I. A. xiv, 56 ; E. I. vii, 9*). And on July 14, in Guntur (*V. R. ii, Guntur 17 ; 180 of 1897 ; E. I. x, 137*). Again on November 27, at Tanjore in his 11th year (*V. R. ii, Tanjore 792 ; 109 of 1910 ; I. A. xi, 244*). Records of him also during the year at Drākshārāma. (*V. R. ii, Godav. 216, 337; 311, 431 of 1893*).

An inscription in Bellary District on February 1, of the W. Chāḷukya Jagadēkamalla II in his 5th year (*696 of 1919*). And in N. Mysore, where the ruler of the Noḷambavāḍi province is named as Vīra Pāṇḍya (*E. C. xi, Dg. 85*). And in N.-W. Mysore (*Ibid viii, Sa. 58 ; Sb. 125, 252*). And in Bellary District. (*V. R. i. Bell. 430 ; 31 of 1904*).

The Hoysala Narasimha I was reigning from Dorasamudra over the Gangavāḍi province, and (so-stated, but hardly in reality) over the Noḷambavāḍi Territory. (*E. C. v. Ak. 55*).

A.D. 1144. On February 12, 1444, a gift by the wife of Gonka II of the Velanāṇḍu family is mentioned in an inscription in Guntur District (*V. R. ii. Guntur 11 ; 174 of 1897 ; E. I. x, 136*). The inscription states that the year was the 12th of Kulottunga-Chōla II's reign.

In Travancore Vīra-Kēraḷa was reigning. (*V. R. iii, Trav. 190-A ; I. A. xxiv, 255*).

A.D. 1145. Kulōttunga-Chōla II reigning in Guntur District. Two records, one of which has date = February 12, 1145. (*V. R. ii, Guntur 5, 11 ; 168 of 1897 ; E. I. x, 136*).

In the Vēṇāḍ country, Travancore, the ruler is named as Kodai-Kēraḷa, probably the same as Vīra-Keraḷa of 1144–45. (*T. A. S. iv. Pt. 1, 18, 20*).

In the Godavari District at Rajahmundry, the Piṭhāpur chief Vishṇuvardhana II ruling in his 21st year. (*V. R. ii, Godav. 79 ; 41 of 1912 ; E. I. iv, 229*).

In Nellore District a village was granted by a local chief Balli-Choḍa son of Kāma, grandson of Venka, and great-grandson of Nanni-Chōḍa. [He was perhaps a Konidēna chief (*see Pedigree of Telugu Chōdas*)]. Balli is mentioned again in a record of A.D. 1166. (*V. R. ii. Nell. 108 ; B. and V. C., p. 354*).

Jagadēkamalla II, W. Chāḷukya king, reigning in N.-W. Mysore. The Banavāsi country ruled by a Kādamba chief Gorava-dēva whose senior wife was Sāntalādēvī, recently deceased. (*E. C. viii. Sb. 67*).

[An inscription, the date of which cannot be determined, but which is vaguely said from palæographic evidence to be of the 11th or 12th century, states that the Kādamba chief Taila of Hāngal, during a cattle-lifting raid on his neighbours, had the effrontery to plunder an agrahāra village, peopled by Brahmans. Villagers were killed. There are two Tailas of Hāngal for the second of whom we have the date 1135. (*Mys. A. A. R. 1923, No. 62*)].

A.D. 1146. [Between May 22 and June 26, 1146 Kulōttunga-Chola II ceased to reign and was succeeded by his son Rājarāja II. The period of Rājarāja's reign saw great changes in Southern India. The power of the Chōlas began to weaken seriously and in consequence a number of ruling families came to the front. The Pāṇḍya princes began to emerge from the obscurity into which they had sunk. The chiefs of the Telugu country grew in strength. The Hoyśala family gained its independence. When, in 1156 the Kaḷachūri Bijjala warred against the Western Chāḷukya king, finally crushed him and seized his throne, there came an end, in the territory south of the Tunga-bhadra river, to alien rule from the north, and most parts of Mysore submitted to the Hoyśala chief, who thus became in his turn a king. The unfortunate W. Chāḷukya princes were also attacked on their north by the Yādava king of Dēvagiri, while the Kākatīya prince Prōla I harassed their eastern possessions. The Pāṇḍya rulers of the Noḷambavāḍi province however preferred for a time to own the intrusive Kaḷachūri as their overlord rather than submit to the Hoyśala].

Two inscriptions near Chicacole dated in Ś. 1068 and 1069 state that the Kalinga-Ganga king Anantavarma-Chōḍaganga gave grants, according to each, in his 72nd year. [This would make his accession to have taken place in 1075–76, but it seems clearly established that his *coronation* at least took place on February 17, 1078. The framers of the record may have counted his reign to have begun when perhaps he may have been associated with his father as co-regent, during the latter's lifetime, or they may have been simply in error in giving him so many years of reign. Note that his successor's reign appears to have begun in A.D. 1142 (*see above*). The old king may have abdicated some years before his death. The question must stand over for future solution.] (*V. R. i. Ganjam 135, 136 ; 387, 388 of 1896*).

More gang-robberies and deaths of villagers in W. Mysore in this and the next year. (*E. C. v. Bl. 142 ; Hn. 108*).

A.D. 1147. Jagadēkamalla II of W. Chāḷulykas reigning on June 12, 1147 at Lakshmēśvar, near Puligerē. His minister was 'Kēśi-Rāja' who ruled the Hāngal province [possibly Jayakēśi II of the Kādambas of Goa] (*E. I. xvi. 31*); also in Bellary on December 25, Sinda chiefs ruling locally. (*211 of 1913 ; 68, 69 of 1904*).

In W. Mysore Hoyśala Narasimha I ruled. (*E. C. vi. Cm. 140*).

And in S. Mysore near Seringapatam. (*Ibid iii. Sr. 70*).

On April 10 and December 25, 1147 records of Kulōttunga Chōla II in Tanjore and Trichinopoly in his 14th and 15th years [probably therefore he abdicated for a time before his death (*see s. v. 1146*, 47)]. (*V. R. ii. Tanjore 698 ; iii. Trich. 892 ; 401 of 1902 ; 83 of 1895 ; E. I. xi. 290*).
Kulōttunga Chōla II is also shown to have been reigning in this year in Guntur District. (*V. R. ii, Guntur 9 ; 172 of 1897*).

A record in N.-W. Mysore of the reign of Jagadēkamalla II contains a pedigree of the Sāntara family chiefs, which gives to the mother of the four brothers who lived about 1077 (Taila, Goggiga, Oḍḍiga and Barmma) a name different from that given to her in another inscription, and also gives a different name to her father, who is 'Rakkasaganga' instead of 'Arumuḷi.' * [The question is discussed by Rice. See notes to the pedigree of the Sāntaras (*below*)]. (*E. C. viii. Nr. 35, 37*).

The Palnāḍ Taluk, Guntur District, was ruled by the Velanānḍu chief Kulōttunga-Chōḍa, Gonka. (*V. R. ii, Guntur, 564 ; 144 of 1913*).

Another portion of the Guntur District was governed by Tribhuvanamalla-Pottapi-Chōḍa, son of Kāma, of the Konidēna branch of the Telugu-Chōḍa chiefs (see pedigree).

(*V. R. ii, Guntur, several records, between Nos. 226 and 262 ; 166 to 202 of 1899*).

A. D. 1148. Records of Rājarāja Chōla II on January 3, in his 3rd year, on August 9 and November 22, 1148 in Trichinopoly and Tanjore districts (76, 79, 92 of 1920 ; 504 of 1918.). In Ongole Taluk, Guntur District, on September 15, an inscription of Kulōttunga-Chōla II, Rājarāja's father, goes far to shew that Kulōttunga lived ; retired after his son's reign began.

(*V. R. ii. Guntur 467 ; B. and V. C., p. 1133*).

December 24, 1148. The Noḷamba tract was ruled by 'Jagadēkamalla' Vira-Pānḍya, subject to the W. Chāḷukya king (*V. R. Bellary, 201 ; 445 of 1914*). Several other records shew that he governed that country till at least A.D. 1160–61.

(*Ibid. 159, 280, 284, 299 ; 88, 92, 107 of 1904 ; 469 of 1914*).

In Ganjam 'Anantavarmadēva' was reigning in this year. This is evidently another name of Kāmārṇava VII of the Kalinga-Gangas. (*V. R. i. Ganjam. 146 ; 390 of 1896*).

In Bellary District the Sinda chief Rāchamalla I ruled under Jagadēkamalla, W. Chāḷukya king, in the latter's 10th year. (*V. R. i. Bell. 93, 119 ; 46, 69 of 1904*).

In Guntur District an inscription mentions a grant of land given by Nanni-Chōḍa of the Konidēna branch of Telugu-Chōḍas. He was son of Tribhuvanamalla-Chōḍa and his wife Mābalādēvī. (*V. R. Guntur 259 ; 199 of 1899*).

A.D. 1149. In Bellary and N.-W. Mysore records of the W. Chāḷukya Jagadēkamalla II on February 21, April 24, and May 9. (*E. C. vii, Sk, 164, 165 ; V. R. i. Bell. 177 ; 479 of 1914*).

In Central Mysore Hoysala Narasimha I ruled under Jagadēkamalla II. (*E.C. xii, Ck. 18,29,40*).

In Tanjore on November 23. Inscription of Rājarāja-Chōla II, reigning in his 4th year. (*V. R. ii. Tan. 207 ; 622 of 1902 ; E. I. viii. 2*).

The country about Erode in Coimbatore District was governed, under the Chōla king, by a Viceroy of the Kongu-Chōla family, Kulōttunga Chōla-Mahārāja. This was his 14th year. This tract had been ruled by members of this family since at least A.D. 1006. (*See above s. v. 1006, 1100, 1118.*) (*V. R. i. Coim. 250 ; 598 of 1905.*)

* According to Nr. 35, the mother of the four Sāntara princes named is Kanchalē who on her marriage to Vira Sāntara was given the name Vira Mahādēvi. Chaṭṭale married a Kāḍava or Pallava Prince and was given the name Kāḍavan Mahādēvi. This Chaṭṭaledēvi obviously had no children and seems to have adopted Goggi or Govinda-Sāntara, her sister's son and lived at the Court of Kanni Sāntara another title Govinda assumed as ruler. Hence the difference in the name of the mother vanishes, Kanchalē or Viramahādēvi being the real mother, Chaṭṭale or Kāḍavan Mahādēvi being the aunt and mother by adoption. The name of the father of Chaṭṭale is similarly *Arumuḷi*, the younger brother of Rakkasaganga, Arumuḷi being the Kannaḍa analogue of the Tamil *Arumoḷi* of the Cholaṣ. Rakkasaganga brought these children up almost from birth and was regarded as father as is usually the case in similar circumstances. There is possibility of confusion in the translation, but reference to the original makes it clear that there is no contradiction.—*Editor.*

The Kalinga country and its dependencies remained under the rule of Madhu-Kāmārṇava VII, who is also called 'Anantavarman II,' and 'Jaṭēśvara.' This was his 4th regnal year. [So in the inscription several other records in Ganjam confirm this].

(V. R. i. Ganjam 261, etc. . . . . ; 383 of 1896, etc...),

Kulōttunga-Chōḍa-Gonka II of Velanaṇḍu in his 17th regnal year gave gifts to the temple at Drākshārāma. *(V. R. ii. Godavari 132, 186 ; 227, 281 of 1893)*.

Tribhuvanamalla-Pottapi-Chōḍa—a Telugu-Chōḍa chief—was ruling at Bāpatla in Guntur District. Two records, one of which is dated = March 25, 1149.

(V. R. ii. Guntur 4, 10 ; 167, 173 of 1897 ; E. I. x. 136).

A.D. 1150. On November 24, 1150, Rājarāja-Chola II reigning in Tanjore in his 5th year. *(V. R. ii. Tanj. 156 ; 165 of 1908 ; E. I. xi, 122)*. Also in the Vengi country at Drākshārāma *(V. R. ii. Godavari, 154 ; 249 of 1893)*.

In Travancore, Vēṇāḍ, Kōdai-Kēraḷa-Tiruvaḍi reigning. *(Trav. A. S. iv, Pt. i, p. 21)*.

An inscription at Drākshārāma *(V. R. ii. Godavari, 187 ; 282 of 1893)* is puzzling.[1] It records a gift to the temple by the Velanāṇḍu chief Kulottunga-Chōḍa-Gonka, in, according to Mr. Rangāchāri, his 'fourth year.' But this chief, Gonka II's rule dates from A.D. 1132. The 'fourth year' probably refers to that of his suzerain Rājarāja Chōla II.

The same Velanāṇḍu chief is also mentioned in this year in another inscription at Drākshārāma, and in another in Guntur District.

(V. R. ii. Godav. 158 ; Guntur 223 ; 253 of 1893 ; 163 of 1899).

In Bapatla, Guntur District, the ruling chief was Rājēndra-Kōna-Lōka of the Kōnamaṇḍala, elsewhere called 'Lōka-Bhūpāla,' son of Bhīma II and the Chāḷukya princess, Rājāmbika.

(V. R. ii, Guntur, 50 ; 213 of 1897).

A.D. 1151. On February 18, 1151, Hoyśala Narasimha I was reigning in Central Mysore. He is also called 'Vishṇuvardhana.' *(E. C. xii, Tm. 9)*.

In N.-W. Mysore the chief Kīrttidēva is mentioned. *(E. C. viii, Sb., 464)*. An inscription dated late in 1151 states that a grandson had been born to the Ganga chief Kīrttidēva-Nanniya-Ganga, his eldest son being the father *(See note on Western-Ganga pedigree ; also Ibid. Sb. 132)*. The chiefs were subject to Jagadēkamalla II of the W. Chāḷukyas.

[Tailapa III of the W. Chāḷukyas came to the throne this year. He was crushed and deposed by Kalachūri Bijjala in 1157].

In Guntur District and at Drākshārāma, Godavari District, Kulōttunga-Chōḍa-Gonka II of Velanāṇḍu was ruling, subject to Rājarāja Chola II reigning in his 6th year. The Chōḍa chief's queen was Sūrāmbā *(V. R. ii. Guntur 31, 40, 48, 51, 53, 833 ; Godavari 169 ; 194, 203, 211, 214, 216 of 1897 ; 264 of 1893)*.

The Konidēna tract south of the Krishna river was ruled by Tribhuvanamalla-Chōḍa, whose son Nanni gave a grant of land in Konidēna. The chief is also called 'Pottapi-Chōḍa. *(V. R. ii. Guntur, 3, 8, 231, 258, 260 ; 166, 171, of 1897 ; 171, 198, 200 of 1899 ; See pedigree of Telugu-Chōḍa chiefs)*.

[1] The puzzle arises from overlooking the doubtful character of the 4th digit in the Śaka date. The figure 2, after 107 is added by the epigraphists doubtfully in brackets. Rangachari's index marks it as doubtful. This record belonging to the time of the same ruler as the one immediately preceding dated in the 7th year equivalent to Śaka 1071, the 4th year of this ruler would fall in Śaka 1057–58. The Śaka date 107 probably stands for 1057 of the era, the 5 having dropped out by some chance.—*Editor*.

A.D. 1152. In Tanjore are inscriptions of Rājarāja Chola II on January 24, and February 14, 1152, reigning in his 6th year (*V. R. ii. Tan. 704, 987 ; 5 of 1899 ; 407 of 1902 ; 5 of 1899 ; E. I. viii, 2, 3*). Also on April 11, in the same regnal year (*521 of 1920*). And in Godavari District in 1152–53 in his 7th year (*V. R. ii. Godav. 131 ; 226 of 1893*). And in Guntur District (*V. R. ii. Guntur 31, 40 ; 194, 203 of 1897*).

On September 11 Kulōttunga-Chōla II is recognized as king in his 20th year, though his successor had been on the throne for six years. This helps to prove that he had abdicated and was now living in retirement. (*V. R. iii. Pudukottai 159 ; 334 of 1914*).

The Velanāṇḍu chief Kulōttunga-Chōḍa-Gonka II ruling in Tenali Taluk of Guntur District. (*V. R. ii. Guntur, 833*).

There were more gang-robberies of cattle, and deaths of villagers in this year in W. Mysore. (*E. C. v, Bl. 143*).

A.D. 1153. Inscription of Rājarāja-Chōla II in his 7th regnal year, bearing date = May 21, 1153. This record fixes his accession as in the year following May 21, 1146 (*See pedigree and notes*). (*V. R. iii, Trichinopoly, 182 ; 597 of 1908 ; E. I. xi, 123*).

There are three inscriptions at Maṇimangalam in Chingleput District dated respectively in the 8th, 12th and 28th years of the Chōla king Rājarāja II. These years are 1153-54, 1157-58 and 1173–74. The first two are quite possible ; in the third there is probably a mistake somewhere. He is declared to have 'taken Madura, Īḷam (Ceylon) and the crowned head of the Pāṇḍya.' These appear to be simply family titles. (*S. I. I. iii. 79, 82, 84*).

In Ongole Taluk, Guntur District, at Drākshārāma and at Chēbrōlu are inscriptions of this year, shewing as local ruler under the Chōla king the Velanāṇḍu chief Kulōttunga-Chōḍa-Ganga, or Gonka II (*V. R. ii, Guntur 26, 83, 341 ; Godavari 133 ; B. and V. C. 928 ; 144, 189 of 1897 ; 228 of 1893*). At Drākshārāma also is a record of this year of the Kōnamaṇḍala chief Bhīma III who was ruling the Vengi tract under Rājarāja Chōla II. (*V. R. ii, Godavari 151 ; 246 of 1893*).

At the end of the year 1153 Hoyśala Narasimha I was ruling central and W. Mysore. (*E.C. v, Cn. 228 ; vi. Kd. 28*).

There are two records of this year in Vizagapatam District of the Kalinga-Ganga king Madhu-Kāmārṇava, alias Anantavarma. (*V. R. iii, Vizag. 222, 224 ; 368, 370 of 1905*).

[Parākrama-Bahu's reign as king of Ceylon began in this year].

A.D. 1154. Rājarāja Chōla II reigning as supreme in Guntur District in his 9th year. (*V. R. ii, Guntur 25, 28, 29, 33 ; 188, 191, 192, 196 of 1897*).

In Guntur District, including the Palnāḍ Taluk, the Velanāṇḍu chief Kulōttunga-Chōḍa-Gonka II was ruling (*V. R. ii, Guntur 522 ; 552 of 1909 ; 831 of 1922*). [In the last noted of these it is stated in the epigraphist's report that the chief's pedigree is given ; but unfortunately the information contained in it is not made available].

A.D. 1155. Rājarāja Chōla II reigning in Guntur District in his 10th year. (*V. R. ii, Guntur 27, 377 ; B. and V. C. 980 ; 190 of 1897*).

In W. Mysore, and also in the east in Kolar District, Hoyśala Narasimha I is soun to be reigning in records of this year. [The latter is specially noticeable as it seems to imply that Chōla supremacy in Kolar District was not now acknowledged]. (*E. C. v, Hn. 57*

At Drākshārāma both the Velanāṇḍu chief Gonka II and the Kōnamaṇḍala chief Malla Rāja are mentioned in inscriptions (*V. R. ii, Godavari, 175, 141 ; 270, 235 of 1893*). Also in 1157–58 (*Ibid. 173 ; 268 of 1893*).

A.D. 1156. Another murderous cattle-stealing raid took place in this year in N.-W. Mysore during the reign of the W. Chāḷukya king Nūrmaḍi-Taila III. The attack was on Korakōḍu village. The inscriptions speak of great slaughter and brave deeds done by defenders. (*E. C. viii, Sb, 175, 176*).

Near Bangalore in Mysore where Hoyśala Narasimha I was ruling there were similar disturbances. Record of deaths during a fight between neighbouring petty chieftains, when a town was sacked. (*E. C. ix, Bn. 112*).

Inscriptions of Rājarāja Chōla II in Guntur in his 10th year. (*V. R. ii, Guntur 24, 30, 58 ; 187, 193, 221 of 1897*).

[This was a fateful year in the history of the W. Chāḷukya kingdom. King Tailapa III had been subjected to great difficulties, as has already been noticed. On the east he was defeated, and his ambitions in that quarter quenched, by the Kākatīya king of Warangal, Prōla I, about A.D. 1155. He had a very powerful noble in his employ named Bijjala of the Kalachūri family, who, after governing a province for some time, was appointed Viceroy of the Baṇavāsi and Noḷambavāḍi countries. He was the Commander-in-Chief of all the Chāḷukya armies. Presumably after Tailapa's defeat at the hands of Prola, Bijjala became all-powerful in Tailapa's kingdom ; so much so that before long he practically usurped the throne. He was in that position in 1157, though Mr. Krishnaswami Aiyangar holds that Tailapa was allowed nominally to continue to reign till 1161]. (*See E. I. v, 9, 24*).

A.D. 1157. Two inscriptions combine to make Bijjala's seizure of the throne (whether actually or only practically) to have taken place between September 25, 1156, and January 17, 1157 (*E. C. vii. Sk. 102, 162*). [A record of 1159 makes December 6, 1156 the latest possible day]. (*Ibid. Sb. 131*).

An inscription in N.-W. Mysore of about March 24, 1157 shews that Tailapa III was still recognized as king there. It relates to more cattle-raids and murders of peasants. (*E. C. viii. Sb. 369*).

In Central Mysore Hoyśala Narasimha I ruled, still acknowledging the W. Chālukya king as his suzerain (*E. C. v. Cn. 246 ; xii, Kg. 1.*) [But the natural result of Bijjala's action was to encourage the Hoyśala chief to attempt to effect his independence]. In the Noḷamba country Vira Pāṇḍya, and later his brother Vijaya Pāṇḍya, were compelled shortly to transfer their allegiance from their Chāḷukya suzerain to the triumphant Kalachūri potentate. (*See also E. I. v. 213*).

An inscription at Drākshārāma, Godavari District, shews the Velanāṇḍu chief Gonka II ruling there. (*V. R. ii, Godav. 173 ; 268 of 1893*).

A.D. 1158. In N. Mysore, in the Sorab Taluk of Shimoga District, there is an inscription of February 1, 1158, describing one of the usual local fights with bands of robbers, and ensuing deaths. The suzerain is mentioned as Kalachūri Bijjala in his 2nd year, as if he were king. (*E. C. viii. Sb. 255*).

In N.-W.. Mysore Bijjala II was now accepted as sovereign instead of the W. Chāḷukya Tailapa III. The Ganga prince Nanniya-Ganga is mentioned. He may possibly have been a grandson of the Nanniya-Ganga who died on August 14, 1122 (*see above*). (*E. C. vii, Sh. 3, 13 ; Sk. 18, 162*).

A *vīrakal* in N. Mysore, Sorab Taluk, witnesses the death of a man when Bijjala II, Kalachūri, besieged the fortress of Gooty (Gutti) with a large army, and 'ruined the town.' [The people of that tract, then though they submitted to the usurper, were not disposed to be very friendly to him]. (*E. C. viii. Sb. 416*).

In W. Mysore Hoyśala Narasimha held his own as ruler (*E. C. v. Ak. 141, 145 ; vi, Tk. 19, 59*). With him, apparently as co-regent or Viceroy, we have mention of his son Baḷḷāḷa II as ruling in this year, as well as in 1154. (*E. C. v. Ak. 154, 157*).

An inscription in Hadagalli Taluk, Bellary District, states that that portion of the Noḷamba province was now ruled by Vira Pāṇḍya, whose uncle Vikrama Pāṇḍya made a gift on April 15, 1158. It mentions as suzerain not Kalachūri Bijjala II but the W. Chālukya prince Jagadēkamalla, probably the prince of that name, son of king Tailapa III, who seems to have ruled some tracts under Bijjala till about 1184. (*V. R. i. Bell. 159 ; 496 of 1914*).

(*For Vīra Pāṇḍya of Uchchangi, ruling in 1152, see ibid 280 ; 88 of 1904*).

Rājarāja Chōla II is seen reigning in Tanjore in his 12th year on March 26, 1158, and in Guntur at the end of the year. (*V. R. ii. Tanjore 213 ; 628 of 1902 ; 114, 115 of 1917 ; E. I. viii. 3*).

A.D. 1159. An inscription in N.-W. Mysore of date = January 5, 1159, gives a pedigree of the W. Chāḷukyas down to Tailapa III. It shews that loyalty to that dynasty still prevailed in parts of the country now ruled by Bijjala Kalachūri. (*E. C. vii. Sk. 123*).

In the same tract another fatal cattle raid took place (*Ibid. 49, 69, 71, 75, 80, 85*). It resulted in many deaths ; or else many such raids took place in this year.

In N.-W. Mysore king Tailapa is still spoken of in terms of loyalty, though an inscription which does so says that 'in his time was king Bijjala'. The Baṇavāsi country was now locally ruled by Kāśyapa Nāyaka, Bijjala's Viceroy (*E. C. viii. Sb. 328*). The date of the record = March 18, 1159. A frank admission, in the same district of Bijjala's supremacy, is given by another record whose date = February 8, 1159 (*Ibid No. 99*). An important inscription of Bijjala's 4th year, also N.-W. Mysore, makes the latest day of his seizure of the W. Chāḷukya throne December 6, 1156. (*E. C. viii. Sb. 131*).

In W. Mysore, Kaḍūr District, Hoyśala Narasimha ruled. An inscription whose date is late in 1159 mentions him and gives a list of the achievements of his father Vishṇuvardhana at length (*E. C. vi, Kd. 69 ; also v, Ak. 119*). Another shews him reigning near Seringapatam, having his residence at Dorasamudra. The date of this last is September 27, A.D. 1159. (*Ibid. iii, Sr. 60*).

In the Kistna District Rājarāja Chola II reigned, in his 14th year. Inscription date = June 26, 1159. This record shews that the last possible day for his accession was June 26, 1146. (*847 of 1917*).

The Śāntara chief of Humcha ruled locally in Sagar Taluk, N.-W. Mysore. It states that Aḷiyā-dēvī, grand-daughter of Taila III Sāntara, had a son Jayakēśi by her husband, a Ganga chief named 'Honna-Ponna.' Aḷiyā gave a gift for a Jain temple erected by her. (*E. C. viii. Sa. 159*).

A.D. 1160. Hoyśala Narasimha ruling in Central Mysore early in the year 1160 (*E. C. ii., Sr. Bel. 138*) ; and late in the year in Hassan District, there is an inscription of his which gives the name of his queen Chāgalā, states that when young he defeated a Kādamba army at Bankāpur in Dhārwār District, and boldly asserts that his father Vishṇuvardhana had taken possession of Kāñchi. (*Ibid. v. Bl. 193*).

An inscription in Sāgar Taluk, Mysore, gives the name of Jagadēva (Sāntara chief of Humcha) as ruling Baṇavāsi and Sāntaḷigē Districts in this year under the W. Chāḷukya prince Bhūlōkamalla, son of the dispossessed king Tailapa III. [It must be assumed then that this prince was placed in charge of these provinces by Bijjala after ejectment of Tailapa and his usurpation of the throne]. The inscription commemorates local disturbances, fighting and slaughter,—the Sāntara chief warring against the Kādamba chief Tailapa, or Tailama.

(*E. C. viii. Sa. 28, 91, 92, 93 ; Mys. A. A. R. 1923, p. 113*).

Bijjala seems also to have placed the Kōgali, Ballakunḍe and Kadambaḷigē tracts under Jagadēkamalla III, another son of the W. Chāḷukya Tailapa III (*See s. v., A.D. 1158*). This is testified to by a record at Bāgali, Bellary District, which mentions Vīra Pānḍya as administering those districts under Jagadēkamalla. (*V. R. i. Bell. 299 ; 107 of 1904*).

A record, which perhaps belongs to this year but is doubtful, gives a pedigree of the W. Chāḷukyas. It states distinctly that Ayyaṇa, son of Daśavarman, reigned after his brother Vikramāditya V and before his younger brother Jayasimha III.

(*E. C. xi. Dg. 35*).

In Tanjore Rājarāja Chōla II was reigning on September 27, 1160, in his 15th year (*V. R. ii. Tan. 707 ; 419 of 1912*). And in South Arcot on January 13, 1160 (*192 of 1918*).

The Baṇavāśi 12000 province was ruled by Sōyidēva, a Kadamba chief of Hāngal, under Kalachūri Bijjala. Pedigree of Sōyidēva is given. He was son of Sāntanṛpa, two ancestors of whom were Bomma and his son Boppa. Sōyidēva married Mālalā-devī, and had a son Mallikhārjuna and a daughter Lachahalā who married Boppa-dēva. [I am unable to identify these personages]. (*E. C. viii. Sb. 346*).

In Bellary District an inscription shews Vīra Pānḍya of Uchchangi locally ruling under Bijjala's Viceroy Jagadēkamalla of the W. Chāḷukyas (*see above s. v., A.D. 1158*).

(*V. R. i. Bell. 299, 107 of 1904*).

In the Pānḍya country in the south Māravarman Srīvallabha came to the throne this year. One of his feudatories was the Kēraḷa Vīra-Ravivarman. He had a son Kulaśēkhara. He was at feud with the Chōlas and was called *Śōlantaka* in token of it. (*49 of 1896 ; 110 of 1907 ; 27, 30, 38 of 1909 ; 97, 111, 318–326 of 1908*).

A.D. 1161. Bijjala II, Kalachūri, reigning in N. Mysore, and Hoyśala Narasimha I in W. Mysore (*E. C. xi. Dg. 84 ; v. Ak. 117*). Both records are of date early in 1161. There is a grant by the former in the N. of Bijapūr at Managōli of September 12, in this year, which shews how extensive were his possessions. (*E. I. v. 9*).

In the Kēraḷa country two inscriptions shew Vira-Ravivarman ruling, subject to the Pānḍya king Maravarman Srīvallabha. (*V. R. iii. Travancore 120, 123*).

At the end of A.D. 1161 an inscription in Anantapur District shews a certain 'Chāḷukya Vikrama' as reigning [This was probably a name adopted for, or by, Bhūlōkamalla, son of Tailapa III, then ruling under Kalachūri Bijjala]. Under him the 'local ruler was Mallidēva-Chōla-Mahārāja of the Niḍugal family of 'lords of Oraiyūr'. The record relates to local improvements in the town of Hemjēru (*15 of 1917*).

A.D. 1162. Kalachūri Bijjana ('Bijjana') II reigning in N.-W. Mysore in his 6th year. On January 17, an inscription shews him as encamped at Baḷḷigāmve (Beḷagāmi) in Shikarpur Taluk. [The date is a sound one, mentioning a solar eclipse]. (*E. C. vii. Sk. 56, 102*).

In the course of the year 1162–63 Bijjala made a state progress to the Southern provinces of the former Chāḷukya kingdom. *(E. I. v. 213).*

Hoyśala Narasimha was ruling in Central, West and South Mysore, with his capital at Dorasamudra. He still adhered to the W. Chāḷukya family as his suzerains, declining to recognize Kalachūri Bijjala, and not as yet ready to proclaim himself independent. One of his inscriptions of this year says that he 'broke the pride of Irungōḷa Chōla' [of the Niḍugal family. This probably refers to an event of his father's reign.]

(E.C. v. Ak. 142, 172 ; Bl, 176 ; iv. Hs, 137 ; vi. Kd. 72 ; xii. Gb, 12 ; Tp. 61, 66).

On April 25, 1162, a gift of a village was made to the family of a brave soldier who had died in a fight between a Sāntara chief Taila, son of Srīvallabha, and a Pāṇḍya Rāja. [Probably Vīra Pāṇḍya then ruling neighbouring districts]. The gift was by Taila.

(Mys. A. A. R. 1923, No. 64, p. 75).

The Noḷambavāḍi province was governed in this year by Tribhuvanmalla Vīra Pāṇḍya under Kalachūri Bijjala. *(V. R. i., Bell, 304; 113 of 1913).*

Rājarāja-Chola II was reigning at Drākshārāma, Godavari District, in his 17th year.

(V. R. ii, Godav. 232 ; 327 of 1893).

In N.-W. Mysore the Koppanāḍ tract on the Tunga river was ruled by Sāntara Mārudēva-who bore the name 'Jagadēka-Vira-Hoyśala', in acknowledgment apparently of Hoyśala overlordship. *(E. C. vi. Kp. 10).*

A. D. 1163. More gifts were made this year to the temple at Drākshārāma by Rājarāja Chola II under whom ruled there the Velanāṇḍu chief Kulōttunga-Rājēndra-Choḍa. The latter had a wife Panḍāmbikā (*V. R. ii. Godavari 134, 138, 143, 161 ; 229, 233, 238, 256 of 1893.*) On December 25, 1163, a record of Rajarāja's 18th year in Trichinopoly District. *(96 of 1920).*

Inscriptions of Kalachūri Bijjala's 7th and 8th years in Sorab Taluk, N. W.-Mysore. One of them mentions his attack on the Gooty (Gutti) fortress. *(E. C. viii. Sb. 287, 449).*

In this year there was a campaign in N.-W. Mysore when three allied chiefs, the Ganga Kīrttideva, Uddharī-Ekkala and Bamma attacked Jagadēva. [It is not possible to identify all these. One of the inscriptions calls Kīrtti a Ganga chief; another calls him 'Lord of Baṇavāśi. He was probably the Kādamba Kīrtti-dēva III. 'Bamma' then would be his nephew Barmma. The name 'Ekkala' looks as if he belonged to the Ganga family. Jagadēva was evidently the Sāntara chief of that name]. *(E. C. viii, Sb, 177, 193).*

Hoyśala Narasimha I ruling in E. Mysore. *(E.C. x. Kl. 177).*

In the Palnāḍ tract, Krishna river, a gift was made to the temple at Chēzarla by a chief called Kēti Reddi of the Manuma-kula. This was probably the Amarāvati chief Kēta II.

(V. R. ii, Guntur 190 ; 157 of 1899).

In Coimbatore the local ruler was the Kongu-Chōla chief Kulōttunga-Chōla (see pedigree of Chōlas ; notes). *(V. R. i. Coim. 22, 124, 250 ; 191 of 1909 ; 158 of 1910 ; 598 of 1905).*

At the end of the year the Noḷamba country was being ruled by Vijaya-Panḍya I, under the W. Chāḷukya Viceroy Jagadēkamalla III, who in his turn was subservient to Kalachūri Bijjala. Vijaya-Pāṇḍya I was son of Rāya-Panḍya and Sōvalādēvi (see pedigree of Noḷamba rulers).

(E. C. xi. Dg. 43).

On January 19, 1163, Kākatīya Pratāpa Rudra I was crowned at Anumakoṇḍa in succession to his father Prōla II, according to the inscription at that place of January 20. It relates the principal events of the reign of Prōla II, saying that he had defeated Gōvinda Rāja (a Western Chāḷukya general, who in 1126–27 was governing Koṇḍapalle near Bezwada and had fought with the Velanāṇḍu chief Gonka II and burnt Vengi); also that Prōla II had been besieged in Anumakoṇḍa by Sāntara Jagadēva but had driven off the invaders. It mentions the death of the W. Chāḷukya king Tailpa III. *(I. A. 1882, p. 9 ; E. I. ix. 256).*

A. D. 1164. Hoyśala Narasimha ruling Central Mysore. Cattle-raids, village fighting and deaths (*E. C. xii. Tp. 32*). Also in W. Mysore. In this record he is said to have 'uprooted the Magara kingdom and established the Chōla kingdom.' [The Hoyśalas consistently supported the Chōlas in these times]. *(E. C. v. Ak. 68).*

In the Bāpatla Taluk, Guntur District, Manma-Chōḍa Gonka III, son of the Velanāṇḍu chief Kulōttunga-Rājēndra-Chōḍa, was ruling. *(V. R. ii. Guntur 142 ; 253 of 1892).*

A. D. 1165. In Narasaraopet Taluk, Guntur District, in this year and in 1169–70, the local ruler was Kulōttunga-Rājēndra-Chōḍa of Velanāṇḍu.

(V. R. ii. Guntur 197, 198 ; 112, 113 of 1893).

On March 22, 1165, Rājarāja-Chōla II is named as in his '18th', really 19th year. [According to this he was alive at this time, but his successor Rājādhirāja II had come to the throne early in 1163. Consequently it must be presumed that Rājarāja II had abdicated,[1] and was living a private life at this time]. *(707, 708 of 1920).* Another inscription at Drāksharāma in the Vengi country calls this year, 'Ś. 1087,' Rājarāja's 20th year.

(V. R. ii. Godavari 121, 122, 130, 141 ; 216, 217, 225, 236 respectively of 1893).

In Central Mysore Narasimha Hoyśala I was reigning early in the year 1165.

(E. C. v. Cn. 210.)

More cattle-raiding and violence, with deaths of villagers, in this year, in N.-W. Mysore, during Kalachūri Bijjala II's 10th year of reign over the W. Chāḷukya territory. *(E. C. viii. Sb. 6.)*

The Sāntaḷigē 1000 tract governed by Śāntara Singi-dēva. Several chiefs raised armies and attacked other chiefs. A *virakal* commemorates deaths in a battle. The inscription implies that the armies were raised under the orders of king Bijjala II. *(E. C. viii. Sa. 114, see also 112, 113).* [Singi was Jagadēva's brother].

In N. Mysore, the Nōḷambavāḍi province was ruled by Vijaya Pāṇḍya of Uchchangi, son of Rāya Pāṇḍya and Sōvalādēvī. The inscription recognizes the W. Chāḷukya Jagadēkamalla III as king, shewing that the people there still clung to their old sovereigns, though they had lost the throne ten years earlier (*E. C. xi. Dg. 5, 77*). Vijaya-Paṇḍya's pedigree is given in Dg. 5.

A. D. 1166. The same Vijaya Pāṇḍya *alias* Kāma ruling Noḷambavāḍi province in N. Mysore. *(E. C. xi. Jl. 8 ; Dg. 39).*

[In this year or the next the power of Bijjala II collapsed. He had fallen in love with the sister of Basava, a Lingayat, who had married the daughter of Bijjala's minister; and in course of time Basava was appointed to be himself minister and commander-in-chief. Basava attained to immense power while Bijjala became careless. Accounts differ as to the mode of the king's death. Some say he was poisoned, some that he was assassinated by three of Basava's followers ('*Mysore and Coorg*,' *Rice*, *79*)].

[1] This presumption would be found unjustifiable in a large number of cases. The usual practice seems to have been to associate the heir-apparent in the administration, and we find these associated with the ruler pretty early in their reign in many cases.—*Editor*.

An inscription of 1173, December 17 (*see below*) makes Bijjala's reign to have ended on a day in the year following December 17, 1166.

An inscription in Madura District of July 23, 1166, mentions Kulaśēkhara-Pāṇḍya (*see below, s. v., A. D. 1167–68*). (*101 of 1908*).

A. D. 1167. Hoyśala Narasimha I was ruling in West, South and East Mysore.

(*E. C. vi. Tk. 18 ; iii. Md. 61 ; v. Bl., 177 ; iv. Ch. 98 ; Hs. 3 ; x. Bp., 8 ; Kl. 93*).

The Kalinga-Ganga king Anantavarman-Rājarāja II came to the throne this year.

(*E. I. vi., 198*).

April 21, 1167, Tribhuvanamalla Malli-deva Chōla-Mahārāja of the Niḍugal family, 'Lord of Orēyūr', ruling his tract in N. Mysore. His wife made a gift on this day (*E. C. xii, Pg. 35, 83*). He ruled also over part of Anantapur District at this time. (*V. R. i, Anant. 139*).

Rajārāja Chōla II was still considered to be reigning in Guntur District, though Rājādhirāja had been on the throne for five years. Rājarāj-'s 21st year is mentioned (*V. R. ii, Guntur 385, 46, 52, 68, 95 ; B. and V. C. 996 ; 156, 209, 215, 231 of 1897*). The local chief was Kulōttunga-Rājēndra-Chōḍa of Velanāṇḍu, son of Gonka II and Sabbāmbikā.

In Tanjore an inscription of the fifth year of Rājādhirāja Chōla II.

(*V. R. ii, Tan. 709 ; 421 of 1912.*)

[Beginning with this year, or perhaps in the year previous, South India was convulsed with war. This struggle is known as the war of Pāṇḍya succession.[1] We gain a great deal of our information from the Singhalese *Mahawaṁśa*, ch. lxxvi (*see the summary of events given in E. R. 1899, §§ 23–38*). There were two claimants to the throne of Madura, Parākrama Pāṇḍya and Kulaśēkhara Pāṇḍya. The former was besieged in Madura by the latter. Parākrama appealed to king Parākrama-Bāhu (1153–1186) of Ceylon for aid, who prepared an expedition. But meanwhile Kulaśēkhara had captured Madura and, having first murdered Parākrama with his wives and children, placed himself on the throne.

The Singhalese armies landed in India under the general Lankāpura. He first attacked and captured the city of Rāmēśvaram, and then proceeded on his march defeating Kulaśēkhara's forces in many places and seizing the towns. Kulaśēkhara took the field, fought a battle against the invaders and was defeated, losing his own camp. Lankāpura advanced to Siruvayal and afterwards took Neṭṭūr. There he heard that Vīra-Pāṇḍya, one of Parākrama's sons who had escaped the massacre, was a fugitive in the Malaiyāḷam country. He sent for him to join him, and that done, Lankāpura again advanced, reduced numbers of petty chieftains and captured Śemponmāri on the border of Pudukoṭṭa State. Kulaśēkhara collected large forces and many minor actions were fought. Then Parākrama Bāhu sent another army from Ceylon to assist Lankāpura, commanded by general Jagad-Vijaya (called 'Jayadhara' in Tamil records). These united armies advanced and were met by Kulaśēkhara, who was again beaten in a pitched battle, his horse being killed under him. Kulaśēkhara took refuge in the Toṇḍamān country.

The victorious Singhalese went to Madura, and there Vīra-Pāṇḍya was placed on the throne by Lankāpura, the local Pāṇḍya chiefs submitting. After a further expedition as far as Pon-Amarāvati, Lankāpura retured to Madura, and the ceremony of Vīra Pāṇḍya's coronation took place. Kulaśēkhara was again defeated in several engagements, and finally took refuge in the Chōla country

[1] *Vide* Mr. S. Krishnaswami Ayyangar's, *South India and Her Muhammadan Invaders*', pp. 2–11. *Mahāwaṁśa*, chs. lxxvi, lxxvii.

By now the whole country was up in arms. Kulaśēkhara was assisted by the Chōla king and by many great chiefs, amongst them 'Pallava Rāya' is mentioned—possibly Ammaiyappan-Pallava-Rāya, father of Perunjinga I, who afterwards came to great power. But these had no success and Kulaśēkhara was again put to flight. Lankāpura then handed over the Pāṇḍya realm to Vīra Pāṇḍya and took all his forces back to Ceylon.

Chōla records allege that Lankāpura's final retirement was brought about by divine aid and given to the Śambuvarāyan chief Edirili-Chōla, who had a son Pallava-Rāya—possibly the leader mentioned above. As to the date of the war it is mentioned in the Ārpākkam grant of 1167–68, and it must have occupied considerable time. Hultzsch dates the invasion of the Singhalese as late in the year 1166. *(J. R. A. S. 1913, p. 519).*

Kulaśēkhara Pāṇḍya is mentioned in an inscription at Tirupattūr, Madura District (101 of 1908). The Ārpākkam grant alluded to is *V. R. i, Chingleput 248 ; 20 of 1899*, of Rājādhirāja's 5th year (1167–68). It describes how Edirili-Chōla Śambuvarāyan begged the High Priest of the Temple to pray earnestly that the Singhalese should be induced to depart, and so the country might be saved. The *Svāmi* did so for 28 days, and at the end of it the invaders left the country. [This shews that the war came to an end in 1167–68]. An inscription of Rājādhirāja's 4th year at Tirukollambūdūr, Tanjore District, also mentions the end of the war describing the Singhalese troops as running into the sea with their noses cut off—and the enthronement of Vikrama Pāṇḍya. [Rājadhirāja's 4th year ended in March 1167]. *(V. R. ii, Tanjore 794 ; 1 of 1899).*

A. D. 1168. January 24. Rājādhirāja Chōla reigning in Tanjore *(504 of 1920 ; E. I. xi, 123).* The inscription states that the date was in this king's '6th' year, but it was actually the 5th. The 6th year began in March, 1168, by Jacobi's fixture.

The Eastern Chāḷukya king Rājarāja II reigning in Guntur District. *(E. R. 1917, C.P.Grant, App. A, No. 23).*

In N.-W. Mysore the Kalachūri king, Rāyamurāri-Sōvidēva, or Sōmēśvara, reigning. *(E. C. vii. Sk. 92).*

A. D. 1169. Rājādhirāja Chola II reigning in Tanjore in his 6th year. The date=March 6, 1169 *(V. R. ii. Tanjore, 163 ; 172 of 1908 ; E. I. xi. 123).* Another inscription of the same on May 30, *(224 of 1917)*, but the number of the regnal year seems to be misquoted. It is admittedly hardly legible.

There are two inscriptions at Drākshārāma, Godavari Disirict, shewing that Rājarāja Chola II was still living—probably retired. *(V. R. ii. Godav. 229, 257 ; 324, 351 of 1893).*

Vijaya Pāṇḍya was ruling the Noḷamba province *(E. C. xi. Dg. 6).* Hoyśala Baḷḷāla (II), son of Narasimha I, mentioned in Central and W. Mysore. He is called 'Giridurgamalla' Baḷḷāla *(E. C. xii. Tp. 91 ; v. Ak. 1).* Narasimha himself was ruling in W. Mysore. *(E. C. vi. Kd. 51).*

On February 1, 1169, an inscription in Tinnevelly District mentions the 37th year of Māravarman Śrivallabha Pāṇḍya, father of the Kulaśēkhara of the great war of 1166–67. [If so he must have been living in retirement.] *(426 of 1916).*

On August 7, 1169, the Nidugal chief Mallidēva Chola Mahārāja ruling locally at Henjēru. It mentions the W. Chaḷukya Jagadēkamalla as his overlord. *(733 of 1917).*

A. D. 1170. On January 15, 1170, the Hoyśala king Narasimha I died. So says an epitaph at Billahaḷḷi in N.-W. Mysore (The *tithi* is giveṇ as 'ba, 10' instead of 'ba. 12'). *(E. C. vii. Ci. 36).* An inscription of March 26, 1170, in S. Mysore also names as ruler Narasimha I, though apparently he had died on January 15 (*E. C. iii, Tn. 136*). He is also named as ruler in West Mysore in 1170–71. (*E. C. v. Hn. 53*).

A private grant of this year in Kaḍūr Taluk, Mysore, gives the name of the ruler as Hoyśala Narasimha I. (*E. C. vi. Kd. 30*).

August 10, 1170. Rājādhirāja Chōla reigning in Tanjore in his 8th year. (*V. R. ii, Tan. 212 ; 627 of 1902.*)

December 25, 1170. Inscription of Kalachūri Sōmēśvara's 3rd year in N.-W. Mysore. He reduced a Changāḷva chief who seemingly had been disaffected. (*E. C. viii. Sb. 345.*)

A. D. 1171. An inscription near Mysore city mentions Hoyśala Baḷḷāḷa II as sovereign. The date appears to be March, 1171, but it is not sound in detail (*E. C. iii. My. 58.*). Another, dated in 'Ś. 1093, Khara' which=A.D. 1171–72, also close to Mysore, mentions Narasimha I as reigning (*E. C. iii. Ml. 52*). Again in W. Mysore an inscription of this year mentions Narasimha as still ruling (*E. C. vi. Kd. 16*). And so does one in S.-E. Mysore whose date is in the autumn of 1171 (*E. C. ix. Kn. 44*). This last mentions another local disturbance—a fight between chiefs and consequent deaths. And another in S. Mysore at the end of 1171 (*E. C. iv. Kr. 53*). [The question of the date of Narasimha's death must stand over for settlement].

In N.-W. Mysore Vijaya-Pāṇḍya, 'defeater of the designs of Rājigā', i.e., of Rājādhirāja Chola, was ruling the Noḷamba province (*E. C. xi, Dg. 32*). [It may be that Vijaya-Pāṇḍya assisted the Singhalese to place Vira Pāṇḍya on the throne of Madura in opposition to the Chōla king who favoured Kulaśēkhara Pāṇḍya].

On the Krishna River at Bezwada, the Velanāṇḍu chief Kulōttunga-Rājēndra-Chōḍa gave lands to a temple. (*V. R. ii, Kistna 111 ; 158 of 1913*).

The Koṇḍapaḍmaṭi chief Buddha Rāja gave a field in the village of Nādiṇḍla, which is not far from Tsandōl, the capital of the Velanāṇḍu chiefs to the Tsandōl temple on which is engraved an inscription relating to it. Buddha's sister Ankama or Akkāmbika had married Velanāṇḍu Rājēndra-Chōḍa. Buddha was vassal to the Chōla king. He is called the ruler of the '*Giripaśchima*' tract, or the 'country west of the hill' (i.e., west of the rock-fortress of Koṇḍavīḍu), also '*Śailapaschātyadīpa*', or 'The light of the west of the hill'. (*E. I. vi. 268*).

A. D. 1172. Two inscriptions of date March 1172, shew Rājarāja-Chōla II still living, and named as if actually reigning. They mention his 26th year, thus confirming the date fixed for his accession, *viz.*, May-June 1146. (*V. R. ii, Guntur 834 ; 704 of 1920*).

An inscription in S. Arcot of date August 21, 1172, names as King Rājādhirāja in his 10th year. This agrees with Jacobi's fixture for his accession as in March 1163 (*340 of 1921 ; E. I. xi, 123*).

[These three records shew either that Rājādhirāja was co-regent with Rājarāja II for several years ; or that Rājarāja retired into private life for several years before his death, but was still being honoured as king].

The Kalachūri king Sōmēśvara, or Sōyidēva, reigning. Other grants at the same place during the next twenty years were made by his brother Śankama, and the Yādava king of Śēuṇadēśa, Bhillama V (*E. I. xv. 315*). Another record of Sōmēśvara in N.-W. Mysore, of which the date is uncertain—the details being quite impossible—mentions as local ruler of the Nāgarakhaṇḍa tract (Shikārpūr Taluk) the Kādamba chief Sōyideva, son of Boppa and Śiri-dēvī (*E. C. viii. Sb. 389, 543*). Yet another of the same reign—dated on September 10, 1172, 6th regnal year (shewing

Sōmēśvara's accession to have taken place on or before September 10, 1167)—names, as local ruler of the Baṇavāsi 12000 province, the Kādamba chief Kīrttidēva III. The latter had Chandragutti in Sōrab Taluk for his residence. (*E. C. viii. Sb. 498 ; Mys. A. A. R. 1923, p. 121*).

Cattle raids on a large scale took place in N.-W. Mysore headed by local chiefs, one of whom was the 'lord of Sāntaḷigē.' There was much bloodshed and many death. (*E. C. vii. Hl. 27, 28*).

In W. Mysore Hoyśala Narasimha I reigned (*E. C. vi. Kd. 66*). The date appears to be December 28, but the week day is wrongly given.

A record in central Mysore whose date is correct, corresponding to December 25, 1172, mentions a local chief of Āsandi, Narasimha, son of Barmma and Gangā-dēvī. Barmma's father was Vaijarasa and his mother Vaijalā-dēvī. Vaijarasa lived in the time of Hoyśala Vinayāditya (1040–1100). Several records mention a curious exploit of his. He was engaged in one of the eternal tribal fights or gang-robberies of the time, and in shooting at a foe his arrow pierced his enemy's eye, killing him, and, passing through the skull, killed a flying kite behind him. (*E. C. vi. Tk. 61, 85*).

In S. Mysore the local ruler was Kulōttunga-Chōla-Changāḷva subject to Hoyśala Narasimha I. (*E. C. iv. Hs. 113*).

In Guntur District grants were made in this year by the Vēlanāṇḍu chief Kulōttunga-Rājēndra-Chōḍa II in the 26th year of Rājarāja Chōla II (so in the record). Rājēndra-Chōḍa was son of Gonka II, of whom it is said that he raised his family to great power and ruled the country from Kāḷahasti (in N. Arcot) to Ganjam [This is probably an exaggeration]. Mention is made of Gonka II's wife Sabbāmbikā. (*V. R. ii. Guntur 1, 2 ; 164, 165 of 1897*).

A. D. 1173. Rājādhirāja Chōla II reigning in Tanjore in his 10th year on February 27, 1173. This helps to confirm the date of his accession as in March 1163. (*V. R. ii. Tan. 919 ; 540 of 1904 ; E. I. ix. 211*).

In May 1173, a record shews Rājarāja Chōla II as still living in his 27th year ; and another names his 28th year which began May–June 1173. (*V. R. ii. Guntur 835, 241 ; 181 of 1899*).

In W. Mysore, in March 1173, Hoyśala Narasimha I was still reigning. Also perhaps in May, though in this second record the week-day does not correspond with the given *tithi*. (*E. C. v. Bl, 25 ; Hn, 154*).

July 22, 1173. Date of coronation of Narasimha I's successor Hoyśala-Baḷḷāḷa II (*V. R. i. Bellary 158 ; 495 of 1914 ; E. C. v, Hn. 119 ; vi. Kd. 4, 136 ; v. Ak. 71*). Another inscription intended to commemorate the event bears a date containing so many errors that it cannot be trusted. This is *E. C. v. Bl. 118*. At the end of the year Baḷḷāḷa is named as ruling. (*E. C. v. Ak. 112 ; Cn. 146*).

In April 1173 the Kalachūri king Rāyamurāri-Sōvidēva, or Sōmēśvara in his (so said but perhaps erroneously) 5th year sent two generals with an army to collect the fixed revenue of the Baṇavāsi 12000 province. The army, being encamped on the east side of the Tungabhadra River, was attacked on all sides by the forces of local chiefs, evidently loyal to their old masters, the Western Chāḷukyas, and a sanguinary battle was fought. The record is a *vīrakal* (*E. C. viii. Sb. 139*). An inscription of December 17, 1173, mentions the day as in this king's 7th year, making his accession subsequent to December 17, 1166 (*E. C. vii. Sk. 236*). Another of his 7th year, but with defective date is in the Kistna District. (*V. R. ii. Kistna 297-B*).

In Kurnool District Velanāṇḍu Rājēndra-Chōḍa was ruling.

(*V. R. ii. Kurnool 357 ; 264 of 1905*).

At Kurugōḍu in the north of Bellary District are two inscriptions, published by Dr. Barnett, of which the dates, though neither is quite accurate, correspond to December 6, 1173, and December 24, 1181. Each proclaims as sovereign the W. Chāḷukya prince Sōmēśvara IV, younger son of king Tailapa III, who had been ousted by Bijjala Kalachūri II sixteen years earlier ; and each stands as public proclamation of the people's loyalty to the Chāḷukya throne—a very bold position to adopt ! The local ruler was Rāchamalla II of the Sinda family, son of Irungōḷa Sinda and his wife Ēchalādēvi. Irungōḷa was son of Rāchamalla I. Rāchamalla II's enemies were the 'Pāṇḍyas' (of Uchchangi) on the south and the 'Telugus' (under the Kākatīyas and Chōlas) on the east.

(*E. I. xiv. 265*).

A. D. 1174. Hoyśala Baḷḷāḷa II reigning in W. and Central Mysore.

(*E. C. v. Bl. 59 ; Ak. 69, 138 ; Hn. 29 ; xii. Tp. 62*).

In S. Mysore Kulōttunga-Chōla-Changāḷva was the local ruler. (*E. C. iv. Hs. 111, 112*).

A. D. 1175. Inscriptions of the Kalachūri king Sōmēśvara reigning in N.-W. Mysore in Shikarpur and Sagar Taluks of Shimoga District and in Bellary District. The date of one corresponds to May 2, 1175, while another was earlier in that year. The Bellary record is at Kurugōḍu, the same place where two years earlier other inscriptions declared the supreme sovereign to be Sōmēśvara IV of the W. Chāḷukyas. [The change of the people's allegiance in these two years is remarkable]. (*E. C. viii. Sa. 66 ; vii. Sk. 75 ; V. R. i. Bell. 108 ; 58 of 1904*).

As opposed to this there is an inscription in Honnāḷi Taluk of the same Shimoga District, Mysore, which makes the supreme lord at that place and in this year the Hoyśala Baḷḷāḷa II.

(*E. C. vii. Hl., 45*).

Baḷḷāla II was also reigning in Coorg (*E. C. i. Coorg No. 65*) ; in W. Mysore (*ibid. vi. Kd. 53*); and in S. Mysore (*ibid. iii. Sr. 138, 146*).

Rājādhirāja Chōla II was reigning in Tanjore on July 26, 1175 (*V. R. ii. Tan. 488 ; 451 of 1912*), and in Trichinopoly (*ibid. Trich. 329 ; 731 of 1909*) ; and in Chittoor District where an inscription of this year mentions his vassal Ammaiyappan–Pallavarāyan (of the Śambuvarāyans of Śengēṇi, of whom we hear more later). (*V. R. i. Chittoor, 339, 345 ; 468, 474 of 1905*).

In Guntur District at Sattanapalle, the local ruler was Rājēndra Chōḍa II of Velanāṇḍu, son of Gonka II. (*V. R. ii. Guntur, 815 ; 49 of 1909*).

A. D. 1176. November 16. Inscription in S. Arcot, shewing Rājādhirāja Chōla II reigning in his 14th year (*537 of 1921*).

Hoyśala Baḷḷāḷa II reigning in Kaḍūr District, Mysore (*Mysore, A. A. R. 1923, p. 36*).

Mallidēva-Chola-Mahārāja of Niḍugal ruling locally in N. Mysore from Henjēru.

(*E. C. xii. Pg. 79*).

In Coorg the local ruler was Vīra-Chōla-Kongāḷva. (*E. C. i. Coorg Ins. S. 33*).

At Bhīmavaram in the Godavari District a gift was made to the temple by the Piṭhāpūr chief Narēndra, son of Vijayāditya III of that family. (*V. R. ii. Godav. 33 ; 474 of 1893*).

A. D. 1177. Kalachūri Sōmēśvara reigning in his 10th year on January 31, 1177, in N.-W. Mysore in Sorab Taluk. An attack by a minor chief on the fortress of Gooty[1] (Gutti) is mentioned

[1] Perhaps Chandragutti may be meant.

(*E. C. viii. Sb. 498*). The date is a sound one. Hence his accession was in the year following January 31, 1167. Another record in Bellary District shews him reigning there in this year, when the Sinda Chief Rāchamalla II made a gift (*V. R. i. Bell. 106 ; 56 of 1904*). In N.-W. Mysore also the Kalachūri prince Śankama is mentioned as ruling in an inscription of this year, which states that 'Uddharē' Tailapa-dēva was besieged in Kuppē by a certain Vikramāditya. There was a battle and slaughter (*E. C. viii. Sb., 174*). Śankama may then have been king. Sōmēśvara had probably retired.

In Central, West and South Mysore we have records of this year of Hoyśala Baḷḷāḷa II, reigning over those parts. (*E. C. xii, Ck. 36 ; V. Bl. 86 ; iii, Md. 44 ; v, Ak. 62*).

Rājādhirāja Chola II was reigning on August 18, 1177, in Tanjore.
(*V. R. ii, Tan. 716 ; 428 of 1912*).

Two inscriptions at Bhīmāvaram, Godavari District, shew that the local ruler was the Piṭhāpur chief Vishṇuvardhana-Mallapa III, then in his 3rd year.
(*V. R. ii, Godav. 45, 46 ; 486, 487 of 1893*).

A record at Kurugōḍ, Bellary District, confirms the fact that the people of that place were now compelled to recognize the Kalachūri king as their overlord (*see above s. v., A.D. 1175*) Kalachūri Śankama, brother of king Sōmēśvara, was ruling there as Viceroy. One of his feudatories, the Sinda Rāchamalla II, made a gift to a temple.
(*V. R. i, Bell. 108 ; 58 of 1904*).

In N. Mysore the Noḷamba chief Vijaya-Pāṇḍya ruled. (*E. C. xi, Dg. 86*).

A. D. 1178. On January 21, 1178, Rājādhirāja Chōla II was reigning in Cuddapah District. By July his reign had ended. (*V. R. i, Cudd. 785 ; 571 of 1907 ; E. I. x, 126*).

The accession of the Chōla king Kulōttunga-Chōla III took place on either 6th, 7th, or 8th, July 1178. He reigned till June 1216. (*E. I. iv, 216, 262 ; viii. 260*).

A record of date May 4, 1178, in N.-W. Mysore mentions the 3rd year of Kalachūri Śankama. It must be taken, then, that his brother Sōmēśvara ceased to reign, and Śankama succeeded him on some day in the year following May 4, 1175. The Kadamba chief Kīrttidēva III was ruling locally. (*E. C. viii, Sb. 431*).

In Central Mysore Hoyśala Baḷḷāḷa II ruled. An inscription of date early in 1178 relates that, apparently owing to some disaffection on the part of Vijaya Pāṇḍya, the ruler of the Noḷambavāḍi province (whose position was most difficult, and who may have definitely accepted as overlord the Kalachūri king and have abandoned any connection with the Hoyśalas) Baḷḷāḷa took the field, attacked and captured the Pāṇḍya's fortress Uchchangi, and seized the person of Vijaya *alias* Kāma, Pāṇḍya (*E. C. iv, Ng. 70*). He restored Vijaya Paṇḍya.
(*E. C. vii, Tk. 10 ; see also ibid. v. Bl. 137*).

There are records of this Vijaya-Pāṇḍya, of this year, in Bellary District.
(*V. R. i, Bell. 176, 201 ; 445, 478 of 1914*).

Hoyśala Baḷḷāḷa II was also supreme in Central and West Mysore and in Anantapur District.
(*E. C. v, Cn. 209 ; Bl. 83, vi. Cm. 21, 22 ; V. R. i. Anant. 97 ; 83 of 1912*).

The Amarāvati country on the Krishna river was now ruled by Kōṭa Kēta II.
(*V. R. ii. Guntur 617 ; 251 of 1897*).

In Vizagapatam District the Kalinga-Gaṅga King Anantavarman Chōḍa-Ganga was reigning.
(*V. R. iii. Vizag. 2 ; 363 of 1905*).

A. D. 1179. Inscriptions of the year 1179 shew Kalachūri Śankama *alias* Niśśankamalla, reigning in N.-W. Mysore (*E. C. vii, Sk. 96, 237*). Another of October 1, 1179, states that that date fell in his 4th regnal year, and makes his accession after October 1, 1175.

(*E. I. xii, 329 ; and xiii, 36.*)

Hoyśala Baḷḷāḷa II ruled central Mysore. An inscription records another violent outbreak when two chiefs attacked one another and fought a battle. (*E. C. iv, Ng. 15 ; xii. Tp. 35.*)

At Koppanāḍu on the Tungabhadra River, N.-W. Mysore, a local chief Bhujabala-Vīra-Sāntara was ruling. His wife Bāchalā-dēvī is mentioned. (*E. C. vi, Kp. 14.*)

From this year forward till A.D. 1210 we hear a great deal of the powerful chief of the Śengēṇi family Ammaiyappan-Śambuva-rāyan, who ruled parts of North and South Arcot under the Chōla king. He has a number of *birudas*, e.g., 'Gaṇḍa-sūriyan', 'Vīra-minḍan', 'Attimallan', 'Pānḍi', 'Rājarāja', 'Vikrama-Chōla', 'Kannuḍai-Perumāḷ.' (*V. R. i, S. Arcot, 373, 374, 997 ; N. Arcot, 341, 26, 414, 422 ; 222, 223, 190 of 1904 ; 301 of 1907 ; 405 of 1905 ; 107, 115 of 1900.*)

A. D. 1180. Four inscriptions in this year of Kulōttunga Chōla III ; the first three on February 13 and 28, and May 15, 1180, in Tanjore, the fourth in Chittor District. The last of these gives the name of a Ganga chief, Śīyaganga-Amarābharaṇa, lord of Kuvalālapura' (Kōlār in E. Mysore), whose wife was Āriyā-Piḷḷai and whose daughter gave a grant to the temple at Kāḷahasti. A later record in 1204 5 calls him 'Tiruvēgambam-Uḍaiyān.' A record of A.D. 1224–25 adds to his name the titles 'Uttama-Chōla' and 'Akaḷanka.' The *Nannūl* was composed by Bhavanandin under his patronage.

It is noteworthy that this last inscription is at Tiruvallam in Chittoor District, and that in 1185–6 and 1188–9 at the same place inscriptions remain mentioning members of the Śambuvarāyan family of Śengēṇi. The latter family seem to have been in possession of the place (*see s. v., A. D. 1179–80*). The Ganga chief was probably a visitor to Tiruvallam.

(*V. R. ii. Tanjore, 157, 166, 715 ; 166, 175 of 1908; 427 of 1912 ; E. I. xi. 123, 124 ; V. R. i. Chittoor, 64, 235 ; 195 of 1892 ; 551 of 1906 ; S. I. I. iii. 122, 207.*)

Hoyśala Baḷḷāḷa II was ruling Central, West, East, South-West, and South-East Mysore. Again a record of cattle robberies and resultant deaths. One inscription relates to a grant by him to Brahmans of a village in the Baṇavāsi province, proving his rule over that country.

(*E. C. iv. Ng. 57 ; v. Bl. 20 ; ix. Cp. 172 ; vi. Cm. 77 ; x. Gd. 41.*)

On July 24, 1180, the Kalachūri prince Āhavamalla's name occurs in an inscription on a stone, so dated, in the Madras Museum (*V. R. ii. Madras 229 ; 292 of 1905*). It is in Kanarese characters. Where it came from is not apparent.

At Drākshārāma the Velanānḍu chief Rājēndra Chōḍa II was ruling.

(*V. R. ii. Godavari, 319 ; 413 of 1893.*)

In N.-W. Mysore the Sinda Rāja Īśvara I was ruling locally under Kalachūri Śankama.

(*E. C. vii. Hl. 50 ; viii. Sb. 43.*)

A. D. 1181. Inscription at Kurugōḍu, published by Dr. Barnett, of date December 24, 1181, mentioning the W. Chāḷukya king Somēśvara (*see above s. v., A. D. 1173–74*).

Kalachūri Āhavamalla's 3rd year is mentioned in an inscription at Baḷḷigāmve in N.-W. Mysore, the date of which = August 9, 1181. It makes his accession as in the year following August 9, 1178. (*E. C. vii. Sk., 119.*)

Hoyśala Baḷḷāḷa II was reigning in Central and South Mysore.

(*E. C. v. Cn. 161 ; iii., Tn. 106.*)

Kulōttunga Chōla III was reigning in S. Arcot on December 11, in Trichinopoly, on September 27, and in Tanjore on October 4, 1181.

(*176 of 1911 ; 81 of 1920 ; 454 of 1912 ; V. R. ii. Tan. 491.*)

Over part of Bellary District ruled (December 25, 1181) the minor chief of the Gutta family of Guttavoḷal who claimed descent from the ancient Guptas. He is here called 'Lord of Ujjain.' This was Vikramāditya II. (*215 of 1918.*)

A. D. 1182. Hoyśala Baḷḷāḷa II ruling in Central, South-West and S.-E. Mysore (*E. C. v. Cn. 150, 254 ; Bl. 137 ; iv. Ng. 32 ; ix. Cp. 160*). His queen Bammalādēvī is mentioned; and his capture of Uchchangi, and the submission to him of its ruler the Noḷamba chief Vijaya Pāṇḍya *alias* Kāma (above, *s. v. A.D. 1178*). (*E. C. ii. Sr. Bel. 124.*)

Kulōttunga Chōla III reigning in Tanjore in his 4th year.

(*V. R. ii. Tan. 774, 1550 ; 1 of 1899 ; 415 of 1904 ; 526 of 1920 ; E. I. viii., 264.*)

Amarāvati on the Krishna ruled by Kōṭa Kēta II, whose pedigree is given in an inscription on a pillar in that place. Buddhist worship at the old stupa was still maintained and Kēta II gave grants in its support (*E. I. vi. 146*). In some other records of the same year Kēta II is stated to have made grants of land. His father Bhīma, and his mother Sabbāmbikā are mentioned. Also his elder brother Kōṭa-Chōḍa. (*V. R ii. Guntur 623, 630, 635, 868–872 ; 257, 264, 269 of 1897.*)

A. D. 1183. Hoyśala Baḷḷaḷa ruling in West Mysore. (*E. C. v. Ak. 79, 88.*)

Kulōttunga III, with the title 'Parakēśari-Vīra-Rājēndra-Chōla' reigning in Tanjore (*V. R. ii. Tan. 167, 169 ; 176, 178 of 1908 ; E. I. xi. 124*). And in Trichinopoly.

(*V. R. iii. Trich. 331 ; 733 of 1909. E. I. xi., 244.*)

At Bhīmavaram, Godavari District, the Piṭhāpūr chief (of E. Chāḷukya descent) Mallappa *alias* Vishṇuvardhana ruling. The date of the beginning of his rule has been held doubtful (*see pedigree notes*). This inscription goes to support the view that it began in A.D. 1174.

(*V. R. Godav. 38 ; 479 of 1893.*)

[About this year a chief named Bamma, or Brahma, succeeded in restoring the W. Chāḷukya sovereignty, and placing Sōmēśvara IV, on the throne of his fathers.]

A. D. 1184. Hoyśala Baḷḷāḷa II reigning in W. Mysore (*E. C. vi. Tk. 15.*)

A. D. 1185. Kulōttunga-Chōla III reigning in Tanjore on January 15, 1185, in his 7th year (*V. R. ii. Tan. 827 ; 386 of 1908 ; E. I. xi. 125*). And in South Arcot on October 15 in his 8th year (*391 of 1921*). And on December 25, in Tanjore in his 8th year (*V. R. ii. Tan. 183 ; 40 of 1914*). Also in Chittoor in his 8th year (*V. R. i. Chit. 22 ; 57 of 1907*) In another of the same regnal year, in N. Arcot, mention is made of the Sengēṇi chief Miṇḍan-Attimallan-Śambuvaraiyan

(*S.I.I. iii. 120.*)

The W. Chāḷukya king Sōmēśvara IV reigning in Anantapur District (*28 of 1917*). [The people of Anantapur now disavowed Kalachūri domination.]

Hoyśala Baḷḷāḷa II ruled large parts of Mysore in the West, South and East of the country. (*E.C. iii, Md. 62 A ; v. Ak, 39, 61, 127 ; vi, Tk, 20 ; Cm. 78 ; Ml, 45, 48 ; Mys. A. R. 1923, p. 41.*)

Kākatiya Rudra I gave a village in this year near Koṇḍapalle, Kistna District, to a temple at Kurnool. This proves that he was reigning as king on the Krishna River, but it does not prove that he was supreme in Kurnool. (*V. R. ii. Kurn. 365 : 273 of 1905.*)

The Velanāṇḍu chief Prithivīśvara's mother Jayāmbikā gave away a village in the Prōlunāḍu, N. of the Godavari River. The pedigree of the family is given, and Dr. Hulzsch published this in 1895 with his examination of the inscription (*E. I. iv. 32; ff.*). The Government epigraphist's note on it is in *E. R.* for 1917, p. 119. (*V. R. ii. Godavari 63 ; 490 of 1893.*)

In part of S. Mysore the Changāḷva chief Kulōttunga-Chōla-Changāḷva ruled locally. (*E. C. iv.Hs., 13.*)

A. D. 1186. Hoyśala Baḷḷaḷā II ruling Central Mysore from Dorasamudra. His capture of Uchchangi is mentioned; and he is stated to have fought a bloody battle against the Ummattūr chief in the South of Mysore. He encouraged agriculture and caused tanks to be dug for storage of water. (*E. C. v. Bl. 175 ; Cn. 152.*)

In the Velanāṇḍu tract, Kistna District, according to an inscription at Piṭhāpur, the local ruler was Prithivīśvara-Gonka Raja. The date = Ś. 1108. (*E. I. iv. 32.*)

A record of Kulōttunga-Chōla III at Chidambaram. The date is the 88th day of his 9th regnal year = October 2 to 4, 1186. [It continues the story of the war when the Singhalese under Lankāpura invaded S. India, which ended with Vira Pāṇḍya being placed on the throne of Madura about the year 1167. Between that date and 1186, probably about 1182, Kulōttunga espoused the cause of Vikrama Pāṇḍya, son of Kulaśēkhara who had been driven from Madura by Lankāpura and the Singhalese. He took the field and fought a battle at Tiruvēḍagam near Madura against the son of Vira Pāṇḍya (now king) who was aided by a body of Singhalese that had been apparently left behind when Lankāpura retired. Kulōttunga defeated these allies, and the inscription says that the islanders were driven into the sea. He then entered Madura, deposed Vīra Pāṇḍya and placed Vikrama Pāṇḍya on the throne so far up to his 9th year. Vīra Pāṇḍya returned to the fight later, and fought Kulōttunga at Neṭṭur but was beaten again. From later inscriptions of his 11th and 19th years we learn that the Kēraḷa king also had joined Vīra Pāṇḍya and that after the allies' defeat, both the Paṇḍya and Kerala kings were forced to submit. Kulōttunga dismissed Vira Pāṇḍya and took his young wife into his harem ; but he forgave the Kēraḷa king and honoured him. Ever since then Kulōttunga Chola III is described in his records as the king 'who took Madura and the crowned head of the Pāṇḍya.'. (*V. R. i. S. Arcot 28 ; 457 of 1902 ; S.I.I. iii. 210 See also the inscription at Śrīrangam of November 12, 1196 S.I I. iii. 217; and V. R. ii. Tanjore 774; 1 of 1899.*)

A. D. 1187. Four records of Kulōttunga Chōla III in this year ; on May 2, May 4 and July 18 at Tanjore, and on October 24 in S. Arcot. (*V. R. ii. Tan. 184, 1004; 41 of 1914 ; 393 of 1907 ; 242 of 1917 ; 425 of 1921 ; E. I. x. 127.*)

Hoyśala Baḷḷāḷa II was ruling in Central Mysore. (*E. C. xii Ck. 9.*)

Sōmēśvara IV now W. Chāḷukya king, reigning in N.-W. Mysore. The Kādamba chief Koṇḍama ruling the Baṇavāśi province under him (*E. C. vii. Sb. 47*). The inscription records cattle-raids and deaths. (*See note above s. v., A.D. 1185–86.*)

In Ganjam the Kalinga king Anantavarama-Rājarāja II was reigning in his 22nd and 23rd years (Ś. 1109, 1110), shewing his accession to have been in A.D. 1166–67. (*V. R. i. Ganjam 331, 416 ; 180, 265 of 1896.*)

A. D. 1188. Kulōttunga Chōla III reigning in his 11th year in N. Arcot. The local chief was Śengēṇi-Ammaiyappan-Kaṇṇuḍai-Perumāḷ *alias* Vikrama-Chola-Śambuvarāyan (*S. I. I. i. No. 132'; iii. No. 61*). Also in Trichinopoly. One Kulōttunga's record at Chidambaram, whose date = November 1–3, 1188, is mentioned above under the remarks regarding the year 1186–87.

It is an inscription of his 11th year, December 15, 1188 (*82 of 1920*), and on December 28, in Tanjore. (*226 of 1917.*)

Hoyśala Baḷḷāḷa II ruling in West and Central Mysore. One of the inscriptions states that the W. Chāḷukya Jagadēkamalla was his suzerain; but this must, so it would seem, be an error, as Jagadēkamalla's brother Sōmēśvara was now reigning king (*E. C. v. Ak. 22, 90; xii, Ck. 20; Mys. A. A. R. 1923, p. 31*). The last of these records gives a date, corresponding to September 30, 1188.

In N.-W. Mysore the Kādamba chief Kāva, or Kāma-dēva, of Hāngal was locally ruling. (*E. C. viii. Sb. 472.*)

In Travancore (Vēṇāḍ) Vīra-Udaiya-Mārtaṇḍa reigned. On November 26, 1188. (*T. A. S. iv. 22.*)

A. D. 1189. Hoyśala Baḷḷāla II, reigning in S.-W. Mysore. His queen Umādēvi is mentioned (*E. C. v. Ak. 57, 93; Ag. 79, 81*). The first of these records credits him with extensive territory, viz., the Noḷambavāḍi, Baṇavāśi, Halāsigē, Huligērē and Beḷvola districts besides the whole of the Gangavāḍi 96,000 country. He was ruling Central Mysore (*E. C. v. Cn. 179; xii. S. i. 104*). On the other hand the W. Chāḷukya king Sōmēsvara IV is said in another record to be ruling the Kuntaḷa-Vishaya, and that Kāmadēva of the Kadambas of Hāngal ruled the Baṇavāśi and Hāngal tracts under him [Note the contradictory assertions of overlordship]. Kāma-dēva's three sons, are mentioned,—Barmma, Sōma and Malla,—by his wife Kālalā, or, as sometimes called, Kētalā-dēvī. Kāma-dēva is said in the inscription, to be grandson of Kīrtti, son of Śāntavarma; which would imply that Kīrtti was another name of Taila II (*E. C. viii. Sb. 179*). Another feudatory of Śōmēśvara's in N.-W. Mysore was the Sinda chief Mallidēva. (*E. C. vii Hl. 46.*)

The Śengēṇi chief Attimallan-Vikrama-Chōla-Śambuvaraiyan was locally ruling in North Arcot District. (*V. R. i. N. Arcot, 26; 405 of 1905; S. I. I. i. 136.*)

More cattle robberies and murders in N.-W. Mysore. (*E. C. vii. Hl. 85.*)

The Sāntara chief Śānteya-dēva gave a grant in Shimoga District, Mysore, in reward to a man for bravery in fight. (*E. C.. viii. Sa. 95.*)

An inscription at Mutgi mentions Kalachūri Bhillama. His relationships to the known Kalachūri princes is not stated. The date is December 25, 1189. (*E. I. xv. 26.*)

[The power of the W. Chāḷukyas, ruined in 1156–57 by Kalachūri Bijjala, was now almost at an end. The Yādāvas of Dēvagiri gained the upper hand, and after Chāḷukya Sōmēśvara IV the latter's dynasty ceased to exist. It fell before the attacks of the Yādavas, the strength of the ambitious Hoyśala, Baḷḷāḷa II, and the growth of the Kākatīya kingdom on the East.]

A. D. 1190. On July 2, 1190, Kulōttunga Chōlla III was reigning in South Arcot in his '13th year' (mistake for 12th year—very natural as the 13th year began July 6–8 that year). (*563 of 1921; E. I. v. 199; S. I. I. iii. 83.*)

In Kulōttunga's 13th year two chiefs bound themselves by a solemn covenant, engraved on a temple wall, to be faithful to the Śengēṇi chief Ammayaippan–Śambuvaraiyan, who is the same as Attimallan-Vikrama-Chōla Śambuvarāyan. (*V. R. i. S. Arcot, 374; 223 of 1904.*)

A. D. 1191. [In 1190 or 1191 the Yādavas of Dēvagiri had pressed southwards and finally crushed the W. Chāḷukya monarchy. Baḷḷāḷa II, Hoyśala, competing with them for the possession of the Chāḷukya dominions, pressed northwards from Mysore, and met the Yādava armies on the banks of the Mālprabha and Krishna rivers, to the north of the Dharwar district. (For a summary see

Ancient India, pp. 251–53.) Successful battles were fought by Baḷḷāḷa at a number of places including Hāngal, Kurugōḍu, Guttivoḷal, Uddharē, at Soraṭur near Gadag, Yelburga, etc. Gadag passed into his hands. (There is an inscription of his there, of date November 21, 1192 ; *I. A. ii. 300.*) On June 23, 1191, an inscription at this place mentions Yādava Bhillamā as supreme (*E. I. iii. 217*). The fall of the fortress of Lakkuṇḍi in Dharwar District into the hands of Baḷḷaḷa apparenty settled the matter. Henceforward the Mālprabha River became the boundary between the two ruling powers, the Yādavas in the north and the Hoysalas in the south—the Western Chāḷukyas and Kalachūris disappear from history. The Noḷambavāḍi province was after this governed directly by the Hoysala king.] Baḷḷāḷa now assumed full imperial titles as an independent sovereign. Mr. Krishnaswami Ayyangar gives a list of these in his *Ancient India*, p. 252.

There are a number of inscriptions of Hoysala Baḷḷāḷa II of this year in Mysore. (*E. C. iii Sr. 57 ; Md, 106 ; iv. Ng. 93 ; Yl. 12 ; v, Bl. 188 ; vi. Mg. 28 ; Kd. 156, 157 ; 38 ; ix Kn. 26.*)

On April 4 and 19 Kulōttunga Chōla III reigning in Conjeeveram. (*620, 390 of 1919.*)

An inscription in N.-W. Mysore of Kāma-dēva of the Kadambas of Hāngal mentions the battle of Uddharē. (*E.C. viii, Sb. 439.*)

A. D. 1192. More records of Hoysala Baḷḷāḷa II in Mysore, and one at Gadag.

(*E.C. ix. Cp. 124 ; iii. Ml. 27, 29 ; v. Ak, 35 ; E.I. vi. 89.*)

An inscription in Cuddapah District, couched in boastful strain, mentions as ruling locally the Telugu-Chōḍa chief Nallasiddha Chōla Mahārāja. He is asserted to have levied tribute from the Chōla king at Kānchī. [Regarding this chief Nallasiddha, see pedigree of Telugul-Chōda chiefs and note attached.] (*V.R. i. Cudd. 495 ; 483 of 1906*)

Kulōttunga-Chōla III reigning in Tanjore. (*490 of 1922*)

An inscription at Kāḷahasti in the 15th year of Kulōttunga Chōla III mentions a gift by Vīra-Rākshasa Yādava-Raja. (*V.R. i Chittoor 66 ; 197 of 1892*)

[He appears to have been chief of Kāḷahasti, and is mentioned in several records. In one of A.D. 1225 he is called 'Śaśikula-Chāḷukki-Vīra-Narasimha-Yādava-Rāja,' and in another of the same year 'Simha *alias* Vīra-Rākshasa-Yādava, son of Yādava-Rāja Tirukāḷatti-dēva.' Another of his *biruḍas* is 'Chāḷukya Nārāyaṇa'; another 'Tani-ninṛu-Venṛa'; another 'ghaṭṭiya-dēva." Both father and son had the title 'Vengi-Vallabha.' Thus he appears to have claimed descent from the Eastern Chāḷukya family. His father must not be confused with members of the Telugu-Chōḍa chiefs, several of whom were called 'Tirukāḷatti,' or 'Tikka', and who ruled further to the north. This Tiru-Kāḷatti is so named from the name of his residence.[1] 'Kaḷatti' = Kāḷahasti. (*V. R. i. Chittoor 69, 101, 102, 122, 111, 120, 139; 197, 200 of 1904; 93, 94, 172, 181–183, 200 of 1903.*)]

[In this year came to the throne the Eastern Kalinga, or Kalinga Ganga king Aṇiyanka-Bhīma. (*E.I. vi. 198.*)]

A. D. 1193. Records of Kulōttunga Chōla III in Tanjore on May 27 and August 23, 1193, and in Chingleput. The last of these mentions the local chief Panchanadivāṇan-Nīlagangaraiyan, 'son of Gaṇda-Gōpāla' (see pedigree, 'Nilaganga-araiyan ').

(*487, 489 of 1922 ; V.R. i. Ching. 858, 809, 870 ; 2, 14 of 1911 ; 279 of 1897.*)

Hoysala Baḷḷāḷa II reigning in Mysore and in Bellary District, where he resided at Bāgali (*E.C. vii, Sk. 105 ; E.R. 1903–4, p. 10*). He paid a visit to the Baṇavaśi province in this year. The

[1] It is hardly likely that the fact of residence is the cause of the name. Tirukāḷatti-dēva must have been his name irrespective of his identification or otherwise with the Telugu-Choḍas of the name.—*Editor.*

province was under the local rule of Ekkalarasa (probably the son of Nanniya-Ganga of the W. Ganga family). An inscription in N.-W. Mysore mentions local raids and slaughter. *(E.C. viii, Sb. 30.)*

A certain Madurāntaka-Pattapi-Chōla *alias* Rāja-Ghaṇḍa-Gopala *alias* Ranganātha is mentioned as having granted some land in Nellore District. His suzerain was the Chōla king. The chief may be Eṛṛasiddha or his cousin (see Telugu-Chōda pedigree).

(V.R. ii. Nellore, 201 ; B. and V.C., p. 423.)

About this time the Chōla king,—who is named 'Kōnērinmai-Koṇḍān' in the inscription in question, and is probably Kulōttunga III, in his 15th year (which if so would be A.D. 1193–94),—extended to his subjects some privileges which they had hitherto been prevented from enjoying by the tyrannical rule of their masters. Amongst others they were now permitted to wear sandals when using the roads, and were allowed to plaster the walls of their mud houses.

(S. I.I. iii. 47 ; E.R. 1904–5, § 43.)

A. D. 1194. Kulōttunga Chōḷa III reigning in Trichinopoly and Tanjore on January 1, March 9 and 31 in his 16th year. *(V. R. iii. Trich., 271 ; Tan. 859, 1239, 654 ; 503 of 1912 ; 418 of 1908 ; 662 of 1909 ; 43 of 1906 ; E. I. ix. 213 ; xi. 125, 246.)*

Hoyśala Baḷḷāḷa II was reigning in most parts of Mysore, including the N.-W. In the Kaḍūr District an inscription states that he had 'raised the north' and laid siege to a town called 'Dusthe' (?) and fought a battle in which deaths occurred, which are commemorated in the record. Another inscription in the same part mentions a local fight—cattle robbery and deaths. He was also reigning in Bellary District, where he had laid siege to Kurugōḍu.

(E. C. vi, Mg. 4, 5 ; Bl. 204 ; Kd. 77 ; v, Ak. 118 ; vii, Sk. 138 ; ix, Ma. 9 ; 217 of 1918 ; Mys. A. A. R, 1923, p. 31.)

A. D. 1195. Kulōttunga Chola III's 17th year, February 13. Inscription near Pondicherry. *(V. R. iii, French Territory 23 ; 395 of 1902 ; E. I. vii, 79.)* Another in his 18th year, November 18, in Tanjore. *(V. R. ii, Tan. 1546 ; 485 of 1912.)*

Hoyśala Baḷḷāḷa II, on the day of a solar eclipse—October 5, 1195—was at Erambaragē, N. of the Tungabhadra River. Erambaragē = Yelburga *(E. C. iii, Tn. 31)*. More cattle raids and deaths this year in W. Mysore *(E. C. vi, Cm. 157, 158)*. Baḷḷāḷa II is said to be residing in his capital 'after having raised the north' *(E. C. vi, Cm. 54, 55 ; v, Ak, 150)*. One inscription of this year mentions Baḷḷāḷa's battles with the Yādava forces from Dēvagiri *(above s. v., A.D. 1191)*. His chief enemy is here stated to be Jaitrapāla who was son of Bhillama. Baḷḷāḷa's capture of Lokkiguṇḍi is mentioned. *(E. C. v, Ak. 5.)*

In N.-W. Mysore the Sinda Rāja Mallidēva ruled locally. *(E. C. vii, Hl. 51.)*

About the Godavari River the Kōnamaṇḍaḷa chiefs Mallidēva and Manma-Satya II ruled locally. They made a grant to the temple at Pithāpur of land near Drākshārāma, the family pedigree is given. *(V. R. ii, Godavary 64 ; 491 of 1893 ; E. I. iv. 83.)*

A. D. 1196. Inscription at Conjeeveram of Kulōttunga-Chōla III's 18th year, date = February 27, 1196 *(558 of 1919)*. Also on September 2 in his 19th year in Tanjore ; and on October 15 and November 12 in Trichinopoly *(V. R. ii, Tan. 504 ; iii, Trich. 129, 477 ; 397 of 1902 ; 47 of 1913 ; 66 of 1892 ; 467 of 1922 ; E. I. vii, 173 ; iv, 219 ; S. I. I., iii, 217)*. The last of these gives a list of his exploits up to date. In Chittoor District, which was part of the Chōla kingdom, the local chief was 'Madhurāntaka-Pottapi-Chōla' perhaps the same as the Gaṇḍagōpāla chief Eṛṛa-Siddha. His wife gave a gift to a temple in this year. *(V. R. i. Chittoor 67 ; 198 of 1892.)*

Hoyśala Baḷḷāḷa II was reigning in Mysore—probably now over the whole of it. One of these records says that he had 'subdued the north as far as the Krishna River.' (*E. C. v, Ak. 16, 104, 178 ; iv, Gu. 27 ; ix, Cp. 72*). One inscription shews that his son Narasimha II was governing in S.-E. Mysore for his father (*E. C. ix, Kn. 67*). There were great local disturbances in the country, tribes fighting against their neighbours as usual. This time a *vīrakal* commemorates a man who died when a regular war took place between the people of the Tagu-nāḍu and those of the Kodagi-nāḍu or Coorg. A battle was fought at Bāḷḷeyahaḷḷi. (*E. C. vi, Cm. 83.*)

July 8, 1196. Date of an inscription in Tinnevelly District of the Pāṇḍya prince Jaṭāvarman Kulaśekhara I, also called 'Rājagambhīra' in his 7th year [He may have succeeded Vikrama Pāṇḍya. Vikrama Pāṇḍya who was placed on the throne of Madura by Kulōttunga Chola III, or he may have been ruling locally a portion of the Pāṇḍya kingdom]. The record proves that the last possible day for the beginning of his rule was July 8, 1190. (*337 of 1916.*)

[The *Mahāwaṁśa* (ch. lxxx) relates some tragic events in Ceylon. About A.D. 1186 the powerful king Parākrama Bāhu I ceased to reign over the island and was succeeded by Vijaya Bāhu who was murdered after a year's reign. The throne was usurped by Mahindu who was killed, after five days, by Kīrtti Niśśanka of the Kalinga race who himself seized the throne. About this year 1196–97 he was murdered. Two royal princes tried to hold the throne, but were ejected after about three months and murdered by a certain Chōḍa-Ganga, nephew of Kīrtti-Niśśanka. Then Chōḍa-Ganga was blinded and deposed, and Līlāvatī, widow of Parākrama Bāhu I, was raised to the throne.

A. D. 1197. Kulōttunga Chola III reigning in Nellore District.

(*V. R. ii. Nell. 527 ; B. and V. C. 824 ; 197 of 1894.*)

Hoyśala Baḷḷāḷa II in Mysore. The second of these records states that Narasimha II, Baḷḷāḷa's son, had defeated the Pāṇḍya, *i.e.*, the Pāṇḍya of Uchchangi who was defeated by Baḷḷāḷa II. (*E. C. v. Ak. 23 ; vi. Tk. 45 ; viii. Sb. 514, 515.*)

In Kulōttunga Chola III's 20th year inscriptions shew that the territorial chiefs subordinate to him were vying with one another in increasing each his power over his neighbour. In one of these, two chiefs, Karikāla-Chola-Āḍaiyūr-Nāḍāḷvān and Śengēṇi-Ammaiyappan-Attimallan *alias* Vikrama-Chōla-Śambuvaraiyan (*above s. v., A. D. 1179*) form a solemn alliance, which is engraved on the temple wall at Chengama in N. Arcot, pledging themselves, in association with Viḍukād-aḷagiya-Perumāḷ, chief of Tagaḍūr in Salem District, to support one another and never to ally themselves with certain other chiefs, of whom Śiyaganga was one.

(*V. R. i. N. A. 414, 422 ; 107, 115 of 1900.*)

At Amarāvati on the Krishna River Kōṭa Kēta II was ruling.

(*V. R. ii. Guntur, 627 ; 261 of 1897.*)

In Travancore Vīra Ravivarman reigned. (*V. R. iii. Trav. 125.*)

A. D. 1198. Kulōttunga-Chōla III reigning in Tanjore on May 3 (*V. R. ii. Tan. 1565 ; 430 of 1904*). And in Trichinopoly at Ratnagiri in November.

(*V. R. iii. Trich. 117 ; 185 of 1914 ; 468 of 1922.*)

Hoyśala Baḷḷāḷa II in Mysore. His defeat of the 'Śeuṇa,' *i.e.*, the Dēvagiri-Yādava king is mentioned. The inscription is mostly concerned with the Ganga chief Ekkala, whose pedigree as given here is entered amongst those of the Western Gangas in the table below (*E. C. viii. Sb. 140 ; v. Bl. 77 ; vii. Sk. 173*). More cattle-raids and murders are mentioned.

In N.-W. Mysore, the Kādamba chief Kāma-dēva ruled locally. (*E. C. viii. Sb. 478.*)

A. D. 1199. In this year the Kākatīya king of Warangal, Gaṇapati who had a very long reign, came to the throne *(See E. R. 1906, § 43)*. An inscription at Bahāl of the Dēvagiri-Yādava king Singhaṇa states that Gaṇapati was 'liberated,' apparently from some confinement, by Singhaṇa's father, Jaitrapāla I, and his kingdom handed over to him. This inscription is of the year A.D. 1222. The Paithān copper-plate record of 1271 confirms it.

(*E. I. iii. 110 ; I. A. xiv. 316 ; xxi, 198.*)

Hoyśala Baḷḷāḷa II reigning in Mysore. (*E. C. iv. Ng. 47 ; viii. Sb. 402 ; xii. Tp. 92.*)

The chief of Tagaḍūr in Salem District Viḍukād-aḷagiya-Perumāḷ (*see above in 1197–98*), son of Rājarāja Adigan (*see pedigree of Adigaimān chiefs*), set up two figures of Yakshas on the Tirumalai Hill. These figures had been set up in long time past by the king or chief Eḷini *alias* Yavanikā, and had been saved from ruin by Rājarāja Adigan *alias* 'Vēgan.' Their territory included parts of the country about the Pālār, Southern Peṇṇār and Kāvērī rivers.

(*E. I. vi. 331-333 ; V. R. ii. Salem 205 ; 8 of 1900 ; E. R. 1906, p. 74 ; 1911, p. 58.*)

In Vizagapatam town a gift was made to a temple by the Velanāṇḍu chief Kulōttunga-Prithivīśvara. (*V. R. iii. Vizag. 61 ; 97 of 1909.*)

[For a note about the state of South India in the latter half of the 12th century A.D., see the remarks of the Government Epigraphist in his Report for 1918–19, p. 98, § 21.]

A. D. 1200. Kulōttunga-Chōla III reigning in Conjeeveram. (*348 of 1919.*)

Hoyśala-Baḷḷāḷa II reigning in Mysore (*E. C. v. Bl., 140 ; vii., Ci., 37 ; iv. Kr. 47 ; xii., Tp. 123 bis*). Another *vīrakal* erected, following a cattle-raid and consequent massacre of villagers.

(*E. C. iii. Md. 23.*)

There was a very severe famine this year in Tanjore District, many people dying of starvation. (*V. R. ii. Tanjore 809 ; 86 of 1911*)

A. D. 1201. Kulōttunga Chōla III 'Kō-nērinmai-koṇḍān' reigning in Chingleput in his 24th year; (August 22. 1201, *232 of 1922*.) And at Karuvūr, Coimbatore District. (*S. I. I. iii.p. 43.*)

At Bezwada on the Krishna river on April 19, 1201, the Nāthavāḍi chief Rudra, brother-in-law of the Kākatīya king Gaṇapathi, was local ruler. (*V. R. ii. Kistna 31 ; E. I. vi., 159.*)

The Prōlunāḍu tract, N. of the Godavari river was ruled in his 9th year by a member of the E. Chāḷukya family, Vishṇuvardhana. He belonged to the Piṭhāpur branch (*E. I. iv., 230 ; V. R. ii. Godav. 52 ; 455 of 1893.*) The record which is at Sarpāvaram, is dated Ś. 1123. It makes his accession as in A.D. 1193-94. Another grant by Mallapa-Vishṇuvardhana III of the Piṭhāpūr branch, probably the same chief, granting the village of Guḍivāḍa in the Prolunāḍu tract to the temple at Piṭhāpūr, is dated June 16, 1202. (*V. R. ii. Godav. 65 ; 492 of 1893 ; E. I. iv. 226.*)

Inscription in Cuddapah District of the Telugu-Chōḍa chief Nalla Siddha, who married Nukkama. Nalla Siddha is called 'Madurāntaka Pottapi Chōda.' He may be the same as Betta II (*see Gaṇḍa-Gōpāla pedigree*). (*V. R. i. Cuddapah 815 ; 601 of 1907.*)

A. D. 1202. For the Piṭhāpūr chief's inscription of June 16, 1202, *see note s.v., A.D. 1201.*

Kulōttunga Chola III reigning in Tanjore on April 26, 1202 (*476 of 1922*) and on December 30, 1202. (*V. R. ii. Tan. 620, 621 ; 380, 381 of 1907 ; E. I. x. 130.*)

Hoyśala-Baḷḷāḷa II reigning in Mysore. Pedigree given of his family from Eṛeyanga. Vishṇuvardhana is said 'by his power to have become first to the Ganga kingdom'—an allusion probably to his capture of Talakāḍ, by which he established his supremacy in Mysore (*E. C. xii., Tp., 128; also E. C. iii., Ml., 10 ; vi., Cm , 104 ; Kd., 148*). In the last of these his feudatory the

Ganga chief of Āsandi, Narasimha, gave a grant. Narasimha was the hero of the arrow exploit. (*See above s. v., A.D. 1172–73.*)

A.D. 1203. Kulōttunga-Chōla III reigning in Tanjore on January 4, 15 and 19, March and July 23, 1203. (*V. R. ii, Tan. 592, 595, 597 ; 479, 482, 484 of 1907 ; 505 of 1918 ; E. I. x. 129.*)

Hoyśala Baḷḷāḷa II reigning in Mysore (*E. C. vi, Kd., 127 ; vii. Hl., 108 ; Sk., 225*). His success in defeating the Kalachūri army is alluded to in the last of these.

A.D. 1204. Kulōttunga-Chōla III reigning in Trichinopoly on February 9, 1204, in his 26th year (*V. R. Trich. 330 ; 732 of 1909*). In S. Arcot on May 3 (*442 of 1921*). And in Tanjore on April 7 and August 24, and in Cuddapah. In the last of these the Telugu-Chōḍa chief, Nalla Siddha, described as son of Madurāntaka-Pottapi-Chōḍa Eṛama-Siddha, exempted some villages from taxation. Nalla Siddha = Betta (*see notes to pedigree*). (*V. R. i. Cudd. 792 ; 578 of 1907.*[1])

Hoyśala Baḷḷāḷa II reigning in Mysore. (*E. C. ix., Cp , 51 ; xi., Hk., 28.*)

In Tinnevelly Jaṭāvarman Kulaśekhara Pāṇḍya ruling on February 26, according to Kielhorn, in his '13th' regnal year. It was actually his 14th year.

(*V. R. iii. Tinn. 472 ; 123 of 1894 ; E. I. vi., 302.*)

Two inscriptions at Beḷgaum (*E I. xiii, 16*) shew that that province was on December 25, 1204, ruled by the Raṭṭa chief of Saundatti, Kārtavīrya IV. His younger brother Mallikārjuna is mentioned.

An inscription of the 27th year of Kulōttunga Chola III (1204-5) at Conjeevaram mentions the chief of Kuvalālapura (Kōlar, Mysore) Śīyagangan-Amarābharaṇa, *alias* Tiruvēgambam-Uḍaiyān. (*See above s. v., A.D. 1297, 1199*). [He has not been identified, but he was evidently a powerful chief and his neighbours were afraid of him.]

A.D. 1205. Hoyśala Baḷḷāḷa II ruling in Mysore. His queen Padmalādēvī mentioned.

(*E. C. iv, Ng. 62 ; vi. Tk. 42 ; xi, Cd. 23 ; Hn. 16.*)

In Tinnevelly an inscription of Jaṭāvarman-Kulaśēkhara-Pāṇḍya on September 19, 1205.)

(*633 of 1916.*)

S. Kanara ruled by the Āḷupa chief Āḷupēndra-Kulaśēkhara.

(*V. R. ii, S. Kan., 124 ; 52 of 1901.*)

The Telugu-Chōḍa chief Tammu Siddhi, younger brother of Nalla, *alias* Betta (*above s. v. A.D. 1204–05 and note*) is stated, in an inscription of this year at Conjeevaram, to have been crowned at Nellore. His father Eṛ-ṛa-Siddhi and his mother Śrī-dēvī are mentioned.

(*V. R. i, Chingleput 317 ; 35 of 1893.*)

A.D. 1206. Kulōttunga-Chōla III reigning in Salem District, in his 29th year on September 5, 1206 (*V. R. ii, Salem 11 ; 418 of 1913.*) In S. Arcot on October 7 (*353 of 1921*). And in Trichinopoly on October 16. (*97 of 1920.*)

Hoyśala Baḷḷāla reigning in Mysore and in Bellary District (*E. C. vi, Kḍ. 130 ; 739 of 1922*). The inscription in Mysore relates to further cattle-raiding and outrages.

A.D. 1207. Kulōttunga-Chōla III reigning in Conjeevaram on July 18, 1207 in his 30th year.

(*453 of 1919.*)

[1] That *Nalla*—or 'Black'—Siddha was another name for Betta is proved by an inscription at Kāvali in Nellore District of A.D 1207 (*B. and V. C. ii., p. 735*) which states that Tammu Siddhi Nalla's (or Betta's) younger brother ruled 'by favour of Nalla,' who had been anointed ; *i.e.* Nalla *alias* Betta preferred to live a monastic life and gave way to his younger brother.

Hoyśala Baḷḷāḷa II reigning in Mysore (*E. C. vii, Sk. 235 ; vi, Kd. 134 ; viii, Sb. 171*). More local raids and robberies and deaths. This time an extensive assault organized by the Kaḍamba chief Kāma or Kāva-dēva, when there seems to have been much murder done. In Rāmnād Jaṭāvarman-Kulaśēkhara-Pāṇḍya I ruling in his 18th year, on September 6, 1207 (*545 of 1922*). [His accession was between May 30 and July 8, 1190.]

The Kōnamaṇḍala chief Satya II, *alias* Manma-Satya ruling locally his tract on the Krishna river in Narasapur Taluk. (*V. R. ii, Kistna 307 ; 517 of 1893.*)

The Telugu-Chōḍa chief Tammu-Siddhi ruling territorially. Grant at Tiruppāśūr, Chingleput District (*E. I. vii, 119*). An inscription at Kāvali, Nellore District, of this year shewing as supreme lord (i.e. of his province) the Telegu-Chōḍa Nalla-Siddhi's brother Tammu Siddhi, who ruled 'by the favour' of Nalla (*see notes to A.D. 1201–02, 1204–5*). [The Tiruppāśūr inscription of the same year contains a passage which might be read to imply that 'Nalla' was the same as the *eldest* brother Manma-Siddhi, and distinctly states that the middle brother Betta waived his right to the chieftainship in favour of the youngest brother Tammu. But I am not sure of the exact meaning of the original][1] (*V. R. ii, Nellore 441 ; B. and V. C. ii, 735 ; 104 of 1892*). There are two inscriptions of Tammu Siddhi at Tiruvālangāḍu, Chittoor District, shewing him as a vassal of Kulōttuṅga Chola III.

(*V. R. i, Chittoor 322, 323 ; 408 of 1896 ; 452 of 1905. See also V. R. i, Chingleput 1116, 1178 ; 104 of 1892 ; 407 of 1896 ; E. I. vii, 119, 152.*)

A.D. 1208. Hoyśala Baḷḷāḷa II reigning in Mysore.

(*E. C. v, Bl. 171 Kb. ; vi, Tk. 68 ; viii, Sb. 28 ; xi, Hr. 18.*)

In this year the Telugu-Chōḍ achief Madurāntaka-Pottapi-Chōḍa-Tirukāḷatti (son of Manma Siddha) made a grant of a village in Nellore District ; and a follower of Nalla Siddha made another grant. (*V. R. ii Nellore 573, 539: B. & V. C. 864, 836.*)

A.D. 1209. On March 24, 1209, the same Tirukāḷatti, who is also called elsewhere 'Tikka I,' gave a gift 'for the merit of his father Manuma-Sitta and of Nalla-Siddha,' at Nandalūr in Cuddappah District, in the 31st year of his suzerain Kulōttunga-Chola III. And a servant of his gave a gift in August in Nellore District.

(*V. R. i, Cuddappah 796; 582 of 1907; V. R. ii, Nellore 300; B. and V.C. 540*)

Hoysala Ballāla II reigning in Mysore (*E. C. v, Ak. 40, 59; vi, Tk. 84; viii, Sb. 377*) And on May 10, 1209, in Bellary District (*261 of 1918.*). On July 18, 1209, on the occasion of an eclipse he gave a grant of a village, being then at 'Vijaya-Samudram' on the Tungabhadra. (*E. C. v, Cn. 172.*)

Kulōttunga Chōla III reigning (on Dec. 21, 1209) in Tanjore.

(*V. R. ii, Tan. 1562; 427 of 1904 E. I. viii, 266.*)

[1] Of Erṛasiddhi and Śrīdēvi were born sons, the eldest of whom was Nallasiddhi who was anointed to the throne. By his favour Tammasiddhi became king (*Kav.* 39). Read in the light of this, the other two (*Ep. Ind.*, Vol. VII, No. 17), could only mean Manmasiddha, the eldest, was anointed and ruled in great fame ; the middle one having been other-worldly in life, and gone to heaven later, Manmasiddha, for the security of the kingdom, gave the kingdom to Tammasiddhi, though younger. This is the meaning of the relevant passages. Three points come out clear from this : (1) Nallasiddha was another name of Manmasiddha, the eldest brother, not of Betta. (2) All three were the sons of Śrīdēvi and (3) Betta was religiously inclined in life and Tammasiddha was nominated to succeed Manuma ; Betta died before Tammasiddha actually succeeded.—*Editor.*

In Travancore (Vēṇāḍ) Vīra-Rāma of Kērala was reigning. *(T. A. S. iv, Pt. ii, p. 66.)*

In Kurnool and Guntūr Districts inscriptions mention as reigning there the Kākatīya King Gaṇapati. In one of them he confirms an earlier grant of land made by a different person. In another a grant of land by Gaṇapati's sister Mēlāmbikā, who had married Rudra, the second son of the Nātavāḍi chief Buddha (*V. R. ii, Kurnool 297; 204 of 1905; 803 of 1922*). [These inscriptions seem to shew that the Kākatīya king had increased his territory to the south by seizing districts that had belonged to the Chōla monarchy.]

[In Ceylon (vide the *Mahāwaṁśa, Ch. lxxx.*) Lilāvati had reigned as queen (*see note above s.v., A.D. 1196, 7*) from A.D. 1197 till she was ejected by Sahāsa-Malla, who seized the throne and began to reign on August 23, 1200. (This date is proclaimed by Dr. Hultzsch to be absolutely certain. See *J. R. A. S. 1913, p. 518*). Two short reigns followed. Then from the mainland came a large army of Tamils under Aṇiyanka who seized the throne, but was murdered after 17 days. Queen Līlāvatī was then again restored by a certain Parākrama and reigned for seven months. Then she was ejected by an army of Tamils under 'Lōkissara' (Lōkēśvara); and Lōkissara reigned for nine months. In A.D. 1211 Līlāvataī was once more made queen of Ceylon, and was again deposed by a Pāṇḍya Prince Parākrama from Madura who seized her throne in 1212 and reigned in Polonnarua for three years.]

A.D. 1210. Kulōttunga Chola III reigning in Conjeevaram on March 8, 1210, in his 32nd year, and in East Mysore in May–June. *(521 of 1919, E. C. x, Mb. 125.)*

In Chingleput District a grant of land was made in the 33rd year of Kulōttunga III by the Chief Panchanadivāṇa-Nīlagangaraiyan-Nallanayan. (This probably means Nallanāyan, son of Nīlagangaraiyan, for whom, see pedigree tables.) *(V. R. i, Chin. 930; 557 of 1912.)*

A.D. 1211. Kulōttunga Chōla III reigning in Trichinopoly on September 29 and December 26, 1211; and in Tanjore on June 6. *(V. R. iii, Trich. 883, 84; 74 of 1895; 152 of 1914; V. R. ii, Tan. 1086; 57 of 1914; E. I. iv. 220.)*

His vassal chief Panchanadivāṇan-Nallanāyan *alias* Chōla-Ganga, gave gifts. *(V.R. i, Chingleput, 929, 931; 556–558 of 1912.)*

Hoyśala Baḷḷāla II reigned in Mysore. Violent cattle-raids and slaughter are recorded. *(E. C. iv, Hg. 25; vi, Kd. 118; viii, Sb. 4, 404.)*

In Nellore District at Rāpūr a temple was built 'for the religious merit of Tikka Kāḷatti Chōḍa-Mahārāja, 'lord of Oreyūr, Lord of Kānchi' Telugu-Chōḍa chief. (These are titles, merely.) *(B. & V. C. iii, 1254; V. R. ii, Nellore 694.)*

At Tiruvallam in N. Arcot, an inscription of Ariya-Piḷḷai, wife of Amarābharaṇan-Śiyaganga alias Tiruvēgambam-Uḍaiyān (*above, s. v., A. D. 1204–5*). Another record calls him 'Lord of Kōlār.' *(V. R. i. N. Arcot, 343; 303 of 1907; see also S.I.I. iii, 122, 207.)*

The Kākatīya King Gaṇapati was reigning in Guntur District on December 25, 1211. *(above, s. v., A. D. 1209–10; 88 of 1917.)*

The Baṇavāśi province was ruled over by Kādamba Kāmadeva. Hoyśala Baḷḷāḷa II for some reason raided into his country and besieged the town of Biraūr. In the fighting which ensued many lives were lost. Inscription on a *Virakal.*

(E. C. viii, Sb. 59. See *below, s. v., A. D. 1213–14.)*

A.D. 1212. Kulōttunga Chōla III reigning in Conjeevaram (*346, 361 of 1919*). One of these of his 34th year bears date = June 18; the other = July 1212, 1. In another inscription of this date and reign Śiya-Ganga, Lord of Kōlār, and son of Chōlēndra-Simha, it is said, built a shrine in Conjeevaram. *(589 of 1919.)*

In this year a solemn compact between contemporary and neighbouring chiefs was made, by which two members of the Vāṇa-Kōvaraiyan family, and a Kāḍavar-aiyar (descendant of the Pallavas) promised to be jointly friends with Aḷagiya-Chōla alias Edirili-Chōla-Śambuvaraiyan, son of Śengēṇi Ammaiyappan, and he with them. *(V. R. ii, Salem 28 ; 435 of 1913.)*

An inscription in Chingleput District, of (probably) August 10, 1212, relates that King Kulōtunga Chola III issued an order levying a new tax, *Ponvari*, and decreed that the waste lands as well as the occupied ones were liable to it. The village assembly refused to pay tax on the waste, and the king arrested and imprisoned all the village authorities, and collected the tax by seizure and sale of a considerable amount of land in the village concerned. [The inscription was engraved[1] on the wall of the temple at Tiruvoṟṟiyūr, evidently as a solemn protest against what was considered an act of despotism.] *(V. R. i. Chin., 1071 ; 202 of 1912.)*

Hoyśala Baḷḷāḷa reigning in Mysore. Local disturbances and massacres. *(E. C. v. Hn., 31 ; viii, Sb. 376, 516.)*

In Nellore Madurāntaka-Pottapi-Nalla-Siddha locally ruling. Inscription at Ātmakūr. *(B. and V. C. i, 219 ; V. R. ii, Nellore, 18.)*

A.D. 1213. That Hoyśala-Baḷḷāḷa II was now in considerable difficulties as regards his hold on territory north of Mysore, conquered by him from the Kalachuri king and threatened by the Dēvagiri-Yādavas, is made clear by an inscription at Gadag in Dharwar District which represents the Yādava Singhaṇa as ruling that country in this year after he had defeated Baḷḷāḷa II as well as from the fact that he, Baḷḷāḷa, had been fighting in the Baṇavasi province in A.D. 1211–12 (*above*). (*I. A. ii, 297*). A little later Singhaṇa had succeeded in conquering and seizing some tracts in North Mysore. *(See below, Inscriptions in Sorab Taluk, Shimoga District, in 1218, 1237, 1241.)*

Kulōttunga Chōla III reigning in Tanjore, Conjeevaram and Trichinopoly on February 26, September 8 and December 16, 1213, in his 35th and 36th year. *(V. R. ii, Tan. 593 ; 480 of 1907. 2 of 1918 ; 435 of 1919 ; V. R. iii, Trich. 275 ; 507 of 1912 ; E. I. x, 133.)*

Hoyśala-Baḷḷāḷa II reigning in W. Mysore, (*E. C. v, Ak. 46*). His queen Umā-dēvī mentioned.

Part of Guntur District was ruled over by the Amarāvati Chief Kōṭa-Kēta II. *(79 of 1917.)*

In the same district the town of Chēbrōlu was in this year given by Kākatīya Gaṇapati, now supreme in that region, to his celebrated general Jaya. *(V. R. ii, Guntur 86 ; 147 of 1897 ; E. I. iii, 95.)*

A gift to a temple commemorated, at Ṭiruppāśūr in Chingleput District, made by a certain 'Yādavarāya Narasimha.' [He is believed to have been the Hoyśala Prince Narasimha, but this seems doubtful—or at any rate not proved.][2] *(V. R. i, Chin. 1177 ; Chittoor 261 ; 406 of 1896 ; 392 of 1911.)*

A.D. 1214. Hoyśala-Baḷḷāḷa II reigning in Mysore. He is called in one record 'the setter up of the Pāṇḍya king'. In another (*E. C. vii, Ci. 64*) he is shewn to have had under him a chief of the Ganga family, Narasimha. *(E. C. xi., Hk. 2 ; vii, Ci, 64 ; Sh. 54 ; iii. Ml. 37 ; xii. Tp. 47.)*

[1] The land involved was granted to the temple. It was not the King but the local governor who did this. The document is translated and its actual significance explained in my work 'Evolution of Hindu Administrative Institutions in South India'.—*Editor*.

[2] This is the Pottappi Prince Yadava Vira-Narasimha of whom there are a large number of inscriptions in the Chingleput District and the Tirupati collection.—*Editor*.

Kulōttunga-Chōla III reigning in Tanjore on January 21, 1214 (533 of 1918). On April 14 (*V. R. ii. Tanjore 216 ; 631 of 1902 ; E. I. viii, 5*). On November 17 (*V. R. ii, Tanjore, 475 ; 659 of 1902*), and in Trichinopoly on June 8. (*60 of 1920.*)

A gift was made in Kāvali Taluk, Nellore District 'for the religious merit' of the Telugu-Chōḍa chief 'Manma-Siddhana, son of Rājēndra Chōḍa [another name of Ēr-ṛa-Siddha], of the race of Karikāla, lord of Oraiyūr (*V. R. ii. Nellore 415 ; B. and V. C. ii, 708*). Another inscription at Ātmakūr in the same district mentions, as ruling chief, Nalla-Siddha. (*B. and V. C. i, 219.*)

In Ramnad an inscription of the 25th year of Jaṭāvarman-Kulaśēkhara-Rājagambhīra-Pāṇḍya whose accession was in 1190. (*V. R. ii. Ramnad, 170 ; I.A. vi. 142 ; xx, 288.*)

A.D. 1215. Kulōttunga-Chōla III reigning in Conjeevaram in his 37th year, on February 15, 1215 (*451 of 1919*). And in Tanjore on April 19. (*512 of 1918.*)

In Vēṇāḍ (Travancore) on February 12, 1215. Record of Rāma-Kēraḷa reigning. (*T. A. S. iv., Pt. I., p. 69.*)

In Anantapur District on a date which may be April, 10, the Dēvagiri-Yādava king 'Simhala' (i.e. Singhaṇa II) was reigning (*345 of 1920*). [This confirms what has gone before, viz., that the Hoyśalas were decisively beaten back from their attempt to seize the W. Chāḷukya territories beyond the Mysore border.]. Another record in Kurnool District, near Kurnool Town, supports this, as it shews a son of Singhaṇa's minister, who was evidently an official of the Yādava king, granting land to a temple there. (*V. R. ii. Kurn. 221.*)

Parākrama Bāhu had reigned over Ceylon for three years, but in this year a prince from Kalinga, named Māgha, invaded the island with a large force, captured Parākrama Bāhu, blinded and deposed him, and seized the throne. He was King of Ceylon for 21 years, under the title Vijaya-Bāhu. (*Mahāwaṁśa, ch. lxxx.*)

In N.-W. Mysore, Shimoga District, the local ruler was the Sinda chief Īśvarā-dēva II son of Malla. (*E. C. vii. Hl. 44.*)

A.D. 1216. [The Chōla throne now passed to Rājarāja III, whose reign was a series of disasters. At the beginning of it he was threatened on all sides. The Kākatīya king, operating from his capital Warangal, had captured large tracts of the Telugu country, and was pressing southwards. The Telugu territory south of the Krishna was ruled by a Telugu-Chōḍa chief, constantly becoming stronger as Chola power weakened. Hoyśala Baḷḷāḷa was very powerful in Mysore though he had been unsuccessful in his attempts over his own northern border. The Pāṇḍya king, an inveterate enemy of the Chōla house, threatened the Chola territories on the south-west. The great local Tamil chieftains, especially the Sengēni family of the Toṇḍamaṇḍalam province, and the Pallava or Kāḍava chief of South-Arcot, Kō-Peruṁ-Singa, were becoming aggressive.

About the time when Rājarāja III came to the Chola throne, the Pāṇḍya throne came into the hands of Māravarman-Sundara-Pāṇḍya I who apparently made it his principal object to overthrow the Chōla Kingdom.]

Kulōttunga Chōla III is mentioned in an inscription in Tanjore as reigning on January 2, 1216, in his 38th year. (*233 of 1917.*)

[Rājarāja Chōla III began to reign on June 27–29, 1216. This is proved by his Tiruvoṟṟiyūr inscription, which is dated on the 43rd day of his 19th year and = 8, 9, or August 10 A.D. 1234. (*Kielhorn., E.I. viii ; 260. V. R. i., Chingleput, 975, 1088; 106, 211 of 1912.*)

In N.-W. Mysore, Sorab Taluk, the Dēvagiri-Yādava king Singhaṇa is recognized as sovereign in his 5th year, which shews that he was steadily encroaching on Hoyśala territory, and working southwards. The date of one record = April 26, 1216. It alludes to cattle-raids and homicide (*E. C. viii, Sb. 507, 398 ; vii, Hl. 48*). The Sinda Rāja Īśvara II ruled under Singhaṇa.

Travancore (Vēṇaḍ) was ruled by the Kērala king Ravi. (*T. A. S. i, 289.*)

In Kādūr District, West Mysore, a gift was made by Harihara-Daṇṇāyaka, lord of Āsandi-nāḍu. (*E. C. vi, Kd. 151.*)

In N.-W. Mysore mention is made of an apparently turbulent chief, possibly one of the Noḷambavāḍi-Pāṇḍya family, called Jagadēva-Pāṇḍya. His minister organized, of course with his master's approval, a cattle-raid on his neighbour's property. (*E. C. viii, Sa. 124, 125.*)

A. D. 1217. An inscription in Tanjore seems to shew that, though Rājarāja III had become Chōla king in the previous year, his predecessor Kulōttunga III was still alive, and retired into private life. Its date is January 15, 1217,[1] and it mentions Kulōttunga's 39th year of reign (*V. R. ii, Tan. 203 ; 618 of 1902 ; E. I. viii, 5*). Another of the same king is dated April 26, 1217 (*24 of 1918.*)

The Baṇavāśi 12000 province and parts of N.-W. Mysore had been conquered by the Dēvagiri- Yādava king Singhaṇa from Hoyśala Baḷḷāḷa II and were now ruled by the former (*E. C. viii, Sb. 135*). Hoyśala Baḷḷāḷa however still held W. Mysore (*E. C. v, Bl. 136, 224*) and S. Mysore (*ibid iii, Md. 38*).

The inscription Sb. 135 referred to has a correct date mentioning a solar eclipse. It = August 4, A. D. 1217. It states that, amongst other successes in war, king Singhaṇa defeated the 'Telunga-Rāya' i.e., Kākatiya Gaṇapati and restored him to his throne. This exploit however does not belong to the reign of Singhaṇa but to that of his father Jaitrapāla I (1191–1210).

Jaṭāvarman Kulaśēkhara-Pāṇḍya I was ruling over Madura on March 29, 1217, in his 27th year. (*V. R. ii, Madura, 152 ; 131 of 1903 ; E. I. viii, 275*)

In Ātmakūr Taluk, Nellore District, the Telugu-Chōḍa chief Eṟṟa-Siddhaya was ruling. (*V. R. ii, Nell. 40 ; B. & V. C. i, 251.*)

A.D. 1218. Hoyśala Baḷḷāḷa II reigning in W. Mysore on January 13, 1218 ; in S. Mysore on January 14 ; and at other times in this year in those parts. Also in N. Mysore (*E. C. v, Hn. 61 ; iv, Hg. 23 ; vi, Kd. 129 ; viii, Sa. 15 ; xi, Dg. 105*). His queen Baichalā-dēvi is mentioned.

Two inscriptions of Rājarāja-Chōla III's second year, in Tanjore. The dates = January 22 and 29, 1218. (*V. R. ii, Tan. 1543, 1510 ; 482 of 1912 ; 505 of 1904 ; E. I. viii, 267.*)

In Tanuku Taluk, south of the Krishna River, the Koḷanu Rāja Kēśavadēva was locally ruling. (*723 of 1920.*)

N.-W. Mysore was under king Singhaṇa of the Dēvagiri Yādavas. An inscription of December 3, 1218, makes this certain. (*E. C. viii, Sb. 256.*)

In Ongole Taluk, Guntur District, the recognized sovereign was Kākatiya Gaṇapati (*V. R. ii, Gun. 370, 464 ; B. & V. C. 972, 1129*). [This testifies to his successful pressing southwards over the territory of the Chōla king.]

[1] The date as given by Kielhorn in *Ep. Ind.* Vol. VIII, No. 5, is January 25, 1217, and it agrees in regard to details with the late Mr. L. D. Swamikkannu Pillai's Ephemeris. I find it as given above in Mr. Sewell's own hand, and leave it as it is.—*Editor.*

In Rājarāja-Chola III's 3rd year a political compact was made by three minor chiefs, and engraved on the temple wall so that it might have binding effect, that each would be a friend to the other, and an enemy to the other's enemies, and that all would be loyal to their king. [Plainly then there was great anxiety in the country as to the future of the Chōla royal house.]

(*V. R. ii, Tan. 1372 ; 23 of 1897 ; S. I. I. i, 497.*)

A.D. 1219. Part of N.-W. Mysore and the Baṇavāśi province were ruled by the Kādamba chief Malli-deva. He was a Kādamba of Hāngal, and his rule began in the previous year (*E. C. viii, Sb. 224, of date January 7, 1219*). The inscription refers to robber-gangs and murders.

In Trichinopoly Rājarāja III was reigning (February 13, 1219) in his 3rd year (*V. R. iii. Trich., 763 ; 136 of 1914*). And in Tanjore on April 19 (*486 of 1922.*)

In Central and West Mysore Hoyśala Baḷḷāḷa supreme. (*E. C. iv, Ng. 29*; *v, Ak. 77.*)

A.D. 1220. Early in 1220 Hoyśala Baḷḷāḷa II was reigning in E. Mysore. This is the latest date known for his reign. (*E. C. ix, Ma. 77 or 78.*)

On April 16, 1220, the new Hoyśala king Narasimha II, son of Baḷḷāḷa II, was crowned (*E. C. v, Cn. 172*). He is mentioned as sovereign on April 11 (*E. C. vii, Ci. 72*), and even on April 3 (*E. C. v, Bl. 85*). He gave his daughter in marriage to the Chōla king Rājarāja III, to whose rescue he came in the troubles which immediately followed.

(*See also E. C. v, Cn. 172 ; E. I. viii, App. ii., p. 13.*)

Rājarāja Chōla III was reigning in Tanjore on January 19, 1220 (*520 of 1922*). And on December 10 and 17 (*45, 47 of 1911*).

Hoyśala Narasimha reigning in N. Mysore, Chitaldroog District, on June 2, 1220. He held the Noḷambavāḍi country against the advancing Dēvagiri-Yādavas. The succession of rulers of the 'Noḷambavāḍi 32000' is given in the inscription (*E. C. xi, Hk. 56*). He was also reigning in W. Mysore. There was some disturbance in the latter country and a battle against a certain Bijjana is mentioned on a *virakal*. (*E. C. v, Bl. 113, 115 ; Ak, 70.*)

In Tinnevelly District Māravarman-Sundara-Pāṇḍya I was reigning, in his 5th year (*353 of 1916*).

A.D. 1221. Hoyśala Narasimha reigning in S.-W. Mysore in his 2nd year.

(*E. C. v, Hn. 106 ; Bl. 154.*)

Rājarāja Chōla III reigning, in his 6th year, in Chittoor and Chingleput (*V. R. i, Chit. 286 ; Ching. 908 ; 273 of 1904 ; 535 of 1912*). In the former mention is made of a battle fought at Uratti between Narasimha, called 'Yādava-Rāya'—a name often given to the Hoyśala kings[1]—and a Kāḍava Rāya. This last was possibly the Kāḍava or Pallava chief Kō-Perunjinga who ruled from Śēndamangalam ; or perhaps the Bāṇa chief who had allied himself with the Pāṇḍya king. In the latter a gift is commemorated by Nīlagangaraiyan-Kaḍakkan-Chōlaganga (*See pedigree of Nilaganga*).

[About this time—the date is not quite certain—the Pāṇḍya king, feeling himself now in sufficient strength, began to make preparations for a grand attack on the Chōla kingdom. He seems

[1] This name has no connection with the Hoyśalas. Vīra-Narasimha Yādava Rāya of Pottappināḍ Chola Viceroy of these parts. The term Yādava Rāya is part of his title and does not seem to mear th family generally as in the case of the Hoyśalas and other South Indian rulers. *Uratti* is proba Chingleput now.—*Editor*.

to have been aided by the Bāṇa chief of a tract about Salem, called the Magadaināḍu—perhaps the 'Makara kingdom' mentioned in some inscriptions (*See E. I. vii, 162*). At first the Pāṇḍya's attack seems to have been successful as his inscriptions (one of them in 1222–23) says that he burnt Tanjore and Karuvūr. But he was thwarted by Narasimha II. The Hoyśala king aware that the Chōla king was very weak and in great danger, and that on all sides the great nobles were rising up and threatening to overthrow him—being moreover his kinsman by marriage—took up arms, and marching southwards interposed between the Pāṇḍya forces, and those of the Chōlas and their supporters.

His march took him to Śrirangam. His inscriptions say that he defeated the chief of a 'Makara' kingdom.

(*See E. C. vi, Cm. 56 ; E. I. vii, 162.*)

[After the first Pāṇḍya success king Sundara's records say that he was anointed as victor at Muḍigonda-Chōlapuram; but he seems afterwards to have made peace with Rājarāja III and retired. It may be that this was forced on him by the Hoyśala advance.]

A.D. 1222. Rājarāja Chōla III was reigning in North Arcot in his 6th year on February 27, 1222, and in Tanjore District on June 13 (*265 of 1921 ; V. R. ii, Tan, 1536 ; 475 of 1912*). Also Drākshārāma, Godāvari District. (*V. R. ii. Godav. 167 ; 162 of 1893.*)

[About this time the Pallava chief Kō-Perunjinga rose against his Chōla sovereign, and a battle was fought at Teḷḷār, after which it would seem that for a time Perunjinga overawed by the intervention of Hoyśala Narasimha, returned to his allegiance.]

In N.-W. Mysore the Dēvagiri-Yādava king Singhaṇa II was reigning (*E. C. vii. Hl. 20*). For a note on the Bahāl inscription of this year see above s.v., A.D. 1199-1200.

[The celebrated Bhāskarāchārya was Singhaṇa's court Astronomer. An inscription gives an account of his family, which belonged to Nasik, or Khandesh. Manōratha is first named. Then his son Mahēśvara who had two sons Śrīpati and Bhāskarāchārya. (*E. I. iii, 340.*)

An inscription at Tiruvoṟṟiyūr Chingleput District, of the 7th year of Rājarāja Chōla III is important in more than one respect. It contains an order issued by 'Narasimha-Yādavarāya, who must be Hoyśala king Narasimha II,[1] and thus shews that his influence in the Chōla kingdom was now so great that he was actually at the time the local ruler at that place, though the sovereign was the Chōla king. [This is quite possible, Rājarāja wanted protection and he may well have entrusted temporarily the government of that territory to the Hoyśala king.] Also it discloses an apparently high-handed and tyrannous act.[2] Certain lands had been granted by former kings tax-free to their holders. Now a long list of taxes is given and Narasimha orders that these hitherto tax free lands are in future to pay all the taxes and to pay them to the Temple treasury.

(*V. R. i. Chingleput 1068 ; 199 of 1912.*)

[1] See Editor's note under A.D. 1221.

[2] This is again a result of misunderstanding. The doubt seems to have been whether the lands concerned were *irangal* or *ningal*, tax-free, or tax payable to some one else. The matter was referred to the king who ruled they were *ningal*. The local officer then laid down the schedule of taxes and made them payable to the temple. There is nothing arbitrary in this and the lands must have been recent gifts, the doubt arising in consequence. The order is not that of the king in person but of reference to the Puravu-vari Register at the headquarters which was the ultimate authority, quite a normal form of procedure—(*see 210 of 1912*).—*Editor*.

Another inscription of the same period affords an example of religious intolerance. It shews that the temple authorities were permitted to levy tax on everyone who professed the Jaina religion.[1]

An inscription of the 7th year of Māravarman-Sundara-Pāṇḍya I states that he had burnt Tanjore and Uraiyūr and 'presented the Chōla kingdom.' This seems to shew that he had warred against the Chōla king, had been partially successful, and had made peace with him. His 7th year=A. D.1222–23. (*V. R. ii. Madura*, 110.)

A record in Kadur District, Mysore, whose date is in autumn of A. D. 1222, commemorates the death of the soldier in a battle when Hoyśala Narasimha II was 'marching against Rangam in the South', i.e. Śrīrangam—which proves that this march took place either in A.D. 1221 or 1222 (*E. C. vi. Cm*, 56). Another record shews that Narasimha II still held the Bellary District in spite of Yādava pressure. It states also that he 'established the Chōla kingdom,' i.e. had successfully prevented the Pāṇḍya attack on it. (*208, 209, 281 of 1918.*)

In Travancore Udaya-Mārttāṇḍa-Tiruvaḍi was reigning. (*T. A. S. i. p. 296.*)

A.D. 1223. In N.-W. Mysore the country was under the Yādava king Singhaṇa. There were two instances of great local raids in this year, a town being plundered in one case, and men killed. (*E. C. vii, Sb. 308 ; vii. Sk. 175.*)

Rājarāja Chōla II was reigning at Kovilūr and in Nannilam Taluk in Tanjore District on February 20, and April 15, 1223 ; and on February 20, in Trichinopoly (*V. R. ii. Tan. 1125 ; 215 of 1908 ; E. I. xi, 127 ; 250 of 1917 ; 91 of 1920*). Yet another inscription close to Tanjore city mentions as sovereign on March 13, 1223 Māravarman-Sundara-Pāṇḍya saying that he had 'presented the Chōla country' (*V.R. ii, Tan. 1455 ; 52 of 1897 ; E. I. vi. 304*). (*See remarks above s.v., A.D. 1222.*)

In Central and S.-W. Mysore Hoyśala-Narasimha II was reigning. A village was granted by the king 'when he was marching on Magara' i. e., the Magadai tract (*see s.v., A.D. 1221–22*) ; the record (which was evidently engraved later) says that the king had defeated 'Pāṇḍya and Makara and the powerful Kāḍavas.' (*E. C. v. Cn. 197, 203.*)

Two records in Bellary District shew Hoyśala Narasimha reigning there (*V. R. i. Bell. 197, 307 ; 38 of 1904 ; 116 of 1913*). His son Sōmēśvara is mentioned in an inscription in Erode Taluk, Coimbatore District. (*V. R. i. Coim. 178 ; 602 of 1905.*)

In Nellore District an inscription mentions, in Rājarāja Chōla's 8th regnal year, a chief Madurāntaka-Pottapi-Chōla Eṟṟa Siddha (not identified see Telugu-Chōḍa pedigree). (*V. R. ii. Nell. 685.*)

In part at least of Guntur the recognized reigning sovereign was Kākatiya Gaṇapati. (*V. R. ii. Gun. 116 ; 241 of 1897.*)

In Travancore the Kēraḷa king Udayamārtāṇḍa was reigning. (*V. R. iii. Trav. 195.*)

A.D. 1224. Hoyśala Narasimha II reigning in W. and S. Mysore (*E. C. vi., Kd. 95 ; iv, Kr. 7*). An inscription of his reign at Harihara in N. Mysore speaks to his having been opposed by the

[1] This seems to refer to the tax called Āśuvigaḷkāśu (Ājīvika-kāśu). There is nothing to warrant that it was taken *from them* as it is included among other general taxes. It is likely that it was intended for feeding and otherwise providing for these mendicants by the community as we sometimes hear of a committee for Udāsīnas (mendicant monks).—*Editor.*

'Kāḍava' and the Pāṇḍya rulers (*E. I. vii, 160. E.C. xi., Dg. 25*). The king is said in this to have had an army of 200,000 infantry, and 12,000 cavalry, and to have defeated the 'Śeuṇa', or the Dēvagiri-Yādava king (alluding to an earlier war); is called the 'Setter-up of the Chōla kingdom,' alluding to recent events when he checked the Pāṇḍya's attack on the Chōla.

In N.-W. Mysore on March 6, Malla-dēva of the Kādamba family of Hāngal was locally ruling in his 6th year. (*E.C. viii, Sb. 180.*)

An inscription in S. Arcot District represents the Pāṇḍya king Māravarman Sundara I as reigning there in his tenth year on June 3. [The date was in his 9th year. Apparently an error in the original]. (*561 of 1921.*)

A grant was made in Rājarāja Chōla's 9th year in Chittoor District 'for the merit of Uttama-Chōlaganga-Amarābharaṇa-Akaḷanka-Sīyaganga, who was also called Tiruvēgambam-Uḍaiyan. (*above s.v., A.D. 1180–81, 1204–05. V.R. i, Chittoor, 235 ; 551 of 1906.*)

A.D. 1225. Rājarāja Chōla III reigning in Mannarguḍi Taluk (Tanjore) and Uḍayarpāḷaiyam Taluk (Trichinopoly) on August 17 and October 24, 1225 (*256 of 1917 ; 77 of 1920*). Against this there is an inscription at Śrirangam on March 28, 1225, which states as then sovereign there the Pāṇḍya king Māravarman-Sundara-Pāṇḍya I, who 'presented the Chōla country.' (*V.R. iii, Trich. 464 ; 53 of 1892 ; E.I. vi. 303 ; I.A. xxi. 344*). [At present it seems difficult to reconcile these statements (*see also below, s.v., A.D. 1227*). There is a record of Sundara Pāṇḍya I's 10th year in Pudukoṭṭai State. (*V.R. iii. Pudu. 385 ; 229 of 1914.*)]

Hoysala Narasimha II was reigning in N.-W. Mysore. *Vīrakal.* More cattle-robberies and murders. (*E. C. vii, Ci. 40.*)

In Chingleput District 'Tikka I' Gaṇḍa-Gōpāla Telugu-Chōḍa chief, is mentioned as then in his 3rd year in an inscription of the ruling Kāḷahasti chief Rājaśraya-Śaśikula-Chāḷukki-Vīra-Narasimha-Yādava-Rāya. (*above s.v., A.D. 1192–93. V.R. i, Chin. 757 ; 659 of 1904.*)

The Kādamba chief of Hāngal, Malla, ruling locally in N.-W. Mysore. Cattle-raids and deaths. (*E.C. viii, Sb. 178.*)

A.D. 1226. Rājarāja Chōla III reigning in his 10th year on April 21 in Pondicherry and in Tanjore in his 11th year on November 30, 1226. (*V. R. iii. French Territory 19 ; Tan. 250 ; E.I. vii. 175 ; 409 of 1908 ; E.I. xi. 128.*)

Hoysala Narasimha II reigning in N.-W., Central and W. Mysore (*E.C. viii, Sa. 126 ; xii. Ck. 42 ; vi. Tk. 2 ; v. Cn. 253.*)

A.D. 1227. Hoysala Narasimha II reigning in Central and West Mysore. His senior queen Padmalā-dēvī mentioned (*E. C. xii. Gb., 11 ; v., Bl., 151*). The latter inscription states that he had protected the Chōla and reduced the Pāṇḍya and the Pallava. [Whatever then the 'Kāḍava' chief of former records may mean, this one certainly points to the 'Pallava' chief Kō-Perujinga as the one intended.]

Rājarāja Chōla III reigning. on May 15 and October 18, 1227, in the Tirutturaipūndi Taluk, Tanjore District (*V. R. ii. Tan. 1527, 1528 ; 466, 467 of 1912.*) Also in Conjeevaram on August 1, in his '11th' year (error for '12th'. *598 of 1919*). And in Uḍaiyārpāḷayam Taluk, Trichinopoly District, on December 27, 1227, in his 12th year (57 of 1920).

In Ramnad Māravarman-Sundara-Pāṇḍya I reigned (*554 of 1922*). And in Pudukoṭṭa, where he is said to have been anointed as a hero at Muḍigoṇḍa-Chōlapuram. (*V. R. iii., Pudukotta 365 ; 322 of 1914.*)

In Guntur District a grant of villages was made by the Telugu-Chōḍa chief Mallidēva 'of the family of Karikāla.' (*V. R. ii. Gun. 339 ; B. and V. C. 924.*)

An inscription on a temple wall in Conjeevaram makes 'Kōnerinmaikonḍān' Sundara-Pāṇḍya on October 13, 1227, remitting certain taxes, as if then in full possession of the city and reigning there (*41 of 1921*). [This requires further examination as the date is based mainly on its being in his 12th regnal year]. [*See above s. v., A.D. 1225.*]

A.D. 1228. Rājarāja Chōla III reigning on April 24, 1228, at Kāḷahasti, Chittoor District (*135 of 1922*). And in Chingleput District on July 5. (*V. R. i. Chin. 975 ; 106 of 1912.*)

Hoyśala Narasimha II reigning in Central and N.-W. Mysore.

(*E. C. v. Cn. 204 ; xii. Tp. 54 ; vii. Hl. 8.*)

[Narasimha II had been in Śrirangam in A.D. 1222 (*above*) and apparently he must have thought the place too valuable to be neglected. Close by Śrirangam is the old city of Kaṇṇanur, and a record of this year at Badanāḷu in Nanjanguḍ Taluk, Mysore (*E. C. iii. Nj. 36*), whose date is clearly March 15, 1228, states that Narasimha's son Sōmēśvara was then residing at Kaṇṇanur. Rice (*iii. Introd., p. 19*) makes the date 1240, but this is an error. It must be assumed therefore that the Hoyśala king held possession of Kaṇṇanūr perhaps from 1222,—certainly from 1228.]

In Nellore District the local ruler was 'Tirukāḷa-Chōḍa' *i.e.* the Telugu-Chōḍa chief Tikka I. (*V. R. ii. Nell. ; 440 ; B. and V. C. 734.*)

A.D. 1229. Hoyśala Narasimha reigning in N.-W. Mysore. No further events related of his reign, except local cattle-raids and deaths (*E. C. vii. Ci. 45*). An inscription of his of the month of March 1223 in central Mysore states that he was then residing at Conjeevaram (*ibid. xii. Tp. 42*). He was also reigning in S. and W. Mysore. (*E. Ci. v. Gu. 19 ; v. Ag. 6.*)

Rājarāja Chōla III reigning in Conjeevaram in his 14th year on August 25, 1229, and on October 7 in Tanjore. (*359 of 1917 ; V. R. ii. Tan. 612 ; 372 of 1907 ; E. I. x. 134.*)

An inscription in Pudukoṭṭa of the 13th year of Māravarman-Sundara-Pāṇḍya I, whose date = April 7, 1229, states that he 'distributed the Chōla country.'

(*V. R. iii. Pudu. 157 ; 332 of 1914.*)

A record at Vriddhāchalam in S. Arcot shews that Kō-Perunjinga, the Pallava chief, recognized as his sovereign the Chōla King Rājaraja III in this year. [He threw over his allegiance later.] It records a grant by Ediriganāyan-Pottapi-Chōḍa (probably one of the Telugu-Chōḍa family) an officer of Perunjinga's bodyguard.

(*V. R. i. S. Arcot 1085 ; 136 of 1900 ; E. I. vii. 160.*)

Local chiefs fighting one another in N.-W. Mysore. Śridhara-Danḍanāyaka (a general) attacked Sāntaḷigē Vīra, son of Bamma. (*E. C. viii. Sa. 141, 146.*)

A.D. 1230. Hoyśala Somēśvara, son of Narasimha II, mentioned in an inscription in Central Mysore. It connects him with his father's exploits, in 'pursuing the Pāṇḍya king' and 'penetrating into the Chōla country.' [He probably accompanied the army in high command.] (*E. C. iv. Ng., 98*). An inscription in W. Mysore shews Narasimha II, reigning there. It mentions his sister Sōvalā-dēvī. (*E. C. vi, Tk. 53.*)

Rājarāja Chōla III was reigning in Conjeevaram, and Tanjore, Salem and S. Arcot districts—records in several places. Dates February 15, 17, May 6, July 3, August 5.

(*408 of 1919 ; 231 of 1917 ; V. R. ii, Salem, 8 ; 415 of 1913 ; 74 of 1922 ; 72 of 1919.*)

In Ramnad on June 10, 1230 Māravarman-Sundara-Pāndya was reigning in his 14th year (*V. R. ii, Ramnad 11 ; 412 of 1914*). And on December 3 in his 15th year in Madura District.

(*V. R. ii, Mad. 57 ; E. I. viii, 276 ; 60 of 1905.*)

In Conjeevaram the local ruler was 'Gaṇḍa-Gōpāla.' Record, dated June 2, 1230. It gives the Chief—i.e., the Telugu-Chōḍa Tikka I—no other titles. (*446 of 1919.*)

A.D. 1231. This year was very eventful in the history of South India. An inscription at Tiruvēndipuram of the 16th year of Rājarāja Chōla (*E. I. vii, 160 f. ; V. R. i. S. Arcot, 329 ; 142 of 1902*) gives very important details as to what occurred.

(*See also V. R. i, S. Arcot, 1085 ; 136 of 1900.*)

Mention has been made of Kō-Perunjinga, the Pallava Chief of Śēndamangalam in South Arcot whom I shall in future call simply Perunjinga, 'Kō' being a prefix signifying royalty. He often bears the title 'Avaniyavana' or 'Avaniyāḷa.' This was the first Perunjinga or Perunjinga I. He had revolted against Rājarāja Chōla III, in A. D. 1221-22 (above) and had been completely checked by Hoyśala Narasimha II. But in this year 1231, or it may be a little earlier, he again rose against his sovereign and this time succeeded in capturing the person of Rājarāja III, and carrying him to Śēndamangalam where the king was imprisoned. Narasimha II, being on friendly terms with Rājarāja and connected with him by marriage, and having been already recognized publicly as 'the establisher of the Chōla kingdom,' owing to his earlier action, declared that he must at all costs maintain this reputation, and fitted out an expedition of rescue. He marched to Pāchchūr near Śrirangam, and thence despatched a strong force under two generals, Appana and Samudra-Gopayya, commanding them to release the Chōla king. The army marched towards Śēndamangalam. On the way they destroyed two villages in the Chidambaram Taluk in which Perunjinga had stayed, and another in which the latter's officer the 'Śōlakōn' had stayed, and fought a pitched battle against the rebel army. In this fight a member of the Singhalese royal family Parākrama Bāhu is said to have lost his life. The victory lay with the Hoyśala army, and the two generals went to Chidambaram and worshipped at the temple there. Thence they marched towards Cuddalore and halted at Tiruppāpuliyūr. Again they destroyed a number of villages in the Villupuram Taluk and some towns on the coast; after which they marched against Śēndamangalam itself. Finding himself outnumbered and in difficulties, Perunjinga submitted to his Hoyśala foe, and released King Rājarāja who was carried triumphantly to his own capital and restored to his dignities.

An inscription at Gaṇapēśvaram in Kistna District of April 7, 1231, mentions as then reigning over that country the Kākatiya King Gaṇapati, who was taking advantage of Chōla weakness and extending his power southward (*E. I. iii, 82 ; I. A. xxi, 197*). His general, Jaya, built a temple at Divi on the sea coast. (*V. R. ii, Kistna, 136 ; 131 of 1893 ; E. I. vii, 82*)

Rājarāja Chōla III reigning in Chingleput, Tanjore and Nellore Districts on March 14, May 17, June 22 and early in 1231, respectively (*137 of 1923 ; 393, 537 of 1922 ; V. R. ii, Nellore, 800 ; B. and. V. C. 1397*) ; also at Conjeevaram on September 7, 1231. (*457 ; 460 of 1919.*)

Records in this year of the Telugu-Chōḍa chief Madhurāntaka-Pottapi Gaṇḍa-Gōpāla, i.e., Tikka, or Tirukāḷatti I (*V. R. i, Chingleput 907 ; 534 of 1912 ; 446 of 1919*). He is stated to have 'taken Kānchi'—a mere boast.

(*See note in E. R. 1920, p. 116 ; and below s.v., A. D. 1232.*)

Hoyśala Narasimha II reigning in Central Mysore (*E. C. v, Cn. 170*). It is noticeable, when observing his position in Chōla territories after his defeat of the Pāṇḍya some years earlier, that gifts to temples near Pudukoṭṭa and at Śrīrangam were made by his servants in 1225 and 1233. *(E. I. iii, 7 ; vii. 160.)*

In N.-W. Mysore the Kādamba chief Malla-dēva was ruling. *(E. C. viii, Sb. 221.)*

In Coimbatore District an inscription of the 25th year of the Kongu-Chōla chief Vīra Rājēndra, whose accession is thus shewn to have taken place in 1207–08. There are many such records duly noted in V. Rangachari's Lists, Vol. I, in Coimbatore. These need not all be noted here. One, No. 443, states that he invaded the Karaivaḷināḍu, in the course of which much damage was done to temples, for which the chief made reparation.

A.D. 1232. Inscriptions of Rājarāja Chōla III in Conjeevaram, South Arcot and Tanjore, in his 16th year, respectively, February 15, and April 14, and March 14, 1232. *(460, of 1919 ; 536 of 1921 ; 76 of 1922 ; 137 of 1923.)*

In N.-W. Mysore, Honnāḷi Taluk, the Dēvagiri-Yādava king Singhaṇa was reigning. *(E. C. vii, Hl. 43.)*

In Central Mysore an inscription of Hoyśala Narasimha II. *(E. C. xii, Ck. 27.)*

Inscription—November 10, 1232,—recording a gift by an official of the Telugu-Chōḍa Chief Madhurāntaka-Pottapi-Chōla-Tirukāḷatti I, who bears the title 'Gaṇḍa-Gōpāla.' It proves that he was a vassal of the Chōla king as the record is dated in the 17th year of Rājarāja III. *(416 of 1919)* *(above s. v., A. D. 1231.)*

A.D. 1233. The same Gaṇḍa-Gōpāla. Record at Conjeevaram. Date = January 18, 1233. *(V. R. i, Chingleput 300 ; 6 of 1893.)*

Rājarāja Chōla III reigning in Conjeevaram and in Tanjore and Trichinopoly districts. *(468 of 1919 ; 526 of 1918 ; V. R. iii, Trich., 263–269 ; 495–501 of 1912 ; 395 of 1919 (which mentions the same Tirukāḷatti I as granting a village (594, 597 of 1919 ; V. R. ii, Tan. 891 ; 515 of 1904 ; E. I. viii, 269).*

Hoyśala Sōmēśvara, son of Narasimha II, at his capital Dorasamudra. Date = July 10, 1233. The inscription mentions him as if reigning, but he did not come to the throne till June 15, 1234, at the earliest. *(E. C. vi, Kd. 12.)*

In Central, and West and in part at least of N. W. Mysore, Hoyśala Narasimha II was reigning. *(E. C. xii, Gb. 45 ; vii, Ci. 52 ; v, Ak. 82.)*

In Sōrāb Taluk, N.-W. Mysore the Dēvagiri-Yādava king Singhaṇa reigned. Tribal fights and great slaughter related. *(E. C. viii, Sb. 403.)*

A.D. 1234. Rājarāja-Chōla III, reigning (Jan. 10, Mar. 27, 1234) in Conjeevaram and Tanjore, and on October 4, in Trichinopoly *(455 of 1919 ; 392 of 1919 ; V. R. iii, Trich. 850 ; 91 of 1914)*. Also in Chingleput on August 8–10, the 43rd day of his 19th year *(211 of 1912)*. And on June 11 in Tanjore District. *(V. R. ii, Tan.,1631 ; 496 of 1904 ; E. I. viii, 269.)*

At the Buddhist stupa at Amarāvati, on the Krishna river, the gift of a lamp was made by Bayyalā, daughter of the Nātavāḍi chief Rudra. This shews that Buddhist worship was still maintained there. *(V. R. ii, Guntur 636 ; 270 of 1897 ; E. I. vi. 157 ; see also V. R. ii, Madras 283.)*

An inscription of Hoyśala Narasimha II in Māṇḍya Taluk, S. Mysore. *(E. C. iii, Md., 121.)*

[He was succeeded by his son Sōmēśvara who came to the throne during the year following June 15, 1234. *(E. C. vi, Tk., 87.)*.]

In Tinnevelly on Nov. 6, 1234, the reigning king was Māravarman-Sundara-Pāṇḍya I. It was his 19th year. *(489 of 1916.)*

A.D. 1235. Rājarāja Chōla III reigning in Trichinopoly District and at Conjeevaram in his 20th year, on July 16 and March 9, 1235. (*39 of 1920 ; 369 of 1919.*)

Inscription in Tinnevelly of the '17th' (*sic.*, but really 19th) year of Māravarman-Sundara-Pāṇḍya I. Date = February 19, 1235 (*V. R. iii, Tinn. 482 ; 133 of 1894 ; E. I. vi, 303*). And on September 3 in his 20th year. (*401 of 1916.*)

In Guntur District, where the Kākatīya king Gaṇapati was now supreme, his general Jaya built the temple at Chebrolu, and gave for its maintenance a village in the Velanāḍu tract. Date = April ?1, 1235. (*V. R. ii, Gun. 88 ; 149 of 1887 ; E. I. vi, 38.*)

In N.-W. Mysore, an inscription of the Devagiri-Yādava king Singhaṇa. (*E. C. viii, Sb. 269.*)

In Travancore, Vīra Ravi Kērala was reigning. (*V. R. iii, Trav. 93-A.*)

Inscription in Salem District shewing as ruler of the country Hoyśala Narasimha II, (*V. R. ii, Salem, 66 ; 201 of 1910*). Another of this year (but no details given) shews Hoyśala Sōmēśvara as reigning king in N. Mysore (*E. C. xi, Jl., 33*). But, again, at this end of 1235 a record in Hassan District, S.-W. Mysore, mentions, as king, Narasimha II (*E. C. v, Cn., 221*). [It would seem probable that Narasimha had abdicated in his son's favour, but was still living.]

A gift was made to a temple during the year at Conjeevaram by the minister of the Telugu-Chōḍa chief Tikka I, during the reign of Rājarāja Chōla III. (*V. R. i, Chinglcput 316 ; 34 of 1893.*)

A.D. 1236. Rājarāja Chōla III reigning in Conjeevaram on February 5, 1236, in his '21st', really 20th year (*560 of 1919*). And on March 5 (437 of 1919). And on December 30, in his 21st year (*596 of 1919*). And on August 13 and 17 (*621 and 622 of 1919*). Also in Tanjore on May 16, in his 20th year (*V. R. ii, Tan., 848 ; 407 of 1908 ; E. I. xi, 129*). And on October 22 in his 21st year. (*247 of 1917.*)

The country about Gudivāda, N. of the Krishna River was governed, by Kākatīya Gaṇapati. (*V. R. ii, Kistna, 227 ; 539 of 1893.*)

In South Mysore, and in the Devangere Taluk of Chitaldroog District in N. Mysore, Hoyśala Sōmēśvara was king (*E. C. iv, Kr. 63 ; xi, Dg. 129*). Also in W. Mysore in Hassan District (*E. C. v, Ak. 123*). In the last, mention is made of his mother Kālaḷādēvī, and his father's sister Sōvalā-dēvī.

The Tirukkōḷūr inscription of Māravarman-Sundara-Pāṇḍya I of the 20th year of his reign describes, in the usual bombastic style of many of these records, the events of his reign; how he invaded Chōla territory, captured and burnt Tanjore and Uraiyūr, visited Chidambaram and there gave back his crown to king Rājarāja Chōla III. [Afterwards he received the Chiefs of the North and South Kongus—probably Perunjinga and Śambuvarāyan[1]—and settled their disputes. Then came a fresh attack by the Chōla forces when a battle was fought in which he was victorious; and

[1] Perunjinga's territory was in South Arcot round Sendamangalam, Tiruvadi and Cuddalore. Śambuvarāyan's territory was in the basin of the Palar with Vrinchipuram and Kanchi as chief towns. Neither has had anything to do with Kongu which lay much to the westward of Dharmapuri in the Salem District. Kongu fell in three divisions: (1) Kongu north of Kaveri, (2) Kongu south of it and (3) Mikongu, Kongu up the hills. Records of this time refer to North and South Kongus alone of these.—*Editor*.

after this he was anointed as a hero at Muḍigoṇḍa-Chōlapuram. [All this seems to have taken place before A.D. 1224. *See above.*] (*See* Prof. Krishnaswami Aiyangar's '*South India*', etc., App., p. 208.)

A.D. 1237. Rājarāja Chōla III reigning in Nellore, in Tanjore (on January 5, January 17 and May 3, 1237), in Conjeevaram (June 10 and October 4), and Chingleput (August 24).

(*V. R. ii, Nellore, 717 ; B. and V. C. 1296 ; V. R. ii, Tanjore, 1105, 1108 ; 195, 198 of 1908 ; E.I. xi, 128 ; 400 of 1919 ; 304, 358 of 1921 ; 481 of 1922.*)

On January 29, 1237, Māravarman Sundara Pāṇḍya was reigning in Tinnevelly.

(*V. R. iii, Tinn. 42 ; 96 of 1907 ; E. I. x, 138.*)

There was more cattle-raiding and slaughter of villagers in Mysore this year. It is mentioned in an inscription of the Dēvagīri-Yādava king Singhaṇa in N.-W. Mysore, of date August 18, 1237.

(*E. C. viii, Sb. 250.*)

Kākatīya Gaṇapati was reigning on the Godāvari river at Drākshārāma, where the Velanāṇḍu Chief Rājēndra-Chōḍa-Gonka ruled locally. (*V. R. ii, Godav. 317 ; 411 of 1893.*)

Hoysala Sōmēsvara was reigning in N. Mysore, where more cattle-raiding took place (*E. C. xi, Hk. 131*). He was also reigning in Central Mysore, where an inscription of this year mentions some local disturbances—A *vīrakal* to a man who fell when the Nāḍāḷvār and other chiefs fought a battle. Sōmēsvara is said to have been 'in the Chōla kingdom', which he 'set up'. Another record says that Sōmēsvara had fought against the Dēvagīri-Yādava prince Krishna-Kandhara (grandson of King Singhana), had penetrated into Chōla territory and had also subdued the Pāṇḍya. (*E. C. iii, Md. 122.*)

A.D. 1238. Rājarāja Chōla III reigning in Conjeevaram on January 6 and 23, February 27 and March 5. (*399, 368, 555, 366 of 1919.*)

An inscription of this year testifies to a gift made by a private person, a Kēraḷa merchant called Rāma, of a village Ammuṇḍi, in the tract north of the Pālār river, which he had bought from the Śambuvaraiyan chief of the Śengēṇi family. It shews that that family owned the land. Ammuṇḍi is in N. Arcot District. (*S. I. I. i. 87.*)

In the same year are two inscriptions of Śengēṇi Ammaiyappan-Aḷagiya-Chōla-Edirili-Śambuvaraiyan (*V. R. i, N. Arcot, 554, 555; 72, 73, of 1887.*) He sold another village for a similar purpose, which was in Vellore Taluk, to the same merchant, here called Ādi-Rāma.

Kākatīya Gaṇapati was reigning in Repalle Taluk, south of the Krishna River.

(*V. R. ii, Guntur, 586 E.*)

An inscription dated in the 23rd year of Māravarman Sundara Pāṇḍya I (1238–39) is in Pudukoṭṭai State. (*V. R. iii, Pudu. 394, 207 of 1914.*)

[According to tradition the Vaishṇava Pontiff Ānandatīrtha was born in this year.

(*E. I. vi. 260.*)]

A.D. 1239. Rājarāja Chola III reigning in Trichinopoly in his 24th year on September 19, and in Conjeeveram on November 15th. (*24 of 1920 ; 606 of 1919.*)

Hoyśala Sōmēśvara reigning in W. Mysore on June 15, in his fifth year; and, during the year, in S. and N.-W. Mysore (*E. C. vi, Tk. 87 ; iii, Tn. 103; iii, Sb. 492*). In the last of these we are told of violent rioting and of the death of a chief.

Māravarman-Sundara-Pāṇḍya II was reigning in Ramnad in his 2nd year on December 7.

(*V. R. ii, Ramnad 268 ; 130 of 1908.*)

Kākatīya Gaṇapati reigning in Ongole Taluk. This shews a still further southward advance made by him (*V. R. ii. Guntur, 413, 415 ; B. and V. C. 1055, 1058*). [Note, however, that he is only given the title 'Mahāmaṇḍalēśvara'.]

A.D. 1240. Rājarāja Chōla III reigning in Conjeevaram on February 12, April 4 and 12, May 12, and August 15 (*611, 612, 615, 559, 388 of 1919*). And in Tanjore on December 13. (*49 of 1911.*)

In this year Hoyśala Sōmēśvara attacked the Telugu-Chōḍa chief Tikka, or Tirukāḷatti I, Ganḍa-Gōpāla. His general was Singaṇa. An inscription in Kaḍūr District, Mysore, states that while Sōmēśvara was on the march, he heard that a son had been born to him. (*E. C. vi, Kadur, 100 ; E. R. 1903–4, p. 54.*)

A.D. 1241. Rājarāja Chōla III reigning in Tanjore on April 5, and on September, and on December 6, 1241. Also in Salem in this year.
(*V. R. ii, Tan. 1238 ; 661 of 1909 ; E. I. xi, 249 ; 75 of 1922 ; V. R. ii, Salem 73; 208 of 1910.*)

King Singhaṇa of the Dēvagiri-Yādavas reigning in N.-W. Mysore, on April 18, 1241. (*E. C. viii, Sb. 387.*)

Hoyśala Sōmēsvara was now residing at Kaṇṇanūr close to Trichinopoly and Śrīrangam in the Chōla country (*E. C. vi, Kd. 83*). [The Hoyśalas had evidently maintained their hold on Kaṇṇanūr and the neighbourhood ever since A.D. 1221 (*see notes above, and s. v. 1222, 1228, 1231, 1235*). In many inscriptions he is said to have made for himself a palace and residence at Kaṇṇanūr in the Chōla country to amuse his mind, and to have re-named the place 'Vikramapura.']

A.D. 1242. Rājarāja Chōla III reigning in Chingleput District, on September 1, 1242 ; and at Conjeevaram in the same district on February 6, March 27, October 21 and December 26 (*111 of 1923 ; 551, 552, 557 of 1919 ; 2 of 1921*). And at Tirumalavāḍi in Uḍaiyārpāḷaiyam Taluk, Trichinopoly District, on July 27 (*25 of 1920*).

Hoyśala Sōmēśvara was reigning in S. Mysore (*E. C. iii, Md. 16 ; iv, Kr. 8, 76*). In *Kr. 8* he is said to be 'in the Chōla country, ruling the kingdom.' [He was certainly at Kaṇṇanūr in the Chōla country, and probably ruled at least some tracts locally.]

In N.-W. Mysore the Dēvagiri-Yādava king Singhaṇa was reigning. There were more local raids and fighting, and siege of a town, in this year. (*E. C. viii, Sb. 217, 425.*)

A gift was made to a temple in Guntur District, Rēpalle Taluk, by Kākatīya Rudra, perhaps Gaṇapati's son. (*V. R. ii, Guntur, 586 F.*)

A.D. 1243. Records of Rājarāja Chōla III in Tanjore District and in Conjeevaram on January 7 and 27, February 28, July 22, October 3.
(*V. R. ii, Tan. 318 ; 291 of 1907 ; E. I. x, 135 ; 511 of 1920 ; 407 of 1919. V. R. ii, Tan. 905 ; 434 of 1908 ; E. I. xi, 130 ; 158 of 1911 ; E. R. 1922, p. 91.*)

In W. Mysore Hoyśala Sōmēśvara reigned. (*E. C. v, Hn. 100.*)

[The old Chōla kingdom now fell to pieces. It will be remembered that the powerful Pallava chief of Śendamangalam, Perunjinga I, had rebelled against his sovereign Rājarāja III, and had captured him, but had been compelled by Narasimha Hoyśala II to release his prisoner. This was in A. D. 1231. Perunjinga I probably died some time during the next twelve years. He was succeeded by another chief of the same name, Perunjinga II. This later Perunjinga in 1243 revolted again, declared his independence, pronounced himself sovereign, and had himself anointed as king. This took place between May 9 and July 30, 1243. His Sanskrit title was 'Avanyavanōdbhava-Rājasimha.'

He seems, however, to have had little success, for inscriptions of subsequent years prove him to have acknowledged as his overlord, at least in some parts of the Chōla realm, the great Telugu-Chōḍa chief of the family that assumed in succession the title 'Ganḍa Gopāla'; while other parts were ruled by the Śambuvaraiyan chief of the Śengēṇi family.

Henceforth the representative of the Chōla family, who is mentioned in inscriptions as reigning, did so only nominally (*E. I. vii, 160 ; S.I.I.. ii, 340 ; E. R. 1903-4, p. 6*). Rājarāja Chōla III seems to have abdicated in 1246, but to have lived till at least 1248 (see below). His successor Rājēndra III was helped to the throne by Hoyśala Sōmēśvara in 1246.

(See *E. I. vii, 169, 176.*)

An inscription in Nellore District mentions the Telugu-Chōḍa chief Madurāntaka-Pottapi-Chōla-Tilaka-Nārāyaṇa-Manuma-Siddha. This was Manma-Siddha (son of Tikka I) afterwards Vijaya-Ganḍagōpāla. This record was during his father's lifetime and rule.

(*B. and V. C. 1258 ; V. R. ii, Nellore, 686.*)

A. D. 1244. Rājarāja Chōla III shewn as reigning in Conjeeveram on September 8, 1244.

(*352 of 1919.*)

An inscription (November 13, 1244), in S. Arcot of Pallava-Perunjinga II, reigning in his second year. (*69 of 1918.*)

At Tirumeyyam in Pudukoṭṭa State an inscription of this year. It states that on a dispute arising between worshippers at the adjoining temples of Śiva and Vishṇu, the people called in the Hoyśala general Appanna, and that he settled it. [It proves Hoyśala overlordships at the time in Pudukoṭṭa.] (*V. R. Puduk. 281 ; 387 of 1906.*)

In Nellore Taluk a record shewing that the local ruler was the Telugu-Chōḍa chief 'Allun-Tirukāḷatti', *i.e.* Tikka I (*B. and V. C. ii. 719 ; V. R. ii, Nell. 427*). Another of the same year alludes to a gift made 'for the merit' of the same chief.

(*V. R. ii. Nell. 729 ; B. and V. C. 1330.*)

The Sindavāḍi country—parts of N.-W. Mysore, Bellary, Dharwar and Bijapur—were ruled over by the Sinda Rāja Bīra-dēva. His capital was at Beḷagutti. (*E. C. viii. Hl. 49.*)

The Kākatiya king Gaṇapati was supreme in Guntur, where he was reigning in security now that the Chōla kingdom was at so low an ebb. At Mōṭupalle on the sea coast (Marco Polo's 'Muṭfili') he gave a decree commanding that, whereas in former times all wrecked ships and their cargoes had been seized by the local authorities and forfeited to the State, henceforth that practice should cease and the cargoes should be left to their owners on payment of custom duty. (*V. R. ii. Guntur 101, 102 ; 600, 601 of 1909 ; E.I. xii, 118 ; Yule's 'Marco Polo' 272, 295, 357.*)

A. D. 1245. Rājarāja Chola III. Inscriptions of his 29th year in Trichinopoly district of February 6 and 12, March 13 and May 19, 1245 (*V. R, iii. Trich. 387, 394, 769 ; 62 of 1903 ; 500 of 1905 ; 142 of 1914 ; 43, 38 of 1920*). Also in Chingleput district on June 26 (*V. R. i. Chin. 754 ; 656 of 1904 ; E. I. viii. 271*) and in Tanjore district on September 9.

(*50, 59 of 1911 ; E. R. 1922, p. 91.*)

Hoyśala Sōmēśvara was reigning in Central Mysore. (*E. C. v, Cn. 221.*)

Kākatīya Gaṇapati supreme in Mārkāpūr Taluk, Kurnool District (*V. R. ii. Kurnool, 338 ; 245 of 1905*). [This seems to shew a further advance on his part.]

At the hill-fortress of Udayagiri in Nellore District the Telugu-Chōḍa chief Tikka I ruled. (*V. R. ii. Nell. 740 ; B. and V. C. 1346.*)

In N.-W. Mysore the Sinda Rāja Bīra-Dēva was ruling. He fought a battle against some local chiefs. (*E. C. vii. Hl. 54, 55.*)

A. D. 1246. [About this time Parākrama Bāhu II, king of Ceylon, who had come to the throne subsequent to the reign of Māgha, usurper from Kalinga, made war against the Tamils who had come over to the island and drove them out, or destroyed them.]

Rājēndra III became Chōla king on a day between March 28 and April 20, 1246 (*E. I. viii. 260*). Three records in Nellore which make his reign begin in 1244 seem to shew that he had been in that year associated with his father Rājarāja III as joint ruler (*B. and V. C. 410, 439, 445*). He was helped to the throne by Hoyśala Sōmēśvara.

Hoyśala Sōmēśvara was ruling in Central and South Mysore (*E. C. v. Cn. 238 ; xii, Tp. 23 ; iii. Md. 62, b*). In the second of these mention is made of local fighting between the 'Kukula Nāḍāḷvār' chief of Kāḍasūr and local leaders.[1] The date of the third is March 4, 1246.

The Kaḷasa country in W. Mysore was ruled by Jākalādēvī, widow of Māru-dēva. (*E. C. vi. Mg. 66, 70.*)

The Telugu-Chōḍa chief Tirukāḷatti, or Tikka I, is said, in an inscription in Nellore district at Annamasamudram, to have 'ruled' in Kānchi (Conjeeveram), where he consecrated a temple. [The 'ruling' may be an exaggeration.] (*V. R. ii. Nell. 7 ; B. and V. C. i. 206.*)

In Guntur district a Parichchēdi chief Bhīma made a gift to a temple. (*138 of 1917.*)

[Mr. Swamikannu Pillai has fixed the date of a record, which purports to be of the 10th year of a Jaṭāvarman Kulaśēkhara Pāṇḍya and is in Tinnevelly taluk, as December 16, 1246. The only year mentioned is the regnal year, and Mr. H. Krishna Sastri believes the record to belong to the reign of Jaṭāvarman Kulaśēkhara I whose 10th year began in A.D. 1199. (*370 of 1916 ; E. R. 1917, p. 93, 110.*)]

A. D. 1247. Inscription of Rājarāja Chōla III (now retired ?) in his 31st year, in Trichinopoly District. Date April 10, 1247 (*55 of 1920*). Another, at Conjeeveram, July 8, 1247 (*566 of 1919*). Regnal year wrongly quoted.

Perunjinga II, Pallava, reigning in S. Arcot in his 4th year on January 19, 1247 (*449 of 1921*), and on December 29, in S. Arcot. (*323 of 1921.*)

Hoyśala Sōmēśvara ruling in S. Mysore (*E.C. iv, Ch. 67.*)

Kākatīya Gaṇapati was reigning in Rajahmundry (*V.R. ii, Godavari 72 ; 506 of 1893.*)

A. D. 1248. Hoyśala Sōmēśvara reigning in W. Mysore. (*E.C. v. Ag. 12.*)

In N. Mysore an inscription of the Dēvagiri-Yādava king Krishna (Kanhara), on September 24, 1248. (*E.C. viii. Sb. 426.*)

Kākatīya Gaṇapati reigning in Rajahmundry (*V. R. ii, Godavari, 84 A*). And in Guntur District (*175 of 1917*). In the latter he is called 'Irmaḍi Gaṇapayya'.

On March 24, 1248, the Niḍugal chief Irungōḷa Chōla II, grandson of Irungōḷa I, was ruling locally in Anantapur District (*V.R. i. Anant. 123 ; 89 of 1913*). A pedigree of these chiefs of

[1] The title in full is Rājēndrachola-Kukula-nāḍaḷva-Kaḍaśūra-Appaya Nāyaka, Kāḍayya Nāyaka. This would mean Kāḍayya Nāyaka, son of Appayya Nāyaka of Kaḍaśūr, who was Kukula Nāḍāḷvār and had the title Rājēndra Choḷa. Kāḍayya would then be chief Kukula nāḍu, Kaḍaśūr being his native village or town.—*Editor.*

Henjēru in N.-E. Mysore, 'Lords of Oraiyūr,' is given in *Pg. 50, E.C. XII.*

(*See above under dates 1128, 1162, 1167 and below 1269, 1285*).

The Telugu-Chōḍa chief Tikka I, here called 'Tikkarasa Gangayya' made a grant in Cuddapah District (*V.R. i. Cudd. 931*). He was ruling also in Nellore District in this year (*B. and V.C. 1231; V.R. ii. Nellore 667*). In the last inscription his younger brother Vijāyaditya is mentioned.

In N.-W. Mysore the Kaḷasa chief Bīra-dēva rose up and made war on the Sāntara chief Bomma of Humcha (Hombuchcha). There was fighting and slaughter, and Bīra plundered Humcha.

(*E.C. viii. Sa. 127, 129.*)

The Nātavāḍi chief Rudra who had married Mailalā-dēvi or Mēlambikā, sister of Kākatīya Gaṇapati, had three sons by her, Rudra, Mahā-dēva, and Mummaḍi Gaṇapa. Each of these brothers gave gifts to temples this year, which are recorded in inscriptions in Kurnool District.

(*V.R. ii, Kurn. 318, 320, 321; 225, 227, 228 of 1905.*)

A. D. 1249. Hoysala Sōmēśvara reigning in W. and Central Mysore. (*E.C. vi. Cm. 20; v. Cn. 238.*)

[A passage in this inscription makes it quite clear that the '*Makara*' kingdom, often mentioned in Hoysala records, does not mean the Pāṇḍya kingdom,—for it calls the king the 'Uprooter of the Makara kingdom and the deliverer of the Pāṇḍya kingdom.']

Rājēndra-Chōla III was reigning in his 3rd year in Tanjore on March 20 and in his 4th year on October 14, 1249 (*V.R. ii. Tan. 703; 406 of 1902; 10 of 1918; E.I. vii. 175*). And in Trichinopoly on September 12, in his 4th year.

(*V.R. iii. Trich. : 361; 596 of 1902; E.I. vii. 6.*)

In Shimoga District, N.-W. Mysore, on June 9, 1249, the Dēvagiri-Yadava king Krishna ('Kannaha') was reigning in his 3rd year—proving his accession to have been in the year following June 9, 1246. (*E.C. viii. Sb. 340.*)

In Tinnevelly inscription of Māravarman-Sundara-Pāṇḍya II on April 25, 1249, in his 11th year. (*V.R. iii. Tinn, 492; 143 of 1894; E.I. vi. 305.*)

Inscription in Tanjore District of Perunjinga Pallava I on July 30, 1249, in his 18th year. As there has been good evidence that Perunjinga II became chief in 1243–44 (*above s.v. A.D. 1247*) this must be a record of Perunjinga I, living in his 18th year but retired (*V.R. ii. Tan. 346; 135 of 1895; E.I. vii. 165*). An inscription of the 7th regnal year of Perunjinga II bears date= October 19, 1249. (*545 of 1921.*)

[An inscription of the 13th century but without date may here be noticed. It is in a village near Avanāśi in the Coimbatore District. A village had been given to the temple by a Kongu-Chōla chief, and the collection of the taxes, a long list of which is given, had been expressly left entirely to the temple authorities. There was a special clause enacted—'No one except the Temple authorities are to be permitted to examine the temple accounts.'

(*99 of 1915; E.R. 1916,p. 121*).]

An inscription at Yēnamanḍala in Guntur district—date A.D. 1249-50—mentions Gaṇapambikā, daughter of Kākatiya Gaṇapati who married Beta, son of Kōṭa-Rudra of Amarāvati. She built a temple there. (*V. R. ii. Guntur 137; 142 of 1913; E. I. iii. 94.*)

On June 8, 1249, the Kākatiya king Gaṇapati seems to have been now firmly settled in Conjeeveram, where his minister Sāmanta Bhōja gave away a village (*V. R. i. Chingleput, 341; 26 of 1890; I. A. xxi, 122, 197*). In Kurnool district, where he was reigning king Gaṇapati gave a tax on salt to a temple in Markapur taluk *(V. R. ii. Kurn. 314 ; 221 of 1905)*. He was reigning in Guntur district at the end of the year 1249. *(805 of 1922.)*

The Telugu-Chōḍa prince Manma-Siddha, who next year succeeded his father Tikka I, made a gift in gratitude for his recovery from illness *(V. R. i. Cuddapah, 812 ; 598 of 1907)*. [It would seem, if the Kākatīya king had captured Conjeeveram, as seems likely from the last noted record, that the Telugu-Chōḍa chief must by now have accepted Gaṇapati as his overlord.]

A. D. 1250. On January 5, 1250, Rājēndra-Chōla III was reigning in Tanjore (nominally) in his 4th year. *(V. R. ii. Tanjore, 1558 ; 423 of 1904.)*

Between August 13 and September 3, 1250, so far as can be gathered from inscriptions, the Telugu-Chōḍa chief Manma-Siddha succeeded his father. He had the family title 'Madhurantaka-Pottapi-Cholā' and called himself 'Vijaya-Gaṇḍagōpāla' and 'Lord of Kānchī.' He seems to have become practically, if not actually, independent; but in some sort was subservient to the Kākatīya king, who had now succeeded in making himself master of Conjeeveram and had crushed out Chōla domination over that region. While Perunjinga's power to the south was weakening that of Manma-Siddha increased.

(E. R. 1900, § 89 ; 1905, § 42 ; 1906, § 44 ; I. A. xxi, 122.)

Kākatīya Gaṇapati of Warangal was in occupation of Conjeeveram. Inscription on a temple there *(V. R. i. Chingleput, 295, 2 of 1893)*. His daughter Gaṇapāmbā, wife of Kōṭa Bēta of Amaravatī-Dharaṇikōta, is described in a record as ruling 6,000 villages S. of the Krishna River *(V. R. ii. Guntur 176 ; 121 of 1893)*. His general Gaṇḍapēṇḍara-Gangayya-Sāhinī of the Kāyashtha family made a gift to a temple in Mārkapūr Taluk, Kurnool District.

(V. R. ii, Kurn. 375 ; 283 of 1905.)

The same Kōṭa Bēta founded a temple and gave a grant for its support in this year in Guntur district. *(V. R. ii. Guntur 137 ; 142 of 1913.)*

An inscription of the 15th regnal year of the Kalingaganga king (or prince) Narasimha I has been reported from Vizagapatam. Its date is said to be Ś. 1172 = A.D. 1250–51 ; and if correct it would make Narasimha's accession to have taken place in A.D. 1236–37.

(V. R. iii. Vizag. 62 ; 98 of 1909.)

[There is some doubt about these accession-dates. They clash with the information derived from other sources *(see J. A. S. B., lxiv. 229, a grant from Puri)*. An inscription at Śrīkurmam in Ganjam District testifies to a gift made by a feudatory of Narasimha I in this year (A.D. 1250–51).

(V. R. i. Gan. 185 ; 307 of 1906.)

In Tinnevelly District on August 12, 1250, Māravarman-Sundara-Pāṇḍya II was reigning in his 13th year. It shews that the latest possible date for his accession was August 12, 1238.

(572 of 1916.)

In Bellary district the Dēvagiri-Yādava king 'Śeuṇa' Khandara (Krishna) was reigning.

(V. R. i. Bell. 261, 276 ; 525 of 1914 ; 84 of 1904 ; Bombay Gaz. 524.)

Hoyśala Sōmēśvara was reigning in Central and W. Mysore (*E. C. v, Ag, 55 ; Cn, 221*) also in Salem district, where a record mentions the date as in his 17th year (*V. R. ii. Salem 69 ; 204 of 1910*). In N.-W. Mysore another battle was fought between neighbouring chiefs.

(E. C. viii. Tl, 25.)

A. D. 1251. On March 27, 1251, Rājēndra-Chōla III was reigning in Tanjore in his 5th year.

(V. R. ii, Tan. 1085; 56 of 1914; E. I. ix, 222.)

Rājarāja Chōla III seems to have been still alive at this date. His 36th year is mentioned in an inscription in Nellore District. (*V. R. ii. Nell. 161.*)

In N. Arcot on September 25, 1251, Vijaya-Gaṇḍagōpāla (Manma-Siddha) was ruling in his 'third' year. (*264 of 1921*), a Vaiḍumba chief, Rājēndra-Chōla, was his vassal. (*V. R. ii. Nellore, 633.*) [The date seems open to doubt.]

South of the Krishna River in the Palnāḍ Taluk, Kākatīya Gaṇapati reigned. (*V. R. ii. Gun. 498 ; 571 of 1909.*)

Central Mysore. Hoyśala Sōmēśvara reigning. (*E. C. xii, Tp. 13.*)

Travancore—(Vēṇāḍ) was reigned over by Vīra-Ravi-Udaiya-Mārttāṇḍa-Varman. (*T. A. S. iv, Pt. I. p. 88.*)

[Jaṭāvarman-Sundara-Pāṇḍya I came to the throne of Madura between April 20 and 28, 1251. (*E. I. xi. 266*).]

A. D. 1252. Inscription at Śrīrangam dated Dec. 25 A. D. 1252 in the 7th year of Rājēndra III. It states that he defeated Hoyśala Sōmēśvara, and presumably drove him out of Kaṇṇanūr, which is close to Śrīrangam and where Sōmēśvara had made his residence. Rājēndra's capital was now at Gangaikoṇḍa-Chōlapuram (*V. R. iii. Trichinopoly 475 ; 64 of 1892 ; E. I. vii, 176*). Another record of the 7th regnal year, otherwise undated, goes further and declares that Sōmēśvara had been reduced to such a humble condition that he himself fastened on Rājēndra's leg an 'anklet of heroes.' [These things must not be taken too literally. Sōmēśvara was Rājēndra's uncle and had helped him to his throne. As to Sōmēśvara's having been driven out of Kaṇṇanūr and Śrīrangam it must be noticed that records of his are found further to the south than that place.]

Hoyśala Sōmēśvara was reigning in Central and West Mysore. (*E.C. v, Cn, 237, 242 ; Ag. 53.*) An inscription shews him at his capital Dorasamudra 'after having marched to Haḷagere and returned.' (*E. C. vi. Kd. 101.*)

In S. Arcot Perūnjinga II (Pallava) was ruling in his 10th year on Oct. 4, 1252. (*459 of 1921.*)

An inscription at Tiruvallam in N. Arcot District is pregnant with information as to the state of the old Chōla kingdom at this time. That tract was locally governed by Aḷagiya-Pallavan-Edirili-Chōla-Śambuvaraiyan of the Śengēṇi family, who proclaims himself here as subject, not to the Chola king but, to the Telugu-Chōḍa Vijaya-Gaṇḍagōpāla, reigning in his 3rd year; who therefore may now be assumed to be *de facto* king in that part. (*V. R. i., N. Arcot, 333 ; 79 of 1889. See also S.I.I., i. Nos. 59, 60, 63 ; iii, p. 123.*)

Jaṭāvarman-Sundara-Pāṇḍya I reigning in Coimbatore District in his second year; and at Nāmakal in Salem district. (*553 of 1905 ; 5 of 1906.*)

Kākatīya Gaṇapati was reigning in Repalle taluk in the Guntur District, and in Kurnool in Markapur taluk (*V. R. ii. Guntur 586–G ; ii, Kurnool 216, 217, 501 ; 223, 224 of 1905*). Another inscription in Kurnool mentions this as Gaṇapati's 54th regnal year, which helps to fix his accession as in 1199. (*V. R. ii. Kurn. 288 ; 195 of 1905.*)

Travancore was ruled over by Vīra-Padmanābha-Mārttāṇḍa-Varman of Kēraḷa. (*V. R. iii. Trav. 226.*)

A. D. 1253. Hoyśala Sōmēśvara reigning in Central, East and South Mysore and in Trichinopoly District at Ratnagiri (*E. C. v., Cn, 236 ; E. C. ix., Bn. 6 ; E. I. iii. 8 ; Bombay Gaz. i, 508 ; E.C. iv. Hg. 111*). In the second of these he is said to be residing in 'Vikramapura, which he had created for his pleasure in the Chōla country.' [Vikramapura is Kaṇṇanūr, from which, therefore, if the inscription records the true facts he had not been expelled as the Chōla records have it. His queen Somalā-dēvī is mentioned. The Ratnagiri inscription bears date = April 13, 1253, and mentions his 21st year. If so his accession was in the year follwing April 13, 1233. But the regnal year may be counted from the date of his independent command in the southern Hoyśala country—not necessarily from the date of his becoming king.] *(V. R. iii. Trichinopoly 108 ; 176 of 1914.)*

In Nellore District an inscription, dated March 1, 1253, in which the sovereign is said to be Rājēndra Chōla III. *(V. R. ii. Nell. 799 ; B. and V. C. 1393.)*

On March 27, 1253, Jaṭāvarman Sundara Pāṇḍya I gave a gift in Tanjore during his occupation of the country *(V.R. ii. Tan. 1506 ; E.I. vi. 306 : 254 of 1904)*. Other records of his are in Trichinopoly District in Uḍaiyārpāḷaiyam Taluk, of dates April 19, and October 29, the first in his second, the second in his third regnal year *(V. R. iii. Trichinopoly 899, 898 ; 90, 89 of 1895 ; E.I. vi. 306.)*. Another, in the same Taluk, bears date = November 8, 1253. *(31 of 1920.)*

Kākatīya Gaṇapati was reigning in Ongole Taluk, Guntur District. *(V.R. ii. Gun. 352 ; B. and V.C. 940.)*

Perunjinga II reigned in Conjeeveram on May 16, 1253. *(353 of 1919.)*

[Between April 30 and July 13, 1253, the Pāṇḍya prince or king Jaṭāvarman Vīra Pāṇḍya's rule, or reign, began. He may have been one of the Pāṇḍya princes who ruled parts of the old Pāṇḍya dominions, but it is clear that he was not reigning in *succession* to Jaṭāvarman Sundara Pāṇḍya I. As otherwise his title would have been 'Māravarman'. Mr. S. Krishnaswami Aiyangar thinks that he was co-regent with the latter *(South India, etc., p. 47)*. His panegyrists give him credit for Sundara's exploits. He is often heard of later.]

A. D. 1254. Kākatīya Gaṇapati reigning in Kurnool, Guntur and Kistna districts *(V.R. ii, Kurn. 262, 264, 324 ; 169, 231 of 1905 ; Gun. 416, 854 ; 160 of 1899 ; B. and V.C. 1064 ; Kistna, 232 ; 543 of 1893.)*. One of the Kurnool records mention a gift made by his minister Gangayya-Sāhini of the Kāyashtha family.

In Bellary District the Devagiri-Yādava king Kannara (Krishna) reigned on June 28, 1254, and on June 16, 1255. *(732, 733 of 1919.)*

Perunjinga II reigned (?) in Conjeeveram on July 20, 1254. *(450 of 1919.)*

Also at Conjeeveram there is an inscription on September 14, 1254, of Vijaya-Gaṇḍagōpāla mentioned as if reigning there *(538 of 1919)*. This was his fifth year and it shews that the last possible day for his accession was September 14, 1250. [It is curious and interesting to find these two rulers mentioned as sovereign in the same city within two months of one another.]

[In this year apparently Jaṭāvarman Sundara Pāṇḍya and Vīra Pāṇḍya broke into open war. First (or perhaps in an earlier year) the Chēra or Kēraḷa army was attacked and beaten and the Kēraḷa king killed. Then, about this year, the Pāṇḍya forces attacked the Hoyśala king. Sundara's inscriptions state that he gained a complete victory, killing a Hoyśala general and putting to flight the Hoyśala king. He attacked Kaṇṇanūr, the Hoyśala's residence, and reduced the country. *(South India, etc., p. 46, 47)*.]

Hoyśala Sōmēśvara's inscriptions of this year are in Central, South-West and South Mysore *(E. C. xii. Tp. 125 ; v, Ak. 108 ; iii. Sr. 110.)*. The last bears date = October 18, 1254, when he was reigning at Dorasamudra. There is an inscription shewing Sōmēśvara's son Narasimha III as reigning at Dorasamudra (Halebīḍ) on November 26, 1254 *(E.C.v. Bl, 125)* and it may be that his father Sōmēśvara had been, as some Pāṇḍya inscriptions state, killed in the fighting at Kaṇṇanūr.

There was more fighting between rival chiefs in N.-W. Mysore in this year.

(E.C. viii. Tl. 177.)

A. D. 1255. Inscription in Tanjore on January 12, 1255, Rajēndra Chōla III, in his 9th year. *(V. R. ii. Tan. : 1553 ; 418 of 1904 ; E. I. viii. 273.)*

Kākatiya Gaṇapati was reigning in Nellore District early in 1255. *(B. and V. C. i. 137.)*

In Dharwar District at Hulgur is an inscription (examined by Dr. Barnett) shewing that country under the rule of the Dēvagiri-Yādava king Krishna ('Kandara') in his 9th regnal year *(E. I. xvi. 334).* The date = February 22, 1255.

[The Hoyśala king Sōmēśvara either died after his flight from Kaṇṇanūr, or was, as Pāṇḍya inscriptions say, killed in the fighting when Sundara-Pāṇḍya attacked him ; and he was succeeded by his eldest son Narasimha III apparently on some day before November 26, 1254, *(see above s. v. 1254).* This however is not quite certain. Narasimha III divided the Hoyśala dominions, himself reigning in the north, while his brother Rāmanātha reigned, almost or wholly, independently in the south. This arrangement seems to have been made in June–July 1255, which is the date arrived at from inscriptions for the beginning of Rāmanātha's reign.

An inscription shews that Narasimha III was in possession of Śrīrangam again in the middle of 1255 *(see E. I. vii. 160 ; iii. 11)* Pāṇḍya inscriptions state that Sundara-Pāṇḍya after the sack of Kaṇṇanūr went to Chidambaram, had himself anointed as a hero and weighed himself against gold, which he distributed ; and then crowned himself king at Śrīrangam. Thence he marched to Perunjinga the Kāṭhaka king's capital Śēndamangalam, seized it and sacked it, but afterwards restored him, and he drove away a Bāna chief and made him flee to the forests. *(E. I. iii. 11.)*

It may be noted here that the political situation in North India had changed entirely against its Hindu rulers. Delhi had been captured by the Muhammadans in A.D. 1193 and these invaders by now dominated all North India,—the 'Slave-King' Nazir-ud-din Mahmud reigning at Delhi.]

In W. Mysore on April 19, 1255, Hoyśala Narasimha III was reigning *(E. C. v. Ag. 38.)* In N.-W. Mysore there was more local fighting and loss of life *(E. C. viii. Sa. 150).* Inscriptions shew that N.-W. Mysore was governed by the Dēvagiri-Yādava king 'Śeuṇa Kānha, [Krishna], the establisher of the Telunga king'—an allusion to the restoration of Kākatiya Gaṇapati by Krishna's great grand-father, Jaitrapāla I about the year A.D. 1199.

(E. C. viii. Sb., 135, 136.)

An inscription in Kurnool District has reference to a gift made by Kāyashtha Gangayya-Sāhini, general of Kākatiya Gaṇapati. He has the titles 'Gaṇḍapēṇḍēra' and 'Maṇḍalika-Brahma-Rākshasa.' *(V. R. ii. Kurn. : 269 ; 176 of 1905.)*

A. D. 1256. In Chingleput District an inscription of February 29, 1256, shews that the then recognized ruler there was Jaṭāvarman Sundara Pāṇḍya I *(209 of 1923).* It shews that cattle raids were prevalent at that time.

In Chittoor District an inscription of the local Kāḷahasti Chief Nalla Siddhi 'of Kānchi,' mentioning as his overlord Vijaya-Gaṇḍagōpala of the Telugu-Chōḍa family in the latter's seventh year. *(V. R. i. Chit. : 141 ; 202 of 1903.)*

On September 11, 1256, an inscription of the 11th year of Rājēndra Chōla III at Kōvilur in Tanjore District *(V. R. ii. Tan. : 1118 ; 208 of 1908 ; E. I. xi. 131).* And at Vallam in the same district, near Tanjore, an inscription which mentions as sovereign the Pallava Perunjinga II, giving him full royal titles *(S.I.I. ii. 340)*. [These records shew how the old Chōla kingdom was now broken up.]

In Tinnevelly Jaṭāvarman Vīra Pāṇḍyā was reigning in his 3rd year on November 9, 1256 *(432 of 1917)*.

In Kurnool Kākatīya Gaṇapati was reigning. *(V. R. ii. Kurn. : 405.)*

In South and West Mysore Hoyśala Sōmēśvara's name is given as reigning, in two inscriptions, though according to other records he had either died, or abdicated in favour of his son Narasimha, two years earlier *(E.C. v. Ak. 166 ; iv. Kr. 9)*. In N.-W. Mysore an inscription mentions as locally ruling a certain Bīrarasa *(E. C. viii. Sb. 561)*. In Coorg the sovereign was Hoyśala Narasimha III *(ibid. i. 6)*.

A. D. 1257. In North Arcot District on January 22, 1257, Jaṭāvarman Vīra Pāṇḍya is said to be reigning in his fourth year *(299 of 1919)*. This record comes from the Tiruvaṇṇāmalai Taluk.

Another inscription of the same year, 1257–58, and in Cheyyār Taluk, North Arcot, registers a gift of land in the 8th year of Vijaya-Gaṇḍagopāla of the Telugu-Chōḍas, by 'Piḷḷaiyār' Rājarāja Śambuvaraiyan. (In some records this chief is called 'Āḷappirandān,' 'Avaniyāḷappirandān,' and 'Pallavāṇḍār.") *(V. R. i. N. Arcot 230 ; 302 of 1912.)*

[The name 'Piḷḷaiyār' may apparently be taken to mean a favourite, or a son, of a king. Nīlagangaraiyar is also called a 'Piḷḷaiyār' of Vijaya-Gaṇḍa-Gōpāla *alias* Manma-Kshamā-Vallabha, and the Government Epigraphist in 1913 expressed the opinion that both Rājarāja Śambuvaraiyar and Nīlagangaraiyar were sons of Vijaya-Gaṇḍa-Gōpāla. The matter must be left over for settlement. All I can say at present is that the brotherhood of these two chiefs does not seem to me to be proved by sufficiently conclusive evidence. [1] That these Śambuvaraiyans were vassals of the Telugu-Chōḍas is shown by records in A.D. 1252, 1273 (*q.v.*).

Vijaya-Gaṇḍa-Gōpāla is described as ruling in Conjeeveram, where there are three records of his of this year whose dates correspond to January 29, September 19, and November 18 (or perhaps December 16), 1257. *(393, 571 and 343 of 1919.)*

In Conjeeveram also is an inscription of date May 3, 1257—the same year—in which the ruler of the country is said to be the Pallava Chief Perunjinga II. The only possible explanation seems to be that both these rival chiefs outwardly affected loyalty to the Chōla king, and were severally supported by their own adherents. *(350 of 1919.)*

Perunjinga II is also represented by another record of March 14, 1257 in South Arcot where he is described as reigning. *(447 of 1921.)*

In Tanjore District on July 19, 1257 an inscription (remission of taxes) of the 12th year of Rājēndra Chōla III, named as reigning there (*V. R. ii. Tan. 1525* ; *531 of 1904* ; *E.I. viii, 273*). But another in Tanjore Taluk of October 7, 1257, mentions, as if reigning there Jaṭāvarman Sundara Pāṇḍya I. *(V.R. ii. Tan. 1460 ; 166 of 1894.)*

In Pudukoṭṭa an inscription commemorates the setting up of an image in a temple in the 23rd year of Hoyśala Sōmēśvara by one of his generals. [This does not necessarily mean that the Hoyśala king was reigning there. And apparently Sōmēśvara was now dead.] *(V. R. iii. Pudu. 262 ; 215 of 1914.)*

[1] See the Genealogical Tables under heading 'Nīlagangaraiyar.' There were several chiefs of that name during the years A. D. 1186 to 1306.

In Trichinopoly District at Śrīrangam the king is stated to be Hoysala Rāmanātha (*V. R. iii, Trich. 478*; *67 of 1892*; *E. I. iii. 9*) in an inscription there of date = January 24, 1257. This would argue that he had driven the Pāṇḍya king Jaṭavarman Sundara I out of the neighbourhood of Kaṇṇanūr subsequent to Sundara's capture of it. But a record at the same place (*V. R. iii. Trich. 460*; *45 of 1891*) gives rise to the supposition that Sundara was firmly established at Śrīrangam after his occupation, for he carried out extensive works there, built several shrines, covered other shrines with gold, built a large hall and made many valuable gifts to the temple. Amongst other gifts was a necklace of emeralds which the inscription states had been looted from Śēndamangalam, the capital of Pallava Perunjinga II. (*E. I .iii. 7, Dr. Hultzsch.*)

In W. Mysore Hoysala Narasimha III was reigning. (*E. C. vi, Cm. 1.*)

In Coimbatore District is an inscription of the second year of a Kongu-Chōla chief Vikrama Chola. Another record shews that he lived till at least A.D. 1263.

(*V. R. i. Coim. 207, 230 ; 555, 578 of 1905.*)

A. D. 1258. In Chingleput District Manma-Siddha II Vijaya-Gaṇḍagōpāla was reigning on April 16, 1258 (*211 of 1923*). Also at Pottapi in Cuddapah District during the year 1258–59 (*V. R. i, Cudd. 857 ; 437 of 1911*). And in Nellore District where there were local disturbances and a revolt put down by him (*V. R. ii. 297, 332 ; B. and V. C. 520, 595*). The first of these in which a mistake was made in the number of Śaka year, the quoted cyclic year being 'Kālayukti' and therefore *Ś 1180*, not *1170* as stated shews that Manma-Siddha II was also known as Nalla-Siddha. At Conjeeveram also Manma-Siddha was reigning on December 28, 1258.

(*428 of 1919.*),

In Salem District at Namakal Jaṭāvarman Sundara Pāṇḍya I reigning in his fifth year when he gave a village. (*13 of 1906.*)

But in Trichinopoly (July 28, 1258) the sovereign named is Jaṭāvarman Vīra Pāṇḍya in his sixth year (*34 of 1920*). The same ruler's seventh year is also mentioned in another record in the same district (*99 of 1920*). The date of the last is September 12, 1259.

Perunjinga II's overlordship is recognized in inscriptions in South Arcot on March 11, April 8, May 13 and July 3, 1258, in his sixteenth regnal year.

(*465 of 1921 ; 96 of 1906 ; E. I. ix. 216 ; 455 of 1921 ; 65 of 1918 ; 38 of 1922.*)

Jaṭāvarman Sundara Pāṇḍya II is named as ruling in Chingleput District on May 27, 1258, in his eighth year. (*V. R. i, Chin. 133 ; 305 of 1909.*)

In N. Mysore Krishna of the Devagīri-Yādavas reigned. (*E. C. xi, Dg. 103.*)

In W. Mysore Hoysala Narasimha III reigned. (*E. C. v, Ak. 109.*)

In N. Arcot near Poḷūr an inscription mentions the Śengēṇi chief Rājagambhīra-Śambuvaraiyar. (*V. R. i, N. Arcot 377; 93 of 1887.*)

In the Palnāḍ Taluk, Guntur District, Kākatiya Gaṇapati was the reigning king.

(*V. R. ii, Gun. 502.*)

A. D. 1259. Jaṭāvarman Sundara Pāṇḍya I named as reigning in Chingleput on February 26, April 29 and June 15, 1259, in his ninth year (*303 of 1921 ; V. R. i, Chin. 167, 168 ; 186, 187 of 1894.*) Also in Salem District (*622 of 1905.*) And at Perambalūr, a few miles N. of Śrīrangam (*V. R. iii, Trichinopoly, 250 ; 8 of 1913*). This last is interesting. It shews that at this period when armies were always on the march the villagers were put to some expense for the maintenance of the troops, and had to ensure their own security. The village council concerned set aside some taxes for the purpose of 'making friendly terms with, and meeting the expenses of, the followers of Sundara-Pāṇḍya.'

In S. Arcot on March 29, 1259, an inscription declares the ruler there to be Jaṭāvarman Vīra Pāṇḍya. (*406 of 1921.*)

In Nellore the reigning king was the Telugu-Chōḍa chief Manma-Siddha Vijaya-Gaṇḍagōpāla (*V. R ii, Nell. 333 ; B. and V. C. 598*). Also on September 13, 1259, in Chingleput District in his tenth year where an inscription records a gift by Perumāḷ Nāchchi, senior queen of Panchanadi-vāṇan-Nilagangaraiyar. (*V. R. i, Chin. 986 ; 117 of 1912.*)

At Rāyakōṭa in Krishnagiri Taluk, Salem District, an inscription shews that the then ruler was Hoyśala Rāmanātha, governing in his sixth year. (*V. R. ii, Salem 120 ; 4 of 1888.*)

An inscription in W. Mysore of this year shews as sovereign Hoyśala Narasimha III, having Dorasamudra for his capital (*E. C. vi, Kd. 92*). Another shews that Narasimha was reigning over Central Mysore. (*E. C. xii, Tp. 28.*)

In Kurnool are inscriptions of the 61st regnal year of Kākatīya Gaṇapati, testifying to gifts made to temples by the Kāyashtha chief 'Gaṇḍapeṇḍēra' Jannigadēva and the Nāthavāḍi chief Kumāra-Gaṇapati. (*V. R. ii, Kurn. 301, 306, 274 ; 208, 213, 181 of 1905.*)

In Mārkāpūr Taluk, Kurnool District, then under the rule of Kōṭa Gaṇapati who was son of Kēta III of Amarāvati and his wife Bayyāmbā or Bayyalā, a gift was made to a temple by a local potentate. (*V. R. ii. Kurn. 311 ; 218 of 1905.*)

Pallava Perunjinga II reigning in S. Arcot in his 17th year on December 26, A.D. 1259 (*320 of 1921*). [Note that in this same year the Pāṇḍya princes held Salem and Chingleput (*see above*).]

In Trichinopoly District a record of November 6, 1259, in Uḍaiyārpāḷaiyam Taluk recognizes Rājēndra Chōla III as sovereign. (*V. R. iii. Trich. 852 ; 93 of 1914.*)

A. D. 1260. In Kurnool and Nellore are records of Kākatīya Gaṇapati in his 62nd year. [This was his last year. His daughter Rudramma was made Queen in her own right in succession to him. She is constantly given male titles, and her period of rule was generally successful and marked by good government.] (*V. R. ii. Kurn. 289 ; Nell. 590 ; 196 of 1905 ; B. and V. C. 1165. See also A. A. R. for 1905-6, p. 168.*) A C. P. grant, with a correct date mentioning a solar eclipse, shews that Gaṇapati was reigning on April 12, 1260. (*E. R. 1917. C. P. No. 4.*)

Perunjinga II is shewn as reigning in Chingleput District on October 31, 1260, at Conjeeveram. (*V. R. i. Chin. 353 ; 38 of 1890 ; E. I. vii, 164-A.*)

Jaṭāvarman Sundara Pāṇḍya I was reigning at Jambukēśvaram, Trichinopoly District, in his tenth year, on April 28, 1260. The inscription states that he had 'uprooted Kēraḷa' (an allusion to his earlier exploits) and was an enemy of Gaṇḍagōpāla, Perunjinga, and Gaṇapati (*V. R. iii. Trich. 417 ; 32 of 1891 ; I. A. xxi, 121 ; xxii, 221 ; E. I. vi, 307*). Also in Chingleput on May 23 (*322 of 1911*).

[Sundara Pāṇḍya I was very active this year, owing probably to the change of crown in the Kākatīya country. He is said to have marched to the North through Perunjingā's country about Chingleput and Vijaya Gāṇḍa-gōpāla's territory, driving the Telugu troops before him as far as Nellore, and defeating Kākatīya Rudramma. At Nellore he had himself crowned for the second time. He did not, apparently, proceed further to the North but returned to Śrīrangam. It is noteworthy that about 40 years later Rashīd-ud-din, writing about the kingdom of Ma'abar, says that it extended across the peninsula from Quilon to Nellore.]

[I cannot refrain from recording here an expression of doubt as to this Northern expedition of Sundara Pāṇḍya I. It would seem almost impossible in the circumstances in which he was placed. It means that he left Śrīrangam, within a few miles of which place resided his enemy Hoyśala Rāmānatha; marched through the country of Perunjinga whose capital, Śēndamangalam, he had recently looted, and who therefore must have been his bitter foe; continued his march through the centre of the territory of Vijaya-Gaṇḍagōpāla,—also hostile to him and to whom, as one of his Śrīrangam inscriptions expresses it, he was as a 'jungle fire to a forest'; and forced his way into the Kākatīya dominions. He could not have had a sufficiently large army to protect his line of communications, about 300 miles long, as well as his base at Śrīrangam; considering that both base and communications were exposed to attack on all sides from the enemy, who surrounded him in front, flank and rear at every point. We have, however, no authority to appeal to, and must accept the assertions of the inscriptions, i.e. of the framers of the inscriptions, whose aim was the glorification of their ruler. Note that Rāmanātha is said to be reigning in Śrīrangam in A.D. 1261 (*below*).]

In W. Mysore Hoysala Narasimha III continued to reign (*E. C. vi. Tk. 3*). Rāmanātha ruled in Salem (*V. R. ii. Salem 67 ; 202 of 1910 ; 4 of 1910*) and is said to have ruled at Śrīrangam. (*E. I. iii. p. 7.*)

An inscription in Markapur Taluk, Kurnool District, mentions Rājēndra Chola III as reigning there in this year. It was evidently engraved by adherents of the Chōla crown, and must not be taken as historically proving Chōla supremacy. (*V. R. ii. Kurn : 294 ; 201 of 1905.*)

On October 23, 1260, Vira Pāṇḍya was reigning (or ruling) in S. Arcot in his 8th year. (*66 of 1918.*)

At Manimangalam, Chingleput District, an inscription mentions a Bāṇa chief as living at the time. [The family, then still existed.] (*V. R. i. Chin. 816 ; 286 of 1897.*)

The Telugu-Chōḍa chief 'Manma-Bhūpati' *i. e.* Manma-Siddha ruling at Guḍivāḍa, N. of the Krishna River (*V. R. ii. Kistna, 239-243*). In his reign, here called, 'Gaṇḍa-Gopāla Vijayāditya' a local chief is mentioned in Nellore District, who was descended from 'Mukkanti-Kāḍuvetti',—*i. e.* of Pallava descent. (*V. R. ii. Nell. 334, 335 ; B. and V.C. 599, 600.*)

A Kolanu-Rāja, Yeṟagaya-dēva, was ruling in the Tanuku Taluk, Kistna District. (*741 of 1920.*)

A. D. 1261. On December 14, 1261, Hoyśala Rāmanātha was reigning at Śrīrangam in his 7th year. Inscription in the Jambukeśvarda temple (*E. I. iii* p. *10 No. ii*). In W. Mysore Hoyśala Narasimha III reigned (*E. C. v. Ag. 42 ; Bl. 74, 98*). And in S. Mysore (*Ibid. iii Tn, 8*c. *Md. 30.*) and in Central Mysore. (*Ibid. xii. ck. 2.*)

Jaṭāvarman Sundara Pāṇḍya I reigning in Tanjore and Trichinopoly districts on May 29 and July 19 and August 31, 1261.
(*V. R. ii, Tan. 688 ; 25 of 1914 ; iii, Trich. 880, 71 ; 71 of 1895 ; 741 of 1909 ; E. I. vi, 308 ; xi, 257.*)

Perunjinga II was ruling in Conjeeveram and in South Arcot District on September 1 and November 28, 1261. (*365 of 1919 ; 316 of 1921.*)

The Kākatīya queen Rudramma reigned in Kurnool District. The record which is one of her second year, calls her 'Rudra-dēva', her masculine name (*V. R. ii, Kurnool, 287 ; 194 of 1905*). And in Guntur District. (*94 of 1917.*)

A. D. 1262. Records in Tanjore of May 21, and October 27, 1262, in Tanjore District name as sovereign Rājēndra Chōla III. *(V. R. ii. Tan : 1123, 1133 ; 214, 223 of 1908.)*

The Dēvagiri-Yādava king Sēvaṇa' Mahādēva now reigning in Bellary District. [He had succeeded his brother Krishna in 1259-60.] *(V. R. i. Bell. 202 ; 446 of 1914.)*

Jaṭāvarman Sundara Pāṇḍya I was reigning in Trichinopoly District on October 23, 1262. *(V. R. iii. Trich. 276 ; 508 of 1912.)*

In the same District at Tiruveḷḷarai and Tiruppattūr, the reigning king is stated to be Hoyśala Rāmanātha. [Thus it is certain that he still retained his hold of Kaṇṇanūr and the neighbourhood.] *(V. R. iii, Trich. 175 ; 590 of 1908 ; 542 of 1905.)*

An inscription in Drāksharāma, Godavari District, mentions Pallava Perunjinga II under his title 'Avanyavanōdbhava', giving him the rank of a sovereign. It also mentions the actual ruler of the country, the Kākatīya king. [This would seem to argue that Perunjinga and Rudramma were on friendly terms.] *(V. R. Godav. 325 ; 419 of 1893 ; E. I. vii, 167.)*. [So far from admitting that Perunjinga had been defeated by Sundara Pāṇḍya I, this inscription says that Perunjinga 'Established the Pāṇḍya country'.]

In Narsapur Taluk, Kistna District the Kōna-Manḍala chief Gaṇapati was ruling. *(V. R. ii, Kistna 310 ; 520 of 1893.)*

The Koṭa chief Gaṇapati ruled locally part of Guntur District. Date = August 13, 1262. *(103 of 1917.)*

A. D. 1263. An inscription of the 11th year of Jaṭāvarman Vīra Pāṇḍya in the Pudukoṭṭai state attributes to him enormous conquests, most of which would appear to be fabulous—He conquered China, Bengal, killed two kings of Ceylon, etc. [There is no mention of such events in the *Mahāwaṁsa.*] *(V. R. iii. Pudu. 91 ; 356 of 1906 ; E. R. 1912, § 39.)*

Vijaya-Gaṇḍagōpāla-Manma-Siddha II, Telugu-Choḍa chief was ruling in Chingleput on March 27, 1263, and during the year in Nellore District. *(230 of 1922 ; V. R. ii. Nell. 442; B. and V. C. 740.)*. And in Kurnool District. *(V. R. ii. Kurn. 364 ; 272 of 1905.)*

A. D. An inscription shews Hoyśala Narasimha III reigning in Central Mysore. *(E. C. xii. Tp. 2.)*

[An interesting record of about this date (impossible to fix the year exactly, but it belongs to the 12th year of Jaṭāvarman Sundara Pāṇḍya I, which expired in April 1263) affords an insight into the conditions of life in the villages in these days. Two villages, evidently after much discussion, came to an agreement. It is arranged between them that the customary raids should not be in future quite so savage as in the past; and that although 'woundings, stabbings and deaths' may take place yet hereafter the fighting men of each village will refrain from molesting the peaceable inhabitants of the village they attack, or from destroying the houses ; and that should such persons be injured or houses be destroyed the guilty party will submit to being fined.] *(V. R. iii. Pudukoṭṭa 135 ; 359 of 1914.)*

A.D. 1264. At Ratnagiri in Trichinopoly District, Jaṭāvarman Sundara Pāṇḍya I gave a grant. *(V. R. iii. Trich. 77 ; 145 of 1914)*. A puzzling inscription at Tiruppārkaḍal in North Arcot makes out that this same Pāṇḍya issued a proclamation from Kaṇṇanūr—a place which we have seen in possession of Hoyśala Rāmanātha *(702 of 1904)*. Another of this king and belonging to this year is at Kāverīpākkam close to Arcot.[1] *(402 of 1905.)*

[1] Another inscription of this year says that Vira Pāṇḍya employed in his army horsemen from the Kanarese country *(134 of 1908)*.

In N. Mysore the Dēvagiri-Yadava king Mahādēva was reigning. A battle between rival chiefs is mentioned. (*E. C. xi. Dg. 87.*)

Queen Rudramma's general Jannigadēva, now called 'Mahārāja', gave a grant of land in Palnāḍ Taluk, Guntur District, for a temple. (*V. R. ii. Gun. 520 ; 550 of 1909.*)

Rājēndra Chōla III recognized as king in Tanjore on January 2, 1264.
(*V. R. ii. Tan. 1629 ; 494 of 1904 ; E. I. viii, 274.*)

A. D. 1265. Hoyśala Narasimha III reigning at Dorasamudra, Mysore, early in the year. (*E. C. vi. Cm., 89*). Another inscription of his reign in Central Mysore states that under the king's orders the Nāḍāḷva chief[1] Chōla-Kukula-Kāḍasūr-Kādaya-Nāyaka made a raid on his neighbour's property (*E. C. xii. Tp. 22*). Narasimha is shewn to be reigning in S.-E. Mysore.
(*E. C. ix. Kn. 80.*)

Jaṭāvarman Vīra Pāṇḍya was reigning in Tinnevelly District on April 27, 1265 (*6 of 1916*). And in Chingleput District on December 11. (*276 of 1910 ; E. R. 1922, p. 92.*)

The Telugu-Chōḍa Vijaya-Gaṇḍagōpāla is represented by three inscriptions at Conjeeveram. (*V. R. i. Chingleput, 342, 350, 351 ; 27, 35, 36 of 1890 ; I. A. xxi. 122 ; xxii. 219 E. I. vii. 128.*)

In Bellary district the Dēvagīri-Yadava king Mahādēva reigned on July 13, 1265, in his 6th year (*V. R. i. Bell. 154 ; 519 of 1914*), and in N. Mysore, where more local fighting and slaughter took place (*E. C. xi. Dg., 100*). At that time in N.-W. Mysore there was still more massacre, chiefs fighting against their neighbours. The local ruler there was the Santaḷige chief Bomma, son of Vīra. (*E. C. viii. Sa., 140.*)

Perunjinga II reigned in South Arcot on July 30, 1265, in his thirteenth year. (*530 of 1920.*)

A. D. 1266. [In the north of India the rule of the Muhammadan 'Slave' kings of Delhi came to an end after a period of seventy years by the usurpation of Ghiyas-ud-dīn Balban. For the last twenty years the country had been desolated by incessant invasions of hordes of Mongols, who had sacked the cities of Lahore and Multan and had devastated Sind.]

Jaṭāvarman Vīra Pāṇḍya reigning in Tinnevelly District. He is stated to have conquered Ceylon and the Chōla and Kongu countries and to have been anointed as a victor at Perumbarra-puliyūr', or Chidambaram, which another record calls 'Tillaimā-nagarī' (*V. R. iii. Tinn. 318 ; 435 of 1905*). He was also reigning in S. Arcot on October 27, 1266 in his fourteenth year.
(*623 of 1920.*)

Rājeñdra Chōla III recognized as sovereign in Tanjore District on January 20 and June 30, 1266.
(*V. R. ii, Tan., 934, 526 ; 555 of 1904 ; 105 of 1897 ; E. I. viii. 274 ; vii, 176.*)

Hoyśala Rāmanātha was reigning in Trichinopoly on March 10, 1266.
(*V. R. iii. Trich. 204 ; 40 of 1913.*)

Mahādēva, Dēvagiri-Yādava king reigned in N. Mysore. He had reduced large tracts.
(*E. C. xi. Dg. 171, 59.*)

[In this year was born the Kēraḷa prince Ravīvarman-Kulaśēkhara-Samgramadhīra whose adventures after he became king in A.D. 1299–1300 are related below.]

A. D. 1267. Hoyśala Narasimha III reigning in S. and E. Mysore.
(*E.C. iv. Kr. 12 ; iii. Md. 123 ; ix. D–B, 31.*)

[1] See Editors' note under 1246.

Rājēndra Chōla reigning in Tanjore District on April 20, 1267 (*V. R. ii. Tan. 991 ; 605 of 1902; E. I. viii. 7*) and on May 8, at Mannārguḍi. (*V. R. ii. Tan. 512 ; 91 of 1897 ; E. I. vii. 177.*)

[Rājēndra III seems to have died about this time, and his death marks the end of the old Chōla kingdom, whose beginning is lost in the mists of antiquity but which was certainly in existence in B.C. 250. Certain Chōla princes are known by name to have lived in 1314 and A.D. 1342—but their relationship to the ancient family is untraceable.]

The Telugu-Chōḍa chief Manma-Siddha-Vijaya-Gaṇḍa-Gōpāla was ruling at Conjeevaram on May 20, 1267 (*568 of 1919*), also on August 7 (*537 of 1919*). In Mārkāpūr Taluk, Kurnool District, his son by Dāmalā-dēvī named Nalla-Siddha gave a grant (*V. R. ii. Kurnool 268 ; 175 of 1905*). And he ruled in Nellore District where an inscription gives him the title 'Vijayāditya' shortened into 'Bijji.' (*V. R. ii. Nell. 336 ; B. L. V. C. 603.*)

Jaṭāvarman Vīra Pāndya reigned in Tinnevelly on November 21, 1267, in his fifteenth year (*437 of 1917*). Two inscriptions of Jaṭāvarman Sundara Pāṇḍya I bear dates = July 1 and 29, 1267 (*V. R. iii. Pudukoṭṭa, 167 ; 342 of 1914 ; 163 of 1916.*). The date of the latter, however, is not perfect.

Hoyśala Rāmanātha was reigning in Trichinopoly District at Ratnagiri in his thirteenth year (*V. R. iii. Trich. 95 ; 163 of 1914.*). And in Salem District. (*Ibid. Salem 7 ; 414 of 1913.*)

Queen Kākatīya Rudramma, here called 'Pratāpa Rudra', gave away a village in Ongole Taluk, Guntur District. (*V. R. ii. Gun. 468 ; B. & V. C. 1135.*)

A. D. 1268. [Between June 10 and 20, 1268 (*E. I. vi. 301*) Māravarman Kulaśēkhara Pāṇḍya I, who was known to the Muhammadan chroniclers as 'Kales Dewar,' came to the throne at Madura. His reign of forty years was disastrous. He partitioned the Pāṇḍya kingdom and this gave rise to dissensions, rivalries and distress amongst his subjects. Finally he was murdered by his own son (*460 of 1916*). From this time forward, if not indeed earlier, we hear of numerous Pāṇḍya princes in the South, often mentioned in inscriptions as if they were kings but who were really viceroys or governors of different tracts. In the decay of the kingdom these princes became practically independent. Wassaf in A.D. 1300 refers to this state of things, and so did Rashid-ud-din in 1310, and in 1292 Marco Polo. (*See below*).]

Perunjīngā II was ruling in his 25th year in S. Arcot on January 29, 1268. (*62 of 1918.*)

Hoyśala Rāmanātha reigning in Salem District in his 14th year (*20 of 1900*); and in Trichinopoly on April 21, 1268, in his 13th year (*41 of 1920*).

A. D. 1268. Hoysala Narasimha III reigining is N., S. and E. Mysore.

(*E. C. xi. Dg, 36 ; Yl ; 9 ; ix, D-B. 8.*)

Kākatiya Rudramma reigning in Nellore District, where her minister gave a gift (*V. R. ii, Nell. 322 B. and V. C. 584.*). And in Nandigāma Taluk, Kistna District, where a grant was made by her general Sāhini Gannama-Nāyuḍu of the Kāyashtha family. (*V. R. ii. Kistna, 278.*)

Vijaya Gaṇḍa-Gōpāla of the Telugu-Chōḍa family ruling in N. Arcot at Kāverippākkam. A gift made by a 'Sāḷukki' chief, perhaps one of the Kāḷahasti Rājas.

(*V. R. i. N. Arcot, 10 ; 389 of 1905.*)

The Dēvagiri-Yādava king Mahādēva was reigning in N. and N.-W. Mysore. There were local disturbances at the time in N. Mysore. The king marched against a certain Kāva-deva, perhaps a Kādamba of Goa, and fighting ensued; and an officer stopped an outbreak at a guard-house. (*E. C. xi, Dg, 79, 102; vii, ci, 21.*)

A. D. 1269. Jaṭāvarman Vīra Pāṇḍya was ruling in Pudukoṭṭa State on July 21,1269, in his seventeenth year. *(V. R. iii, Pudu. 321 ; 278 of 1914.)*

Kākatīya Rudramma, called 'Rudradēva Mahārāja', reigned in Guntur District, Date-October 31, 1269. *(155 of 1917.)*

In Vizagapatam District a Matsya chief, Arjuna I, son of Jayanta I, ruled locally and gave a village to Brahmans (April 6). A C. P. record gives the pedigree of the family for 23 generations. *(V. R. iii, Vizag. 51, 130, 190; 302, 362 of 1899; E. I. v, 106.)*

Perunjinga was ruling in S. Arcot in his 27th year on November 2, 1269. *(70 of 1918.)*

Central and South Mysore were under Hoyśala Narasimha III *(E. C. iv, Ng, 48, 49 ; xii, Tm, 49 ; iii, Tn, 97)*. There was fighting between chiefs in N.-W. Mysore *(E. C. viii. Sa. 128.)* Hoyśala Rāmanātha reigned in Trichinopoly District at Ratnagiri in his 15th year *(V. R. iii. Trich. 126 ; 44 of 1913.)*. [That Narasimha ruled over South Mysore seems to shew that Rāmanātha's portion of the kingdom was very small, and confined to the extreme south.]

An inscription in Salem District, Āttur Taluk, commemorates a gift by Jaṭāvarman Sundara Pāṇḍya I; but does not necessarily imply that he was ruling there, or even alive at the time. *(V. R. ii. Salem, 22 ; 429 of 1913.)*

In Nellore District a village was granted by the Telugu-Chōḍa chief Manma-Siddha II, here called 'Bhīma Rāja Siddhaya.' *(V. R. ii Nellore, 338 ; B. and V. C. 605.)*

Irungoḷa-Chola II, the Niḍugal Rāja of Heṁjeru *(N.-E. Mysore)* raided the Tumkur District in Mysore. *(E. C. xii. Tm, 49.)*

A. D. 1270. Vijaya-Gaṇḍagōpāla of the Telugu-Chōḍa family ruling in Conjeeveram on January 27, February 10 and November 25, 1270.

(501, 429 of 1919 ; V. R. i. Chingleput 920, 547 of 1912 ; 637 of 1919.)

Hoyśala Ramanātha reigning in Kaṇṇanūr, close to Śrīrangam, on March 24 and June 15,1270 *(E. I., iii, 10 ; E. R. 1911, § 47)*. Hoysala Narasimha reigning in West Mysore. *(E. C. v. Bl, 92.)*

Kākatīya Rudramma reigning in Guntur and Kurnool districts *(761 of 1922 ; V. R. ii. Kurn. 339 ; 246 of 1905)*. In the latter the queen is called 'Rudrayya-dēva Mahārāja.'

The Kalasa country in W. Mysore was ruled by a lady Kālalā-Mahādēvi. *(E. C. vi. Mg. 71.)*

A chief named Bommarasa, perhaps of the Sāntara family, ruled a tract in N.-W. Mysore. *(See above s. v. A. D. 1248 and below 1275.)* *(E. c. viii, Sa, 137.)*

The Dēvagiri-Yādava king Rāmachandra came to the throne on a day between September 24, 1270, and March 19, 1271. *(E. C. vii. Sk, 122, 140, 141.)*

A. D. 1271. Hoyśala Rāmanātha was reigning at Kaṇṇanūr, close to Śrīrangam on July 16, 1271 *(E. R. iii. p. 10, No. V)*. And in Trichinopoly on June 5 and during the year. *(V. R. iii. Trich. 426 ; 33 of 1891 ; 21 of 1920.)*

Vijaya-Gaṇḍa-Gōpāla of the Telugu Chōḍas was ruling in Chingleput District on August 12, 1271 *(V. R. i. Chin. 1112 ; 243 of 1912)*. And at Conjeeveram in the same district on January 25, February 13, and May 31. *(405, 503, 492 of 1919.)*

The Kākatīya queen Rudramma ('Rudradēva') reigning in Guntur District on March 26. *(660 of 1920.)*

Māravarman Kulaśēkhara reigning in Tinnevelly District in his fourth year on July 31 and September 19, 1271. *(483, 636 of 1917.)*

The Kalinga-Ganga king Bhānudēva I, son of Narasimha and grandson of Ānanga Bhīma II, reigning in Vizagapatam District. *(V. R. iii. Vizag. 5 ; 358 of 1905.)*

A. D. 1272. Hoyśala Narasimha III reigning in W. Mysore on February 15, 1272. [Date correct; lunar eclipse mentioned.] *(E. C. vi, Kd. 124, 125).* He is given the title 'Establisher of the Chōla kingdom', alluding to Rājēndra III having been helped to the throne by Narasimha's father Hoyśala Sōmēśvara.

In Guntur District the Parichchēdin chief Bhīma Rāja gave a gift to a temple on August 20, 1272. *(137 of 1917.)*

The Dēvagiri-Yādava king Rāmachandra was now reigning as is proved by the Thānā copper-plate grant *(E. I. xiii. 198).* N.-W. Mysore was ruled by him. *(E. C. viii. Sb., 137.)*

A gift was made to a temple in Kurnool District by the Kāyastha chief 'Gaṇḍapenḍēra'—Tripurāri. *(V. R. ii. Kurn. 341 ; 248 of 1905.)*

A. D. 1273. A gift of land was made in this year in Kurnool District by the Kāyastha Chief Ambadēva grandson of the Kākatīya king Gaṇapati's general Gangayya Sāhiuī.

(V. R. ii. Kurn. : 261 ; 168 of 1905.)

Kākatīya Rudramma was reigning in Nellore early in the year.

(V. R. ii. Nell. 133 ; B, and V. C. 393.)

At Conjeeveram Vijaya-Gaṇḍāgōpāla was reigning on April 29, 1273, in his 23rd year.

(409 of 1919.)

A prince of Eastern Chāḷukya descent Vijayāditya II gave a gift at Śrīkūrmam, Ganjam District on a date believed by Dr. Hultzsch to correspond with October 23, 1273. The Śaka year 1195 is stated. (See *Pedigree*). Mr. V. Rangachari says that this record 'confirms the tradition that Nannaya Bhaṭṭa first translated the *Mahābhārata* in Rājarāja-Narēndra's court.'

(V. R. i. Ganjam 230 ; 352 of 1896 ; E. I. v. 32, 36.)

Panchanadivāṇan-Nīlagangaraiyan *(see Geneol. Table)* is mentioned in a record of the '24th' year of Vijaya-Gaṇḍagōpāla, corresponding to November 1, 1273. The regnal year should be '23rd'.

(V. R. i. Chingleput 920, 861, 862, 870 ; 547 of 1912 ; 5, 6, 14 of 1911.)

Hoyśala Rāmanātha was reigning in Trichinopoly on May 8, 1273. *(46 of 1920.)*

In S. Mysore Hoyśala Narasimha III was reigning. *(E. C. iv. Ch., 203.)*

Māravarman Kulaśēkhara Pāṇḍya I reigning in Ramnad in his 6th year. *(540 of 1922.)*

Jaṭāvarman Sundara Pāṇḍya gave a gift to a temple in Coimbatore District in his 23rd year.

(548, 617 of 1905.)

A. D. 1274. Hoyśala Ramanātha was reigning in Salem District in his 20th year *(V. R. ii. Salem 129, 132 ; 26, 29 of 1900).* [About this time his elder brother, Narasimha III reunited in his own person the Hoyśala kingdom, thus reducing Rāmanātha to the position of viceroy in the south. Rāmanātha lived till at least 1295.] On April 23, and May 9, 1274, Rāmanātha was ruling in Trichinopoly District *(20, 47 of 1920.)* And on September 24 in S. Arcot. *(560 of 1921.)*

In S. Mysore Hoyśala Narasimha III reigned *(E. C. iv. Ch., 131).* His son Kumāra Mallidēva is mentioned as granting land in W. Mysore and setting up images. *(E. C. v. Bl., 150.)*

A. D. · Kākatiya-Rudramma reigning in Guntur District on April 9, 1274. *(179 of 1917.)*

Pallava Perunjinga II ruling on February 10, 1274, at Tirukachchūr in Chingleput Taluk in his 31st year. (The inscription is not clear throughout, but only the last figure '1'. It was however his 31st year.) *(V.R. i, Chin. 162 ; 181 of 1904.)*

In the same district near Conjeeveram at Tennēri an inscription of September 3, 1274, makes the Telugu-Chōḍa Vijaya-Gaṇḍa-Gōpāla ruling there in his 25th year. The record shews that the latest possible date for his accession was September 3, 1250. *(229 of 1922.)*

A. D. 1275. Hoyśala Narasimha III reigning in S. and W. Mysore (*E.C. iv, Ch. 142 ; v, Ag., 54 ; vi, Kd. 143*). The Bellary District was now ruled by Hoyśala Rāmanātha, Narasimha's younger brother, as viceroy. *(V.R. i, Bell. 192, 193 ; 33, 34 of 1904 ; E.R. 1903-4, p. 10.)*

In Chingleput District, near Madras, Vijaya-Gaṇḍagōpāla ruled in his 26th year. A gift made by a chief Lankēśvara with the prefix to his name 'Panchanadivāṇan' (*V.R. i, Chin. 857, 909 ; 1 of 1911 ; 536 of 1912*). (See Genealogical Tables under head 'Nīlagangaraiyan'.)

On May 8, 1275 Jaṭavarman Vīra-Pāṇḍya was ruling in Tanjore District in his 22nd year *(67, 73 of 1911 ; E.R. 1922, p. 92.)*

On April 1, 1275. Māravarman Kulaśēkhara was reigning in Trichinopoly District. A Bāṇa chief, to whom is given the affix 'Piḷḷai', is mentioned as governing the Kōnāḍ tract. 'Piḷḷai' or 'Piḷḷaiyār' here probably means a favourite, or a vassal (*above, s.v. A.D. 1257*). *(357 of 1922.)*

The Coimbatore District, or part of it, was ruled by a Kongu-Chola chief Vikrama-Chōla III, this being his second year. *(V.R. i, Coimbatore, 186 ; 610 of 1905.)*

An inscription in Nellore District mentions the Kākatīya queen Rudramma—'Maharaja'—as reigning there, but gives her only the title 'Mahāmaṇḍalēśvara', which is not a royal title. The same is the case with an inscription of Kākatīya Gaṇapati in the same district, of date A.D. 1239 (*above*). There are other instances also. It looks as if the people of Nellore were doubtful as to the Kākatīya rule being permanent. *(V.R. ii, Nellore, 396 ; B. & V.C. iii, 1013.)*

Kēta Rudra (possibly grandson of Rudra) of the Amarāvati family of 'Kōṭa' chiefs locally ruling in Guntur District. *(V.R. ii, Guntur, 271 ; 152 of 1899.)*

The Sāntara chief Bomma of Humcha was ruling in N.-W. Mysore (*E.C. viii, Sa. 134*). There were local disturbances and battles.

The Kalinga-Ganga king Narasimha II came to the throne between May 22 and September 19, 1275, according to two inscriptions whose dates are reliable.
(367 of 1896 ; J.A.S.B. lxv, 229 ; V.R. i, Ganjam, 245. Other records are scattered between Nos. 150 and 253. Their results sometimes vary.)

A. D. 1276. In this year the Devagīri-Yādava king Sēuṇa Rāmachandra made a determined effort to crush the Hoyśala dynasty. He sent a large army under his son-in-law Harapāla and general Sāluva Tikkama into N. Mysore and they marched down to the attack of the Hoyśala capital Dorasamudra, or Haḷēbīḍu. Irungoḷa-Chōla II of the Niḍugal family, who ruled over a tract in N.-E. Mysore in the north of Śira taluk, aided the Sēuṇa invader, as did several other chiefs. The Hoyśala's defending army, commanded by Baḷḷāḷa, son of Narasimha III, met them at Beḷavāḍi in Hassan District, near the capital, and a great battle was fought there on April 25, 1276. The Sēuṇa army was defeated and driven back beyond the Dummi river with great slaughter.

(E.C. v, Bl. 164, 165, 167, 120.)

There is an inscription of Yādava Rāmachandra in Bellary District dated = March 17, 1276. (*717 of 1919*). In North Mysore he gave away a village for a Brahman *Agrahara* (*E.C..xi, Dg. 70*). He was also ruling in N.-W. Mysore. *(E.C. viii, Sa. 69, 70.)*

Hoyśala-Narasimha III is represented by two inscriptions in S. and S.-W. Mysore.

(E.C. iv, Ch. 103 ; v, Cn. 269.)

Near the Krishna River in Narasapur taluk, the local ruler was the Kōna chief Gaṇapati.
(*V.R. ii, Kistna, 313 ; 523 of 1893.*)

[Between August 10 and 25, 1276 Jaṭavarman Sundara Pāṇḍya II Kodaṇḍa-Rāma, began to rule (*See Pedigree notes*). This is the prince mentioned by Wassaf and Marco Polo (*s.v., A.D. 1292*). Wassaf says that he employed as his agent at Kāyal for the importation of horses from Arabia a Muhammadan, named Taki-ud-dīn Abdur Rahmān.]

(*See 418 of 1909 ; 432 of 1913 ; 529, 570 of 1920 ; and Yule's Marco Polo ii, 269, 305–311.*)

In Guntur District Kākatīya Rudramma was reigning on November 13. (*718 of 1920.*)

A. D. 1277. Hoyśala Narasimha III reigning in S. Mysore on March 9, 1277 (*E. C. iii. My. 51.*) Other records in the same locality. (*E. C. iii. Md. 70 ; Tn. 78 and in S. E. Mysore ix. Kn. 72.*)

In Chingleput District the Telugu-Chōḍa Manma-Siddha Vijaya-Gaṇḍagōpāla was reigning on October 31, 1277. (*110 of 1923.*)

In Anantapur District on June 7, an inscription of the Niḍugal Chief Irungōḷa or Irugona Chōla-Mahārāja. (*40 of 1917.*)

The Kākatīya queen Rudramma reigning at Chēbrōlu near the Krishna River.
(*V. R. ii. Guntur 110 ; 609 of 1909.*)

In N.-W. Mysore mention of a battle between two chiefs. Hōsaguṇḍa Bommarasa was ruling locally (*above s. v. 1270–71 ; E. C. viii. Nr. 20.*). The reigning king there was a Yādava Rāmachandra of Dēvagiri (*vii. Ci. 2.*). It would appear from this that the Hoyśala success over the Yādava invaders had only been temporary. (*See remarks s.v. A.D. 1279.*)

A Parichchēdi family chief Bhima Rāja and his brother Uttam Bhima made gifts to a temple in Guntur District (*136 of 1917*). [The date of this, however, is not satisfactory.]

The Kaḷaśa Country in W. Mysore was ruled by Kālalā-Mahādēvī. (*E. C. vi. Mg. 67, 71.*)

In Vizagapatam the Kalinga-Ganga King Anantavarma Bhānudēva I was reigning in his 18th year the only date given is Ś. 1200, which may be either A.D. 1277–78 or 1278–79.
(*V. R. iii. Vizag. 81 ; 253 of 1899.*)

A. D. 1278. In Trichinopoly on January 5, 1278, Māravarman Kulaśēkhara Pāṇḍya I is recognized as king, this being in his 10th year (*V. R. iii. Trich. 410 ; 25 of 1901 ; E. I. vi 309*). This seems to shew that the Hoyśalas and Pāṇḍyas were now living in amity at this time, for a record of the same year shews that Hoyśala Rāmanātha who ruled in W. Mysore was residing in Kaṇṇanūr close to Trichinopoly. (*E. C. v. Ak. 149.*)

[About this time the Pallava Perunjinga II, whose influence about South Arcot and Chingleput had been powerful enough to prevent the Pāṇḍyas from getting much hold on that country, died or ceased to reign, and thereafter Pāṇḍya influence greatly increased there and in the neighbourhood.] Perunjinga's last known date is one of this year at Chidambaram. He had reigned 36 years. (*E. I. vii. 165.*)

Hoyśala Narasimha reigning in S., W. and E. Mysore. (*E.C. iv. Ch. 201; vi. Tk. 80; x. Mr. 38.*)

There was fighting in N.-W. Mysore in this year when a local chief Immaḍi-Baḷḷaha (or Vallabha or Baḷḷāla)[1] attacked Narasimha (*E. C. viii. Nr. 9.*) Nr. 11 also mentions this chief.
(*E. C. xii. Tp. 22, 23.*)

In N.-W. Mysore on March 30, 1278, 'Kāvarasa', probably Kāmadēva of the Kādambas of Hangal, was locally ruling. (*E. C. viii. Sb. 187.*)

[1] *Editor*

Kākatiya Rudramma was reigning in Vinukonḍa Taluk, Guntur District, on July 2, 1278. (*V. R. ii. Gun. 856, 857, 863 ; 532, 533 of 1913*). All these records belonging to the same day.

The Telugu-Chōḍa Manma-Siddha II Vijaya-Ganḍagōpāla reigning in Cuddapah District in his 29th year. (*V. R. i. Cudd. 692 ; 417 of 1911.*)

The Matsya chief Mankāditya II made a gift to the temple at Simhāchalam. (*V. R. iii. Vizagapatam, 143 ; 315 of 1899.*)

A. D. 1279. Hoyśala Narasimha III, reigning in W. Mysore, granted a village in the Konganād tract over which he ruled (*E. C. v, Ag. 21*). He also reigned in S., Central and W. Mysore on March 29, 1279 and on other days (*E. C. iv. Ch. 17 ; vi. Tk. 9 ; v. Bl. 187, 166 ; iii. Tn. 84*). One of these mentions a fight at Solēur. The inscription is difficult to understand but it seems to imply that the fight took place when the Gajapati (king) united with Hoyśala Rāmanātha, which might mean that the Kākatīya queen Rudramma was trying to induce Ramanātha to rebel against his elder brother Narasimha III. The inscription however is defaced in part. One of the inscriptions says that for some reason Narasimha arrested his own general Chikka-Kētaya, a fight followed.

One inscription seems to shew that Rāmanātha was now governing Central Mysore. But this may not actually have been the case. It is unwise to judge by a solitary record. (*E. C. xii. Tm., 56.*)

Rāmanātha was governing Trichinopoly on November 30, A.D. 1279. (*23 of 1920.*)

Kakatiya Rudramma was reigning in Nellore District. (*V. R. ii. Nell., 57.*)

Vijaya-Ganḍagōpāla was reigning in Chingleput District in his 30th year. No date specified. A gift made by Panchanadivāṇan-Nīlagangaraiyan (*above s. v. A. D. 1273*). (*V. R. i. Chin., 850, 860, 862, 882 ; 3, 4, 6 of 1911 ; 662 of 1904.*)

Kālalā-Mahādēvi ruled the Kaḷasa tracts in W. Mysore. (*E. C. vi. Mg., 72.*)

In N. Mysore the Yādava king of Dēvagiri Rāmachandra ruled. Date = September 21, 1279. (*E. C. xi. Jl., 30.*)

A. D. 1280. Hoyśala Narasimha III was reigning in W. Mysore (*E. C. v. Bl., 89*). And in W. Mysore (*ibid. Bl., 155.*)

Kākatīya Rudramma reigning in Kistna District. She is called 'Pratāpa Rudra' (*834 of 1922*). And in Guntur District at Ongole. (*V. R. ii. Gun., 402 ; B and V. C. 1032.*)

The Yādava king of Dēvagiri, Rāmachandra, reigning in N. Mysore. The inscription states that his general Sāḷuva Tikkama plundered Dorasamudra (*but see above s. v. A. D. 1276 ; E. C. xi. Dg. 59*). He was reigning in N.-W. Mysore (*E. C. vii. Ci., 24 ; viii. Sb., 275.*). The date of the last seems to be December 26 1280. He reigned also in Bellary District on February 12, 1280. (*205 of 1918.*)

An inscription in Nellore District early in 1280, of the Telugu-Chōḍa chief Tirukāḷatti-dēva, to whom is given the affix 'Irumuḍi' (='Immaḍi') (*V. R. ii. Nellore, 196 ; B. and V. C. 417*). He was son of Manma-Siddha Vijaya-Ganḍagōpāla.

A record in Coimbatore District mentions the fifteenth year of a chief with a Pānḍya name—'Vīra Pānḍya,' and a Chōla title—'Rājakēsari'. He may have belonged to the Kongu-Chōla line of rulers, and have assumed a Pānḍya name since that of Chola had lost its old significance with the fall of the Chōla kingdom. His rule must have begun in A.D. 1266–67. Many records of his time are noted in the Coimbatore District. (*V. R. i. Coim. 196 ; 544 of 1905.*)

A. D. 1281. Hoysala Narasimha III reigning in S. Mysore. *(E. C. iv. Ch., 8.)*

The Telugu-Chōḷa Vijaya-Gaṇḍagōpāla ruling in Conjeeveram on September 18, 1281, in his 31st year. [The regnal year was probably wrongly calculated, as the latest date for expiry of his 31st year was September 3 in that year.] *(500 of 1919.)*

Kulaśēkhara Pāṇḍya I was reigning in Madura on September 21, 1281, in his fourteenth year. *(V. R. ii. Mad. 197 ; E. I. xi. 263.)*

The Kaḷasa country in W. Mysore was ruled Kālalā-Mahādēvī. *(E. C. vi. Mg., 73.)*

Naraharitīrtha, founder of the Dvaita school of philosophy and disciple of the Vaishṇava pontiff Ānandatīrtha, was governor of Kalinga. He built a shrine in this year. *(E. I. vi. 260.)*

In N.-W. Mysore, where the local ruler was Bīrarasa there was another of the perennial outbreaks of savage local wars. In this case fifty groups of villages (*naḍus*) in combination fought against another such group. A town was besieged and there was much slaughter. *(E. C. viii. Nr., 20.)*

A. D. 1282. The Yādava king Rāmachandra of Dēvagiri was reigning in Bellary District on April 26, 1282 (*247 of 1918*). Another record of his eleventh year in N.-W. Mysore (*E. C. viii. Sb., 160*). Others in Bellary district of dates = April 23, and May 9,–94 (*224 of 1918 ; V. R. i. Bell. 213 ; 486 of 1914*). In April of 1282 there was more severe fighting in N.-W. Mysore when the town of Hosaguṇḍa was besieged by a local chief Tammarasa, son of Bommarasa during king Rāmachandra's reign (*E. C. viii. Sa., 84, 85, 86 ; Sb., 218*). Rāmachandra was also reigning in N.-W. Mysore. *(ibid. Sb., 57 ; vii. Ci., 23.)*

In W. and E. Mysore the reigning king was Hoysala Narasimha III (*E. C. v. Hn, 47 ; ix. Ma, 71*).

Inscription of the Kalinga king Narasimha II dated in his seventh year, in Vizagapatam District (*V. R. iii. Vizag : 3 ; 364 of 1905*).

In Chingleput District the Telugu-Chōḍa Manma-Siddha II, Vijaya-Gaṇḍagōpāla, was ruling. in his 33rd year (*V. R. i. Chin. 836 ; 222 of 1910*).

A. D. 1283. [Mr. Swamikannu Pillai has fixed the date for the beginning of the rule (or reign) of Māravarman Vikrama Pāṇḍya as between January 12 and August 29, 1283. He was probably one of the Pāṇḍya princes who ruled a province. The king at Madura was Māravarman Kulaśēkhara I at this time. Jatāvarman Sundara Pāṇḍya II whose rule began in 1276 was certainly alive as we have a record of his at Siddhalingamaḍam in South Arcot in 1289 (*V. R. i. S. Arcot 821; 418 of 1909; 432 of 1913*) and Māravarman Vikrama Pāṇḍya is also mentioned as being at the same place in his 6th year, or August 29, 1288 (*V. R. i. S. Arcot 813 ; 410 of 1909*). There are many inscriptions of these and other Paṇḍya princes. At present they seem confusing but future research will doubtless solve the problem. What must be remembered is that the governorship of the Pāṇḍya realm had been divided into different portions. It remains to work out the divisions and their several rulers over the whole country from Madras to Cape Comorin, excluding Mysore.]

Māravarman Sundara Pāṇḍya ruling in Chingleput District in his fourteenth year on March 1 and April 11, 1283. *(342, 343 of 191 ; E. R. 1922, p. 92.)*

Jatāvarman Sundara Pāṇḍya ruling in Tanjore District, in his seventh year, on December 29, 1283. *(114, 115 of 1911 ; E. R. 1922, p. 92.)*

Hoysala Narasimha III reigning in S.-E. Mysore. *(E. C. ix, Kn. 82.)*

King Rāmachandra of the Yādavās of Dēvagiri reigning in N.-W. Mysore (*E. C. viii, Sa, 63. ; Sb, 189).*

Upēndra II, a prince of Eastern Chāḷukya descent made a gift to the temple at Simhāchalam (*V. R. iii. Vizagapatam 127 ; 299 of 1899.)*

A. D. 1284. Māravarman Sundara Pāṇḍya (a prince) ruling in Chingleput District in his fourteenth year on February 14, 1284. (*344 of 1911 ; E. R. 1922, p. 92.)*

Yādava Rāmachandra of Dēvagiri reigning in N. and N.-W. Mysore, more local fighting and siege of the town of Kuppe. (*E. C. viii, Sb, 31 ; vii. Sk, 122, 140, 141.)*

Hoyśala Narasimha III reigning in Central Mysore (*E. C. iv, Ng, 38)*. And in W. Mysore where open warfare existed between opposing groups of villages (*nadus*). (*E. C. vi. Cm, 117–119.)*

A. D. 1285. Hoyśala Narasimha III reigning in W. Mysore and in Coorg (*E. C, v. Ag, 37 ; Suppt Belur, 244 ; i, Coorg, 7.)*. Narasimha claims to have reduced Irungōḷa-Chōla of the Niḍugal family, who had become refractory. (*E. C. v. Ak, 151.)*

The Śāntara chief Rāya-Baḷḷaha ruling the Kaḷasa country in W. Mysore (*E. C. vi. Mg. 69.)*

Early in 1285 the Telugu-Chōḍa Manma-Gaṇḍagōpāla is said to be ruling in Nellore District in his third year. This may be Manma III governing as a Viceroy under his grandfather of the same name ; or the regnal year may be wrong and the ruler intended may be his grandfather Manma Vijaya-Gaṇḍagōpāla in his 36th year. (*V. R. ii. Nellore 25, 505 ; B and V. C. i. 231, ii. 794.)*

On July 23, 1285, Jaṭāvarman Sundara Pāṇḍya II ruling in his 10th year in S. Arcot (*V.R. i. S. Arcot 324; 137 of 1902*). And in Cuddapah District at Nandalūr.

(*V. R. i. Cudd. 805, 807; 591, 593 of 1907.)*

A D. 1286. Jaṭāvarman Sundara Pāṇḍya ruling in Cuddapah District at Nandalūr on September 30, 1286 in his 10th year (*V. R. i. Cudd. 806 ; 592 of 1907*) and in Tanjore District on May 28, 1286. (*68 of 1911; E. R. 1922, p. 92.)*

Early in 1286 Hoyśala Narasimha III was reigning in Central and N. Mysore (*E.C. xii, Tp, 123 ; xi, Cd. 12, 32*). There is an epitaph dated in this year noting the death of a man who fell in a fight when Narasimha III marched to the attack on the fort of Niḍugal and destroyed Bāgēyakēra. (*E. C. v, Ak, 151.)*

In N.-W. Mysore Yādava Rāmachandra of Dēvagiri reigned. His hostility to the Hoyśala family is mentioned (*E. C. vii, Hl. 17*). Another record of the same king, also in N.-W. Mysore and of date = May 5, 1286. It mentions his 16th year. (*E. C. viii, Sb, 208.)*

In Central Mysore is an inscription of February 10, 1286, which shews that Hoyśala Baḷḷāla III, son of Narasimha III, was ruling there, probably as viceroy. (*E. C. xii, Tp, 40.)*

In E. Mysore the ruler was Hoyśala Rāmanātha. Inscription in Kolar District.

(*E. C. x, Kl. 27.)*

The Matsya chief Annama, *alias* Gōpālavardhana, gave a gift to the temple at Simhāchalam. (*V. R. iii Viz. 186; 358 of 1899.)*

A. D. 1287. Hoyśala Narasimha III reigning in W. and N.-W. Mysore (*E. C. vi, Cm. 44; v. Ak. 9; vii Sh, 61, 62*). There were the usual cattle raids and deaths of villagers this year (*E. C. vi, Tk. 48*). In E. and Central Mysore Rāmanātha ruled as viceroy for his brother.

(*E. C. ix, Dv. 53; x, Kl. 139; xii, Tm, 27, 28, 29, 33.)*

Yādava Rāmachandra reigning in Bellary District on July 25, 1287 in his 17th year.

(*718 of 1919.)*

Māravarman Kulaśēkhara Pāṇḍya I of Madura reigning on June 20, 1287. Record in Tinnevelly District (*460 of 1916*). In Ramnad on August 27, a record of Jaṭāvarman Sundara Pāṇḍya II in his 12th year (*V. R. ii, Ramnad. 152; 575 of 1902; E. I. viii, 279*). In South Arcot an inscription of this year of Māravarman Vikrama Pāṇḍya (*54 of 1905*). Records of this last prince allege of him that he conquered Kākatīya Gaṇapati (probably an error for Rudramma and Vījaya-Gaṇḍagōpāla. [This is almost certainly an empty boast.] One of his inscriptions gives him the full titles of an Emperor. (*below, s.v. A. D. 1291–92.*)

The country in Cuddaph District included in the divisions of the Rēnāḍu, Ghanḍikōta, Mulikināḍu, Pottapīnāḍu, etc., was ruled by Ambadēva-Mahārāja who had the titles 'Gaṇḍapeṇḍēra' and 'Maṇḍalika-Brahmarākshasa'. He was grandson of Gangasāhini, the general of the Kākatiya queen Rudramma (*V. R. i. Cudd. 654–849, a number of inscriptions; 406–423 of 1911; 618–623 of 1907*). Another member of his family was Jannigadēva, called 'Mahārāja of Panugal'.

(*V. R. i. Cudd. 923. See Pedigree of Kāyastha family.*)

A. D. 1288. Hoysala Rāmanātha was ruling in his 33rd year in E. Mysore (*E. C. x, Bp, 59 Mr. 98; Sp. 36; Kl. 92, 99; ix. Dv. 24*). In S.-E. Mysore, Narasimha III reigned.

(*E. C. ix Cp. 66; Kn, 77, 78.*)

Yādava Rāmachandra of Dēvagiri reigned in N. Mysore, where an inscription records an attack on a town (*E. C. xi, Dg. 81*). And in N.-W. Mysore (*V ii Hl, 12; viii, Sb, 128, 247*). The date of the last of these is November 27, 1288.

In Kurnool the Kāyastha chief Ambadēva was ruling locally.

(*V. R. ii, Kurn. 335; 242 of 1905.*)

Kākatīya Rudramma was reigning in Guntur District on October 27, 1288. (*130 of 1917.*)

An inscription of the 13th year of Jaṭāvarman Sundara Pāṇḍya II in the Chingleput District states that he quelled some disturbances there. The persons injured appealed for protection to the 'Pottapi-Raja' (evidently one of the Telugu-Chōḍa family). The property of the offenders was confiscated (*315 of 1909*). [This shews that the influence of the Pāṇḍya princes was spreading northwards along the east coast districts and renders intelligible the assertion of Marco Polo who was on the coast in this year that the Coromandel Coast was ruled by a Pāṇḍya prince. Polo could not of course know exactly the topographical limits of Pāṇḍya power. It must be noted also that there are six records of Pāṇḍya princes at Nandalūr in Cuddapah District belonging to the years 1286 to 1293 (*588–594 of 1907*).]

[Attention must be directed now to affairs in Ceylon, where king Bhuvanēka Bāhu died in A.D. 1288 after a reign of eleven years. The *Mahāwamśa* relates (ch. xc) that subsequent to his death 'the five brethren who governed the Pāṇḍya kingdom' sent an army to the island. The Tamils laid waste the country on every side and seizing a fortress took the Tooth-Relic of Buddha and all the solid wealth that was there' and returned to the mainland. The new king of Ceylon Parākrama-Bāhu III (*1288–93*) himself went, properly escorted, and presented himself before the Pāṇḍya king (Māravarman Kulaśēkhara I), and prayed for the return of the relic. His prayer was granted and the relic was thus restored to the people of Ceylon.]

A.D. 1289. Kākatīya Rudramma reigning, on November 28, 1289, under the title 'Rudradēva,' in Guntur District. (*V.R. ii. Gun. 860; 536 of 1913*)

Jaṭāvarman Sundara Pāṇḍya II, was ruling in Salem District on August 1, 1289, in his 13th year (*V.R. ii, Salem 127; 24 of 1900; E.I. vi; 310*). Another inscription of his, of date June 3, in the same district (*V.R. ii, Salem 25 ; 432 of 1913*). Another, of August 5, is in Chingleput District. (*Ibid. Chin. 979 ; 110 of 1912 ; E.I. ix, 259.*)

The Yādava king of Dēvagiri, Rāmachandra, ruling in N.-W. Mysore on April 3, 1289. The regnal year given is '20.' Apparently it should be '19.'

(*E. C. viii, Sb. 209. Compare Sb. 31 and 208 for year of accession.*)

Hoyśala Narasimha was reigning in W. Mysore from Dorasamudra (*E.C. v, Cn. 232 ; vi, Cm. 11*). The first of these records says that 'Rāmanātha-dēva, raising an army, came out to fight . . .' with whom cannot be gathered ; but the inscriptions of the last few years shew that Mysore was in a very disturbed state at this period.

In E. Mysore in the Kōlār District Hoyśala Rāmanātha was ruling. (*E.C. x, Mb. 44, a.*)

In N.-W. Mysore one of the local rulers was the Kādamba chief Kāva-dēva. There was cattle-raiding and consequent deaths in this tract in this year. (*E.C. viii, Sb. 503.*)

In Ramnad Māravarman Kulaśēkhara Pāṇḍya I was reigning on June 27, 1289, in his 22nd year. (*V. R. ii, Ram. 125 ; 107 of 1903 ; E.I. viii, 277.*)

A.D. 1290. Rāmachandra of Dēvagiri continued to reign in N.-W. Mysore (*E.C. viii, Sb. 113, 192*). More cattle raiding recounted.

In E. Mysore, Hoyśala Rāmanātha ruled on July 12, 1290. (*E.C. x, Mb. 100 ; Ct. 84.*)

In S. Mysore Hoyśala Narasimha III reigned, after having taken over the Government of that province from his brother Rāmanātha who formerly ruled there. (*E.C. iv, Yl. 56 ; iii, Tn. 27 58*). He was also reigning in N.-W. Mysore. (*E.C. vii, Hl. 90.*)

Tinnevelly was reigned over by Māravarman Kulaśēkhara Pāṇḍya I. Record of his 22nd year there on January 30, and another on April 21 ; another on October 30, 1290 (*81, 110, 17 of 1916*). He reigned in Madura district, also. (*V.R. ii, Mad. 33 ; 447 of 1906 ; E.I. ix, 223.*)

Jaṭāvarman Sundara Pāṇḍya II was reigning in Salem District on May 15, 1290 in his 14th year (*V. R. ii, Salem 126; 23 of 1900 E. I. vi, 312*). And in Tanjore on August 9. (*V. R. ii, Tan. 1124; 294 of 1908; E. I. xi, 136*). There is an inscription of his in Cuddapah District also, at Nandalūr, whose date is February 20, 1920. (*V. R. i. Cudd, 804; 590 of 1907.*)

At Simhachalam, Vizagapatam District the Kalinga-Ganga king Narasimha II reigned in 1290–91, and in 1291–92, which was his 15th year.

(*V. R. ii, Vizag. 120, 125, 185; 292, 297, 357 of 1899.*)

In Kurnool District the Kāyastha chief 'Gaṇḍapeṇḍēra' Ambadēva was in power locally. He remitted some taxes (*V. R. ii. Kurn. 267, 360, 174, 268 of 1905*). Kākatiya Pratāpa Rudra II was his overlord. (*V. R. ii, Kurnool, 409.*)

[We must here take note of what we learn from the chronicle of Marco Polo the Venetian traveller, who was at Kayal on the gulf of Manaar in 1288 and 1293, about the state of Southern India at this period. And before doing so it will be well to note that, if we may judge, what the daily life of the peasant population of South India was by the revelations made in numberless inscriptions in Mysore, and the neighbouring districts, it would appear to have been very difficult. For as soon as anyone became possessed of some sort of wealth by his breeding of cattle he was attacked by his neighbours, who united in gangs and proceeded to rob him of all he had acquired. And not only did these robbers take the cattle, but they were in the habit of sacking the villages and carrying off the young women. We also learn from these records that these crimes were not confined to a man's immediate neighbours, but that fighting was incessant. Groups of villages combined to attack other groups, and the inhabitants of a whole *nāḍu* set forth to rob and slaughter the dwellers in another *naḍu*. In fact as it is well known, robbery and murder were elevated into a romance, and poems were written describing the bravery and heroism of these savage marauders.

(*See 'Notes and Cautions', above*).

It is appropriate here also to note that men could not travel in safety from one place to another because of the danger of death at the hands of the Thugs, who also elevated the wholesale murder of innocent people into a fine art. Vincent Smith has well described the system of Thuggee in his *Oxford History of India*, p. 666-67. In the year of which we are treating, A.D. 1290-91, Sultan Jalal-ud-din Khilji became king of Delhi, and since it is related of him that he arrested and deported 1,000 Thugs in an endeavour to put an end to their horrible practices, we know that Thuggee must have been a curse to the country in his time. In the course of the centuries it grew worse and worse till the British Government sternly put it down in the first half of the 19th century. It may tend to an appreciation of what Thuggee really meant to the inhabitants of India if I repeat one sentence of V. Smith's remarks on the subject—' One man confessed to having been concerned in the murder of 719 persons ' (*op. cit., p. 666*).

Nor was the sea safe for travel on trade. Marco Polo found that piracy abounded to an immense extent in those seas. To use his own words (*Yule's Edit. III cap. xxiv-xxv*) ' From this kingdom of Malabar and from . . . . . . Gujarat there go forth every year more than a hundred corsair vessels . . . . These pirates . . . stay out the whole summer . . . . No merchant-ship can escape them . . . . When any corsair sights a vessel a signal is made . . . and then the whole of them make for this, and seize the merchants and plunder them.' Of the Gujarat pirates he says that they are the ' most desperate pirates in existence ' ; and that they and the pirates of Malabar were protected by the local chiefs.

The trade in horses, brought by sea to Kāyal in those days by Arab dealers and seamen, and sold to the leading Rājahs in South India, suffered greatly from these pirates. The western coast of Malabar proper was especially dangerous.

To Marco Polo and to the Muhammadans generally ' Malabar ' or ' Ma'abar ' meant apparently the whole of Southern India. They got their information from west coast traders and Musalman settlers, and did not distinguish between the west coast Malabar proper and the east coast which the English have learnt to call the Coromandel Coast. Thus in ch. xvi Marco Polo writes of the body of St. Thomas lying ' in a certain city of the province of Ma'abar,' and he repeats this description in ch.. xviii. He tells us that ' in this province there are five kings who are own brothers ' and that at this end i.e., at the southern end, presumably about Kāyal, the name of the king was 'Sonder-Bandi-Devar', Sundara Pāṇḍya-deva, i. e. (probably) Jaṭāvarman Sundara Pāṇḍya II, 1276 to 1293. Wassaf, writing somewhat later, says that *Malabar* extended from Cape Comorin to Nellore (' Kaulam to Nilawar').[1]

[Marco Polo, Wassaf and Rashid-ud-dīn all agree the old Pāṇḍya kingdom was now broken up, and that different provinces in the south were ruled by different Pāṇḍya princes jointly called the Five Brothers in accordance with ancient legend.]

[1] Mr. Sewell is here confounding Malibar and Ma'bar of Wassaf. The first according to this author extended from Khor to Kúlam and was 800 parasangs (p. 31). Ma'bar extends in length from Kúlam to Nilawar (Nellore), nearly 800 parasangs (p. 32.)

See Wassaf in *Elliot III. and S. Ind. and Her Muhammadan Invaders*, p. 71.—*Editor*.

A. D. 1291. Māravarman Kulaśēkhara Pāṇḍya I reigning in Madura on June 1, 1291, in his 23rd year (*740 of 1919*). And at Tanjore on June 28, where two records calling him 'Bhuvanēka Vīra' place the day as in his '22nd' year—a mistake for 24th. (*260, 263 of 1917.*)

In Chingleput District Jaṭāvarman Sundara Pāṇḍya II was reigning on August 18 in his 15th year. (*305 of 1921.*)

In S. Arcot Māravarman Vikrama Pāṇḍya ruled. The inscription gives him full imperial titles. (*116 of 1900.*)

Hoyśala Narasimha III reigned in N.-W. Mysore on April 16, 1291. (*E. C. vii, Sh. 78.*) And in S. Mysore (no details of date are given). (*E. C. iv. Kr. 10.*)

Hoyśala Rāmanātha is stated in a laudatory record to have been reigning as an Emperor in his own right. This is in E. Mysore. But it also states that a battle had taken place in which two of Rāmanātha's ministers were engaged; and this would give rise to the impression that he rebelled against the succession to the throne of his nephew Baḷḷāḷa III. (*E. C. x, Kl, 234, 239.*) Three more of his inscriptions in E. Mysore. (*Ibid. x, M, 43 ; Bp, 68a ; ix, D, 45.*)

Hoyśala Baḷḷāḷa III represented as reigning in W. Mysore on November 18, 1291. The date correctly stated. His capital Dorasmudra is named (*E. C. vi, Kd, 49*). He was crowned on January 31, 1292 (*E. C. vi, Cm, 36*). Narasimha had probably died before November 18, 1291. Another record of Baḷḷāḷa III names him as reigning in S. E. Mysore on December 18, 1291. (*E. C. ix. Kn. 64.*[1])

Kākatīya 'Pratāpa Rudra,' i. e., Rudramma reigning in Guntur District. She seems to have died in this year. Mention made of Manuma-Gaṇḍagōpāla. This may be Manma-Siddha II, whose reign came to an end in this year, or his grandson Manma Siddha III, son of Nalla Siddha. Manma Siddha III succeeded his grandfather (*V, R. ii. Guntur, 275 ; 204 of 1899*). Manma Siddha II, Vijaya-Gaṇḍagōpāla is represented by an inscription of this year at Conjeevaram (*E. I. xiii, 194. See E. R. 1920, p. 119 ; E. I, vi, 274 vii, 129 ; xiii, 194*). Rudramma's daughter's son 'Kumāra" Pratāpa Rudra was ruling in the Palnāḍ Taluk, Guntur District in this year. (*V. R. ii. Guntur, 514 ; 548 of 1909.*)

Amba-dēva of the Kāyastha family was ruling locally in Kurnool District. He claims to have 'established at Nellore Manmagaṇḍagōpāla who had been deprived of his kingdom', and to have destroyed a Kāḍava-Rāja. (*V. R. ii. Kurn: 266 ; 173 of 1905.*)

A. D. 1292. In Central Mysore Gaṇēśa Chōla-Mahārāja of Niḍugal was ruling locally. A pedigree of the family is given. (*E. C. xii. Pg. 53.*)

Severe famine this year in North India.

Hoyśala Baḷḷāḷa III, now king, reigning in S. Mysore on February 20, 1292 (*E. C. iii. Nj 103*). And in W. Mysore (*V. Bl, 18*). And in the S. E. This last inscription is of date about June-July, 1291. It speaks of an 'incursion by the forces of Rāmanātha', who was Baḷḷāḷa III's uncle. This supports the idea mooted above (*s. v. 1291–92*) that Rāmanātha opposed his nephew's succession by force of arms. (*E. C. ix. Kn. 28.*)

Hoyśala Rāmanātha is recognized as ruling in E. Mysore in his 37th and 38th regnal year. (*E.C. ix, Nl, 38b ; x, Sp, 62.*)

[1] This reference is not given by Sewell; but has been put in by me. This seems the record intended as the date agrees according to L. D. S. Pillai's Indian Ephemeris.—*Editor.*

There was fighting between local chiefs in N.-W. Mysore (*E. C. viii, Sa, 89, 97*). Another record (*Sa, 110*) mentions a fight, perhaps the same, between a certain Koṭi-Nāyaka and some other minor chiefs.

Yādava Rāmachandra of Devagiri was reigning in N.-W. Mysore on June 12, 1292 in his 23rd year. (*E. C. viii, Sb, 198.*)

Sundara Pāṇḍya was ruling in his 15th year in S. Arcot on March 26, 1292. (*570 of 1920.*)

Kākatīya Pratāpa Rudra, called also 'Kumāra-Rudra', ruling in Guntur and Kistna districts. (*V. R. ii, Gun. 143, 145, 206 ; Kistna 146 ; 545 of 1909 ; 126 of 1897 ; 254, 256 of 1892.*)

In Vizagapatam District at Simhāchalam the Matsya chief Jayanta II was ruling on July 26. And a gift was made there by the chief Arjuna, alias Narasimha Vardhana for the merit of his younger brother Annama-Gōpālavardhana. (*V. R. iii, Vizag. 130, 133 ; 302, 305 of 1899.*)

A.D. 1293. Hoyśala Rāmanātha continued to rule in E. Mysore, this being his 38th year (*E. C. x, Mr. 99 ; Kl, 18*). In August–September 1293, his son 'Manjeya-*Māguttar*' made a grant for the health of his father, establishing a festival to take place once a month. Another to the same purpose was made in 1295, the inscription which mentions it calling the prince '*Mavuttar*' (*E. C. x, Bp, 23, 25a. See also ibid. 27.*)

Hoyśala Baḷḷāḷa III was reigning in S.-E. Mysore, where there was local fighting and slaughter (*E. C. ix, Kn, 107*). And in S. Mysore (*Ibid. iv, Hg. 15*).

In Tinnevelly District Māravarman Kulaśēkhara Pāṇḍya I was reigning on November 18, 1293. (*V. R. iii, Tinn., 483 ; 134 of 1894 ; E. I. vi, 309.*)

Jaṭāvarman Sundara Pāṇḍya II was ruling at Nandalūr in Cuddapah District in his 17th year, on March 14 and 18, 1293 (*V. R. i, Cudd. 808, 802 ; 588, 594 of 1907*). And in South Arcot district on March 22 (*405 of 1921*). Wassaf records the death of this prince during the Hijra year ending on December 20, 1293. Mr. Swamikannu Pillai has, on the strength of several inscriptions, established the existence of another Jaṭāvarman Sundara Paṇḍya, whose rule began in the year following February 8, 1293.

Kākatīya Pratāpa Rudra II ruling in Guntur District, Ongole Taluk. (*V. R. ii, Gun. 379 454 ; B. & V.C. 983, 1115.*)

The Kalinga-Ganga king Narasimha II was reigning in Ganjam District on May 21, 1293, in his 18th year, when a gift was made at Śrīkūrmam by the sage Naraharitīrtha (*V. R. i, Ganjam 245, 367 of 1896*). Several inscriptions combine with this to prove that this king came to the throne in the year following May 22, 1276. (*V. R. i, Gan. 201, 213, 234, 237, 241.*)

Marco Polo's second visit to Kāyal on the Gulf of Manaar took place in this year (*See Oxford History of India, p. 215*).

A.D. 1294. Kākatīya Pratāpa Rudra II ruling in Guntur District (*V. R. ii, Gun. 307*). This was early in 1294. Also in Kurnool district (*V. R. ii, Kurnool 272 ; 179 of 1905*). Here he claims to have defeated ('cut off the head of') Manma-Gaṇḍagōpāla, the Telugu-Chōḍa chief. [This is confusing ; but it is noticeable that the Kāyastha chief Ambadēva in 1291–92 claimed to have 'established' this same Manma, and it may be that there was some disturbance at the time—Manma being defeated by Pratāpa Rudra and afterwards assisted to regain his authority by Ambadēva.] Pratāpa Rudra was also ruling in Nellore. (*V. R. ii, Nell. 357 ; B. & V.C. 630.*)

Hoyśala Rāmanātha was ruling E. Mysore early in 1294, and in June–July of that year (*E. C. ix Ht, 151 ; Bn, 100 ; x, Ct, 88*). It was his 39th and 40th year. Hoyśala Baḷḷāḷa III reigning in S. Mysore. (*E. C. iv, Ch, 44.*)

Yādava Rāmachandra supreme in N.-W. Mysore. More violent raids on a large scale, carried out by a number of villages composing a *nāḍu* and ruining the inhabitants of another such group. The defenders were robbed of the crops they had grown.

(*E.C. viii, Sb. 502 ; vii, Hl, 29.*)

Inscription at Conjeeveram. The date is not very sound but is probably February 13, 1294. This was in the 3rd year of the Telugu-Chōḍa Chief Manma Siddha III, Vira Gaṇḍa-gōpāla. (*603 of 1919.*)

In Tinnevelly District, Māravarman Kulaśekhara Pāṇḍya I reigning in his 27th year on December 10, 1294. (*V. R. iii. Tinn. 486 ; 137 of 1894 ; E.I. vi, 308.*)

[This year saw the first advance of the Delhi Muhammadans towards the Dekhan and the south. Sultan Jalāl-ud-dīn Khilji of Delhi had a nephew Alāu-d-dīn, who obtained permission from his uncle to make an expedition into Malwa. Concealing his movements from the Sultan he invaded the Dekhan in force and compelled Yādava Rāmachandra of Devagiri to surrender the province of Ellichpur. He collected enormous booty and returned. He effected a meeting in 1296 between himself and his uncle at Karā near Allahabad and there murdered him. The Sultan's head was struck off and displayed to the troops, and Alāu-d-dīn seized the throne of Delhi. He raised a great army of 475,000 men. His success against Rāmachandra was partly due to the absence from Dēvagiri, the Yādava capital, of the king's eldest son Śankara with a large body of troops, forming an army that was intended for the conquest of the Hoyśala dominions in the south. Rāmachandra defended himself with courage and ability, but the city was unprepared for a siege and it was captured. Negotiations followed, Rāmachandra playing for time till Sankara could return to his assistance. When eventually the prince and his army arrived a battle was fought, and victory was almost in the hands of the Hindus when their troops were thrown into a panic by the arrival on the scene of a fresh body of Muhammadan soldiers which they mistook for the advance party of a great army. Śankara's forces broke and fled, and Rāmachandra was forced to submit. Ferishtah's description of the amount of treasure made over to the victor sounds almost fabulous. It was certainly sufficient to enrich Alāu-d-dīn and he spent it lavishly in securing his sovereignty and preparing for further war. Having now learned something of the wealth that might be obtained by the sack of the royal cities and the ancient temples in South India the Muhammadan rulers never again withheld their hand. Alāu-d-dīn made repeated raids on the Dekhan. Alāu-d-dīn, viewed in some aspects, was a monster of cruelty. He murdered the families of those who had been loyal to his uncle, sparing neither the women nor the children. Annoyed by the presence near Delhi of a large number of Mongol settlers he slaughtered from 15,000 to 30,000 of them. As regards his policy towards the Hindus he ordered his ministers to 'grind them down and deprive them of their wealth and property.' He took half of the gross produce of the cultivated lands, and commanded that the peasants should only be left just enough to enable them to live. He governed by a system of espionage and ferocious punishments.]

A.D. 1295. There are two inscriptions of Yādava Rāmachandra in this year in N.-W. Mysore. (*E. C. vii, Ci, 26 ; viii., Sb. 124.*)

Kākatīya Pratāpa Rudra reigning in the Nandigama taluk, Kistna District. (*V.R. ii. Kistna, 252.*)

An inscription at Teṅkarai in Madura District combines mention of the 28th year of Māravarman Kulaśēkhara Pāṇḍya I and that of the 10th year of Jaṭāvarman Sundara Pāṇḍya II. The date is November 27, 1295. (*V.R. ii. Mad. 195 ; 124 of 1910.*)

About this time Kulaśēkhara associated with himself in the government his illegitimate son Vīra Pāṇḍya to the exclusion of his legitimate son Sundara; and this led to bitter hatred between the two brothers, which culminated in tragedy later.

In this year Parākrama Bahu IV king of Ceylon came to Madura and obtained from Kulaśēkhara Pāṇḍya the return of the Tooth Relic of Buddha, which he carried back to the island. (*above, s. v. A. D. 1288 ; Mahāwamśa, ch. xc.*)

A.D. 1296. In July 1296 Alāu-d-dīn Khilji became sultan of Delhi. (*above, s. v. A. D. 1294.*)

Hoyśala Baḷḷāḷa III was reigning in W. Mysore on August 8, 1296, in his 6th year. (The date has a wrong week day, however, and cannot quite be trusted, but the year, month and tithi give the result stated.) (*E. C. vi. Cm. 36 ; Tk. 88.*)

The Kalinga-Ganga king Narasimha II reigning in Vizagapatam District at Simhāchalam (*V.R. iii, Vizag. 145 ; 317 of 1899*). At the same place a gift was made to the temple by the wife of Jayanta of the Matsya family. (*V. R. iii, Vizag. 132 ; 304 of 1899.*)

Kākatīya Pratāpa Rudra was reigning in Kurnool District. (*V.R. ii, Kurn. 376 ; 45 of 1909.*)

In Nellore, a gift is mentioned as having been made by the Telugu-Choḍa chief Ranganātha *alias* Raja-Gaṇḍagōpāla in the 6th year of Vijaya-Gaṇḍagōpāla. The date, which is quite accurate = December 26, 1296 (*V. R. ii, Nell. 543 ; B. and V. C. 841 ; 194 of 1894*). [The inscription should be further examined. This Ranganātha seems to be the same as Manma-Siddha III.—Rāja-Gaṇḍagōpāla. His grandfather Vijaya-Gaṇḍagōpāla had ceased to reign in 1290–91, the reign having begun in 1250. It seems possible that a mistake has been made in the reading of the record, and that it may refer to the 6th year of Manma-Siddha III.]

A.D. 1297. Mr. Krishnaswami Aiyangar quotes this year as being the one in which an embassy was sent to China by the Pāṇḍya Jaṭāvarman Sundara II, whose ambassador was Fakru-d-dīn Ahamad, son of Jamālu-d-dīn the Arab chief who supplied the Pāṇḍya ruler with horses from Arabia. Jamāl's brother Takiu-d-dīn lived at Kāyal on the Gulf of Manaar. Fakru-d-din stayed four years in China and died on board ship on his return voyage in 1305. He was buried near his uncle Takiu-d-dīn who had died in 1303. At this time there were numbers of Musalman traders and others in South India, and Ibn Batuta tells us that under Hoyśala Baḷḷāḷa III there served a force of 20,000 of them.

In this year the Telugu-Chōḍa Manma-Siddha III took possession of Conjeeveram as a vassal of the Kākatīya king Pratāpa Rudra II (*E. I. vii, 128 ; 213 of 1892*). He was ruling in the Guntur District (*V. R. ii, Gun. 308 ; 213 of 1892.*)

Hoyśala Baḷḷāḷa III was ruling in W. Mysore (*E. C. v, Ak, 120*). Hoyśala Viśvanātha had about 1294–5 succeeded his father Rāmanātha and now ruled in Salem District (*V. R. ii, Salem, 104, 105 ; 204, 205 of 1911*). And in E. and S.-E. Mysore (*E. C. x, Ct, 45 ; ix. Ht, 136, 138*). [But the actual sovereign was his cousin Baḷḷāḷa III.]

Narasimha II, Kalinga-Ganga king, reigning in Vizagapatam District in his 23rd year. (*V. R. iii, Vizag. 128 ; 138, 300, 310 of 1899.*)

Kākatīya Pratāpa Rudra II was reigning in Guntur District.

(*V. R. ii, Gun. 414, 497, 499 ; B. and V. C. 1057 ; 570, 572 of 1909.*)

The Kaḷasa country in W. Mysore was locally ruled by Vīra Pāṇḍya. (*E. C. vi, Mg. 68.*)

A.D. 1298. Kākatīya Pratāpa Rudra reigning in Ongole Taluk and at Bezwada.

(*V. R. ii, Guntur 375 ; B. and V. C. 978 ; Kistna 58 ; 306 of 1892.*)

A gift was made to the Simhāchalam temple by the Matsya chief Jayantika, or Jayanta.

(*V. R. iii, Vizag. 144 ; 316 of 1899.*)

An order is mentioned as having been made in Coorg by Hariharadēva, probably the Changāḷva chief Harihara. (*E. C. i, Coorg, 59.*)

On July 5, 1298, Māravarman Kulaśēkhara Pāṇḍya I was reigning in Madura.

(*V. R. ii Mad. 35 ; E. I. ix, 224.*)

A.D. 1299. Hoyśala Baḷḷāḷa III reigning in S.-E. and in N.-W. Mysore (*E. C. ix, Kn, 76, viii, Sa, 96*). The latter inscription mentions the customary attack of one local chief on another, with accompanying deaths of fighting men.

In Nellore District 'Rāja Gaṇḍagōpāla' was ruling. This was the Telugu-Chōḍa chief Manma Siddha III, who bore that title. (*B. and V. C. i, 460, 832; V. R. ii, Nell. 266, 534.*)

[The Kērala king Ravivarman-Kulaśekhara-Saṃgrāmadhīra came to the throne this year. He was born in 1266 (*see above*). He governed from Kollam (Quilon).

Alāu-d-dīn Khilji of Delhi invaded Orissa in this year, but to no great effect]

The Kalinga-Ganga king Narasimha II reigning in Vizagapatam District in his 25th year.

(*V. R. iii. Vizag. 131 ; 303 of 1899.*)

Kākatīya Pratāpa Rudra reigning in Guntur District. (*V. R. ii. Gun. 583 ; 565 of 1909.*)

A.D. 1300. Hoyśala Baḷḷāḷa III reigning in Mysore. An inscription of this year states that he captured Hosaguṇḍa, an unidentified place, 'marched on the Gangeya-Sāhani' and plundered the country (*E. C. viii, Sa, 45*). [Apparently Viśvanātha attempted by armed force to oust Baḷḷāḷa, and Baḷḷāḷa attacked that part of Mysore which had been in some measure under Viśvanātha's father Rāmanātha's influence. This plundering of the country shews clearly who it was that suffered most from these dynastic wars. The armies on the march ruined and despoiled the peasant population. This must always have been the case.]

Māravarman Kulaśēkhara Pāṇḍya reigning in Tinnevelly (*416, 417, 552 of 1916*). The dates are respectively May 7, March 17 and November 23, 1300.

A.D. 1301. The same king, June 7, 1301. Record in Tinnevelly (*V. R. iii, Tinn. 44 ; 98 of 1907*). And in Tanjore on July 8 (*V. R. ii. Tan. 477; 661 of 1902 E. I. viii, 277*). Another Tanjore record of September 10, 1301 (*see Ind. Ant. 1913; p. 172*) alludes to the confusion in the country and the general distress caused by Kulaśēkhara's partitioning of the Pāṇḍya kingdom amongst the princes of his house. It would appear that these princes abused their position and harried the people each ruler attempting to make himself stronger than his neighbour. When the king abolished this arrangement and re-assumed sovereignty in his own person over the whole realm the people took heart and returned to the homes which they had been driven to desert.

(*V. R. ii, Tanjore, 657; 46 of 1906.*)

Inscription in South Arcot District of Jaṭāvarman Vīra Pāṇḍya Kulaśēkhara's illegitimate son, date November 12, 1301. The 5th regnal year (*430 of 1921*). This record is in Tirukoyilūr Taluk. Another inscription in Chidambaram Taluk of the same district shews that Jaṭāvarman

Sundara Pāṇḍya II, the king's legitimate son and heir, was ruling there on December 26, 1301. The regnal year stated is the 24th, but it was actually his 26th year. *(529 of 1920.)*

Hoyśala Baḷḷāḷa III was reigning in E. Mysore in this year, where there are six inscriptions of his. *(E. C. ix, Bn, 65 ; Nl, 38 ; Cp, 36; x, Mr, 67, 71, 100.)*

A.D. 1302. The Telugu Chōḍa chief 'Ranganātha-Rāja Gaṇḍagōpāla' i.e. Manma-Siddha III ruling in Nellore District on January 10, 1302. It belongs to his 12th regnal year (*V. R. Nell. 532. B. and V. C. 829*). [According to this his accession must have taken place before January 10, 1291. There is a little confusion at present as to the exact time of his accession owing to conflicting results derived from his inscription dates (*see above,* A.D. *1296*)].

Jaṭāvarman Vīra Pāṇḍya ruling in Tanjore District at Nannilam, in his 6th year, on September 1302. *(V. R. ii, Tan. 842; 401 of 1908; E. I, xi, 137.)*

Hoyśala Baḷḷāḷa III reigning in S., N. and N.-W. Mysore. In the north there was fighting 'when Kandali-dēva came marching to Hoḷalkere.' Kandali was some local chief, seemingly, trying to raid and plunder his neighbour's property. In the north-west there was more local fighting by armies of chiefs, of whom it appears that one was encouraged by the king (*E. C. iv. Ch. 191 ; xi. Hk. 106 ; viii. Nr. 27*). Another inscription (*viii. Sa. 101*) shews that in the autumn of A.D. 1302 Baḷḷāḷa III 'marched and encamped at Baṇavāsi,' and a battle was fought (perhaps against the Kādamba chief of Baṇavāsi) at Kadambaḷigē-nāḍu.

In Guntur district Kākatīya Pratāpa Rudra II was reigning in Palnāḍ Taluk.

(V. R. ii. Gun. 519 ; 549 of 1909.)

In S. Kanara, the Āḷupa chief Bankidēva-Āḷupēndra was ruling from Mangalore.

(V. R. ii. S. Kan. 87 ; 17 of 1901.)

A.D. 1303. [In this year Alāu-d-dīn Khilji, Sultan of Delhi, sent an expedition against Kākatīya Pratāpa Rudra II of Warangal, which, however, failed.]

Kākatīya Pratāpa Rudra II was reigning in Guntur district on February 18, 1303. *(173 of 1917.)*

A.D. 1304. A village in Chingleput district was given away by the chief Panchanadivāṇan Tiruvēgamban-Nīlagangaraiyan on July 8, 1304, in the 37th year of king Māravarman Kulaśēkhara Pāṇḍya I. In 1273 (*see above*) this Nīlaganga owned Vijayagaṇḍagōpāla as his sovereign (*V. R. i. Chin. 928 ; 555 of 1912*). [There were several Nīlagangaraiyas (*see Genealogical Table*].

An interesting copper-plate inscription found in Nellore district throws light on the life of the merchants at this date. It belongs to the year 1304–05. A body of merchants in that part of the country had combined to make certain rules for trade. One of their number turned traitor to them, and was murdered. This trades union then gave this document to the murderer, by which they found themselves in gratitude to allow him to carry on his merchandise in future free of duty.

(E. R. C. P. 10 of App. A. 1918–19.)

More fighting in N.-W. Mysore. A battle mentioned. *(E. C. viii. Nr. 12.)*

In E. Mysore Hoyśala Baḷḷāḷa III reigned. *(E. C. ix. Bn. 53.)*

Kākatīya Pratāpa Rudra reigning in Guntur district, Palnāḍ Taluk.

(V. R. ii. Gun. 486 ; 561 of 1909.)

A.D. 1305. Early in A.D. 1305 Hoyśala Baḷḷāḷa III attacked Rāmachandra of Dēvagiri, and a battle was fought. *(E. C. viii. Sa. 156.)*

Māravarman Kulaśēkhara Pāṇḍya I reigning in S. Arcot on April 28, 1905, in his 37th year (*539 of 1921*). And in Tinnevelly on October 31, in his 38th year (*19 of 1916.*)

A.D. 1306. The only inscriptions of this year are five, in N. and S.-E. Mysore, shewing Hoyśala Baḷḷāḷa III reigning there. (*E. C. ix. Bn. 76 ; Kn. 81 ; Ma. 55 ; D–B. 52, 60 ; xi. Hk. 136.*)

[In this year according to Ferishta (but in 1307 according to Amīr Khusrū and in 1308 according to Barni) Alāu-d-dīn Khilji of Delhi, who had given high command to his infamous favourite Malik Kāfur, sent him south again to attack Rāmachandra of Dēvagiri. Malik Kāfur laid waste the country up to the gates of Dēvagiri, and compelled Rāmachandra (whom the Musalman chroniclers call 'Ram Deo') to sue for terms. On his submission he sent him a prisoner to Delhi, where the sultan received him kindly, and after six months, honourably released him. (For an account of this expedition and the later ones of Malik Kāfur into South India, see Krishnaswami Aiyangar's '*South India, etc.*,' pp. 74 ff.). This defeat of the Yādava king by the encroaching Muhammadans must have terrified the inhabitants of Mysore and the neighbourhood, but there was worse to follow.]

A.D. 1307. Hoyśala Baḷḷāḷa reigning in W., N.-W. and E. and S.-E. Mysore.

(*E. C. v. Bl., 163 ; viii. Sa., 62 ; x., Mr., 83 ; ix. Cp., 76.*)

A Kādamba chief Kāva-dēva raided some country in N.-W. Mysore. (*E. C. viii. Sa., 32.*)

The Kalinga-Ganga king Bhānu-dēva II was reigning in Vizagapatam district in his 3rd year. (*V. R. iii. Vizag. 155, 157 ; 327, 329 of 1899.*)

Kākatīya Pratāpa Rudra was reigning in Kurnool district. (*V. R. ii, Kurn. 512.*)

A.D. 1308. Māravarman Kulaśēkhara was reigning in N. Arcot, Chingleput and Tanjore districts in this, his 40th, year; which makes it clear that he had got completely the upper hand of the great chiefs who had been ruling in the two former districts for several years since the downfall of the Chōla dynasty—*viz.*, the families of the Telugu-Choḍas, the Śengēṇis, and that of the Pallava Perunjinga. The dates are respectively = January 18, February 24, and March 18, 1308. (*476 of 1920 ; V. R. i, Chin. 503 ; 134 of 1896 ; E. I. vi, 300 ; V. R. ii. Tan. 930 ; 551 of 1904 ; E. I. viii, 276.*)

Kākatiya Pratāpa Rudra was reigning in Cuddapah and Kurnool districts.

(*V. R. i. Cudd. 130 ; 616 of 1907 ; Kurn. 353, 533 ; 260 of 1905.*)

Hoyśala Baḷḷāḷa III reigning in East Mysore. (*E. C. ix. Bn., 134.*)

A.D. 1309. Hoyśala Baḷḷāḷa in North-West Mysore, ruling from Dorasamudra.

(*E. C. vii, Sh. 19.*)

Māravarman Kulaśēkhara Paṇḍya I reigning in Madura on June 9, in his 41st year; and on July 13, in his 42nd year. (*V. R. ii. Mad. 342 ; 431 of 1907 ; 339 of 1918.*)

Gift made to a temple in Cuddapah district by a chief named Brahmmidēva, 'grandson of Brahmmidēva and Bhōgalādēvī.' (Unidentified). (*V. R. i. Cudd. 607 ; 506 of 1906*)

[Towards the end of this year Sultan Alāu-d-dīn of Delhi again despatched Malik Kāfur to attack the Hindus in the south. He was ordered to capture the fortress of Warangal and bring about the submission of Kākatīya Pratāpa Rudra II. The Muhammadan army marched across the Dekhan and at one point were assisted by the now humble Yādava Rāmachandra of Dēvagiri. As soon as they reached what they believed to be the border of the dominions of the Kākatīya king, they began proceedings by burning a town and massacring the inhabitants. They marched on Warangal, seized Hanumakonḍa and laid close siege to the capital.]

A.D. 1310. [The siege of Warangal was carried on with such vigour that in March 1310 Pratāpa Rudra was reduced to extremities and compelled to submit. Moderate terms, for which he begged, were refused him and Malik Kāfur, on being asked what the King was expected to surrender, replied that he demanded not only the king's treasures but the wealth of his whole country. Eventually the conqueror took the entire property and movable possessions of Pratāpa Rudra and left for Delhi, carrying with him, so say the Muhammadan chroniclers, 1,000 camels laden with treasure.

A little later in the year trouble broke out in the Pāṇḍya kingdom at Madura. It has already been mentioned above that Kulaśēkhara Pāṇḍya's two sons, Sundara Pāṇḍya, the legitimate son and rightful heir to the throne, and Vīra Pāṇḍya, the king's favourite (but himself illegitimate) had borne bitter enmity towards one another. This had been the case ever since 1296.

Some time before the end of May 1310 Sundara Pāṇḍya, enraged at his father's having openly nominated Vīra Pāṇḍya as his successor on the throne went to the length of killing the king and seizing the crown. Open war then broke out between the two brothers each of whom had his supporters; and about November of that year, after an action in which Vīra Pāṇḍya had been beaten, Sundara Pāṇḍya suffered an overwhelming defeat in his turn and was so hard pressed that he fled for protection to the Muhammadans.

Alāu-d-dīn now found the moment favourable for a great movement which would finally crush the whole of South India and bring that country into subjection to Delhi. The Yādva kingdom of Dēvagiri and the Kākatīya kingdom of Warangal had been conquered. There remained only two considerable kingdoms in the south to be reduced, the Hoyśala throne of Dorasamudra and the Pāṇḍya dominion of Madura. But there was an equally powerful attraction in the hoarded wealth of the great Hindu sacred places. These he resolved, should be systematically plundered, and the people, if possible, converted to the true faith of Islam.

He accordingly despatched Malik Kāfur on this mission with a great army. The general left Delhi in Nevember 1310 and marched towards Dēvagiri].

There is an inscription in Hassan Taluk, W. Mysore, recording the death of a soldier who died fighting against the 'Turks'. Its date, as given, would be February 5, A. D. 1310. But I cannot help believing that an error has been made in the year stated possibly by the original compiler of the record—because it was in February 1311[1] that Malik Kāfur reached Dorasamudra. *(E. C. v. Hn, 51)*

Two inscriptions recognize Pratāpa Rudra, Kākatiya as reigning in Nellore and Guntur Districts in 1310–11 *(V. R. ii. Nell. 94 B. and V. C. 333; V. R, ii. Gun; 384; B. and V. C. 994.)*

An inscription of Hoyśala Ballāla III in N. Mysore. *(E. C, xi, Cd, 7.)*

A.D. 1311. Two records shewing Kākatiya Pratāpa Rudra reigning in Kurnool and on the Krishna river in Palnāḍ Taluk. *(V. R. ii, Kurn. 397; Gun. 582; 564 of 1909.)*

[The Mussalman forces under Malik Kāfur reached Devagiri on February 4, 1911, according to Amīr Khusrū's chronicle; and there Malik Kāfur learned that, owing to the war in the Pāṇḍya country between the princes Sundara and Vīra, Hoysala Ballāla III had collected an army and left his capital with a view of himself seizing Madura and the Pāṇḍya dominions. Malik Kāfur determined therefore to proceed at once to the reduction of Ballāla's capital hoping to succeed in his venture before the Mysorean army could effect its return. He left Dēvagiri on February 8 and reached Dorasamudra on the 25th. But meanwhile Ballāla III, who could not have gone far to the south before the news reached him of the Muhammadan invasion, had returned and was then in his capital. He found Malik Kāfur's force overwhelmingly strong, so much so that resistance

[1] 5th Shawwal A. H. 711 – Thursday, 25th February 1311 is the actual date. *Editor.*

would be useless, and was induced to surrender. He was compelled to abandon all his possessions and treasures which were seized by his conqueror, and after twelve days' stay in the city Malik Kāfur despatched them and also the person of king Vīra Baḷḷāḷa's son Baḷḷala, as a prisoner and a hostage, to Delhi.

Then Malik Kāfur set forth, bent on further plunder and on the reduction of Vīra Pāṇḍya. He stormed and sacked several places whose names as stated in the Muhammadan chronicles are unintelligible, and attempted to capture Vīra Pāṇḍya in person. The prince, however, eluded him and fled from place to place, the Muhammadans following in constant pursuit, and at one time he took refuge in the jungles. On that Malik Kāfur returned to the place he had last started from—'Kandur' probably Kaṇṇanūr near Srīrangam and there learned that immense treasures existed at a place which Amīr Khusru calls 'Brahmastpuri', and which Mr. Krishnaswami Aiyangar believes to be perhaps Chidambaram. Here was a very holy and very rich Hindu temple. This Malik Kāfur destroyed. He massacred the inhabitants ruthlessly, killing the Brahman priests, and seizing all the temple treasures. Then, in April 1311 he marched to Madura, reaching it on April 14, he found the place empty, and here also he wrecked and burned the temples and sacked the city.

(Mr. Krishnaswami Aiyangar has gone very fully into the history of these invasions in his volume *South India etc.*, pp. 91–131, which readers would do well to consult.)

Malik Kāfur returned to Delhi on October 18, 1311 bringing with him, so the chroniclers say, 312 elephants laden with spoil, 12,000 horses, 96,000 *mans* of gold, and many boxes of pearls and precious stones.

This terrible inroad made an immense impression on the minds of all the Hindu inhabitants of South India. For it must be remembered that, although fighting had been incessant there throughout the centuries, it had been only between Hindus, and that whatever suffering was entailed on the mass of the population it did not touch the Brahman priests or the temples. Dynasties might be wiped out for ever, the chiefs killed, the country devastated, but the temples and the persons of the Brahmans were inviolate, and these temples were immensely wealthy. For many centuries the civil rulers had lavished on them the revenues of innumerable villages, laid enforced taxes for their support on the people and presented them with all kinds of valuables, precious stones and gold in quantities. And, whatever slaughter of the people went on, the Brahman remained untouchable. The deadliest curse that could be pronounced on a man was, as is evidenced by the inscriptions, that his punishment hereafter should be like that awarded by the high gods to a man who had killed a Brahman.[1] And yet now there came down on the Hindus those masses of marauding foreigners, sacking the cities, slaughtering the people, destroying the ancient fanes and killing even the sacred Brahmans, in the name and for the glory of God. The thing was monstrous—unheard of. The result was that the whole of Southern India was convulsed by this catastrophe; the one hope in men's minds was that some Hindu Power would arise to defend the country from any such disaster in future; and when, a few years later, certain princes took the lead, they were enthusiastically supported by almost all parties. This paved the way for the establishment on solid ground of the empire of Vijayanagar.]

[1] As an instance of how the temples were enriched and maintained readers may refer to the Tanjore temple inscription of May A.D. 1012 noted above.

A.D. 1312. Three inscriptions shew that Kākatīya Pratāpa Rudra continued to reign in Kurnool and Nellore districts. (*V. R. ii, Kurn. 23, 326 ; Nell. 586 ; 233 of 1905 ; B. and V. C. 1158.*)

[In the state of confusion to which South India had now been brought, the way lay open for any strong ruler to increase his strength by conquest. The Chōla kingdom had long since practically perished. At Madura there was chaos, the city having been sacked.]

Vīra Pāṇḍya had been driven to flight by Malik Kāfur, and Sundara Pāṇḍya was negligible. The Yādavas and Hoyśalas had been reduced, and the only sovereign left with any real power was the Kākatīya Pratāpa Rudra II. Accordingly, the Kēraḷa king of the West Coast Ravivarman-Kulaśēkhara-Samgrāmadhīra seized his opportunity and marched eastwards, bent on conquest. He seized Madura, and prevented Vīra Pāṇḍya's return thither, and thus became temporarily lord of the Pāṇḍya kingdom. Proceeding forwards, Ravivarman invaded the Chōla country and seized Conjeeveram ejecting thence the Telugu Chōḍa prince Manma-Siddha III, Rāya-Gaṇḍagōpāla. An inscription of his in that city records the fact that he gave a gift to the temple there, and states that he was crowned there a second time, he being then in the 46th year of his age. As he was born in A.D. 1266–67, this coronation ' on the banks of the Vēgāvati ' took place in 1312–13.

(*34 of 1890 ; E. I. iv. 145, viii. 8 ; V. R. i. Chingleput, 349*)

This is supported by an inscription of the same king at Tiruvadi in S. Arcot of A.D. 1313–14 (*q. v.*).

In this year, 1312, the Yādava king Śamkara withheld the tribute promised to the Sultan of Delhi by his father Rāmachandra, and Aḷaud-dīn sent Malik Kāfur again to Devagiri. The capital was seized and king Śamkara made prisoner and put to death. Malik Kāfur remained for some time at Dēvagiri, collecting tribute and ravaging the neighbouring country. (*Bombay Gazet. p. 533.*)

A.D. 1313. An inscription at Tiruvadi in S. Arcot, the date of which = December 29, 1313, confirms the assertion made above that Ravivarman was crowned at Conjeeveram in the 46th year of his age. It adds the information that the day in question, December 29, 1313, was in the king's 4th year, and tells us that his first coronation as Kēraḷa king took place in the year following December 29, 1309 (*V. R. i. S. Arcot, 295 ; 34 of 1903 ; E. I. viii. 8 ; vii. 130*). Ravivarman's conquest of the Pāṇḍya king is also confirmed by an inscription at Poonamallee close to Madras (*V. R. i. Chingleput 848 ; 34 of 1911*) which though undated and not containing a definite assertion to that effect, displays the emblem of the Chēra *aṁkuśa* (elephant goad) with underneath it, symbolically, the Pāṇḍya fish. (*E. R. 1911, p. 79*)

There are several records of the Kākatīya king Pratāpa Rudra II, dated in this year in Kurnool, Nellore, Cuddapah and Guntur districts. The first two mentioned are of date = February 1 and 26, 1313 (*V. R. ii. Kurn. 463, 472 ; Nell. 438, 72 ; i, Cudd., 586, 587, 18 ; ii. Gun. 546 ; 27, 36 of 1915 ; B. and V. C. 730, 296 ; 328, 329 of 1905 ; 585 of 1909*). In one of these a servant of his claims to have reduced the fortress of Gaṇḍikōṭa, and another states that the king appointed Gonkayya Reḍḍi to be governor of that place.

Hoyśala Baḷḷāḷa III recognized as reigning in Central, N. and N.-W. Mysore from Dorasamudra. The 3rd of these says that he was ruling ' after the Turuka War ', i.e. after Malik Kāfur's raid. (*E. C. xii. Mi. 3 ; xi. Hr. 87 ; vii. Sh. 68.*)

On May 6, 1313, the Hoyśala prince Vīra Baḷḷāḷa, who had been carried captive by Malik Kāfur to Delhi as a hostage, but had been released by the Sultan arrived home again at Dorasamudra and was received by the people with great rejoicings. (*E. C. vii. Sh. 68.*)

A.D. 1314. Kākatīya Pratāpa Rudra reigning in Guntur district, Palnāḍ taluk (*V. R. ii. Gun. 547 ; 586 of 1909*). A local chief who had fought against the Muhammadans is honoured by the title 'Rescuer of the Kākatīya family.' Other records, the first of which is of date = June 19, 1314, are in Guntur and Nellore districts. (*V. R. ii. Gun. 547, 329 ; 131 of 1917 ; B. and V. C. 901*)

A certain Bukka Rāya is mentioned as a local chief in the Nellore District in this year. (*V. R. ii. Nell. 366 ; B. and V. C., p. 642.*)

Jaṭāvarman Sundara Pāṇḍya, the legitimate son of Kulaśēkhara I whom he killed, reigning in S. Arcot on January 26, 1314, in his 11th year ; which makes his seizure of the throne as in the year following January 26, 1303. (*571 of 1920.*)

Hoyśala Baḷḷāḷa III reigning on March 21, 1314, in W. Mysore and in most other parts of Mysore—seven inscriptions.

(*E. C. v. Hn., 181, 182 ; vii. Ht., 76 ; ix. Ht., 139 ; Cp., 30 ; xii. Mi., 63 ; Ck., 26.*)

A.D. 1315. Māravarman Kulaśēkhara Pāṇḍya II ruling in Tanjore District on December 8, 1315. (*517 of 1922.*)

Hoyśala Baḷḷāḷa III reigning in East and South Mysore.

(*E. C. ix. Ma., 15, 39, 58 ; Ht., 159 ; iv. Gu., 58.*)

Kākatīya Pratāpa Rudra II reigning from Warangal, in Cuddapah, Nellore and Guntur districts. The last of these calls him 'Mahāmaṇḍalēśvara Mūrurāyalagaṇḍa.'

(*V. R. i. Cudd., 879 ; ii. Nell. 270 ; Gun., 423 ; 432 of 1911 ; B. and V. C., 455, 1079.*)

In S. Kanara the Āḷupa chief Ṣōyidēva Āḷupēndra was ruling.

(*V. R. ii. S. Kan. 175 ; 157 of 1901.*)

An inscription of Ravivarman-Kulaśēkhara-Samgrāmadhira of Kērala at Conjeeveram, where he had been crowned, apparently as usurper of the Chōla throne (*see above* A.D. *1312–13*). It states that he had conquered the Pāṇḍya and Chōla kingdoms, and that Vīra Pāṇḍya had been driven to the forests. (*34 of 1890 ; E. I. iv. 145 ; vii. 130 ; V. R. i. Chingleput, 349.*)

A.D. 1316. Māravarman-Kulaśēkhara-Pāṇḍya II ruling in Trichinopoly District, in his 2nd year, on January 2, 1316. (*103 of 1920.*)

In Nellore District an inscription (the date is correct and = March 4, 1316) of the 27th regnal year of Ranganātha-Rājagōpāla, i.e., Manma-Siddha III. (*V. R. ii. Nell., 546 ; B. and V. C. 844.*)

Kākatiya Pratāpa Rudra reigning in the Palnāḍ Taluk, Guntur District (*V. R. ii. Gun. 521 ; 551 of 1909*) and in Nellore District. (*V. R. ii. Nell., 552.*)

Hoyśala Baḷḷāḷa III reigning in S. Mysore. (*E. C. iii. Ml., 12 ; Md., 100 ; iv. Ch. 116, 137.*)

[The Kākatīya king of Warangal, Pratāpa Rudra II, now with greatly diminished wealth in consequence of Malik Kāfur's raid, strengthened himself sufficiently to attack his neighbours. He evidently objected strongly to the Kēraḷa king's seizure of Conjeeveram, and to that city he marched early in 1316. The details of the war that ensued are unknown but Pratāpa Rudra succeeded in driving out Ravivarman and his following, and in seizing the place on some day between March 25 and June 11, 1316. This success was due to the Kākatīya general Muppiḍi-Nāyaka. This officer installed as governor of Conjeeveram a certain 'Māna-vīra,' whom Dr. Hultzsch believes to have been Manma-Siddha-Gaṇḍa-Gōpāla of the Telugu-Chōḍa family.[1] If this be so, his appointment

[1] This belief is partly based on the fact that the Aruḷāḷa temple inscription referred to states that the revenues of the granted villages were ordered to be paid ' in the coinage of Gaṇḍa-Gōpāla.'

meant that he was reinstated in the post which he held before Ravivarman ejected him in 1312, but that he now held it as a vassal and officer of the Kākatīya king.]

These dates are derived from an inscription at the Aruḷāḷa temple at Conjeeveram, which describes Muppiḍi-Nāyaka's entry into the city as in the year 'Nala', which began on March 25, and mentions two grants of village revenues made by him to the temple on June 11 and 16, 1316.

(*V. R. i. Chingleput, 325 ; 43 of 1893 ; E. I. vii. 128.*)

[In this year Hoyśala Baḷḷāḷa III, who had ruled his country from Beḷūr or Honnūr since Malik Kāfur's destruction of Dorasamudra, the capital, returned to the city which meanwhile had been rebuilt. One inscription of the following year would seem to imply that he marched thither from Kaṇṇanūr, but this is not certain. (*E. C. xii. Ck., 4 ; below.*)

Another event of the year was the death of Sultan Alāu-d-dīn of Delhi, which was immediately followed by the murder of Malik Kāfur, the scourge of South India. Malik Kafūr had attempted to become all-powerful by throwing into prison the king's sons, but on his assassination, the nobles released one of the sons Kutbu-d-dīn Mubārak Khān and placed him on the throne.

Another event of the year was the revolt against the suzerainty of Delhi by Harapāla, the brother-in-law of the Yādava king Singhaṇa of Dēvagiri, who for a time was successful.

A.D. 1317. Hoyśala Baḷḷāḷa III reigning in Central Mysore, where an inscription states that a fight took place 'when the king was marching from Kaṇṇanūr.' (*E. C. xii. Ck. 4*). Other records of this king shew him reigning in Anantapur district and in East Mysore. The date of the first of these = February 17, 1317. It mentions his son Tipparasa Bhairava.

(*738 of 1917 ; ix. Md., 59 ; x. Kl., 173.*)

Kākatīya Pratāpa Rudra was reigning in Guntur district on May 19, 1317 (*715 of 1920*). And on the Godavari river (*V. R. ii. Godav., 12 ; 501 of 1893*). And in Guntur district.

(*V. R. ii, Gun., 330 ; B. and V. C. 902.*)

In Travancore the regining Kēraḷa king was now Vīra-Udaiya-Mārttāṇḍavarman, successor of Ravivarman-Kulaśēkhara now dead. [He may have lost his life when defeated at Conjeeveram by Muppiḍi-Nāyaka, but there is no proof of this.] (*T. A. S. iv. Pt. i, p. 89.*)

The Pāṇḍya king Maravarman Kulaśēkhara II reigning on July 23, 1317 and on September 2, in his 4th year (*V. R. iii. Trichinopoly, 804 ; 75 of 1892 ; E. I. vi, 313 ; 107 of 1916*). He was reigning also in Tanjore on September 24, in the same regnal year. (*509, 510 of 1920.*)

In Tinnevelly district the ruler was Jaṭāvarman Vīra Pāṇḍya, in his 21st year on October 31, 1317. (*639 of 1916.*)

A.D. 1318. [The result of the Yādava Harapāla's revolt against the Sultan of Delhi was tragic. Mubārak sent an army under Khusru Khān to chastise the rebel. Harapāla fled, was pursued and captured, and Khusrū Khān with inhuman ferocity caused him to be flayed alive. His decapitated head was set up over the gate of the city. Thus the whole Yādava country, as far south at least as the Tungabhadra river and even beyond it, passed into Musalman hands. The capital was renamed Daulatābād.]

In Mysore Hoyśala Baḷḷāḷa continued to reign.

(*E. C. v, Ak., 113 ; ix, Cp. 10, 76 ; xii, Tm., 63.*)

In Ramnad Jaṭāvarman Vīra Pāṇḍya ruled on May 3, 1318. The regnal year is given as '23,' but this would differ from some other records as to his date of accession.

(*V. R. ii. Ramnad, 266 ; 128 of 1908.*)

Kākatīya Pratāpa Rudra II reigning in Kurnool and Guntur districts (*V. R. ii. Kurn.*, *498 ; 652 of 1920*). The commander of his army was Sōmaya Venkan. (*V. R. ii. Gun.*, *827.*)

The Vaishṇava pontiff Ānandatīrtha died this year and was succeeded by his disciple Padmanābhatīrtha, who held the office for six years, when, in 1324, he was succeeded by Naraharitīrtha. (*E. I. vi. 260.*)

A.D. 1319. Hoysala Baḷḷāḷa reigning in Mysore.

(*E. C. v, Ak., 165 ; ix, Kn., 68, 69 ; Cp., 12 ; Nl., 57 ; xii. Mi., 28.*)

Kākatīya Pratāpa Rudra II reigning in Guntur district. (*V. R. ii, Gun., 500 ; 573 of 1909.*)

[The Malabar coast, being now open to attack by the Muhammadans of the north owing to the fall of the Yādava kingdom and the weakness of the Pāṇḍya and Kēraḷa rulers, was raided by Khusru Khān from Delhi. He returned to his master the Sultan laden with treasure looted from the merchants and the Hindu temples.]

Māravarman Kulaśēkhara Pāṇḍya II reigning at Gangaikoṇḍa-Chōlapuram on March 5, 1319, in his 5th year. (*V.R. iii, Trichinopoly, 807 : 78 of 1892 ; E.I. vi, 313.*)

A.D. 1320. Kākatiya Pratāpa Rudra II reigning in Kurnool from Warangal on January 26, 1320 (*V. R. ii, Kur. 548, 271 ; 178 of 1905*). And on March 16 in Nellore district (*V. R. ii, Nell. 326, 327 ; B. and V. C. 589, 590*). And in Guntur district.

(*V.R. ii, Gun. 331, 332 ; B. and V. C. 903, 905.*)

Māravarman Kulaśēkhara Pāṇḍya II reigning in Trichinopoly district on January 12.

(*V.R. iii, Trich. 72 ; 742 of 1909 ; E.I. xi, 264.*)

March 15, 1320, is Kielhorn's fixture for the date of the Koṭṭayam plates of the Syrian Christians, which name Vīra Rāghava as reigning king in Travancore ; but this fixture needs some confirmation. (*V.R. iii, Trav. 91 ; E.I. ii, 83 ; iv, 270 ; I.A. vi, 83.*)

Hoysala Baḷḷāḷa III reigning in Mysore and in Anantapur district. The first of these records bears date = September 1, 1320, and mentions fighting between the royal troops and some local chiefs. Another also mentions a fierce battle—perhaps the same.

(*772 of 1917 ; E.C. viii, Sa. 135 ; Nr. 19 ; iv, Gu. 69 ; ix, Cp, 31.*)

A.D. 1321. Māravarman Kulaśēkhara Pāṇḍya II reigning in Tinnevelly district on February 5, 1321 [the inscription seems to err in the number of his regnal year]. (*415 of 1917*). Another of September 30 (?) (*V. R. iii, Tinn. 88 ; 126 of 1907 ; E. I. x, 146*). Another of November 14. (*V. R. iii, Tinn : 471 ; 122 of 1894 ; E.I. vi, 312.*) The last two were executed in this king's 8th year.

Hoysala Baḷḷāḷa II reigning in E. Mysore (*E. C. x, Kl, 124 b, 128*). The Kalinga-Ganga king Bhānudēva II, 'Vīrādhivīra,' reigning in Ganjam district. (*V.R. i, Gan. 180 ; 302 of 1896.*)

Kākatiya Pratāpa Rudra II reigning in Guntur district. (*V.R. ii, Gun. 272 ; 153 of 1899.*)

[In March 1321, Mubārak Khilji, sultan of Delhi, was murdered, and Malik Khusru said to have been a participator in the crime. The house of Khilji was now completely eradicated, no scion of the royal stock having been left in existence. The nobles had to fill the throne and they elected to that honour a Karaunian Turk of high birth who had had a local government. This was Ghāzī Malik. He was made sultan and assumed the name of Ghiyāsu-d-dīn Tughlak. He captured Malik Khusru and executed him. The new sultan despatched his son Ulugh, or Jūnā Khan, otherwise known as Muhammad Tughlak, with orders to subdue the Kākatīya king of Warangal and to seize his dominions on the East Coast. Warangal was duly besieged, Pratāpa Rudra making a stout defence ;

but the invading army was attacked by a severe epidemic and what remained of it was marched homewards, to the great relief of the Hindus.]

A.D. 1322. An inscription in Nellore district engraved on copper-plates bears date = October 15, 1322, and mentions as king Pratāpa Rudra II. It should be compared with a record of a similar nature in A.D. 1304 (above), since it is of importance as revealing something of the life of the times. The same body of merchants who openly rewarded a man in 1304 for killing one of their number whom they believed to have been a traitor to their guild, now in 1322 publicly reward another man for having murdered two toll-collectors, and present to him a document, intended to be permanent, as a token of their satisfaction and approval *(E.R. 1919, C. P. No. 11)*. Another record in Nellore district shews Pratāpa Rudra reigning there in this year and in Guntur district.

(V.R. ii, Nell. 311 ; Gun. 105 ; B. and V. C. 561 ; 604 of 1909.)

Jaṭāvarman Vīra Pāṇḍya ruling in Tinnevelly District in his 26th year on April 29, 1322, This makes the beginning of his rule as from a day between December 17, 1296 and April 29, 1297. *(546 of 1911 ; E. R., 1922, p. 92.)* Mr. Swamikannu Pillay identifies him as the Vīra Pāṇḍya of the Muhammadan invasion of Madura,—natural son of Kulaśēkhara Pāṇḍya I.

Jaṭāvarman Parākrama Pāṇḍya is also represented as now ruling in part at least of Tinnevelly District in his 8th year.

(V. R. iii, Tinn. 259 ; 487 of 1909 ; E. I. ix, 226 ; E. R. 1910, p. 97.)

In this year the Śengēṇi chief 'Veṇṛumāṇkoṇḍa' Śambuvaraiyan began to govern the family territories about North and South Arcot and Chingleput.

(See E. I. xi, 251 ; V. R. i, N. Arcot 548 ; 24 of 1897 ; 42 of 1921 ; E. R. 1903, p. 16.)

A.D. 1323. Hoyśala Baḷḷaḷa III reigning in Anantapur District and in E. Mysore. The first of these records bears date = March 18, 1323 and records local disturbances, a battle, and a victory gained over a chief. The week-day is however wrongly stated.

(771, 796 of 1917 ; E. C. x, Kl, 10.)

Jaṭāvarman Parākrama Pāṇḍya ruling in Pudukoṭṭa on August 27, 1323 in his 9th year. Mr. Swamikannu Pillai finds his rule to have begun between April 15 and August 10, 1315.

(V. R. iii, Pudukotta, 128 ; 352 of 1914.)

[In this year Warangal was again attacked by forces from Delhi, and the Kākatīya king Pratāpa Rudra II was made prisoner and sent to Delhi. The kingdom, though now shrunk, was not annexed by the sultan ; and Pratāpa Rudra's son Krishna *alias* Vīrabhadra became king.]

A.D. 1324. At Rajahmundry on the Godaveri river a Muhammadan mosque was consecrated on September 12, 1324, 'in the reign of the Emperor Muhammad Tughlak'. Muhammad was however, then only a prince—son of the Emperor Ghiāsu-d-din. *(V. R. ii, Godaveri, 82.)*

In S. Kanara the Āḷupa chief Śoyidēva was ruling. *(V. R. ii, S. Kan. 205 ; 92 of 1901.)*

[In this year Naraharitīrtha, who had been governor under the king of Kalinga, became supreme Vaishṇava pontiff. *(E. I. vi, 260.)*]

Jaṭāvarman Parākrama Pāṇḍya ruling in Tanjore in his 10th year on December 31, 1324.

(160 of 1911 ; E. R. 1922, p. 93.)

Piracy abounded on the coasts of S. India at this time. Ibn Batuta fell a victim to it. Hindu pirates seized the ship on which he sailed when on a voyage from Quilon to Honawar and he was stripped of all his possessions, and landed with nothing to wear even, but one pair of trousers. *(Ind : Ant : 1923, Supp. Piracy in Eastern Waters, p. 14.)*

A.D. 1325-26. [Ghiāsu-d-dīn Tughlak of Delhi and his young son Mahmūd were killed by an 'accident' carefully arranged by his son Muhammad Tughlak, *alias* Junā; who seated himself on the throne. 'He occupied the throne for twenty-six years of tyranny as atrocious as any on record in the sad annals of human devilry' (*V. Smith, Oxford History of India,' p. 237*). In A.D. 1326 he compelled the inhabitants of Delhi to quit the place and travel to Dēvagiri which he fixed on as his capital, a journey of 600 miles.[1] Immense numbers died on the way. Ibn Batuta says that two men who ventured to remain were slaughtered by the sultan's orders, and that a blind man was dragged on the ground along the road till his body rotted and fell to pieces.

A.D. 1326. Hoyśala Baḷḷāḷa III ruling in South Mysore. (*E. C. ix, Cp. 98.*)

A.D. 1327. The same ruler in W. Mysore (*E. C. vi, Kp. 11*). And in S. Mysore. (*Ibid. iv, Hg. 98.*)

A.D. 1327. [In this year Muhammad Tughlak sent an expedition to the South in order to bring the country into complete subjection to him. The first objective was the Hoyśala kingdom with its capital Dorasamudra, where Baḷḷāḷa III was reigning. The expedition was successful. The Hindus could not put up a substantial resistance and the city of Dorasamudra was ruthlessly looted and destroyed. Baḷḷāḷa retired to Tonnūr near Seringapatam and finally to Tiruvaṇṇāmalai in N. Arcot, where he established himself strongly. The Musalman forces then occupied the Toṇḍamaṇḍalam country and Musalman governors were placed over Mysore and Madura.[2]

The *Kōyiloḷugu* chronicle describes the panic that ensued when, after the sack of Dorasamudra, the Muhammadan army arrived at Śrīrangam (A.D. 1327). The temple authorities removed the image of Ranganātha and conveyed it by a circuitous route to the Western coast; thence to Mēlukōṭ in Mysore and from there to the Tirupati sacred hill in Chittoor District. There it was kept safe till 1371, when Kampana II of Vijayanagar conquered and pacified the Toṇḍamaṇḍalam and other districts and his general Gopana brought the image back to Śrīrangam in triumph. (*E. I. vi, 322.*)

The downfall of the Warangal kingdom enabled a hitherto minor chief, ruling at the formidable hill fortress of Koṇḍavīḍ, south of the Krishna river in Guntur district, named Prōla or Prōlaya Vēma Reḍḍi to establish himself there as a quasi-independent lord of the neighbouring tract. He is widely remembered as having constructed a great set of steps cut in the hill side and leading up to the temples at Śrīśailam and Ahōbilam. He is said to have seized the government of the Amarāvati tract from the officers of the now dispossessed Kākatīya king. A quaintly worded inscription of A.D. 1344, very suggestive of the state of the country, describes him as ruling for a long time 'enjoying what was left of the country after its enjoyment by the Brahmans'. (*E. I. xi, p. 313.*)

A.D. 1328. Hoyśala Baḷḷāḷa III continued to reign in Mysore, but from his new capital in N. Arcot, Tiruvaṇṇāmalai (*E. C. ix, D.-B, 14, 18 Dv, 1, 60 ; Ht, 124; iv, Yl, 39; vi, Kp, 13; xi, Cd, 4*). Also in Anantapur District. (*V. R. i. Anant. 70; 81 of 1912.*)

A.D. 1330. Kākatīya Pratāpa Rudra said to be reigning in Nellore District on January 5, 1330, on the day of a lunar eclipse. (*V. R. ii, Nell. 299; B. and V. C. 538.*)

[This is his latest known date.

[1] This is hardly a fair statement. Muhammad changed his capital and ordered his courtiers to build houses for themselves. People were not asked to move out now. It is some years later when the inhabitants of Delhi pestered him with letters of abuse that he ordered the inhabitants to move out of Delhi as a measure of mad vengeance. See Cambridge History of India, Vol. III.—*Editor*.

[2] The invasion of 1327 was no more than a raid. Vira Baḷḷāḷa removed to Tiruvannamalai as a better centre for his efforts at organising resistance. See Mr. Sewell's remarks under A.D. *1330*.—*Editor*.

It shews that the people in Nellore were loyal to the dynasty, but as a matter of fact Pratāpa Rudra's reign had come to an end in 1323, when he was sent prisoner to Delhi.]

Hoyśala Baḷḷāḷa III ruling in W. Mysore. (*E. C. v, Ak. 66.*)

[The existence of a number of inscriptions of this king down to his death in 1342 seems to shew that after the sack of Śrīrangam the Muhammadan armies retired northwards and paid little attention to the condition of the Mysore country, while they left a Muhammadan governor at Madura.]

A.D. 1331. Hoyśala Baḷḷāḷa III reigning in Central, East and South Mysore.
(*E. C. v. Ak, 31, which mentions the Muhammadan invasion ix, Cp, 71; Ht, 97; xii, Gb, 30.*)

A.D. 1332. The same king in east and south Mysore. (*E. C. ix, Bn, 61, 63; iii, Ml, 113.*)

Māravarman Kulaśēkhara Pāṇḍya II reigning in Trichinopoly on October 22, 1332.
(*V. R. iii, Trich. 233; 29 of 1913.*)

A.D. 1333. Hoyśala Baḷḷāḷa III reigning in Mysore.
(*E. C. iii, Ml, 104; x, Gd, 16; xii, Tp, 83.*)

Mādhavatīrtha, disciple of Ānandatīrtha became Vaishṇava pontiff about this time.
(*E. I. vi, 260.*)

A.D. 1334. Hoyśala Baḷḷāḷa III reigning in Mysore (*E. C. iv, Kr, 40; viii. Sb, 494; ix, Bn, 44 ; Cp, 7 ; Ht, 96*). The second of these inscriptions says that the king sent his general, Kāmayya, with an army and laid siege to Kuppe, and a battle was fought. The reason for this course is not stated.

A.D. 1334-35. [Jalālu-d-dīn Ahsan Shāh who had been left as governor of Madura when the army from Delhi retired northwards, and who had ruled there since, thinking himself sufficiently free from interference from Delhi, declared his independence either in 1334 or 1335, and proclaimed himself sultan of Madura.

Prior to this, probably in 1334, Sultan Muhammad Tughlak's nephew Bahāu-d-dīn Gushtasp rebelled, and the sultan marched southwards to punish him. Bahāu-d-dīn fled for refuge to Kampli in Bellary district on the Tungabhadra river. A little to the west of this place, on the north side of the river, is the small hill-fortress of Ānegundi, and it would seem to have been in this place that the Hindus made a stand. Their Raja held out against a siege till the garrison were reduced to starvation, when in desperation his wives threw themselves on to a funeral-pyre and committed suicide, while the Raja and the surviving soldiers sallied forth and were all slain. The sultan seized eleven of his sons and forced them to become Muhammadans. Meanwhile Bahāu-d-dīn had succeeded in escaping into the Hoyśala country, but was pursued and captured. Muhammad Tughlak caused him to be flayed alive, and he had his flesh cooked and sent to his wife. His skin was stuffed with straw, and was sent to be exhibited about the country.

Nuniz, writing about 200 years later, says that the sultan found it advisable to restore the captured fortress to the Hindus and raised to be chiefs of it two brothers who had been respectively minister and treasurer to the dead Raja. These were named Harihara and Bukka. They raised their power into an empire and built the magnificent city of Vijayanagar. That they were enabled to do so is proof positive that the Muhammadans had retired from the neighbourhood of Ānegundi, which is just across the river opposite the new city. The city was built round the old village of Hampe on the south bank.

Another account of this family of five brothers sons of Sangama, a Yādava chief of the Lunar race, for five there certainly were, the others being Kampana I, Mārapa and Mudappa, is contained in

Mr. Krishnaswami Aiyangar's suggestion that they were separately employed some by Baḷḷāḷa III as governors of different provinces of his kingdom (*'South India etc. . . .' p. 180*). Harihara governed on the West coast and is the same as the 'Horaib' or Hariyab mentioned by Ibn Batuta as ruling at Honawar. Bukka ruled at Dorasamudra and Penukoṇḍa. An inscription of date A.D. 1353 describes Bukka as being a 'Mahāmaṇḍalēśvara' (great lord) ruling 'in the Hoyśala country.' (*J.B.B.R.A.S., xii. 338, 342*). Kampana I is the same as 'Kapraz' or 'Kampraz' mentioned by Musalman writers as ruling between Bijapur and Gulbarga. Mārapa ruled over the Āraga tract in N.-W. Mysore. Muddapa governed at Mulbāgal in S.-E. Mysore. Mr. H. Krishna Sāstri, in his excellent monograph on '*The First Vijayanagar Dynasty etc. . . .*' in the Archæological Survey of India *Annual Report for 1907–8, p. 235*, to a certain extent supports this view.

[Whatever the truth may be as to their origin, it is certain that these five brothers raised the whole of south India into determined opposition to the Muhammadans. Forts were built; armies were raised, and the people, thoroughly alarmed by the savage inroads made on their country, flocked to the leaders' standards, with such success that further invasions were stayed. It may be due to the fact that the whole mass of Hindus in the Hoyśala dominions were roused against him that Muhammad Tughlak refrained from marching across Mysore against his rebellious subjects at Madura.]

An inscription at Paṇaiyūr in Pudukoṭṭa State mentions this year as the 9th regnal year of 'Muhammad Sultan,' proving that Muhammad Tughlak's viceroy Jalālu-d-dīn Āhsan Shāh had been governing that country since A.D. 1327 (*see above*). (*S. Krishnaswami Aiyangar, 'South India, etc. . . .' p. 153*, where it is stated that a number of inscriptions which quote the Hijra year have been found in the district of Ramnad).

A.D. 1335. The Śengēṇi chief Veṅrumaṇkoṇḍa Śambuvaraiyan ruling in his 14th year, part of S. Arcot district. The inscription mentions the irruption of the Muhammadans, and the resulting ruin of the country. (*V. R. i. S. Arcot, 1048 ; 434 of 1903.*)

Hoyśala Baḷḷāḷa III reigning in S. and S.-E. Mysore. (*E. C. iv. Ch., 66 ; ix. Cp., 178.*)

Māravarman-Kulaśekhara Pāṇḍya II ruling in Trichinopoly on April 7, 1335. (*52 of 1920.*)

The Reddi chief of Koṇḍavīḍ, Prōlaya Vēma, here called 'Vēmayya Reḍḍi,' issued a C.-P. grant of lands. He makes a number of claims of successes, e.g. He 'defeated the king of Gujarat,' 'captured Raichūr,' etc. (*E. R. 1919 App. A., C.-P. No. 5.*)

A.D. 1336. Harihara Rāya the eldest of the five brothers sons of Sangama who had established themselves at Vijayanagar on the Tungabhadra river, gave a village in Nellore district as an *agrahāra* to a Brahman. The importance of the inscription lies in the fact that it mentions the coronation of the new king which took place on April 18, 1336.[1]

(*V. R. ii. Nell., 189 ; B. and V. C., C.-P. No. 15 ; i. 109 ; E. C. x. Bg. 70.*)

[1] The two inscriptions under reference are copper-plate grants conveying *agrahāras* to Brahmans, one in the Kolar District and the other in South Nellore. They are of the same date, and seem otherwise to be different versions of the same grant. The Nellore inscription uses the expression *paṭṭābhishēka-uttaraṭaḥ-parastāt*, after the festival of the coronation. The date given is the date of the grant and not of his coronation, which, on the basis of this grant, must already have taken place. The corresponding passage in the other grant, Bg. 70, is *phalābhishēkotsavataḥ-purastāt-Pampā Virūpāksha-Mahēśvarasya* before the *phalābhishēka* of the Mahēśvara-Virūpaksha at Pampā. This puts an entirely different complexion on the occasion of the grant. This is not the place to discuss the whole bearing of the grants ; but in both the grants, Harihara is definitely stated to be ruling in Anegundi already, and reference to his coronation at Hampi would be out of place in the same grant.—*Editor.*

Hoysala Ballāla III reigning in S. Kanara (*V. R. ii. S. Kan. 140 ; 122 of 1901*). Mr. V. Rangāchāri notes that the inscription implies that the Ālupa chief had been dispossessed by the Hoysala king. He was also reigning in E. Mysore (*E. C. ix. Bn. 110 ; Ht. 134, 137*). The first of these says he was ruling with Dorasamudra as his capital.

Māravarman-Kulaśēkhara-Pāṇḍya II named as reigning in Madura in his 21st year on July 5, 1336 (*741 of 1919*). [The record is interesting as it shews that some of the Madura people at least clung to their old Pāṇḍya rulers, though they had been governed by a Muhammadan for ten years].

A.D. 1337. Hoysala Ballāla III reigning in Mysore, east and south-east.

(*E. C. iii. Tn, 83, Ml., 109 ; ix. Kn. 30 ; Bn. 60.*)

A.D. 1338. The same king. Inscriptions in E., W. and S. Mysore.

(*E. C. x. Bp. 10 ; vi. Kp. 12 ; iv. Hs. 82.*)

A.D. 1339. At Conjeeveram a record of June 20 shewing Veṅrumāṅkoṇḍa Śambuvaraiyan of the Śengēṇi family ruling there in his 18th year. Coupled with 24 of 1897 it fixes his accession as between May 11 and June 20, 1322 (*48 of 1921*). He was also ruling in N. Arcot on May 10 (*202 of 1921*). And on February 19 in Conjeeveram (*42 of 1921*). And in Chingleput district.

(*V. R. i. Chin. 426 ; 46 of 1900.*)

Hoysala Ballāla III reigning in E. Mysore from Dorasamudra (*E. C. ix. Bn. 117*). Another record of this year says that he was residing then at 'Vijaya-Virupākshapura' (*E. C. ix. Ht. 43.*) Mr. S. Krishnaswami Aiyangar (*South India, etc., p. 171*) believes this place to be identical with both Hospett and Hampe-Vijayanagar, the whole forming a great fortress, with Hospet as a salient. (Hospett was also called 'Hosadurga' and 'Hosaviḍu'). If this identification is correct it proves that Ballāla III supported Harihara I.

Māravarman Parākrama Pāṇḍya ruling in Tanjore on July 30, 1339 in his 5th year. Coupled with 78 of 1918 this makes the beginning of his rule as on a day between April 21 and July 30, 1335.

(*509 of 1918.*)

The Matsya chief Jayanta II made a gift to the Simhāchalam temple.

(*V. R. iii. Vizagapatam, 115 ; 287 of 1899.*)

A.D. 1340. Hoysala Ballāla III reigning in Anantapur district on September 2, 1340. (*780 of 1917*). And in E. Mysore, his capital being Tiruvaṇṇāmalai in N. Arcot district.

(*E. C. ix. Bn. 31 ; Ma. 13, 19 ; Dv. 54.*)

With the Hoysala king reigning from Tiruvaṇṇāmalai it is curious that an inscription at Chengama, a few miles distant, of this year 'Ś, 1262' mentions a gift of land made in the 6th year of Māravarman Parākrama Pāṇḍya.

(*Inscriptions at Tiruvaṇṇāmalai of Ś. 1262 mentioning Hoysala Ballāla III as sovereign V. R. i. N. Arcot, 454, 464 ; 499, 509 of 1902. Inscription at Chengama of the Pāṇḍya prince, ibid., 420 ; 113 of 1900.*)

At Bādāmi, Dharwar District, an inscription of February 29, 1340 states that a certain Nāyaka chief constructed a fort there by order of the new 'great ruler' (*Mahāmaṇḍalēśvara*) Hariyappa (= Harihara I) 'lord of the Eastern and Western Oceans'. [It is possible that the record itself was composed at a somewhat later date than that of the construction of the fort. Hence the use of the grand title. At any rate it shews that Harihara's authority extended to country north of the Tungabhadra river.] (*I.A., i. 63.*)

Early in October apparently, an inscription (imperfect as to date, since the week day does not suit the given tithi) near Bangalore in E. Mysore mentions Harihara I of Vijayanagar as ruling there. (*E.C. ix. Nl. 19.*)

[This is important, as it shews (i) that Harihara's power was spreading widely; and (ii) that since Hoyśala Baḷḷāḷa III undoubtedly was king at that place, he must have countenanced Harihara's establishing himself further north as a great lord, and supported him by allowing him to rule locally in the very heart of the Hoyśala kingdom. It gives colour to the theory of the Government Epigraphist that in some way Harihara and his brothers were connected with the Hoyśala royal house.]

A.D. 1341. Māravarman Parākrama Pāṇḍya reigning in Trichinopoly, in his 6th year, on February 11, 1341. (*100 of 1920.*)

Hoyśala Baḷḷāḷa III reigning in Central, E. and S.-E. Mysore.

(*E.C. xii. Si. 10; x. Mr. 82; ix. Cp. 185.*)

Rājanārāyana-Śambuvarāyan of the Śengeṇi family ruling in S. Arcot in his 4th year, on (?) September 14, 1341. (The date is not a perfect one.) (*48 of 1922.*)

The Kalinga-Gaṇga King Narasimha III made a gift to the temple at Simhāchalam.

(*V. R. iii. Vizagapatam, 158; 330 of 1899.*)

[There was a terrible famine in the Dekkan in this year, so severe that cannibalism became prevalent.] (*I.A. 1923, p. 229.*)

In this year Ghiyāsu-d-dīn Dhamaghani became sultan of Madura. He was guilty of horrible cruelties to the Hindus, of which we hear from an eye-witness, Ibn Batuta, who so far from being prejudiced was an honoured guest of the sultan. He was with the Sultan during a march through a forest, where a number of Hindu workers were engaged in clearing a road. He writes 'every infidel found in the forest was taken prisoner. They sharpened stakes at both ends and made their captives carry them on their shoulders. Each was accompanied by his wife and children and they were thus led to the camp. . . . The next morning the Hindu prisoners were divided into four sections and taken to each of the four gates. There, on the stakes that they had carried, the prisoners were impaled. Afterwards their wives were killed and tied by the hair to these pales. Little children were massacred on the bosoms of their mothers. . . . this is shameful conduct such as I have not known any other sovereign guilty of . . . . . . He gives another instance which he witnessed while one day at food with Ghīyāsu-d-din—' an infidel was brought before him accompanied by his wife and son aged seven years. The sultan made a sign with his hand to the executioners to cut off the head of this man; then he said to them in Arabic "and the son and the wife." They cut off their heads and I turned my eyes away. When I looked again I saw their heads lying on the ground.' He relates other such atrocities also. Small wonder that Ibn Batuta found himself 'disgusted with the town of Madura' and took his departure.

Ghiyasud-d-din died of disease in A. D. 1342, to the relief of all parties. He was succeeded by Alāu-d-din Udauji, as sultan of Madura.

A.D. 1342. Prior to September 8, in this year, there are inscriptions of Hoyśala Baḷḷāḷa III in E. Mysore (*E.C. ix, Bn. 21, 24, 129; Hl. 90, 135; Dv. 21, 46*). One of these bears date July 3, and one even as late as September 5. The inscription next noted shews that he was killed on September 8. Later inscriptions mentioning 'Baḷḷāḷa as reigning must refer to his son and successor Bāḷḷāḷa IV, *alias* Virūpāksha.

September 8, 1342. On this day according to an inscription, a *vīrakal* at Bidare in Kaḍūr Taluk, Mysore, the old Hoyśala king Bāḷḷāḷa III was killed at 80 years of age.

(*E.C. vi, Kd., 75.*)

[The occurrence and what led to it are recorded by Ibn Batuta. But a preliminary note about place names must be inserted before we turn to the narrative. The inscription just noticed says, according to Rice's rendering, that Baḷḷāḷa III met his death fighting against the Muhammadans at 'Beribi'. Mr. S. Krishnaswami Aiyangar, who has examined the original record, tells us ('*South India, etc. . . .*' *p. 173*) that this is a misreading. The name of the place as given was 'Chirichira-pali' and this is the Kanarese pronunciation of Trichinopoly. Ibn Batuta says that the battle took place 'near the town of Cobban', i.e. Koppam. This is now, no doubt rightly, declared to mean Kaṇṇanūr near Trichinopoly, which is also called 'Kaṇṇanūr-Koppam.]

Thus the story becomes more clear. Ghiyāsu-d-dīn was in possession of Kaṇṇanūr, and king Baḷḷāḷa, who had an army of 100,000 men, attacked him there and fought a battle which was successful, the Muhammadan garrison only numbering 6,000. Closely besieged the defenders treated for terms, and, during the delay caused by negotiations, made a sudden sally, devoting their lives in the belief that they would all be slain. The Hindus, taken unawares, fought with them in confused fashion when suddenly Ghiyāsu-d-din the sultan appeared on the scene with a relieving force and the Hindus were completely defeated. The aged Hoyśala monarch was taken prisoner and brought before Ghiyāsu-d-dın who 'Extorted from him his wealth, elephants and horses and all his property and had him killed and flayed. His skin was stuffed with straw and hung up on the wall of Madura'—where, says Ibn Batuta 'I saw it suspended'.

Such was the end of Baḷḷāḷa III on September 8, 1342. It is mentioned in an inscription on a *Virakal* at Mālūr in Kolār District, Mysore (*E. C. x, Mr, 82*). He was succeeded by his son Baḷḷāḷa IV, *alias* Virūpāksha, whose accession therefore took place on the same day. The new king continued the struggle against the Madura Muhammadans. He is mentioned as reigning on September 14, 1342 in an inscription in E. Mysore.

(*E. C. x. K. 22 See. also E. C. vi, Cm, 45 ; and ix Bn, II ; Ht, 147.*)

On January 30 and on February 15, 1342 the Śengēṇi chief Rājanārāyana Śambuvarāyan was ruling in S. Arcot in his 5th year. (*49, 52 of 1922.*)

An inscription at Hoyśala Baḷḷāḷa's capital in N. Arcot, Tiruvaṇṇāmalai, of date August 23, 1342, mentions a certain Tribhuvana Vīra Chōla, probably a prince of the old Chōla dynasty now of no power. He may have been the same as the chief of that name alluded to in a record at Tiruvallam in N. Arcot District of date in 1314–15. (*E I. vii. App. 869, 870 ; 3 of 1890. V. R. i. N. Arcot, 477 ; 522 of 1902 ; E. I. iv. 70 ; viii. pp. 7, 8 ; I. A. xxiii, 298.*)

A.D. 1343. Hoyśala Virūpāksha-Baḷḷāḷa IV was crowned on August 11, 1343 (*E. C. vi, Cm, 105*). [The date however has a wrong week day.]

Māravarman Parākrama Pāṇḍya was reigning in Tanjore on April 30, 1343 in his 8th year.

(*525 of 1918.*)

A Kalinga-Ganga queen, wife of Narasimha III, made a gift to the temple at Srīkūrmam. She is also mentioned in some other inscription.

(*V. R. i. Ganjam 186, 187, 221, 222 ; 308, 309, 343, 344 of 1896.*)

Māravarman Vīra Pāṇḍya was ruling in Chingleput District on October 19, 1343 in his 10th year. (*277 of 1910 ; E R. 1922, p. 92.*)

A.D. 1344. The Śengēṇi chief Rājānārāyaṇa-Śambuvarāyan ruling in Conjeeveram on July 30, 1344 in his 7th year *(49 of 1921)*. [This and the record 30 of 1890 show his accession to have taken place between July 31, 1337 and March 24, 1338.]

There is a record of this year, a copper-plate grant from the Muḷbāgal Taluk of Kolar District, E. Mysore—which would seem to be of doubtful genuineness, though I cannot pass it over without notice. Harihara I of Vijayanagar was reigning in that year, but the document mentions Bukka I as reigning and it gives him full imperial titles. Moreover it would have us to believe that the Hoyśala dominions had been completely wrested from Hoyśala Virūpāksha and were now governed from Vijayanagar. It is quite true that this was the case a little later, but I think that the document should be further examined[1] before its contents are accepted as historically accurate. *(E. C. x. Mb, 158.)*

[There was, so we gather from inscriptions, a great combination of Hindu rulers in this year sworn to drive the Muhammadans out of South India once for all. It was headed by Harihara I of Vijayanagar. As to exactly what took place we are left in the dark for want of any detailed account. But it seems that the Kākatīya prince Krishna, *alias* Virabhadra, son of Pratāpa Rudra II, took part in it; and so did Prōlaya Vēma the Reḍḍi chief of Konḍavīḍ, for he is said to have restored the Brahman villages—*Agrahārams*—which had been taken away from them by the Muhammadans during his father's lifetime (*E. I. viii. 9, Madras Museum plates—of date March 18, 1345*). Ferishtah (*Briggs' Edition, I, 427*) states that Kākatīya Krishna induced the Hoyśala king Baḷḷāḷa IV to join the confederation. The sultan Muhammad Tughlak was at that time involved in a series of expeditions to put down rebellions in other parts, and apparently no great resistance was offered to the Hindus. One result was that the Kākatīya capital Warangal was freed from Muhammadan control.

It should be noted here that from the date of the tragical death of the old sovereign of the Mysoreans, Baḷḷāḷa III, in 1342 the Hoyśala kingdom seems to have gone to pieces. Baḷḷāḷa III had had a large army under his command, and Virūpāksha his successor should, it would be thought,

[1] A careful examination of Mb. 158 referred to by Mr. Sewell shows that the grant is dated on Tuesday, the 23rd March 1344. This grant describes the family of these five brothers almost in the same manner as the other copper-plate grants of 1336 referred to by Mr. Sewell on page 185. In these latter Harihara I, while actively taking part in the transactions in Hampi, is clearly described as ruling from Anegundi, which must be taken to be his capital. In this document which is almost exactly eight years later, Bukka is said to be ruling from Vidyānagari, called after Vidyāraṇya. The actual conquests are described as though they were conquests made, not by Bukka alone specifically, but by the brothers as a whole. In regard to the imperial titles that Mr. Sewell refers to, excepting one or two terms, such as Rājādhirāja and Rāja-Paramēśvara, none of the others could be regarded as at all imperial in their character. Even these are applied to subordinate rulers in a number of other inscriptions. It cannot therefore be said that these are imperial titles necessarily. There is no specific reference to Virūpaksha Baḷḷāḷa, the son of Virā Baḷḷāḷa III in documents beyond A.D. 1343. The reference in Bn. 120 in the next page is of a vague and indefinite character 'in the time of Baḷḷāḷarāya', which cannot strictly be interpreted as referring specifically to the administration of Baḷḷāḷa IV. It looks as though this Baḷḷāḷa IV had been disabled, or suffered from some other kind of adversity, subsequent to A.D. 1343. These brothers apparently went about doing what they had begun doing, thoroughly, and in an united effort without any partition of spheres. One of the two of Harihara's grants has reference to Chandragirirājya, and the other one to Penugonda, and here is one of Bukka's referring to the rājya of Gutti. While therefore we may regard that, during this period of transition, these brothers had their own governments, they carried on their wars and administration without any regard to separate and exclusive demarcation of boundaries. As a matter of fact, formal assumption of an imperial position does not appear to have taken place till the time of Harihara II, son of Bukka. If the genuineness of these copper-plate grants is to be called into question, it must be on other grounds than this discrepancy as Mr. Sewell seems to fear. There seems to be no discrepancy in fact.—*Editor*.

have been able to attain some power by its aid. I can only suppose that the army leaders had no great confidence in the new king, believed themselves hopelessly beaten, and gave him no solid support. After a few more years we hear no more of the Hoyśala monarchy, and the whole of his country, with the exception of one or two small fragments came under the power of Harihara and his brethren at Vijayanagar. The history of the period would go to shew that from the beginning of Harihara's access to power he and his family were supported and encouraged by the Hoyśala king as forming a strong bulwark against the Muhammadans in the Dekkan. This alone would account for Harihara's success, for the whole country to his south was on friendly terms with him.]

A.D. 1345. The inscription of Prōlaya-Vēma Reḍḍi noted above (*s.v.*, A.D. *1344*) whose date is March 18, 1345 shews that he was now ruling at Amarāvati, or Dharaṇikōṭa. [Kākatīya Pratāpa Rudra had been reigning over the Guntur District where Vēma's fortress Konḍavīḍ was and the ancient town of Dharaṇikōṭa; and it seems probable that the strength of the Reḍḍi chief at this time was owing to the Kākatīyas having abandoned those possessions when the Muhammadans drove them from Warangal in 1323.] In 1345 Vēma Reḍḍi decorated the temple at Amarāvati.

(*V. R. ii. Guntur, 634 ; 268 of 1897 ; E. I. iii. 10 ; V. R. ii. Kistna, 11 ; E. I. viii. 9.*)

About this time there are a number of records in Ganjam District of the Kalinga-Ganga king Narasimha III 'Vīrādhi-Vīra.' (*V. R. i. Gan. 178 . . . 236 ; 300 . . . 358 of 1896.*)

A.D. 1346. Prōlaya-Vēma Reḍḍi of Konḍavīḍ ruling part of Kurnool District. Inscription mentioning his son Annavōta Reḍḍi. (*V. R. ii. Kurn. 284 ; 191 of 1905.*)

In Chingleput District the Śengēṇi chief Rājanārāyaṇa-Sambuvarāyan ruled in his 9th year. (*V. R. i. Chin. 345, 96 ; S. Arcot, 799 ; 30 of 1890 ; 268, 396 of 1909*). Another record gives this chief the names 'Mallinātha' and 'Jiyadēva.' (*86 of 1921.*)

An inscription in Bangalore District, Mysore, shews that on October 6, 1346, the Vijayanagar brother's Harihara and Bukka, whose names are coupled together therein, were ruling there (*E. C. ix. Bn., 59*). Another of August 18 mentions Harihara as ruling in Mālūr Taluk, Kōlār District. (*E. C. x. Mr. 61.*)

The five Vijayanagar brothers, Harihara, Kampaṇa I, Bukka I, Mārapa, and Muddapa jointly gave a grant of villages to Brahmans at Śringēri in Kaḍūr District, W. Mysore, on March 9, 1346. It calls Harihara 'conqueror of the earth from the eastern to the western Ocean' (*E. C. vi, Sg, 1 ; Arch. Ann. Rep. 1907-8, p. 236*). Harihara and Muddapa are mentioned together in an inscription (earlier than April 23, 1346) in Kolar District, Mysore. (*E. C. x. Mr. 39.*)

Harīhara I of Vijayanagar ruling in N.-W. Mysore on November 15, 1346. His title is 'Mahāmanḍalēśvara'. The grant is by a minor chief called the 'Pānḍya Chakravarti' (*E. C. viii, Tl, 154 Arch: Ann: Rep: p. 1907-8, p. 238 n. 4*). Mr. Krishna Sāstri suggests that this Pānḍya chief may have belonged to the Āḷupa family, some of whom bore that title.

Hoyśala Baḷḷāḷa IV is mentioned in an inscription in the Bangalore District, Mysore. This is the latest record known to exist of the Hoyśala dynasty. (*E. C. ix, Bn, 120.*)

[During this year when Muhammad Tughlak was absent from Dēvagiri, putting down a revolt in Gujarat, the people at the capital revolted against him and set up a king of their own, Nasiru-d-din Ismail Khān. The Sultan returned but before he could do anything of importance he was again compelled to go to Gujarat, leaving Ismail Khān at Dēvagiri].

A.D. 1347. Harihara I reigning in the 'Gutti-rajya' and governing from Vijayanagar (*E. R. 1921, App. A, C-P. 9*). Another of his records bears date October 29, 1347 (but the date is not quite perfect). This is in S.-E. Mysore (*E. C. ix, Bn, 97*). Another on December 1, in S.-E. Mysore.

(*E. C. ix, Dv, 50.*)

The Koṇḍavīḍu Reḍḍi chief Annavōta, here called 'Annamma,' gave a gift to a temple in Markapur Taluk, Kurnool District. (*V. R. ii, Kurn. 343 ; 250 of 1905.*)

[Very important occurrences at Dēvagiri-Daulatabad. Nāsīru-d-din Ismail Khān, being left there when Muhammad Tughlak went to Gujarat, drove out of the capital the remaining royal troops and, while himself retiring into the background, raised up an officer Alāu-d-din Hasan Gango Bāhmanī to rule the place. The rebellion against Tughlak rule having completely freed the place, this Hasan Gango was, with the goodwill of all the chiefs and populace declared to be an independent ruler of Daulatābād and its dependencies and he was crowned king on, according to the *Burhān-i Ma'asir*, December 3, 1347. He was a fierce and bigoted Muslim, and slaughtered the 'infidel' Hindus ruthlessly. Alāu-d-dīn's title 'Bāhman' is derived, so says V. Smith, from an early Persian king so-called from whom he claimed descent, viz. the king known to the Romans as 'Artaxerxes Longimanus' and to the Jews 'Ahasuerus'. He began by reducing a number of fortresses in the Dekhan, Sāgar, Mudhol, Miraj, Kiṭṭur Kolhāpūr, Goa, etc . . .

(*I. A, 1899.*)

He was the first of a powerful Dynasty, with their capital at Kulbarga, known as that of the Bahmanis, which ruled most part of the Dekhan for a century and a half. The effect of this change was widely felt in Southern India. For one thing it greatly strengthened the power of Harihara and his brothers as it gave them time for consolidation of the new Hindu kingdom.

Inscriptions shew that the territories governed by Harihara and his four brothers were now widely extended. (*See Mr. H. Krishna Sastri in Arch. Ann. Rep. 1907-8, p. 239.*)

A.D. 1349. Inscription at Simhāchalam of the Matsya chief Jayantika-dēva and his queen Chengamā. The date is not clear but it belongs to the period 1348-1357.

(*V. R. iii, Vizagapatam, 142; 314 of 1899.*)

Māravarman Parākrama Pāṇḍya in his 14th year ruling at Virddhāchalam in S. Arcot on April 20, 1349. (*78 of 1918.*)

A.D. 1350. A C-P. grant of Anavēma, Reḍḍi chief of Koṇḍavīḍu (*V. R. ii, Kistna, 102*), from Koṇḍapalli near Bezwada, shewing that he governed north as well as south of that river.

A.D. 1351. Bukka I, then prince, ruling in S.-E. Mysore, under Harihara I of Vijayanagar.

(*E. C. ix, Cp, 13 ; Kn, 40.*)

[At this period Akshōbhyatīrtha, disciple of Ānandatīrtha was Vaishṇava pontiff (*E. I. vi. 260*). He was a contemporary of Mādhavāchārya-Vidyāraṇya, who assisted the five Vijayanagar brothers.]

Rājanārayaṇa-Śambuvarāya ruling in Chingleput District, in his 14th year, on August 19, 1351.

(*302 of 1921.*)

[Muhammad Tughlak of Delhi died in March 1351, and was succeeded by Firoz Tughlak, who was enthroned in his camp on the Indus on March 23, 1351. He was more humane than his predecessors, since he abolished the tortures which had been freely applied to their subjects ; but in his war with Bengal in 1353 he was merciless and is said by his historians to have caused the death of 180,000 Hindus. He enumerates the tortures the use of which he reprobates, and it is as well to make a note of these, as the system throws light on the manner in which government was carried on in those days. They are 'amputation of hands and feet, ears and noses; tearing out the eyes, pouring molten lead into the throat, crushing the bones with mallets . . . driving iron nails into the hands, feet, etc. . . .'. 'These', says Firoz, 'and many similar tortures were practised'. He himself, as we learn from his own words, dealt very harshly with the Hindu 'infidels'. He alludes with satisfaction to his having decapitated the leaders of one Hindu sect; and when he heard of some new Hindu temples having been constructed, he, 'under divine guidance', destroyed these buildings, killed the Brahman leaders, and flogged the common folk. Learning that the Hindus were enjoying the pleasures of a fair in one town he had the leaders and promoters put to death, and erected a mosque on the ruins of the temples. On one occasion a Brahman who had dared to follow the rites of his religion in public was burned alive. Nevertheless, though led away by religious zeal and fanaticism he seems personally to have been kind and charitable; and it must be placed to his credit that he founded a hospital.

A.D. 1352. An inscription shews Kampana II, son of Bukka I of Vijayanagar ruling in North Arcot District on September 24, 1352. *(297 of 1919.)*

A record of this year 1352–53, 'Nandana', shews Rājanārāyaṇa-Śambuvarāya ruling at Arpākkam in Chingleput District in his 16th year. *(140 of 1923.)*

That the old Hoyśala capital Dorasamudra was now a stronghold of the new Vijayanagar kingdom is proved by an inscription in Anantapur District of this year, which states that Bukka I was governing Dorasamudra and Penukoṇḍa.

(V. R. i. Anant. 103; 522 of 1906.)

Prince Sāyaṇa or Sāvaṇa of Vijayanagar is mentioned in an inscription in Cuddapah District as ruling at Udayagiri (in Nellore). This is probably Sāvana I, son of Kampana I, but might be Sāvana son of Mārapa (*V. R. i, Cudd, 604; 503 of 1906*). This record shews that the great hill-fortress of Udayagiri had passed from the possession of the Reḍḍi chiefs into that of Harihara I of Vijayanagar between 1346 (*above where the Reḍḍi chief is seen ruling in Kurnool*) and 1352. The Reḍḍis had ruled there since the downfall of the Kakatiyas in 1323.

A.D. 1353. An inscription at Tiruvoṟṟiyūr in Chingleput District shews the same prince ruling there in 1353–54 in his 7th year. His rule must therefore date from 1347–48. He must have been appointed by Harihara I, and his rule may have perhaps encroached on that of the Śambuvarāyan family (*V. R. i. Chin. 1082; 213 of 1912*). Another record in Cuddapah District shews him in authority there in this year (*V. R. i, Cudd. 601; 500 of 1906*). His father Kampana I and his mother Mangadēvī are mentioned in it.

Kampana II was ruling at Kadiri in Anantapūr District for his father Bukka I. His general Gōpana made a gift to a temple there. *(V. R. i, Anant. 104; 523 of 1906.)*

In Ongole Taluk, Guntur District, Annavōta Reḍḍi of Koṇḍaviḍ was ruling.

(V. R. ii. Gun. 405; B. and V. C. 1037.)

An inscription in S. Arcot makes Māravarman Vīra Pāṇḍya ruling there in his 19th year in 1353. Judging by the dates of records and regnal years, this 'Vīra' may be the same as 'Parākrama', whose rule began in 1335, 1353 being in his 19th year. *(494, 495 of 1921.)*

In Ganjam the Kalinga-Ganga king Bhānudeva III was reigning in his 3rd year.

(V. R. i. Gan. 214; 336 of 1896.)

A.D. 1354. The same king reigning in the same district. *(V. R. i. Gan. 193; 315 of 1896.)*

An inscription at Gōrantla in Anantapur District mentions Sāluva Mangi and his (?) son Narasimha in 1354–55. The latter built a temple there. The Saluva family were rising into importance at this time. (*V. R. i. Anant. 49 ; 92 of 1912 ; E. I. vii. 74.*)

Bukka I of Vijayanagar reigning in Central and N. Mysore. The date of the first of these records is May 20, 1354. It seems that he had moved his capital from Dorasamudra to Vijayanagar, where he was ruling 'from his jewelled throne'. This was probably due to the sickness or death of his elder brother Harihara, then the reigning king, who died, so far as can be gathered, in this year (*E. C. xii, Pg. 74 ; xi, Dg. 67*). King Harihara I's last known record[1] is one in Sorab taluk N.-W. Mysore, the date of which is early in A.D. 1354, and in which the king is called the 'Suratāla' (sultan) of Hindu kings (*E. C. viii. Sb., 104*). It is pretty evident that there must have been some rivalry as to the succession on his death and that Bukka I went to Vijayanagar, or to Hōsapattana (Hospett) a few miles distant, in order to strengthen his position as against Kampana I's sons Sāvana I and Sangama II, the latter of whom was absent at his government in the east. The Bitragunta grant of May 31, 1356 (*see below*), mentions Sangama II as giving a grant of a village to Brahmans on the anniversary of his father Kampana I's death, but it does not positively name Sangama as king. And all the evidence goes to shew that Bukka II ousted his nephews and seized the throne.

Virūpanna I or Virūpāksha I, son of Bukka I, was in 1354 ruling the Penukonda province while Bukka was at Hospett. Virūpāksha strongly fortified the already strong hill-fortress at Penukonda (*E. I. vi. 322 ; V. R. i. Anantapur, 161 ; 339 of 1901*). His minister Anantarasa is named as his executive in the work. He was also minister to king Bukka in 1364, and to Bhāskara Bhavadūra in 1369.

In Chittoor District Kampana II, son of Bukka was ruling in this year 1354–55.

(*V. R. i. Chit. 260 ; 577 of 1906.*)

A.D. 1355. An inscription of May 18, 1355 and another in 1356–57 in N. Mysore shew Bukka I to have been then ruling there from Hospett. The former mentions a general Mallinātha and says that he had gained victories over the 'Turuka, Sēuna, Telinga, Pāndya and Hoyśala rulers'. This need not be taken too seriously as proof of many wars and victories having actually taken place, but it serves to shew that Vijayanagar power was spreading in many directions.

(*E. C. xi, Cd. 2, 3.*)

A.D. 1356. Bukka I reigning in E. Mysore. (*E. C. x, Kl. 222.*)

Annavōta, Reddi chief of Kondavidu was ruling at Tripurāntakam in Kurnool District.

(*V. R. ii, Kurn. 278 ; 185 of 1905.*)

Upēndra III of the Panchahārala branch of the E. Chālukyas made a gift to the temple at Simhāchalam. (*V. R. iii, Vizagapatam, 122 ; 294 of 1899.*)

The Bitragunta grant in Nellore District by Sangama II of Vijayanagar on the anniversary, May 31, 1356, of his father Kampana I's death has been already noticed above. Mr. H. Krishna Sastri is satisfied that it was the first anniversary, and therefore we may take it that Kampana I died on May 31, 1355 (*V. R. i, Nellore, 273, 274. B. and V. C., C.-P. grants No. 20, p. 181 ; E. I. iii, 21, 118 ; viii, 12*). The plate contains a laudation of Sangama's spiritual preceptor

[1] Bn. 101 with a date corresponding to Monday, February 8, 1361, refers itself to the time of Ariyappa Udaiyar. It is a stone inscription in mixed Tamil and Grantha characters. It is just possible that this record refers to Prince Harihara, Bukka's son ; but there is no lead therefor.—*Editor.*

13

Śrīkanṭhanātha, and a pedigree of the family of Mādhavāchārya the celebrated minister of the first Vijayanagar kings.

A.D. 1357. Early in the year. Inscription shewing Bukka I reigning in W. Mysore.

(*E. C. v. Ag. 68.*)

A.D. 1358. The same king reigning in E. Mysore (*E. C. ix. Dv. 27*). And in S. Mysore.

(*E. C. iii, Ml. 22.*)

An inscription at Tirukkaḷākkuḍi in Tinnevelly District of Māravarman Vīra Paṇḍya's 31st year, has been thought to have been dated September 7, 1358. It mentions the sufferings undergone by the priests and worshippers in consequence of the harsh rule of the Muhammadan sultans of Madura, and the relief experienced when Kampana II of Vijayanagar 'destroyed the Tulukkan.' On this foundation the theory has been raised that Kampana turned the Musalman sultan out of Madura before that date in 1358; and this theory is said also to receive support from an entry in my 'Lists of Antiquities' published forty years ago. I think now that there is good reason to suppose that the date of the record was really August 30, A.D. 1364, and that the Pāndya prince mentioned was that Māravarman Vīra Pāndya *alias* Parākrama whose rule seems to have begun in A.D. 1335.

(*See above, s. v. A. D. 1353. 64 of 1916 ; E. R. 1916 § 33.*)

Alāu-d-dīn Bahmanī died on February 20. 1358, and was succeeded by his eldest son Muhammad. Early in Muhammad's reign it was discovered that the Hindus of the Vijyanagar and Kākatiya kingdoms were melting down large quantities of Bahmanī coins. Muhammad pretended to take offence at this and made war on Warangal, now ruled by Kākatīya Vināyaka, son of Pratāpa Rudra II. He plundered the country and only retired on receiving a large indemnity.

The Koṇḍavīḍu Reddi chief Annavota confirmed in this year the order passed in 1244 by Kākatiya Gaṇapati decreeing that foreign ships wrecked on the coast should not be held confiscated to the State, but that they and their cargoes should merely be held liable to pay customs duty.

(*V. R. ii. Guntur, 102, 103 ; 258 of 1897 ; 601, 602, of 1909 : E. R. 1910, p. 118.*)

A.D. 1359. Bukka I of Vijayanagar reigning in E. and W. Mysore (*E. C. ix. Nl. 23 ; vi. Mg. 25*). And in S. Kanara. (*V. R. ii. S. Kan. 157 ; 139 of 1901.*)

His sovereignty was now recognized over large regions. Some of the principal provinces were the *Udayagiri-rājya* in Nellore and Cuddapah, then called the 'Pāka-vishaya' and the 'Muliki-dēśa'; the *Penukoṇḍa-rājya*, which later included the Gutti-rājya, i.e Bellary, Anantapur, and parts of N. Mysore; the *Āraga-, Male, or Maleha-rājya*, which included the Baṇavāsi 12000, Chandragutti and Goa; the *Muḷuvāyi-rājya*, comprising large parts of Mysore, and later of Salem and S. Arcot Districts; the *Barkūr-and-Mangaḷūru-rājya*, also called the *Tuḷu-rājya*, on the west coast; and the *Rājagambhīra-rājya*, by which in my opinion is meant not the old Pāṇḍya kingdom as has sometimes been supposed but the possessions of Rājagambhīra-Śambuvarāyan of the Śengēṇi family about the S. Arcot District. (*Arch. Ann. Rep. 1907–8, p. 239 ; I. A. 1914, p. 7.*)

Bukka's son Kampana II ruled over N. Arcot (February 22). (*304, 305 of 1919.*)

An inscription of this year in Kolar District, Mysore, mentions a chief Kāṭṭaya-Nāyaka, son of Kampana, son of 'Kaṭṭāri-Sāḷuva Bukka' (*E. C. x., Bp. 31*). He has not been identified.

A.D. 1360. Bukka I reigning in E. Mysore (*E. C. x. Ct., 75*). Another record, shewing him reigning in W. Mysore, mentions his eldest son 'Tippanna,' who had captured Uchchangi. [This name 'Tippanna' is not otherwise known as a name of a son of Bukka I. It may, perhaps, be a local name for Harihara II.] (*E. C. v. Hn. 19.*) Bukka I was also reigning in S. Kanara. (*V. R. ii. S. Kan. 150, 156 ; 132, 138 of 1901.*)

A.D. 1361. Prof. E. Hultzsch published a list of the inscriptions then known relating to Bukka I's son Kampana II (*E. I. vi. 322*). From the first of these it is clear that he was ruling in N. Arcot and Chingleput Districts in A.D. 1361–2. His general was Gōpana. [Kampana succeeded in bringing into subjection the Śengēṇi-Sambuvarayan chief who had ruled those countries. He warred against him and took him prisoner (*See below s.v., A.D. 1363*).] Kampana was ruling in Chittoor District this year, over the 'Pulināḍu' tract on September 7, 1361. (*V. R. i. Chittoor, 178 ; 309 of 1912.*)

Another record in the Chittoor District names as then ruling that country Kampana II's cousin Sāyana I, son of Kampana I. (*Ibid. Chitt. 127 ; 188 of 1903.*)

Kampana II recognized as ruling in E. Mysore (*E. C. x, Kl. 203*). He was ruling from Muḷbāgal ('Muḷuvāyil'). Also he was ruling in Chingleput (*V.R. i, Chin. 485 ; 250 of 1901*). His father Bukka I was reigning over Kurnool. (*V.R. ii, Kurn. 519.*)

Annavōta, the Reḍḍi chief of Konḍavīḍu, who ruled at Amarāvati on the Krishna river was in this year defeated by two leaders, brothers, sons of Kākatīya-Pratāpa-Rudra's general Singa. These were Anapōtanīḍu and Madanīḍu. Annavōta seems to have been ejected and to have been succeeded by his brother Anavēma. (*Amaravati inscription. E.I. viii, 9; 258 of 1897.*)

[The poet Śrinātha flourished at the court of Anavēma Reḍḍi.]

A.D. 1362. An inscription in S. Arcot mentions a chief of the Sāluva family, Mangu-Mahārāja, as receiving an order from Kampana II's general Gopana, and acting on it. Mangu was son of Gunḍa. (*52 of 1905 ; E.R. 1904–5, p. 57.*)

Kampana II was ruling in E. Mysore (*E.C. x, Ct. 95; Kl. 101; Mb. 58*). And in Trichinopoly (*V.R. iii, Trich. 803–D*). And in S. Arcot on December 19, 1362. (*351 of 1921.*)

Virūpanna, son of Bukka I of Vijayanagar gave a grant of land in N.-W. Mysore. He is described as 'ruling with a settled reign in the Āraga kingdom,' *i.e.* the Baṇavāśi, etc., territory. (*E.C. viii, Tl. 20, 37.*)

Sāvana ruled in Cuddapah district. (*V.R. i, Cudd. 605 ; 504 of 1906.*)

A Javanese poet of this date mentions Buddhist monks residing 'at the six monasteries at Kānchipura'—which would seem to shew that Buddhism was still alive at this time in Conjevaram. (*Memoirs of the Batavian Soc. of Arts LIV, 1902.*)

A.D. 1363. Kampana II ruling in N. Arcot on October 20, 1363 (*228, 266 of 1919 ; 203 of 1921*). And in E. Mysore. (*E.C. ix, Bn. 81.*)

Bukka I spoken of as ruling in S. Mysore, his minister being Basavayya (*E. C. iv, Ch. 117, 113*). Also in N.-W. Mysore where his son Virūpanna ruled the 'Malē-rājya,' or hill-tracts towards the Western ghāts. (*E.C. viii, Tl, 197.*)

Kampana II had warred against and defeated the Śengēṇi chief Veṅṟumāṇkonḍa-Śambuvarāyan whom he took prisoner. So says an inscription at Māḍam in N. Arcot District, which relates the capture as having been made by the son of Kampana's minister Sōmaya (this was in 1361). He erected a gōpura in honour of the capture and of the conquest of the Rājagambhīran-malai. (*267 of 1919.*) [*See note above s.v., A.D. 1359.* It is just possible that the Veṅṟumāṇkonḍa may be the chief whose rule began in 1322, but he had been succeeded in 1337 by Rājanārāyaṇa. He might however have been living a retired life since then. Or, again, the chief who was captured may have been a younger man not otherwise heard of.]

A gift was made on October 12, 1363 to a temple at Conjevaram by a servant of Sāyana II, son of Kampana I of Vijayanagar. *(523 of 1919.)*

A.D. 1364. Kampana II was now in great power in Conjevaram. He reinstated worship in the Rājasimhēśvara temple there which had been abandoned since about the 12th century, and restored the lands belonging to it which had been sold. *(S.I.I. i. 117, 120, 123 ; Nos. 86, 87, 88.)*

Sāvana I of Vijayanagar, son of Kampana I ruling in Nellore (*V. R. ii, Nell. 550 ; B. and V.C. 847*). In E. Mysore Mallappa, or Mallinātha son of Bukka I was governing. *(E.C. ix, An. 82.)*

A Kōna-Maṇḍala chief named Bhīma Vallabha (II) mentioned as governing in Narasapur taluk, Kistna district. *(V.R. ii, Kist. 312 ; 522 of 1893.)*

[In this year Muhammad Shāh Bahmanī again attacked Warangal, the capital of the Kākatīya kings. He defeated the defenders and made prisoner their Raja Vinayaka, grandson of Pratāpa Rudra II. He put him to death in a horrible manner. He caused a great furnace to be constructed, and when it was heated he had Vināyaka shot from a machine like a catapult into the flames, where he perished miserably. In his retirement the Sultan was so harassed by the Hindus that only a small portion of his force succeeded in returning to Kulbarga, the Sultan himself being wounded. Hearing of this atrocity Bukka I of Vijayanagar attempted to enlist the assistance of the Sultan of Delhi, Firoz Tughlak, against Muhammad Shāh, but in vain. Further war between Gulbarga and Warangal ended by the submission of the Hindus, when great indemnities were forced upon them, and Golkonda and its dependencies were ceded to the Bahmanī king, who was further enriched by the presentation to him of a throne of great value set with precious stones. (*See Firishtah.*)]

The Tirukaḷākkuḍi inscription, whose date is not satisfactory but which may be intended for August 30, 1364, has been alluded to above (*s. v., A. D. 1358*). If this date be accepted as correct it proves that earlier than that day the Vijayanagar prince Kampana II in the course of his southern campaigns had defeated the sultan of Madura and brought to an end the rule there of the Musalmans That he actually did so is well established—the only question being as to the precise date. Musalman leaders in Madura are heard of for a few years longer, but so far as can be gathered their power was now at an end.

A.D. 1365. Bukka I of Vijayanagar reigning in S. Kanara (*V. R. ii, S. Kan. 159 ; 141 of 1901*). And in Anantapur District on October 24. *(27 of 1917.)*

Kampana II, his son, was ruling in E. Mysore (*E. C. ix, Bn. 67*). And in Chingleput and Chittoor (*V. R. i, Chin. 458 ; Chit. 307 ; 18 of 1899 ; 440 of 1905 ; S. I. I. i, Nos. 86, 87*). And in N. Arcot on July 6, 1365. *(266 of 1919.)*

A.D. 1366. Bukka I reigning in S. Kanara. *(V. R. ii S. Kan. 238 ; 117 of 1901.)*

Kampana II, his son, ruling in N. Arcot on December 27, 1366 (*243 of 1919*). And in Chingleput (*V. R. i, Chin. 348, 737 ; 33 of 1890 ; 639 of 1904*). And in Coimbatore (*ibid. i, Coim. 329 ; 246 of 1913*). And in Kolar District, Mysore (*163 of 1892*). And in N. Arcot (*21 of 1899*). [For a valuable note on the two princes Kampana by Dr. E. Hultzsch see *E. I. vi, 322.*]

[War now broke out between Gulbarga and Vijayanagar. Muhammad Shāh Bahmanī on one occasion jeeringly issued an order for payment of a reward to some singers by an order on the

Vijayanagar king's treasury. Bukka I construed this into an insult that could only be wiped out by blood. He therefore took the field and advanced with a large army by stages to Adoni, Muḍkal and Raichūr. He captured Raichūr and slaughtered the Musalman residents there.

Muhammad Shāh started on his march, according to Firishtah, in January 1366, and advanced to the Krishna river, which he crossed with a small body of cavalry. Bukka Rāya in alarm tried to retreat, but could only get a short distance because of bad weather and the hindrance caused by muddy ground—black cotton soil in which the elephants sank— ; and Muhammad's attack was completely successful, Bukka being forced to fly to Adoni. Muhammad then set to work to kill all the Hindus left in and about the camp, and is said to have slain 70,000 men, women and children.

After a short rest the Bāhmanī king led his army across the Tungabhadra into Vijayanagar territory, and a great battle was fought on July 23, 1366, resulting in a victory for the Muhammadans. Firishtah says that Muhammad Shāh then 'gave orders to resume the massacre of the unbelievers . . . pregnant women and children at the breast did not escape the sword. After a time peace was made, but not till Muhammad Shāh had, so says Firishtah, slain 500,000 Hindus and so wasted the districts that for several decades they did not recover their natural population. (For full details see '*A Forgotten Empire*', *pp. 33–39.*)]

A.D. 1367. Bukka I reigning in many districts in Mysore (*E.C. v. Ak. 115 ; ix, D-B. 39 ; Ht. 117 ; Bn. 27 ; x, Mr. 79 ; xi, Dg. 78*). And in Anantapur district. (*779 of 1917 ; 671 of 1922.*)

Bukka's son Kumāra Kampana II ruling at Conjevaram on February 11 and April 11, 1367 (*33 of 1890 ; E.I. vi, 325 ; 27 of 1921*). And in N. Arcot on January 13. (*298 of 1919.*)

Bukka's son Virūpanna governing the Āraga tract in N.-W. Mysore and the country about Gooty (Gutti). (*E.C. viii, Nr. 34.*)

An inscription in E. Mysore mentions as ruler there in this year 'Rajēndra Voḍeya, son of Bukka-Oḍeyar.' [It is doubtful who is meant by this name.] (*E C. x, Kl. 134.*)

Jaṭāvarman Parākrama Pāṇḍya ruling in Tanjore District, in his 10th year, on December 29, 1367. (*159 of 1911 ; E.R. 1922, p. 93.*)

A.D. 1368. Kampana II, son of Bukka I ruling in Chingleput District (*152 of 1923 ; V. R. i, Ching., 277, 291, 1079 ; 29 of 1888 ; 230 of 1910, 210 of 1912*). And in N. Arcot (*V. R. i, N. Arcot, 264 ; 250 of 1896*). And in S. Mysore, where on May 27, he settled the affairs of the temple at Tagaḍūr. (*E.C. iii, Nj. 117 ; iv, Gu. 46, Yl. 64.*)

Bukka I reigning in E. Mysore as supreme (*E.C. ix, Ma. 18*). And in S. Mysore his minister being a Brahman, Basavayya. A certain Ganapa Timma ('Ganapatima') is stated to be 'governing the south side of the Kāvērī river in the country of . . . Vishṇuvardhana Hoyśala.' [Who this was, if a prince so-named, is not known, but the title may perhaps be merely honorific for any member of the Hoyśala family, which was evidently well-remembered.] (*E. C. iv, Ch. 113.*)

Bukka was also reigning in N.-W. Mysore. An inscription there gives him full imperial titles. (*E. C. vii, Sk. 281.*)

August 15, 1368. Date of a document known as 'Rāmānujacharya's Śāsana', his name being mentioned in it. It states that Bukka I settled a dispute between rival religious factions in Central Mysore. (*E. C. ii, Sr., Bel. 136.*)

Virūpanna, son of Bukka I ruling the Araga tract in N.-W. Mysore. (*E.C. viii, Tl. 30.*)

A.D. 1369. Bukka I reigning in S.-E. and E. Mysore (*E.C. x, Kl. 12 ; ix, Cp. 150*). And in Hampe-Vijayanagar, called 'Hastināvati'. (*E. C. vi, Kp. 6.*)

Kampana II his son, ruling in E. and S. Mysore for his father (*E.C. ix, Ht. 103*). And in N. and S. Arcot (*V.R. i, N. Arcot, 661 ; 108, 110 of 1921. S. Arcot, 351, 936 ; 701, 159 of 1904 ; 227 of 1906*). In the latter case his son Jommana or Jammana is said to be ruling. He was also ruling in Chingleput on February 11, 1369. (*V. R. i, Chin. 1077 ; 208 of 1912.*)

Bukka's son Bhāskara 'Bhavadūra' (evidently a title borrowed from the Muhammadan 'Bahadur') ruling the Udayagiri province (Nellore District). This is a record of October 15, 1369, apparently. [Note that in 1358 the Śrīrangam plates say that the Telugu country was then ruled by Mummaḍi Nayaka ; but I am not satisfied as to the genuineness of this document and have not tabulated it with the other known inscriptions of that year.]

(*E. I. xiv. 97, V. R. i, Cuddapah, 12; 91 of 1913.*)

A.D. 1370. Bukka I reigning in Cuddapah District. (*V. R. i, Cudd. 20.*)

Kampana II, his son, ruling in Chingleput District (*V.R. i, Chin. 739, 1064 ; 641 of 1904 ; 195 of 1912*). On October 14, 1370 a record shews him ruling in S. Arcot (*373 of 1921*). And another of December 31, 1370 states that he was ruling in N. Arcot. This is confirmed by others.

(*375 of 1921 ; V.R. i, N. Arcot, 7, 214, 738 ; 386 of 1905 ; 56 of 1900 ; 78 of 1908.*)

In Kurnool District a certain chief named Gunḍa, probably of the Śaḷuva family, granted land for a temple. (*V. R. ii, Kurn. 631.*)

Virūpanna, son of Bukka I granted land for a temple in the Kaḷasa-nāḍu in W. Mysore.

(*E. C. vi, Mg. 52.*)

About this time the poet Śrīnātha flourished at the court of Vēma Reḍḍi of Konḍavīdu.

(*E. I. viii. 8.*)

A.D. 1371. [For a note as to the date of Kampana II's victory over the Muhammadan sultan of Madura see above *s. v.* A. D. 1365. This date is somewhat uncertain, but it seems to be a fact that the image of Ranganātha-swāmi, which had been secretly carried away from Srīrangam by devoted Hindu priests when the Muhammadans seized that place and Madura in 1327, was brought back in triumph by general Gōpana in 1371. An inscription at the Ranaganātha temple at Srīrangam mentions the event. The image had been taken to Triupati in Chittoor District in 1327. It is certain, therefore, that Kampana's victory and the suppression of Muhammadan rule must have taken place considerably earlier than 1371. Some time must have elapsed after that victory for Hindu rule to be so firmly established that the priests would consider it safe to bring back the image. And moreover after its removal from Tirupati it was kept for some time at Jinji. I have given my reasons above (*s. v. A. D. 1364*) for thinking that Kampana's driving out of the Musalman governors of Madura must have taken place about A.D. 1364.]

(*E. I. vi, 322 ; V. R. iii, Trichinopoly, 466 ; 55 of 1892. E. R. 1903–4, p. 12 ; 18 of 1899.*)

Bukka I reigning in S. Kanara (*V. R. ii, S. Kan. 147 ; 129 of 1901*), and in N.-W. and E. Mysore. (*E. C. viii, Tl, 119 ; Sb, 17 ; x, C-B, 63.*)

Kampana II ruling in Chingleput on May 4, 1371 (*V. R. ii, Madras, 310 ; 511 of 1913*) and in Ramnad (*V. R. ii, Ram. 124, 129 ; 106, 111 of 1903*). And in N. Arcot (*V. R. i, N. Arcot, 232-A ; 293 of 1895 ; E. I. vi, 326*). His rule over Ramnad shews that he was practically master of all South India by this time.

Jaṭāvarman Parākrama Panḍya ruling in his 15th year at Kōṭṭaru, near Nāgarkoyil in Travancore. (*V. R. iii, Trav. 5 ; E. I. vii, 121 ; xi, 228.*)

Anavēma Reḍḍi of Konḍavīḍu, son of Prolaya-Vēma ruling that country. One record says that he immediately succeeded his eldest brother Annavōta. Two inscriptions of April 30 and December 27, 1371. *(C-P. Nos. 9, 15 of 1922–23.)*

A.D. 1372. Bukka I of Vijayanagar reigning in N.-W. Mysore (*E. C. viii, Sb, 199*). And in Bellary District (*259 of 1918*). And in S. Kanara (*V. R. ii, S. Kan. 66*).

Kampana II, his son, ruling on November 26, 1372 in S. Arcot (*V. R. i, S. Arcot, 928, 1061 ; 13 of 1903 ; 29 of 1905 ; 45 of 1922*). He made a gift in Tanjore District (*V. R. ii, Tan. 2 ; 617 of 1902*). On March 7 a record of his in S. Mysore (*E. C. iv. Gu. 32 ; E. I. vi, 326*). Another in N. Arcot (*V. R. i, N. Arcot 656 ; 696 of 1904*). And in Chingleput. *(V. R. i, Chin. 1186.)*

A.D. 1373. Grant by Anavēma Reḍḍi of Konḍavīḍu, Guntur District (but date not quite accurate) at Naḍupūru. It gives pedigree of the family. *(E. I. iii, 286 ; E. R. 1920, App. A, C-P. 6.)*

Bukka I reigning in S. Kanara. *(V. R. ii, S. Kan. 179 ; 161 of 1901.)*

Kampana II ruling in E. Mysore (*E. C. x, Kl, 205*). And in S. Arcot and Chittoor Districts. *(V. R. i, S. Arcot, 520 ; Chitt. 343 ; 162 of 1906 ; 472 of 1905.)*

A.D. 1374. Bukka I reigning in Chingleput District. A long list of taxes mentioned in the inscription, payable to the temple authorities. It shews that there was a tax imposed on anyone entering the village from outside (*V. R. i, Chin. 689 ; 324 of 1911*). Also in E. Mysore (*E. C. ix, Nl, 533*). And in N.-W. Mysore. *(E. C. viii, Sb, 115.)*

Kampana II was ruling in Ramnad, at Tirupullāṇi (*V. R. ii, Ram. 132 ; 114 of 1903*). And on July 7 and September 1 in Chingleput District (*ibid. i, Chin. 343, 725, 732 ; 28 of 1890 ; 634 of 1904 ; 267 of 1912 ; E. I. vi, 325*). And in Pudukoṭṭa (*V. R. iii, Pudu. 380 ; 244 of 1914*). And in Trichinopoly District (*ibid. iii, Trich. 602 ; 282 of 1903*). And in N. Arcot. *(V. R. i, N. Arcot, 11 ; 390 of 1905.)*

Judging by the inscription at Tirumalai near Pōḷur in N. Arcot District, Kampana II had died before December 11, 1374 ; but the details of this date in the record are not quite satisfactory. It mentions as chief ruler there Jammana, the son of Kampana II (*S. I. I. i, p. 103 ; No. 72 ; V. R. i, N. Arcot 390 ; 87 of 1887*). [If the date is accepted Kampana II died on a day between September 1 and December 11, 1374.] *(See I. A. xxiv, p. 3.)*

Jammana, son of Kampana II and grandson of Bukka I is mentioned as ruler in N. Arcot in A.D. 1374–75 (*V. R. i. N. Arcot 529 ; 573 of 1902*). And in S. Arcot. *(Ibid., S. Arcot 348 ; 224 of 1906.)*

In S. Mysore ' Nanjanna,' son of Kampana II, is mentioned as in this year giving a village to Brahmans. He may be the same as, or a brother of Jammana, mentioned above. *(E. C. iii. Nj. 108.)*

In Travancore the Kēraḷa king Ādityavarma-Sarvānganātha erected a shrine at Trivandrum, where there are three records of the year 1374–75. *(V. R. iii. Trav. 204 ; T. A. S. i. 171.)*

A.D. 1375. A son of Bukka I of Vijayanagar was ruling in S.-E. Mysore (*E. C. ix. Kn. 93.*) The name of the son is illegible.

Bukka I was reigning in E. Mysore. *(E. C. ix. Dv. 13.)*

Jammana, son of Kampana II and grandson of Bukka I, was ruling in E. Mysore. *(E. C. x. Ct., 94.)*

[On April 21, 1375, according to Firishtah, Muhammad Shāh Bāhmanī died, and was succeeded by Mujāhīd, his eldest son. Muhammad has been already noticed for the ferocity with which he carried out his campaigns. Another instance is shewn by his method of putting down gang-robbery and violence. He did so by wholesale massacre,—'near 8,000 heads were brought to Kulbarga and piled up in heaps near the city.' It can hardly be supposed that all these heads were actually those of dacoits themselves. Nevertheless, in spite of these defects he had his virtues, according to Firishtah. The *Burhān-i-Ma'āsir* credits him with none.

Early in the reign of Mujāhīd Bāhmanī war broke out between him and Bukka I of Vijayanagar, owing to a dispute as to whether the Krishna or the Tungabhadra rivers was to be the boundary of the two kingdoms. At this time Bukka's kingdom, now grown into an empire, included the Tuḷu districts on the west, and from Beḷgaum to the eastern sea, the Kākatīya family still, however, ruling the northern portion of the east coast. The whole of southern India, except the most southerly portion in Tinnevelly, which was ruled by the Pāṇḍya princes, acknowledged him as sovereign *de facto*. Granting that Mujāhīd began to reign in April 1375, and that, according to the accounts on which we have to depend, some time elapsed before he started on his expedition; then, since we are informed that when he marched his elephants, crossed the two great rivers, and since it is clear that they could only have done so when the river-beds were almost empty of water in the dry season, we cannot suppose that this march took place in the hot weather of 1375. And it can only be in the hot weather of 1376.]

A.D. 1376. Bukka I reigning in N.-W. Mysore (*E. C. vii. Sk. 57 ; viii. Sb. 106*). And in Chingleput (*V. R. i. Chin. 193 E. ; 490 ; 255 of 1901*). And in E. Mysore. (*E. C. ix. An. 29.*)

An inscription in Salem district is puzzling, as it seems to mention Kampana II of Vijayanagar as ruling there on January 3, 1376 (so Mr. Swamikannu Pillai). But the details of the date are irregular. I can only note it and pass on.

(*See above s. v. 1374 for note of Kampana's death. V. R. ii. Salem 24 ; 431 of 1913.*)

The Kalinga-Ganga king Bhānudēva III reigning in Vizagapatam district in his 31st year. (*V. R. iii. Vizag. 196 ; 268 of 1899.*)

[Mujahid Bāhmanī probably began his campaign against Vijayanagar in the hot weather of this year. He crossed the Krishna and Tungabhadra rivers with a large army and 500 elephants and arrived at Adoni. I follow broadly Firishtah's narrative, but have no space for details. (See *Firishtah*, and summary given in '*A Forgotten Empire*,' *p. 39 f.*) 'By slow marches and with great caution' he advanced towards Vijayanagar. We are told that Bukka Rāya fled but managed to re-enter his capital six months later. This takes us to the year 1377.]

A.D. 1377. The Hebbasūru inscription in S. Mysore records a grant of a village to Brahmans made by Harihara II of Vijayanagar in order that Bukka I, his father, 'might obtain union with Śiva'. The date is February 24, 1377. And this probably means that king Bukka I died on that day. But it may mean only that the king was then very ill, and he may have died shortly before or after that date (*E. C. iv. Yd. 46*). It seems, however, from another C.-P. grant noted in the (*Mysore Arch. Ann. Report for 1914-15, p. 57*) that Bukka's death did actually take place on February 24, 1377[1]. Another record (*E. C. xii. Si. 52*) which apparently makes Bukka reigning on August 29,

[1] The actual expression used is that Bukka had attained to 'Śivasāyujya' which implies he was already dead. The grant of the *agrahāra* by the son was for his attaining to Siva's grace by the destruction of his sins. This means that Bukka was dead on the date February 24, 1377, and might have died sometime before. The date given is the date of the grant *when Harihara was the ruler*. If it be taken as the date of Bukka's death, the grant would be without date, and Harihara could not then be described as being on the throne, as he is.—*Editor*.

1377 does not really do so; a vīrakal was erected on that day in honour of a woman who had become *satī* at an earlier date when Bukka I was reigning—a very different thing.

Bukka I was succeeded by his son Harihara II.

Harihara II was reigning in N.-W. Mysore (*E. C. vii, Sk, 35; viii, Tl, 16*). And in Nellore District on June 21, 1377 (*V. R. ii, Nell. 369; B and V. C. 647*). And in N. Arcot (*V. R. i, N. Arcot 215, 518; 57 of 1900; 562 of 1902*). The date of the last is July 27.

In Central Mysore Bukka II was ruling as viceroy for his father Harihara II.

(*E. C. xii, Pg, 92.*)

Virūpanna or Virūpāksha, son of Bukka I, was governing the Āraga tract in N.-W. Mysore.

(*E. C. viii, Tl. 125.*)

One of the Bukkas of Vijayanagar was ruling in S. Kanara in A.D. 1377-78 later than March 10, 1377. But no details are given. (*V. R. ii, S. Kan. 69.*)

The Koṇḍavīḍu Reḍḍi chief Anavēma made a gift. (*V. R. ii. Godavari, 16, 505 of 1893.*)

[Mujāhid, early in the year 1377 was inside the outer defences of the city of Vijayanagar and close to the citadel, where he destroyed a temple. He was then savagely attacked by the infuriated populace, and very nearly lost his life. A battle that was fought ended favourably for the Musalmans, but one of the Hindu king's brothers arrived at the capital with a force described as one of '20,000 horse and a vast army of foot'. This is probably a gross exaggeration, made to exonerate Mujahid from any blame attaching to him for the wise course which he adopted namely to retire. But he did retire and attacked Adoni, laying siege to the fortress for nine months. A prolonged drought caused great distress to the garrison but at last there was heavy rainfall. This points to the autumn season of 1377. Mujahid was advised to abandon the siege, and did so. He retired to Mudkal, and while there was assassinated on April 17, 1378 (for details see '*A Forgotten Empire*', p. 42 f).

With reference to the death of Bukka I having taken place on February 24, 1377, this must have been at the time when Mujāhīd was before Vijayanagar city, and it is curious that the Muhammadan historians do not allude to it.]

A.D. 1378. Harihara II of Vijayanagar reigning in N.-W. Mysore (*E. C. viii, Sb, 200*). And in Central Mysore (*E. C. v, Cn, 256*). And in E. Mysore (*E. C. x, Ct, 68; Sd, 112*). And in Chingleput (*V. R. i, Chin. 347*). And in S. Kanara (*V. R. ii, S. Kan. 144, 173; 126, 155 of 1901*). One of these bears date June 11, 1378. Also in S. Arcot (*V. R. i, S. Arcot, 926; 27 of 1905*). Harihara II assumed full imperial titles.

Anavēma Reḍḍi of Koṇḍavīḍu built a hall at Śrīśailam in this year. Inscription date = January 6, 1378 (*V. R. ii, Kurnool 456; 20 of 1915*). He has the title 'Jaganobbagaṇḍa'.

[Mujahid Bahmanī was assassinated by Dāud Khān on April 17. He was succeeded by Muhammad Shāh II. Harihara II taking advantage of this, crossed the Tungabhadra river and invested Raichūr. After this peace was made.]

The Kalinga-Ganga king Narasimha IV reigning in Vizagapatam District.

(*V. R. iii, Vizag. 85, 91; 257, 263 of 1899.*)

Prince Virūpanna I of Vijayanagar ruling the Āraga tract in N.-W. Mysore. (*E. C. vi, Kp, 30.*)

A.D. 1379. Harihara II reigning in S. Kanara on April 18. (*V. R. ii, S. Kan. 101; 59 of 1901.*) And in N.-W. Mysore (*E. C. viii, Hl, 84; viii, Sb, 196*). And in N., Central and E. Mysore.

(*E. C. xi, Dg, 34; xii. Si, 76; ix. Ht, 113.*)

The Kalinga-Ganga king Narasimha IV reigning in Ganjam District in his 3rd year. (*V. R. Ganjam 204, 207; 326, 329 of 1896.*)

Virūpanna I of Vijayanagar ruling in N.-W. Mysore. (*E. C. viii Tl, 14.*)

There was a rising in the Konkan in this year against the rule of king Harihara, which was suppressed by his general Baichappa. (*E. I. xv. p. 12.*)

An inscription on a rock in Coimbatore District mentions Prince Ṣāvanna of Vijayanagar, which prince of that name cannot be determined. (*V. R. i, Coim. 469; 169 of 1909.*)

A.D. 1380. Harihara II of Vijayanagar reigning in N.-W. Mysore. The death of general Baichappa in the Konkan rising is mentioned (*E. C. viii, Sb., 152*). And in Central Mysore on October 29. The Nagasandra C.-P. grant tells how the fortress of Adoni was captured from the Muhammadans by Channappa, son of the prince Mallinātha and nephew of Harihara II. Channappa presented the fortress to the king, and was appointed its governor (*E. C. xii. Kg. 43*). Harihara II was reigning also in E. Mysore (*E. C. ix, An., 49; Bn., 73*). And in S. Mysore (*E. C. iv. Ch., 64*). And in S. Kanara (*V. R. ii. S. Kanara, 153; 135 of 1901*). And in Chingleput district. (*V. R. i. Chin., 1074; 205 of 1912.*)

Anavēma Reḍḍi of Konḍavīḍu ruling in the Amalāpuram taluk of Godavari District on February 6. (*V. R. ii. Godav., 18; E. I. iii. 59.*)

About this time Kumāragiri Reḍḍi of Konḍavīḍu, son of Annavòta ḍivided his territory and handed over the Rajahmundry tract to his minister Kāṭayya Vēma, who was also his brother-in-law. Kāṭayya established himself as independent at Rajahmundry. (*E. I. viii. 9.*)

A.D. 1381. Harihara II of Vijiyanagar reigning on January 21, in N. Arcot (*122 of 1921*). And on April 29, in S. Mysore (*E. C. iii, Ml., 21, 76*). And in W. Mysore (*E. C. v, Bl., 52; Hn., 36*).

Anavēma Reḍḍi of Konḍavīḍu carried out improvements at the temple at Drākshārāma. (*V. R. ii. Godavari, 352; 446 of 1893.*)

In Tanjore, Bukka II son of king Harihara II of Vijayanagar granted land to a temple. (*V. R. ii. Tanjore, 1505; 253 of 1894.*)

A.D. 1382. Harihara II regining in Cuddapah district. His son Dēva Rāya ruling Udayagiri province (*V. R. i. Cudd., 413; 404 of 1904*). And on April 28, 1382 in S. Kanara (*V. R. ii. S. Kan., 192; 174 of 1901*). And in W. Mysore (*E. C. v. Bl., 75*). And in N. Arcot (*V. R. i. N. Arcot, 621; 422 of 1905*). And in Chingleput district (*V. R. i. Chin., 1065; 196 of 1912*). Bukka II, son of Harihara II, ruling in E. Mysore (*E. C. ix, Ht., 154*). Virūpanna I (or II ?) ruling in Tanjore. (*V. R. ii. Tan., 547; 654 of 1902.*)

Gift in the reign of Harihara II by Iruga, son of the Vijayanagar general Baichayya, to a Jain temple. (*V. R. i. Chingleput, 451; 41 of 1890.*)

Virūpanna II, son of Harihara II ruling in N. Arcot (*V. R. i. N. Arcot 265; 251 of 1906*). And in the Āraga tract in N.-W. Mysore (*E. C. vi. Kp., 31*). In this last inscription the prince is called 'Chikka-Rāya, son of Harihara-Rāya, son of Bukka-Raya.'

A.D. 1383. Harihara II of Vijayanagar reigning on March 7, in N. Arcot (*251 of 1919*). And in N.-W. Mysore. (*E. C. viii. Sb., 428.*)

Gifts made in Vizagapatam district by Tārādēvī, queen of the Kalinga king Bhānudēva III and Birijādēvī, queen of Narasimha III. (*V. R. iii. Vizag., 97, 98; 267, 270 of 1899.*)

A.D. 1384. Harihara II of Vijayanagar reigning in Salem district on April 6 (*V. R. ii, Salem, 23 ; 430 of 1913*). And in N.-W. and E. Mysore (*E. C. viii, Tl., 147 ; ix, An., 32 ; x. Kl., 67, 80.*)

Virūpāksha II, son of Harihara II, ruling in Tanjore (*V. R. ii. Tan., 741 ; 58 of 1913*). And in Trichinopoly. (*Ibid. iii. Trich., 531 ; 665 of 1909.*)

An inscription in Central Mysore whose date is in the autumn of 1384 relates the death of Śāḷuva Rāma, a chief who was killed in battle when the army of king Harihara II 'went to the Warangal country' and when 'the Turukas came and attacked Kottakoṇḍa' (N.-W. of Warangal). [This may refer to an event of the year 1364 when the Bāhmanī forces finally destroyed the Kākatīya kingdom of Warangal—and when very likely they attacked Kottakoṇḍa while on the march thither. But we have no information, so far as I know, that king Harihara had on that occasion sent an army to assist the Kakatīya king and had fought against Muhammad Bāhmani's forces at Kottakoṇḍa.] (*E. C. xii, Ck., 15.*)

A.D. 1385. Harihara II reigning at Conjevaram on June 8 (*V. R. i, Chingleput 346 ; 31 of 1890*). And in Kurnool district. (*Ibid. ii. Kurn., 362 ; 270 of 1905.*)

Virūpāksha II, son of Harihara II, ruling in Tanjore District on February 5. (*V.R. ii, Tan. 765, 837 ; 75 of 1913 ; 396 of 1908.*)

Vēma Reḍḍi, son of Kāṭama Reḍḍi of the Reḍḍi family of Rajahmundry ruling in the Krishna District (*V.R. ii, Kistna 311 ; 521 of 1893*). Kāṭama or Kāṭayya had been minister to Kumāragiri, the Reḍḍi chief of Koṇḍaviḍu, and he had married Kumāragiri's sister Mallāmbika. In gratitude for his assistance Kumāragiri made over to him his territory about Rajahmundry.

A.D. 1386. Harihara II reigning in N.-W. Mysore on May 15 (*Mys. Arch. Ann. Rep. 1923, p. 90*). And in N. Mysore (*E.C. xi, Hk, 127*). And in W. Mysore (*E.C. vi, Kp. 34*). And in S. Kanara (*V. R. ii. S. Kan. 84, 145 ; 27, 127 of 1901*). And in Coimbatore (*V.R. i, Coim. 314 ; 179 of 1910*). And in Kurnool (*V. R. ii, Kurn. 350 ; 257 of 1905*). Where an inscription shews that Bhāskara-Bhavadūra, his brother, was ruling the Eastern provinces with his capital at Udayagiri.

Virupāksha, son of Harihara II was ruling for his father in South Arcot. (*V.R. 1903–4, p. 12 ; V.R. i. S. Arcot, 385 ; 234 of 1904.*)

Iruga, son of the Vijayanagar general Baichayya, built the Gāṇigitti Jain temple at the capital, Hampe ; on the wall of which is an inscription to that effect, bearing date February 16, 1386. (*S.I.I. i, 155; V.R. i, Bellary, 334 ; 17 of 1889.*)

Prince Vīra Bhūpati, son of Bukka II and grandson of Harihara II, is mentioned in an inscription of date=December 13, 1386 on the Kumāraswāmi temple on the Sandūr hill near Vijayanagar (*742 of 1922*). This prince may be the same as prince Ōbaladēva mentioned in A.D. 1387–8.

Harihara II's son Bukka II was ruling for his father in E. Mysore. (*E.C. ix, Bn.139.*)

Kāṭayya-Vēma III of the Rajahmundry Reḍḍis gave a gift to the Simhāchalam temple for the merit of his father Kāṭama II and his mother Doḍḍāmbikā (*V.R. iii, Vizagapatam, 105 ; 277 of 1899*). He also made a gift to the temple at Amarāvati. (*V.R. ii, Guntur, 625 ; 259 of 1897.*)

A.D. 1387. Harihara II of Vijayanagar reigning in N.-W., Central and West Mysore (*E.C. viii, Sb. 512 ; xii, Tm. 39 ; v, Bl. 63*). And in Chingleput District (*V.R. i, Chin. 895 ; 675 of 1904*). And in N. Arcot (*Ibid. i, N. Arcot 149 ; 29 of 1911*). And in S. Kanara (*Ibid. ii, 172 ;*

154 of 1901). The last record says that he ruled from Dorasamudra, the old Hoyśala capital, thus preserving the traditions of that dynasty.

At Simhāchalam in Vizagapatam District the Kalinga-Ganga king Narasimha IV made a gift to the temple. (*V.R. iii, Vizag. 181 ; 353 of 1899.*)

Prince Ōbaladēva, son of Bukka II, and grandson of Harihara II mentioned in a record in Chingleput District. (*V.R. i, Chin. 1167 ; 342 of 1909.*)

Prince Virūpāksha II, son of Harihara II, gave a village in Tanjore District. Śoraikkāvūr C-P. grant (*V.R. ii, Tan. 625-A ; E.I. iii, 298*). The date = March 20, 1387.

A.D. 1388. Virūpāksha II ruling in N. Arcot. His cousin Jammana, son of Kampana II gave a grant in memory of his deceased father (*V.R. i, N. Arcot, 528 ; 572 of 1902*). He was also ruling in Chingleput (*Ibid. i, Chin. 193 B and C*). And in N. Arcot. (*Ibid. i, N. Arcot 250 ; 236 of 1906.*)

Harihara II of Vijayanagar reigning in S., N.-W. and Central Mysore (*E.C. iii, Ml. 20. viii, Sb. 483 ; xii, Tp. 9*). Also in S. Kanara. (*V.R. ii. S. Kan. 182 ; 164 of 1901.*)

Prince Bukka II of Vijayanagar ruling on January 23, 1388 for his father Harihara II in Anantapur District (*819 of 1917*). And in E. Mysore (*E. C. x, Gd. 6*). The last inscription says that he resided at Penukoṇḍa. Another inscription in E. Mysore of the end of the year states that Bukka then had his residence at Muḷbāgaḷ. (*E.C. x, Bp. 17.*)

Annadēva of the Koṇḍavīḍu Reḍḍi chief's family gave a grant of a village in Mārkāpūr taluk, Kurnool District. (*V.R. ii, Kurn. 347 ; 254 of 1905.*)

A.D. 1389. Harihara II reigning in S. Kanara (*V.R. ii, S. Kan 126, 156 ; 55, 156 of 1901*). And in N.-W. Mysore. (*E.C. viii, Sb. 116.*)

Virūpāksha II, prince of Vijayanagar, gave a village in S. Arcot on July 6, 1389. The week-day stated is, however, wrong (*328 of 1917*). Another record of his of October 1? in S. Arcot (*510 of 1921*). He also ruled in N. Arcot District. (*V. R. i. N. Arcot 437 ; 483 of 1902.*)

Bukka II, son of Harihara II, governing E. Mysore for his father. (*E. C. x. Mb. 11.*)

The Kalinga-Ganga king Narasimha IV reigning in Vizagapatam District. Gifts by his mother Tārā-devī and his grandmother Birijādēvī. (*V. R. iii. Vizag. 159 ; 331 of 1899.*)

A.D. 1390. Harihara II reigning in N.-W. Mysore on October 9 (*E. C. vii. Sk. 313 ; Hl. 6*). And in E. Mysore. (*E. C. x. Kl. 105.*)

Virūpāksha II, his son, ruling in Trichinopoly District about February 25 (*V. R. iii. Trichinopoly 102 ; 170 of 1914*). [Mr. V. Rangāchāri equates the date to March 24, but I think this is a mistake.] Virūpāksha was also ruling in N. Arcot. (*V. R. i. N. Arcot, 253 ; 239 of 1906.*)

In Travancore the Kērala king Mārttāṇḍa-varman was ruling on October 2 (*V. R. iii ; Trav. 176–A ; I. A. ii. 361*). [Kielhorn settled the date ; but I find the details not quite satisfactory.]

There was a terrible famine in this year, long remembered as the 'Pramōda famine.' One of Virūpāksha's inscriptions noted above says that it was so disastrous that 'innumerable skulls were rolling about.' (*E. R. 1907, p. 82 ; 239 of 1906.*)

A.D. 1391. Harihara II reigning in S. Mysore. (*E. C. iv. Yd. 1.*)

Kāṭayya-Vēma III, Reḍḍi chief of Rajahmundry, son of Kāṭayya II, ruling at Piṭhāpuram. The record gives a pedigree of his family. (*V. R. ii. Godavari, 66 ; 493 of 1893 ; E. I. iv. 328.*)

A.D. 1392. Harihara II reigning in S. Kanara 'from Dorasamudra' (*V. R. ii. S. Kan. 169 ; 151 of 1901*). And in Anantapur District (*V. R. i. Anant. 160 ; 338 of 1901*). And in W., E. and S. Mysore (*E. C. vi. Kp., 49 ; x. Bg. 15 ; Gd., 68 ; iii. Ml., 47*). And in Coimbatore. (*V. R. i. Coim. 330 ; 247 of 1913.*)

Virūpāksha II ruling for his father Harihara II in N. Arcot (*V. R. i. N. Arcot 736 ; 76 of 1908*). (*For a valuable note on this prince and others see E. I. viii. 298, 306.*)

A.D. 1393. Harihara II reigning in N.-W. Mysore (*E. C. viii. Sb. 134*). And in Conjevaram (*E I. iii. 229*). And in S. Kanara (*V. R. ii. S. Kan. 177 ; 159 of 1901*). And in Chingleput. (*ibid. i. Chin : 344 ; 29 of 1890.*)

Virūpāksha, son of Harihara II, ruling for his father on June 12 in Tanjore (*476 of 1918 ; V. R. ii. Tan : 542. ; 649 of 1902*). This last mentions the famine in the year 'Pramōda.'

A.D. 1394. Harihara II reigning in N.-W. and N.-E. Mysore (*E. C. viii. Tl. 173, 201 ; vii. Ci. 13*). And in S. Kanara (*V. R. ii. S. Kan. 183, 233 ; 165, 112 of 1901*). And in Kurnool. (*V. R. ii. Kurn. 610–c.*)

Bukka II, son of Harihara II, gave a gift in Salem District. (*V. R. ii. Salem, 115 ; 208 of 1911.*)

A.D. 1395. Harihara II reigning in many parts of Mysore (*E. C. viii. Sb. 103 ; xii. Tp. 44*). This last mentions a war with the Bāhmani Muhammadans, in which the general 'Bāichappa' distinguished himself in a battle which ended with Harihara capturing Rangiṇi (*E. C. ix. Cp. 37 ; v. Bl. 61, 62 ; x. Sp. 54*). Bukka II was viceroy in E. Mysore, residing at Muḷbāgal. Harihara II was also reigning in S. Kanara. (*V. R. ii. S. Kan : 167 ; 149 of 1901.*)

Virūpāksha II, son of Harihara II was ruling in S. Arcot (*V. R. ii, S. Arcot, 554 ; 194 of 1906.*)

A.D. 1396. Harihara II reigning in Chingleput (*V. R. i, Chin. 835 ; 221 of 1910*). A long list of taxes is mentioned. He was ruling in N.-W. Mysore on June 21. The inscription which gives this date mentions the battle of Rangini (*above, s. v. A. D. 1395*) and the valour of general Bāichappa (*E. C. vii. Hl. 71; viii, Sb, 121 ; vii. Sk, 241*). Another record of June 21, lunar eclipse. (*E.C. viii Tl, 8.*). He was reigning in W. Mysore (*E. C. v. Hn, 786*). And in S. Kanara. (*V. R. ii. S. Kan. 86 ; 26 of 1901.*)

Prince Dēva Rāya I, his son, was ruling in Cuddapah District (*V. R. i. Cudd : 9 A.*). And at Udayagiri in Nellore District. (*V. R. i. Cudd. 11*).

Prince Virūpāksha was ruling N. Arcot District on April 13, 1396 (*V. R. i. N. Arcot, 419) 112 of 1900 ; E. I. vi. 329*). And on June 30 he was in authority in South Arcot, his minister being Nanjanna. (*474, 475 of 1921.*)

The great 'Durga-Dēvī' famine, which lasted 12 years and the severity of which has never been forgotten, began this year.

A.D. 1397. [Muhammad Shāh Bāhmanī II died this year and was succeeded by his son Ghiyāsu-d-din, who was at once blinded and deposed. His brother Shamsu-d-dīn took the throne and was also overthrown, blinded and deposed ; and the throne was seized by Firoz, cousin of Muhammad II. For full details regarding the Bāhmanī dynasty see Major I. S. King's translation of the *Burhan-i-Ma'asir* in the *Indian Antiquary* for 1899–1900, which has also an excellent map.]

Harihara II of Vijayanagar 'governing the Hoyśala country' and generally in Mysore (*E. C. iv. Ch, 114 ; x, Kl, 248 ; iii, Tn, 134*). Another record in N.-W. Mysore says that he was 'protecting the Āraga kingdom' (*E. C, viii, Tl, 146, 160*). He was reigning over Chittoor District on July 8, 1397 (*312 of 1922*). And in Coimbatore District. (*V. R. i, Coim. 343 ; 18 of 1910.*)

Harihara II's son Dēva Rāya I ruling in N. Arcot. (*V. R. i, N. Arcot 268 ; 254 of 1906.*)

Virūpāksha II, son of king Harihara, ruling in Chingleput District.
(*V. R. . i, Chin. 530 ; 299 of 1910..*)

Bukka II, another son, was governing in E. Mysore. (*E. C. x, Mb, 74.*)

Prince Nārāyaṇa son of Mallinātha who was brother of king Harihara II, gave on July 29 a grant of a village in S. Mysore to Brahmans. (*E. C. iii. Tn, 64 ; E. I. vi 327.*)

A.D. 1398. [Invasion of N. India in this year by the Amīr Tīmūr, or Taimūr of Samarkhand —'Tamerlane' in English literature. He won his way to Delhi, killing the Hindu inhabitants mercilessly. He had 100,000 prisoners murdered in cold blood : and after he captured Delhi he renewed the slaughter of the townsfolk; when he retired he carried off multitudes of women and children. This was only a wanton raid as he had no intention of remaining in Hindustan.]

Harihara II of Vijayanagar reigning in Mysore (*E. C. v.Cn, 195 ; x. mb, 29*). And in Chingleput District. (*217 of 1916.*)

Virūpāksha II, his son, ruling in Tanjore (400 of 1918). And in Chingleput.
(*V. R. i. Chin. 572 ; 353 of 1911.*)

Rācha Vēma, brother of Śrīgiri of the Reḍḍis of Konḍavīḍu constructed an irrigation work this year in Nellore Taluk. (*V. R. ii, Nell, 305 ; B and V. C. 549.*)

[In the cold weather of A. D. 1398 when the cotton-soil plains were passable, Bukka II, son of Harihara, was permitted by his father to make a raid northwards into Bāhmanī territory with the object of seizing possession of the tract between the Tungabhadra and Krishna rivers, including Raichūr and Muḍkal. Firoz Shāh advanced to meet him and found the Hindu army encamped close to the Krishna river. One night a Muhammadan Kāzi proposed to the sultan that he (the Kāzi) should cross the river disguised, mingle with the Hindus of the royal enclosure, and find some means of assassinating prince Bukka, or one of the princes. He was completely successful, stabbing to death prince Bukka's young son and escaping in the confusion which ensued. In the morning Firoz, having crossed the river in the night, attacked the Vijayanagar camp. Bukka II, prostrate with grief, made a feeble attempt to oppose his enemy and finally fled, carrying off the body of his son to Vijayanagar. Immense slaughter followed and Firoz retired with great booty from the plundered camp. About the middle of 1399 peace was made, Firoz accepting a large sum as indemnity.]

A.D. 1399. Harihara II reigning in Nellore District in his 25th year on May 11, 1399 (*V. R. ii. Nell. 548 ; B. and V. C., 846*). And in Mysore (*E. C. viii. Tl. 215 ; v. Cn. 175*). And in Salem District (*V. R. ii. Salem, 221 ; 664 of 1905*). And in Chingleput on October 15 (*E. I. iii. 113, 116 ; V. R. i. Chin. 703-A*). Harihara's son, Bukka II, was ruling in E. Mysore on March 19.
(*Mys. A. A. R. 1923, p. 62.*)

Prince Dēva Rāya I, son of king Harihara, ruling in Guntur District.
(*V. R. ii. Gun. 111-B.*)

Virūpāksha II, son of king Harihara, ruling in N. Arcot District. (*106 of 1921.*)

A.D. 1400. Harihara II of Vijayanagar reigning in Chingleput District (*V. R. i. Chin 891, 671 of 1904*). And in Mysore (*E. C. ix. Kn. 97 ; viii. Sb. 173*). And in S. Kanara.
(*V. R. ii. S. Kan. 14.*)

Prince Bukka II ruling Chingleput District for his father. (*V. R. i. Chin. 230 ; 344 of 1908.*)

A.D. 1401. Harihara II reigning in E. Mysore (*E. C. ix. Ht. 118*). The Āraga tract in N.-W. Mysore was governed under Harihara II by a certain Jannarasa (*E. C. viii. Tl. 31*). Harihara reigning in Chittoor District. (*V. R. i. Chit. 131 ; 192 of 1903.*)

Pārvati-dēvī, queen of the Kalinga king Narasimha IV gave a gift to a temple. (*V. R. iii. Vizag. 86 ; 258 of 1899.*)

A.D. 1402. Harihara II reigning in Mysore (*E. C. vii. Sk. 302 ; iv. Kr. 21, 22*) and in S. Kanara. (*V. R. ii. S. Kan. 151, 152, 300 ; 133, 134, 90 of 1901.*)

Prince Bukka II ruling for his father in Tanjore District. (*V. R. ii. Tan. 710 ; 422 of 1912 ; E. R. 1912, p. 118.*)

In Tinnevelly District Jaṭilavarman Kulaśēkhara Pāṇḍya II was ruling in his 7th year. His accession had taken place in 1396–97. (*V. R. iii. Tinn. 290.*)

A.D. 1403. Harihara II reigning in Mysore (*E. C. xii. Si. 95 ; vi. Kp. 51, 52 ; viii. Sb. 117 ; x. Ct. 86*). The date of the last = May 18, 1403. He also was reigning in Chingleput District (*V. R. i. Chin. 884 ; 664 of 1904 ; 661 of 1919*). The date of this last = February 14, 1403.

Prince Bukka II was ruling North and South Arcot for his father on April 16 and October 12, 1403. (*257, 117 of 1919 ; V. R. i. Chin. 524 ; 293 of 1910.*)

Prince Dēva Rāya I ruled for his father in Salem District. (*V. R. ii. Salem, 222 ; 665 of 1905.*)

In Vizagapatam District a *Gōpura* of a temple was built by a chief called Chōḍa or Chōḍēndra. (*V. R. iii. Vizag. 22 ; 210 of 1899.*)

An inscription of this year at Pulipparakōyil in Chingleput District gives a long list of taxes imposed by the temple trustees (*V. R. i. Chin. 524 ; 293 of 1910*). A later one at the same place of A.D. 1417 (*q. v. below*) shews that the residents were dissatisfied.

A.D. 1404. Harihara II reigning in Mysore (*E. C. viii. Tl. 133*). The date of this is early in the year. Another of May 10, 1404 (*ibid. x. Kl. 73*). Another of March 26 (*E. C. viii. Tl. 9*). Building of a hall at the temple of Śrīśailam in Kurnool District during the year,—Harihara being king (*V. R. ii. Kurn. 447, 489-0 ; 11 of 1915*). [The date of the earlier of these last requires further investigation since Mr. Swamikannu Pillai's interpretation of it (*January 29, 1405*) conflicts with the assertion made (*E. C. viii. Tl. 129*) that king Harihara II died in August A.D. 1404.]

August 16, A.D. 1404 = date of death of king Harihara II (*E. C. viii. Tl. 129 ; ii. Sr.-Bel. 126 ; E. I. xv. 13*). The first of these dates works out correctly. The second has, apparently (the word may have been misread) the week-day given as Monday (*Sōma*—) whereas it was Saturday (*Saurē*—) ; and the wrong fortnight is quoted.[1] [On Harihara's death a struggle seemingly arose between his sons, the succession being disputed.]

[1] In regard to the date of death of Harihara II, the decisive record is E.C. VIII, Tl. 129. This gives the date of death of the king, equal correctly to August 16, A.D. 1404, according to Mr. Sewell. It gives the date of grant of the *agrahāra* by a minister Viṭṭhala, a fortnight after, called *Mukta-Hariharapura*, the city of Harihara 'released from life's bondage'. This grant was made when Harihara had died, and in consequence of it, on Saka 1326 expired, in Tāraṇa, Asviyuja Śu, *Sōmavāra*-Monday, 15th September 1404. The last part of the grant was the provision of a goldsmith, a carpenter and a metaller for the service of the village. This was provided for on *Kārttika*, Ba. 3.—Tuesday, 21st October 1404, which is the date of the record on stone. In regard to the first date Mr. Sewell finds it correct to August 16, 1404. Mr. Rice gives the equivalent as August 31, 1404. According to Mr. Swamikkannu Pillai's Ephemeris, both of them would be wrong in detail.

The Śrīśailam record refers to the completion of a building ordered by Harihara, after his death, and the date has reference to the actual completion of the work.—*Editor*.

On October 27, 1404 an inscription in N.-W. Mysore, in the same part of the country as the first of the two just quoted, viz., Tl. 129, names Harihara's son Virūpāksha as king, giving him full imperial titles (*E. C. viii. Tl. 13*), and so does another of November 29, in the same tract also giving him imperial titles. (*E. C. viii. Tl. 196.*)

But an inscription of October 5, again in the same tract, names Bukka II as 'Sovereign of the whole kingdom' and 'sitting on the throne of Vijayanagar.'

(*E. C. viii. Tl. 11 ; E. I. xv. 13.*)

[Since these records all come from the same taluk it cannot be supposed that the brothers were at the same time recognized, each as sovereign, by rival factions—a supposition that might have been entertained if the records came from different provinces—and therefore the solution must be that from August 16 for a short time Bukka II was king, but that between October 5 and 27 Virūpāksha had succeeded in ejecting him and gaining the throne. Since an inscription of July 27, 1405 (*below*) in the same taluk again mentions Bukka II as king and thereafter, it is certain that he was king ; we have to assume that Virūpāksha did enjoy a short reign and was ejected from the throne by Bukka II some time before July 1405. Virūpāksha is said to have been guilty of great cruelty and oppression during the brief period of his reign (*E. I. xv. 14*).]

Bukka II ruling Chingleput District some time during A.D. 1404.

(*V. R. i. Chin. 575 ; 359 of 1911.*)

Pedda Kōmaṭi Vēma of Koṇḍavīḍu mentioned as granting a village in this year.

(*E. R. 1920., App. A., C-P. No. 13.*)

A.D. 1405. About April–May, 1405, Bukka II of Vijayanagar consecrated a temple near Vellore and gave gifts (*S.I.I. i. 78*). He is recognized as sovereign on July 27 in inscriptions in N.-W. and S. Mysore (*see above ; E. C. iii. Ml. 19 ; viii. Tl. 12*). And in W. Mysore on November 4 (*E. C. v. Bl. 56*). Another record of his during the year is in Trichinopoly District (*V. R. iii. Trich. 229 ; 25 of 1913. See also E. R. 1904–5, p. 57*). Another in Chingleput District (*V. R. i. Chin. 528, 888 ; 297 of 1910 ; 668 of 1904*). Another in Mysore in September. (*E. C. viii. Tl. 126.*)

Dēva Rāya I was apparently ruling in Chittoor District for his brother Bukka II in May–June, and on August 5, 1405. (*313, 320 of 1922.*)

On January 1, 1405 Pedda Kōmaṭi Vēma Reḍḍi of Koṇḍavīḍu gave land to a temple.

(*V. R. ii. Guntur, 604–A.*)

A.D. 1406. Bukka II of Vijayanagar reigning in Tanjore District on February 26 (*217 of 1917*). And at Conjevaram on March 26 (*12 of 1893 ; E. I. vi. 329*). And in S. Mysore on May 20 (*E. C. iii. Md. 28*). And in N. Arcot in May or June (*V. R. i. N. Arcot 594 ; 351 of 887*). And in S. Arcot on August 17 (*370 of 1917*). And at other times of the year in South Kanara (*V. R. ii. S. Kan. 116 ; 41 of 1901*). And in Chingleput (*V. R. i. Chin. 171, 172, 308 ; 57, 58 of 1909 ; 12 of 1893*). And in Kurnool. (*V. R. Kurn. 184.*)

Deva-Rāya I, brother of king Bukka, ruling in Chittoor District on April 14 and 19, 1406.

(*319, 321 of 1922.*)

Bukka II died some time between August and November 1406. And his successor, his younger brother Dēva Rāya I, was crowned king of Vijayanagar on November 5. [The other brother Virūpāksha is not heard of again.] (*E. I. xv. 8, the Anbil grant ; E. C. v. Hn. 133 ; I. A. 1909, p. 91 ; V. R. i. Cuddapah 159 ; 345 of 1905 ; I. A. xxiv. p. 204*). There is a record of king Dēva Rāya I in E. Mysore whose date = November 25, 1406. (*E. C. x. Kl. 94.*)

The *Arch. Ann. Rep.* Calcutta for 1905–6, p. 169, mentions king Dēva Rāya I's son Harihara III as governing the country on the bank of the Bhavānī river, Coimbatore District.

The Koṇḍavīḍu Reḍḍi chief Mallaya, son of Śrīgiri, son of Pina Kōmaṭi, granted to a Brahman the hereditary right of priesthood in this year. (*V. R. ii. Nellore 321, a C.P. grant.*)

Shortly after Dēva Rāya came to the throne a Bēḍar chief in W. Mysore gave trouble. He 'slaughtered people all over the country, carrying off prisoners and causing great disturbances and famine.' The king ordered his viceroy in the Āraga tract, Vīranna son of Bommanna, to quell the rising, and this gave rise to a battle. The revolt, or whatever it was, was crushed.

(*E. I. xv. 14.*)

[Shortly after his coronation Dēva Rāya was induced by the representations of a certain Brahman to send to Muḍkal and bring to his palace from there a beautiful girl, the daughter of a farmer, for his harem. This involving an expedition into enemy territory he sent a body of 5,000 cavalry for the purpose. Hearing of this, and exasperated by several years delay in paying the arranged tribute to him, Sultan Firoz Bāhmanī in the winter of 1406 moved in great force towards Vijayanagar and attacked the city. Desultory fighting occurred in the suburbs, and the Sultan was compelled to withdraw his force a short distance. The country around was plundered and wasted by his army. Then he took Bankapūr and threatened Adoni. Dēva Rāya, reduced to great straits, bought of the Sultan peace by presenting him with his own daughter as a bride. Firoz accepted the bride, made peace, visited Vijayanagar in person and was received with honour in the Hindu capital. The farmer's daughter was taken by Firoz and married to his eldest son Hasan Khān.

(For details as given by Firishtah see '*A Forgotten Empire*' *p. 57 f.*)

A.D. 1407. Dēva Rāya I of Vijayanagar reigning in Anantapur District on May 21, and in Kurnool (*401 of 1928 ; V.R. ii, Kurn. 252*). And in Mysore (*Mys. A.A.R. 1923, p. 72 ; E.C. viii, Tl. 122, 131 ; xii, Si. 101 ; ix, Dv. 32*). And in S. Arcot.

(*V.R. i. S. Arcot, 800 ; 397 of 1909.*)

'Bhūpati-Rāya,' *i.e.* Bukka III, son of Dēva Rāya I, ruling in N. Arcot.

(*V.R. i, N. Arcot, 735 ; 75 of 1908.*)

Another son of Dēva Rāya I, Rāmachandra ruled in S. Mysore.

(*E.C. ix, Kn. 2 ; I.-A. 1909, p. 91.*)

A chief named Viśvēśvara, claiming to be of Chāḷukya descent, built a hall at a temple in Vizagapatam District. (*V.R. iii, Vizag. 28 ; 216 of 1899.*)

A.D. 1408. Dēva-Rāya I of Vijayanagar reigning in Mysore on August 7 and at other times (*E.C. x, Mb. 175 ; viii, Sb. 107, 261 ; ix, Bn. 122 ; vi, Kp. 26*). And in Chingleput District on October 29 (*486 of 1920*). And in Coimbatore District (*V.R. i, Coim. 344 ; 19 of 1910*). And in S. Kanara. (*V.R. ii, S. Kan. 241.*)

In E. Mysore an inscription mentions a gift made 'for the merit of Harihara Rāya'—probably Harihara III son of king Dēva-Rāya I. (*E.C. x, Gd. 59.*)

Gift of lands to a temple in Nellore District by Malla Reḍḍi III of Koṇḍavīḍu, son of Śrīgiri, who was son of Pina Kōmaṭi, who was son of Malla I, brother of Prōlaya Vēma (*V.R. ii, Nellore 289–292 ; B. and V. C. 502–515*). An inscription at Koṇḍavīḍu mentions Pedda Kōmaṭi Reḍḍi.

(*V.R. ii, Guntur 217 ; 538 of 1909.*)

A.D. 1409. Dēva-Rāya I of Vijayanagar reigning in Cuddapah District (*V.R. i, Cudd. 551; 467 of 1906*). And in Nellore District (*V. R. ii, Nell. 41, 193 ; B. and V. C. 414*). And in N.

Arcot (*V. R. i, N. Arcot 403; 248 of 1909*) where his son Vijaya Bhūpati *alias* Bukka III made a grant. And in Chingleput (*V. R. i, Chin. 1093; 224 of 1912*). And in Bellary (*Ibid. i, Bell. 371*). And in Cuddapah (*Ibid. i, Cudd. 551; 467 of 1906*). And in S. Kanara.

(*V. R. ii, S. Kan. 37.*)

In Tinnevelly District an inscription of 14th year of Māravarman Kulaśēkhara Pāṇḍya whose accession took place in A.D. 1396. (*V. R. iii, Tinn. 331; 528 of 1911.*)

In Salem an inscription of Prince Vijaya Bukka III. (*V. R. ii, Salem, 215; 658 of 1905.*)

A.D. 1410. Dēva-Rāya I reigning in Mysore (*E. C. xi, Dg. 23; viii, Sa. 8; ix, Bn. 16; vi, Mg. 85; E. I. xiv, 68*). This last shews that prince Bukka III, 'Vijaya-Bhūpati,' was viceroy at Mulbāgal. An inscription in South Arcot shews that 'Bhūpati-Uḍaiyar' *alias* 'Vīra Bhūpati' was ruling that country. This may be Dēva Rāya's nephew, son of Bukka II, or may be the same as Vijaya Bhūpati (*452 of 1921; 388 of 1922*). Dēva-Rāya was also reigning over South Kanara (*V. R. ii, S. Kan. 92; 81 of 1901*). In N. Arcot 'Bhūpati-Uḍaiyar' was ruling for king Dēva-Rāya I. (*V. R. i, N. Arcot 722; 62 of 1908.*)

That prince Vijaya-Bhūpati, was ruling on March 20, in Chittoor District, near Punganūr (*V. R. i, Chittoor 213; 324 of 1912*). On September 8, he founded an *agrahāra* village for Brahmans near Palmanēr (*ibid. i, Chittoor 174-A; C-P. No. 6 of 1912–13*). This mentions his mother Hēmāmbikā, queen of Dēva Rāya I, who was the daughter of Nūka Bhūpāla, i.e. the Reḍḍi chief Nalla Nunka or Nūka who had married Vēmasāni the sister of Anavēma Reḍḍi of Konḍaviḍu.

On February 21, an inscription of Sūramāmbikā, wife of Pedda Kōmaṭi Vēma Reḍḍi of Konḍavīḍu. It says that that chief 'ruled for a long time, enjoying what was left of the kingdom after enjoyment by the Brahmans' (*V. R. ii, Guntur, 803; 162 of 1899*). The record is on a pillar in front of the temple at Phirangipuram. (*E. I. xi, 313.*)

Kāṭama Vēma Reḍḍi III of Rajahmundry made a gift of a village. The record mentions his former master Kumāragiri of Konḍavīḍu, and his (Kāṭama's) son Kumāragiri.

(*V. R. ii, Kurnool, 598; 84 of 1915.*)

A.D. 1411. Dēva Rāya I of Vijayangar reigning in Mysore (*E. C. viii, Sb. 26*). And in Bellary District. (*V. R. i, Bell. 372; 25 of 1904.*)

Prince Harihara III, son of Dēva Rāya I, mentioned in an inscription in Coimbatore district.

(*V. R. i. Coim. 429; 132 of 1909.*)

Prince Vijaya-Bukka III, son of Dēva Rāya I. A prayer for success to his arms, March 27. Inscription in Mysore (*E. C. ix. Ht. 149*). Another in Salem district calls him 'Vijaya-Rāya.'

(*V. R. ii. Salem 216; 659 of 1905.*)

Prince Vīra-Mallanna, or Mallapa, son of Dēva Rāya I granted a village in N. Mysore, in memory of his mother Mallayavve. (*E. C. xi. Cd. 14.*)

Prince Vīra-Bhūpati, son of Bukka II, ruling in Tanjore for his uncle, king Dēva-Rāya I.

(*V. R. ii. Tan: 742; 52 of 1913.*)

Pedda Kōmaṭi-Vēma of Konḍavīḍu ruling in Guntur district.

(*E. R. 1920, App. A., C.-P., No. 14.*)

Kāṭama-Vēma II of the Reḍḍi family of Rajahmundry, mentioned as minister of the Konḍavīḍu Reḍḍi chief Kumāragiri, whose sister, Mallāmbikā he had married, granted a village in the Kōnadēśa, or Godavari delta. (*V. R. ii. Godav. 17; E. I. iv. 318.*)

A.D. 1412. Dēva Rāya I of Vijayanagar ruling in Mysore on April 25, August 8 and November 5 or a day or two later (*E. C. ix. Kn. 74 ; Ht. 63 ; An. 44 ; viii. Sb. 467*). And in S. Kanara. (*V. R. ii. S. Kan. 138 ; 120 of 1901.*)

Prince Harihara, son of Dēva-Rāya I, ruling in Coimbatore district. (*V. R. i. Coim. 248, 429 ; 596 of 1905 ; 132 of 1909.*)

Pedda Kómaṭi Vēma, Reḍḍi chief of Konḍavīḍu gave away a village in the Vēlanānḍu country. (*V. R. ii. Madras, 196 ; C.-P. 6 of 1908–09.*)

Severe famine in the Dekhan, described by Firishtah, this year. (*I. A. 1923, p. 230.*)

A.D. 1413. Dēva-Rāya I reigning on August 19, in Mysore (*E. C. x. Cl. 81*). And in Guntūr district on March 6. (*798 of 1922.*)

His son Vijaya-Bhūpati, Bukka III, ruling N. Arcot district for his father. (*V. R. i. N. Arcot, 524 ; 568 of 1902.*)

A.D. 1414. Dēva-Rāya I reigning in Mysore on April 7 (*E. C. ix. Cp. 148*). Another in Mysore mentions Baichappa who had been the minister of Harihara I of Vijayanagar and of Bukka I. The text is somewhat obscure. (*E. C. v. Bl. 14.*)

'Kumāra Vijaya-Bhūpati,' i.e. Bukka III son of Dēva Rāya I ruling in Chingleput district for his father (*V. R. i. Chin. 231 ; 345 of 1908*). On September 24, an inscription in Central Mysore seems to shew him ruling there also. (*E. C. xii. Pg. 88.*)

Prince Harihara III ruling in E. Mysore and in Trichinopoly District for his father (*E. C. x. Cl., 95 A ; V. R. iii, Trich., 475 ; C.-P. 27 of 1905*). He was in authority in Coimbatore district, as is shewn by the Śrīrangam C.-P. record. (*E. I. xvi, 222.*)

Kāṭayya Vēma Reḍḍi III of Rajahmundry ruling on October 28, 1414, the tract N. of the Godavari river. He built a hall at the temple at Drākshārāma. (*V. R. ii. Godav., 50, 328 ; 453, 422 of 1893 ; E. I. iv. 328.*)

A.D. 1415. Dēva-Rāya I of Vijayanagar reigning in Mysore (*E. C. xii, Mi., 83 ; viii, Tl., 217 ; iii. Ng., 178*). The date of the first is April 24. Of the last October 4. Also in Nellore district (*V. R. ii. Nell., 106 ; B. and V. C. 350*). And in S. Kanara (*Ibid. S. Kan., 161, 165 ; 143, 147 of 1901*).

Vira Bhūpatī, his nephew, granted land to a temple in Tanjore district. (*V. R. ii. Tan., 1460-B.*)

Vēmaya-Rācha-Vēmana, son of Pedda Kōmaṭi Vēma of the Reḍḍi family of Konḍavīḍu, dug an irrigation channel. (*V. R. ii. Guntur, 766 ; 543 of 1909.*)

In Tinnevelly district an inscription of the 31st year of Parākrama Pānḍya, implying his accession in A.D. 1385–86. [This chief or king is not otherwise known.] (*V. R. iii. Tinn., 337 ; 203 of 1895.*)

A.D. 1416. Dēva-Rāya I of Vijayanagar reigning in Mysore (*E. C. vii, Sk., 252 ; x. Mb., 7 ; vi. Sg., 29 ; viii, Sb., 168 ; ix, Cp., 169*). And in Nellore district, where his son Rāmachandra was ruling as viceroy over the Udayagiri province (*V. R. ii. Nell., 363 ; B. and V. C. 636*). And in S. Kanara (*V. R. ii. S. Kan , 190 ; 172 of 1901*). And in N. Arcot (*Ibid., N. Arcot 406, 251 of 1909.*)

His son Bukka III was ruling, late in the year, in W. Mysore. (*E. C. v. Hn., 18.*)

On January 10, Vīra Bhūpati, nephew of Dēva-Rāya I, was ruling in S. Arcot, and made a gift for the health of the king. (*335 of 1921.*)

Allāda Reḍḍi of the Rājahmundry branch 'B' of the Reḍḍis of Koṇḍaviḍu (*see pedigree and notes*), who had been minister to Kāṭayya Vēma Reḍḍi III of the Rajahmundry branch 'A' and who ruled the Amalāpuram tract, fought against the Koṇḍavīḍu Reḍḍi chief Pedda Kōmaṭi Vēma. An inscription of Allāda's (*V. R. ii. Godavari, 14 ; 503 of 1893*). Another in Narasapur taluk, Kistna district. (*V. R. ii. Kistna, 305, 306 ; 515, 516 of 1893.*)

A servant of Kāṭayya Vēma III of the Rajahmundry Reḍḍi chiefs (branch 'A,') built a hall at the temple at Drākshārāma. (*V. R. ii. Godavari, 349 ; 443 of 1893 ; E. I. iv, 328.*)

A.D. 1417. Dēva-Rāya I of Vijayanagar reigning in Mysore (*E. C. vii, Sk., 37 ; x. Kl., 83 ; iii. Md., 103 ; ix. Cp., 58 ; viii, Tl., 148*). And in Anantapur district (*V. R. i. Anant., 107, 194 ; 526 of 1906*). And in S. Kanara (*Ibid. ii. S. Kan., 96 ; 83 of 1891*). And in Salem district. (*Ibid. ii. Salem, 116 ; 209 of 1911.*)

Allāda Reḍḍi of branch 'B' of the Reḍḍis of Rajahmundry, at Drākshārāma. (*V. R. ii. Godavari, 351 ; 445 of 1893.*)

Vijaya Bukka III, prince of Vijayanagar and son of king Dēva-Rāya I, ruling in E. Mysore. (*E. C. x, Bp., 61.*)

Prince Harihara III, son of Dēva-Raya I is said in an inscription in Chitaldroog taluk, N.-W. Mysore, to have marched to the west and seized the town of Kārēyapaṭnam. (*E. C. xi, Hr., 52.*)

[About this time Firoz Shāh Bāhmanī again waged war on the Hindus and advanced as far as Rajahmundry on the Godavari but he does not seem to have been very successful. The Vēmāvaram C.-P. grant alleges that Allāda Reḍḍi of Rajahmundry defeated 'Alp Khān', a Muhammadan general. About the middle of A.D. 1417 he attacked and laid close siege to Pāngal, a strong fort about 60 miles east of Raichur, but the Hindu defenders made a gallant night attack on the enemy and Firoz was completely defeated and compelled to retire. Such is the account given in the *Burhān-i-Ma'āsir*. Firishta says that the seige lasted two years, and was raised because a pestilence broke out in Firoz's army and he had to abandon his enterprise in consequence. (*I A. 1889, p. 188 ; Firishta, Scott's Edit., i., 90.*)]

An inscription in Chingleput District at Pulippara Kōyil states that the people of the village had complained against unlawful taxation and oppression of them by the temple authorities, and the temple trustees confess that they wronged the inhabitants by the excess of their demands, and make some sort of reparation. (*V.R. i, Chin. 525 ; 294 of 1910 ; E.R., 1911, p. 83. See above s.v. A.D. 1403.*)

A.D. 1418. Dēva Rāya I of Vijayanagar reigning in Mysore (*E.C. viii, Sb. 119 ; ix, An. 4 ; Mys. A.A.R. 1923, p. 91*). And in S. Kanara. (*V.R. ii, S. Kan. 85 ; 22 of 1901.*)

Vijaya-Bukka, i.e. Bukka III, son of Dēva Rāya, ruling in S. Arcot. (*564 of 1902.*)

In Tanjore District an inscription on January 12, 1418, of Kōnērinmaikoṇḍān Vikrama Pāṇḍya in his 17th year. (*See Pāṇḍya Genealogical Table—Notes. V.R. ii, Tan. 3 ; 612 of 1902.*)

A.D. 1419. Dēva Raya I reigning in Mysore on November 18 (*E. C. viii, Sa. 35 ; vi, Mg. 47*). And in Chingleput on March 12, (*148 of 1923. V. R. i, Chin. 838 ; 224 of 1910*). And in Bellary District on November 19. (*283 of 1918.*)

An inscription of one of the Reḍḍi chiefs of Koṇḍāvīḍu who was called 'Vēma, son of Komaṭi.' There were two such. (*E.R. 1920, C-P. 7 of App. A.*)

[When Firoz Bāhmanī retired in confusion from his camp before Pāngal, owing to disease attacking the army (*see above, A.D. 1417*) after his two years' seige of the place he was attacked while retreating, by a strong force despatched by Dēva Rāya I of Vijayanagar, and defeated. The Hindus revenged themselves by a massacre of the Muhammadans, and ravaged the Bāhmani territory, but were driven out eventually by Firoz's brother. (*Firishta, Scott, i. 90.*)]

A.D. 1420. Dēva Rāya I reigning in Mysore in October and on June 12 (*E.C. viii, Sa. 74 ; zii, Ml. 80*). And in S. Kanara. (*V.R. ii, S. Kan. 178 ; 160 of 1901.*)

Vīra-Bhūpati, son of Prince Bukka II of Vijayanagar, ruling in Tanjore District. (*V.R. ii. Tan. 546 ; 653 of 1902.*)

[About this time the family of the Reḍḍis of Koṇḍavīḍu disappears from history. Koṇḍaviḍu fell into the hands of the Gajapati king of Orissa, and remained a possession of the Orissa kings till 1516 when it was captured by Krishṇadēva Rāya of Vijayanagar. (*E.I. viii. 8*).

A.D. 1421. Dēvā Rāya I reigning in Mysore (*E.C. viii, Sb. 118, 120 ; Tl. 144*). And in Pudukoṭṭai State (*V.R. iii, Pudu. 180 ; 158 of 1907*). And in Chingleput. (*Ibid. i, Chin. 780 ; 355 of 1908.*)

Prince Mallappa of Vijayanagar, son of Dēva Rāya I, governing in E. Mysore for his father. (*E.C. ix, An. 86.*)

In 1420 or 1421 Nicolo Conti visited Vijayanagar and has left us a graphic account of the grandeur of the city, which is well worth study. (*' A Forgotten Empire,' p. 81.*)

A.D. 1422. Dēva Rāya I of Vijayanagar died on some day before August 3, 1422. On August 2, his son, Prince Harihara, granted a village as an *agrahāra* to Brahmans ' in order that Dēva Rāya Mahārāja might attain to the world of merit.' (*E.C. iv, Gu., 24 ; Ch. 159 ; E.I. xv. 14.*)

These two inscriptions bear the same date, and give the same information. They may both refer to the gift of one village, or the prince may have dedicated two villages on the same day. Dēva Rāya I was succeeded by his son Vijaya-Bukka, or Bukka III, who had a very short reign.

Bukka III was ruling in Mysore early in 1422. The inscription referred to calls him ' Vijaya-Mahārāya '—a title which does not necessarily imply that his father was dead (*E. C. x. Sd., 1*). He seems to have been reigning as king on August 17 and on September 21 (*E. C. ix. An., 79 ; vii. Sk., 93*). The latter record in W. Mysore gives him full royal titles as sovereign. Also on October 14 (*E. C. x. Kl., 178 ; see also ibid. viii. Sb., 461*). He was reigning also in Kurnool District. (*V. R. ii. Kurnool, 348 ; 255 of 1905.*)

Another inscription of prince Harihara III in Mysore. (*E. C. iv. Ch., 144.*)

Inscriptions of Reḍḍi chiefs of Rajahmundry in Godavari District. (*V. R. ii. Godav. 11, 15; 500, 504 of 1893*). Annavota was ruling in Narasapur Taluk. (*Ibid. ii. Kistna 304 ; 514 of 1893.*)

In Ramnad Jaṭāvarman Vikrama Pāṇḍya was ruling in his 22nd year on December 16. His accession was in 1401. (*V. R. ii. Ramnad, 262 ; 124 of 1908 ; E. I. xi. 139.*)

In Vizagapatam District an inscription mentions a chief Nrisimha, said to be of Chāḷukya descent. He married Vīramā. (*V. R. iii. Vizag. 30, 31 ; 218, 219 of 1899.*)

The inscription at Tenkāśi reported on in the *Travancore Arch. Sur. I*, p. 44, shews that Arikēśari Parākrama Pāṇḍya began to rule in that country in June–July 1422. He is spoken of as being ' born in (the asterism) Mrigaśiras.' He lived till A.D. 1463–64. There are a number of inscriptions of his time existing. He has other names—' Mānābharaṇa,' ' Mānakavacha,' ' Mānabhūsha.' He is perhaps the Mānābhūsha who is said to have been defeated by the Tuḷuva Narasa Nāyaka in the period when the latter was serving under Śāḷuva Narasimha, then minister to the king at Vijayanagar, before the fall of the first dynasty. (*T. A. S. I. 44, 95, 126 ; 514 of 1909 ; 172, 178, 188, 199 of 1895 ; E. R. 1905, p. 56 ; 1906, p. 72 ; 1910, p. 100 ; 1918, p. 158.*)

[Firoz Shāh Bāhmanī died, so far as can be gathered from Firishta's history, on September 24, 1422, and was succeeded by his brother Ahmad Shah I, who ousted the rightful heir, Firoz's eldest son Hasan. He at once made preparations for an attack on Vijayanagar and on the Hindus generally. The account of his doings in the *Burhān-i-Ma'āsir* is rather confused. Firishta's narrative is clearer, and is here shortly summarized. Hearing of Ahmad Shah's activity Bukka Rāya III[1] obtained help from Warangal and the combined armies encamped on the bank of the Tungabhadra. The Bāhmanī army encamped, facing them, on the north bank. The Warangal troops withdrew and deserted their allies. Some Muhammadan leaders crossed the river at night and attacked Bukka-Rāya's own camp, where the king was asleep. Utterly surprised he took refuge in a thick plantation of sugarcane. He had some interesting experiences as he was quite alone and undressed, and passed unrecognized by his own soldiers; but at last he made himself known to some officers, and then taking command withdrew his whole force to the capital. Ahmad Shāh then crossed the river with his entire army, and leaving Vijayanagar to itself spread himself over the country, slaughtering the inhabitants and desolating the villages.

Firishta is quite clear as to Ahmad's conduct. He says that whereas the former Shāh Muhammad had promised to spare the lives of the innocent when he was at war Shāh Ahmad 'overran the open country, and wherever he came put to death men, women and children. . . . . . Laying aside all humanity, whenever the number slain amounted to 20,000 he halted three days and made a festival in celebration of his bloody work. He broke down the idol temples and destroyed the colleges of Brahmans.'

Afterwards Ahmad Shāh marched to Vijayanagar and besieged it so straitly that Bukka Rāya was compelled to sue for peace. Terms were arranged, based on payment of heavy tribute, and the king's son conveyed this to the Shāh's camp. The Hindu prince was received honourably and the Bāhmani invaders returned to their own country. (*Scott's 'Firishta' I, p. 99.*)]

A great famine this year in the Dekhan. (*ibid. p. 102.*)

Some inscriptions in Madura and Tinnevelly Districts of a Pāṇḍya ruler named 'Māravarman-Kōnērinmaikoṇḍān-Kaliyugarāman-Tirunelvēlipperumāḷ-Vīra-Pāṇḍya,' shew that his accession took place in A.D. 1422–23, and as that is the year of accession of Arikēsari-Parākrama-Pāṇḍya, (*above*) it is reasonble to suppose that the two may have been the same.

(*86 of 1905 ; 172, 178 of 1895.*)

A.D. 1423. Bukka Rāya III of Vijayanagar seems to have died this year, after a very short reign of a few months. He was succeeded by his son Dēva Rāya II, who had the titles 'Gajabēnṭekāra', 'Prauḍha Pratāpa', and 'Vijaya-Rāya'.

There are two inscriptions of Dēva-Rāya II, in which the week-day is wrongly given but the other details afford the dates February 10 and 25, 1423. He may, on those days, have been king. He certainly was heir to the throne. (*E. C. viii., Tl, 14 ; Sb, 565.*)

Dēva-Rāya II had some Muhammadan subjects, amongst them his servant Āhmad Khān.

(*V. R. i, Bellary 356 ; 18 of 1904.*)

A.D. 1424. Dēva-Rāya II reigning in N. Arcot. The Satyamangalam C.-P. grant, whose date is June 26, 1424, and who calls the king a 'Suratrāṇa' (sultan) says that he had a brother called Prauḍha Pratapa Dēva-Rāya'. [There has been much discussion as to whether there were

[1] Firishta calls the Vijayanagar king, 'Dewul Roy,' for Dēva-Rāya, in error. It is almost certain that Bukka III was the hero of the episode referred to, though it may have been his son Dēva-Rāya II.

two brothers, each called 'Dēva-Rāya'; or whether there was only one actual Dēva-Raya, i.e. the king, and a brother Srīgirindra who was also styled 'Dēva-Rāya', that being in his case a complimentary title. I am inclined to the latter view, and have framed my notes on the history of the times accordingly.] (*V. R. i. N. Arcot 564 ; E. R. 1890, p .2 ; E. I. iii. 35. See also V. R. i. Chingleput 885 ; 665 of 1904 ; and the late T. A. Gopinatha Rao in E. I. xv. 16.*)

Dēva Rāya II reigning in S. Kanara (*V. R. ii, S. Kan. 82, 197,198, 298 ; 25, 179, 180 of 1901.*)

Prince Śrīgirīndra brother of Dēva Rāya II ruling a tract in N. Arcot on November 3. (*V. R. ii, Madras, 189, l. N. Arcot 625, E. I. viii. 306.*)

An inscription of A.D 1424–25 in Tanjore records a grant made to a temple by Vijaya-Rāya. This may refer to Dēva-Rāya II, the title 'Vijaya' being honorific, or to a gift made in an earlier year by Bukka III. (*V. R. ii, Tan. 1460-A.*)

Dēva Rāya II reigning in Chingleput District (*V. R. i. Chin. 961 ; 367 of 1911*). And in N. Mysore on November 6. (*E. C. xi, Dg. 29.*)

Firishta states that in this year 1424–25 Āhmad Shāh Bāhmani marched against Warangal in revenge for its king having allied himself with Vijayanagar. He halted at Golkonda and sent forward his general to Warangal, who succeeded in gaining possession of the fortress and killing its ruler, taking immense treasures back with him. The sultan then retired to Gulbarga. (*Scott's Edit., p. 103.*)

A.D. 1425. Dēva Rāya II reigning in Mysore (*E. C, viii, Tl, 163 ; ix, Kn, 59 ; Dv, 8i.*). The date of the last November 25, 1425, is accurate in all details.

In Godavari District a gift made 'for the merit of' Akāda Reḍḍi of Rajahmundry branch 'B' in the genealogical table. (*V. R. ii, Godav. 61 ; 497 of 1983,*)

Dēva Rāya II reigning in Tanjore District (*V. R. ii, Tan. 907 ; 519 of 1904*). And in Cuddapah. (*Ibid. i. Cudd. 597 ; 496 of 1906.*)

Prince Śrīgirīndra brother of Dēva Rāya II, inscription in N. Arcot (*V. R. i. N. Arcot, 723; 63 of 1918*). An inscription in S. Mysore says that Prince 'Pārvati', i.e. Śrīgiri, jumped a ditch on his horse when out boar-hunting. (*E. C. iv, Ch. 195.*)

A.D. 1426. Dēva Raya II reigning in S. Arcot on April 6 (*133 of 1919*). And in Bellary (*V. R. i, Bell. 399 ; 32 of 1889*). And in Mysore (*E. C. iii, Tn. 55 : ix, cp. 162 ; Ht. 114 ; x. Bp. 83. xii, Tm. 11*). And in N. Arcot (*V. R. i, N. Arcot, 602 ; 49 of 1887*). [The date of this last is a sound one : February 27, 1426.] (*Ibid. i. N. Arcot 614-A.*) And in S. Kanara (*V. R. ii, S. Kan. 227 ; 86 of 1901*). And in Chingleput (*V. R. i, Chin. 684 ; 319 of 1911*). And in Nellore (*V. R. ii, Nell. 797 ; B. and V. C. 1391*). He built a Jain temple at Hampe, the capital (*S. I. I. i. 160*). In this last he is called '*Abhinava*-Vīra-Dēva-Rāya', the first portion of the name shewing him to have been then a young man.

Prince Vīra-Pārvati, *alias* Śrīgirīndra, gave a grant in S. Mysore. (*E. C. iv, ch, 105.*)

A temple was built in 1426 in Nellore District by Śāluva Śamburāya. (*See Pedigree of a branch of the Śāluva family. Below. V. R.ii, Nell. 606 : B and V. C. iii., pp. 1184, 1202.*)

A.D. 1427. Dēva-Rāya II of Vijayanagar reigning in Chingleput District. An inscription at Tiruvoṟṟiyūr gives an interesting list of taxes enforceable (*V. R. i. Chin. 829, 1095, 1190 ; 215 of 1910 ; 226 of 1912*). Also reigning in Mysore (*E. C. ix. An. 64 ; vi. Kp. 27*). And in Chittoor District (*V. R. i. Chitt. 276, 350 ; 389 of 1911 ; 479 of 1905*). And in Salem District (*V. R. ii. Salem,*

223 ; 666 of 1905) where mention is made of his minister Lakkanna. And in Trichinopoly District (*E. I. xvii. 110*). This last record shews that the old names of districts still persisted in use. The north bank of the Kāvēri river was in the 'Rājarāja-vaḷanāḍu,' while the south bank belonged to the 'Rājagambhīra-vaḷanāḍu'.

A.D. 1428. Dēva Rāya II reigning in Nellore District (*V. R. ii. Nell. 83, 571–A ; B. and V. C. 319*). And in Mysore, where a grant was made by the minister Lakkanna (*E. C. x. Kl. 104*). And in S. Kanara. (*V. R. ii. S. Kan. 291 ; 104 of 1901.*)

The Triplicane plates mention, as ruling, 'Pratāpa Dēva Rāya' brother of king Devā-Rāya II. I have already given my opinion that this was a name applied to Śrīgirīndra. (*E. I. xiii. 1.*)

In part of Vizagapatam District a local chief Nrisimha, descended from the ancient Chāḷukya family was ruling. (*V. R. iii. Vizag. 26 ; 214 of 1899.*)

Dēva Rāya II, reigning in S. Arcot, remedied a serious wrong, according to an inscription gratefully engraved on the wall of the temple at Chidambaram. His official had been fleecing the people, and enforcing the payment of unjust taxes demanded by the temple-officials and others.[1] The hardship and suffering was felt so severely that the people deserted their homes and worship in the temple ceased. The king, being appealed to, after enquiry ordered restoration to be made. It is significant that this condemnation of the conduct of the temple authorities was actually engraved on the temple wall. (*V. R. i. S. Arcot, 168 ; 376 of 1913.*)

A.D. 1429. Dēva Rāya II reigning in Nellore (*V. R. ii. Nell. 23-A, 107 ; B. and V. C. 352*). And in Mysore (*E. C. iv. Yl. 69 ; viii. Sb. 24 ; ix. An. 1 ; xii. Kg. 18*). The date of the last = March 6, 1429. He was also reigning in S. Arcot (*V. R. i. S. Arcot, 433 ; 72 of 1903*). And in Cuddapah (*V. R. i. Cudd. 626*). And in S. Kanara, where there is an inscription of this year at Muḍabidri (*V. R. ii. S. Kan. 103, 108 ; 28, 133 of 1901*). And in Tanjore (*V. R. ii. Tan. 1507 ; 255 of 1904*). And in Trichinopoly (*V. R. iii. Trich. 234 ; 30 of 1913*). This gives a long list of taxes imposed. And in N. Arcot. (*270 of 1921.*)

[There seems to have been a great deal of local oppression of the people at this period, as is shewn by the following two inscriptions, one in Tanjore District, and one in South Arcot.]

(i) On a temple wall at Tiruvaigāvūr, Tanjore, an inscription of date = October 29, 1429 declares that 'since the time of the Hoyśalas,' for about a century the people had been paying taxes to the temple-authorities but not to the crown. The temple-authorities seem to have leased out the right to collect taxes—'collections were not made by any one single person'—and there was such grinding tyranny and oppression that 'the whole district was brought to ruin.' At last, naturally after a great deal of negotiation, the people got the list of admittedly payable taxes fixed, and the result was engraved on the temple wall. A long list of taxes is given. There was a poll-tax on every one, a trade-tax on every trade, a house-tax on every house and every shed, in addition to land-taxes and tolls. (*V. R. ii. Tanjore, 1088 ; 59 of 1914 ; E. R. 1915, pp. 106–108.*)

(ii) April 24, 1429. Inscription in S. Arcot, Dēva-Raya II reigning. The people there had suffered so much at the hands of the king's tax-collectors that a compact was entered into between

[1] Mr. Sewell is here confounding issues. The question is one of confusion of rights between temple and public lands. The temples suffered by official appropriation or misappropriation resulting from the confusion of invasion, or enemy occupation. This was enquired into and set right. For the correct exposition of this and matters noted under 1429, see my *Sir W. Meyer Lectures* in the Press.—*Editor.*

the rival *Valangai* and *Iḍangai* castes that these bodies would chastise any man who assisted a collector or helped him with his accounts. Moreover no shelter was ever to be given to a collector; and if any member of those castes broke this agreement in any way he should be stabbed and killed.

(*92 of 1918, see also 216 of 1917.*)

A.D. 1430. Dēva-Rāya II of Vijayanagar reigning in Mysore. He had, so says the first of these records, 10,000 Musalman cavalry in his army—probably from the north with a certain number of mercenaries from Bāhmanī territory (*E. C. iii, Sr., 15 ; x. Bp., 72 ; xi, Cd., 29*)—which mentions Dēva-Rāya's elder sister as having married Śāḷuva Tippa, and thus proves the growing importance of the Sāḷuva family (*E. C. viii, Sk., 40*). He was also reigning in N. Arcot (*V. R. i, N. Arcot 695 ; 87 of 1908*). And in S. Kanara (*V. R. ii, S. Kan., 3, 73, 137, 166 ; 119, 148 of 1901*). And in Chingleput (*207 of 1922*). And in Cuddapah (*V. R. i. Cudd. 139*). And in Salem.

(*V. R. ii. Salem, 88 ; 193 of 1910.*)

This year, or perhaps 1429, is the probable year of accession of the Gajapati king of Orissa Kapilēndra or Kapilēśvara, who seized the throne and established a new dynasty fixing his capital at Cuttack. When fully established, his dominions extended as far south as the river Krishna.

(*V. R. i, Ganjam 162, 191, 195 ; and ii, Kistna, 60 ; 284, 313, 317 of 1896 ; 308 of 1892.*)

In Tinnevelly this year began to rule Aḷagan-Perumaḷ-Kumāra-Kulaśēkhara Pāṇḍya (*see Pāṇḍya genealogical table, notes*). [He was ruling some part of the south at the same time as Arikē-śari Parākrama Pāṇḍya was ruling another part. These matters must be worked out hereafter, defining the separate divisions of the country governed by the Pāṇḍyas.] Kulaśēkhara had a son Parākrama who built the *Gōpura* of a temple at Tenkāśi. (*T. A. S. i, 53 ; 278 of 1908 ; 198 of 1895.*)

A.D. 1431. Dēva-Rāya II reigning in Mysore (*E. C. ix, Bn., 127 ; viii. Nr., 1 ; Sa., 51 ; x. Mb., 96 ; Mr., 3*). In the last of these the Śāḷuva chief Gōpa, son of Tippa, was locally ruling (*vii. Sh. 71, iii, Sr. 7, whose date = October 7, 1431*). And in S. Kanara at Barakūr.

(*V. R. ii. S. Kan., 139, 191 ; 121, 173 of 1901.*)

The Reḍḍi chief of Rajahmundry, Allāda-Doḍḍa, granted a village.

(*V. R. ii. Godavari 359 ; E. R. v. 53.*)

The Jain colossus of Gōmata at Kārkaḷa was set up in this year by Vīra Pāṇḍya, chief of Kaḷasa, son of Bhairava. His family was allied to the Sāntara family of Humcha.

(*E. I. viii 122 ; V. R. ii. S. Kan., 208 ; 63 of 1901 ; I. A. ii. 353 ; E. I. vii, 109.*)

A.D. 1432. Dēva-Rāya II reigning in S.-E. Mysore, where an inscription records a local raid, highway robbery, and a death (*E. C. ix, Cp., 149*) ; more disturbances and fighting in N.-W. Mysore (*E. C. viii, Tl., 23*). Other inscriptions of the year (*E. C. x. Gd., 17 ; ix, D.-B. 62 ; viii, Sb., 497 ; v, Cn., 241 ; vii. Ci., 73 bis*). And in Nellore district (*V. R. ii. Nell., 80*). And in Anantapur district (*765 of 1917*). And in N. Arcot (*V. R. i. N. Arcot, 379 ; 95 of 1887*). This is dated October 24, 1432.

The Jain colossus at Kārkaḷa was dedicated and consecrated on February 13, this year.

(*above s. v. A.D. 1431*)

A.D. 1433. Dēva-Rāya II reigning in Mysore (*E. C. ix. An., 35 ; Ht., 155*). And in Bellary district (*V. R. i. Bell., 359, 377 ; 21 of 1904*). And in Chingleput (*200 of 1916*). And in Trichinopoly on June 19 (*44 of 1920*). And in Cuddapah (*V. R. i. Cudd., 820 ; 606 of 1907*). And in S. Kanara (*V. R. ii. S. Kan., 98, 195 ; 56, 177 of 1901*). And in Tanjore.

(*V. R. ii. Tan., 712 ; 424 of 1912.*)

In Rāmnād Māravarman Vīra Pāṇḍya was ruling in his 12th year. He began to rule, therefore, in 1422–23. (*V. R. ii. Ram.*, *138 ; 86 of 1905.*)

A.D. 1434. An inscription of date = June 7, 1434 shews the Reḍḍi chief Allāda, or Allaya, Doḍḍa ruling at Rajahmundry. (*E. I. xiii, 237.*)

Dēva Rāya II reigning in Trichinopoly district (*V. R. iii, Trich.*, *449, 450 ; 3, 5 of 1888 ; C.-P. 19, 20 of 1905–6*). He was reigning in Mysore (*E. C. viii. Sb.*, *126 ; xi. Mk.*, *32*). The date of the last, mentioning a solar eclipse is correct and = June 7, 1434. Also in Cuddapah (*V. R. i. Cudd.*, *642*). And in Chingleput. (*202 of 1923.*)

Mallāmbikā, wife of the Rajahmundry Reḍḍi chief Kaṭayya-Vēma III, gave a grant of land to the temple at Bhīmavaram. (*V. R. ii, Godavari, 20 ; 461 of 1893.*)

A.D. 1435. [On February 27, this year Āhmad Shāh Bāhmanī died, and was succeeded by his son Alāu-d-din II. The latter's younger brother Muhammad Khān rebelled but was pacified and forgiven, and was given the government of a province in Telingana which included Raichūr and Warangal (*I. A.*, *1899, p. 238*). Dēva Rāya II sent an expedition to attempt the capture of the town of Muḍkal. It was successful for a time and the place was occupied ; but when Alāu-d-din attacked in turn and besieged the Hindus in Muḍkal they were compelled to submit and make terms, promising heavy tribute as indemnity.] Dēva Rāya was reigning in Chittoor District. (*V. R. i, Chitt. 132, 325; 193 of 1903; 454 of 1905.*)

A.D. 1436. Dēva Rāya II reigning in S. Kanara (*V. R. ii, S. Kan. 22, 26, 230 ; 109 of 1901*). And in South Arcot (*V. R. i, S. Arcot, 271; 153 of 1902*). And in Chingleput (*V. R. i, Chin. 84; 272 of 1912*). And in Mysore (*E. C. viii, Sb. 490*). He was also ruling Ānegundi fortress, north of the Tungabhadra river immediately opposite the city of Vijayanagar. (*V. R. i, Bell, p. 301, Ānegundi inscriptions b.*)

A.D. 1437. Dēva Rāya II reigning in Mysore (*E. C. iii, Nj, 109; viii, Tl, 175 ; ix. Cp, 147 : xii Tp, 137 ; Mys. A. A. R. 1921. p. 29*). And in N. Arcot (*V. R. i, N. Arcot 525 ; 569 of 1902*). And in S. Kanara (*V. R. ii, S. Kan. 95; 85 of 1901*). And in Cuddapah District (*V. R. i, Cudd. 637,*)

In Travancore the reigning king was Vīra-Rāma-Mārthāṇḍavarman. (*T. A. S. i, p. 299. See Kēraḷa kings' pedigree, notes.*)

A.D. 1438. Dēva-Rāya II reigning in Rāmnad, when a gift was made for the merit of his minister Lakkanna's brother Mādanna. (*V. R. ii, Ram. 205; 141 of 1903.*)

A.D. 1439. Dēva-Rāya II, called Gajabeṭegāra,' reigning in S. Kanara (*V. R. ii, S. Kan. 141, 146; 123, 128 of 1901*). His servant Āhmad Khān dug a well this year. (*V. R. i, Bell. 356; 18 of 1904.*)

In Travancore Vīra-Rāma-Mārthāṇḍa-Varman was reigning. (*V. R. iii, Trav. 108 T. A. S. i. 299.*)

In Tinnevelly Vīra Pāṇḍya was ruling in his 19th year. This is the same as the Vīra Pāṇḍya noted above in A.D. 1422, and identical with Arikēśari-Parākrama-Pāṇḍya, whose accession was in 1422 (*V. R.i ii, Tinn. 325; 178 of 1895*). Another local ruler in Tinnevelly District was the 'Chēra, Udaya-Mārttāṇḍa' perhaps the same as Rāma-Mārttāṇḍa ruling this year in Travancore. (*V. R. iii, Tinn. 124-A.*)

A.D. 1440. Dēvā Rāya II reigning in Mysore, with Vīra Pāṇḍya ruling the Kaḷasa country (*above* A.D. *1431 ; E. C. vi, Mg. 42*). A victory is mentioned gained by his general Mādanna (*E. C. x, Mb. 101*). A local leader in E. Mysore made a gift to the god Chokkanātha in order that king Dēva Rāya 'might be seated on the throne' (*E. C. ix, Bn. 8*). He was also reigning in Trichinopoly District, where a gift was made 'for the merit of the king's general Lakkanna,' 'lord of the Southern Ocean' (*V. R. iii, Trich. 230 ; 26 of 1913*). And in Coimbatore (*V. R. i, Coim. 113 ; 583 of 1903*). And in Cuddapah (*V. R. i, Cudd. 317*). Lakkanna was also in power in Tanjore where he was governing for King Dēva Rāya.

(*V. R. ii. Tanjore 945, 946; 566, 567 of 1904 ; E. R. 1904-5, p. 57.* For a note about him in power in Madura see *I. A. January 1914.*)

A.D. 1441. Dēva Rāya II reigning in Mysore on June 19, 1441 (*E. C. viii, Sa. 68*). And in Kurnool (*V. R. ii, Kurn. 361; 269 of 1905*). And in Coimbatore (*V. R. i, Coim. 111; 581 of 1903*). And in Salem District (*Ibid. ii, Salem 91 ; 196 of 1910*). And in S. Kanara (*V. R. ii, S. Kan. 10*). And in N. Arcot. (*V. R. i, N. Arcot 654; 694 of 1904.*)

In Tinnevelly a record of Vīra Paṇḍya in his twentieth year ; i.e., Arikēsari Parākrama Paṇḍya whose accession was in 1422–23. (*Above s. v. 1439. V. R. iii, Tinn. 319; 172 of 1895.*)

A.D. 1442. Dēva Rāya II reigning in Mysore (*E. C. viii. Sb, 489 ; vii. Sk, 240*). The date of the latter is October 15, 1442. Also in N. Arcot, where Sāḷuva Tippaya made over some taxes to a temple (*V. R. i. N. Arcot, 663 ; 703 of 1904*). And in Cuddapah.

(*V. R. i. Cudd. 41.*)

In the Godavari district a local ruler Ayyappa Māharāja of the Vatsa family is mentioned.

(*V. R. ii. Godav. 59 ; 495 of 1893.*)

[About this time, according to Abdul Razzak's chronicle, king Dēva-Raya took great pains for better organization of his army. He entertained Musalman soldiers, gave their leaders jaghirs, erected a mosque for them at the capital, and commanded that they be allowed to practise their religion undisturbed, etc. His army consisted of 2,000 Musalman and 60,000 Hindu archers, 80,000 horse, and 200,000 foot.

Abdul Razzak was at Calicut from November 1442 to April 1443, and while he was there king Dēva-Rāya's brother, probably Śrīgirīndra made a desperate attempt to gain the throne. He carried out a carefully arranged plan whereby numbers of the king's officers and guards were privately murdered in a hall in the palace at Vijayanagar, and then he went to the king in person and tried to induce him to enter the same hall. On Dēva Rāya's refusal the prince stabbed him and believing him dead ascended a portico and proclaimed himself king, saying that his brother had been slain. Dēva Rāya however recovered, and, by way of his harem, went to the portico and cried out to the people that he was alive. Whereupon the courtiers threw themselves on the traitor-prince and killed him.

(*See 'A Forgotten Empire,' p. 72. Arch. Ann. Rep. Calcutta 1905–6, p. 169.*)

A.D. 1443. Dēva-Rāya II reigning in S. Arcot on November 4.

(*230 of 1916 ; V. R. i. S. Arcot 344 ; 55 of 1905.*)

[Abdul Razzāk, the chronicler, had an interview with king Dēva-Rāya II about December, 1443. To continue shortly his narrative—when Alāu-d-dīn Bāhmanī heard of the abortive attempt on Dēva-Rāya's life he thought it well to attack the Hindu king once more, and made preparations to that end. Dēva Rāya received information of these preparations and at once took the field, sending an army under command of his general Lakkanna into Kulbarga territory. Muḍkal was taken, Raichūr besieged, and the country was devastated as far as Bijapur. The Bāhmanī army under Malik-al-Tijar marched to Raichūr and battle was joined. During the fight Dēva Rāya's eldest son, Mallikhārjuna was wounded, and Malik-al-Tijar was made prisoner by the Hindus. Hard fighting followed, but eventually peace was made. This was earlier than December 1443].

There is an inscription of Dēva-Rāya's general Lakkanna in Tanjore district, in which he is described as 'lord of the southern ocean.' (*V. R. ii. Tan. 894 ; 100 of 1911.*)

Prof. Kielhorn examined three inscriptions of this year, between March 13 and July 28 in the Tinnevelly, Madura, and S. Arcot districts, which shew 'Māravarman-Vīra-Pāṇḍya as locally ruling. (*E. I. ix. 229—' M.'*)

A.D. 1444. Dēva-Rāya II reigning in Trichinopoly (*V. R. iii. Trich. 70 ; 740 of 1909*), and in S. Kanara (*ibid. ii. S. Kan. 7, 15*). And at Drākshārāma, Godavari district (*ibid. ii. Godav. 348 ; 442 of 1893*). And in Mysore (*E. C. x. Bp, 11*). And in Guntur district (*V. R. ii. Gun. 457 ; B. and V. C. 1121*). The details of the date in this last are impossible.

A.D. 1445. Dēva-Rāya II reigning in S. Kanara (*V. R. ii. S. Kan. 75*), and in Mysore on April 22, (*E. C. viii. Tl. 200*), and on May 7. (*Ibid. xii. Tm. 37.*)

In Tinnevelly district is an inscription of the 23rd year of Māravarman Vīra Pāṇḍya, *alias* Arikēśari Parākrama, shewing his accession to have been in 1422. (*422 of 1917.*)

A.D. 1446. Dēva Rāya II reigning on January 2 in Mysore (*E. C. x. Gd. 50*), and on March 10 and 18 in S. Arcot. (*68 of 1918 ; 32 of 1922.*)

Dēva Rāya II died on May 24, 1446. The Śravaṇa-Beḷgoḷa record of this is worded—'In the evil year *Kshaya*, in the wretched second month Vaiśākha, on a miserable Tuesday in the dark fortnight, on the fourteenth day' (*E. C. i. Sr. Bel. 125 ; I. A. xxv. 1896, p. 346*). The accession of his son Mallikhārjuna by queen Ponnalā-dēvī therefore took place on that day. Like his father he received the appellation '*Gaja-veṭṭai-kāra*'—'he who witnessed the elephant hunt.' His minister was Śāḷuva Tirumala or Timmana whose family now rose to great eminence. Tirumala was son of Gunḍa III and brother of Narasimha, who later on usurped the throne.[1]

An inscription in S. Arcot of date = September 30, 1446 states that the king's officials had been forcing the people to give them presents at the beginning of each reign. 'In consequence of this all the ryots were harassed and went away to other places, abandoning their homes. Worship and festivals at the temples ceased. The country became full of disease. All people [that remained] either died or suffered.' The king, being appealed to, put a stop to these extortions. (*476 of 1921 ; E.R. 1905, p. 58.*)

An inscription in Tanjore, whose date = June 29, 1446, names as king 'Pratāpa Dēva-Rāya.' This may refer to Dēva Rāya II, the gift commemorated having been made by one of his officers; or it may refer to Mallikhārjuna who was also so-called. (*V.R. ii. 1356; 35 of 1891; S.I.I. ii. 338.*)

At Kuttālam in Tinnevelly District on April 10, 1446, Vīra-Pāṇḍya was locally ruling. See also in last year (*452 of 1917*). Repairs or additions to the Tenkāśi temple in Tinnevelly District were carried out by Arikēśari-Parākrama. [These two inscriptions help to shew that the two Princes named were one and the same.] (*V.R. iii, Tinn. 343 ; 507 of 1909 ; T.A.S.I. 102.*)

[1] Mr. Sewell has not noted any authority for this statement. There were a number of Tirumalas, two of these being of the family of the Sāḷuvas. One of them was Narasimha's brother; another Pratāpa Deva Rāya's cousin. The minister however seems a different man, son of a chieftain of Nagamangala in Mysore (*E.C. Mys. I. Se. 89, 86 and 133*). The elder brother of Sāḷuva Narasimha is under reference in *E.C.X. Bp. 24* as governor of the locality. The other Tirumala of the Sāḷuva family referred to as Gopa Timma also is under reference, in No. 67 of 1903 and 59 of 1892. See the *A Little Known Chapter of Vijayanagar History*, pp. 22–25.—*Editor.*

[There is said to have been a combined attack on the new king of Vijayanagar early in his reign by the Bāhmani king Muhammad III, and the king of Orissa, Kapilēśvara Gajapati, which was repulsed by Sāḷuva Narasimha. So says the drama *Gangādasa-pratāpa-vilāsa*, but the assertion needs corroboration.] (*'Sources of Vijayanagar History', p. 65.*)

A.D. 1447. Remission of taxes by King Mallikhārjuna in Chingleput District (*102 of 1923*). He was reigning in N. Arcot District. (*435 of 1922*)

Mallikhārjuna reigning in Mysore in April (*E.C. vi, Kp. 32*) ; and on September (*E.C. iii, Ml. 86*), and on August 17 (*E.C. vii, Sk. 239*) and on November 19 (*E.C. iii, Sr. 11 ; xii, Pg. 69*). He was also known as 'Immaḍi-Dēva-Rāya'.

Virūpāksha III, brother of King Mallikhārjuna, was ruling in parts of Mysore. (*E.C. iii, Ml. 121 ; ix, Dv. 38.*)

An inscription of May 16, 1447, (at Śambūr-Vaḍagarai, of Arikēsari-Parākrama-Pāṇḍya, ruling in his 25th year (*see above s.v. A.D. 1422, and below A.D. 1458.*) (*T.A.S.I. pp. 255–256, Nos. B.C.D.*)

There were serious local disturbances in Anantapur District. One chief, with '1000 horse and 100,000 foot' (so says a *vīrakal*), attacked another chief. 500 men were killed. (*33 of 1917.*)

A.D. 1448. Mallikhārjuna reigning in December in Mysore (*E.C. viii, Sb. 473*). And in Chingleput District. (*V.R. i, Chin. 502 ; 133 of 1896.*)

A.D. 1449. Mallikhārjuna reigning in Mysore on February 18, 1449. The date is a sound one. It mentions the death of Dēva-Rāya II (*E.C. viii, Sb. 18*). And in N. Arcot on August 2 (*V.R. i, N. Arcot, 381 ; 97 of 1887 ; S.I.I. i. 110*). And in S. Kanara (*V. R. ii, S. Kan. 163 ; 145 of 1901*). And in Chittoor. (*V.R. i, Chit. 342 ; 471 of 1905.*)

At Tenkāśi in Tinnevelly District, on November 2, 1449, Jaṭilavarman-Parākrama-Pāṇḍya was ruling in his 28th year. He is probably, as already stated, identical with Arikēśari-Parākrama. (*V.R. iii, Tinn. 376 ; 5 of 1912.*)

A.D. 1450. An inscription at Suchindram of the same Parākrama-Pāṇḍya date of which = April 15, 1450. (*T.A.S.I., p. 281, 'y'.*)

Mallikhārjuna reigning in Mysore on October 11, 1450 (*Mys. A.A.R. 1923, p. 77*). And in S. Arcot (*154 of 1919*). And in Chittoor District (*V.R. i, Chit. 341 ; 470 of 1905*). And in Tanjore (*524 of 1920*). And in Bellary, where he is called 'Immaḍi-Prauḍhadēva (*V.R. i, Bell. 374 ; 24 of 1904*). [Some inscriptions shorten 'Immaḍi-Dēva-Rāya' into 'Dēva Rāya,' and cause confusion in so doing, leading some to interpret them as records of his predecessor (*e.g. E.C. viii, Nr. 67 ; See E.R. 1903–4 notes*). Mallikhārjuna was also reigning at Conjevaram. (*645 of 1919.*)

Several records about this time and later mention the powerful nobles of the Sāḷuva family. (*V.R. i, Chittoor, 10–15 ; 249–254 of 1904 ; S.I.I. ii, 117–119.*)

A.D. 1451. Mallikhārjuna of Vijayanagar reigning in Mysore (*E. C. viii. Sb. 566*). And in S. Kanara (*V. R. ii, S. Kan. 104 ; 29 of 1901*). And in N. Arcot (*V. R. i, N. Arcot, 398 ; 67 of 1907*). And in Chingleput (*V. R. i, Chin. 900 ; 680 of 1904*). And in Kurnool (*V. R. ii, Kurn. 601*). A record of date December 13, 1451 shews that cattle-robbery and violence, leading to death, was prevalent in Shimoga taluk, N.-W. Mysore. (*Mys. A. A. R., 1923, p. 86.*)

A.D. 1452. Mallikhārjuna reigning in Tanjore on April 3 (*448 of 1922*). And in S. Kanara (*V. R. ii, S. Kan. 16, 39*). And in Chingleput. (*V. R. i, Chin. 526 ; 295 of 1910.*)

In Tinnevelly District inscriptions of 'Jaṭilavarman-Parākrama-Pāṇḍya' on July 19 and of 'Arikēśari Parākrama-Pāṇḍya' on November 13.

(*V. R. iii, Tinn. 377 ; 6 of 1912 ; E. R. 1922, p. 94 ; 507 of 1917.*)

A.D. 1453. Sāḷuva Tirumalayya or Timma in power in Trichinopoly.

(*V. R. iii, Trich. 392 ; 67 of 1902 ; see also 593, 594 of 1902 and I. A. 1914, p. 13.*)

An inscription in the Madura country shews that in this year a chief of the Bāṇa stock, Urangāvillidāsan-Māvali-Vāṇarāya was ruling at the old Pāṇḍya capital in this year.

(*T. A. S. i, p. 53.*)

This was the accession year of the Pāṇḍya prince Jaṭilavarman Parākrama *alias* Srīvallabha who was 'born in Ārdrā,' or 'Tiruvādirai.'

A.D. 1454. Mallikhārjuna reigning in S. Kanara (*V. R. ii, S. Kan. 11, 25*). And in N.-W. Mysore, where there were more cattle-raids and consequent deaths.

(*E. C. viii, Sb. 167.*)

Jaṭilavarman-Parākrama-Pāṇḍya, *alias* (?) Arikēśari Parākrama ruling at Tenkāśi on November 7 in his 33rd year. (*V. R. iii, Tinn. 378 ; 7 of 1912 ; E. R. 1922, p. 94.*)

A.D. 1455. Mallikhārjuna reigning in Trichinopoly (*V. R. iii, Trich. 710 ; 474 of 1908*). And in N. Arcot (*Ibid. i, N. Arcot 4, 374 ; 383 of 1905 ; 346 of 1912*). And in Mysore.

(*E. C. viii, Nr. 65.*)

An inscription in the Kistna District shews that the Gajapati king of Orissa was then ruling the country about Bezwada and Koṇḍapalle. King Kapilēśvara's officer Rahutarāya or Rautarāya, who had 'defeated two Turushka princes,' gave to a temple at Bezwada a village near Koṇḍapalle.

(*V. R. ii, Kistna, 60 ; I. A. xx, 390.*)

Sāḷuva Tirumala remitted some taxes in Tanjore District, shewing that he was locally ruling there (*V. R. ii, Tan. 1312 ; 73 of 1888 ; S. I. I. ii, p. 109, 117*). Śāḷuva Narasimha, son of Guṇḍa, gave a village near Tirupati in N. Arcot ; he was therefore also ruling locally in that tract.

(*V. R. i, Chit. 14 ; 253 of 1904.*)

Jaṭilavarman-Parākrama-Pāṇḍya was ruling in Tinnevelly on March 24 (*467 of 1917*). Māravarman Vīra Pāṇḍya ruling at Tenkāśi on July 20, 1455 in his 13th year.

(*V. R iii, Tinn. 387 ; 196 of 1895 ; E. I. viii, 282 ; see also V. R. i. S. Arcot, 319 ; 57 of 1903.*)

A.D. 1456. Śāḷuva Tirumala, son of Gōpa or Goppa, made many gifts to the temple at Śrīśailam. (*V. R. ii, Kurn. 489-H.*)

Mallikhārjuna reigning in S. Arcot (*V. R. i. S. Arcot, 383, 479, 732 ; 232 of 1904 ; 26 of 1905 ; 304 of 1910*). The last of these mentions Śāḷuva Narasimha. Mallikhārjuna was also reigning in Chingleput. (*V. R. i, Chin. 366 ; 4 of 1906.*)

A.D. 1457. Mallikhārjuna reigning in Mysore on July 1. (*E. C. iv, Ng. 91.*)

In Ramnad is an inscription, of date = January 16, shewing Māravarman-Vīra Pāṇḍya ruling there in his 14th year. His rule had begun in A.D. 1443 (*V. R. ii, Ramnad, 155 ; 578 of 1902 ; E. I. viii, 283*). Another record of his 14th year on March 12. (*V. R. i. S. Arcot, 319 ; 57 of 1903.*)

Śāḷuva Narasimha was ruling locally in N. Arcot. (*107 of 1921.*)

In S. Kanara a chief Abhinava Pāṇḍya of Humcha is mentioned, who was a Jain by religion and 'belonged to the family of Jinadatta.' (*V. R. ii. S. Kan. 215 ; 70 of 1901.*)

A.D. 1458. Mallikhārjuna reigning in Tanjore District. The inscription calls him 'Prauḍhadēva' (*452 of 1922*). And in Kurnool on February 4 (*V. R. ii. Kurn. 458, 461 ; 22, 25 of 1915*).

And in Mysore on December 2 (*E. C. iii. Sr. 89, 133 ; v. Hn. 16*). And in Pudukoṭṭah State (*V. R. iii. Puduk. 324 ; 281 of 1914*). And in S. Kanara.

(*V. R. ii. S. Kan. 143, 162 ; 125, 144 of 1901.*)

At Tirupati in Chittoor District is an inscription mentioning 'Ahōbala-rāja Kampaya Mahārāja'; evidently a chief of distinction but not yet identified.

(*V. R. i. Chit. 9–H ; 60 of 1889.*)

An inscription at Śāmbūr-Vaḍagarai in Travancore mentions Parakrāma, *alias* Śrīvallabha Pāṇḍya, nephew of Arikēśari Parākrama Pāṇḍya, ruling in his 5th year on September 29, 1458; shewing his accession to have been in the year following September 29, 1453.

(*T. A. S. I. 263–' I' ; compare V. R. iii. Trav. 132.*)

Alāu-d-dīn Bāhmanī died in H. 862, says Firishta, i.e. in the year beginning in November 1457, and was succeeded by Humāyūn Shāh, one of the most ferocious wretches that have ever disgraced a throne. His horrible atrocities, as related by the chronicler, need not here be mentioned in detail. (*See Firishta, Scott's Edit. I. 140f.*)

Humāyūn put down the rebellion of a relative, and then attacked some Telugu fortresses, amongst others Devarakoṇḍa where he suffered a defeat, the defenders being assisted by troops from Orissa. (*I. A., 1899, 244.*)

A.D. 1459. Mallikhārjuna reigning in Kurnool District (*V. R. ii. Kurn. 517*). And in Cuddapah (*Ibid. i. Cudd. 516*). And in N. Arcot, where a gift was made for the merit of (Śāḷuva) Narasimha (*Ibid. i. N. Arcot 13 ; 392 of 1905*). And in Mysore.

(*E. C. viii. Sa 1.*)

Warangal was now in possession of the Orissa king Kapilēśvara (*110 of 1902, E. R. 1902, §7*). The inscription which is on a pillar at the gate of the fort at Warangal, says that 'the son of Kapilēndra Gajapati' took the fort. Koṇḍaviḍu and the neighbouring country had been occupied by him since about 1420.

Two inscriptions in Maṇḍya taluk, S. Mysore, shew that king Mallikhārjuna and his viceroy in the N.-E. coast provinces, Śāḷuva Narasimha, were together at Penukoṇḍa, consulting 'on the affairs of Narasimha's territories.' Apparently they were perturbed by Kapilēśvara's successes which seemed threatening. (*E. C. iii. Md. 12, 59.*)

In Tinnevelly are three records of Arikēśari-Parākrama-Pāṇḍya, one of which bears date = June 13, 1459. (*V. R. iii. Tinn. 356, 390 ; 199 of 1895 ; 520 of 1909 ; 533 of 1917*)

A.D. 1460. Mallikhārjuna reigning in Trichinopoly. (*V. R. iii. Trich. 231 ; 27 of 1913.*)

Two records of Jaṭilavarman-Parākrama-Pāṇḍya, i.e. Arikēśari-Parākrama, of dates = January 5, in his 38th year and November 1, 1460, in his 39th year—both in Tinnevelly District.

(*535, 568 of 1917.*)

A.D. 1461. Mallikhārjuna reigning in S. Kanara and Madras (*V. R. ii. S. Kan : 164 ; 146 of 1901 ; ibid. ii. Madras, 192*). And in Mysore. (*E. C. viii. Sb., 562.*)

Jaṭilavarman-Parākrama-Pāṇḍya ruling in Tinnevelly District in his 40th year on August 30.

(*3 of 1912 ; E. R. 1922, p. 94.*)

[In this year the cruel Humāyūn Shāh Bāhmanī died and was succeeded by his son Nizām, a boy only 8 years old. Taking advantage of this king Kapilēśvara of Orissa marched, by way of Rajahmundry, 'says Firishta, plundering and wasting the country, but was defeated and driven back. (*I. A., 1899, 277. Firishta, Scott's Edit. i., 143*)]

A.D. 1462. Mallikhārjuna reigning in Trichinopoly District (*V. R. iii. Trich. 458 ; C.-P. No. 28 of 1905*). An inscription in Mysore, of about April 1462, seems to shew that the whole power there was in the hands of Śāḷuva Narasimha. (*E. C. x. Bp. 24.*)

Arikēsari-Parākrama Pāṇḍya ruling in Tinnevelly District. (*V. R. iii. Tinn. 362, 367 ; 526, 531 of 1909.*)

Prince Virūpāksha III, brother of king Mallikhārjuna, mentioned in an inscription in Nellore District. (*V. R. ii, Nell. 32 ; B. and V. C. 242.*)

Sāḷuva Narasimha mentioned in an inscription at Tirupati, Chittoor District; also in another Saḷuva Timma, son of Guṇḍa, and elder brother of Narasimha (*V. R. i, Chitt. 9 Q, 10 ; 69 of 1889 ; 249 of 1904*). [The date of the last is A.D. 1463–64.] Narasimha is mentioned in a record in Chingleput District. (*V. R. i, Chin. 1113 ; 244 of 1912.*)

A.D. 1463. Mallikhārjuna reigning in S. Kanara (*V. R. ii, S. Kan. 181 ; 163 of 1901*). And in Mysore (*E. C. viii, Nr. 68, 69*). And in Salem District. (*V. R. ii, Salem, 103 ; 203 of 1911.*)

Arikēśari-Parākrama-Pāṇḍya ruling on July 28, 1463 in his 42nd year. An inscription in Tinnevelly District, mentioning 'Perumāḷ-Māran-Parākrama *alias* Parākrama Pāṇḍya', states that that chief died in this year. This was probably the same Arikesari-Parākrama. (*V. R. iii, Tinn. 342 ; 506 of 1909.*)

April 29, 1463. On this day a festival was held, perhaps in all parts of the Vijayanagar kingdom, it being the name-giving day of a son who was born to king Mallikhārjuna. It was celebrated in the Sāntaḷige tract in N.-W. Mysore, where the king gave a grant of land in commemoration of the event. As this young prince is said to have been only one year old when his father died this record helps to confirm the date given for the king's death. (*E. C. viii, Tl, 206.*)

The Bāhmanī kingdom was greatly disturbed at this time. No sooner was the attack from Orissa in 1461 repelled than the sultan of Malwa attacked Gulbarga. A great battle was fought which ended favourably to the invader; but on a contingent from Gujarat arriving to assist the Dekhānis the tables were turned and the army of Mālwa was driven back. Suddenly young Nizam Shāh the Bāhmanī Sultan died, and his brother Muhammad, then only nine years old, succeeded.

A.D. 1464. Mallikhārjuna reigning on March 9 in Mysore (*E. C. ix, Kn. 36*). And in Tanjore District in 1464–65. (*V. R. ii, Tan. 1624 ; 489 of 1904.*)

Several inscriptions go to shew that the Gajapati king of Orissa, Purushōttama, came to the throne in A.D. 1464–65 (*V. R. i, Ganjam, 152, 225, 243, 244 ; 274, 347, 365, 366 of 1896*). Thus Ś. 1392 (A.D. 1470–71) is named as his 7th year; Ś. 1417 (A.D. 1495) is named as his 32nd year; and so on.[1]

Arikēśari-Parākrama-Pāṇḍya ruling in Tinnevelly District, on March 2. (*518 of 1917.*)

At the village of Munnūr in Tiṇḍivānam Taluk, S. Arcot District, are two inscriptions, one a copy of the other, which mention as ruler 'Dakshina-Kapilēśvara-Kumāra-Mahāpātra, son of Ambīra', which last name is believed to mean Ham-vīra. This Kapilēśvara is said in the record to have been 'Parīksha' or viceroy of Koṇḍavīḍu, but now in 1464 to be viceroy of a number of places including Trichinopoly and even Chandragiri. Ambīra is evidently the chief called by

[1] The late Mr. R. D. Banerji gives the date of accession of Purushottama as in the year 1470. (See his History of Orissa, I. 303.)—*Editor*.

Firishta 'Ambur Ray'. Mr. H. Krishna Sāstri considers (*E. R., 1919, § 47*) that this conclusively proves that the new king of Orissa carried out an invasion far to his south and west about this time. If so the success of his arms must have seriously frightened the rulers of the Vijayanagar kingdom, and largely curtailed their dominions (*51, 92 of 1919*). And yet in 1466 we find Sāḷuva Narasimha recognized as the ruler in this same village in S. Arcot, under the Vijayanagar king (*53 of 1919*). Hence the only safe conclusion to adopt is that the expedition so far to the south, of the Orissa force from Koṇḍavīḍ, was merely a sudden raid, followed by speedy withdrawal.

A.D. 1465. June 18. A grant made for the merit of Mallikārjuna of Vijayanagar in Mysore (*E. C. ix, Bp. 18*). He was reigning in Conjevaram in this year (*V. R. i, Chingleput, 352; 37 of 1890; I. A., xxi, 321*). And in Cuddapah District (*V. R. i, Cudd. 336*). And on July 14 in S. Mysore. (*E. C. iii, Ml. 64.*)

In Tinnevelly District Perumāḷ-Kulaśēkhara-Pāṇḍya, i.e. Śrīvallabha was reigning in his 36th year. His accession had been in 1430. (*V. R. iii, Tinn. 366; 530 of 1909.*)

Mallikārjuna died this year, and his son being only one year old, the king's brother Virūpāksha III was raised to the throne. He was crowned on November 1465. (*Śrīsailam plates, E. I. xv, 8, 24*)

The Śāḷuva family chiefs were now in great power. Narasimha practically ruled the Vijayanagar kingdom. His cousin Parvata was ruling at Tirupati in Chittoor District (*V. R. i. Chit. 12; 251 of 1904; I. A., 1914, p. 12*). [Records of Narasimha are found over the whole eastern and central dominions of Vijayanagar, from as early as A.D. 1462, but not on the west coast, where Mr. Krishna Sāstri thinks the Kaḷasa chiefs were growing in strength.]

A.D. 1466. On October 23, king Virūpāksha III gave a grant in W. Mysore (*E. C. v. Bl. 135*).

Śāḷuva Narasimha mentioned as ruler in E. Mysore, where, on December 22, he granted 13 villages to a temple (*E. C. x. Kl. 33*). Also in S. Arcot on December 7. (*53 of 1919.*)

In Tinnevelly Jaṭilavarman Kulaśēkhara, *alias* Śrīvallabha *alias* Kumāra Kulaśēkhara, Pāṇḍya was ruling on November 8, 1466 in his 36th year, which shews his accession to have been on or after November 9, 1430 (*476 of 1917*). On June 26 an inscription of Jaṭilavarman Kulōttunga Pāṇḍya, 'born in Jyēshṭhā' asterism. He was one of the four brothers of Arikēśari Parākrama. This record being in his 43rd year, his installation dates from June 27, 1423. (*569 of 1917.*)

A.D. 1467. Virūpāksha III reigning on July 31 in Mysore (*E. C. ix. Dv. 56*). And in Anantapur on December 28 (*V. R. i. Anant. 83; 576 of 1912*). Also in Mysore on August 22 (*E. C. iii. Sr. 139*). And in Conjevaram on August 19 (*658 of 1919*). And in Bellary on November 9. (*V. R. i. Bell. 60; C.-P. 2 of 1914.*)

Śāḷuva Narasimha gave certain final orders about worship in the temple at Tirupati in Chittoor District (*762 of 1916; V. R. i. Chitt. 11; 250 of 1904*). He gave away five villages to the temple on November 28. His father Guṇḍa is mentioned.

Jaṭilavarman Kulaśēkhara Pāṇḍya ruling in Tinnevelly in his 38th year, shewing the latest possible date for his installation to have been November 28, 1430 (*see above under A.D. 1466*). These two records shew that he began to rule between November 9 and 28, 1430 (*649 of 1917*). Another of his records shews him ruling on May 23, 1467, in his 37th year (*453 of 1917*). Others of his in the same district. (*471, 477 of 1917.*)

A.D. 1468. Virūpāksha III reigning in E. Mysore on February 22. A gift was made by a private person 'for the merit of Narasimha', Śāḷuva, (*E. C. x. Mb. 20*). On the same day in Kurnool Śāḷuva Parvatayya, Narasimha's cousin, gave lands to a temple (*V. R. ii. Kurn. 469 ; 33 of 1915*). Another record of Virūpāksha III is in N.-W. Mysore, Date March 9. It mentions fighting between local chiefs (*E. C. viii. Tl. 143*). He was reigning also in Vellore (*V. R. i. N. Arcot 533 ; 4 of 1896*). This last mentions young prince Rajaśēkhara, son of Mallikārjuna and nephew of Virūpāksha III, then about five years old.

In Tinnevelly records of Jaṭila Kulaśēkhara Pāṇḍya on March 16 in his 38th year, October 6 and October 12 in his 39th year (*643, 526, 419 of 1917*). And of Jaṭila Arikēśari Parākrama Pāṇḍya on August 19. [The regnal year here stated appears to be in error.] (*541 of 1917.*)

The rule of Aḷagan-Perumāl-Parakrama-Paṇḍya who was born under the constellation Dhanishṭhā (Tamil 'Aviṭṭam') began in this year. (*T. A. S. I. 351.*)

A.D. 1469. Virūpāksha III of Vijayanagar reigning in E. Mysore (*E. C. x. Mb. 147*), and near Seringapatam. (*E. C. iii. Sr. 86.*)

Śāḷuva Narasimha ruling in N. Arcot District. (*V. R. i. N. Arcot, 710 ; 75 of 1900.*)

Jaṭilavarman-Kumāra-Kulaśēkhara ruling in Tinnevelly on March 22 in his 39th year. (*645 of 1917.*)

Another Pāṇḍya prince Bhuvanēka-Vīra-Samarakolāhala mentioned in this year (*V. R. i. Chin. 340 ; 25 of 1890 ; E. R. 1907, § 57 ; 1909, § 31 ; I. A., 1914, p. 13*). And another two years later (see below) named Aḷagan-Perumāḷ Śrīvallabha.

An inscription on a bell in Tinnevelly District names as ruler the Travancore prince Ādityavarman. (*V. R. iii. Tinn. 282, 283 ; I. A. ii. 360 ; E. I. iv. 146, n. 2.*)

In the autumn of 1469 Muhammad Shāh Bāhmanī III despatched an expedition to the Konkan to reduce certain refractory chiefs. Mallik-al-Tījar Mahmūd Gāwān commanded the Gulburga army.

There was trouble about now also in Trichinopoly where a local chief Kampa, claiming descent from the Cholas, opposed Sāḷuva Tirumala in his government of the country.

The Gajapati king of Orissa, now in possession of Koṇḍavīḍu and other fortresses, is said to have marched southwards along the Coromandel coast as fār as Conjevaram (*E. R. 1906-7, p. 56*). This expedition has been assigned to this year, but it may possibly refer to the southward raid alluded to above (*s. v. A. D.* 1464).

A.D. 1470. [Mahmūd Gāwān commanding the Bāhmanī king's army captured several places on the west coast including Goa which he took from the king of Vijayanagar. He devastated the country far and wide. Muhammad Shāh III then sent Nizām-ul-Mulkh Bahri to the east and seized Rajáhmundry and Koṇḍavīḍu, and Koṇḍapallī from the king of Orissa. (*So the 'Burhān-i-ma'āsir', I. A., 1899, 285.*)]

The Gajapati king Purushōttama reigning in his 7th year in Ś. 1373=A. D. 1470–71 or 1471–72. (*V. R. i. Ganjam 152, 243, 244 ; 274, 365, 366 of 1896.*)

Virūpāksha III of Vijayanagar reigning in Mysore on May 23 (*E. C. xii, Gb, 29*). And in Chingleput (*V. R. i. Chin. 354 ; 39 of 1890*). And in Tanjore (*V. R. ii. Tan. 1548 ; 487 of 1912*). Here he is 'called' Vīra Pratāpa Dēva Rāya. His minister Śāḷuva Narasimha was ruling for his master in S. Arcot. (*V. R. i, S. Arcot, 862 ; 1 of 1905 ; 8 of 1922.*)

Mention of the then very young Vijayanagar prince Rājaśēkhara, aged about seven years. (*121 of 1921.*)

A.D. 1471. Virūpāksha III reigning early in the year in S. Arcot (*461 of 1921*). [I base this on the month 'Kumbha' stated in the Epigraphist's List, *E. R. 1921–22*, p. 40. But Mr. Swamikannu Pillai (p. 88) says that the month was Simha. If he means that the true reading of the original is 'Simha' then the date of this inscription is August 27 A.D. 1470]. Virūpāksha was also reigning in Chingleput (*V. R. i, Chin. 865 ; 9 of 1911*). And in N. Arcot on July 21, 1471 (*120 of 1921*). And in S. Kanara. (*V. R. ii. S. Kan. 105, 176 ; 30, 158 of 1901.*)

Aḷagan-Perumāḷ-Srīvallabha-Pāṇḍya ruling in Tinnevelly. (*V. R. iii. Tinn. 298 ; 278 of 1908.*)

Sāḷuva Narasimha minister of the Vijayanagar king (whose name is not mentioned) ruling at Tirupati. (*V. R. i. Chitt. 9-O ; 67 of 1889.*)

A.D. 1472. Virūpāksha III reigning in Conjevaram on January, 92, 1472 (*613 of 1919*). And in Mysore (*E. C. viii. Sa, 60*). And in S. Arcot. (*V. R. i. S. Arcot, 596 ; 93 of 1906.*)

Śaḷuva Narasimha ruling for the king in E. Mysore (*E. C. x. Bp, 19*). And in S. Arcot (*118 of 1919*). And in N. Arcot. (*V. R. N. Arcot, 598 ; 45 of 1887.*)

Purushōttama Gajapati king of Orissa reigning in Vizagapatam District. (*V. R. iii, Vizag. 113 ; 285 of 1899.*)

[In this year Muhammad Shāh Bāhmanī III, hearing that the governor of the fort at Beḷgaum had marched to try and recover Goa for the kingdom of Vijayanagar, collected his forces and captured Beḷgaum after a siege. The sultan then returned to Gulbarga. Firishta (*Scott's Edit. 156 ff.*) devotes much space to the relationship at this period between Muhammad Shāh and his minister and general Khwāja Jahan Mahmūd Gāwān emphasizing the devotion of the latter and the affection felt for him by the king. Muhammad Shāh added Beḷgaum to Mahmud Gāwān's Jāghīr.]

A.D. 1473. Several inscriptions in Tinnevelly of Kumāra-Kulaśēkhāra-Paṇḍya whose accession was in 1430 ; viz. in his '42nd' year on April 17 [it was really his 43rd year] ; and in his 43rd year and 44th year. (*6456 of 1917 ; V. R. iii. Tinn. 359, 360, 382 ; 523, 524 of 1909 ; 11 of 1912.*)

A.D. 1474. Mention of Śāḷuva Tippa in Negapatam Taluk, Tanjore District, on January 3, when he gave away a village to a temple. This was probably the chief who married a sister of Deva-Rāya II, king of Vijayanagar. (*482 of 1922.*)

A great famine this year in the Dekhan, lasting two years. (*Firishta, Scott's Edit : i. 162.*)

Jaṭilavarman-Kulaśēkhara-Pāṇḍya, whose accession was in 1430, ruling in Tinnevelly on January 3, in his 44th year (*565 of 1917*). And on February 18. (*544 of 1917.*)

Two records in Travancore State, of correct date = October 13, 1474, mention the seventh year of Parākrama, *alias* Vīra-Pāṇḍya, who was born under the constellation Dhaṅishṭhā (Tamil 'Aviṭṭam'). His accession was in A.D. 1468. Another record of the same bears date = February 5, 1475. (*T.A.S. i, pp. 256, 260, E.F.G.*)

A.D. 1475. Virūpāksha III of Vijayanagar reigning in Mysore. (*E.C. viii, Sb., 527 ; ix, Ma., 44.*)

Śāḷuva Narasimha ruling for the king in Chittoor District. (*V.R.i , Chitt. 9, G ; 59 of 1889.*)

A.D. 1476. [The Hindu population of Koṇḍapalli fortress in the Krishna District revolted in this year, or a year or two later against the Bāhmanī governor and murdered him. They asked for aid from Orissa which was given, Gajapati troops advancing as far as Rajahmundry on the Godavari river, where the Bāhmanī governor was Nizām-ul-Mulkh Bahri, and besieging the place. Muhammad Sultān came to the rescue of the garrison and the Gajapati army was compelled to retire. The accounts given in the *Burhān-i-Ma'āsir* and by Firishta differ in details, but both agree that the Bāhmanī king in the end retained possession of Koṇḍapalli. The *Burhān-i-Ma'āsir* states that Muhammad Shāh took savage vengeance in 1477 on the people of Koṇḍapalli—destroying a temple and erecting a mosque in its place, and killing the Brahman priests. It is very difficult to get a clear story with accurate dates as to the events of this or of the next three or four years, as the Muhammadan chroniclers differ in essentials.]

An inscription in Salem District (*V.R. ii, Salem 90 ; 195 of 1910*) professing to be of the Śaka year 1398 (A.D. 1476–77) should be re-examined. It records a gift made in that year and mentions Mallikārjuna of Vijayanagar as reigning. But Mallikārjuna had died in 1465.

Virūpāksha III, reigning in S. Kanara. (*V.R. ii, S. Kan. 114, 180 ; 39, 162 of 1901.*)

In Madura this year was ruling a chief of the old Bāṇa stock, Sundara-Tōḷ-uḍaiyān I, son of Tiru-Mālirunjolai-Māvali-Vāṇa (*T.A.S. i, p. 53*). His father was alive in 1477.

Śāḷuva Tirumala, brother of Śāḷuva Narasimha remitted taxes in a part of Tanjore District, shewing that he ruled there as viceroy of Vijayanagar. (*534 of 1922.*)

A.D. 1477. [About this time, or may be a little later, Muhammad Bahmanī made Nizām-ul-Mulkh Bāhri his viceroy in the Telingana tracts of Rajahmundry, Bellaṁkoṇḍa, Koṇḍapalli, etc., and placed Azīm Khān in charge of Warangal.]

Śāḷuva Narasimha ruling in Cuddapah for Virūpāksha III.[1] (*V.R. i, Cudd. 653 ; 405 of 1911.*)

In Ramnad a gift to a temple was made by Tirumāl-Irunjoḷai-Mahābali-Bāṇa, ruling in Madura. (*V.R. ii, Ram. 178-C.*)

A.D. 1478. [About this time (the date is doubtful) Firishta states that Muhammad Bāhmanī III marched to the capital of Orissa slaughtering the inhabitants and devastating the country as he went (*Scott's Edit., p. 163*). He was bought off by rich presents, and returned southwards to Koṇḍapalli, where, as related above (*s.v., A.D. 1476*) he captured that place and slew the priests of the temple. After which he halted three years at Rājahmundry.]

A grant was made in Mysore 'for the *dharma*' of Śāḷuva Narasimha. The king is not mentioned (*E.C. ix, Cp. 158*). He was also ruling for the king in S. Arcot (*408 of 1921*). And in North Arcot. (*402 of 1912.*)

Virūpāksha III reigning in Mysore. (*E.C. v, Cn. 153 ; x Bp., 69.*)

A.D. 1479. [According to Barros (*Dec. I, vii, c. 10*) there was a great massacre of Muhammadans in this year at Honawar, then in possession of Vijayanagar. There was a great trade in Arab horses at that place, and when it was reported at the Hindu capital that the Musalman traders had been selling horses for the army of the Bāhmanī Sultan, orders were issued that the hostile traders should be slain. These were carried out to such effect that 10,000 'Moors' lost their lives.]

A.D. 1480. [About this time (the exact date is doubtful) Firishta tells us that the Bāhmanı Sultan Muhammad III received information concerning the richness and grandeur of the temples at the Hindu city of Kānchī, Conjevaram, and, being only ten days' journey from that place, viz., at 'Ghonḍpore'[2] which Brigg's Edition renders as 'Koṇḍapalli', he made a forced march to Kānchī (*Firishta, Scott's Edit.:, I. 166, 167*). The *Burhan-i-Ma'āsir's* story goes that the Sultan, hearing that a rebellion had broken out amongst his subjects at Koṇḍaviḍu, assembled an army and marched

[1] Neither of the authorities cited has reference to Virūpāksha III in the original.—*Editor*.

[2] If Firishta's 'Ghonḍpore' was really Kondapalli the Sultan would have had to travel about 300 miles to reach Conjevaram, too far for 'a ten-days' journey', and especially so in a hostile country, and with a very small force.

to that place in November, 1480. Having invested it the rebels pleaded for mercy alleging that they had been misled by certain ambitious nobles. Muhammad forgave them, but ever afterwards cherished a belief that Malik-al-Tijar Mahmūd Gāwān had turned against him and was a traitor. The Sultan then went to Malūr (a place I am unable to identify—it cannot be Malūr in Kolar District, Mysore) and Śāḷuva Narasimha fled before him. *Then* it was that the Sultan heard of the richness of the Kānchī temples, and, selecting a small body of troops, he rode hastily to that city, his army following him and surrounding the town. He arrived there on March 12, 1481.]

Virūpāksha III of Vijayanagar reigning in Chingleput District.

(V.R. i, Chin. 759 ; 661 of 1904.)

In Travancore State an inscription of date May 11, 1480, shewing Kēraḷa Mārttānda reigning there. *(V.R. iii, Trav. 227 ; E. I. iv, 204.)*

In Tinnevelly on November 26, Parakrāma Pāṇḍya was ruling in his 13th year.

(548 of 1917.)

The rule of Kulaśēkhara-Pāṇḍya who was born under the constellation Krittikā began between January 12, and August 1, 1480. *(T. A. S. i, p. 46 ; 542, 618 of 1917.)*

A.D. 1481. [On April 5, Sultan Muhammad Bāhmanī summoned to court his old and faithful minister Mahmud Gāwān and there, declaring him to be a traitor, he caused him to be put to death. All authorities are agreed as to the date. This tragedy had a double effect. Very shortly after this Muhammad III died, stricken with remorse when he discovered his error; and almost all his nobles turned against the Sultan, so that the Bāhmanī kingdom broke up.]

Śāḷuva Narasimha ruling in Mysore. *(E. C. ix, Kn. 8.)*

Śāḷuva Sangama mentioned in an inscription in Trichinopoly District.

(V. R. iii, Trich. 359 ; 594 of 1902.)

At Śrīrangam is an inscription of this year of a 'Chōla-Nārāyaṇa' chief.

(30 of 1891 ; I. A. 1914, p. 13, note.)

A.D. 1482. Virūpāksha III reigning near Trichinopoly.

(V. R. iii, Trich. 812 ; 83 of 1892.)

Śāḷuva Narasimha ruling for Virūpāksha III in North Arcot—Gift made by a certain Nāgama Nāyaka *(V.R. i ; N. Arcot 601 ; S.I.I. i, p. 132 ; 48 of 1887)*. And in South Arcot *(ibid i, S. Arcot, 1005 ; 198 of 1904)*. His agent Narasa Nāyaka is mentioned.

[On March 26, 1482 Muhammad Shāh Bāhmanī died, and was nominally succeeded by his son Mahmūd Shāh. But he had no power, and one after another his nobles deserted him and established their independence.]

A.D. 1483. An inscription in North Arcot mentions, on April 14, 1483, 'Dēva-Rāya, son of Mallikārjuna' of Vijayanagar,—probably another name of prince Rājaśēkhara. *(309 of 1919.)*

A.D. 1484. In E. Mysore Śāḷuva Narasimha ruling for the king who is not mentioned.

(E. C. ix, Ma., 32 ; iv, Ng. 59.)

And in Chingleput District, where Nāgama Nāyaka, is mentioned.

(318 of 1909 : E. R. 1910, p. 113.)

In Tinnevelly District on November 26, 1484 an inscription of 'Parākrama Pāṇḍya' ruling in his eleventh year. This would make the beginning of his rule as in 1473–74. He is not therefore the prince of that name who began to rule in 1468. One other record of his is at Śankaranāyanār-kōvil of date A.D. 1506–07, mentioning his 33rd year. *(520, 521, 551 of 1917.)*

A.D. 1485. Inscription mentioning Dēpanna-Voḍeyār of Ummattūr in S. Mysore, son of Immaḍi-Rāya. (*E. C. iv, Ch. 127.*)

An inscription mentioning—' Kumāra-Mallikārjuna ' of Vijayanagar on July 13, 1485, has been commented on by the Government Epigraphist, who points out that since this cannot be the king of that name it may be some prince of the family. (*473 of 1921 ; E. R. 1922, p. 111.*)

Virūpāksha shewn to be reigning in S. Arcot during some part of the year (*V. R. i, S. Arcot, 801 ; 398 of 1909*). And in E. Mysore on July 29. (*E. C. x, Mb. 104.*)

[The powerful Minister of Virūpāksha III of Vijayanagar, Śāḷuva Narasimha, usurped the throne in this year dispossessing king Virūpāksha III. It is difficult to arrive at the exact truth. Nuniz, writing about seventy years later, says (*A Forgotten Empire, pp. 305 f*) that Virūpāksha had two sons,—that the eldest son murdered his father and was in turn murdered by his own brother ' Padearao ' (Prauḍha-dēva-Rāya). Then that Śāḷuva Narasimha, supported by the nobles who were tired of the misgovernment of the recent kings, went to the palace in force. The young king fled, and Narasimha was raised to the throne amidst great rejoicings. I have stated my opinion (*J. R. A. S. 1915, pp. 383 f.*) that this event occurred after July 29, 1485—(basing this date on the last-noted record)—and before November 1, 1486, on which day the Sītakallu inscription noticed below gives Narasimha full imperial titles as a reigning sovereign. This period may be shortened by an examination of the details of the two inscriptions 593 of 1902 and 31 of 1901, a summary of whose contents has not reached me.] (*See E. C. x, Mb. 104 ; xii, Tm. 54.*)

An inscription of September 9, 1485, shews Narasimha ruling (as Viceroy possibly) in Anantapur District. (*710 of 1917.*)

A.D. 1486. At Sītakallu in Tumkur District, Mysore. Inscription of date = November 1, 1486, mentioning Śāḷuva Narasimha as king—giving him full imperial titles and saying that he was seated on the diamond throne in Vijayanagar (*E. C. xii, Tm. 54*). Another inscription of his in Cuddapah District. (*V. R. i, Cudd. 588.*)

Śāḷuva Sangama made a grant of land in Trichinopoly District in this year (no details of date available), his overlord being mentioned as ' Prauḍha-dēva, son of Virūpāksha ' (III). (*V. R. iii, Trich. 358 ; 593 of 1902.*)

Parākrama-Pāṇḍya, said to be in his second year of office, mentioned in two inscriptions in Trichinopoly and Ramnad. (*V. R. iii, Tinn. 365 ; ii, Ram. 178–D ; 529 of 1909.*)

A.D. 1487. Śāḷuva Narasimha, now king in Vijayanagar, reigning on April 29, in Chingleput District. (*648 of 1919 ; 235 of 1922.*)

A.D. 1488. Śāḷuva Narasimha reigning in S. Arcot District on July 27. (*308 of 1921.*)

Gift by a ' feudatory of Mahābali-Bāṇa ' in Madura District, shewing that the Bāṇa chief was ruling there. (*V. R. ii, Madura 170 ; 44 of 1908.*)

A.D. 1489. Nanja-Rāja, Rāja of Ummattūr in S. Mysore, son of Immaḍi, ruling in that tract and in the Dhārāpuram country in Coimbatore District. (*E. C. iv, Gu. 9 ; 108, 109 of 1920.*)

The Gajapati king of Orissa at this date was Purushōttama, who to a certain extent, relieved his country from attacks by the Bāhmanī king. (*E. I. xiii, 155.*)

[This year saw the beginning of the end of the Bāhmanī kingdom. Muhammad Shāh had encouraged all kinds of Asiatics to come to the Dekhan, and Firishta says that numbers of Georgians, Circassians, Calmucks and other Turkish tribes were imported. The Turks looked to Yusuf Ādil Shāh, said to be of Ottoman descent as their leader. He was appointed viceroy of

Bījāpur. The Dekhanis and Abyssinians were headed by Nizām-ul-mulkh Bāhri, and there was great rivalry between the two nobles. Before long there occurred riots and disturbances in the city (Gulbarga) and several thousand men lost their lives. Then Yusaf Ādil retired to Bījāpur, and became practically independent in 1489, but did not openly proclaim himself so. Nizām-ul-mulkh Bāhri having been slain, his son Malik Ahmad took up a strong position, founded the city of Ahmadnagar and assumed the title of Ahmad Nizām Shāh in the same year. A little later Qāsim Barīd raised his standard as sovereign at Bīdar. Imād Shāh of Berar had become independent already in 1485. Qutb Shāh at Golkonda, like the Ādil Shāh did not at once renounce his allegiance to the Bāhmanī throne, but became independent in 1512. Thus the Bāhmanī kingdom broke up into five separate states.]

A.D. 1490. An inscription at the temple at Tagaḍūr in S. Mysore names as ruler the Ummattur chief Nanja-Rāja, son of Immaḍi-Rāya (*E.C. iii. Nj, 118*). These chiefs made a bid for independence, and 20 years later Krishnadēva Rāya of Vijayanagar had to crush them.

A.D. 1491. In Tinnevelly District a record of Jaṭāvarman-Parākrama-Kulaśēkhara-Pāṇḍya ruling in his eleventh year on February 13. He was 'born in Krittikā' and began to rule in 1480. (*502, 503, 524 of 1917.*)

Another inscription in the same district mentions another Parākrama-Pāṇḍya ruling in 1491–92 in his second year. (*V.R. iii, Tinn. 304-D.*)

In Kurnool a record of a grant by Timma-Rāja, minister to prince Immaḍi-Narasimha, son of king Narasimha who had usurped the throne of Vijayanagar. (*V.R. ii, Kurn. 602.*)

A.D. 1492. [Some time in this year, or at least on a day earlier than January 27, 1493, Śāḷuva Narasimha, sovereign of Vijayanagar died and was succeeded by the elder of his two sons; but this young prince was almost immediately murdered by a certain Timmarasa. Then the minister Narasa Nāyaka, keeping all the power in his own hands, raised to the throne the younger brother Tamma-dēva or Tammayya (= *Dharma*) who was given the title of 'Immaḍi-Narasimha' and who is recognized as being king in an inscription of date = January 27, 1493, in Mysore.

(*E.C. vi, Mg. 50, 54, 56 ; J.R.A.S. 1915, p. 386. See also V.R. iii, Trichinopoly, 66 ; 736 of 1909.*)

Nuniz says that Immaḍi Narasimha was practically kept in confinement at Penukoṇḍa by Narasa Nāyaka with 20,000 men stationed there to guard him and prevent his escape, while the minister governed the kingdom at the capital. (*A Forgotten Empire, p. 310.*)

By this time Yusuf Ādil Shāh of Bījāpūr had become possessed of the forts of Muḍkal and Raichūr on the north side of the Tungabhadra; and Narasimha, urged, according to Firishta, by Qāsim Barīd of Bīdar, sent an army into that country and took both those places. But a little later in a pitched battle the Bījāpur Sultan retook them and the neighbouring tracts in April–May 1493.]

Immaḍi Narasimha named as reigning in A.D. 1492–93 in an inscription in Kurnool. (*V.R. ii, Kurn. 516.*)

There are three inscriptions in the year 1492–93 of the Ummattūr chief Nanja-Rāja, and one of Immaḍi-Dēpanna in S. Mysore and in Coimbatore District.

(*E.C. iv, Gu. 2 ; Ch. 192 ; Yd. 41 ; 179 of 1920.*)

In this year in April Yusuf Ādil Shāh of Bījāpur advanced to the south and defeated an army of Narasimha of Vijayanagar. The Shāh then seized the territory of Muḍkal and Raichūr. Narasimha's son died of wounds received in action in this battle. The disputed tracts remained in possession of Bījāpur.

A.D. 1493. Immaḍi Narasimha reigning in Cuddapah District. Gift by a servant of the minister Narasa-Nāyaka (*V.R. i, Cudd. 618 ; 516 of 1906*). The inscription naming him king on January 27, 1493 has already been noticed. He was reigning in E. Mysore on May 14 (*E.C. vi, Mg. 50.*), and on September 25. (*E.C. x, Gd. 80.*)

Some puzzling records in the Doḍ-Baḷḷāpur Taluk of E. Mysore should be further examined. One mentions a prince Śāḷuva-Dēpanna son of Immaḍi Narasimha[1] as ruling there. [But king Immaḍi Narasimha was himself very young in 1493.]

(*E.C. ix, D-B. 42 and 45.*)

A.D. 1494. Another similar inscription shewing 'Śulliri-Dēvappa-Nāyaka,' son of Immaḍi-Narasimha,[2] making a gift to a temple in Central Mysore. (*E.C. xii, Kg. 26.*)

Immaḍi-Narasimha was reigning in Chittoor District at Kottakōṭa near Madanapalli, where a mosque was built this year,—proving that there were numerous Muhammadan residents there at the time. (*V.R. i, Chit. 158 ; 438 of 1914.*)

Jaṭilavarman-Parākrama-Kulaśēkhara-Pāṇḍya, 'born in Krittikā,' ruling in Tinnevelly District in his 15th year. (*V.R. ii, Tinn. 379, 380, 278-W ; 8, 9 of 1912.*)

A.D. 1495. The same ruler mentioned in an inscription whose date = March 6, 1495, (*T.A.S. i, 265*) ; and March 11. (*8 of 1912 ; E.R. 1922, p. 93.*)

Immaḍi-Narasimha reigning in Mysore (*E.C. ix. Bn. 123 ; Ht. 23 ; x, Kl. 34 ; ix, Dv. 66 ; Ma. 31*). And in North Arcot. (*V.R. i, N. Arcot, 597 ; 44 of 1887.*)

Two of these dates shew him reigning in August, 1495.

In Ganjam District an inscription of the 32nd year of the Gajapati king of Orissa, Purushōttama. (*V.R. i, Ganjam, 225 ; 347 of 1896.*)

A.D. 1496. Immaḍi-Narasimha reigning in Mysore on February 14 and March 15. (*E.C. x, Kl. 1 ; xii, Mi., 33*). The last of these mentions his minister and general Narasa-Nāyaka. An inscription at Hanche a village near Mysore City mentions as reigning on September 19 the '*Mahāmanḍalēśvara* Narasimha-deva.' (*E.C. iii, My., 33.*)

Travancore was, on June 22, under the rule of Jayasimha, *alias* Vīra-Kēraḷa-Varman, residing in Quilon. (*T.A S. ii, p. 26 ; V.R. iii, Trav. 53.*)

A.D. 1497. Immaḍi Narasimha reigning in Anantapur District (*V.R. i, Anant. 39*). And in Cuddapah. (*ibid. i, Cudd. 508.*)

Jaṭilavarman-Parākrama-Kulaśēkhara Pāṇḍya (*sec s.v., A.D. 1494, etc. . . .*) ruling in Tinnevelly in his 18th year on August 1, 1497. (*502, 504, 508 of 1917.*)

[In this year Vasco da Gama, the Portuguese adventurer, with three vessels, doubled the Cape and discovered the open sea-route from Europe to India and the East.]

The Ummattūr chief Channa-Nanja-Rāja ruling in South Mysore.

(*E.C. iv, Gu. 11 ; V.R. i, Coimbatore 259 ; 441 of 1906.*)

[1] The two inscriptions, Nos. 42 and 45, are copies of one record. The grant is dated Śaka 1415, Pramadi in 45 but Sarvajit in 42 which is wrong. The corresponding English date is December 18, 1493, during the governorship of Tippūr Simē by Sāḷuvaya Devapa Nāyaka, son Sāḷuva Immaḍi Rāya Mahārāya. The village Bhairāpura was granted to Tipparasayya, son of Singappayya by Baiyapa Gauda, son of Bayyaṇa Gauḍa, the Nāḍ-prabhu of Hullakaḍi, on *Makara-Sankrānti* to be enjoyed as an exclusive agrahāra by him and his descendants. Makara-Sankrānti fell in that year on Saturday, December 28, 10 days later than the date of the grant. The ruler under reference was ruler of a sub-division and was the son of Sāḷuva Immaḍi Rāya which need not mean Immaḍi Narasimha.—*Editor.*

[2] The name is not Immaḍi-Narasimha in the original Kanarese even in this case.—*Editor.*

A.D. 1498. [Vasco da Gama seized and plundered on the coast of Africa a small vessel belonging to a Muhammadan which had a rich cargo. This act of piracy roused the people against him. *(See Castanheda, Kerr. ii, 336 ; I.A. 1923. Suppl., p. 18.)*

On August 26, 1498, he arrived at Calicut on the west coast of India. This was the first appearance of the Portuguese in India in any force. He shortly afterwards returned to Lisbon.

Ādil Shāh of Bijāpur obtained possession of Kulbarga and Sāgar in 1498.

Immaḍi Narasimha reigning in Anantapur District in March, 1498 *(719 of 1917 ; 429 of 1920)*. And in Cuddapah District *(V.R. i, Cudd. 400)*. One inscription, noted in *E.R.* 1904–5, § 44, mentions the king's minister Narasa-Nāyaka as being not so much his minister as his partner *(pampu)*. It shews what power Narasa-Nāyaka had acquired.

Narasa-Nāyaka granted a village in Mysore on December 13.

(E.C. iii, Nj. 16; I.A. xxvi. 330.)

A.D. 1499. Immaḍi-Narasimha reigning in Mysore in April and June. One inscription calls him by his name 'Tammaya-dēva' *(E.C. x, Mr. 5 ; ix, Cp. 52)*. And in North Arcot *(25 of 1919)*. And in South Kanara *(V.R. ii, S. Kan., 184 ; 166 of 1901 ; E.I. vii, 79)*. And in Ramnad.

(V.R. ii, Ram. 203, 216, 227 ; 139, 151 of 1903 ; 89 of 1908.)

The Ummattūr chief of South Mysore, Nanja-Rāja, is represented as ruling part of Coimbatore District. *(V.R. i, Coim. 31, 175, 373 ; 200 of 1909 ; 315 of 1908 ; 579 of 1893.)*

Jaṭilavarman-Parākrama-Kulaśēkhara-Pāṇḍya ruling in Tinnevelly District in his 20th year, November 14, 1499. *(505 of 1917 ; V.R. iii, Tinn. 388 ; 197 of 1895.)*

In Madura Muttarasa-Tirumalai-Māvalivāṇa, a chief of the old Bāṇa family, ruling Madura. *(T.A.S., i. 53.)*

A.D. 1500. [The Portuguese under Cabral arrived on October 29, 1500, at Calicut. They attacked and robbed the Moorish vessels on the Malabar coast. Quarrels with the resident merchants and with the 'Zamorin' *(Samurī)* followed, and much blood was shed on both sides. The Portuguese detested all 'Moors' but behaved generously to the Hindus. The Māppilla (Moplah) merchants opposed the foreigners, and slew many of them, thus provoking the latter to revenge themselves, and in doing so the Portuguese used no mercy and were guilty of horrid cruelties. They established a factory at Calicut.

In Guntur District is an inscription of date = November 5, 1500, shewing the Gajapati king Vīra Rudra, son of Purushōttama, reigning over that country. [The Gajapati king was then in possession of Udayagiri and Koṇḍavīḍu.] *(802 of 1922 ; V.R. ii, Gun. 98-A.)*

Parākrama-Kulaśēkhara-Pāṇḍya ruling in Tinnevelly in his 21st year on October 2, 1500. *(516 of 1917.)*

A.D. 1501. Immaḍi Narasimha reigning in Trichinopoly and Salem Districts, where he is called Tammaya-dēva, and in Chingleput under the name 'Dharma-Rāya' *(V.R. iii, Trich. 530 ; 664 of 1909 ; 173 of 1919 ; V.R. ii, Salem, 203 ; 155 of 1905)*. Another record of his of this year is in Cuddapah District, where it mentions a gift made 'for the merit of Narasa Nāyaka, the king's minister *(V.R. i, Cudd. 829 ; 615 of 1907)*. The same king, but called 'Vīra Narasimha' was reigning in South Kanara *(V.R. ii, S. Kan. 170 ; 152 of 1901 ; 615 of 1907 ; E.I., vii. 80)* and in Kurnool. *(V.R. ii. Kurn. 16.)*

Jaṭilavarman-Parākrama-Kulaśēkhara-Pāṇḍya ruling in Tinnevelly in his 22nd year on November 27, 1501. *(534 of 1917.)*

In Ramnad the farmers were so harassed by the unendurable amount of taxation imposed on them that they sold their lands and left their homes. (*50 of 1916.*)

[The Portuguese in this year fought an Arab fleet and sunk their ships. They were befriended by the Rāja of Cochin.]

A.D. 1502. [Vasco da Gama returned to Calicut, this time as an open enemy, in consequence of the massacre of the Portuguese that had taken place there. He seized a large ship filled with Muhammadan travellers and burned it with all on board, some 300 men and 30 women (*Castanheda, Kerr's 'Voyages' i. 435*). He also bombarded the town of Calicut and burned the ships belonging to the Chief of the place.]

Immaḍi Narasimha reigning on October 1, in Mysore. (*E.C. viii, Nr. 73 ; iii, Nj. 88.*)

Kulaśēkhara-Pāṇḍya ruling in Tinnevelly on August 11, in his 23rd year. (*527 of 1917.*)

A.D. 1503. Immaḍi Narasimha reigning in Kurnool on August 7 (*V.R. ii, Kurn. 551, 552 ; 166 of 1913*). And in Mysore on December 29 (*E.C. xii, Mi. 59*). And in South Arcot (*368 of 1917 ; V.R. i, South Arcot 136 ; 344 of 1913*). Mention made, March 13, of the minister Narasa-Nāyaka. (*E.C. xii, Mi. 106.*)

In Ganjam District the king of Orissa Gajapati Pratāpa Rudra was reigning. [He afterwards fought, with disastrous result, against Krishnadēva Rāya of Vijayanagar.]

(*V.R. i, Gan. 224 ; 346 of 1896.*)

In South Mysore gift by Mahādēva, brother of the Changāḷva chief Nanja (*E.C. iv, Hs. 63*). The inscription gives a pedigree of the family for four generations.

The Chief of Calicut, in revenge for the loss of his ships and jealous of the Cochin Raja's support of the Portuguese, made war on Cochin, drove the Raja from his capital, and compelled the Portuguese to retire. Later in the year Albuquerque arrived at Cochin, expelled the Calicut force, and established a factory there, which he fortified.

A curious inscription, commented on by Dr. Hultzsch (*E. R. 1902*, §7), praises a certain 'Chittapa Khan', for having taken Warangal fortress from the Muhammadans. He seems to have been a Hindu, but to have been given a Muhammadan title. (*108 of 1902.*)

A.D. 1504. Immaḍi Narasimha reigning on April 26 in Salem. The inscription calls him 'Dharma-Rāya' (*V. R. ii, Salem 5 ; 412 of 1913*). The king gave a village in Chittoor District on August, 25 (*V. R. i, Chitt : 371 ; E. I. vii, 74—the Dēvulapalli plates*). He was reigning in N. Arcot on September 25, 1504 (*V. R. i, N. Arcot, 196 ; 395 of 1912*). And in Mysore on October 23, where an inscription calls him simply 'Narasinga-Rāya.' (*E. C. x, Gd. 38.*)

[Amīr Barīd of the Barīd Shāhs of Ahmadābād succeeded his father in this year.]

Inscription in S. Mysore mentioning a grant by Nanja Rāja, probably the Changāḷva chief of that name. (*E. C. iv, Gu. 6.*)

[At Cochin Albuquerque succeeded in patching up a treaty with the *Samuri* (Zamorin) of Calicut. But shortly afterwards some Portuguese seized a Calicut boat, and then the new Portuguese fort at Cochin was attacked, but without success. Lopo Soares blockaded the town. The Portuguese, however, did not treat the Hindus of Cochin well and there was much antagonism between them, and violent outbreaks.]

A.D. 1505. Immaḍi Narasimha reigning in N. Arcot on February 2 and on February 28, 1505 (*V. R. i, N. Arcot 197, 155 ; 396, 354 of 1912*). [This inscription states the day as being in the year 'Raktākshi' which = A. D. 1504–05, and the details given suit the date February, 28, 1505 ;

but the number of the Śaka year is wrongly stated as 'Ś. 1429', which would = A. D. 1507–08. In my opinion a mistake has been made in the number of the Śaka year, either in the original or the copy which should read '1426' and would then correspond with Raktākshi. It is easier to imagine a mistake in the number than in the name. I hold that this king was alive on this February 28 (*J. R. A. S., 1915, p. 394*). Mr. Swamikannu Pillai has examined a record of this king which professes to make him alive on February 11, 1506, but he has announced that the details of the date are unsatisfactory.]

An inscription in Cuddapah (*V. R. i, Cudd. 462*) shews 'Sāḷuva Narasimha' alive and reigning in the year Krōdhana, but again quotes a wrong Śaka year. And since the ruler's name is ambiguous it cannot be assumed that Immaḍi Narasimha was meant.

[On some day, then, subsequent to February 28 and before August 14, 1505 (*see the inscription next noted*) the king of Vijayanagar Immaḍi Narasimha was treacherously assassinated by a 'captain', to use Nuniz's phrase—who with other nobles had planned the deed in order to raise the minister Narasa-Nāyaka to the throne. I translate Nuniz's version of the captain's name 'Codemerade' into 'Kondama-Raja', who is heard of in some inscriptions. The vacant throne was now seized by the minister Narasa-Nāyaka, son of Iśvara of a Tuluva family who established the very powerful third dynasty of Vijayanagar. I must note, however, that Prof. Krishnaswami Aiyangar has expressed the opinion that possibly Narasa Nāyaka did not himself seize the throne, but that it was his son Vīra Narasimha who did so ('*A Little Known Chapter of Vijayanagar History*', *p. 70.*) ('*A Forgotten Empire*', *pp. 311-14.*)

Very shortly after the murder of Immadi Narasimha, Narasa-Nāyaka died and Vīra Narasimha became king.]

An inscription in E. Mysore shews that Vīra Narasimha was king on August 14, 1505. The date given is a sound one (*E. C. x, Gd. 77*). He was reigning in S. Arcot in Ś. 1427, A. D. 1505–06 (*V. R. i, S. Arcot, 863-B*). And in Kurnool on October, 16 (*V. R. ii, Kurn. 381, 556 ; 54 of 1915 ; 171 of 1913*). The date of the last of these two is doubtful in detail.

A record in Mysore notifies a gift made in A. D. 1505–06 'for the prosperity of Narasimha Mahārāja and Narasimha-Nāyaka'. This might have been engraved after the beginning of Ś. 1427, i.e., after March 6, A.D. 1505 and if so we should have to assume that Immaḍi Narasimha was murdered on some day later than that March 6. It may be so, but this is not the place for a full discussion. (*E.C. x, Mb. 242.*)

[In A.D. 1505 the king of Portugal appointed Almeida as his viceroy on the Indian coast. He attacked Honore which belonged to Vijayanagar, with a fleet and 1,500 soldiers, burning some ships there on October 16.]

A.D. 1506. 'Immaḍi-Narasa-Nāyaka' mentioned as reigning over Vijayanagar on February 5, 1506. This must be intended for Vīra-Narasa, son of Narasa-Nāyaka, since Immaḍi Narasimha, equally with his own father Narasimha, was not called 'Nāyaka'. (*330 of 1921.*)

To a certain extent this is supported by another record in Mysore which mentions 'Sāluva Immaḍi Narasimha' as reigning on some day (details of date illegible) in Ś. 1427 ; but the date cannot be depended upon. (*E. C. ix, Ht. 121.*)

Vīra Narasimha was reigning in Trichinopoly District on July 17, 1506 (*V.R. iii, Trich. 79 ; 147 of 1914*). And in Cuddapah, in 1506–07, where an inscription calls him 'Immaḍi-Rāya-Dēvarāya' (*V.R. i Cudd. 62*). He sent an expedition against the Kaḷasa country

(*E.C. vi, Mg. 41*). Varthema says that he attacked the Musalmans at Goa. The *kongudēśa-rājakkaḷ* says that he tried to put down a rebellion by the chief of Ummattūr but was not successful.

In Tinnevelly District Parākrama Pāṇḍya was ruling. (*V.R. iii, Tinn. 304-A.*)

The Ummattūr chief Chikka-Rāya Malla-rāja, son of Dēvanna gave on December 15, a grant in the reign of 'Bhujabala Vīra Narasimha'. 'Bhujabala' is the origin of the name 'Busbalrao' given to Vīra Narāsimha by Nuniz in his chronicle ('*A Forgotten Empire*', *p. 314*).

(*E. C. iii, Ml. 95.*)

A.D. 1507. Vīra Narasimha reigning in Mysore on January 13, 1507. The exploits of his father Narasa are related in somewhat fanciful fashion. Vīra Narasimha's mother Tippāji mentioned (*E. C. viii, Nr. 64*). And during the year in S. Arcot.

(*V. R. i, S. Arcot, 597 ; 94 of 1906.*)

Taxation in villages was excessive at this period. Four records at Dēvikāpuram in N. Arcot give details of 33 separate taxes levied, 32 of which were enforced by the temple and one by the Crown. (*353, 355, 395, 396 of 1912.*)

An inscription in Coimbatore District of the Ummattūr Rāja Nanjanna-Uḍaiyār. His son was 'Chikka' Ganga Rāja. (*V. R. i, Coim. 353 ; 210 of 1909.*)

[The Portuguese at Cochin were attacked this year by a fleet said to be manned by both Muhammadans and Hindus. Several actions were fought. De Brito was beseiged in Cannanore but was saved by a Portuguese fleet commanded by Da Cunha. Almeida succeeded in destroying the Zamorin's fort at Ponnāni.]

A.D. 1508. Vīra Narasimha reigning in Cuddapah (*V. R. i, Cudd. 565 ; 389 of 1904*). And in Mysore on January 3 (*E. C. ix, Bn. 52*). And, early in 1508 in Chingleput, where the Kuḍiyantāṇḍal C. P. grant gives him full royal titles. (*E. I. xiv, 231.*)

Parākrama-Kulaśēkhara ruling in the south on January 12. This is the chief who was born in Krittika. (*618 of 1917.*)

In Coimbatore a record of the Ummattūr chief Chikka, son of Nanja.

(*V. R. i, Coim. 30, 326 ; 199 of 1909 ; 23 of 1910.*)

An inscription in Bellary District mentions Āraviṭi Timmaya, son of Rāma and grandson of Bukka. This was Timma Rāja uncle of that 'Aḷiya' Rāma Raja who was destined to become very prominent in the later history of the Vijayanagar Empire ; the date is April 15, 1508. (*689 of 1920.*)

[Almeida visited Cannanore, and at Dabhōl was guilty of a terrible massacre of the inhabitants.]

A.D. 1509. Vīra Narasimha, reigning in Salem District on January 26, 1509 (*V. R. ii, Salem 1 ; 408 of 1913*). And on April 5, in E. Mysore (*The Tēki grant ; E. C. x, Mr. 6*). And on April 17, at Conjevaram (*601 of 1919*). And on July 22, in S. Arcot—if the date be accepted as such, but though that is the day corresponding to the named tithi, etc., week day does not correspond with the one mentioned in the record (*289 of 1915*). The Tāḍpatri record (*V. R. i, Anantapur, 207 ; 342 of 1892*) shews that Vīra Narasimha was reigning, and the date has been stated to be May 4, 1509, but I have not been able to prove it. An inscription in S. Kanara of the year 1509-10 records gift of a village by 'Narasimha Rāya', who may have been Vīra Narasimha. But this is not certain.

(*V. R. ii, S. Kan. 9.*)

An inscription in Bellary District shews Vīra Narasimha's brother and successor Krishnadēva Rāya reigning on July 26, 1509. (*703 of 1919.*)

And this seems to prove that Vīra Narasimha died on some day between (certainly) April 17, or (possibly) July 22, and July 26, 1509.

Krishnadēva Rāya was reigning as king (we may now call him Emperor) of Vijayanagar in the month Kārttika of Ś. 1431 = October 14 to November 13, 1509. Inscription at Pulivēṇḍla in Cuddapah District. (*V. R. i, Cudd. 627 ; 491 of 1906 ; Arch. Ann. Rep. for 1908, p. 175.*)

[Nuniz relates a painful story—whether true or not will never be known—of the last act of Vīra Narasimha. Nuniz was told that on his deathbed the king sent for his minister Śāḷuva Timma and commanded that the king's own young son, then only eight years old, should be placed on the throne; and to this end he ordered the minister to put out the eyes of his (the king's) brother Krishnadēva Rāya and bring them to him, so that Krishnadēva should never become king. Śāḷuva Timma tore the eyes out of a she-goat and presented them to his sovereign, who then died happy. Whereupon Krishnadēva was raised to be king in his stead.

(*' A Forgotten Empire ', 314–15.*)

Afonso d'Albuquerque was made viceroy to the king of Portugal in supersession of Almeida. Lopes de Sequeira was governor of the seas East of Cape Comorin.]

Krishnadēva Rāya reigning in some part of the year 1509–10 in S. Kanara.

(*V. R. ii, S. Kan. 36.*)

Pratāpa Rudra Gajapati of Orissa ruling Udayagiri fort and neighbourhood in Nellore District. (*E. R. 1921, App. A, C. P. 21.*)

In E. Mysore an inscription mentions ' Virūpāksha-Rāya ' as governing the country,—probably locally. It is not known who this was. (*E. C. ix, Ht., 76.*)

Jaṭilavarman-Parākrama-Pāṇḍya ruling in Tinnevelly District on January 3, 1509, in his 30th year. This may be the same as the Kulaśekhara who was ' born in Krittikā ; but if so there would seem to be a mistake of perhaps a few days in the date as it would make January 3, 1480, the last possible day for his accession, and this would not quite agree with the results obtained from other records. (*12 of 1912 ; E. R. 1922, p. 94 ; see the Pedigree Table of Pāṇḍyas.*)

A.D. 1510. Krishnadēva Rāya was crowned king, or Emperor, of Vijayanagar, which now embraced the whole of Southern India with a few local exceptions (there are no records naming him as king in Tinnevelly District), on January 23, 1510 (*Hampe temple inscription, E. I. i, 361*). His minister was Śāḷuva Timma.

Inscriptions shew Krishnadēva Rāya reigning in Mysore on March 11, 1510 (*E. C. xii, Mi. 58*). And on the same day in Conjevaram (*411 of 1919*). This record says that a gift was made by a private person of land made over to him by ' Narasimha Mahārāya,' who may be identical with Śāḷuva Vīra Narasimha *alias* Chellapa or Sellapa of whom we hear in other records, and who was Krishnadēva Rāya's viceroy in the south. (*Below. s. v. 1530.*)

Krishnadēva Rāya was reigning in Mysore on September 17, and October 14 (*E. C. ix, D.-B.* 1 *x, Gd. 28 ; C.-B., 4*) ; and on December 16. (*E.C. xii, Mi. 64.*)

Other records of the same year shew him reigning in Anantapur, Guntur, Chittoor, Ramnad, and Cuddapah districts (*717 of 1917 ; V.R. ii, Gun. 371 ; B. and V.C. 974 ; 348 of 1922 ; V.R. ii, Ram. 229, 230 ; 91, 92 of 1908 ; V.R. i, Cudd. 399, 563 ; 387 of 1904*). The Rāmnād inscriptions referred to record gifts of land and villages to a temple ' for the merit of Chellapa *alias* Vīra Narasimha '. In Chingleput, another inscription similarly records the grant of a village ' for the merit ' of the same person (*V.R. i, Chin. 240 ; 256 of 1910 ;* see *Mr. Krishnaswami Aiyangar's introduction to Mr. Satyanatha Aiyar's* 'History of the Nayakas of Madura', *p. 8 ; and the former's* 'Sources of Vijayanagar History' *Introd. pp. 12, 13, and Text 158, 162*).

[N.B.—*It is unnecessary henceforth to refer to all the inscriptions which mention the names of Vijayanagar kings. They are very numerous and the periods of the kings' reigns are now well-known. Attention will therefore be called only to those of historical importance.*]

Pratāpa Rudra Gajapati of Orissa reigning in Vizagapatam District.

(*V.R. iii, Vizag. 198 ; 377 of 1905.*)

[Yusuf Ādil Shāh of Bījāpūr died this year and was succeeded by his son Ismāīl Ādil Shāh.]

[On January 4, 1510, Albuquerque attacked the Zamorin's palace at Calicut and burned it, but in the end was repulsed and withdrew to Cochin. On February 28, the Portuguese took Goa from the Muhammadans. It was retaken on May 20, by the Bījāpūr army, and was again seized by the Portuguese on November 10. Several thousand inhabitants, men and women, were killed. A Portuguese embassy visited King Krishna Rāya, asking his help against the Ādil Shāh: and in return Krishna Raja sent envoys to Goa, and granted permission to the Portuguese to erect a fort at Bhaṭkal, one of his reasons being to increase the trade in horses for the supply of his army.

(' *A Forgotten Empire*', *pp. 126–128.*)

When he came to the throne Krishnadēva's first precaution was, says Nuniz (' *A Forgotten Empire,' p. 325*), to immure his nephew, Tirumala, son of Vīra Narasimha and the rightful heir to the throne, as well as his own three brothers in the fortress of Chandragiri, where shortly afterwards Tirumala died.]

Krishnadēva remitted the tax on marriages which had been previously enforced on all brides and bridegrooms. It existed at least as far back as the eleventh century A.D., and is alluded to in the Leiden grant (*Tamil and Sanskrit inscriptions, 204, 224*). The inscription which records this remission mentions as locally ruling in Cuddapah District the Chief Minister Śāḷuva Timmaya and others. (*V.R. Cudd. 563 ; 387 of 1904. Cf. Cudd. 399.*)

A.D. 1511. Either in this year or in 1512, Krishnadēva made war against and defeated the refractory chief of Ummattūr in S. Mysore, Nanja Rāja. These chiefs claimed to be Lords of Penukonḍa. Krishnadēva captured Śivanasamudra from them, and then the whole of the south of Mysore submitted to him (*E.I. vii, 17*). [This victory over the Ummattūr chief has been misplaced in Nuniz's chronicle. He makes out that it occurred after Krishnadēva's campaign against Simhāchalam, which he calls 'Symamdari' (for Simhādri). There is however no doubt that it was the king's first exploit before he marched to attack the Gajapati king at Udayagiri. Nuniz states that the country governed by the Ummattūr chief was 'the land of a lord,' which land was called 'Catuir.' Mr. Krishnaswami Aiyangar's excellent article on the subject in the *Hindustan Review*, 1917, makes it clear to my mind that, as he suggests, 'Catuir' is a rendering of 'Kādava', and that it really referred to the name of the Ummattūr chief's ancestry, or to the ancestry of other chiefs in alliance with him, viz., those who claimed to belong to the family of the 'Kāḍava' chief Perunjinga. Nuniz's description of the operations which led to Krishnadēva's capture of the Kāḍava's chief city is similar to that given in the *Krishnarājavijayamu* when dealing with the capture of Śivanasamudram.][1]

[Albuquerque went to Malacca and was guilty of much wanton bloodshed there. Goa was again attacked by the Ādil Shāh but was relieved.]

[1] See also the Telugu poem *Pārijātāpaharaṇamu* dedicated to Krishna himself.—*Editor.*

A.D. 1512. An inscription in Chittoor District mentions Krishnadēva's queen Chinnāji. (*V.R. i, Chit. 9-M ; 65 of 1889.*)

The Ummattūr chief Chikka Rāya, son of Nanja Rāja, mentioned in a record in Coimbatore district. (*V.R. i, Coim. 326 ; 23 of 1910.*)

[Krishnadēva Rāya sent an expedition to recapture the fortress of Raichūr from the Bījāpūr Sultan, and after a time it was successful and the place passed into the hands of the Vijayanagar king and remained in his possession for some years. But we hear of it as being again held by Bījapūr when Krishnadēva attacked it in 1520. (*'A Forgotten Empire', p. 325 f.*)

In this year Quli Quṭb Shāh of Golkonda became independent Sultan of Golkonda. As Qutb-ul-Mulkh, he had been governor of the Telingana provinces of the Bāhmanī kingdom, and he had remained loyal to his sovereign, lately bereft of all power, till this year.]

A.D. 1513. [In this year Krishnadēva Rāya, after elaborate preparations and the collection of large forces, set out on a campaign against Pratāpa Rudra Gajapati of Orissa with the intention of capturing from him the group of fortresses south of and near the Krishna river, namely, Udayagiri, Koṇḍavīḍu, Koṇḍapalli, Vinukoṇḍa, Bellamkoṇḍa and others which had passed into the possession of the kings of Orissa during the previous half century. He marched first to Udayagiri and besieged it (*E.I. vii, 18. A 'Forgotten Empire,' 130, 316*). Nuniz says that his army was composed of 800 elephants and 34,000 foot. He lay before Udayagiri for a year and a half, making approaches and roads.]

While besieging Udayagiri, Krishnadēva held the surrounding country, and he gave a village in the Polur taluk, Nellore District, to a temple. (*V.R. ii, Nell. 636 ; B. and V.C. 1316.*)

The *gōpura* of the Viṭṭhalaswami temple at Hampe was built this year by Krishnadēva and his two queens (*V.R. i, Bellary, 337*). And he gave six villages to the temple of Rāmachandra. (*ibid. 349, 350*).

Gift by Śāḷuva Gōvinda (*V.R. i, Anantapur 205 ; 340 of 1892*). A peace was patched up between the Portuguese and the chief of Calicut and a factory was established there.

A.D. 1514. The fortress of Udayagiri was captured early in this year, and there Krishnadēva Rāya made prisoners of an uncle and an aunt of the king of Orissa, whom he treated with all honour. The uncle's name was Tirumala Kānta *alias* Rāghava Rāya. The Gajapati king fled to Koṇḍavīḍu and was pursued thither. Krishnadēva was encamped at Udayagiri, after its fall, on June 9, 1514. An inscription on a rock at the fortress gives the date and the name of the prince taken prisoner (*V.R. ii, Nellore 791 ; B. and V.C. 1386*). He carried away from Udayagiri an image of Krishna and erected it at the capital after his return thither, and gave some villages to temples (*V.R. ii, Nellore 788 ; 203 of 1892 ; B. and V.C. 1382*). In his summary of these two records, Mr. V. Rangacharya is in error in calling Tirumala Kānta the 'nephew' of the Gajapati king. The inscriptions distinctly call him uncle.

An inscription in South Arcot of February 12, 1514, alludes to excessive taxation of the people and the consequent abandonment of their homes by the villagers. This led to a revision of the taxes. (*246 of 1916.*)

Krishnadēva's governor of Udayagiri, Rāyasam Koṇḍamarasa gave a grant on August 20, 1514. (*V.R. ii, Nellore 617 ; B. and V.C. 1197.*)

The king's erection of the image of Krishna, which he had brought from Udayagiri, at Vijayanagar is mentioned in inscriptions. (*V.R. i, Bellary 392, 393, 419 ; 25, 26 of 1889 ; 498 of 1907.*)

Other grants of this governor have been found (*V.R. ii, Nellore 298, 584, 730 ; B. and V.C. 536, 1156, 1330*). One bears date about May 1514.

[In 1514 A.D., the Ādil Shāh, Sultan of Bījapūr, was successful in several campaigns against the rival Sultans of the Dekhan.]

A.D. 1515. [At the beginning of this year, Krishnadēva Rāya marched with a large army against Pratāpa Rudra Gajapati. He began by besieging the Koṇḍavīḍu hill fortress, south of the Krishna river, to which the Gajapati king had fled from Udayagīri. In the course of his operations he captured a number of fortresses, Addanki, Vinukoṇḍa, Bellamkoṇḍa and others. He stormed Koṇḍavīḍu, captured the stronghold on June 23, 1515 (*Pillar inscription at Mangaḷagiri, V.R. ii, Guntur 148 ; 257 of 1892*), and made prisoners of Prince Vīrabhadra Gajapati, son of Pratāpa Rudra, a certain Nariharipātra, son of Hammīrapātra, and many other Hindu chiefs, and also seized two Musalman chiefs who apparently were resident at Koṇḍavīḍu. (It is to be noted here that, according to Muhammadan accounts, Quli Quṭb Shāh of Golkonda had about this time, after considerable difficulty, captured Koṇḍavīḍu in the course of a campaign against the Gajapati king. It is impossible in a work like the present, to attempt a reconciliation of all accounts that conflict).]

While at Koṇḍavīḍu Krishnadēva visited Amarāvati on the Krishna river, weighed himself against gold, and made some munificent gifts to the temple of Amarēśvara. Two inscriptions record this and mention his queens Tirumalādēvi and Chinnādēvī (*V.R. ii, Guntur 632, 638 ; 266, 272 of 1897*). He was at Amarāvati on July 8.

His capture of Koṇḍavīḍu is noted in a number of inscriptions.

(*V.R. ii, Guntur, 148 ; 257 of 1892 ; E.I. vi, 108 ff ; B. and V.C. i, 125.*)

After his capture of the Krishna fortresses Krishnadēva Rāya visited Śrīśailam and Ahōbilam, where he gave gifts and benefited the temples on July 25 and December 21.

(*V.R. ii, Kurnool 454, 455 ; 578 ; 18, 19, 64 of 1915.*)

At Pērūr near Guḍivāḍa are two records of this year and 1520 stating that Nādēnḍla Appanna, son of Timmaya and nephew of Śāḷuva Timma, the king's minister, was made governor of Vinukoṇḍa, Gutti and Amaravāti by Krishnadēva Raya ; and that Appanna's brother Gōpanna was made governor of Koṇḍavīḍu (*V.R. ii, Kistna, 234-D., 234-E ; E.I. vi, 230*). At one time the two governors seem to have changed places.

After his capture of Koṇḍavīḍu and visit to Amarāvati, Krishnadēva moved to Bezwada and laid siege to Koṇḍapalli, a strong hill-fortress north of the Krishna River. The place fell into his hands, and Nuniz says that it was *there* that Krishnadēva made prisoners of the wife 'and one of the sons' of Pratāpa Rudra Gajapati, whom he sent to Vijayanagar. It would seem then that this young prince was not the prince Vīrabhadra but another son of the king of Orissa. Vīrabhadra apparently was treated kindly by Krishnadēva, for an inscription, whose date = October 19, 1515, shews him as Nāyaka of a small tract in Mysore, and as making a grant by permission of Krishnadēva and 'for the merit' of Krishnadēva and Vīrabhadra's father king Pratāpa Rudra. He must have been sent into the Mysore country very shortly after his capture.

(*Inscription at Malebennūr in N. Mysore. E.C. xi, Dg., 107.*)

[From Koṇḍapalli Krishnadēva marched northwards into Gajapati territory, capturing a number of places till he got as far as Simhāchalam ; whence, having the Gajapati king now completely conquered and holding his queen as hostage, he returned to Vijayanagar, entered into a treaty with Pratāpa Rudra, made peace, and married his (the Gajapati king's daughter). This carries the story into A.D. 1516.]

[The Portuguese viceroy Albuquerque died in 1515, and Lopes Soares was appointed viceroy of Goa in his stead.]

A.D. 1516. A long inscription at Tiruvaṇṇāmalai in N. Arcot gives a list of Krishnadēva's triumphs to date. (*V.R. i, N. Arcot 530 ; 574 of 1902.*)

Early in the year Koṇḍamarasa, governor of Udayagiri, granted a village to a temple (*V.R. ii, Nellore 610 ; B. and V.C. 1187*). He settled certain boundary questions about the territories of Koṇḍavīḍu and Koṇḍapalli. (*325 of 1919.*)

Śaḷuva Gōvinda mentioned in a record in Cuddapah District. (*V.R. i, Cudd. 156 ; 342 of 1905.*)

Krishnadēva built this year the 100-pillared hall at the temple of Viṭṭhalaswāmi at the capital. (*711, 712, 713 of 1922; V.R. i, Bellary, 344, 345.*)

The king made a grant in Hassan District, Mysore on June 29, 1516 ' when he was returning ' home after his successes in his war against the king of Orissa, and after he had set up a pillar of victory on the bank of the Krishna river. (*E.C. v, Hn. 13.*)

A grant was made, in the Kāḍūr District, W. Mysore, by a local chief Bhairarasa, ruling the Kaḷasa country on July 13, 1516, in gratitude to heaven for his escape from the threatening approach to his country of a great Vijayanagar army which had been encamped at Mangalore, but had retired. (*E.C. vi, Mg. 41, 39.*)

That Krishnadēva's arms really reached as far as Simhāchalam is shewn by his inscriptions of the year A.D. 1516 in Vizagapatam District. (*V. R. iii, Vizag. 71, 72, 73 ; 243, 244, 245 of 1899.*)

He visited Kāḷahasti in 1516 and erected there a 100-pillared hall at the temple. (*V. R. i, Chittoor, 135 ; 196 of 1903.*)

In an inscription of this year in Mysore he is given the titles of the Śāḷuva family, to which he did not belong. This is also noticeable in a few other cases. (*E. C. v. H. N. 19.*)

In Cuddapah District an inscription records a gift made ' for the merit of ' Krishnadēva and Śāḷuva Govinda. (*V .R. i, Cudd. 156 ; 342 of 1905.*)

A.D. 1517. A long inscription at Śēndamangalam in South Arcot District gives a list of Krishnadēva's triumphs up to date (*V. R. i, S. Arcot, 435 ; 74 of 1903*). In Cuddapah District mention made of his minister Śāḷuva Timma, *alias* Appājī. (*V. R. i, Cudd. 32, 44.*)

A fragmentary (broken) inscription in Coimbatore District seems to shew that the defeated Ummattūr chief Nanja still held rule over a tract there. (*V.R. i, Coim. 284 ; 208 of 1909.*)

In Anantapūr District a record stating that a gift was made to a temple by Rāyasam Koṇḍamarasa, governor of Udayagiri (*above, A.D. 1514*), in order that king Krishnadēva might be blessed with children. The king's son Tirumala was born shortly before or after this event. (*V.R. i, Anant. 47 ; 87 of 1912.*)

A pedigree of Krishnadēva's family, Tuḷuvas, is given in an inscription. (*E. C. iv, Gun. 30.*)

The king's minister, Śaḷuva Timma, gave a grant on November 4, 1517, at Kāḷahasti in Chittoor District. (*113 of 1922.*)

An inscription in Ramnad mentions the Bāṇa chief ' Mahābali-Vāṇāda-Rāya-Nāyaka '. (*V. R. ii. Ram. 131 ; 113 of 1903.*)

The Kaḷasa and Kārkaḷa tracts 'above and below the ghats' were ruled in this year by the (? Sāntara) chief Immaḍi-Bhairarasa subject to the Vijayanagar king.

(*E. C. vi, Mg. 62.*)

Śāḷuva Timma mentioned as a great lord ruling in E. Mysore 'in the time of Tirumala-dēva' son of Krishnadēva-Raya. (*V. R. i. Cuddapah, 123 ; E. C. ix, Ma. 82.*)

A.D. 1525. Krishnadēva Rāya gave a village near the capital to the Mādhva teacher Vyāsatīrtha. (*E. R. 1904–5, p. 59.*)

[Nothern India was convulsed at this time by the invasion of the Mughals under Bābur of Samarkhand, who crossed the frontier and attacked Hindustan.]

A.D. 1526. An inscription at Atti in N. Arcot District of August 20, mentions the grant of that village made by king Krishnadēva Rāya while 'encamped on the bank of the Krishnavēṇi river.' The government epigraphist suggests that he was on the lower Krishna engaged in trying to come to terms with the Gajapati king; but it seems equally likely that it refers to the upper reaches of the river and Krishnadēva's camp near Raichūr.

(*V. R. i, N. Arcot, 227 ; 299 of 1912.*)

[The Mughal Emperor Bābur, pursuing his victorious career, fought and won a great battle at Pānīpat, and captured Agra and Delhi, the Sultan Ibrahim Lodi being slain. Bābur was proclaimed Pādshāh on April 25, and established the Mughal Empire.]

An inscription in Nellore District of a date early in the year 1526 represents Krishnadēva Rāya's brother Achyuta-Rāya as 'seated on the diamond throne of Vijayanagar.' This was not actually the case, though Achyuta may have represented the king or may have been his viceroy or Delegate. (*V. R. ii, Nell. 509 ; B. and V. C. 802.*)

In Travancore Bhūtala-Udaya-Mārttāṇḍa protected Christian fishermen who had been molested by their Hindu rivals. (*V. R. iii, Trav. 40–B.*)

A.D. 1527. Grant of a village in Udayagiri-rājyam by Rāyasam Ayyapa—probably of the family of the Governor of Udayagiri, Rāyasam Koṇḍama.

(*V. R. ii, Nellore 350 ; B. and V. C. 615.*)

[Bābur was joined this year at Delhi by his son Humāyūn.]

Several inscriptions of Krishnadēva Rāya in this year in Bellary, Coimbatore, Chittoor and Chingleput Districts and in Mysore.

A.D. 1528. Inscriptions of Krishnadēva Rāya in Bellary, Chingleput, Kurnool, Madura and S. Kanara Districts and in Mysore.

An inscription in Central Mysore commemorates a remission of taxes by Krishnadēva Rāya's 'dear son,' Singapa Nāyaka.[1] The expression son—*piḷḷai*—is only a metaphor meaning a valued public servant or friend. Several records noted above in earlier years use a similar expression. (*E. C. xii, Ck. 37.*)

[1] Harsan III is dated Sarvadhāri, Śrāvaṇa. Ba. 5 = Monday, July 6, 1528 is a grant by some Nāyaka, a relative presumably of Singappa Nāyaka, son of Venkaṭādri and grandson of Krishṇa Rāya. It was a grant to God Mādhava in the local temple made in the auspicious—Sankrānti. This could only be Dakshināyana Sankrānti which fell on Monday, June 29th, preceding.

Chikkanāyakanahalli 37 is of date Saka 1450, Vaiśaka Ba. 30, Sōmavāra, Sūryoparāga = 18th May 1528, Monday, on which there was an eclipse of the sun. Here Singappa is referred to as a dear son of Krishnadēva Rāya Mahārāya. The two Singappa's are not the same—while the latter may in some sense be son, or simple favourite, the former may have had no connection as Krishna is not referred to with any distinctive royal appellation—*Editor*.

In E. Mysore an inscription mentions Prince Achyuta of Vijayanagar as ruling that country. *(E. C. x, Sd. 15.)*

An inscription of this year at Muṭṭatti in Hassan Taluk, Mysore, requires some examination and explanation. It purports to record a grant made by Singappa-Nāyaka[1] (note the other inscription of this chief in the same year—*above*), son of Venkatādri and grandson of Krishnadēva Rāya. We know of no son or grandson of this king bearing those names, and the king himself was not much above forty years of age in 1528; for Nuniz says that he was only 'over twenty' in 1509. *(E. C. v, Hn. 111.)*

[Bābur attacked Rājputāna and captured Chandēri fort and Ranthambor.

The Portuguese at Goa assisted Burhān-Nizām-Shāh of Ahmadnagar against Bahādur Shāh of Gujarāt, and destroyed a Gujarāt fleet.]

A.D. 1529. Inscription in Mysore, of date March 15, representing Achyuta-Rāya of Vijayanagar as 'ruling the kingdom'—evidently as viceroy for the king, his brother. *(E. C. xii, Gb. 32.)*

Krishnadēva Rāya was reigning in Chingleput and Bellary Districts on April 15 and 23, and in Kurnool on April 29 (The *Udayambākkam Grant, E. I. xiv, 168 ; I. 398 ; V. R. i, Bell. 366 ; Chin. 468 ; Kurn. 549 ; 233 of 1901 ; 164 of 1913*). And in N. Arcot on June 26 (*V. R. i, N. Arcot 240 ; 294 of 1912*). And in Nellore District on 28 July (*V. R. ii, Nell. 113 ; B. and V. C. i, 362*). And at Conjevaram on October 17 (*512 of 1919*). And in Kurnool District on October 27. *(V. R. ii, Kurn. 451 ; 15 of 1915.)*

[About this time or a little earlier Krishnadēva Rāya appointed Visvanātha Nāyaka his viceroy in Madura, in succession to the latter's father Nāgama, whose behaviour had displeased the king.]

An inscription, which unfortunately in the absence of certain details cannot be verified, but of which the given details correspond to November 11, 1529, represents Achyuta-Rāya, brother of Krishnadēva Rāya, as ruling in Mysore. It may be assumed, from the analogy of other records noted above, that Achyuta was ruling then as viceroy, and it may be that Krishnadēva was still alive on that day. But this is not certain. *(E.C. viii. Sb. 39.)*

The Kaḍalāḍi C.P. grant of Achyuta Rāya distinctly states that on December 28, 1529, Krishnadēva Rāya was dead (*E.I. xiv. 310 ; V.R. i, N. Arcot, 373*). It seems certain therefore that Krishnadēva's death occurred between October 27 and December 28, 1529.

Achyuta-Rāya's minister was Rāmabhaṭlu. His chief general was Salakam (or Chālukya ?) Tirumala, whose sister was one of the queens. Rāmabhaṭlu is mentioned in an inscription in Coimbatore (*V.R. i, Coim. 325 ; 22 of 1910*). [Nuniz calls Krishnadēva's minister Śāḷuva Timma, 'Salvatinica', and Achyuta's minister 'Salvanay' (Śaḷuva Nāyaka). He asserts. ('*A Forgotten Empire*', *p. 361*) that Krishnadēva, believing that Śāḷuva Timma had poisoned prince Tirumala, the king's son, had the minister blinded.]

A.D. 1530. [Immediately on Krishnadēva's death, Ismāīl Ādil Shah took up arms and marched to recover Raichūr and the Doab country generally, which was given up to him by king Achyuta who, Nuniz says, was a man of weak character, 'very negligent of the things which most concern the welfare of the kingdom' and 'given over to vice and tyranny' ('*A Forgotten Empire*,' *367, 369*). Nuniz gives an interesting list of Achyuta's principal nobles and governors. *(Ibid. p. 384, f.)*

[1] Please see note on p. 244.

Achyuta-Rāya reigning earlier than March 1530. Inscriptions in Chingleput District and N. Arcot (*V.R. i, Chin. 825 ; N. Arcot 195 ; 295 of 1917 ; 394 of 1912*). There are a number of his inscriptions of this year in the Madras Districts and Mysore including Ramnad, but none in Tinnevelly.

On March 14, he was reigning in Anantapur. (*453 of 1920*). And during the year ending in March 1530 in N. Arcot (*V.R. i, N. Arcot, 195 ; 394 of 1912*). And on April 12, in Mysore (*E.C. ix, D.-B. 30*). These sufficiently establish the period of his accession.

Vīra Narasimha *alias* Chellapa, the Vijayanagar governor of the South has been already mentioned (*s.v. 1510*). At Uraṭṭūr in Chingleput District is an inscription of A.D. 1530–31, commemorating a gift made 'for his merit' (*V.R. Chin. 240 ; 256 of 1910*). His exploits are related in the Achyutarāyābhyudayam (See Krishnaswami Aiyangar's *Sources of Vijayanagar History*, p. 158 *f*).

The Sāntāra (?) chief Bhairarasa was ruling the Kārkaḷa country below the ghats of Western Mysore. (*E.C. vi, Kp. 47.*)

In December 1530 the Mughal leader Bābur died, and his son Humāyūn succeeded him.

[The Portuguese, finding their trade greatly hampered by the piracy so prevalent on the west coast, looted a number of coast towns in the belief that they were the abode of the pirates.]

A.D. 1531. Many inscriptions of king Achyuta-Rāya in Chingleput, S. Arcot, Anantapur and Bellary Districts, in the Pudukoṭṭai State, and in Mysore, in this year.

War between Ismāīl Ādil Shāh of Bijapūr and Burhān Nizam Shah of Ahmadnagar, in which the former was victorious.

An inscription of date = March 20, 1531, states that one of the Golkonda Sultan's officers, who was a 'friend' of his master's, established near Koṇḍapalli (Kristna District) certain charitable institutions and gave for their maintenance two villages. (*V. R. ii, Kistna, 103 ; 152 of 1893.*)

[Śāḷuva Narasimha, *alias* Chellapa, allied with Tumbichi Nāyaka and the Tiruvaḍi-Raja of Vēṇād (Travancore) Udaya-Mārttāṇḍa, took up arms about this time, threw over the overlordship of Vijayanagar and attempted to drive out the Pāṇḍya ruler Jaṭilavarman-Śrīvallabha. They were attacked and defeated by a Vijayanagar general, and Chellapa fled for refuge to Travancore. The Vijayanagar generals were Salakam-Tirumala, Nāgama Nāyaka of Madura and his son Viśvanātha Nāyaka.]

A.D. 1532. Many inscriptions of Achyuta-Rāya—unimportant.

The image of Narasimha was set up this year in the court of the temple of Viṭṭhalaswami at Hampe by the Mādhva teacher Vyāsatīrtha. (*710 of 1922.*)

Achyuta-Rāya visited Conjevaram this year and had himself weighed against pearls which he distributed in gifts (*V.R. i, Anantapur 87 ; 580 of 1912*). He was in Conjevaram on May 21, 1532. (*541 of 1919.*)

[In this year the Portuguese continued their attacks on coast towns near Goa, and compelled the people of Bombay and Thānā to pay large sums.]

A.D. 1533. Many records—unimportant—of Achyuta-Rāya.

His son Venkaṭādri is mentioned in an inscription of October 29, 1533, in Anantapur District. (*V.R. i, Anant. 81 ; 574 of 1912.*)

An inscription mentioning Kānchirāya-Rangayya Chōla-Mahāraja—one of a line of chiefs of former years akin to the Chōla-Mahārājās of Niḍugal. (*V. R. i, Cuddapah 509 ; 479 of 1906.*)

Achyuta was at Conjevaram on January 20. (*543 of 1919.*)

The *Achyutābhyudāyam* (*'Sources of Vijayanagar History' p. 159*) says that after king Achyuta had been weighed against pearls in Conjevaram, hearing that his rebellious viceroy Chellapa after his defeat by Vijayanagar troops had taken refuge in Travancore, sent his general, the 'son of Salaka', to the south to reduce the refractory leaders. A battle was fought 'near the mountains' when Chellapa was completely defeated. He and the Tiruvaḍi-Rāja were taken prisoners and presented to Achyuta, who commanded that the Raja should be punished, and the Pāṇḍya Prince restored to his 'ancestral territories'. This Pāṇḍya Prince was Jaṭilavarman-Kulaśēkhara-Śrīvallabha, who, having freed his country received the title 'Irandakālam-Eḍutta'—'he who brought back the old times.'

A village in Nellore was granted by Salakam-Tirumala, king Achyuta's brother-in-law (*V. R. ii, Nell. 233; B and V. C. 432*). He is also mentioned in a record in Anantapur District in this year. (*V. R. i, Anant. 10; 51 of 1912.*)

Grant of land at Cape Comorin by Bhūtala-Udayamārttaṇḍa of Travancore. (*V. R. iii, Trav. 39.*)

A.D. 1534. A number of unimportant inscriptions of Achyuta-Rāya.

This is the year of accession of the Pāṇḍya Prince Jaṭilavarman-Kulaśēkhara-Śrīvallabha 'who brought back the old times,' and was son of Āhava-Rāma (*see Pedigree Table and Notes*). He had been aided by Achyuta-Rāya (*above*). (*525 of 1909; E.R. 1910, p. 101; T.A.S. i, 56 see also 650 of 1917.*)

On February 28, 1534, a grant was made in Anantapur District on the occasion of Achyuta-Rāya performing the *Lakshahoma* ceremony. (*V. R. i, Anant. 144; 179 of 1913.*)

An inscription in Madras District mentions Achyuta's minister Salakam-Timma. (*V. R. ii, Madras 185; C. P. 11 of 1905–06.*)

In the Ramnad a gift made 'for the merit of Viśvanātha-Nāyaka,' who later on founded the Nāyaka dynasty of Madura. (*V. R. ii, Ramnad 251; 113 of 1908.*)

[The Portuguese erected a fort at Diu, and again fought against and defeated the Zamorin of Calicut; who after this ceased from his opposition to the foreigners.

War broke out between the Sultans of Bijāpūr and Golkonda; in the course of which Muhammad Quṭb Shāh of Golkonda is said to have behaved brutally to the prisoners he had captured, cutting off their noses and ears. (*Firishta, Scott's Edit. i, 257.*)

Ismāil Ādil Shāh died this year on August 13. Assad Khān was made Regent for the new Sultan Malū, son of Ismāil, who, after a few months, being found incompetent, was deposed and blinded, his brother Ibrahim Ādil being raised to the throne.]

A.D. 1535. A number of inscriptions, of no historical importance, shewing Achyuta-Rāya reigning.

[According to Firishta, the new Sultan of Bijāpūr, Ibrahim Ādil Shāh was invited by Achyuta to visit Vijayanagar and he did so, accompanied by Assad Khān.]

Jaṭilavarman Śrīvallabha was ruling in Tinnevelly District (*V. R. iii, Tinn. 361; 525 of 1909*). He is called 'Irandakālam-Eḍutta'—'he who brought back the old times.'

The Government of Madura was in the hands of Viśvanātha Nāyaka. (*113 of 1908; E. R. 1909, p. 119.*)

In Ramnad District, a gift by Sundara-Tōḷ-Uḍaiyār, the Bāṇa chief. (*585 of 1902; 121 of 1903.*)

A.D. 1536. Many unimportant records of king Achyuta.

In an inscription in Bellary District mention is made of his son the 'Chikka Rāya.' This was Venkaṭādri. (*V. R. i, Bellary 319 ; 5 of 1904.*)

[The Portuguese built a fort at Cranganore. The Governor of Goa, da Cunha, attempting to seize territory was opposed by Assad Khān and compelled to retire.]

A.D. 1537. [I pass over many records of Achyuta, which are not important.]

Jaṭilavarman Śrīvallabha was ruling in Tinnevelly on November 21, in his third year. (*577 of 1917 ; V. R. iii, Tinn. 391 ; 200 of 1895.*)

In Travancore a record of Bhūtala Ravivarman of Kērala as ruler. (*V. R. iii, Trav. 163.*)

In Ramnad District a gift by the Bāṇa chief Sundara-Toḷ-Uḍaiyār. (*587 of 1902.*)

From an inscription in Tinnevelly, it would appear that king Achyuta's nephew Sadāśiva, afterwards himself king, was ruling in the south as viceroy, the governor under him being Viṭṭhala. (*V. R. iii, Tinn. 287 ; C. P. 6 of 1905/6.*)

A.D. 1538. A number of inscriptions in Mysore and Madras districts shew Achyuta-Rāya reigning imperially. Two of these alone require notice. One (*V. R. ii, Madura 6 ; 1 of 1894*) shews that he was recognized as sovereign in Madura, over which Viśvanātha Nāyaka ruled. The other shews him as equally supreme in Ramnad. (*V. R. ii, Ram. 259 ; 121 of 1908.*)

A.D. 1539. Achyuta's supremacy apparent over all South India. But in Tinnevelly an inscription shews a local Pāṇḍya ruler, Māravarman-Sundara-Pāṇḍya III, then in his eighth year of office. (*V. R. iii, Tinn. 251 ; 18 of 1912.*)

A.D. 1540. Many inscriptions of Achyuta. One, in Central Mysore, shews that Sadāśiva, Achyuta's nephew, was ruling there as viceroy. (*E. C. xii, Mi. 66.*)

[There was a terrible famine in this year which reduced many of the inhabitants of the eastern districts to cannibalism, while numbers drowned themselves. Joao de Castro relates that two-thirds of the population of the Vijayanagar Empire perished of starvation. (*I. A. 1923 ; p. 232.*)

In 1540 Quli Quṭb Shāh of Golkonda made war on Orissa and inflicted a severe defeat on the Gajapati king in a battle near Rajahmundry. The king of Orissa sued for peace and ceded to Golkonda the whole of the territory between the Godavari and Krishna rivers.

The Portuguese concluded a treaty in this year with the Sultan of Bijapūr, Ibrahīm Ādil Shāh, and with Burhān Nizām Shāh of Ahmednagar, and the Zamorin of Calicut.

The Mughal Emperor Humāyūn was defeated by the Afghān Shīr Shāh who rebelled. Humāyun fled to Persia where he took refuge till restored to the throne in 1555. Meanwhile Shīr Shāh made himself master of Delhi.]

A.D. 1541. Amongst Achyuta's records of this year are two dated October 31 and November 5, 1541, shewing him then reigning (*B. and V.C. i, 91 ; 49 of 1917*). An inscription in Chittoor District mentions his son, Prince Venkaṭādri. (*V.R. i, Chit. 264 ; 373 of 1911.*)

In Tinnevelly District on October 23, Jaṭillavarman-Śrīvallabha-Pāṇḍya 'who brought back the old times' was reigning in his seventh year, shewing his accession to have been in the year preceding October 24, 1535.

Achyuta's minister at Penukoṇḍa and in Coimbatore was Rāmabhaṭlu. (*V.R. i, Anantapur, 141, 142 ; 176, 177 of 1913 ; ibid., Coim. 325 ; 22 of 1910.*)

A.D. 1542. This year saw the end of Achyuta's reign and the beginning of Sadāśiva's at Vijayanagar ; but with, apparently, the former's son Venkaṭādri on the throne for two or three days. It is necessary to examine the dates given in inscriptions relating to these rulers.

We have records shewing Achyuta as on throne on January 29, 1542 (*165 of 1922 at Kālahasti*); on March 19 (*E.C. vi, Kd. 160 in West Mysore*); on April 5, near Penukoṇḍa (*V.R. i, Anantapur 142; 177 of 1913*); on May 17, in W. Mysore (*E.C. vi, Mg. 64*); on May 29 also in W. Mysore (*ibid. vi, Kd. 158*); on June 24 in E. Mysore (*ibid. x, Mr. 32*); and on June 25 at Conjevaram. (*614 of 1919.*)

[One date, perhaps of August 11, 1542, in S. Arcot, which seems to shew Achyuta as reigning then, cannot be trusted to as evidence, as the details of the date are insufficient for verification.]

There are records shewing Sadāśiva reigning at Bādāmi on June 27, 1542 (*I.A. 1881, p. 63, No. LXXXVIII*); and in October of the same year (*B. and V.C. iii. 1377; V.R. ii, Nellore, 782*) at Udayagiri.

There is a record of 'Venkaṭa' on September 7, 1542, which represents him as 'Mahārāja'. This is in E. Mysore (*E.C. x, Mr. 62*); and another on January 1, 1543, also in E. Mysore. [*But see below.*] (*E.C. x, Sd. 52.*)

Putting all these together, if the dates are accepted and the inscriptions are truthful, we should conclude that king Achyuta died about June 25 or 26, 1542, and was succeeded by his son Venkaṭādri (*see E.I. xiv. 341*), but that the latter was at once ousted and the throne seized for Sadāśiva by that prince's supporters; so that by June 27, he was king. It seems clear that the succession was disputed. Venkaṭādri, the rightful heir, was supported by the 'Salakam' (Chāḷukya? family) chiefs; but the three powerful brothers, chiefs of the Āravīḍu family, Rāma, Tirumala and Venkaṭādri, probably knowing that Sadāśiva was a prince of weak character, and that the whole power would be in their hands, succeeded in displacing him and raising Sadāśiva to the throne. The inscription in Mysore which names, as ruling there on January 1, 1543, 'Venkaṭapati' may possibly refer to Venkaṭādri, the youngest of the three Āravīḍu brothers, and not to the prince of that name, son of Achyuta the king (*E.C. x, Sd. 52*) and the same with the inscription of September 7, 1542.

There is an inscription which requires notice in Anantapur District (*800 of 1917*). It says that the son of the Daḷavāy made a grant to a temple in gratitude for divine answer to his prayer that Sadāśiva's 'accession to the throne might be permanent.' The date of this is April 29, 1542. Here is one of those historical puzzles whose solution awaits further research.[1] The exact meaning of the words used in the record must be elucidated, and comparison made between it and the originals of the other records quoted above. Then alone will the truth become apparent.

[In the Dekhan there was again war in this year between the Musalman Sultans. Burhān Nizām Shah and Amīr Barīd of Bīdar in alliance attacked Ibrahīm Ādil Shāh of Bijāpūr. They 'spread fire and slaughter' through the latter's country, says Firishta (*Scott's Edit., p. 269*), and burned and laid waste the suburbs of Bījāpur city. In his turn, when he gained the ascendancy Ibrahīm 'took ample revenge . . . burning and destroying the territories of his enemies.']

The Kaḷasa-Kārkaḷa tracts of Western Mysore were being governed by Pāṇḍyappa, son-in-law of Bhairarasa, *alias* Vīra-Pāṇḍya. (*E. C. vi., Mg. 64.*)

[1] The details of the date given are Śaka 1565 *Śobhakrit*, Vaiśākha, Śu. di. 15. These according to Swamikannu Pillai's Ephemeris = Thursday, 19th April, 1543. Mr. Sewell's date in the previous year would be correct for *Śubhakrit*, not the next year *Śobhakrit*, the year in the record.—*Editor*.

An inscription in Kurnool District mentions Āravīti-Ahōbala, or Aubala of Nandyāl. (*V. R. ii. Kurn. 106.*)

A. D. 1543. There are inscriptions shewing Sadāśiva as king early in the year; one on April 30 and one on August 6 (*337 of 1917 ; 331 of 1922 ; 269 of 1921 ; 213 of 1916*). These are in S. Arcot, N. Arcot, Chittoor and Chingleput Districts.

In this year Tirumala, brother of Aḷiya-Rāma, was ruling at the Udayagiri fortress. (*B. and V. C. ii. 793.*)

Accession year in Tinnevelly of Jaṭilavarman-Kulaśēkhara-Parākrama-Pāṇḍya, elder son of Abhirāma. (*T. A. S. i. 48, 103, 266, 271, 274, 277 of 1908—records at Tenkāśi ; E. R. 1909, § 32.*)

Āravīṭi-Aubala, son of Narasinga, gave a grant (*see last year's note*). (*V. R. ii, Kurnool, 243 ; 160 of 1905.*)

[Rāma-Rāya, practically ruler of Vijayanagar, urged to action by Burhān Nizām Shāh, attacked Raichur, then a possession of the Ādil Shāh.

Quli-Quṭb Shāh of Golkonda was assassinated this year, and was succeeded by Jamshīd, who blinded his elder brother.]

A. D. 1544. A number of records shewing Sadāśiva on throne.

The Āravīḍu family in great power. Mention of Aubala, Chinna Timmayya, Chinna Aubala, Kōnēṭi Aubala (*E. C. iv. Ch. 121 ; V. R. ii, Kurnool, 177, 28, 610-B, 51, 55, 61, 67 ; 671, 674, 678, 700, 770 of 1917*). Viṭṭhala mentioned in Tanjore and Mysore. (*V. R. ii. Tan. 1243 ; 273 of 1991 ; E. C. xi. Hr. 29 ;* see also *V. R. i. Cuddapah, 624.*)

Abhirāma Parākrama Pāṇḍya ruling in Tinnevelly in his tenth year. (*V. R. iii., Tinn. 291.*)

Venkaṭādri, brother of Aḷiya Rāma-Rāja of Vijayanagar, remitted some taxes in Kurnool. Mention of Timma, grandson of Bukka of Āravīḍu. (*V. R. ii. Kurn. 558, 614, 610-A.*)

Mention of the Changāḷva chief Śrīkanṭha or Chennaya ruling in Coorg. (*E. C. i. Coorg. 26.*)

Two records in Cuddapah mention Kōnēṭi-Chinna-Timma, son of Pedda Konḍa of Āravīḍu. (*V. R. i, Cud. 537, 538.*)

A. D. 1545. Excluding unimportant records of king Sadāśiva, we have one which is very valuable as regards the end of young prince Venkaṭādri.

An inscription of June 24, 1545, mentions Sadāśiva as reigning, and expressly states that he was placed on the throne by his brother-in-law Aḷiya Rāma, who, it truthfully declares, was 'the ruler of the Karnāṭa Kingdom.' It also says that on king Achyuta's death, his son Venkaṭadēva came to the throne but 'soon died'. (*E.C. iv, Ng. 58.*)

Rāma-Rāja-Viṭṭhala-Rāja of Vijayanagar gave away two villages in Tanjore District—Sadāśiva reigning. (*140 of 1895, V. R. ii. Tan. 351.*)

On February 1 and Ooctber 4, 1545, Jaṭilavarman-Śrīvallabha-Pāṇḍya was ruling in Tinnevelly in his tenth year. He was the Pāṇḍya prince who brought back the old times.' (*543, 511 of 658, 662, 663, 666 of 1917.*)

Another Tinnevelly record names Jaṭilavarman-Kulaśēkhara-Pāṇḍya as ruling there on July 8 in his second year. He was son of Abhirāma-Pāṇḍya and was also called 'Parākrama' (*386 of 1917. See also 389 of 1917*). Another one, in which he is called 'Kōnērimaikonḍān', makes him ruling there on September 29, 1545, in his third year (*657 of 1917*), and another of his third year is dated October 1, 1545. (*V. R. iii. Travancore 145, 146 ; T. A. S. i, 103, 266.*)

It is noticeable that Sadāśiva's supremacy was recognized in Ramnad in this year.

(2 of 1923 ; Tam. and Sans. Mss., 108-9 ; V. R. ii. Ramnad, 166.)

And, for the first time in history, Vijayanagar overlordship is recognized in Tinnevelly in A.D. 1546. *(V. R. iii, Tinn 275.)*

A gift was made in Chingleput District 'for the merit of Chinna Timma of the Āravīḍu family, son of Timma and grandson of Rāma. This Chinna Timma was Aḷiya Rāma's cousin *(V. R. i, Chin. 717 ; 250 of 1910)*. In the Cuddapah District in this year an inscription mentions Chinna Timma son of Rāma of the same family. This may possibly be Aḷiya Rāma's son of that name, but, from the date, is more probably his uncle.

(V. R. i, Cud. 547.)

[The Portuguese in this year made a treaty with Ibrahim Ādil Shāh of Bījāpur by which, in return for surrendering to him the person of the rebel prince Abdullah, they were given the small territories of Salsette and Bardes. They took Abdullah as far as Cannanore and then brought him back to Goa.]

A.D. 1546. [*From here forward I omit all unimportant records of Sadāśiva. There are many every year.*]

In Tinnevelly on May 20, 1546. Inscription of Jaṭilavarman-Kulaśēkhara-Pāṇḍya in his 3rd year,—elder son of Abhirām-Parākrama *(388 of 1917)*. There is another of his, apparently of date = February 26, but the date is not quite perfect. *(T. A. S. i. 266.)*

Some Madura records are said to shew that up to this year at least and for some years past that city was under the immediate rule of Sundara-Tōḷ-Uḍaiyān II—Māvalivāṇa of the old Bāṇa stock. *(T. A. S. vi. 53.)*

Viṭṭhala of Āravīḍu, son of Timma, son of Rāma mentioned in an inscription in Tinnevelly. He was cousin of Aḷiya Rāma. He invaded Travancore.

(V. R. iii, Tinn. 275 ; 129 of 1905 ; see I. A. 1914, 230.)

[The Portuguese attacked and burned some towns in Gujarāt in this year.]

A.D. 1547. Records in Nellore and Kurnool record remission of taxes by Aḷiya-Rāma and other members of his family, shewing the extent of his power. *(V. R. ii, Nell. 616 ; B. and V.C. 1195 ; V. R. ii, Kurnool, 59, 66, 211, 390 . . . 395, 414, 419, 421, 424, 429, 525, 532, 565, 572, 577, 611, 627, 629, 633.)*

In Tinnevelly an inscription of the fourth year of Jaṭilavarman-Kulaśēkhara-Parākrama-Pāṇḍya the date of which = June 9, 1547 *(397 of 1917)*. One of August 28, 1547, mentions (probably in error) his fifth year. *(525 of 1917.)*

[The Portuguese in 1547 broke away from their treaty of 1545 with Ibrahim Ādil Shāh and concluded a triple alliance with Vijayanagar and Ahmadnagar for the purpose of conquering the Bījāpur kingdom. In 1548 they again made a treaty with Ibrahim Ādil.]

Aḷiya Rāma Rāya's brother Venkaṭādri was in a position of authority in the Kurnool District where he granted the revenues of a village to Brahmans.

(V. R. ii, Kurnool. 228.)

The Ghanḍikōṭa tract in Cuddapah District was apparently governed by *Nandyāl Timma.*

(V. R. i, Cud. 25 ; 318 of 1895.)

The Kērala-Rāja Bhūtala-Vīra-Rāmavarman was ruling in Travancore.

(V. R. iii, Trav. 148 ; 64 of 1896.)

In Tinnevelly inscriptions of the fourth and fifth year of Perumāl-Parākrama-Pāṇḍya. The Śaka year is the same in each case. He was eldest son of Abhirāma Parākrama.

(*V. R. iii, Tinn. 294, 297 ; 274 of 1908 ; 660 of 1917.*)

A.D. 1548. The same Pāṇḍya Rāja ruling on March 27, at Tenkāśi in his fifth year (*587 of 1917*). And on August 15, October 24, November 25 and December 8 in his sixth year (*566, 531, 532, 562 of 1917*). His brother Śālivāṭipati, here called 'Tirunelvēli-Perumāḷ,' is also mentioned on December 3, 1548. (*451 of 1917.*)

Nandyāl Chinna Aubala, 'son of Narasinga and grandson of Singa' gave a grant in aid of worship at the Ahōbilam temple in Kurnool (*V. R. ii, Kurn. 595 ; 81 of 1915*). His brother Nārapa granted a village in Cuddapah. (*V. R. i, Cud. 395.*)

A.D. 1549. Records of Jaṭilavarman-Parākrama, eldest son of Abhirāma-Pāṇḍya on (?) February 8 and 13 and on June 17, July 20 and September 7 (*V. R. ii, Tinn. 278-M ; 472, 536, 545, 553, 583 of 1917*). In the first of these a wrong *nakshatra* is quoted. Hence the doubt as to the exact day. [The record of July 20, being in this chief's seventh year, shews that his accession took place on or before July 20, 1543, while a record (*see below* of July 19, 1551), which is placed in his eighth year shews that it must have taken place on or after July 20, 1543. The two together prove his day of accession as July 20, 1543.]

(*See also 567 of 1917 ; and V. R. iii, Travan. 137 ; T.A.S. i. 48, 268.*)

One of the Āravīḍu family chiefs, Koṇḍa, son of Chinna-Timma, gave a grant of revenue-taxes to a temple in Cuddapah. It is difficult to fix precisely which 'Koṇḍa' this was.

(*V. R. i, Cud. 515, 517 ; 471 of 1906.*)

[War broke out again this year between the Portuguese (with whom was allied the Raja of Cochin) and the Zamorin of Calicut. The Portuguese were defeated at Bardeḷa.

Sevappa-Nāyaka, whose wife's sister had been one of king Achyuta's queens, was made Governor of Tanjore.]

A.D. 1550. Inscriptions in Tinnevelly District shew that Sadāśiva was acknowledged here as supreme overlord (*599, 609 ; 373 of 1916*) ; while the local ruler was Jaṭilavarman-Kulaśēkhara, eldest son of Abhirāma-Parākrama, for whom we have dates March 26, April (?) and June 16, in his seventh year and August 21, in his eighth year (*573, 659 of 1917 ; V. R. iii, Travancore. 138, 231 ; T.A.S. i. 271 ; 563 of 1917*). The latest of these mentions an order given by this chief's younger brother, Vīraveṇbāmālai-Kulaśēkhara *alias* Śālivāṭipati. (*See also 564 of 1917 and 276 of 1908.*)

This Śālivāṭipati's beginning of rule took place, as gathered from records, between June 14 and 27, 1550. He was crowned in 1552. (*T. A. S. i. 56; V. R. iii, Tinnevelly 302.*)

The Āraga-Rājya in N.-W. Mysore was ruled, under Vijayanagar, by Keḷadi Sadāśiva-Nāyaka. (*E. C. viii, Nr. 77.*)

[Ibrahim Quṭb Shāh of Golkonda became Sultan in this year on his brother Jamshīd's death. While a prince he had stayed as a guest of the king's at Vijayanagar. Aḷiya-Rāma, anxious to make friends with him, gave him an estate, and to that end seized a property which he had already bestowed upon one Āmbur Khān and turned the latter out of it. Āmbur Khān quarrelled with Ibrahim, on this grievance, in the streets of Vijayanagar, and the two fought a duel which resulted in Āmbur Khān's death.]

A.D. 1551. July 19. Jaṭilavarman-Kulaśēkhara-Pāṇḍya ruling in Tinnevelly in his eighth year. This was the last day of his eighth year (*See above, s.v. 1549 ; 532 of 1909 ; 450 of 1917*). Another of his eighth year, whose date = September 3, 1551, seems to quote the wrong regnal year (*466 of 1917*). So also does another whose date = January 4, 1551, but which quotes the seventh regnal year (*554 of 1917*). The same ruler is mentioned in an inscription of October 5, 1551, in his ninth regnal year (*540 of 1917*). One record (*508 of 1909 ; E. R. 1910, p. 102*) affixes to his name the *biruda* 'Śeḷiyan, Ponnin-Pāṇḍya.'

Varatunga-Rāma-Pāṇḍya, a prince, son of Parākrama and grandson of Abhirama, gave a village in Ramnad to Brahmans. (*V. R. ii, Ramnad, 180 ; T. A. S. i. p. 106.*)

A grant was made to Brahmans in this year on June 15, at Bevinahalli, a village close to Madras, by Aḷiya-Rāma, king Sadāśiva's minister, at the request of Ain-ul-Mulkh, who is called 'Ainama-Malukka, in the original, probably the chief whom Firishta calls 'Mallik Ain-ul-Mulkh Gilāni' (*Briggs's Edn, iii. p. 381*). The grant mentions, Mailāpur-Mādarasa' and as Mailāpur is a suburb of modern Madras the origin of the name 'Madras' is here believed to have been disclosed.[1] (*E. I. xiv, 210.*)

Aḷiya-Rāma's brother Tirumala of Āraviḍu was now ruling in Central Mysore. He is given royal titles. (*E. C. ix, Nl, 42.*)

Tirumala was also ruling at Udayagiri. (*B. and V. C. No. 104.*)

[Rāma-Rāja of Vijayanagar and Burhān Nizām Shāh made an alliance this year against Bījāpur, and took Raichūr and Muḍkal, thus restoring the Raichūr Dōāb to the Hindu monarchy. Rāma-Rāja's brother Tirumala seems to have become jealous of his powerful brother's supremacy and to have become refractory. He was besieged by Rāma-Rāja in Adoni and on capitulating, was afterwards pardoned.]

[According to Hunter, with whom Burgess agrees, it was in this year that the Telugu chief Mukunda-Bāhubalēndra usurped the throne of the Gajapatis of Orissa.]

A.D. 1552. April 25. Kulaśēkhara-Sālivāṭipati-Pāṇḍya ruling in Tinnevelly. His *birudas* are 'Vīraveṇbāmālai,' 'Vrīhivritīśvara,' 'Ponnan,' and 'Vīravēl.' The record belongs to his second regnal year (*513 of 1917 ; T.A.S. i. 56, 104, 272*). He was crowned in 1552–53.

(*V. R. iii. Tinn., 344 ; 508 of 1909 ; E. R. 1918, p. 60 ; V. R. iii, Trav. 139.*)

Keḷadi Sadāśiva was ruling the Āraga tract on the Western Ghats under the Vijayanagar king. (*E. C. viii, Nr. 5.*)

The Kaḷasa country of Mysore was governed by Bhairarasa.

(*E. C. vi, Mg. 40 ; and ibid. 39.*)

A.D. 1553. A grant was made in Udayagiri (Nellore District) by Timma of the Āraviḍu family, son of Kōnēṭi-Rāya, and Aḷiya Rāma Rāja's cousin. (*V. R. ii, Nell. 773 ; B and V.C. 1363.*)

Sālivāṭipati-Pāṇḍya ruling in Tenkāśi in his third year. Date = June 2, 1553 (*557 of 1917 ; 281 of 1908*). Another record of his fixes July 8, 1553, as in his fourth year, (*387 of 1917*). Another of his fourth year bears date December 2. (*559 of 1917. See also V. R. iii, Tinn., 302, 304-F.*)

[1] It is matter for regret that Mr. Sewell should have been misled into thinking Bēvinahaḷḷi to be a village near Madras. Bēvinahaḷḷi and the two other villages going into it are said to have belonged to Rauḍakundiya *Sīma*, in Keḷavaḍi *nāḍ*, in Hastināvati *vaḷita* ; in the division of Hastināvati (Anegondi-Hampi), in the sub-division Kaḷavaḍi (Keḷadi in Mysore), and the district of Rauḍakundi. The villages may have been in Mysore-Bellary border. *Mailāpurada-Mādarasa* is almost certainly the name of a *Kannaḍa Brahman* and probably belonged to Mailapur, a neighbouring village on the border of which one of the boundary stones was planted (l. 278 of the Ins.). It is very doubtful if the name could have had any association with Mailapur-San Thome, near modern Madras. See *Journal of Indian History*, Vol. VII, pp. 103–104.—*Editor*.

An *agrahāra* village was founded in this year by Varatunga-Rāma, son of Kulaśēkhara Parākrama-Pāṇḍya, then a prince. (*T. A. S. i. 59, 106, 113, 116.*)

[The Portuguese attacked and burned some more towns on the Malabar Coast. Aḷiya Rāma Rāya's brother Venkaṭādri defeated Ain-ul-Mulkh, a leader who had revolted against the Bījāpur Sultan. (*Forg. Emp., p. 190.*)]

A.D. 1554. 'Vīraveṇbāmālai'-Kulaśēkhara, *alias* Sālivāṭipati-Pāṇḍya ruling in Tinnevelly in his fifth year on June 27. This shews that the last possible day for the accession was June 27, 1550. (*543 of 1917.*)

There are several records in this year of the Āravīḍu family. 'Timma, son of Kōnēṭi, and grandson of Pedda-Koṇḍa' built a hall at a temple in the capital. (*V. R. i. Bellary 327 ; 13 of 1904.*) A village in Kurnool District was given to a temple by 'Timma, son of Rāma-Rāja-Kōnēṭi-Rāja' (*V. R. ii. Kurn. 240 ; 157 of 1905*). In the same district land was granted to 'Aubala, son of Kōnēṭi, and grandson of Pedda-Koṇḍa' (*V. R. ii. Kurn. 579, 580 ; 65 of 1915*). 'Rāma-Rāja Viṭṭhala-Rāja-Tirumala-Rāja' granted a village in Central Mysore (*E. C. xii. Mi. 78*). 'Nandyāl Pedda Vīrayya' granted a village in Kurnool District (*V. R. ii. Kurn. 214*). 'Rāma-Rāja-Viṭṭhala-Raja' granted a village in Mysore. (*E. C. xii. Pg. 39.*)

A.D. 1555. 'Vīraveṇbāmālai'-Sālivāṭipati-Pāṇḍya ruling in Tinnevelly District on March 20 and April 5 in his fifth year (*575, 538 of 1917*). Both these are at Tenkāśi, and each of them mentions Sālivāṭipati's nephew Guṇarāma. An inscription at Gangaikoṇḍān near Tinnevelly names as ruler there Māravarman-Sundara-Pāṇḍya, on June 1, 1555, in his twenty-fourth year. His period of rule had begun in the year following June 1, 1531. (*V. R. iii. Tinn. 405 ; 171 of 1905.*)

In S. Kanara the Āḷupa chief Bhujabala-Kavi-Āḷupēndra was ruling. (*V. R. ii. S. Kan. 189 ; 171 of 1901.*)

In W. Mysore mention of Immaḍi-Pāṇḍya governing Keravase, and Bhairarasa, son of Bomma, governing the Kaḷasa country. (*E. C. vi, Mg. 60.*)

[The Mughal Emperor Humāyūn was restored to the throne of Delhi this year. But he died the following year.

The Portuguese attempted to place their friend Prince Abdullah (*see above s.v. A.D. 1545*) on the throne of Bījāpur, but they were opposed by Sultan Ibrahim Ādil aided by a contingent of troops sent to his aid from Vijayanagar by Aḷiya-Rāma Rāja, and several fights took place. The war lasted for more than a year, and the Portuguese failed to carry out their plan.]

A.D. 1556. [Humāyūn's death took place in January 1556. In the following month Akbar was enthroned. It is advisable to note that Akbar's internal policy was in theory much the same as in the far-gone days of the Maurya Chandragupta, viz. the cultivators must be compelled to cultivate whether they will or no, in order that the emperor's treasury should be enriched. The holders of land were at first to be encouraged to do their best; but the Government officials were to see to it that no ryot was lazy, and no excuses were to be accepted. Labour was compulsory. As to the land-taxes, the emperor is said to have in practice seized for the crown about one-third of the gross produce—though he laid it down as a religious principle that it was lawful for a Musalman ruler to take the whole property, as well as the person, of every 'infidel' Hindu, and distribute it amongst the followers of Islam—making the Hindus slaves. His practice was milder than his theory. (*J.R.A.S., Jan. 1922, p. 19.*)]

In Tinnevelly District on October 1, 1556, Vīravenbāmālai-Sālivāṭipati-Pāṇḍya was ruling according to an inscription, in his 'sixth' year (*620 of 1917*). [The regnal year was actually the seventh.]

Keḷadi-Sadāśiva-Nāyaka was governing part of N.-W. Mysore. (*E. C. vii, Sk. 55.*)

'Rama-Raja Tirumala' of Āravīḍu gave a grant in Central Mysore (*E. C. xii, Si. 31*); and 'Rama-Rāja-Viṭhala-Rāja-Tirumala granted a village to Brahmans in N. Mysore.

(*Ibid. xi, Mk. 4, 6.*)

'Ahōbala (Aubala) Rāja, son of Rāma-Rāja Kōnēṭi-Rāja' built a *gōpura* and a *maṇḍapa* at the Viṭṭhalaswāmi temple at Hampe-Vijayanagar (*V. R. i, Bellary 348*). And 'Tirumala, son of Viṭthala, son of Rāma', remitted taxes in the Rāyadrūg tract (Bellary District).

(*V. R. i, Bell. 451, 452 ; 104, 105 of 1913.*)

Rāma-Rāja Tirumalarāja granted a village in Central Mysore—Sadāśiva reigning.

(*E. C. xii, Pg, 40.*)

The British Museum plates of Sadāśiva, dated 1556, differing from others, state that Achyuta's brother Ranga, father of Sadāśiva, was the elder brother and Achyuta the younger. (*E. I. iv, 1.*)

A.D. 1557. [Ibrahīm Ādil Shāh of Bījāpur died in this year from a complication of disorders. He put to death several physicians who had tried, but failed, to cure him. He was succeeded by his son Ali Ādil Shāh, who at once tried to establish, for political reasons, a solid friendship with Rāma-Rāja at Vijayanagar. He visited the Hindu capital, and was outwardly received with all honour; but Rāma-Rāja offended him on his departure, by not attending him out of the city. The event increased Rāma-Rāya's sense of his own importance, and irritated the Sultan.]

In Tinnevelly on April 26, Vīravenbāmālai-Sālivāṭipati-Pāṇḍya was ruling in his 7th year (*481 of 1917*). Two of his records, of dates = July 22 and 24, also mention them as in his 7th year, thus disagreeing with the fixture June 14–27, 1550, for his accession (*529, 572 of 1917*). [These inscriptions require examination.]

'Obala, son of Kōnēṭi and grandson of Rāma-Rāja Koṇḍa' of Āravīḍu gave a grant of villages in S. Arcot (*V. R. i, S. Arcot 391 ; 66 of 1906*). And 'Chinna Aubalēśvara of Nandyāl, son of Aubalēśvara and grandson of Aubala', gave a gift at Ghaṇḍikōṭa in Cuddapah District.

(*V. R. i, Cudd. 164 ; 485 of 1906.*)

'Parakrama-Pāṇḍya' (i.e. Kulaśēkhara-Parākrama whose accession was in 1543) gave a grant of a village in Tinnevelly District in his '16th' (should be 14th or 15th) year.

(*V. R. iii, Tinn. 304-I.*)

A.D. 1558. [The Portuguese Franciscan friars at Mailāpur and S. Thomé near Madras, according to Couto (*see 'A Forgotten Empire', p. 193*) destroyed some temples and thereby roused the indignation of the Brahmans and the Hindus generally. Aḷiya-Rāma went in person to S. Thomé and held an enquiry, but, finding that the foreign priests were all very poor, he let them alone.

A combined army of forces from Vijayanagar and Bījāpur, in alliance, attacked the dominions of Husain Nizām Shāh of Ahmadnagar. They laid waste the country, says Firishta, 'in such a manner that from Porundeh to Khiber and from Ahmadnagar to Dowlatabad, not a mark of population was to be seen. The infidels of Beejanuggur (Vijayanagar), who for many years had been wishing for such an event, left no cruelty unpractised. They insulted the honour of Mussulman women, destroyed the mosques, etc.' Ibrahim-Quṭb-Shāh joined the allies in this attack on Ahmadnagar, and ceded to Vijayanagar the fortresses of Kōvilkonda, Pāngal and Guntūr.]

An important inscription in S.-E. Mysore gives pedigrees of the Vijayanagar royal family and of the Āraviḍu family. *(E. C. ix, Cp. 186.)*

In Tinnevelly 'Vīraveṇbamālai-Kulaśēkhara-Pāṇḍya, alias Sālivāṭipati, was ruling in his 8th year on April 4, 1558 *(403 of 1917)*; and on June 3 *(530 of 1917)*. *(Also V.R. iii Tinn. 293.)*

At Madura Viśvanātha Nāyaka ruled locally. *(I.A. 1914, p. 15.)*

Aḷiya Rāma-Rāya of Vijayanagar had in his employ, as indeed was necessary, a Muhammadan agent, Dilawār-Khān. *(E.C. x. Kl. 147.)*

A.D. 1559. [Viśvanātha Nāyaka of Madura and Śevappa-Nāyaka of Tanjore effected an arrangement by which Śevappa ceded Trichinopoly to Viśvanātha and Viśvanātha ceded Vallam to Śevappa. Luiz de Mello left Goa and wasted the country as far as Mangalore, where he fired the town and slaughtered the inhabitants.]

The same Pāṇḍya prince mentioned above, Sālivāṭipati continued to rule in the Tinnevelly country. There are records of him of date = June 13 and November 5 in his '9th' year. [They must be examined with reference to the regnal year stated, as the last one disagrees with a fixture in June 1550 for his accession.]

Tirumala, brother of Aḷiya-Rāma, was in authority in Nellore District, and in Mysore, and in Anantapur District.

(V.R. ii, Nell. 484 ; B. and V.C. 880 ; E.C. xi, Cl, 54 ; V.R. i, Anant. 41.)

A.D. 1560. The same Pāṇḍya prince ruling on January 14 and March 20, 1560, in Tinnevelly District. [Here again the given regnal year clashes with some in other inscriptions.]

(326 of 1918 ; 592, 593, 594 of 1917.)

Viśvanātha-Nāyaka, ruling in Madura, had a general in command of his army by name Āryanātha. *(V.R. iii, Tinn. 455 ; 622 of 1915.)*

A.D. 1561. Another record of the same Pāṇḍya prince, Sālivāṭipati, on February 2, 1561, in which the regnal year is stated, apparently in error, as the '9th'. *(579 of 1917.)*

Two other Pāṇḍya inscriptions mention the year A.D. 1561–62 as being the 13th year of 'Kulaśēkhara Ativīra-Rāma-Pāṇḍya' in Rāmnād and of 'Dharma-Perumāḷ Kulaśēkhara Pāṇḍya' in Tinnevelly. *(V.R. ii, Ramnad, 168–B ; iii. Tinn. 255 ; 483 of 1909.)*

'Rāma-Rāja-Koṇḍa-Raja' of Āraviḍu gave a grant to a temple at Kampli.

(V.R. i, Bellary, 362.)

A.D. 1562. 'Vīraveṇbāmālai'-Kulaśēkhara, younger son of Abhirāma-Pāṇḍya (i.e. Sālivāṭipati) ruling on September 6, 1562, in his 12th year. [This again disagrees with other records which mention the regnal year.] *(546 of 1917)*. Another, of date = September 5, similarly disagrees. The '12th' regnal year is stated. *(537 of 1917.)*

An inscription of June 12, 1562, states that the Vinukoṇḍa province *(Sīma)* was given by Rāma-Rāja Tirumala to Koṇḍa-Rāja. *(V.R. ii, Guntūr 883 ; 530 of 1913.)*

Sultan Husāin Nizām Shah of Ahmadnagar, after his disastrous war against Bījāpur, Vijayanagar, and Golkonda now made friends with the Sultan of Golkonda, Ibrahīm Quṭb Shāh and attacked the other two states, but without success.

A.D. 1563. 'Jaṭilavarman-Tirunelvēli-Perumāḷ-Kulaśēkhara-Pāṇḍya' (i.e. Sālivāṭipati) ruling on May 22 in Tinnevelly in his 13th year *(515 of 1917)*. Another of his records at Tenkāśi of this year mentions a day in his '12th' year. [Again some confusion.]

(V.R. iii, Tinn. 363 ; 527 of 1909.)

The Changāḷva chief Vīra-Raja-Uḍaiyār was locally ruling in S. Mysore. (*E.C. iv, Hs. 49.*)

An inscription in W. Mysore, in the Hassan tract, says that the village to which it belonged was in an estate which had been given by king Sadāśiva to Aḷiya Rāma-Rāja. Another mentions Seringapatam as in the same estate, which therefore included a considerable tract of country.

(*E C. v, Hn. 2, 15 ; iii, My. 50.*)

'Nandyāl Aubala, son of Kōnēṭi, son of Pedda Koṇḍa' of the Āraviḍu family gave a grant of village revenues to the temple at Ahōbilam on August 6, 1563.

(*V.R. ii, Kurnool, 586, 596 ; 72, 82 of 1915.*)

A.D. 1564. The Pāṇḍya Ruler Sūlivāṭipati seems to have died in June 1563, and to have been succeeded by his son Ativīrarāma Pāṇḍya-Śrīvallabha, also called 'Aḷagan-Śivalavēl', who was crowned on April 16, 1564. (*T.A.S. i, 56, 105 ; V.R. iii, Tinn. 345 ; 509 of 1909.*)

An inscription from N.-W. Mysore, referring to Aḷiya Rāma-Rāja gives him full imperial titles and describes him as 'seated on the jewelled throne' of Vijayanagar. The date of this C.-P. grant is December 18, 1564, only a month before the total destruction of Vijayanagar and the death of Rāma-Rāja at Talikōta. (*E.C. vii, Ci., 62.*)

[The Portuguese were at war in this year with the Rāja of Cannanore. They behaved with great brutality, capturing ships and killing the sailors whom they made prisoners.]

('*Forgotten Empire*', *p. 195.*)

A.D. 1565. Aḷiya-Rāma-Rāja's success in grasping the whole power at Vijayanagar while he kept Sadaśiva-Rāya, the real Emperor, virtually a prisoner, had so intoxicated him with a sense of his own importance that, in the course of the past year, he had alienated his dangerous Musalman neighbours in the Dekhan, each of whom considered himself insulted by the Hindu ruler's overbearing conduct. Firishta makes this very clear. The result was that Ali Ādil Shāh conceived the possibility of an united attack by all the four Dekhāni powers in alliance on the kingdom and city of Vijayanagar, with the object of accomplishing the complete overthrow of the Hindu empire. He sent an embassy first to Husain Nizām Shāh and gained his approval of the plan, which was ratified by intermarriages between the younger members of the two families. The Golkonda and Bidar Sultans also agreed to join in this holy war.

The Musalmani forces from all four States met at Bijāpur, and began their march on December 25, 1564. They pushed forward to the village of Talikōta,[1] where a great battle was fought on January 23, 1565, with the armies of Vijayanagar, which had been rapidly collected from all quarters and were

[1] A Kannaḍa Bakhair known as the Bakhair of Rāmarāya gives an account of the battle of Talikoṭa differing in essential particulars from the account of Firishṭa. Without going into the full details, this Bakhair makes it doubtful whether the battle should any more be called the battle of Talikoṭa. Talikoṭa is twenty-five miles from the north bank of the Krishna, where the Ahmadnagar army camped for the time. According to this Bakhair, the Vijayanagar army after crossing the Tungabhadra made a short camp at a place called Tāvarēkere, from which they advanced, and Rāmarāya made his camp at a place called Rākshasatangaḍi, from which he sent out the divisions under his two brothers to oppose the Bijapur and Golkonda divisions respectively, the centre being placed over against the Ahmadnagar army. One feature of the description of the battle is the effort made to cross the Krishna and the defence of the fords by Vijayanagar. The battle joined after the Muhammadan armies had crossed the Krishna, and therefore is some little way from the south bank of the river. It would be more appropriate to call it the battle of Rākshasatangaḍi, where the main camp of the Vijayanagar army lay and from which that army operated as occasion demanded by movements of various kinds. The need for calling it Rākshasatangaḍi is made necessary by Grant Duff referring to the battle in a corrupt form of that name Rakshitagunḍi in his standard work, *History of the Mahrattas*. For the whole of this discussion, see a paper presented by the Editor to the Indian Historical Records Commission in its Poona Session, 1925. Tāvarēkere is next stage to Kanakagiri on the Vijayanagar-Mudgal Road. The Survey of India Atlas, Sheet 56, marks the battle on this side of the Krishna

led by the three Āravīḍu brothers in person,—Rāma-Rāja in the centre, Tirumala on the left and Venkaṭādri on the right. Firishta says that the Hindu army numbered nearly a million men. By all accounts, Rāma-Rāja, now a very old man, behaved with great gallantry, but by a series of accidents and some mismanagement, his enemies succeeded in breaking his line and making him a prisoner. He was taken to Husāin Nizām Shāh who at once had him decapitated.

To put the result in as few words as possible, since this is not the place for a descriptive story, the armies of Vijayanagar broke and fled. They were closely pursued up to the walls of the capital, and massacred in numbers. The chronicler relates that 'according to the best authorities' more than 100,000 Hindus lost their lives. Then the city was entered and completely sacked. King Sadaśiva and his family and the surviving Āravīḍu brothers, Tirumala and Venkaṭādri fled for safety to Penukoṇḍa, carrying with them enormous treasure. The helpless citizens of the city were slain or deprived of all their possessions; and the invaders settled down to their task of deliberately destroying the whole city. So that after a time it was totally reduced to ruins—a condition in which it has ever since remained.

To realize the extent of this disaster it would be well for the reader to note what the city had been when at the height of its prosperity only a few years earlier, and for this purpose to read the accounts given of its wealth and grandeur by Abdur Razzāk in the fifteenth century and by Paes about A.D. 1520 (*'A Forgotten Empire', pp. 81 f, 253 f*). And for details of the event and of what followed, refer to pp. 196-213 of the same work.

Firishtah says that the plunder of the wealthy citizens was so great that 'every private man in the allied [conquering] army became rich.' And in addition to this the whole country around the capital was devastated. It must be remembered that Vijayanagar had been a city protected by seven lines of fortification, the outer walls measuring twenty-eight miles in circumference. The loot and destruction were increased by the violence of the scum of the population and by hordes of bandits.

Sadāsiva, however, though he and his supporters retired to Penukoṇḍa and Chandragiri, was still sovereign in South India subsequent to his defeat. Inscriptions naming him as on the throne later in the year 1565 have been found in Mysore. Their dates correspond to October 20 and November 7 in that year (*E.C. ix, Ht. 88; x, Gd. 52*). Tirumala of Āravīḍu remained as minister to the puppet-king, with all the power in his hands. His son Rāma is mentioned as being in a position of some authority in Anantapur District in 1565–6. (*V.R. i, Anant. 155; 333 of 1901.*)

A.D. 1566. Records of king Sadāśiva on February 19, 1566, and on other days (*Mys. A.A.R. 1923, p. 83; V.R. ii, Guntur 354; B and V.C. 946; E.C. viii, Nr. 1; ix, An. 16*). One of these shews a member of the Āraviḍu family, Rangappa, governing the fortress of Koṇḍavīḍu. Another shews the Keḷadi chief Sadāśiva ruling the Āraga tract.

In Tinnevelly Ativīrarāma-Śrīvallabha-Pāṇḍya was ruling in his 3rd year on May 31—a date which shews that his accession took place on or after June 1, 1563. Others of his records naming his 3rd year bear dates = June 19 and 27, 1566, and these disagree with one that makes June 13, 1563, his latest possible day of accession. [These records all require careful examination if it is considered necessary to fix the date of accession. He was son of Sālivāṭipati.]

(*501, 571, 491 of 1917; also V.R. iii, Travan., 141; T.A.S. 274–8.*)

between Mudgal and the river—that is on the road from Tävarĕkere through Mudgal to Talikota and Bijapur. Somewhere about this locality Rākshasatangaḍi must have been. See Survey of India Atlas, Sheets 56 and 57. —*Editor.*

A.D. 1567. The same Pāṇḍya chief ruling in Tinnevelly District on January 24 in his '3rd' year; and on August 22 in his '5th' year (*617, 494 of 1917*). And another of his '5th' year. (*V.R. iii, Tinn. 392, 393 ; 201, 202 of 1895. Also 558 of 1917. V.R. iii, Travancore, 141 ; T.A.S. i. 274.*)

[Mukunda-Bahubalēndra, the Telugu usurper of the Gajapati kingdom of Orissa, was overthrown by Sulaimān Kararānī of Bengal in 1567 or 1568 (Hijra 975).]

On April 9 and 19, 1567, Tirumala-Rāya, Sadāśiva's minister and practical ruler of the kingdom, gave land and villages in Kurnool to Brahmans. (*V.R. ii, Kurn. 10, 47, 48 ; 137 of 1913.*)

In Tinnevelly District king Sadāśiva of Vijayanagar gave villages to a temple at the request of Krishnappa-Nāyaka of Madura (*V.R. iii, Tinn. 407-A ; E.I. ix, 328*). Sadāśiva is mentioned in records in Kurnool and Mysore as still reigning (*V.R. ii, Kurn. 246, 400 ; 163 of 1905 ; E.C. xii, Kg. 32*). Also in Anantapur, Chittoor, and N. Arcot Districts (*V.R. i, Anant. 159 ; Chittoor 35, 97 ; N. Arcot 317, 409, 562 ; 337 of 1901 ; 63 of 1907 ; 301 of 1904 ; 38, 39, 40 of 1887 ; 169 of 1922*). In one of these in N. Arcot a gift was made by the ruler Tirumala at the request of Chinna Bomma Nāyaka of Vellore.

A.D. 1568. There are several records shewing Sadāśiva reigning in this year.
(*E.C. vi, Cm. 24 ; xi, Hk. 6, 7 ; Hr. 47 ; V.R. ii, Kurnool 534–7 ; ii, Guntur 115 ; 240 of 1897.*)

In Tinnevelly District inscriptions of the 5th year of Ativīrarāma-Pāṇḍya on January 27 and July 19, and during the year.

(*490, 589 of 1917 ; V.R. iii, Tinn. 369, 370, 371 ; 533, 534, 535 of 1909.*)

In S. Mysore the Changālva chief Vīradēva, son of Śrīkaṇṭha, was locally ruling.
(*E.C. iv, Hs. 24.*)

A.D. 1569. Sadāśiva still reigning in this year (*V.R. ii, Kurnool 49, 249 ; i, Chittoor 98 ; Coimbatore 320 ; 138 of 1913 ; 302 of 1904 ; 166 of 1905 ; 15 of 1910 ; E.C. vi, Kd. 18*). In Central Mysore an inscription describes Tirumala as reigning king, giving him full imperial titles, but these are probably honorific.

Inscriptions of Ativīrarāma-Śrīvallabha-Pāṇḍya, one of them dated on January 7, in his 6th year and another on March 7, in his 7th year, whose date = March 7, 1569, raise further difficulty as to the date of his accession. (*407, 492, 496 of 1917.*)

[Murtazā Nizām Shāh, now Sultan of Ahmadnagar in succession to his father Husain, who died on June 7, 1565, shortly after the destruction of Vijayanagar, quarrelled with Ali Adil Shāh of Bijāpur and attacked his territory, seizing Dharwar.

The Portuguese attacked and burned the town of Honawar.]

A.D. 1570. Sadāśiva is named as king in inscriptions in Mysore and in Nellore District (*E.C. iv, Ch. 79 ; V.R. ii, Nellore 478 ; B. and V. C. 868*). The first of these shews him as reigning on March 24, 1570, the second on March 29.

Ativīrarāma-Śrīvallabha-Pāṇḍya was ruling in Tinnevelly in his 7th year on February 28, and in his 8th year on December 14. (*See above, and 409 495 of 1917.*)

Kumāra-Krishnappa-Nāyaka of Madura is mentioned in an inscription in Tinnevelly District. (*V.R. iii, Tinn. 287-A.*)

[There was a very severe famine in this year on the Western Coast.

The Portuguese attacked Kalyān and burned the suburbs. Indignant at this outrage, the Sultans of Bijāpur and Ahmadnagar again made friends, and allied themselves with the Zamorin of

Calicut. They advanced against the Portuguese and besieged Goa, but a peace was patched up between Bijāpur and Goa. The Ahmadnagar force attacked Chaul, but also made peace and withdrew.

The date of king Sadāśiva's death is not known. He may have died in 1570, or may have survived in retirement. Some records mention him in 1575, 1576 and 1577 (*see below*). But Tirumala of Āravīḍu became king of Vijayanagar in this year; by usurpation if the late king had left any descendants, which is not certainly known, or by election if the throne was vacant. He established the Fourth Vijayanagar dynasty.]

A.D. 1571. Tirumala of Āravīḍu was now actually king of Vijayanagar (*E.I. xvi, 244*). He ruled from Penukoṇḍa, as is stated in an inscription commemorating a gift of a village to Brahmans in N.-W. Mysore by Keḷadi Sadāsiva-Rāya's grandson Rāma-Rāja-Nāyaka (*E.C. viii, Sb. 55*). Records of Tirumala shewing him reigning this year are found in Kurnool and Chittoor and Cuddapah Districts and in S.-E. Mysore (*V.R. i, Cudd. 678 ; Chitt. 368 ; ii, Kurn. 74 ; 497 of 1905 ; E.C. xi, Tm. 1 ; ix, Cp. 99*). Keḷadi Rāma is mentioned in an inscription in N.-W. Mysore.

(*E.C. viii. Sa. 21.*)

[The Zamorin of Calicut besieged Chāliyam in this year which was defended by Jorge de Castro for the Portuguese. He took the fort and destroyed it. The Portuguese attacked Dabhōl but were defeated and driven back with heavy losses.]

Ativīrarāma-Śrīvallabha-Pāṇḍya is represented by two inscriptions of January 7, and May 4, 1571, the former being in his 8th year. (*328 of 1918 ; V.R. iii, Tinnevelly, 278-P ; T.A.S. i, 277.*)

A.D. 1572. [Ibrahim Kutb Shāh of Golkonda warred against the Gajapati king of Orissa, who held Rajahmundry and neighbouring forts. The Hindus were severely beaten near Rajahmundry and the Golkonda troops captured the town and held it and the surrounding country.]

On January 26, 1572, king Tirumala of Vijayanagar granted a village to Brahmans in Cuddapah District (*V.R. i, Cudd. 845 ; V.R. i, Chittor, 168-A ; C.P. 1 of 1913 ; E.I. xvi. 244*). The Maṭla chief Tirumala is mentioned in the inscription.

A grant was made during the year by Śrīranga I, son of king Tirumala in Guntur District (*806 of 1922*). Śrīranga was also governing in Kurnool. Under him was one of the Āravīḍu family by name Ōbala, as his Daḷavāy (*V.R. ii, Kurn. 630*). Another of Śrīranga's records of this year is in Guntur District (*V.R. ii, Gun. 130-L*); and another shews him in authority in Chingleput District on July 9, 1572. (*185 of 1922.*)

There are several inscriptions in this year of Ativīrarāma-Śrīvallabha-Pāṇḍya in Tinnevelly District, whose dates = March 3, April 17, June 20, July 31, August 4, October 27 and December 19. The confusion of regnal years is troublesome. April 17 is placed in his '10th' year, but June 20 is said to be in his '9th' year. The later ones are all '10th.'

(*499, 500, 585, 595 597, 598, 601, of 1917.*)

At this time in Nellore District the relations between Hindus and Muhammadans seem to have been, at least in some measure, friendly; for an inscription at Vavvēru relates that a Musalman named Muhammad Miyā constructed a fountain 'for the religious merit of' Prince Śrīranga, son of king Tirumala. (*B. and V.C. ii. 885 ; V.R. ii, Nell. 486.*)

A.D. 1573. King Tirumala reigning at Penukoṇḍa about October or November. (*698 of 1917.*) His son Śrīranga ruling in Anantapur, Cuddapah, Nellore and in Central Mysore.

(*823 of 1917 ; V.R. i, Cudd. 783 ; ii, Nell., 526 ; B.* and *V.C. 822 ; E.C. xii, Ck. 8.*)

In Tinnevelly, inscriptions of Ativīrarāma-Śrīvallabha-Pāṇḍya in his 10th year on March 9 and 13 and April 6 (*V.R. Travancore, 142 ; T.A.S. i. 279 : 596, 602 of 1917*). One of June 12—regnal year doubtful (*603 of 1917*) and one of November 6 in his 11th year.

(*487 of 1917.*)

Another Pāṇḍya prince mentioned in Tinnevelly District in his second year. This was Kulaśēkhara-Perumāḷ-Parākrama-Pāṇḍya-Māran-Aḷagiya-Śokkanār.

(*V.R. iii, Tinn. 254 ; 482 of 1909.*)

In N.-W Mysore the Keḷadi chief Rāma-Rāja-Nāyaka was ruling locally. (*E.C. viii, Tl. 19.*)

[Jorge de Castro was beheaded this year by order of the king of Portugal, as punishment for his loss of Chāliyam in 1571.]

Nandyāla Narasimha of the Āravīḍu family gave a grant this year in Kurnool District.

(*V.R. ii, Kurn. 105.*)

A.D. 1574. Śrīranga I, son of king Tirumala of Vijayanagar, was ruling in S. Arcot, Kurnool and Guntur Districts (*355 of 1921 ; V.R. ii, Kurnool, 619 ; Guntur, 765 ; 542 of 1909*). In the Kurnool record mention is made of Kumāra-Chinna-Aubala of Āravīḍu.

An inscription in Tinnevelly shews Ativīrarāma-Śrīvallabha-Pāṇḍya ruling there on February 11, 1574. Another of his, of date = July 22, places that day as in his 12th year, and therefore agrees with the fixture June 1 to 13, 1563, for his accession. (*574 of 1911 ; 599 of 1917.*)

Vīrappa-Nāyaka of Madura gave land to Muhammadans for the site of a Mosque.

(*77 of 1905.*)

A.D. 1575. Prince Śrīranga I of Vijayanagar ruling in Guntur District, in E. Mysore, in Chingleput, in Nellore and in Bellary Districts (*162 of 1917 ; 383 of 1919 ; V.R. ii, Nell. 688 ; B. and V.C. 1259 ; V.R. i, Bell. 61 ; E.I. xi. 326 ; E.C. x, Cl. 65 ; C.-B. 27, 28*). The Bellary District record is from Mārēḍapalli. It credits Śrīranga with having captured Koṇḍavīḍu, Udayagiri and Vinukoṇḍa, but it would appear that these are mere titles derived from the victories of Krishnadeva-Rāya sixty years previously ; for at this time the Muhammadans were in great power in that country, as is shewn by an inscription in Guntur District in 1576. (*q.v.*)

An interesting inscription in S. Arcot shews that political feelings there were not in a settled state for it describes king Sadāśiva of Vijayanagar as reigning there in this year, though Tirumala had ousted him from the throne at least four years earlier (*5 of 1919*). [It is of course just possible that Sadāśiva survived his dethronement and lived some years in retirement. The inscription should receive careful examination.]

A.D. 1576. A record in E. Mysore also seems to mention Sadāśiva as still on the throne, but most of it is said to be illegible and it cannot be depended upon. It may be that it refers to some grant made in an earlier year when Sadāśiva was reigning. (*E. C. x, Cl. 82.*)

Prince Śrīranga I is named as ruling at Penukoṇḍa (*V. R. i, Anantapur 171 ; C.-P. 23 of 1911*). And in N. Arcot on January 28, when a gift was made to a temple at the request of Chinna-Bomma-Nāyaka of Vellore (*V. R. i, N. Arcot 565 ; 41 of 1887*). He is also named as reigning in this year in S. Arcot, Mysore and Guntur. The last one, of date = October 7, comes from the taluk of Guntur. But another, whose date = October 26, in the same taluk, names, as then ruling, Ibrahim Kuṭb Shāh of Golkonda and refers to orders given by him. It would seem that Guntur was actually under Muhammadan rule, but that the country people clung to the Hindu crown.

(*134 of 1917 ; E. C. iv, Gu. 21 ; 89, 93 of 1917.*)

In Tinnevelly Ativīrarāman Śrīvallabha-Pāṇḍya was ruling in his 14th year, on August 8. *(488 of 1917.)*

Achyutappa-Nāyaka was ruling in Tanjore. *(E. I. xii, 340.)*

[A massacre of Portuguese took place this year in Dabhōl.]

A.D. 1577. An inscription of this year or 1578 (S. 1500) again names Sadāśiva of Vijayanagar as reigning (*see above s. v. 1570, 1575, 1576*). *(V. R. ii, Kurnool 97.)*

Prince Śrīranga I ruling in Guntur District (*V. R. ii, Gun. 130-A ; 113 of 1917*). The date of the latter is April 2, 1577. And in Central Mysore where he is distinctly stated to be 'sitting on the diamond throne'. (*E. C. xii, Mi. 37.*) And in Anantapur (*391 of 1920*) and in Tinnevelly, where a gift made by Periya-Vīrappa-Nāyaka of Madura for the merit of his father Krishnappa-Nāyaka is said to have been made under Śrīranga's rule—shewing that the Madura Nāyakas acknowledged the king of Vijayanagar as their overlord. *(V. R. iii, Tinn. 406 ; 16 of 1912.)*

Keḷadi Rāma-Rāja-Nāyaka was ruling, probably for his grandfather Keḷadi-Sadāśiva in the Āraga country of W. Mysore. *(E. C. viii, Sb. 475 ; Tl. 5.)*

Ativīrarāma-Pāṇḍya was now in his 15th year, ruling in Tinnevelly. *(406 of 1917.)*

The Travancore State Government epigraphist notes two records there of this year ; one of the 5th year of Parākrama Pāṇḍya who probably was Aḷagan-Śokkanār, and one of the 17th year of a Māravarman Sundara, whose rule began, therefore, in 1561-62. *(T. A. S. i, 24, 25.)*

[The Portuguese fitted out an expedition against the Thanadar of Dabhōl.]

A.D. 1578. Śrīranga I of Vijayanagar reigning in Chingleput and Tinnevelly Districts and in Mysore on March 31, May 16 and November 9. *(209, 663 of 1916 ; E. C. x, Mr. 41 ; v, Bl. 1.)*

Another inscription in the Mālūr taluk (*E. C. x, Mr. 57*) asserts positively that on March 8, 1578, the reigning king of Vijayanagar was Tirumala (father of Śrīranga I). Tirumala died, then, later than March 8 in this year and Śrīranga I became king in succession to him. Śrīranga is also mentioned as reigning in Chingleput and Cuddapah Districts (*V. R. i, Chin. 767, 1152 ; Cudd. 56, 167 ; 255, 327 of 1909 ; 488 of 1906*). In one of the Cuddapah records No. 167, Narasimha of Nandyāl is mentioned.

Gifts by Vīrappa Nāyaka I and Viśvanātha Nāyaka of Madura, brothers. *(98 of 1903 ; 663 of 1916.)*

Achyutappa-Nāyaka of Tanjore, son of Śevvappa-Nāyaka was ruling in Tanjore. *(V. R. ii, Tan 1371 ; 22 of 1897 ; SII ii. 498.)*

[Orissa was declared annexed to the Mughal empire of Delhi by the Emperor Akbar.]

A.D. 1579. Śrīranga I of Vijayanagar reigning in S. Arcot and Nellore Districts and in Mysore. *(490 of 1921 ; V. R. ii, Nell. 374 ; B and V. C. 657 ; E. C. ix, Nl. 49 ; X, Bp. 77.)*

Local disturbances in Mysore. A town besieged and plundered with slaughter of the inhabitants. *(E. C. viii, Sb. 301.)*

A.D. 1580. Records of king Śrīranga I reigning in Mysore, Guntur and S. Kanara. *(E. C. v, Bl. 12 ; x, Kl. 153 ; V. R. ii, Gun. 297 ; S. Kan. 188 ; 235 of 1892 ; 170 of 1901.)*

An important record in the Guntur District of date = A. D, 1592 relates that in 1580 (Ś. 1502) Ibrahim Kuṭb Shāh of Golkonda sent an army, commanded by his son Muhammad Kuli, and seized the fortresses of Udayagiri, Vinukoṇḍa, Bellamkoṇḍa, Tangēḍa and Koṇḍavīḍu. *(V. R. ii, Guntur, 764, 541 of 1909 ; E. R. 1910, p.119.) (See below s.v A. D. 1592.)*

[Ali Ādil Shāh of Bijāpur was murdered on April 11, 1580, by an eunuch.]

A.D. 1581. Inscriptions of king Śrīranga I in Kurnool and Anantapur Districts.

(V. R. ii, Kurn. 388, 416 ; i, Anant. 143 ; 178 of 1913.)

[According to Firishta, the whole of the Telugu country having been for a long time subject to the depredations of robbers, dacoits, and murderers (probably Thugs), Ibrahim Kuṭb Shāh of Golkonda, now supreme in that territory, took strong measures to repress the evil, and was so successful that 'merchants and travellers could travel night and day without going in caravans, in perfect security.' *(Scott's Edit., i. 408.)*]

Muhammad Kuli Kuṭb Shāh now became Sultan of Golkonda, Ibrahim having died.

A.D. 1582. Inscriptions of king Śrīranga I in Conjevaram (May 27 and October 21); in Chingleput (June 5); in Nellore and Kurnool Districts. He ruled the Vijayanagar kingdom from Penukoṇḍa.

(479, 58 of 1919 ; 194 of 1922 ; V. R. ii, Nell. 491 ; Kurn. 103 ; B and V.C. 892.)

Achyutappa-Nāyaka of Tanjore, son of Śevvappa, ruling in Ramnad (*V.R. ii, Ram. 136 ; 84 of 1905*). He was in power also in N. Arcot as he was able to give away land there. He completed the building of the tower at the temple at Tiruvaṇṇāmalai, which had been begun by Krishnadēva-Raya. *(E. R. 1904–5, p. 57 f.)*

At Tenkāśi Ativīrarāma-Śrīvallabha-Pāṇḍya was ruling on September 21 in his 20th year. The inscription registers a gift by prince Abhirāma-Varatungarāma, son of Kulaśēkhara-Parākrama.

(600 of 1917 ; T. A. S. i. 117.)

A.D. 1583. This Varatungarāma gave away a village (*V. R. ii, Madura, 80 A, the Daḷavāy Agraharam C.-P. grant.*)

An inscription of December 4, shews Śrīranga I of Vijayanagar reigning in Anantapur District from Penukoṇḍa (*732 of 1916*); and in Conjevaram on October 22. *(586 of 1919.)*

Venkaṭapati I, Śrīranga I's brother, was ruling in Central Mysore.

(E. C. xii, Si. 3.)

Ativīrarama-Śrīvallabha-Pāṇḍya, *alias* Aḷagan-Perumaḷ, ruling in Tinnevelly District in his 21st year. His contemporary Periya-Vīrappa-Nāyaka of Madura mentioned. (*V. R. iii. Tinn. 364; ii, Madura, 70 ; Rammad, 173 ; 528 of 1909 ; 35 of 1908 ; I. A. 1916, p. 90 ; T. A. S. i, 57, 61, etc.*)

[The Portuguese destroyed several Hindu temples in Salsette. In revenge the Hindus destroyed the Christian churches. This was followed by a merciless massacre of Hindus and Muhammadans by the Portuguese.]

The Pudukoṭṭa plates of date Ś. 1505, speak of a battle fought at Vallamprakāra, or Vallam, between Ativīrarāma-Pāṇḍya and Varatunga on one side, and Achyutappa Nāyaka of Tanjore and Vīrappa-Nāyaka on the other, which ended in the flight of the Tanjoreans. But it is not easy to decide on the date of the battle nor why it was fought.

(See T. A. S. i. 57, 59, 84, 105, etc. ; E. R. 1906, App. A, No. 7.)

A.D. 1584. Several inscriptions of Śrīranga I of Vijayanagar, ruling from Penukoṇḍa, in Mysore, and in Kurnool, Madras, Chingleput, Cuddapah and S. Arcot Districts, the latest of which is November 7, 1584 (*E.C. v, Bl. 212 ; x, Gd. 25 ; V.R. ii, Kurn. 584 ; Madras 329 ; 25, 31 of 1921 ; V.R. i, Cudd. 534 ; 70 of 1915 ; 237 of 1903 ; 9 of 1922 ; 697 of 1917*). One of the Kurnool inscriptions mentions a conferring of temple privileges at the Vaishnava temple at Ahōbilam on a Maṭla chief in commemoration of his grandfather having helped to drive away from the temple, the Golkonda invaders under Ibrahim Kuṭb Shāh after the latter had, in conjunction with the Haṇḍē chiefs of Anantapur, who were Śaivas, occupied the temple for seven years.

(*V.R. ii, Kurn. 584 ; 70 of 1915.*)

A.D. 1585. Śrīranga reigning in Kurnool, S. Arcot, and Mysore (*V.R. ii, Kurn. 222 ; 262 of 1916 ; E.C. x, Sd. 51*). The S. Arcot record bears date=October 25. The Mysore one is of a date late in the year, in month 'Dhanus'. This was Śrīranga I's last year.

Ativīrarāma-Śrīvallabha-Pāṇḍya ruling in Tinnevelly on November 19, in his 23rd year.

(*410 of 1917.*)

[The Mughal Emperor Akbar sent an army this year to the Dekhan to impose his authority there.

The Portugese erected a new fort at Ponnani.]

A.D. 1586. Venkaṭapati I of Vijayanagar came to the throne early in this year in succession to Śrīranga I. An inscription of date early in the year names him as sovereign (*V.R. ii, Kurn. 585 ; 71 of 1915*). Other records of his are in Mysore, on April 15 (*E.C. iii, Nj. 141*). And on March 11, a grant by the Changāḷva chief, Piriya Rāja (*E.C. iv, Hs. 41, 71*). And in Nellore (*V.R. ii, Nell, 774, 775 ; B. and V. C. 1365, 1367*). And in Anantapur (*728 of 1917*). In Madura during his reign he granted a village at the request of Periya-Vīrappa-Nāyaka of Madura *alias* 'Vīrabhūpa', son of Krishnappa and grandson of Viśvanatha Nāyaka (*V.R. ii, Madura 80—the Daḷavāy Agrahāram plates ; E.I. xii. 159*). In the British Museum is a C.-P. grant of this king dated October 14, 1586 (*E.I. xiii. 225*). Venkaṭapati I marrried Bayamā, daughter of one of the nobles, Jagga Rāya.[1] He reigned till 1614–15.

There is an inscription of this year of April 3 shewing Ativīrarāma Śrivallabha-Pāṇḍya ruling in Tinnevelly. (*325 of 1918.*)

That the Golkonda Sultan was in power in Nellore District is proved by an inscription which in itself is very interesting as shewing the goodwill existing there between Muhammadans and Hindus. A certain Lāl Khān granted some lands to Brahmans 'for the religious merit of Muhammad-Kuli-Shāh of Golkonda.' (*V.R. ii, Nellore, 381 ; B. and V. C. 667.*)

This was the accession year of Abhirāma-Varatunga *alias* Vīra Pāṇḍya in Madura, who was also called 'Aḷagan-Perumāl-Ativīrarāma.'

(*605 of 1917 ; V.R. ii, Madura 80—A.-B. ; T. A. S. i, 117.*)

A.D. 1587. Venkaṭapati I of Vijayanagar reigning on August 3 in Conjevaram (*531 of 1919*). And in Kurnool and Mysore. (*V.R. ii, Kurn. 109 ; E.C. vii, Sh. 83 ; vi, Cm. 79.*)

In Cuddapah District at Siddhavaṭṭam, the village council gave 100 *bigas* of land to a Muhammadan Pīr-Jādah-Saheb. (*V.R. i, Cudd. 932, 933.*)

There appears to be some mistake in an inscription reported from S. Kanara District 'Ś. 1508 Sarvajit'=A.D. 1587–88, which represents king Sadāśiva of Vijayanagar as still reigning. The original should be examined. (*V.R. ii, S. Kanara, 158 ; 140 of 1901.*)

Two records of Ativīrarāma-Pāṇḍya *alias* Aḷagan-Perumāḷ in Tinnevelly District differ from one another in the matter of his regnal year. Both quote the year Sarvajit. One (*V.R. ii, Tinn. 256 ; 484 of 1909*) calls it his 24th year. The other (*ibid, Tinn. 304–E.*) calls it his 26th year. A day in Sarvajit would have been either in his 24th or 25th year.

[1] The actual name of this queen was Koṇḍama, daughter of Gobbūri Oba and sister of Jaggarāya, according to the *Rāmarājīyamu*. See *Sources of Vijayanagar History*, p. 243, Ext. 79.—*Editor*.

A.D. 1588. Venkaṭapati I of Vijayanagar reigning in N. Arcot and Ramnad, and in Conjevaram and Erode (*163 of 1921; V. R. ii, Ram. 223; 587 of 1919; 13 of 1891*). And in Chidambaram.

(*V. R. i, S. Arcot 127 to 165; 335 to 373 of 1913. His records of this year are scattered between these numbers.*)

This seems to have been the year of the coronation of Varatungarāma Pāṇḍya *alias* 'Vīra', 'Abhirāma', 'Vēlvīrarāma', or 'Sundarēśvara', who was 'born in Pushya nakshatra' and began to rule in 1586. The inscription recording it mentions the battle of Vallam (*see above, s. v. A. D. 1583*).

(*T. A. S. i. 56, 115; V. R. Tinnevelly 291, 292, 348; 272 of 1908; 512 of 1909.*)

The Changāḷva chief Piriya-Rāja, son of Śrīkaṇṭha ruling in S. Mysore. (*E. C. iv, Hs. 15.*)

Bhairarasa, 'son of Gummata-dēvī', chief of Kaḷasa ruling the Koppa tract on the upper Tungabhadra River in W. Mysore. (*E. C. vi, Kp. 57.*)

[Mirān Nizām Shāh having slain his own father Murtazā, came to the throne in Ahmadnagar. He was long remembered for his cruelty and debauchery. He murdered many of the royal family. Firishta writes of him—'It was frequently his custom in fits of intoxication to ride through the city with his drunken associates, and put persons to death though not guilty of any crime.'

The Portuguese devastated the west coast of Ceylon.]

A.D. 1589. Venkatapati I of Vijayanagar reigning in Kurnool and Mysore (*V. R. ii, Kurn. 500; E. C. xi, Hr. 88; xii, Ck. 39*). And in S. Arcot (*36 of 1905*).

[Mirān Nizām Shāh of Ahmadnagar was deposed and slain. Firishta describes the terrible events at the city, where there seems to have been an orgy of slaughter. One of the rebel leaders 'commanded his adherents to murder the foreigners of every rank and occupation in the city and to plunder and burn their dwellings. The soldiers and their followers . . . put to death indiscriminately the noble, the rich, the master and the servant, the merchant, the pilgrim and the travelling stranger. Their houses were set on fire . . . virgins . . . were dragged by the hair into the assemblies of the drunken. . . . In the space of seven days nearly a thousand foreigners were murdered.' (*Scott's Edit. p. 392.*)

Muhammad Kuli Khān of Golkonda moved his capital to Haidarabād.]

An inscription of date = March 16, 1589, in Ganjam District states that the Muhammadan General of the Sultan of Golkonda dug a tank for irrigation purposes. He is said to command '84 forts of the Āndhra-Trilinga-Madhyama' country (*V. R. i. Ganjam, 15; 187 of 1913*). It also says that the 'Utkala' country (i.e., Kalinga, Rajahmundry and Saurāshtra) was ruled by Śāḷuva Narasimha—'a relation', says Mr. V. Rangacharya, 'of Bahubalēndra apparently. A chief who lived after Mukundadeva's usurpation which took place in 1551.'

In Maṇḍya Taluk, Mysore a grant was made on March 8 by 'Rāma and Tirumala, sons of Tirumala Rāja 'Mahāmaṇḍalēśvara.' [I am unable to identify these chiefs.] [1]

(*E. C. iii, Md. 25.*)

A.D. 1590. Venkaṭapati I of Vijayanagar reigning in Kurnool from Penukoṇḍa (*V. R. ii. Kurn. 582; 68 of 1915*). And in Tinnevelly District. (*Ibid. iii, Tinn. 457.*)

On October 9, in Tinnevelly at Tenkāśi a record of Abhirāmasundara Varatungarāma-Paṇḍya in his 4th year. This makes his accession as in the year following October 9, 1586. (*605 of 1917.*)

[1] Tirumala must have been the last viceroy of Seringapatam, son of Rama, the emperor's elder brother. Rama and Tirumala, the sons of this, must be Princes of the Seringapatam viceroy—*Editor.*

[After the murder of Mirān Nizām Shāh of Ahmadnagar in 1588 his nephew Ismail became Sultan. He was in this year deposed, and his father Burhān-Nizām-Shāh made Sultan in his place. A Bijāpur army was defeated by forces from Ahmadnagar.]

A.D. 1591. Venkaṭapati I of Vijayanagar reigning in Bellary District. Inscription at Kampli on the Tungabhadra river, shewing that, in spite of the destruction of the capital, he was recognized as king in the near neighbourhood (*717 of 1922*). Another record of his reign is at Conjevaram, bearing date December 21 (*421 of 1919*). Another of June 26 is *C.-P. 6 of 1922–23.*

Two inscriptions in Tinnevelly District of Ativīrarāma-Śrīvallabha-Pāṇḍya, of dates = March 12, 1591, in his 28th year and June 13 in his 29th year, shew that his accession was after March 12 and earlier than June 13, 1563. (*482, 485 of 1917.*)

The Changāḷva chief Piriya-Rāja, son of Śrīkaṇṭha, gave grants in S. Mysore.

(*E.C. iv, Hs. 103, 121.*)

[The Portuguese Governor André Furtada brought many West-coast towns to submission.]

A.D. 1592. Venkaṭapati I of Vijayanagar reigning in Mysore; in Chingleput on April 2; in Conjevaram on May 18; in N. and S. Arcot during the year 1592–93. An inscription at Virinchipuram in N. Arcot is noticeable in that it gives Venkaṭapati only the title of a great lord—'Mahāmaṇḍalēśvara'—and accords him Śāḷuva family titles.

(*E.C. x, Bg. 38 : xi, Hr. 6 ; 208 of 1916 ; 381 of 1919 ; V.R. i, N. Arcot, 6, 614 ; 385 of 1905 ; 61 of 1887 ; 258 of 1916 ; S.I.I. i. 78, No. 58.*)

Keḷadi Venkaṭappa-Nāyaka, a feudatory of Vijayanagar, gave a grant in Shimoga Taluk, Mysore, on September 30. (*Mys. A.A.R. 1923, No. 108, p. 105.*)

In Cuddapah, a local 'Chōḷa-Mahārāja,' Gangādhara, granted land. (*V.R. i, Cudd. 465.*)

An inscription at Amīnābād in Guntur District relates that in A.D. 1580 (*see above*) Ibrahim Kuṭb Shāh of Golconda sent an army and seized strong fortresses of Udayagiri (whence 'Venkaṭa-Rāzu,' i.e., Venkaṭapati I of Vijayanagar, was expelled), Vinukoṇḍa, Bellaṁkoṇḍa, and Tangēḍa with their dependent territories. Afterwards he took Koṇḍavīḍu, the principal stronghold, and made his son Muhammad Kuli Governor thereof. In 1592, a number of local leaders, including some Muhammadan Zamindars, raised a rebellion. An army was sent, crossed the Krishna River, and marched through the country 'punishing the wicked and protecting the good.' [It should be noticed that the inscription was engraved on the wall of the temple of Durga, probably under compulsion by the Golkonda Commander.] (*V.R. ii, Guntur, 764 ; 541 of 1909 ; E.R. 1910, p. 119.*)

[Burhān Nizam Shāh of Ahmadnagar besieged the Portuguese in Chaul; but the siege was raised.]

A.D. 1593. Venkaṭapati I of Vijayanagar reigning in Mysore, Chingleput, Anantapur and Tinnevelly.

(*E.C. iv, Ch. 30 ; xii, Mi. 21 ; 10 of 1921—date August 29—322 of 1920 ; V.R. iii, Tinn. 285.*)

In Cuddapah district, Nandyāl Obala-Rāja mentioned in an inscription.

(*V.R. i, Cudd. 432 ; 377 of 1904.*)

A C.-P. grant of two villages in Ramnād district to Brahmans by Prince Abhirāma-Ativīrarāma-Pāṇḍya, son of Ativīrarāma *alias* Jaṭilavarman-Śrīvallabha, then in this 30th year. Date, Ś. 1515. (*V.R. ii, Ramnad 66 ; C.P. 1 of 1912.*)

In the Krishna River tract, Mangaḷagiri and Nizāmpatam were ruled by Sultan Muhammad Kuli II of Golkonda. (*V.R. ii, Gun. 150 ; 259 of 1902.*)

[The Mughal Emperor Akbar despatched an army to reduce the Muhammadan Sultans of the Dekhan who disputed his sovereignty.]

A.D. 1594. Venkaṭapati I reigning on July 27 in Chingleput (*190, 191 of 1922*). His nephew Śrīranga II ruling in Tinnevelly district. (*V.R. iii, Tinn. 117 ; 187 of 1895.*)

[The Portuguese seized three ships belonging to Calicut. They built another fort at Korlai.]

A.D. 1595. Venkaṭapati I reigning in Conjevaram on August 9, and in S. Arcot (*382 of 1919 ; 129 of 1917*) and in Tinnevelly. (*615 of 1915.*)

Travancore was ruled by Vīra Ravivarman. (*V.R. iii, Trav. 193, T.A.S. I. 176.*)

In Tinnevelly, Taṭāvarman-Abhirāma-Varatungarāma-Pāṇḍya was ruling in his tenth year. (*V.R. iii, Tinn. 295 ; 615 of 1915 ; 275 of 1908.*)

In Madura District Ativīrarāma Pāṇḍya gave away a village in the 33rd year of the dynasty. He is described as 'sitting on the lion-throne of Vallabha-Narēndra.'

(*V.R. ii, Madura, 92 ; T. A. S. i. 133.*)

[Burhān Nizām Shāh of Ahmadnagar died this year and was succeeded by his son, Ibrahim, who was killed four months later in a battle fought against Ibrahim Ādil Shāh of Bijapur. The nobles were divided as to the succession. Queen Chānd-Bibī of Bijāpur, great-aunt of Ibrahim Nizām Shā's infant son, Bahādur, returned to Ahmadnagar and assisted in placing the child on the throne. But the emperor Akbar's son Murād appeared on the scene and besieged the city. Chānd-Bībī made a gallant defence, and when forces from Bijāpur and Golkonda approached to attack him, Murād retired, after receiving the cession of some districts in Berar which belonged to Ahmadnagar.]

A.D. 1596. Venkaṭapati I of Vijayanagar reigning in Chingleput on November 14.

(*198 of 1922.*)

An inscription in Tinnevelly names this year erroneously as the '39th' regnal year of Aḷagan-Perumāḷ-Atīvīrarāma-Paṇḍya *alias* 'Śivaladēva.' (*V.R. iii, Tinn. 315 ; 515 of 1909.*)

[Fighting between the Dekhāni Sultans and the Mughal Emperor continued. Ahmadnagar was again besieged, and the town surrounding the fort was sacked by the troops from Delhi. Chānd-Bībī succeeded in holding the fort.]

A.D. 1597. Venkaṭapati I reigning in Chingleput on May 9, and in Madura, and S. Arcot Districts (*7 of 1921 ; V.R. ii, Madura, 91 ; 329 of 1917*). The last two mention Muttu-Krishnappa-Nāyaka of Madura as contemporary.

An inscription of March 16, shews Ativīrarāma Śrīvallabha, son of Kulaśēkhara-Śālivāṭipati Pāṇḍya, ruling in Tinnevelly. (*484 of 1917.*)

[The Mughal armies gained many victories in the Dekhan ; and Akbar subdued Orissa.]

A.D. 1598. Venkaṭapati I reigning in Tanjore on August 28, in Kurnool and in Tinnevelly. (*398 of 1918 ; C. P. 14 of 1906 ; V.R. ii, Kurn. 236 ; iii, Tinn. 64 ; 280 ; C. P. 9 of 1913 ; E.I. xvi, 287, 329.*)

Kumāra-Krishnappa-Nāyaka of Madura is mentioned in both these Tinnevelly inscriptions.

The Kaḷasa chief Pāṇḍyappa, son of Bhairarasa, gave gifts for the upkeep of a Jaina Basti at Koppa on the Tunga River in N.-W. Mysore near the ghats. (*E.C. vi, Kp. 50.*)

[Akbar left Delhi in person to lead his armies against the Dekhāni Sultans.]

A.D. 1599. Venkaṭapati's nephew Śrīranga II, prince of Vijayanagar, ruling in Mysore on July 8. Gift made of two villages to a soldier for war services. (*Mys. A.A.R. 1923, p. 44.*)

[Akbar of Delhi arrived at Burhānpur. The Mughal army besieged Ahmadnagar. The heroic queen Chānd-Bībī of Bijāpur was murdered in Ahmadnagar by her own soldiers.

The Portuguese induced a West Coast pirate to surrender on promise of his life being spared, and on his doing so, beheaded him at Goa.]

A.D. 1600. Venkaṭapati I of Vijayanagar reigning in Mysore. *(E.C. xii, Pg. 85.)*

In Travancore, an inscription of Ativīrarāma-Śrīvallabha-Pāṇḍya shewing him ruling there. *(V.R. iii, Trav. 98.)*

On August 6, an inscription shewing Muhammad Kuli Kuṭb Shāh II of Golkonda ruling in Guntur District. *(841 of 1922.)*

In Cuddapah District the Maṭla chief Anantadēva 'Choḷa-Mahārāja' made a gift of land. *(V. R. i, Cudd. 681, 682.)*

A Changāḷva chief Rudragaṇa, 'son of Kulōttunga-Changāḷva-Chengaya, gave a grant for the merit of his father Śrīkanṭha'. Thus Śrīkanṭha was another name of Chengaya. *(E. C. iv, Hs. 104.)*

[Severe famine in the Dekhan in this year.] *(I. A. 1923, p. 234.)*

The State of Ahmadnagar was finally seized by the Emperor Akbar and annexed. The Nizām Shāhi dynasty came to an end, and the young king Bahādur and the royal family were sent as prisoners to Gwalior. The Dekhan generaly submitted to Akbar, whose son Danyāl was made viceroy. He married the daughter of Ibrahim Ādil Shāh of Bījapur.

Continued struggles between Portuguese and Dutch in various places where they had established trading factories.

On December 31, 1600 Queen Elizabeth of England granted the first Charter to the 'London company of merchants trading to the East Indies'.

A.D. 1601. Venkatapati I of Vijayanagar reigning in Kurnool (*V. R. ii, Kurn. 439*). And on May 9, in N. Arcot, on which day a grant was made at the request of the Vellore chief Lingappa, son of Chinna-Bomma Nāyaka (*The Viḷappakkam Plates ; V. R. i, N. Arcot, 663 A ; E. I. iv, 269.*) In this record the king is said to have warred against the Golkonda Sultans.

Inscription at Trivandrum of June 20, 1601, Kollam Āṇḍu 776, states that on that day the Kēraḷa king Ravivarman V performed the *Tulāpurusha* ceremony at the temple, weighing himself against gold and distributing it ; and that he built a manṭapa in memory of it. *(V. R. iii, Trav. 213 ; T. A. S. ii, 28 ; ibid. i, p. 175.)*

A.D. 1602. Venkaṭapati I of Vijayanagar reigning in Nellore, Kurnool, Madura, Anantapur and Madras Districts, and in Mysore. *(V. R. ii, Nell. 54, 625 ; B. and V. C., C. P. No. 5 ; V. R. ii, Kurn. 111, 188 ; Madura 71 ; 36 of 1908 ; 382 of 1920 ; V. R. ii, Madras 328 ; 236 of 1903 ; E. C. xii, Mi. 6.)*

An inscription of January 9 shews Ativīrarāma Pāṇḍya ruling in Tinnevelly. The date however seems confused as regards the regnal year. *(V. R. iii, Tinn. 278—R.)*

[The Mughal Emperor Akbar was proclaimed 'king of the Dekhan'.]

A.D. 1603. Venkaṭapati I of Vijayanagar reigning in Kurnool District (*V. R. ii, Kurn. 458 ; 32 of 1915*). And in Tiṇḍivanam. *(31 of 1905 ; V. R. i, S. Arcot, 467.)*

[The Dutch, now in some strength, blockaded the Portuguese at Goa with a large fleet, and began a struggle between the two nations which lasted for a long time.]

A.D. 1604. Venkaṭapati I reigning in Anantapur on December 29, and in Mysore (*736 of 1917 ; E. C. iii, Ml. 111*). And in Coimbatore. *(356 of 1901 ; V. R. i, Coim. 483.)*

Muhammad Kuli Kuṭb Shāh of Golkonda reigning in Ganjam and Vizagapatam Districts. The Ganjam inscription, which is at Śrīkūrmam, mentions the Shāh's defeat of the Orissa usurper Mukunda Bahubalēndra, the Telugu chief, who was driven over the border. The Vizagapatam record tells the same story. (*V. R. i, Ganjam, 250 ; 372 of 1906 ; ibid. iii, Vizag. 194 ; 373 of 1905.*)

Ativīrarāma-Pāṇḍya ruling in Tinnevelly in his 42nd year. (*399 of 1917.*)

A.D. 1605. Venkaṭapati I of Vijayanagar reigning in Mysore, and in Madras and Chingleput Districts. (*E. C. x, Bg. 20 ; xii, Si. 61 ; V. R. ii, Madras, 190 ; 379 of 1919.*)

In Tinnevelly District Ativīrarāma-Śrīvallabha-Pāṇḍya, called 'Aḷagan-Perumāḷ' ruling, on June 27, in his 42nd year (*405 of 1917*). And on June 16, also in his 42nd year (*580 of 1917*). The regnal year was, however, apparently 43rd, not 42nd.

A.D. 1606. [The Mughal Emperor Akbar died on January 27, 1606; and was succeeded by his son Prince Abūl-Muzaffar-Salīm, who assumed the title of Jahangīr.]

Inscription of Venkaṭapati I of Vijayanagar in North Mysore. (*E.C. xi, Cd. 80.*)

The Keḷadi chief Venkaṭappa-Nāyaka ruling locally in N.-W. Mysore above the ghats. (*E.C. viii, Sd. 123.*)

Gift to the Rāmēśvaram temple by the Dalavāy Sētupati-Kātta, the first of the Ṣētupati ruling family. (*V.R. ii, Ramnad, 106 ; C-P. 11 of 1911.*)

A.D. 1607. Another gift at Rāmēśvaram by the same, who here has the title 'Tirumalai-Uḍaiyan'. (*V.R. ii, Ramnad, 110.*)

[Malik Ambar, minister of Murtazā-Nizām-Shāh of Ahmadnagar, acquired great power and defied the Mughal Emperor.]

Vīra-Ravi Ravivarman ruling the Kēraḷa country. (*T.A.S. i. 186.*)

A.D. 1608. Venkaṭapati I of Vijayanagar reigning in East Mysore and in Chingleput District. (*E.C. x, Kl. 241 ; 197 of 1922.*)

In Madura, Muttu-Vīrappa-Nayaka was ruling. A shrine was built at Rāmēśvaram in this year and the inscription regarding it quotes him as sovereign, proving the subordination to Madura of the Ramnad Sētupatis. (*V.R. ii, Ram. 95 ; 102 of 1903.*)

A.D. 1609. Venkaṭapati I reigning in Mysore on March 26, and on other days in the year; and on June 16, in Kurnool. He is stated to be ruling with Penukoṇḍa as his capital (*E.C. xii, Si. 1 ; vi, Mg. 63 ; ix, Hl. 119 ; x, Sd. 5 ; V.R. ii, Kurn. 581 ; 67 of 1915*). In Mg. 63, the chief, Bhairarasa, son of Bhairarasa, is shewn to be ruling the Kaḷasa country. He is given the prefix of 'Sāntara.'

In Madura, Muttu-Vīrappa-Nāyaka was ruling (*E.R. 1905, App. A. 9*). He acknowledges the Vijayanagar king as his overlord. He himself was overlord to the Ramnad Śētupatis. (*V.R. ii, Madura, 60-B, 95 ; I. A. 1916, p. 132 ; Tamil and Sans. Inscriptions, No. 23 ; 87 of 1905.*)

An inscription of Venkaṭapati I's reign in Chingleput District of date January 9, 1609, mentions Gobbūri-Ōba-Rāja, who is believed to be, probably, the king's brother-in-law Ōba-Rāja,[1] who is alluded to by Barradas in his account of the Chandragiri Palace tragedy of 1615-16. ('*Forgotten Empire*', *p. 222-3. 92 of 1923 ; V.R. i, Ching. 710, 1157 ; 243 of 1910 ; 332 of 1909.*)

[Malik Ambar came to open war with the Mughal forces at Ahmadnagar who were

[1] It is more likely this is the father-in-law as the son is distinguished by being named *Chinna* Oba. Queen Koṇḍama was the daughter of Gobbūri Oba. His sons were Jagga and Chinna Oba. See extract 79 from the *Rāmarājīyamu, Sources of Vijayanagar History* and *Journal of Indian History* v. 164, ff.—*Editor.*

commanded by Prince Khān-Jahān, afterwards the Emperor Shāh-Jahan. Malik Ambar defeated the prince and became master for a time of almost all the Dekhan. He invaded Gujarat, and plundered Surat, but retired. The Dutch built a fort at Pulicat, north of Madras.]

A.D. 1610. [Malik Ambar gained possession of Berar.]

Venkaṭapati I of Vijayanagar reigning in Mysore and in Chingleput District (*E.C. vii, Tl. 166 ; ix, D-B, 49 ; iv, Ch. 194 ; 188 of 1922*). The first of the Mysore records mentions Venkaṭappa or Venkaṭādri-Nāyaka as governing the Āraga country in N.-W. Mysore. Vīrappa Nāyaka ruling in Madura. (*Tam.* and *Sans. Ins. p. 109.*)

A.D. 1611. [The English Capt. Hippon of the ship 'Globe' visited the West Coast and attempted to establish factories at 'Pettipollee' (English for Peddapalli, 36 miles West of Masulipatam, afterwards known as Nizampatam). He opened trade and founded an Agency at Masulipatam.]

A.D. 1612. Venkaṭapati I of Vijayanagar reigning in Mysore and in Nellore district.

(*E.C. iii, Tri. 62 ; xii, Si. 84 ; V.R. ii, Nell. 36, 707 ; B. and V.C. i, 245 ; iii, 1286.*)

Muttu-Vīrappa-Nāyaka of Madura ruling in Tinnevelly. (*V.R. iii, Tinn. 34 35 ; 122, 123 of 1907 ; I.A. 1916, 132.*)

The Changāḷva chief, 'Vīrapa, son of Vīra Rājaya son of 'Śiīkanṭha' gave a gift in S. Mysore. (*E.C. iv, Hs. 118, 119.*)

[The Mughal viceroy of Gujarat drove out the English merchants trading in Surat; but later, the Emperor Jahangīr granted permission to the English to establish a factory there and at Ahmadabad, Kambay and Gogha. The Portuguese attacked the English factory at Surat. On October 28, an English fleet of armed merchant-ships under Captain Best fought and defeated the Portuguese; and thereafter the English factory at Surat was firmly established.

Muhammad Kuli Kuṭb Shāh of Golkonda died this year and was succeeded by his brother Abdullah.]

A.D. 1613. Venkaṭapati I reigning from Penukoṇḍa (*C.-P. 7 of 1922-23*). And in Mysore and in Chittoor and Tinnevelly Districts.

(*E.C. iv, Ch. 135 ; E.R. 1922, App. A, No. 9 ; 452 of 1916 ; E.I. xiii. 231.*)

Keḷadi Venkaṭappa-Nāyaka made a grant to the temple at Uḍipi in S. Kanara.

(*V.R. ii, S. Kan. 231 ; 110 of 1901.*)

A.D. 1614. Venkaṭapati I of Vijayanagar reigning, in June or July, in Mysore (*E.C. x, Kl. 157 ; iii, Sr. 157*). And, during the year in Kurnool District (*V.R. ii, Kurn. 380 ; 286 of 1905*). On October 10, 1614, an inscription in Central Mysore represents the country as being governed by king Venkaṭapati I's nephew Śrīranga (*E.C. xii, Pg. 94*); and another in East Mysore says that country was under the rule of Rāma who is represented as 'sitting on the diamond-throne (of Vijayanagar) at Penukoṇḍa' (*E.C. ix, An. 47*). The date of this last record is November 6, 1614.

The tragic events which disturbed the Vijayanagar monarchy are fully described by the Chronicler, Barradas, and are detailed in '*A Forgotten Empire*' p. 222, f. It is necessary here to summarize and synchronize them, shortly.

Barradas's letter was written on *December 12, 1616*, and he relates that war had been going on for two years between rival factions since prince Rāma II, surviving son of Śrīranga II, had been placed on the throne. The record in E. Mysore noted above makes Rāma II was on the throne on November 6, 1614. The inscription mentioned as found in Central Mysore makes Rāma II's predecessor, Śrīranga II, ruling on October 10, 1614. He had been a short time on the throne when he was killed. King Venkaṭapati was on the throne in June or *July 1614*. Thus we must assume that Venkaṭapati died after (say) July, and before October 10, when Śrīranga was king, and that Śrīranga's cruel death took place after *October 10*, and before *November 6*, when Rāma II was king.

The following summary of events is shortened from Barradas's story.

Venkaṭapati I, had married Bayamā the daughter[1] of Gobbūri Jagga Rāya, one of the great nobles. When on his death-bed the king forced his nephew Śrīranga II, greatly against the latter's will, to become king in his stead, and Śrīranga was accordingly proclaimed. Three days later Venkaṭapati I died, aged 67. Śrīranga's accession was opposed by Jagga-Rāya, Timma-Nāyaka, and another noble whom Barradas calls 'Maca Rāya.' One day, on their declaration that they desired to do homage to king Śrīranga, they were admitted to an audience in the palace at Chandragiri. Once in with their followers they broke into open rebellion, seized the person of the king, proclaimed him deposed and placed Jagga-Raya's nephew on the throne. A certain 'captain' Ēchama, who was loyal to king Śrīranga collected troops, and tried in several ways to effect the king's escape. Their attempts failed, but Ēchama by a clever stratagem managed to get Śrīranga's second son Rāma out of the palace and into safety in his camp. Jagga-Rāya then sent his brother 'Chinaobraya' (probably Chinna Obala Raya, or Aubala) to the palace with orders that king Śrīranga must either kill himself or be killed. The king, under compulsion beheaded the queen and slew his youngest son and a daughter. The king's eldest son beheaded his own wife; and then both Śrīranga and his son fell on their own swords and so died. Chinna Obala afterwards killed the king's youngest daughter.

Hearing of all this Ēchama challenged Jagga-Rāya, and after 'some time', the two forces met in a pitched battle in which Jagga-Rāya was defeated and fled. Ēchama plundered Jagga-Rāya's camp and recovered the royal insignia and an immense treasure, part of which consisted of precious stones worth a million pounds. He then enthroned the rescued Prince Rāma, son of Śrīranga, as king.

Both Ēchama and Jagga-Rāya strengthened their armies and called for adherents. Many of the nobles joined Ēchama, while others joined Jagga Rāya. Amongst these the Madura Nāyaka took the side of Jagga Rāya (Travancore was then an appanage of Madura); while the Tanjore Nāyaka joined Ēchama.[2]

(*For contination see below s.v, A.D. 1616.*)

A.D. 1615. There is a confusing inscription in a village near Udayagiri, which, while asserting that in Śaka 1537 (A.D. 1615–16)—no mention being made of the cyclic year's name—Venkaṭapati I gave away a village, adds that it was granted while Timmaya-Dēva was 'seated on the diamond throne at Penukonḍa.' Venkaṭapati may have given the village in A.D. 1614, since Ś. 1537 *current*=A.D. 1614–15. Who 'Timmaya' was is not known.[3]

(*V.R. ii, Nellore, 764; B. and V.C. 1359.*)

[1] See note on p. 269. Konḍama, familiarly Bayama, was Gobbūri Jagga's sister.—*Editor*.

[2] For a fuller exposition of Barradas' letter and other Portuguese, etc., sources, see article of Father Heras in the *Journal of Ind. Hist.* V, noted above; for the relationship of Jagga and other details of the transactions as a whole, relevant extracts from contemporary works in *Sources of Vijayanagar History*. The place of the massacre seems to have been Penukonda, and not Chandragiri or Vellore.—*Editor*.

[3] This seems to refer to Tirumala Rāya, father of Venkaṭa, who gave the *Amara* (Service-fief) to the donor.—*Editor*.

Keḷadi Venkaṭappa-Nāyaka was ruling in N.-W. Mysore (*E.C. viii, Tl, 97*). And in S. Kanara. (*V.R. ii, S. Kan. 50.*)

The Changāḷva chief Virājaiya, son of Śrīkanṭha, made a grant in S. Mysore (*E.C. iv, Hs. 56.*)

In Tinnevelly, Varaguṇa-Śrīvallabha-Kulaśēkhara was ruling. He performed a *yāga* ceremony at Tenkāśi and was consequently known by the title 'Sōmāśiyār Dikshitar'. (*V.R. iii, Tinn. 393–A ; T.A.S. i, 147 ; 268 of 1908.*)

[A Portuguese fleet attacked an English fleet but was driven off. A combination of Dekhāni Muhammadans from Bijāpur, Ahmadnagar and Golkonda was defeated by a Mughal army under Prince Khurram, sent by the Emperor Jahāngīr.]

The Portuguese effected a treaty with Jahāngīr by which the Dutch and English merchants were to be expelled from the Empire. In their turn the Portuguese were to destroy the bands of pirates that harassed the coasts, especially on the West.

Louis XIII of France granted a Charter to a French Company for promoting trade in the East.

The dwellers in the town of S. Thomé close to modern Madras begged the Portuguese viceroy, Manuel de Frias, to take possession of it, which he did. A Portuguese fleet made the capture secure. Evidently the townsfolk were apprehensive, considering the disturbed state of the country. (*See below s.v. A.D. 1616.*)]

A.D. 1616. [Southern India was greatly disturbed by the fighting amongst the Vijayanagar factions. Barradas, writing on December 12, 1616, says, 'there are now assembled in the field in the large open plains of Trinchenepali (Trichinopoly) not only the hundred thousand men that each party has, but as many as a million of soldiers.']

An inscription in N. Arcot (*112 of 1921*), as reported, of date[1] 'Ś. 1538. Nala' (=A.D. 1616–17) appears to make Venkaṭapati I of Vijayanagar still on the throne. [It seems to require examination, as it would entirely contradict the story told by Barradas. (*above s.v. A.D. 1614.*)]

Keḷadi Venkaṭappa-Nāyaka ruled locally in N. W. Mysore. (*E.C. viii, Nr. 79 ; Tl. 53.*)

In Tinnevelly Muttu Virappa Nāyaka of Madura was recognized as overlord. (*V.R. iii, Tinn. 1 ; 556 of 1911.*)

Śivalamāra-Varaguṇa-Kulaśēkhara-Pāṇḍya-Sōmayāji gave a grant in Travancore in his 3rd year. (*V. R. iii, Trav. 127 ; T. A S. i, 148*)

[Surat was made the chief English factory in India. Others were started at Calicut and Cranganore. The Danes established a factory at Tanjore.

Prince Khurram proceeded with his campaign to crush the rebellious Malik Ambar and the Dekhānis generally.]

A.D. 1617. Rāma II of Vijayanagar, called 'Rāmachandra', recognized as sovereign in Mysore. (*E. C. x, Bg. 40, 75.*)

An inscription at Vīranna-Kanupūr, Nellore District, quoting the year 'Pingala' but giving a wrong Śaka year, seems to represent Venkaṭapati I of Vijayanagar as still reigning. But it is just possible from the wording of it that the date may be that on which a grant which had been *previously* granted by that king was now assigned for a particular object. So it is not conclusive to prove that Venkaṭapati was alive in A.D. 1617–18. (*V. R. ii, Nellore 263 ; B. and V. C. i, 454.*)

[1] The date given Śaka 1538, Nala, Āvaṇi 5 - Sun., August 4, 1616.—*Editor.*

[Malik Ambar was forced to submit to prince Khurram, who was given the title 'Shāh Jahān'. There was some fighting at Mangalore between the townsfolk and the Portuguese.]

In Travancore Vīra-Kēraḷa-Rāmavarman-Tiruvaḍi ruled (*T. A. S. i, 55.*)

A.D. 1619. Rāma II of Vijayanagar reigning in E. Mysore. (*E. C. x, Kl. 204.*)

Grant made by an agent of Muttu-Vīrappa-Nāyaka of Madura, who is said to be a feudatory of Rāma II of Vijayanagar (*V. R. i, Coimbatore, 73*). [The date is not very clear.]

A.D. 1620. Rāma II of Vijayanagar reigning in N. Arcot (*11 of 1896 ; V. R. i, N. Arcot 635 ; Chingleput, 1211*). And in Mysore, where mention is made of the locally ruling prince Chāma-Rāja VII, son of Narasa. (*E. C. iii, Sr. 36.*)

An inscription on a rock near Mysore city (*E. C. iii, My. 17*) makes the then ruler of the country, Vīra-Rāghava-Rāya, and gives him full imperial titles.

[An English factory was established at Pulicat, alongside the Dutch one.

Malik Ambar, becoming again refractory, was attacked and defeated by a Mughal Army. In the course of the war a Mahratta leader, Shāhji Bhonsla, greatly distinguished himself fighting on the side of the Mughals.

Raghunātha-Nāyaka of Tanjore granted the port of Tranquebar to the Danes.

There was another naval fight between Portuguese and English.]

A.D. 1621. Rāma II of Vijayanagar reigning in Mysore (*E. C. vii, Sh. 27*). And in Chingleput. (*V. R. i, Chin. 1195, E. C. iii, Md. 17.*)

Keḷadi Venkaṭappa-Nāyaka ruling in W. Mysore. (*E. C. vi, Sg. 5 ; viii, Sa. 54.*)

[Prince Shāh-Jahān, greatly aided by Mahratta troops, again defeated Malik Ambar. In Shāh-Jahān's absence his mother Nūr Jahān plotted to deprive him of the throne and to make his younger brother Shāhryār Emperor. At this time the Persians conquered and annexed Kandahar ; and the Emperor Jahāngīr ordered Shāh Jahān to proceed thither and recapture it, but in consequence of the family and Court intrigues, the prince refused to go. Jahāngīr, influenced by Nūr Jahān, confiscated Shāh Jahān's estates and deprived him of his command.]

A.D. 1622. Rāma II of Vijayanagar reigning on March 3, in Coimbatore District (*239 of 1920*). And in Kurnool. (*V. R. ii, Kurn. 379 ; 285 of 1905.*)

[There was a terrible famine in this year in South India. A Jesuit Missionary describes the sufferings of the people.] (*I. A. 1923, p. 234.*)

[Prince Shāh-Jahān threw off his allegiance to his father and proclaimed himself Emperor of Hindustan. He marched in force to Delhi, but was defeated by the imperial troops and returned to the Dekhan. He was again defeated. Then he attacked Orissa, and afterwards Bengal. Prince Khusru, his elder brother, died, leaving a son Dāwar Baksh.]

[The Hindu nobles were fighting amongst themselves near Pulicat. The English factory was withdrawn from that place.]

A.D. 1623. Rāma II reigning in Mysore from Penukoṇḍa (*E. C. iii, Tn. 62 ; xii, Ck. 1 ; ix, Cp. 182*). In Trichinopoly District Rāma II's Viceroy was Pedda Venkaṭa II of the Āraviḍu family. (*V. R. iii, Trich. 300 ; 1 of 1913.*)

Muttu-Vīrappa of Madura ruling at Ambasamudram. (*309 of 1916.*)

Shāh Jahān marched to attack Agra, but was defeated and retired into Golkonda territory.

About this time, during Jahāngīr's reign William Hawkins wrote, describing the injustice and oppression of Mughal rule in India in his day, and the ruthlessness with which the treasury was enriched—' A man cannot continue half a year in his living but it is taken from him and given unto another; or else the king taketh it for himself (if it be rich ground and likely to yield much) making exchange for a worse place. . . . By this means he racketh the poor to get from them what he can.'

(Purchas, *his pilgrimes, iii. 221.*)

A.D. 1624. Rāma II of Vijayanagar reigning in Kurnool District.

(*V. R. ii, Kurn. 423 ; 53 of 1915.*)

Keḷadi Venkaṭappa Nāyaka ruling in N.-W. Mysore. (*E. C. viii, Tl. 82, 83, 66.*)

Chāma Rāja VII of Mysore ruling in the neighbourhood of Mysore town. (*E. C. iv, Hg. 21.*)

Kūttan Sētupati Kātta built two *manṭapams* at the temple at Rāmēśvaram.

(*V. R. ii, Ramnad, 81 ; Tam. and Sans. Ins., p. 60.*)

[Prince Shāh Jahān again attacked Orissa, but was beaten back and retired to the Dekhan.]

A.D. 1625. Rāma II reigning in Chingleput District. (*V. R. i, Ching. 588 ; 616 of 1904.*)

[Shāh-Jahān, finding further resistance useless, submitted to the Emperor his father, and was forgiven. The prince's elder brother Parvīz died this year.

The Rāja of Venkaṭagiri gave some ground to the English merchants to enable them to establish a trading factory at Ārumugam (*Anglicē* ' Armagaon ') N. of Pulikat.]

A.D. 1626. Rāma II of Vijayanagar reigning in Mysore and in Anantapur District. The date of the former is March 5, 1626. (*E. C. xii, Si. 54 ; 376 of 1920 ; E. R. 1921, p. 106.*)

[Sultan Ibrahim Ādil Shāh of Bijāpur died this year and was succeeded by his son Muhammad, under whom the Mahrattas rose to great power.]

A.D. 1627. Keḷadi Venkaṭappa Nāyaka, on April 10, gave land for support of a mosque—shewing much religious toleration (*E. C. viii, Tl. 38, 39*). Also gave land in S. Kanara.

(*V. R. ii, S. Kan. 59.*)

[The Mughal Emperor Jahāngīr died this year. The rightful heir was Dāwar Baksh son of the Emperor's eldest son Khusru, now deceased, but Nūr Jahān tried to secure the throne for her youngest son Shāhryār. The nobles took sides and fought, and Shāhryār was defeated.]

Sivājī, son of Shāhjī Bhonsla the Mahratta leader was born on May 6, 1627.

A.D. 1628. Rāma II of Vijayanagar reigning in Mysore and in Anantapur District.

(*E. C. ix, Bn. 1 ; iv, Yd. 34 ; 374 of 1920.*)

[Shāh Jahān put to death most of the members of the royal family, except Dāwar Baksh whom he exiled to Persia, and Shāhryār whom he blinded. Having got rid of all rivals he mounted the throne and was crowned. All the nobles, however, were not satisfied. Khān Jahān Lodi, viceroy of the Dekhan, became disaffected.

The chiefs in power at Masulipatam gave some trouble to the English merchants there, and the factory was abandoned. The factory at Armagaon was provided with 12 guns for defence.]

A.D. 1629. Rāma II of Vijayanagar reigning in E. Mysore (*E.C. x, Mb. 62*), and in Madura District. (*V.R. ii, Mad. 5 ; 3 of 1894.*)

[Shāh Jahān granted a *firmān* to the English merchants at Surat. Rebellion against him of Khān Jahān Lodi, who was defeated and fled to the Punjāb.

Shāhjī Bhonsla, with a large force of Mahrattas, joined the Mughal army and received a high command.

A disastrous famine in the Dekhan and the north of the present Madras Presidency. Letters from English residents in Masulipatam and Armagaon speak of its horrors. Cannibalism was of common occurrence.]

A.D. 1630. Keḷadi Vīrabhadra Nāyaka ruling in N.-W. Mysore. (*E.C. viii, Tl. 51, 58; Sb. 451.*)

Rāma II of Vijayanagar reigning in S.-E. Mysore in the month Vaiśākha of Ś. 1552 in the year Pramōda = April 1630 (*E.C. x, Kl. 164, 165*). Another inscription of the same year and month in S.-E. Mysore names 'Śrīranga' as ruler, giving him all royal titles and describing him as 'sitting on the diamond throne at Ghanagiri' (Chandragiri).[1] This Śrīranga was probably Śrīranga III, then a viceroy for King Rāma, the titles given being exaggerated. (*E.C. ix, Ma. 1.*)

Rāma II of Vijayanagar seems to have died during the year. He was succeeded by Pedda Venkaṭa II, grandson of Aḷiya-Rāma-Rāya.

[The terrible famine lasted into this year.]

The war between the Mughals and the Dekhāni forces of Malik Ambar continued.

An English traveller in this year (Peter Mundy) states that at this time the country was 'swarming with rebels and thieves.' (*Oxford Hist. of India, p. 416.*)

A.D. 1631. Pedda Venkaṭa II of Vijayanagar now on the throne. (*E.C. x, Kl. 251.*)

The Keḷadi chief Vīrabhadra-Nāyaka, grandson of Venkaṭappa I, ruling in N.-W. Mysore and S. Kanara. (*E.C. viii, Sa. 41; V.R. ii, S. Kan. 297; Mys. A.A.R. 1923, pp. 82, 109.*)

In S.-W. Mysore Kanthīrava-Narasa Rāja of Mysore ruled. (*E.C. v, Cn. 122.*)

[The famine continued.

Khān Jahān Lodi continued to obstruct the Mughal imperial troops in the Dekhan and was severely defeated.

Muhammad Ádil Shāh of Bijāpur refused to accept the supremacy of the Mughal Emperor, and was besieged by the latter's troops; but the siege had to be raised in consequence of the attackers suffering from an outbreak of disease, and difficulties of supply caused by the famine.

Murtazā Nizām Shāh of Ahmadnagar was murdered. His son Husain was raised to the throne but only reigned for one year.

The Emperor Shāh Jahān, hearing that at Hūghli the Portuguese had been forcibly compelling the townsfolk to abandon Islām and embrace Christianity, ordered the total destruction of the foreigners.]

A.D. 1632. Venkaṭa II of Vijayanagar reigning in Chingleput District. (*V.R. i, Ching. 1199.*)
Keḷadi Vīrabhadra Nāyaka ruling in N.-W. Mysore. (*E.C. viii, Tl. 94.*)

[A Mughal army attacked the Portuguese in Hūghli to punish them for their attempt to make the people Christians by force, and the town was captured after a three months' siege, during which ten thousand men, women and children of the town lost their lives.

Shāh-Jahān, in a fanatical mood, destroyed 76 Hindu temples at Benares.

The English factory at Masulipatam was re-established by permission of Abdullah Kuṭb Shāh of Golkonda.]

A.D. 1633. Pedda Venkaṭa II, or Venkaṭapati, of Vijayanagar was reigning in Anantapur and Chingleput Districts and in North Arcot. (*V. R. i, Anant. 100; E. R. 1918, App. A, No. 17; V. R. i, Ching. 1213, 1215; N. Arcot 549; 65 of 1887, 94 of 1912.*)

[1] Ghanagiri is Penukonda equivalent in meaning; the words being Sanskrit and Telugu respectively.—*Editor.*

Chāma Rāja VII, ruling in Mysore. *(E. C. iii, Tn. 13.)*

Keḷadi Vīrabhadra Nāyaka ruling in N.-W. Mysore. *(E. C. viii, Tl. 181.)*

[Husain Nizām Shāh of Ahmadnagar was captured by the Mughals and imprisoned at Gwalior.]

A.D. 1634. Pedda Venkaṭa II of Vijayanagar reigning in Tinnevelly in April.
(The Kuniyūr plates : V. R. iii, Tinn. 76-A ; E. I. xii, 236 ; E. R. 1901, p. 6.)

Chāma Rāja VII of Mysore ruling at Sravaṇa-Beḷgoḷa. *(E. C. ii, Sr.-Bel. 84, 140.)*

[The Emperor Shāh Jahān invaded the Dekhan and 'laid waste the country of Bijāpur without mercy' *(Firishta, Scott's Edit., p. 340)*. He gave permission to an English company to reside and trade in Bengal.]

A.D. 1635. Pedda Venkaṭa II of Vijayanagar reigning in Chingleput District. *(201 of 1922.)*

Keḷadi Vīrabhadra Nāyaka ruling in N.-W. Mysore. *(E. C. viii, Tl. 62, 84.)*

Travancore threatened by Tirumala Nāyaka of Madura. *(Trav. State Manual, p. 302.)*

[Shāh Jahān brought to an end the Dekhāni kingdom of Ahmadnagar, which for several years had lain under the influence of the Mahratta Shāhjī, who held all the power in the state while setting up puppet kings of the former reigning family. The devastation of Bijāpur territory was continued. Three armies converged on the unhappy people who were ruled by the Ādil Shāhs. It is related that in one village alone 2,000 men were killed, and from another a population of 2,000 was bodily carried off into slavery, the women as well as the men being sold.]

A.D. 1636. Pedda Venkaṭa II of Vijayanagar reigning in Mysore from Penukoṇḍa *(E. C. xii, Ck. 19)*. And in Nellore and N. Arcot Districts *(V. R. ii, Nell. 452, 652 ; B. and V. C. 753, 1212 ; V. R. i, N. Arcot 325-A ; I. A. xiii, 125 ; Tam. and Sans. Inscriptions 186 ; 118 of 1921)*. The last noted record *(118 of 1921)* is noticeable in that it calls the king 'Ānaigondi Venkaṭapati,' or Venkaṭapati of Ānegundi, the fortress immediately to the North of Vijayanagar, and separated from the capital by the Tungabhadra river. It is the modern home of the descendants of the former royal family.

In Tinnevelly District the recognized overlord was Tirumala Nāyaka of Madura, who had by this time thrown over his allegiance to Vijayanagar. *(V. R. iii, Tinn. 1-A.)*

[Abdullah Kuṭb Shāh of Golkonda finally submitted to Shāh Jahān, who succeeded in reducing the other Dekhāni kingdoms and appointed prince Aurangzīb to be his 'governor of the Dekhan'.]

A.D. 1637. Pedda Venkaṭa II reigning in E. Mysore. *(E. C. x, Kl. 246.)*

Tirumala Nāyaka of Madura ruling at Trichinopoly.
(V. R. iii, Trich. 200 ; Lists of Antiquities p. 203.)

[Shāhjī Bhonsla, under the instructions of the Emperor Shāh Jahān, entered the service of Muhammad Ādil Shāh at Bījāpur, and was sent in high command to Mysore.

The Portuguese in Goa were besieged by the Dutch.]

A.D. 1638. Pedda Venkaṭa II of Vijayanagar reigning in Anantapur. *(807 of 1917.)*

The Keḷadi chief Vīrabhadra Nāyaka gave a gift in S. Kanara. *(V. R. ii, S. Kan. 273.)*

The Changāḷva chief Vīra Rājayya, son of Nanjuṇḍa, gave a grant in S. Mysore.
(E. C. iv, Yd. 19, 20.)

[The Dutch blockade of Goa continued.

Bijāpur troops attacked and captured Bangalore, defeating the Mysore Rāja Immaḍi Rāja.]

A.D. 1639. Pedda Venkaṭa II of Vijayanagar reigning in Anantapur.

(*V. R. i, Anant. 170 ; C.P. 17 of 1911.*)

Mysore was now ruled by Kanṭhīrava Narasa Raja I, nominally under Vijayanagar.

(*E. C. iii, Nj. 198.*)

[The Factors of the English Trading Company on the East Cost, finding that Armagaon was unsatisfactory as a settlement, sought for one a little further south and obtained permission from the local governor Naique, Dāmarla Venkaṭādri Nāyaka, to build a fort north of S. Thomé close to the sea. This was the foundation of the city of Madras. The English at Armagaon had found the people miserably poor, owing to the continual oppression by the ' Naique of the place, who himself was in great difficulties, being driven to commandeer supplies for himself and his sovereign owing to the aggression of the Muhammadans. Corrupt village headmen added to the oppression of the people and left them destitute. The Agent at Masulipatam wrote to the Hon. Company in London in October 1639 that trade was at a standstill because (to quote him in modern English) 'the Naik so pillages and despoils the merchants that they are not able to comply with their contracts.' Dāmarla Venkaṭādri encouraged the English to build a new fort for his own purposes, which are set forth in the same letter, one of them being 'that the fort, being made substantial and strong may be able to defend his person on occasions against his insulting neighbours.' Indeed he promised himself to construct the fort, but when he began to do so it was found that his intention was merely to construct a stockade ('*Vestiges of Old Madras*,' Love, *i, 1620*). The building of the fort was therefore proceeded with. It was named 'Fort St. George.']

A.D. 1640. Pedda Venkaṭa II of Vijayanagar reigning in Anantapur and in E. Mysore (*361 of 1920 ; E. C. x, Sd. 31*). He is also recognized as sovereign in name in S. Mysore, but Kanṭhīrava-Narasa of Mysore was evidently the actual ruler there. (*E. C. iv, Gu. 10, 50.*)

Keḷadi Vīrabhadra ruling the Āraga tract in N.-W. Mysore. (*E.C. viii, Tl, 3, 4, 165.*)

[A very serious famine in the Dekhan which lasted several years. (*I. A. 1923 p. 237.*)

The Nāyakas of Madura and Tanjore were now quasi-independent, and the Vijayanagar Prince Śrīranga was sent to compel them to submission ; but Tirumala Nāyaka of Madura obtained aid from Golkonda and repelled the royal troops. The Tanjore chief Raghunātha Nāyaka, after an attack on the Gingi Fort, submitted to the suzerain.]

A.D. 1641. Keḷadi Vīrabhadra Nāyaka ruling in part of N.-W. Mysore and S. Kanara (*E. C. viii, Tl. 43, 44, 45, 63, 88, 101, 182 ; vii, Sh. 2 ; V. R. ii, S. Kan. 55 ; Mys. A. A. R. 1923, p. 92*). And in the next year. (*E. C. viii, Tl. 41, 42, 49, 53.*)

Grant by Prince Śrīranga III of Vijayanagar, great-grandson of Aḷiya Rāma, gave a grant on E. Mysore October 24, 1641 (*E. C. x, Kl, 225*). He was adopted by Gōpāla of the same dynasty.

Abdulla Kuṭb Shāh of Golkonda ruling in Nellore district.

(*V.R. ii, Nell. 353 ; B. and V. C. 624.*)

The Changāḷva chief Vīra Raja was attacked in his own capital Piriyapaṭṭana, west of Mysore City, by Kanṭhīrava-Narasa I of Mysore. He defended himself to the end, but, when driven to extremity, he slew his own wives and children and was himself killed.

(*Rice E. C. iv, Introd. p. 18.*)

A.D. 1642. Pedda Venkaṭa II of Vijayanagar reigning in Conjevaram (*502 of 1919*). He died this year in October.

Tirumala Nāyaka of Madura, practically independent, ruling at Trichinopoly and in Coimbatore district. *(V. R. iii, Trich. 610 ; 290 of 1903 ; i, Coimb. 374.)*

[Śrīranga III succeeded Pedda Venkaṭa II as king of Vijayanagar. His power was greatly restricted, and confusion reigned in the country. The Muhammadan power in the north was overwhelming and aggressive, and the great Nāyaka of Madura threw over his allegiance to the crown. Troops from Golkonda drove the Hindu Nāyaka away from his government about Armagaon.

On September 20, 1642, the Factors of Fort St. George at Madras wrote to the Directors in London complaining of the difficulties they had to contend with owing to the rapacity of the Nāyaka of Tanjore who ruled over S. Thomé town. They say that he 'puts in almost monthly (to him that will give most) a new governor.'

(Love's '*Vestiges of Old Madras,*' *p. 45.*)]

Abdullah Kuṭb Shāh of Golkonda captured Udayagiri, the great hill-fortress in Nellore District, his general being Ghāzi Ali. *(V.R. ii, Nell. 790 ; B. and V.C. 1385.)*

Kanṭhīrava-Rāja of Mysore reigning in Trichinopoly. *(E.C. v, Cn. 163.)*

A.D. 1643. Śrīranga III of Vijayanagar reigning in Kurnool District from Penukoṇḍa *(691 of 1917)*. And at Chidambaram *(V R. i, S. Arcot, 63 ; 271 of 1913)*. And in S. Mysore on March 10. *(E.C. iv, Yd. 5.)*

Keḷadi Venkaṭappa Nāyaka gave away land in S. Kanara. *(V.R. ii, S. Kan. 57.)*

[Prince Aurangzīb was in this year deprived of all his power in the Dekhan by Shāh Jahān, the Emperor, his father. But on his submission and his expressed wish to retire from public life he was restored.]

Fights both on land and sea between Portuguese and Dutch continued.

The Madras merchants were greatly perturbed at the state of Southern India at this time. The Muhammadans had pressed down as far as Nellore. Śrīranga III was almost powerless. The great Southern Nāyakas, rivals of one another, had become independent, and the ruler of Mysore was king in all save the name. Faction-fighting raged everywhere. The Madras Factors wrote to the Directors in London in January—'This country being all in broils, the old king of Karnāṭa being dead ; so is the Naik of Armagaon, whose country is all in the hands of the Moors............ The war drawing so near has caused us to bring ashore four small pieces of ordnance.' Armagaon is about 45 miles N. of Madras. ('*Vestiges, etc.......*', Love, *i. 53.*)

A.D. 1644. Vijaya Rāghava Nāyaka of Tanjore ruling there. *(V.R. ii, Tan. 68 ; 614 of 1909.)*

[The Bijāpur Muhammadans greatly increasing in strength in Mysore and a Golkonda army besieging Gingi. The army of Bijāpur then attacked the army of Golkonda, and the fortress of Gingi was captured by the former, the Kuṭb Shāhi forces retiring.]

In July the Factors at Madras reported that the Dutch merchants in Pulicat, 22 miles N. of Madras, were besieged 'by the Moors.' ('*Vestiges, etc......*', Love, *i. 62.*)

A.D. 1645. Śrīranga III of Vijayanagar reigning in W. Mysore, E. Mysore and Anantapur *(E.C. v, Hn. 41 ; x, Mb. 60; V.R. i, Anant. 69 ; 80 of 1912)* ; and in N. Arcot *(The Kaḷḷakūrichi Grant, E.I. vii, 545, App)*. In the last of these, mention is made of Kōnēṭi Obala Rāja of Nandyāl.

[Śrīranga III confirmed the grant of Madras to the English Company and added some more land surrounding it.]

Keḷadi Vīrabhadra Nāyaka ruling in N.-W. Mysore. *(E.C. viii, Tl. 40.)*

[In gratitude to the English Surgeon Boughton for saving the life of a royal princess, the Emperor Shāh Jahān granted permission to the English Company of merchants to trade, free of customs-duty, throughout the Empire.]

A.D. 1646. The Golkonda Sultan, Abdullah Kuṭb Shāh reigning in Cuddapah District.

(*V.R. i, Cudd. 344.*)

[Śivājī Bhonsla, son of Shāhjī Bhonsla, now 20 years old seized a fort in the Dekhan, on pretence of holding it for Bijāpur.

The Golkonda army captured the royal residence of the Vijayanagar king, the Chandragiri fort and palace, and also seized the town of Chingleput. King Śrīranga III fled for safety to Bednūr.] [1]

In February 1646, the Madras merchants report that 'this country is at present full of wars and troubles, for the king (of Vijayanagar) and three of his Naiks are at variance, and the king of Bijapūr's army is come into the country on one side, and the king of Golkonda on the other—both against this (the Vijayanagar) king.' The Golkonda general Mir Jumla, however befriended the English at Fort St. George. ('*Vestiges, etc.......*', Love, *i, 76.*)

A.D. 1647. [A very severe famine in Southern India. It had begun in Madura in the previous year, and now spread (*I.A. 1923 p. 237*). It was the cause of much suffering at Madras and the Factors there begged for some tons of rice to save the lives of the poor of the place. In a letter written in October they report that in the (now very small) settlements of Madras, 4000 persons had died of starvation, and in Pulicat and S. Thomé together, 30,000.]

('*Vestiges, etc.......*', Love, *i, 75.*)

Śivājī broke out this year into open rebellion against his father Shāhji, and seized the latter's Jāghīr and several forts.

The Dutch established a centre of trade at Sadras, South of Madras]

Śrīranga III of Vijayanagar reigning in Nellore and Kurnool Districts—Nominally.

(*V.R. ii, Nell. 647 ; B. and V.C. i, 44 ; V.R. ii, Kurn. 544.*)

Kanṭhīrava Narasa I of Mysore ruling. (*E.C. v, Ag. 64 ; ix, Cp. 23.*)

[Mīr Jumla, acting for the Mughal Prince Aurangzīb formed a camp near Madras for the blockade of the Portuguese settlement at S. Thomè. The English merchants assisted Mīr Jumla; but they only had 33 soldiers, ('*Vestiges, etc. . .* ' Love, *pp. 79, 80*). The state of the country at this time was terrible. Besides the horrors of the famine there were the rival armies of the Mughals, Bijāpur, Golkonda, Vijayanagar, Madura and Tanjore, each opposed to the other, living on the country and impoverishing the cultivators.]

A.D. 1648. Tirumala Nāyaka of Madura made a grant of lands in Tinnevelly District.

(*V.R. iii, Tinn. 139-A.*)

Kanṭhīrava Narasa ruling in S.-W. Mysore, where the Bijāpur leaders had built a fort.

(*E.C. v, Cn. 165.*)

[The famine increased in severity and a great part of the population of Coimbatore died of starvation.

Śivājī, with a large Mahratta force supporting him, openly rebelled against the Ādil Shāhi Sultan of Bijāpur, and established himself as a leading chief, with Kalyān for his capital.

[1] See, for this period and the evidence of British Factory Record, *Journal of Indian History*, vol. ix part ii. 'The Rise of the Mahratta Power in the South.'—*Editor.*

The Madras Factors thus describe the state of affairs in September 1648.— 'The body of this Kingdom is harried by two foreign nations. . . . . with powerful armies, watching all advantages upon each other; yet both strive to make a prey of this miserable or divided people. These are the Golkonda and Bijāpur Moors, the latter of whom have brought in 8,000 freebooters, who receive no pay but plunder what they can, whose incursions, robberies and devastations have brought about a desolation on a great part of the country round about.' (*' Vestiges, etc. . . .'* Love, *i, 98*)]

A D. 1649. Śrīranga III of Vijayanagar reigning in East Mysore (nominally). (*E.C. ix, Ht, 71.*)

[Muhammad Ādil Shāh of Bijāpur tried to stop Śivājī's aggressions by seizing the person of Shāhjī, but the Emperor Shāh Jahān had Shāhjī released. Śivājī continued his career, unmoved.]

A.D. 1650. Kanṭhīrava Narasa Nāyaka of Mysore reigning at Seringapatam. (*E.C. v, Cn. 185.*)

Part of the Nellore Dislrict about Kandukūr was given as a *Mokhasa* to a Mahratta leader, Rāghōjī Pantulu. (*V.R. ii, Nell. 315 ; B. and V.C. 569.*)

A.D. 1651. [The Portuguese at S. Thomè and the English at Madras made an amicable arrrangement for their mutual advantage (*' Vestiges'*, Love, *i, 101*). An English factory was established at Hughli, near Calcutta.]

A.D. 1652. [Cromwell, now Dictator of England, declared war on the Dutch, and this led to fighting between the foreign settlers in India.]

In Tinnevelly Varaguṇa-Rāma-Pāṇḍya-Kulaśēkhara-Dikshitar was ruling.

(*V.R. iii, Tinn. 288.*)

A.D. 1653. Kanṭhīrava-Narasa of Mysore reigning. (*E.C. iii, Nj. 106.*)

In N.-W. Mysore, the Bijāpur Sultan was now supreme. His Dewān constructed a tank for irrigation purposes at Hosahaḷḷi. The inscription states that the people of the country were living in terror of hordes of robbers who frequented the jungles to the South. (*E.C. vii, Ci. 43.*)

The Mahratta Shāhjī had been granted, ten years earlier, a large territory in Mysore as his private estate. An inscription in East Mysore seems to shew that it was governed by his eldest son Sambājī, to whom is given the Royal title 'Rājādhirāja' (*E.C. x, Mb. 154*). Sambājī or Sambhōjī was elder brother of Śivājī.

Fort St. George, now a considerable town, was made the presidential head-quarters.

A.D. 1654. Sambājī Bhonsla was governing in East Mysore, a large part of which now formed the jāghīr of his father Shāhjī. (*E.C. x, Kl. 193.*)

[Mīr Jumla, in command of the Golkonda army close to Fort St. George, was attacked by the army of the Mughal Emperor. The Madras merchants wrote, almost in despair, in September 1654—' It has been no small misery that this poor ...... country has suffered, any time these ten years almost ... our Navāb [Mīr Jumla] is lately up in arms against the king of Golkonda, his master. ...... What the issue of these things will be, the Almighty only knows.'

(*' Vestiges, etc.,'* Love, *i. 115.*)

Peace was proclaimed between England and Holland.

Muhammad Ādil Shāh of Bijāpur marched to attack Goa but was repulsed. Peace was made in December.

The garrison of Fort St. George consisted of only 26 English soldiers.

(*' Vestiges,' p. 121.*)]

A.D. 1655. Śrīranga III, of Vijayanagar recognized as severeign in Salem District.

(*312 of 1919.*)

Kanṭhīrava Narasa I of Mysore reigning in South Mysore and Coimbatore District.
(E.C. iv, Hg. 49 ; V.R. i, Coimb. 150 ; 170 of 1910.)

Several records in Coimbatore from 1655 onwards prove that the Rāja of Mysore had considerably reduced the power of Tirumala Nāyaka of Madura. *(V.R. i, Coim. 299, 303, 305, 375–77.)*

[Prince Aurangzīb assisted Mīr Jumla in his rebellion against the Sultan of Golkonda.]

A.D. 1656. An inscription of Vijaya-Rāghava Nāyaka of Tanjore. *(E.R. 1922, App. A. No. 10.)*

[Fighting between Hindus and Muhammadans of Golkonda close to Madras, where houses were burnt in the suburbs. Abdulla Kuṭb Shāh of Golkonda, overcome by the strength of the Mughal Emperor and the rebel Mīr Jumla combined, submitted to become tributary to Delhi.

[Muhammad Ādil Shāh of Bijāpur died and the succession was disputed, Ali Ādil eventually obtaining the throne. But Mughal troops occupied Bijāpur territory.]

A.D. 1657. Inscription noting a grant in Tinnevelly District, of land by Ranga Krishna Muttu Vīrappa Nāyaka III of Madura, son of Chokkanātha. *(V. R. iii, Tinn. 304–L.)*

Gift at Rāmēsvaram by the Sētupati chief Tirumalai Raghunātha.
(V.R. ii, Ramnad, 105 ; C.—P. 10 of 1911.)

[Fort St. George was besieged by the Muhammadans for seven months. There were only a dozen Englishmen in the fort who could bear arms, and the Factors organized a small body of militia to assist in the defence.] *('Vestiges', Love, i. 167, 170.)*

[Prince Aurangzīb captured Kalyān from the Sultan of Bijāpur, after which peace was made. The Mughal princes revolted against their father the Emperor Shāh Jahān, who was seriously ill.]

A.D. 1658. Inscription at Tiruchchengōḍu of Tirumala Nāyaka of Madura.
(V.R. ii, Salem, 196 ; 650 of 1905.)

Śrīranga III of Vijayanagar recognized as supreme in Chingleput District.
(V.R. i, Ching. 1201.)

Record at Rāmēśvaram of a gift to the temple by the Sētupati chief Raghunātha Tirumalai.
(V.R. ii, Ramnad, 112 ; E.R. 1911. App. A. No. 10.)

[Aurangzīb triumphed over his brothers, entered Delhi and on June 11, made his father the Emperor Shāh Jahān a prisoner. The eldest brother Dārā Shekoh fled to Lahore. Aurangzīb imprisoned his brother Murād, and seized the throne. Shāh Jahān survived some years and lived in retirement. Aurangzīb thus became Emperor. He was proclaimed on July 30.]

A.D. 1659. Śrīranga III of Vijayanagar reigning in West Mysore *(E.C. v, Bl. 80, 196)*. And in Coimbatore (20 of 1910).

[Another severe famine in the Madura country. The Jesuit priests reported the death of 10,000 Christians in one tract alone.] *(I.A. 1923, p. 237.)*

Tirumala Nāyaka of Madura died on February 16, 1659, according to local chronicles. His successor Muttu Vīrappa ruled for 4 months. Chokkanātha Nāyaka then became ruler of Madura.

The Bijāpur Muhammadans attacked and took Tanjore and Vallam, with great slaughter. Famine and pestilence spread over the country.

Aurangzīb captured his elder brother Dārā Shēkoh and put him to death in prison. Another of his elder brothers, Shuja, opposed Aurangzīb, fought him, was defeated, and fled.

Śivājī, opposed by a Bijāpur army commanded by Afzūl Khān, pretended to temporize with his opponent and treacherously stabbed him to death. Then he defeated his foes and seized more forts.

The Muhammadan settlers in Cuddapah District were on good terms with the Hindus there and sometimes made presents of gold to the temples, and helped with irrigation works.

(*V. R. i, Cudd. 183, 247.*)

Under Aurangzīb the crown took half the peasants' crops, Akbar having only taken one-third. Aurangzīb insisted on all his officials seeing that every cultivator worked hard. They were to be watched and encouraged if industrious, but an idle peasant was to be made to work by the use of force and the whip. (*Zarab.*)

(*J. R. A. S. January, 1922. pp. 19 f. Mr W. H. Moreland.*)

In N.-W. Mysore a grant by Keḷadi Śivappa Nāyaka. (*E. C. viii, Tl. 81.*)

A.D. 1660. In Bellary District an inscription mentioning Venkatapati of Vijayanagar as ruling —perhaps Śrīranga III's brother, or son. (*273 of 1918.*)

Śrīranga III reigning in W. Mysore. (*E. C. v, Bl. 81, 82.*)

While Abdulla Kuṭb Shāh of Golkonda was ruling in Nellore District, a temple was destroyed and a mosque erected in its place. (*V. R. ii, Nell. 787; B. and V. C. 1381.*)

[The Sultan of Bijāpur tried to make a strong combination of Dekhāni states to overthrow the troublesome Mahrattas.

The Dutch seized Negapatam.]

A.D. 1661. Śrīranga III of Vijayanagar reigning in E. Mysore. (*E. C. ix, Ht. 79.*)

In Ramnad grants were made in honour of Chokkanātha Nāyaka of Madura, now chief.

(*V. R. ii, Ramnad, 150, 151.*)

[Aurangzīb killed many of the survivors of the Mughal royal family.

Ali Ādil Shāh of Bijāpur recovered some forts which had been taken by Śivājī for the Mahrattas.

Bombay Island was ceded to England on the marriage of Charles II of England with Catherine of Braganza, but occupation of it was withheld for four years.

The Dutch took Quilon on the West Coast.

The merchants at Fort St. George were now in great straits. They wrote to the Directors ' we have 5 or 6 armies within the compass of 100 miles about us', and that they had to see carefully to their defence. ('*Vestiges, etc.*,' Love, *i, 197.*)]

A.D. 1662. Śrīranga III of Vijayanagar reigning in W. Mysore. (*E. C. v, Ag. 83.*)

Inscriptions of Doḍḍadēva Rāja of the Mysore royal family ruling in Mysore. These would seem to shew that after Kanṭhīrava Narasa's death in 1659, Doddadēva and not his brother Kempadēva had succeeded; but I have not dared in my Pedigree Table to alter Mr. S. Krishnaswami Aiyangar's fixtures.

(*E. C. v, Cn. 156 ; iii, Md. 114 ; Tn. 23 ; iv, Kr.67 ; ix, Kn. 94 ; xii, Kg. 33, 87, 38.*)

Keḷadi Bhadrappa Nāyaka, son of Śivappa, ruling in N.-W. Mysore.

(*E. C. viii, Tl. 76, 85, 145.*)

Sambājī, son of the Mahratta Shāhjī Bhonsla ruling in E. Mysore, near Kolar,—probably for his father who was still alive, and whose personal estate (*jāghīr*) included Bangalore.

(*E. C. x, Kl. 219.*)

Chokkanātha Nāyaka of Madura, son of Muttu Vīrappa, made a grant of land to the Śrīrangam temple, in the reign of Śrīranga III of Vijayanagar.

(*V. R. iii, Trichinopoly, 442.*)

[The Golkonda Muhammadans attacked and seized the Dutch settlement at S. Thomé, close to Madras. The Madras merchants thereupon wrote to the Directors in London begging to be supplied with good muskets for purposes of defence. They stated that when they set out to examine their stock of arms the muskets were found so rusty with disuse that they burst on being fired.] (*'Vestiges, etc.,'* Love, *p. 211.*)

The Dutch drove the Portuguese out of Cranganore and Cochin, leaving the Portuguese possessions reduced to Goa and Diū.

A.D. 1663. Śrīranga III of Vijayanagar reigning (but with little power) in South and West Mysore (*E.C. iii, Sr. 13 ; vi, Cm. 153 ; v. Hn. 39, 40*). The first of these is a C.-P. document at Seringapatam. It mentions as ruler ' Dēva Rāja Uḍaiyār ', i.e., Doḍḍa Dēva Rāja of Mysore. In the last Śrīranga is called ' son of Gōpāla ' whereas in reality he was Gōpāla's adopted son.

(*See also E.C. i, Tn. 23 ; Mys. A.A.R. 1917, p. 59.*)

Chokkalinga Nāyaka of Madura was ruling in Salem District.

(*V.R. ii, Salem ; 200 ; 654 of 1905.*)

[On January 8, 1663, the Rāja of Cochin handed over the fort there to the Dutch and ceded certain islands to them in return for a promise of their protection of the royal family of Cochin. The Rāja and the Dutch settlers formed an alliance against their joint enemies.

South India was terribly disturbed from now onwards. The Nāyakas of Madura and Tanjore were constantly at war with one another, and the armies of Bijāpur made descents on the country with intent to conquer all the Hindu rulers. About 1663 the forces of Bijāpur ruined the country about Trichinopoly until they were bought off by Chokkanātha of Madura. They destroyed the suburbs, seized the crops, and burned the villages. A little later, Chokkanātha attacked Mysore, but unsuccessfully.]

This cession by the Rāja of Cochin is embodied, as well as the other terms of the treaty, in the Pāḷaiyam plates (*V.R. iii, Cochin 1 ; T.A.S. i, No. iv, p. 27*) whose date is March 22, 1663.

A.D. 1664. Abdullah Kuṭb Shāh of Golkonda reigning supreme in Chingleput District near Conjevaram ; and in Guntur District (*80 of 1923 ; E.R. 1923, p. 125 ; 128 of 1917*). The date of the last = June 15, 1664.

Śrīranga III of Vijayanagar reigning in West Mysore. (*E.C. v, Mj. 21 ; xii, Kg. 46.*)

Keḷadi Sōmaśēkhara Nāyaka ruling locally in N.-W. Mysore.

(*E. C. viii, Tl. 53, 80, 86, 92, 96.*)

Doḍḍa Dēva Rāja of Mysore ruling in Central Mysore, but subordinate to Śrīranga III of Vijayanagar. (*E.C. xii, Kg. 46.*)

[Śivājī, the Mahratta chief, extended his conquests and attacked and plundered the town of Surat. The fort, however held out. Śivājī stripped the townsfolk and resident merchants of all their wealth, personally ordering the heads of those who attempted to conceal it, to be struck off. The place was the richest sea-port in India.

In reply the Muhammadan forces of Bijāpur retaliated and laid waste large tracts of country ruled by the Mahrattas. (*Firishta, Scott's Edition ii, 10, 11 ; For the Surat Factors' report of the event, written at the time, see I.A. li, 1–6.*)

[Śivājī's father Shāhjī Bhonsla died this year, and Śivājī assumed the title of ' Rāja '. He defeated a Bijāpur army and plundered Ahmadnagar.

The Portuguese refused to deliver up Bombay to the English or to fulfil the terms of the treaty. This gave rise to serious disputes.

Chokkanātha of Madura attacked Vijayarāghava Nāyaka of Tanjore, but was beaten off, and lost Vallam. Then Chokkanātha fought a campaign against the Sētupati chief Tirumalai, and captured Pudukōṭṭa and other places, but was eventually forced to retire.]

(*R.S.A. Nayaks, pp. 158 f.*)

A.D. 1665. Śrīranga III of Vijayanagar reigning in Mysore and Coimbatore (*E.C. x, Gd. 3 ; V.R. i, Coimb. 396, 434*). The two Coimbatore C.-P. grants referred to, shew that Chokkanātha Nāyaka of Madura was ruling there.

In N.-W. Mysore and S. Kanara the Keḷadi chief Sōmaśēkhara Nāyaka was ruling.

(*E.C. viii, Tl. 7, 55, 48–50 ; V.R. ii, S. Kan. 272.*)

[Bombay island, but not its dependencies, was handed over by the Portuguese to the English.

Śivājī nominally submitted to the Mughal Emperor Aurangzīb, and assisted him in his fight against Bijāpur.

Abdullah Kuṭb Shāh of Golkonda aided Bījāpur against Aurangzīb, and incurred the Emperor's displeasure.]

A.D. 1666. Grant of a village as an *agrahāra* by Chikka Dēva-Rāya of Mysore.

(*E.C. iv, Yd. 54.*)

Keḷadi Sōmaśēkhara Nāyaka gave a grant of land on May 8 in Shimoga Taluk, Mysore (*Mys. A.A.R. 1923, p. 99*). On the bank of the Tungabhadra river in N.-W. Mysore the Keḷadi chief Bhadrappa was ruling. (*E.C. viii, Tl 156.*)

In E. Mysore, probably in Shāhjī Bhonsla's *jāghīr*, Jayitā Bhāi, wife of Śivājī's son Sambājı, gave a grant. (*E.C. x, Kl. 227.*)

[Second plunder of Surat town by Śivājī's Mahrattas.] (*Firishta, Scott's Edition. ii. 18.*)

A combined army of Mughals and Mahrattas invested Bijāpur and took several outlying places.

Śivājī and his son Sambājī went to the Court of the Emperor Aurangzib, but were coldly received, and were practically kept in restraint—the Emperor, knowing Śivājı's character and reputation, being naturally anxious for his own safety. Śivājī escaped and went to Rājgarh.

A.D. 1667. Śrīranga III of Vijayanagar reigning in E. Mysore from his palace at Chandragiri. (The date, however, of the inscription in question is not sound.) (*E. C. ix, Ma. 2.*)

In N.-W. Mysore the Keḷadi chief Sōmaśēkhara Nāyaka I was ruling.

(*E. C. viii. Tl. 78 ; Mys. A. A. R. 1923, p. 93.*)

Doḍḍa Dēva Rāja of Mysore ruling in S. Mysore. (*E. C. iv, Yd. 43.*)

In Tinnevelly Chokkanātha Nāyaka of Madura was ruling. (*652 of 1917.*)

In Ramnad a gift made 'for the merit of' Tirumalai-Raghunātha-Hirāṇyagarbhayājī, son of Daḷavāi Sētupati Kātta. (*V. R. ii, Ram. 113 ; T. and S. i, No. 7.*)

[Aurangzīb confirmed Śivājī's title of 'Rāja'.

The Emperor's son Muazzam was made governor of the Dekhan.]

A.D. 1668. Grants by Keḷadi Sōmaśēkhara Nāyaka I in N.-W. Mysore.

(*E. C. viii, Tl. 98, 99 ; vii, Sh. 81.*)

Chokkanātha Nāyaka of Madura ruling at Tiruchchengōḍ. (*649 of 1905.*)

[Śivājī obtained the support of the Kuṭb Shāh of Golkonda and seized several forts belonging to Bijāpur.

The French established a factory at Trincomalee, but were turned out by the Dutch.]

A.D. 1669. Doḍḍa Dēva Rāja of Mysore ruling in South, S.-W. and Central Mysore (*E. C. iv, Hs. 139 ; v, Cn. 155 ; xii, Tp. 72*). The first of these mentions his son Kanṭhīrava Narasa II. He ruled in Coimbatore District also. (*V. R. i. Coimb. 306, 308, 309 ; 181 of 1910.*)

In N. W. Mysore Keḷadi Sōmaśēkhara Nāyaka continued to rule. (*E. C. viii, Tl. 50, 74, 75.*)

[The Emperor Aurangzīb came to terms with Ali Ādil Shah of Bijāpur. Śivājī compelled both Bijāpur and Golkonda to pay tribute to him.]

The Dutch succeeded in capturing S. Thomé, close to Madras, from the Portuguese.

Fort St. George was attacked by a local Naik, but the siege was raised, the Muhammadans intervening on behalf of the English.

A.D. 1670. Śrīranga III of Vijayanagar reigning in Central Mysore. (*E. C. xii, Pg. 46.*)

In S. Mysore grant of a village by Kanṭhīrava Narasa II, son of Doḍḍa Dēva Rāja. (*E. C. iv, Hg. 119, 120.*)

[The Mahrattas continued their devastation and plunder of the Dekhan country. At Rāmghir the soldiers carried off some of the wives of the inhabitants.]

(*Firishta, Scott ii, p. 32. Contemporary records.*)

The Emperor Aurangzīb declared his intention of stamping out the religion of the Hindus in his dominions and many fine old Hindu temples were destroyed.

Śrīranga III of Vijayanagar is not much heard of after 1670. He was a fugitive and is believed to have died some time between 1670 and 1677.

Śivājī again plundered Surat town and again failed to take the fort.

The English Factors at Madras agreed to pay to the Sultan of Golkonda 1,200 pagodas rent for the area on which the increasing town now stood. This after the Golkonda troops had blockaded the town.

[Severe faminine in this year in South India.]

A.D. 1671. Doḍḍa Dēva Rāja II of Mysore reigning in Central and S. E. Mysore. (*E. C. xii, Kg. 4, 5 ; ix, Kn. 95.*)

In N.-W. Mysore, grants in April, and on May 1, and August 10, by Keḷadi Sōmaśēkhara Nāyaka. [Some time between August 10, 1671 and August 1672, he was assassinated and the Keḷadi country was governed for a time by his widow Chennamājī.]

(*E. C. viii, Tl. 71 ; Sa. 39 ; vii, Sh. 3*)

[Śivājī seized more forts in the Dekhan.]

A. D. 1672. Doḍḍa Dēva Rāja of Mysore reigning (*E. C. v, Cn. 273*). On December 12, 1672, his son Kanṭhīrava Narasa II gave a grant in South Mysore (*E. C. iv, Hg. 57*). Dodda Dēva is believed to have died in 1672–3.

Keḷadi Chennamājī, widow of Sōmaśēkhara Nāyaka ruling in North-West Mysore (*E. C. vii, Sk. 213 ; viii, Sa. 16–18 ; Tl, 100, 69, 118*). The date of the last of these is about August 19, 1672.

(*See remarks above, s. v. A. D. 1671.*)

[The French now declared war against the English and began operations by seizing S. Thomè, close to Madras, then garrisoned by Golkonda troops. At the same time the Dutch blockaded the coast.]

A. D. 1673. Chikka Dēva Rāya of Mysore reigning in South Mysore (*E. C. iii. Tn, 54*). And in Salem district. (*Lists of Antiquities, i, 194.*)

Keḷadi Chennamājī, widow of the late Nāyaka, ruling in North-West Mysore. (*E. C. viii, Tl. 67, 68.*)

In Ramnad a gift made by Tirumalai-Sētupati-Kātta. (*V. R. ii, Ram. 280.*)

Saādat-ullā-Khān was governing the Kurnool district for the Sultan of Golkonda. He was a Nawāb and a Saiyid. (*V. R. ii, Kurn. 194.*)

War between Madura and Tanjore, Chokkanātha of Madura captured Vallam and Tanjore, and Vijayarāghava of Tanjore was killed. Muttu Aḷagiri Nāyaka was made ruler of Tanjore. (*R. S. A. Nayaks, 163.*)

Khān Jahān's army in the Dekhan was defected by an army from Bijāpur.

[Śivājī increased his power by conquering the Konkans and Sātāra. His government was very oppressive. Dr. Fryer wrote in 1673. "It is a general calamity . . . . to hear the complaints of the poor people that remain (in North Kanara), or rather are compelled to endure the slavery of Śivājī". The headmen were forced to take up land at double the old rates and if they refused, were imprisoned and tortured. "They have now in prison Brahmans whose flesh they tear with pincers heated red-hot," and inflict floggings on them, etc. . . . . . .

The Dutch besieged the French in S. Thomé.]

A. D. 1674. Keḷadi Chennamājī ruling in North-West Mysore and in South Kanara. (*E. C. viii, Tl. 73, 184 ; Sa, 53 ; Mys. A. A. R, 1923, p. 89 ; V. R. ii, S. Kan., 6, 70.*)

Chikka Dēva Rāya of Mysore reigning in Central Mysore. (*E. C. xii, Kg, 7.*)

Chokkanātha Nāyaka of Madura ruling in Trichinopoly (*V. R. iii, Trich. 492—K—Q*). He is now sometimes called "Karnāṭaka Chakravarti" ('Emperor of the Carnatic') as if he had taken the place of the Vijayanagar king. (*Mys. A. A. R. 1912, p. 57.*)

Some inscriptions in East Mysore shew that at least a portion of the community was loyal to the now defunct Vijayanagar kingdom. They name King Śrīranga III as still reigning from his capital Chandragiri though he was actually a fugitive. (*E. C. ix, Ma. 5, 29, 30.*)

[Chikka Dēva Rāya of Mysore has the reputation of having been very tyrannous in the matter of taxation of the farmers. Besides maintaining all the old taxes, he is said to have invented twenty new ones. Three of these are worthy of notice. (i) He added a permanent 2 per cent tax on to the land assessment to reimburse the treasury for loss owing to defective coins. (ii) It was the practice in Mysore for a proprietor of a village held on payment of a fixed annual sum to the State, if his actual receipts fell short of the amount of his dues, to levy a contribution on all his farmers to recoup his own loss. Chikka Dēva improved on this by fixing as a permanent extra land-tax, in addition to the assessment, the largest sum ever so levied. (iii) Farmers who sold their grain locally had always been free from payment of tolls on roads which they did not use. To compensate for this Chikka Dēva imposed a tax on every plough in the country.

Śivājī was crowned as 'Mahārāja' this year on June 6. He again attacked Bijāpur.

His half brother Ekōji or Venkājī seized Tanjore from its Nāyaka ruler and established a new Tanjore-Maharatta dynasty which ruled the country for a century and a half.

The Dutch captured S. Thomé and ceded it to Golkonda.

The French purchased Pondicherry from the Muhammadan Governor of Gingi.]

A.D. 1675. An inscription of this year shews Chikka Dēva Rāya of Mysore reigning. He is credited in it with a victory over Chokkanātha of Madura, another over the Keḷadi chief, and three victories over Muhammadans. (*E.C. iv, Ch. 92.*)

[Famine in the Madura country this year. (*I.A. 1923, p. 239.*)]

A.D. 1676. Chikkadēva Rāya of Mysore reigning in S. Mysore and in Coimbatore District. (*E.C. iv, Ch. 138 ; V.R. i, Coimbatore 74, 300 ; 209 of 1909.*)

Ēkōjī or Venkājī, now ruling at Tanjore, confirmed the gift of Negapatam to the Dutch merchants made by Vijaya Rāghava Nāyaka of Tanjore. The grant was engraved on a silver plate. (*V.R. ii, Tanjore, 893–H.*)

[Śivājī, allied with Abul Hasan of the Golkonda Kuṭb Shāhi family, marched to the conquest of the Carnatic, in defiance of the Mughal Emperor.

Muhammad Sultan, eldest son of the Emperor Aurangzīb died of poison this year. He is said to have been put to death by his father's orders.

The French at Pondicherry raised a small military force of 300 men.

The English Agent at Fort St. George complained to the Directors that the Hindu rulers and their ministers were 'pillaging and squeezing the people'. 'The government of the country', they wrote, 'is now in bad hands, nothing but fraud and oppression'.

(' *Vestiges* ' etc., Love, *i, 356.*)]

A.D. 1677. Chikkadēva Rāya of Mysore reigning in S.-W. Mysore. (*E.C. v, Ag. 2.*)

Keḷadi Chennamājī ruling in N.-W. Mysore. (*E.C. viii, Tl. 77.*)

[The Famine in Madura continued.

Śivājī seized the fortress of Gingi in S. Arcot. He also besieged Vellore in N. Arcot district and took the fort. He captured the country about Bellary, Cuddapah and Kurnool, and obtained possession of his father Shāhjī's *jāghīr* in Mysore, levying *chauth* on the beaten tracts.]

A.D. 1678. Chikkadēva Rāya of Mysore reigning in South Mysore. (*E.C. iv, Kr. 45.*)

Keḷadi Chennamājī ruling in N.-W. Mysore. (*E.C. viii, Tl. 179.*)

In Madura, Muttu Vīrappa's son Aḷagiri or Aḷagādri is mentioned in an inscription (*Lists of Antiquities I. List of copper-plate records, No. 10*). Aḷagiri was brother to Chokkanātha. The record acknowledges the suzerainty of Vijayanagar in the person of Śrīranga III ; who however was now a fugitive at Ikkēri, having been defeated by Chikkadēva of Mysore as noted in a record of 1679 (*q. v., below*). (*V.R. Madura, 157.*)

[Śivājī and his brother Ēkōjī, alias Venkājī, were now in possession of Tanjore, where Ēkōjī was left as ruler. Śivājī swept over Mysore, to the ruin of the inhabitants.]

A.D. 1679. Chikkadēva Rāja of Mysore reigning, on April 7, in Salem district (*316 of 1917*). And at Seringapatam (*E.C. iii, Sr. 151*). He is said, in the latter inscription, to have defeated Chokkanātha of Madura, and the Keḷadi chief, who came against him in alliance with the Muhammadans, from Bijāpur and to have captured Tumkūr and other places. (*R.S.A. Nayaks, p. 172.*)

'Muddaḷagādri Nāyaka' (i.e., Aḷagiri) gave a grant of land revenue.

(*Mysore, A.A.R. 1917, p. 57.*)

Rāṇī Chennamājī of Keḷadi was ruling in N.-W. Mysore. (*E.C. viii, Tl. 64.*)

[The war between the Mughal Emperor Aurangzīb and the Mahrattas continued.]

A.D. 1680. At Rāmēśvaram, a grant by Raghunātha Sētupati Kātta early in the year.

(*T. and S. i, Sētupati Grant, No. 8.*)

[Aurangzīb continued his destruction of Hindu temples, especially in Rajputana. Over 250 temples were razed to the ground and the sacred images broken up.

Śivājī died this year, and was succeeded by his elder son Sambājī, who immediately imprisoned his brother Rājā Rām]. Before his death Śivājī had completely laid waste the country about the Jālnā.

An inscription in E. Mysore shews Sambājī as in possession of the hill fort of Nandi.

(*E. C. x, C B, 32.*)

A.D. 1681. Śrīranga Rāya (perhaps the grandson of Śrīranga Rāya III of Vijayanagar) ruling in E. Mysore. (*E. C. ix, Ma. 8.*)

Keḷadi Chennamājī ruling in N.-W. Mysore.

(*E. C. viii, Tl. 89; Mys. A. A. R., 1923, p. 96, E. C. vii, Sk. 82.*)

[Prince Akbar, son of the Emperor Aurangzīb, revolted against his father and took refuge with Sambājī, now Mahārāja of the Mahrattas in succession to Śivājī; but had to flee to Persia, where he died in A. D. 1706.

Aurangzīb sent a large army to the Dekhan to reduce the Mahrattas.

The village and fort of Madras had by now become a place of refuge for the afflicted people of the country, and had grown in 40 years into a city. Being threatened, in 1681, with an attack, and the garrison being absurdly small, the Indian residents of Madras volunteered to raise a militia force of 215 men and to maintain it at their own expense. This was followed by the similar raising of another corps of 150 men. These offers were gratefully accepted by the English merchants. (‘*Vestiges*’, Love, *i, 439.*).]

A.D. 1682. Chikkadēva Rāya of Mysore reigning in Central Mysore. (*E. C. xii, Gb.* 52.)

Sētupati Raghunātha Tēvan ruling in Ramnad. (*416 of 1914.*)

[Madura at this time was ruled by Ranga-Krishna Muttu-Vīrappa Nāyaka, but he had lost much territory to the Mysore King and to the Tanjore Mahrattas. Some tracts had been seized by predatory *Maṛavar* chiefs. ‘The country was a prey to complete anarchy and universal pillage, foreign enemies occupying the forts and robber chiefs being masters of the rural areas, and carrying on their brigandage with impunity.’ (*Madura District Manual, 1896, p. 53.*)]

A.D. 1683. Keḷadi Chennamājī ruling in S. Kanara. (*V. R. ii, S. Kan. 274.*)

[The army of the Mughal prince Muazzam, operating in the Konkan, was forced back to Ahmadnagar by Sambājī and his Mahrattas. The Portuguese, who joined the Mughals in their attack on the Mahrattas, were also driven back.

The misgovernment and tyranny of the Mahratta Ēkōjī or Venkājī at Tanjore is dwelt on in letters from the missionary Jesuits resident there. He is said to have taken four-fifths of all the agricultural produce of the country, demanding payment in money and not in kind. One of the Jesuit fathers wrote that ‘as he (Ēkōjī) takes care to fix the price himself much beyond that which the proprietors could realize, the result is that the sale of the *entire* produce does not suffice to pay the entire contribution.’ In such cases the proprietors were sometimes subjected to ‘barbarous tortures’ The writer adds that the tyranny was ‘frightful and revolting’, but that things were even worse in the Kingdom of Gingi . . . . ‘I cannot find words to express all that is horrible in it.’

Letter of Jean de Britto, 1683, R. S. A., ‘Nāyaks . . .’ 291.)

A.D. 1684. Grant in Ramnad by Sētupaṭi Kātta Raghunātha Tēvan.

(*T. and S. I., Setupati, Grant, No. 9.*)

[Mughal armies attacked Bijāpur and Golkonda. Bijāpur was closely invested by Aurangzīb in person.]

A. D. 1685. Chikkadēva Rāya of Mysore reigning with capital at Seringapatam. (*E. C. iii, Ml. 61.*)

Ēkōjī, or Venkāji, reigning at Tanjore on April 5, 1685. (*540 of 1918.*)

[Aurangzīb halted at Shōlapūr. Sambājī, alarmed at the Emperor's actions, entered into an alliance with Golkonda. The city of Hyderabad was looted. Golkonda was invested. Bijāpur was closely besieged. In October ministers Madana and Akkana were murdered by the mob. Golkonda capitulated and the Sultan Abūl Hasan submitted to the Emperor.]

A.D. 1686. Keḷadi Channamāji ruling in N.-W. Mysore. (*E.C. viii, Sb. 548.*)

Ranga-Krishna Muttu-Virappa of Madura ruling in Trichinopoly District (*V.R. iii, Trich. 249*). Chokkanātha's widow Mangammāḷ repaired a channel near Trichinopoly. (*V.R. iii, Trich. 800 ; 71 of 1890.*)

Chikkadēva Rāya of Mysore reigning. A C.-P. grant at the Ranganātha temple at Seringapatam gives a long and wordy pedigree of the family. (*E.C. iii, Sr. 14.*)

[Aurangzīb attacked Bijāpur and captured the city. He seized the person of the young Sultan Sikandar Ādil Shāh and imprisoned him. Sikandar never recovered his freedom and died about A.D. 1700. The kingdom of Bijāpur thus came to an end, and was annexed to Delhi.]

A.D. 1687. Keḷadi Channamājī ruling in N.-W. Mysore. (*E.C. viii, Tl. 180.*)

[Aurangzīb went to Golkonda and finally seized the kingdom, which became a province of the Mughal Emperor.

His son, Prince Muazzam, was arrested on an accusation of treachery and was imprisoned for seven years.]

A.D. 1688. Keḷadi Channamājī ruling in N.-W. Mysore. (*E.C. viii, Tl. 61.*)

Some records of the Maṭla chief Muttu Venkaṭa Rāma 'Chōḍa-Mahārāja,' son of Kumāra Ananta. (*V.R. i, Cuddapah 656, 657, 663, 681, 863–A ; E.R. 1907-8, C.–P. 3, 4.*)

[After the annexation to Delhi of the kingdoms of Bijāpur and Golkonda, those countries were for a time a prey to anarchy. Rebellions were hatched and the country-folk were oppressed and persecuted by bands of lawless soldiery.

Aurangzīb renewed the charter to the merchants of Madras.

The Emperor proceeded against the Mahrattas. He seized Sambāji's Mysore *jaghīr*, and his army marched to Poonamallee and Wandewash.

Ēkōjī being now dead, Tanjore was ruled by his eldest son Shāhjī who submitted to Aurangzīb and became a tributary of the Mughal Empire.

Ghāzi-ud-dīn was created governor of the Dekhan by Aurangzīb.]

A.D. 1689. [Madras had by now become a place of refuge, and from having been 50 years earlier a fishing village, was now a city of 400,000 inhabitants.

Aurangzīb captured Sambājī, the Mahratta leader, tortured him and put him to death, making Sambājī's brother Rājā Rām Mahārāja of the Mahrattas. He sent Sambāji's young son Shāhjī to the Mughal camp at Bijāpur.

The English merchants at Masulipatam and Vizagapatam were murdered by Mughals. At Madras a French fleet was driven away northwards by English and Dutch ships. At Cuddalore the construction of Fort St. David was begun.]

A.D. 1690. Venkaṭa, son of Śrīranga III of Vijayanagar, recognized as suzerain (but only in name) in the Bellary District. (*V.R. i, Bell. 363.*)

Keḷadi Channamājī ruling in N.-W. Mysore. (*E.C. viii, Tl. 90.*)

[Several sea-fights took place between the French and English in India, the two nations in Europe being at open war.

Ghāzi-ud-dīn Khān, governor of the Dekhan, entered the territories adjoining Hyderabad and laid waste large tracts of land. (*Firishta, Scott's Edit., ii, 73.*)

A.D. 1691. Keḷadi Channamājī ruling in N.-W. Mysore. (*E.C. vii, Sk. 79.*)

Mangammāḷ, Queen-Dowager of Madura ruling in Trichinopoly. (*V.R. iii, Trich. 783.*)

A.D. 1692. In Tinnevelly a grant for maintenance of a mosque was made by Vijaya-Ranga Chokkanātha, son of the deceased Rāja Muttu-Vīrappa of Madura. The overlordship of Vijayanagar, in the person of Śrīranga, grandson of Śrīranga III, is recognized. The real ruler of Madura was Mangammāḷ, young Chokkanātha's grandmother.

(*V.R. iii, Tinn. 463., E.R. 1888, App. ii, No. 12 ; 1906, App. A. No. 25.*)

[The Mahrattas ravaged the country in many localities.]

The fortress of Gingi was besieged by prince Kām Baksh, son of the Emperor Aurangzīb, and Zulfiqar Khān, governor of the Dekhan. The Mahratta garrison made a stout resistance and drove off the enemy. But Zulfiqar Khān sat down before Gingi for three years, making a pretence of fighting, but really in communication with the Mahratta defenders.

The Emperor created Zulfiqar Khān ' Navāb of the Carnatic ' (Karnāṭaka).

A.D. 1693. Gift of land near Madura by the Rāṇi Mangammāḷ. She was ruling also in Trichinopoly. (*V. R. ii, Madura 379 ; iii, Trich. 455 ; 733 of 1905 ; C. P. No. 25 of 1905.*)

[Madura now paid tribute to Delhi.

The Dekhani Mughals were defeated by the Mahrattas.

The French abandoned Pondicherry to the Dutch.]

A.D. 1694. Keḷadi Channamājī settled a matter of tolls in N.-W. Mysore. (*E. C. viii, Tl. 46.*)

A.D. 1695. An inscription in Tinnevelly District, of date July 11, of Prince Vijayaranga Chokkanātha of Madura, who was apparently ruling a tract under his grandmother Mangammāḷ.

(*E. R. 1918–19, App. A, C.-P. 1, 2 ; V. R. iii, Tinn. 129.*)

Chikkadēva Rājā of Mysore ruling at Avanāśi. (*V. R. i, Coimbatore 35.*)

[Prince Muazzam of Delhi was released from imprisonment by Aurangzīb and appointed governor of Kābul.

Aurangzīb turned against the foreigners. He ordered the imprisonment of the English Factors of Surat, the siege of Bombay, and an attack on Madras.]

A.D. 1696. [Near Gingi, the Mahrattas defeated a Mughal force under Ali Mardān Khān.]

Aurangzīb is recognized as reigning in Chittoor District. (*322 of 1922.*)

[The Portuguese made a treaty of peace with the Zamorin of Calicut.]

A.D. 1697. Aurangzīb also acknowledged as reigning in Kurnool District at Nandikōṭkūr.

(*V.R. ii, Kurn. 386.*)

[The half-hearted siege of Gingi continued.]

A.D. 1698. A temple in N. Mysore, which had been destroyed by the forces of the ' Dilli Pātasāha ' Aurangzīb two years earlier, was restored. (*E. C. xi, Dg. 164.*)

Chikkadēva Rāja of Mysore reigning in S.-E. Mysore. (*E. C. ix, Nl. 65.*)

Keḷadi Basavaṇṇa, or Basapa I, ruling the Âraga country in N.-W. Mysore, Channamāji having died in 1697. (*E. C. viii, Tl. 178.*)

Queen Mangammāḷ of Madura granted a village near Trichinopoly.

(*Mys. A. A. R. 1917, p. 57.*)

[At Gingi after six years' siege so-called, Zulfiqar Khān allowed the Mahratta Commander Rājā Rām, brother of Sambājī I, to escape, and then stormed and captured the fortress. Rājā Rām returned to Sātāra, the Mahratta capital. Late in the year, in December, Aurangzīb's army appeared before Sātāra.]

A.D. 1699. Chikkadēva Rāja of Mysore reigning. (*E. C. xii, Mi. 16 ; Tm. 45.*)

[Sātāra besieged by the Mughal army. Rājā Rām fled to Bengal.

Chikkadēva of Mysore sent an embassy to Aurangzīb, which was received with honour.

Foundation of Fort William in Calcutta.

The Danes at Tranquebar were attacked by Shāhjī of Tanjore.]

A.D. 1700. In Tinnevelly District a grant by Ranga-Krishna Muttu-Vīrappa of Madura—said to be 'in the reign of Narasimhadēva at Ghanagiri' or Chandragiri, (Penugonda—*Editor*). [The document should receive further examination.] (*'Lists of Antiquities II, No. 168.'*)

Queen Mangammāḷ of Madura issued a C.-P. grant. (*V. R. ii, Madura 4.*)

[Sātāra was captured by Aurangzīb, and several other Mahratta fortresses. Rājā Rām of Sātāra died of disease.]

A.D. 1701. Grants by Mangammāḷ of Madura, acknowledging as Suzerain, Venkaṭa (perhaps Venkaṭa IV) of Vijayanagar.

(*E. R. 1911, App. A, 3, 19 ; and pp. 89, 90 of the Report. V. R. ii, Madura 94.*)

A.D. 1702. Keḷadi Basavappa Nāyaka ruling in N.-W. Mysore.

(*E.C. viii, Tl. 79, 106, 110, 117, 136.*)

[Dāūd Khān now Navāb of the Carnatic in succession to Zulfiqar Khān, invested Madras. The English merchants informed him that if he persisted they were prepared to defend the place by force, whereupon the Navāb gave way, and visited Madras in friendly fashion. The Madras Records say that when he was entertained he drank to excess.

(*'Vestiges' etc.*, Love. *ii. 19.*)]

A.D. 1704. Vijayaranga Chokkanātha Nāyaka of Madura ruling on April 1, in Coimbatore District. (*281 of 1920.*)

Queen Mangammāḷ of Madura ruling in Tanjore District.

(*V.R. ii, Tan. 1005, 394 of 1907 ; I.A. 1917, 156.*)

[A contemporary writer, Dulpat Roy, a Bondela officer, thus describes the state of the country in the Dekhan, speaking specially of Hyderabad and Bijāpur territory. The holders of estates (jāghirdārs) 'did not consider the ease of the farmers, but oppressed them for money by every mode of avarice that they could devise......The ancient territories of the Dekhan were not less troubled by the tyranny of governors......The jāghīrdārs were obliged, not only to supply their own necessities, but furnish large bribes to the civil officers about the Court......The parties sent everywhere to collect supplies......were guilty of every sort of excess.' In addition to this, certain collectors 'forced millions from the farmers and accounted only for small sums with the royal treasury......the farmers thus oppressed left off cultivating more ground than would barely subsist them, and in their turn became plunderers.' (*Firishta, Scott's Edit., ii, 107.*)]

A.D. 1705. Kanṭhīrava-Narasa III of Mysore, who succeeded Chikkadēva, now reigning at Seringapatam. *(E.C. ix, Bn. 118.)*

A.D. 1706. Grant by Mangammāḷ of Madura, in which the overlordship of Venkaṭa IV of Vijayanagar is recognized. *(V.R. iii, Tinnevelly, 462.)*

[Mahratta inroads and wanton plunder by Mahratta banditti had become so frequent that, says a contemporary witness, ' the necessaries of life are exceedingly scarce.']

(Firishta, Scott's Edit., ii. 120.)

A.D. 1707. Keḷadi Basavappa Nāyaka ruling in N.-W. Mysore.

(E.C. viii, Tl.93 ; Mys. A. A.R. 1923, p. 100.)

An inscription in Kurnool District names as reigning sovereign the ' Sulan Padshāh ', i. e. the Mughal Emperor. *(V.R. ii, Kurnool 502.)*

Grant by the Sētupati Vijaya Raghunātha Katta at Ramēsvaram. *(Mys. A.A.R. 1912, p, 55.)*

[Death of the Emperor Aurangzīb, aged 89. He was succeeded by prince Muazzam, who took the title ' Shāh Ālam ', and is known as ' Shāh Ālam I.']

The Mahratta Shāhjī, or Sāhuji II, who had been kept in confinement by Aurangzib since his father Sambājī's execution, was allowed to escape. He went to Sātāra, which was then held by the regent Tārā Bāī, and obtained possession of the fort by intrigue.

Fort William at Calcutta was armed and garrisoned by 125 soldiers.

A proof that the people of Madras were afforded protection and were well treated is given by an incident that took place this year. Some of the Hindu residents made trouble as they disliked being taxed for town improvements. They were told by the English Factors that they were at liberty to leave the town if they so desired. But none of them did so. (' *Vestiges* ', Love, *ii, 112.)*

A.D. 1708. In reign of Venkaṭa IV of Vijayanagar, ruling at Chandragiri, Vijayaranga Chokkanātha of Madura gave a grant of lands. *(E.R. 1915 App. A. 4 ; Mys. A.A.R. 1912, p. 55.)*

Keḷadi Basavappa Nāyaka ruling in N.-W. Mysore. *(E.C. viii, Tl. 60.)*

[Sāhujī or Shāhjī fought against Tārā Bāī's party at Sātāra, was successful, and ascended the throne as Mahārāja of the Mahrattas.

Dāūd Khān, Navāb of the Carnatic, gave several villages, including Ennore and Nungumbaukum to the English at Madras.]

A.D. 1709. Keḷadi Basavappa Nāyaka ruling in N.-W. Mysore. *(E.C. viii, Tl. 91, 95.)*

[Very heavy floods in South India, followed by a drought of several years' duration.

Tārā Bāī's party at Sātāra fought against Sāhujī and gained a victory. Sāhujī then made a compact with the Mughal leaders.]

A.D. 1710. Vijayaranga Chokkanātha ruling at Madura, under the overlordship of Vijayanagar. *(E.I. xvi, 88.)*

[Saādat Ullah Khān was created Navāb of the Carnatic. He persistently tried to seize villages now belonging to the English at Madras.]

A.D. 1711. Keḷadi Basavappa ruling in N.-W. Mysore in this year and in 1712.

(E.C. viii, Tl. 59, 72, 189.)

A.D. 1712. Vijayaranga Chokkanātha of Madura ruling there on March 8. In spite of the suffering of the people owing to the famine, he increased their taxation and did nothing to help them. One man, in despair, threw himself from a tower and was killed. Then at last the Nāyaka reduced the taxation. *(6 of 1915 ; T. & S.I. p. 110, No. 24 ; V.R. ii, Madura 60—C. 78.)*

Three records in E. Mysore speak of the reigning king there as Śrīranga of Vijayanagar, ruling from Chandragiri [1] ('Ghanagiri'). Evidently some classes of the people were loyal to the old regime, now defunct. *(E.C. ix, Ma. 3, 4, 42.)*

A sluice for irrigation was constructed by the Maṭla chief Perumāḷḷa, son of Venkaṭa-Krishna Chōḷa-Mahārāja, in Cuddapah District. *(V.R. i, Cudd. 705 ; 430 of 1911.)*

[Death of the Mughal Emperor Shāh Ālam I alias Bahādur Shāh, formerly Prince Muazzam. Civil war ensued between his four sons. The three younger were killed in battle. Jahāndar, the eldest, secured the throne. But his nephew Farrukhśiyar took up arms and opposed him.

At Sātāra Prince Sambhājī II, nephew of the reigning king Shāhūjī, seized Kohlapur and proclaimed himself as Rāja there, independent of his uncle. Shāhūjī was not strong enough to oppose him. Henceforth there were two separate Mahratta dynasties. Sambhājī II's mother Tārā Bāi was imprisoned.]

A.D. 1713. Muttu Vijaya Raghunātha Sētupati Kātta made a gift at Rāmēśvaram. *(V.R. ii, Ramnad 104 ; C. P. 9 of 1911.)*

[Farrukhśiyar defeated Jahāndar Shāh and put him to death. He also put to death Zulfiqar Khān. Farrukhśiyar then ascended the throne of Delhi. He had his own brother blinded with red-hot irons.

Nizām-ul-Mulkh Āsaf Jāh was appointed Subahdār of the Dekhan. The office became hereditary and he founded a dynasty, whose chief was known as 'The Nizām.'

Indecisive fighting between him and Shāhūjī of Sātāra.

Farrukhśiyar, behaved with brutal cruelty, killing and torturing numbers of his former opponents. *(See Firishta. Scott's edit., ii, Pt. v, p. 133.)*

A.D. 1714. Doḍḍa Krishna Rāja II of Mysore now reigning. Inscription at Āttur in Salem District. *(V.R. ii, Salem 54.)*

Grant at Rāmēśvaram by Vijaya Raghunātha Sētupati Kātta, son of Raghunātha. *(T. & S.I. Sētupati grant 10.)*

[Bālājī Viśvanāth appointed 'Pēshwa' by Sāhūjī of Sātāra. He became very powerful, the office became hereditary, and he established a dynasty of Mahratta Pēshwas who ruled the country, keeping the real Mahārāja and his family in a state of semi-confinement.

At Bombay the country people suffered so severely at the hands of their Muhammadan rulers that when the English Directors secured a concession of the island of Divi, they anticipated that the island would soon be inhabited by numbers of refugees—as indeed was the case.]

A.D. 1715. Vijayaranga Chokkanātha Nayaka of Madura ruling in Tinnevelly District. *(V. R. iii, Tinn. 456.)*

[At the Mughal Court at Delhi, Surgeon Hamilton came into favour with the Emperor in consequence of his having cured him of an illness.]

Farrukhśiyar put down a rebellion of the Sikhs and in doing so was guilty of fiendish cruelties. *(Firishta, Scott's Edit., ii, 133.)*

A.D. 1716. Vijayaranga Chokkanātha of Madura ruling at Śrīrangam, under the nominal suzerainty of Śrīranga of Vijayanagar. *(Lists of Antiquities, ii, C.-P. No. 50.)*

[1] Ghanagiri is Penugonda, its Telugu equivalent. Chandragiri never had this alternative designation.—*Editor.*

A.D. 1717. Grant by the same V. R. Chokkanātha in Chingleput District. *(V. R. ii, Madura* 89. *A. C. P. grant in Madras Museum.)*

Doḍḍa Krishna Rāja reigning in W. Mysore. *(E. C. v, Bl. 29.)*

Sarfōjī of the Mahratta family of Tanjore repaired a temple. *(V. R. ii, Tan. 914 ; 535 of 1904.)*

In Cuddapah a mosque built by Abdul Nabi Khān, Subahdār of Cuddapah under the Nizām of Haidarābād. *(V. R. i, Cudd. 45.)*

[Some troops serving under the Navāb of the Carnatic in Madras became unruly and were ejected from Madras.]

A.D. 1718. Doḍḍa Krishna Rāja II of Mysore reigning in Salem *(V. R. ii, Sal. 113).* And in S. Mysore. *(E. C. iii, Tn. 18.)*

Sarfōjī and Tukājī of the Mahratta dynasty of Tanjore ruling together (' reigning as kings '). *(V. R. ii, Tan. 1302 ; C.-P. grant.)*

A.D. 1719. Doḍḍa Krishna Rāja II of Mysore reigning in Central Mysore. *(E. C. xii, Tm. 46.)*

Keḷadi Somaśēkhara Nāyaka ruling in N.-W. Mysore. *(E. C. vii, Sk. 42 ; vi, Kp. 46.)*

The Maṭla chief Kumārai Ananta ruling in Cuddapah District. *(V. R. i, Cudd. 706, 707.)*

[On February 25, the Emperor Farrukhśiyar was deposed, blinded and imprisoned and then murdered by a body of rebels headed by two brothers, Sayyids. The Emperor's cousin Rafīu-d Darajāt was placed on the throne but died of consumption in June. Then his brother Rafīu-d Daula was raised to the throne but died within a few months. Then another cousin Roshan Akhtar, son of Jahān Shāh, was made Emperor under the title ' Muhammad Shāh '.

The Nizām Āsaf Jāh was removed from his post of Subahdār of the Dekhan as he opposed the successful rebels.]

A.D. 1720. Doḍḍa Krishna II of Mysore reigning. *(E. C. xii, Tm. 47, 48 ; ix, Nl. 70.)*

[The Nizām Āsaf Jāh took up arms against the new Emperor Muhammad Shāh, in revolt against the murderers of Farrukhśiyar. He won several battles.

The Mahratta Pēshwa Bālājī Viśvanāth died this year, and was succeeded by his son Bāji Rao I.]

A.D. 1722. Doḍḍa Krishna Rāja II of Mysore reigning. *(E. C. iii, Sr. 64 ; App. A. C.-P. No. 1 of 1911 ; E. C. ii, Sr. Bel. 83.)*

[Nizām Āsaf Jāh was made Wazīr to the Emperor Muhammad Shāh, but did not work cordially with him.]

A.D. 1723. Keḷadi Sōmaśēkhara Nāyaka ruling in N.-W. Mysore. *(E. C viii, Tl. 6, 183, 186.)*

Doḍḍa Krishna Raja of Mysore reigning. *(E. C. ii, Sr–Bel. 83.)*

[Nizām Āsaf Jāh resigned his office of Wazīr and returned to the Dekhan. The Emperor made Mubāriz Khān Subahdār of the Dekhan in place of Āsaf Jāh, and instructed the former to raise an army for defence against Āsaf.]

A.D. 1724. [Āsaf Jāh fought against Mubāriz Khān, defeated and killed him. Then he threw off all semblance of allegiance to the Emperor, and declared himself independent at Haidarābād.]

Vijaya Ranga Chokkanātha of Maduṛa ruling under the nominal suzerainty of Vijayanagar. *(V. R. iii, Tinn. 461.)*

A.D. 1725. Doḍḍa Krishna Rāja of Mysore reigning in S. Mysore. *(E. C. iii, Tn. 59.)*

A.D. 1726. Vijaya Ranga Chokkanātha of Madura ruling in Trichinopoly District. *(V. R. iii, Trich. 782.)*

[Bājī Rao, Mahratta Pēshwa of Sātāra, invaded Mysore and levied a contribution from Seringapatam. He retired without having gained much advantage beyond ruining the peasantry on his march.]

A.D. 1727. [Bājī Rao fought against Āsaf Jāh of Haidarābād, and at one place defeated him.]

A.D. 1728. Vijaya-Ranga Chokkanātha Nāyaka of Madura reigning at Trichinopoly. *(V. R. iii, Trich. 563 ; 697 of 1909.)*

A.D. 1729. A grant by a local magnate of a village near Dinḍigul, in Madura district in the time, so it is stated, of Vijaya Ranga Chokkanātha (of Madura) who was 'Viceroy' of Śrīranga of Vijayanagar. *(V. R. ii, Madura, 3—A ; T. and S. I., p. 117, No. 27.)*

[By a surprise attack the Pēshwa Bājī Rao defeated the Rāja of Kolhapur, Sambhājī II, and took prisoner the Rāṇi Tāra Bāi, carrying her to Sātāra.]

A.D. 1730. Tūkājī, the Mahratta Rāja of Tanjore, ruling his country. *(521 of 1918.)*

Severe famine in Tanjore. Great loss of life by starvation, and pestilence owing to the dead remaining unburied or unburned. Letter of Father Beschi. *(I. A. 1923, p. 241.)*

[The Mahratta States, Sātāra and Kolhāpur, came to terms and agreed that they should be separate and independent. Their boundaries were settled.]

A.D. 1731. Vijaya Ranga Chokkanātha of Madura ruiling in Trichinopoly. *(Lists of Antiquities II, No. 56. V. R. ii, Tinn. 464.)*

[Death of Doḍḍa Krishna Raja of Mysore. He was the last survivor of his line. A member of the Hemmanhaḷḷi family, Chāma Rāja VIII, was placed on the throne, but was kept virtually a prisoner.]

Death also of Vijaya Ranga Chokkanātha Nāyaka of Madura. He left no issue. His widow Mīnākshi became Regent for her adopted son Vijaya-Kumara. Insurrections occurred and there was general turmoil.

M. Dupleix arrived from France and took office as head of the French community at Chandanagore (Chandranagar).]

A.D. 1732. Chāma Rāja VIII of Mysore reigning in E. Mysore. *(E. C. ix, Ma. 37.)*

[Death of Saādat Ullah Khān, Navāb of the Carnatic, alias Muhammad Sayyid. He was succeeded by his nephew Dost Ali Khān. A younger brother of Dost Ali, named Bakir Ali, was made governor of Vellore.]

A.D. 1733. Grants in Trichinopoly district by Queen Mīnākshi of the Madura Nāyaka dynasty. *(V. R. iii, Trich. 440, 784 ; Lists of Antiquities I, 267, 268 ; II, C. P. No. 49.)*

[Famine very severe in Chingleput district.

More fighting in the Konkan. The Mahrattas compelled the city of Ahmadābād to pay them large sums of money in addition to enforced *Chauth*. (One-quarter of the land-revenue assessment).]

A.D. 1734. [Chāma Rāja VIII of Mysore was deposed by the Daḷavay, and a child of three years, Immaḍi Krishna III was placed on the throne. He never had any power at all, but was kept on the throne as nominal Rāja till 1761.

Two coast forts in Malabar were ceded to the English.]

Grant by Immaḍi Krishna III (infant) Rāja of Mysore. *(V.R. ii, Salem, 202.)*

Gift of villages by Kumāra-Muttu-Vijaya-Raghunātha, now the Sētupati chief ruling in Ramnad. He was brother of Nātchiyār, the wife of the Sētupati Tāṇḍa Tēvan II, who had been killed in 1734 by Bhavāni-Śamkara, illegitimate son of the Sētupati Raghunātha-Tevan.

(V. R. ii, Ramnad, 119 ; T. and S. I. Sētupati grant, No. 14.)

A.D. 1735. [The Mahrattas ravaged the country governed by the Navāb of Arcot (or of the Carnatic) at the instigation of Āsaf Jāh, Subahdār of the Dekhan. The villages were ruined in large numbers.]

A.D. 1736. Gifts by the Sētupati chief Muthu-Kumāra-Vijaya-Raghunātha.

(V.R. ii, Madura 82 ; Ramnad 120 ; Lists of Antiquities, ii, C.-P. No. 23.)

Inscription of Immaḍi Krishna Rāja of Mysore,—an infant five years old.

(E.C. v, Bl. 64.)

[In Persia Tahmasp Kuli Khān was proclaimed Shāh. He is generally known in India as Nadir Shāh. He at once marched on Kandahar, and took possession of it after two years of war.

The Pēshwa Bājī Rao seized many Districts in the Dekhan, and in alarm, Nizām Āsaf Jāh, Subahdār of the Dekhan became reconciled to the Emperor at Delhi.

Chanda Sahib became Dewān to his father-in-law Dost Ali, Navāb of the Carnatic. He seized and held Trichinopoly and became its governor, imprisoning Queen Mīnākshī of Madura who had ruled for four years in the absence of heirs to the late Rāja. The queen took poison and died. And so came to an end the rule of the Nāyakas of Madura, the whole of their country falling into the Navāb's hands.]

A.D. 1737. [The Pēshwa Bājī Rao marched to attack Delhi but when near the city he retired. Nizām Āsaf Jāh advanced to meet him on his retirement.

The sufferings of the people in the neighbourhood of Madras at this time were very great. The agent of the British Company wrote to the Directors that the people were harassed and oppressed by their own rulers, and were the prey of dacoits and thugs. 'The exactions of the Havildars have been so vexatious and intolerable . . . that several towns and villages have been deserted by the inhabitants. In a word the confusion and disorder of the country is exceeding great.' (*'Vestiges'*, Love, *ii, 278.*)

A.D. 1738. Immaḍi Krishna Rāja, now seven years old, reigning as Rāja in Central Mysore.

(E.C. xii, Mi. 56.)

[Āsaf Jāh's army from Haidarābād was attacked near Bhōpāl by Bājī Rao and his Mahrattas. The Nizām was defeated and forced to come to terms, paying fifty lakhs of rupees and ceding some territory.

The Mahrattas occupied half the dominions of the Barīd Shāh of Ahmadābād. They attacked the Portuguese in the Konkan, took several forts and besieged Mahim.

In Tanjore Bābā Sahib, the Mahratta chief, died and was succeeded by his brother Sāhūjī. He was opposed by hostile factions, and sought aid from the French.

Chanda Sahib at Madura was aided by the French, who at this time were growing stronger.

In the North-West of India Nadir Shāh, having occupied Kābul, advanced to Peshawar.]

A.D. 1739. [Nadir Shāh swept over the North-West of India and captured Lahore. On March 19, he seized and sacked the imperial city of Delhi, which was given over to loot and massacre. Thousands of the inhabitants were slaughtered. A contemporary writer describes the horrors of the occupation (*Firishta, Scott's Edition, ii, Pt. v, p. 209 f*). 'The streets streamed with blood and the bodies of the dead obstructed the passages.' Besides the uncontrolled looting by the soldiers, the merchants and richer classes were ordered to pay large sums. The various portions of the city were handed over to revenue-farmers. 'In place of ten they extorted thirty or forty thousand rupees. The first sum was paid to the treasury, and the rest was embezzled by these infernal wretches.' The Vizier's Dewan, who had already paid the conqueror's demand, was threatened with tortures on failure to pay a much larger sum—tortures so horrible that to avoid them he stabbed himself to death. Numbers of other citizens followed his example. In many places the city was set on fire. Nadir, after ruining the capital marched away, carrying with him the peacock throne set with diamonds, and booty estimated at from 80 to 145 millions of pounds in value.]

The Mahrattas seized Mahim, Bassein and other forts.

The pirate-leader Angria captured Chaul, and threatened Bombay, anchoring off the island of Elephanta.

A.D. 1740. [The Mahrattas under Rāghōjī Bhonsla, 50,000 strong, invaded the Karnāṭaka and in a pitched battle at Dāmalcheruvu, the Navāb Dost Ali and his eldest son were killed. Safdar Ali, his second son, succeeded him as Navāb, and tried to buy off the Mahratta invaders.

Bājī Rao, the Pēshwa, died this year and was succeeded by his son Bālājī-Bājī Rao.

Several of the ruling families of the south, in fear of the Mahrattas, fled to the French at Pondicherry for refuge. The Navāb Safdar Ali favoured the French cause as against the English. Nevertheless, he sent his family for safety to Madras.

Dissensions at Tanjore. Pratāpa Simha, illegitimate son of Tūkājī the former Rāja, made overtures to the French with the object of turning out Sāhūjī, the ruling Raja.

In December 1740, the Mahrattas invested the town of Trichinopoly, pillaged the neighbouring districts—ruining the peasantry,—and sacked Negapatam on the East coast.]

A.D. 1741. [Chanda Sahib surrendered Trichinopoly to the Mahrattas, and the town was ruthlessly sacked. Morari Rao was left there as governor under the Pēshwa. Chanda Sahib was taken prisoner to Sātāra.]

Disturbance in Haidarābād, where Nāzir Jang, son of the Nizām Āsaf Jāh, rebelled against his father, but was defeated and taken prisoner.

At Tanjore Pratāpa Simha was successful in deposing the Raja Sāhūjī and taking his place. Sāhūjī went for help to the English.

[The French made peace with Rāghōjī Bhonsla.]

A.D. 1742. An inscription in Bellary district shews that at least some people remained loyal to the now-defunct Empire of Vijayanagar, for it names a Venkaṭapati as reigning. (*745 of 1922.*)

[At Delhi, the Mughal Emperor Muhammad Shāh, in fear of the Mahrattas, made friends with the French.

Rāghōjī Bhonsla, having looted part of the Karnāṭaka (Carnatic) two years earlier, now attacked Bengal. The Pēshwa Bālājī Rao sent aid to Muhammad Shāh against Rāghojī.

Ghulām Murtazā Ali of Vellore, who had married a cousin daughter of his uncle, the Navāb Dost Ali, rebelled against his brother-in-law, Safdar Ali, the ruling Navāb, and killed him. Murtazā proclaimed himself Navāb, but revolts ensued. The Nizām marched against him with

120,000 men, seized Murtazā's son, Sahib Jadda, a minor, and drove off the Mahrattas who had marched to the attack of Vellore. He deposed Murtazā and made Sayyid Muhammad alias Saādat-Ullah Khān II, infant son of Safdar Ali, 'Navāb of Arcot,' abolishing the title 'Navāb of the Karnāṭaka'. Sahib Jadda was murdered.

More villages were granted to the English at Madras.]

A.D. 1743. [The Mahrattas retired from the Karnāṭaka.]

A.D. 1744. Immaḍi Krishna Rāja of Mysore reigning on April 15. (*Mys. A.A.R. 1923, p. 66.*)

Gift to the Uḍipi temple by the Keḷadi chief Basavaṇṇa Nāyaka. (*V.R. ii, S. Kanara, 240.*)

Gift by the Sētupati chief of Ramnad, Muttu-Kumāra Vijaya Raghunātha, son of Muttu-Vijaya Raghunātha, and grandson of the chief of the same name who was known as "Hiraṇya-garbhayājī." (*V.R. ii, Ramnad, 281.*)

[France and England, in Europe, at open war. Some fighting by sea on the coast of India. The European garrison available at Madras was so small that the councillors at Madras wrote to the Directors in London saying that they were 'ashamed to turn out guards when the great men of the country came' to visit them.] ('*Vestiges*,' Love, *ii, 299.*)

The Navāb of Arcot, Muhammad Saādat-Ulla Khān II, was assassinated. As Subahdār of the Dekhan, the Nizām Āsaf Jāh appointed Anwaru-d-dīn, who had been guardian to the young Navāb, to be Navāb of Arcot.

A.D. 1745. [Anwaru-d-dīn went to Pondicherry and used his good offices to prevent the French and English from fighting and destroying one another.]

A.D. 1746. [Madras was attacked by the French by land and sea, and the small garrison was compelled to surrender. The Navāb Anwaru-d-dīn's son, Māhfuz Khan, then attacked the French in an attempt to assist the English, but failed. Before this the French had agreed to withdraw on payment of a small ransom, but after the Navāb's interference they broke this agreement and seized Madras.

Nāsīr Jang, son of Āsaf Jāh of the Dekhan, exacted tribute from the Raja of Mysore.]

A.D. 1747. [The French attacked Cuddalore, but were driven off by the English fleet.

Nadir Shāh of Persia, who was guilty of terrible atrocities, was murdered. An Ābdāli chief, Āhmad Khān, founded a new dynasty and kingdom under the name of 'Durānī'.]

A.D. 1748. [Death of the Mugal Emperor Muhammad Shah and accession of his son Āhmad Shāh. He had no real power.

Death of Nizām-ul-Mulkh Āsaf Jāh of Haidarābād. He was succeeded by his second son Nāsir Jang, the eldest son Ghāziu-d-dīn Khān being employed in high office in Delhi.

French and English fighting one another.]

A.D. 1749. Immaḍi, or Chikka, Krishna Rajā ruling, in April, in S. Mysore. (*E.C. iii, Tn. 63.*) (*See Pedigree of the Dynasty of Mysore and footnote.*)

[Anwaru-d-dīn, Navāb of Arcot, attacked an allied force of the French under Dupleix, Chanda Sahib and Muzaffar Jang at Ambūr, and lost his life in the battle. The Mughal Emperor had no power at this time and the French, acting independently, proclaimed Chanda Sahib, Navāb of the Carnatic; while Muzaffar Jang, ignoring the claims of Nāsir Jang, assumed the rank of Subahdār of the Dekhan. The English took the side of Nāsir Jang, as Nizām, and of Muhammad Ali, son of Anwaru-d-dīn as Navāb of the Carnatic. Muhammad Ali is often spoken of as 'Navāb Wālājāh', and as 'the Company's Nabob'.

Shāhujī of Sātāra died, after adopting as his heir Rāma Rāja, son of his cousin Śivājī II, and committing him to the care of the Pēshwa, Bālājī Rao, who retained all the power.

Haidar Ali was given a command by the Rāja of Mysore.

The English received the territory of Dēvikoṭṭa as reward for their help to Rājā Sāhujī, or Sāyāji of Tanjore in recovering his throne from the usurper Pratāpa Simha after the latter had ruled for eight years.

The French attacked Trichinopoly and Tanjore, in alliance with Chanda Sahib, and Sāhujī made a treaty with them.

Madras was restored by the French to the English under the Treaty of Aix-la-Chapelle.]

A.D. 1750. Immaḍi Krishna Rāja reigning in S. Mysore.

(E.C. iv, Ch. 55 ; ix, Dv. 69.)

[Navāb Nāsir Jang of Haidarābād, assisted by 600 English, marched on Gingi and defeated Chanda Sahib and Muzaffar Jang. He then proclaimed Muhammad Ali, Navab of Arcot. Muhammad Ali was, however, attacked shortly afterwards by the French under Bussy and by Chanda Sahib, who again took Gingi.

Shortly afterwards Nāsir Jang was, on December 16, shot and killed by the Navab of Kurnool; and the French then proclaimed as Subahdār of the Dekhan Muzaffar Jang.]

A.D. 1751. [Muzaffar Jang was killed by the Navāb of Kurnool.

Muhammad Ali,—the opposition of the French and Chanda Sahib being very strong—shut himself up in Trichinopoly, where he was besieged. In place of Muzaffar Jang, Salābat Jang, brother of Nāsir Jang was, with French assistance, proclaimed Subahdār of the Dekhan. Salabat thereupon gave to the French the fortress of Konḍaviḍu and the country about Narasapatam and Nizāmpatam near the River Krishna.

The Pēshwa attacked Salābat Jang and Bussy, but was defeated. Afterwards peace was made.

Captain, afterwards Lord, Clive occupied Arcot, to defend it for Muhammad Ali, but was besieged there by Chanda Sahib.]

A.D. 1752. The Vijayanagar dynasty still recognized as supreme in an inscription in Bellary district, which, on December 2, names Venkaṭapati as ruling. *(719 of 1922.)*

[Chanda Sahib being in straits, the French sent him for safety to the Tanjore Mahratta General who however caused him to be executed.

Clive defeated the French in a small engagement.

Salābat Jang made peace with the Pēshwa and Rāghōjī Bhonsla, but his Dewan began to intrigue against French influence.]

A.D. 1753. [The French induced Salābat Jang to dismiss his Dewan and make a new appointment to that post. He also made several more concessions to the French, giving them Ellore, Rajahmundry and Chicacōl, in return for their promise of support, and for the expenses of their army.

The English and Muhammad Ali now stood opposed to the French, the Mahrattas and the Mysore Rāja, who was irritated at being deprived of Trichinopoly.

The Mahrattas attacked Fort St. David at Cuddalore.

At Vellore there was fighting between Ghulām Murtāzā Ali of Arcot and Abdul Wahāb, son of Anwaru-d-dīn of Haidarabad. The latter was defeated.

Trichinopoly was besieged by the French and their allies, but held out under Clive, who was assisted by a force from Tanjore.]

A.D. 1754. An inscription in Tinnevelly district mentions a Pāṇḍya prince Kulaśēkhara Dikshita, alias Śivala (Śrīvallabha) Varaguṇarāma, who had the title 'Iṛandakalameḍutta'—'He who brought back the old time.' It states that two armies made offerings to the deity at Kuttālam. These were probably a detachment of the Pēshwa's Mahrattas and the forces of Tanjore, who were opposed to one another. *(V. R. ii Tinn, 340, 341 ; T. A. S. i, 149.)*

[The Dekhāni Mahrattas were now fighting at Tanjore against their kinsmen, the Mahrattas of Tanjore, and engagements were fought near Tanjore, the Tanjore garrison beating their opponents.

At Delhi, the Mughal Emperor Āhmad Shāh was deposed and blinded, and the undoubtedly rightful heir, Ālamgīr II, son of Jahāndar Shāh, was raised to the throne. He made Navāb Ghāziu-d-dīn his Wazīr.

Dupleix was recalled to France. Bussy obtained some power in Haidarābād.

On February 15, the English suffered a severe defeat. A convoy was proceeding to Trichinopoly when it was attacked by Morari Rao and captured, the English battalion losing a third of its strength.]

A.D. 1755. Inscription of a Maṭla chief Venkaṭarāma II, 'Chōḷa-Mahārāja,' son of Tiruvēngadanātha. *(Several records of these Maṭla chiefs, are scattered between. V. R. i, Cuddapah 864 and 936.)*

[The *pirate* Angria's stronghold Śuvarṇadrūg ('Severndroog') was captured from him by Commander James of the English navy.]

A.D. 1756. Inscription of Immaḍi Krishna Rāja of Mysore reigning in Coimbatore district from Seringapatam. *(V. R. i, Coim, 32 ; 201 of 1909.)*

[Delhi was captured by the Afghan chief Āhmad Shāh Durānī, and completely sacked. A contemporary witness states that the city 'was for many days given up to the merciless plunder of the soldiery. . . Such was their cruelty . . . that numbers of the unfortunate inhabitants put themselves to death with their women' *(Firishta, Scott's Edit, ii, 232)*. A little later there was 'a general massacre of the unhappy inhabitants of Muttra' (Mathurā).

A revolt took place in Madura against the governor Mahfūz Khān, brother of Muhammad Ali, Navāb of Arcot. The revolt was put down with the aid of the English, and Mahfūz Khān was left as governor.

Gooty (Gutti), now in possession of the Mahratta, Morari Rao, was attacked by Salābat Jang, Subahdār of the Dekhan and the French, but the fort held out and the French retired.

Calcutta was attacked and captured by Sirāju-d-Daula, Navāb of Bengal. A number of English prisoners were suffocated while in confinement in a small prison, which was ever after remembered as 'The Black Hole of Calcutta.' One hundred and twenty-three lives were lost out of a total of 146.]

A.D. 1757. The French under Bussy seized the town of Bobbili in Vizagapatam district assisted thereto by the now-unimportant Raja Śrī Rāma of Vijayanagar (Vizianagaram) who was murdered by servants of the local Paḷegār.

In Bengal Sirāju-d-Daula the Navāb with 68,000 men was completely defeated by 3,000 English under Clive at the battle of Plassey. Sirāju-d-Daula was put to death by Mīrān, son of Mīr Jafar. Mīr Jafar was made Subahdār of Bengal in his place, and ceded the 24-Parganas to the English.

[The districts about Tinnevelly were pacified by the English officer, Capt. Calliaud.

Seringapatam, where Haidar Ali now practically ruled, though nominally serving the Rāja of Mysore, was invested by a force of 60,000 Mahrattas under the immediate command of the Pēshwa, Bālājī Rao; but they were bought off and retired.

Capt. Calliaud occupied Madura; and an officer in the English army Muhammad Yusuf Khān took Shōlavandān. Māhfūz Khān, who had been governor of Madura, was removed and granted a pension.

Haidar Ali took up arms against the English and seized Shōlavandān, but the English recaptured the place. Haidar then plundered the surrounding country.]

A.D. 1758. An inscription in S. Mysore records an agreement made between the Rāja of Mysore, Krishna Rāja III, and the Rāja of Kaḷalē 'through the medium of Haidar Ali Bahādur and Khaṇḍē Rao', by which, the Rāja of Kaḷalē was made Commander-in-Chief and was given permission to build a fort. *(E. C. iv, Nj. 267.)*

[Clive was made Governor and Commander-in-Chief in Calcutta, and sent a force of 500 Europeans and 2,000 Indians to assist the English of Madras in their defensive operations against the French in the Northern Sarkārs.

Māhfūz Khān, resenting his removal from Madura, collected a small army and started out to ravage the country in the neighbourhood.

The French Commander Lally landed at Pondicherry and at once attacked the English at Fort St. David in Cuddalore, capturing the fort and town, and seizing also Negapatam. This so seriously alarmed the Mahratta Rāja of Tanjore, Sāhūjı, that he applied for help to the English. This help was accorded to him and Lally was made to retire. The French captured Trinomali, Karunguḷi and other places, but were ejected from Rajahmundry by the English after five years of occupation. Lally, at the end of the year, left Conjevaram and attacked Fort St. George, Madras.

The Mahrattas, in alliance with Ghulām Murtazā Ali Khān, son-in-law of the late Navab of Arcot, vainly attempted to seize Tirupati.]

An inscription in Tanjore District names apparently as still ruling as Rāja of Tanjore, Pratāpa Simha. Probably he had been left by Sāhūjī, the present Rāja, to rule part of the country. At any rate this inscription and the next one seem to shew that Pratāpa Simha had accepted office in Tanjore under Sāhūjī. *(Ep. Rep. 1921, App. A, C. P. 15.)*

A.D. 1759. Another similar inscription of Pratāpa Simha ruling in Tanjore. *(Ep. Rep. 1921, App. A, C. P. 14.)*

Immaḍi Krishna Rāja reigning in E. Mysore. Haidar Ali paid a sum of money to the king's treasury and the king gave a village to a Muhammadan *faqīr*. *(E. C. ix, An. 90; Cp. 32.)*

[The English at Madras were attacked (January 2) by the French. The English were assisted by forces sent by Abdul Wahāb and Najībullah, brothers of the Navāb of Arcot, by Sāhūji Rāja of Tanjore and by Murtazā Ali of Vellore. After some fighting the English fleet appeared off Madras and Lally at once raised the siege (February 27).

Masulipatam was captured from the French by Colonel Forde, the Marquis de Conflans capitulating.

Lally now proclaimed Chanda Sahib's son, Rājā Sahib, Navāb of Arcot, and had him crowned. This put an end at once to any friendship between the French and the Subahdār of the Dekhan, Salābat Jang, who had always opposed Chanda Sahib's claim—a claim manifestly unfounded. He concluded that the English would be more useful to him than the French, and made a treaty with Madras by which the English engaged not to assist the Subahdār's enemies, and the Subahdār in consideration of this support gave them, in '*inam*,' eight districts, some of which had been formerly in possession of the French, with jurisdiction over the districts of Koṇḍavīḍu and Nizāmpatam.

Mir Jafar of Bengal gave Clive a tract of land as a *jāghīr*.

Mahfūz Khan, the Navāb of Arcot's brother, received a *jāghīr*, and, for safety and peace, took up his residence in Madras.

The Mahrattas again invaded Mysore, but retired on payment of ransom for a town they had taken.

Indecisive fighting between the French and the English took place, ending in December with the English capturing Wandewash and Karunguḷi, and making prisoner of the French Commander, Bussy.

The Mughal Emperor Ālamgīr II was murdered and was succeeded by his son Shāh Ālam II who was hostile to the English. Hindustān was again invaded by Āhmad Shāh Durānī, whereupon all branches of the Mahratta power united and attempted to drive away the invaders. One of their armies was defeated in the Rohilla country in October–November.]

A.D. 1760. Inscriptions of this year of Immaḍi Krishna Rāja of Mysore and Haidar Ali Bahādur. (*Mys. A.A.R. 1923, p. 41 ; E.C. iv. Kr. 18 ; V.R. i, p. 551, 553.*)

[Lally, after the British success at Wandewash, retired to Pondicherry, which was promptly surrounded by British troops and was attacked in force in October. Cuddalore, Chidambaram, and many other places which had been held by the French capitulated to the English. Lally then appealed for aid to Haidar Ali, who took the field and fought several engagements against the English. But later, both he and the French were beaten in the open field, and Karūr was taken by the English. Haidar thereupon retired.

Haidar Ali occupied S. Kanara.

In the North of India in January, the Mahrattas under Holkar were completely defeated by the army of the Afghans and Rohillas. In July the main Mahratta force seized Delhi and did great damage to some of its most beautiful palaces and shrines. In December after heavy fighting, the Mahratta army retired to Pānīpat.

A contemporary Indian chronicler, referring to the ruin inflicted on the country in Central India owing to the merciless treatment of the peaceful inhabitants by the Mahratta and Muhammadan soldiery, wrote that in Behar the people were 'so much disgusted . . . . . . who before were anxious for the success of the Vizier that they changed their wishes into prayers for the success of the English, who had never molested them.' (*Firishta, Scott's Edit., p. 432.*)]

A.D. 1761. Records of Immaḍi Krishna and Haidar Ali in Mysore.

(*E.C. iv, Yd. 17 ; ix, Cp. 166.*)

[Haidar Ali in this year entered openly upon the Government of Mysore, and took all power out of the hands of the Rāja.

Pondicherry, the French headquarters, was captured by the English, and its fortifications destroyed. By April the English had practically crushed down French power in Southern India.

At Haidarābād Nizām Ali, brother of the Subahdār Salābat Jang, revolted, seized and imprisoned the Subahdār, and proclaimed himself ruler of the Dekhan in his stead. He held that office for the next forty years.

A great and decisive battle was fought at Pānipat between the invading army of the Durānīs and the Mahratta main body. The Mahrattas were completely defeated and the Pēshwa's son Vishvas Rao was killed, with 40,000 of his men. The Pēshwa Bālājī Rao died broken-hearted.

Lord Clive tried in vain to free the English in India from political complications and the constant necessity for interference with the various rulers of the country. His desire was that 'the English should attend solely to commerce, which was their proper sphere and their whole aim in these parts.'

The Emperor Shāh Ālam II, unable to defend himself against Durānī armies, gave himself up to the English and was protected by them.

Mādhava Rao, son of Bālājī Rao, was made Pēshwa at Sātāra, Vishvas Rao being dead. The British made an agreement with him, and the Mahratta sovereign Rajā Rām was left undisturbed.]

A.D. 1762. Inscriptions of Immaḍi Krishna Rāja of Mysore, shewing him reigning.

(*E.C. iv, Ch. 81 ; Ng. 7 ; v, Hn. 132 ; xii, Tp. 112.*)

[Salābat Jang, Subahdār of the Dekhan, was murdered, and his brother Nizām Ali permanently secured his place ; a success which he signalized by destroying a number of Hindu temples.

Muhammad Ali, Navāb of Arcot, appealed to the English for help in settling a dispute about tribute between him and Sāhujī of Tanjore.

Śivājī Bhonsla became Rāja of Kolhāpur, having been adopted by Jījī Bāi, widow of Sambhājī. The government was carried on by the Rāṇi.]

A.D. 1763. Immaḍi Krishṇa Rāja of Mysore reigning. (*E.C. iv, Yl. ix, Nl. 51 ; xii, Ck. 45.*) In a grant given by Haidar Ali to a *faqir*, Haidar is given full imperial titles—' Rājādhirāja-Rāja-paramēśvaram as if he were sovereign (*E.C. ix, Cp. 146*). Immaḍi Krishṇa Rāja was also ruling in Coimbatore district. (*Lists of Antiquities, ii, C.P. No. 171.*)

[Haidar Ali captured Beḍnūr, ravaged the western tracts and took Sunda, whose Rāja fled for protection to Goa.

The Mahrattas under Raghunāth Rao, brother of the Pēshwa Bālājī Rao, defeated the Subahdār of the Dekhan, Nizām Ali, near the Godavari River.

Peace was proclaimed between France and England in Europe, and it was agreed that the French factories in India taken by the English should be restored, but that the French should not fortify them ; similarly places taken from the English by the French should be restored ;—Muhammad Ali, ' the Company's Nabob ', to be Navāb of Arcot. The Navāb then granted certain of his districts, including most of the modern district of Chingleput, to the English.]

A.D. 1764. ' Chikka ' (or Immaḍi) Krishṇa Raja of Mysore reigning. (*E.C. xii, Kg. 36.*)

[The Navāb of Bengal attacked Patna. In a battle at Baksar (Buxar), he was completely defeated by the English.

This victory laid Bengal at the feet of the English. Lord Clive arrived at Calcutta, having been created Viscount, and was made Governor. The Emperor Shāh Ālam II placed himself under British protection. Allahabad and Chunār were captured from the Navāb Vizier of Oudh. The Navāb of Bengal was given a pension. The Emperor was assigned certain districts including Allahabad and was granted a large annuity from the revenues of Bengal. In return he confirmed the right of the Company to the territory now in their possession. He thus practically became a pensioner of the Company. The Dīwāni of the whole of Bengal, Bihār and Orissa was assigned to the Company.]

A.D. 1765. Haidar Ali made a grant to a temple in South Kanara (*V.R. ii, S. Kan., 257*). [The Mahrattas retired from Mysore, Haidar permitting them to retain the places they had lost.

Tuljājī, son of Pratāpa Simha, became Rāja of Tanjore.]

A.D. 1766. [The 'Northern Sarkars,' i.e., the modern districts of Ganjam, Vizagapatam, Godavari, Krishna and Guntūr were ceded to the Company by the Nizam of Haidarābād, in return for a payment to him of 9 lakhs of rupees a year as rent, and a promise of military help from the English.

A Treaty was made between Haidar Ali and the Pēshwa. This was immediately followed by a secret Treaty between the same rulers.

Two English battalions joined the Subahdār, Nizām Ali, for an attack on Bangalore, held by Haidar.

Immaḍi Krishṇa Rāja of Mysore died and was succeeded by his son, Nanja Rāja who was placed on the throne by Haidar Ali.

Haidar then invaded Malabar and seized Calicut.

The unfortunate French Commander Lally, who had failed to conquer the English in India, was beheaded in Paris.]

A.D. 1767. Haidar Ali ruling, with full titles as sovereign, in Mysore. (*E.C. ix, Cp. 18, 114.*)

[Haidar persuaded the Nizām to abandon the British and come over to his side. He did so, and together, Haidar having bought off the Mahrattas, they opened a campaign. This resulted in their being defeated at Trinomali and Āmbur, whence they retreated into Mysore.]

A.D. 1768. [The Nizām having openly broken his contract with the English, a British force marched on Warangal; whereupon Nizām Ali submitted, broke his alliance with Haidar, revoked all grants ever made by the Subah to Haidar, handed over to the English the administration of the Karnāṭaka country above the Ghāts, and acknowledged Muhammad Ali as Navāb of Arcot.

The English then conquered from Haidar the districts of Salem, Krishṇagiri, Venkaṭagiri, Muḷbāgal, Kolār and Hōsūr. In August, Haidar proposed terms of peace which were refused, and the war continued, the English being defeated in two minor actions.]

A.D. 1769. An inscription of the Sētupati of Ramnad, 'Muttu Rāmalinga,' dated on November 5 (*T.A.S. i, 7, 13*). A C.-P. grant of 'Hiraṇyagarbha Raghunātha Sētupati Kātta' (*V.R. ii, Madura 81*). Both donors are the same person.

[Haidar advanced, seized Karūr and Erode and with a force of 6,000 cavalry boldly marched to St. Thomas Mount, a few miles from Madras. There he proposed a Treaty with the English, by which there should be a mutual restoration of captured places and a defensive alliance. The treaty was signed, and so ended the first Mysore War.]

A.D. 1770. Gift by the Sētupati Muttu Ramalinga alias Vijaya Raghunātha.

(*V.R. ii, Ramnad 103 ; C.-P. 7 of 1911.*)

An inscription shewing two Muhammadans holding a jāghīr in Mysore. (*E.C. x, Bg. 32.*)

[A very severe famine in Bengal, in which a large proportion of the people perished from starvation.

In August a Treaty of perpetual friendship was concluded between the English Government and Haidar Ali.

The Pēshwa sent a large body of horse and foot against Haidar, but retired owing to sickness.

Nanja Rāja of Mysore was strangled by order of Haidar Ali, and his brother Beṭṭada Chāma Rāja IX, was placed on the throne, but kept without power.]

A.D. 1771. Grant of land by Tuljājī, (called ' Tulaśi ') of the Tanjore Mahratta dynasty. (*V.R. ii, Tan. 1460—1.*)

An inscription of the Ramnad Sētupati, Muttu Rāmalinga. (*T.A.S. v, 7, 13.*)

[The Navāb of Arcot and the Rāja of Tanjore quarrelled about payment of tribute, and the English helped the Navāb. Tanjore was invested and then peace was made, contrary to the wishes of the English leaders.

The Mahratta main advance against Mysore became so threatening that Haidar Ali shut himself up in Seringapatam, which was invested. As before, Haidar bought off the Mahrattas by payment of a large sum of money, nominally in tribute. The Mahrattas then moved on Bangalore. Haidar appealed to the English for help under the Treaty of 1769, but, influenced by the Navāb Muhammad Ali, the English declined to assist him.]

A.D. 1772. [Muhammad Ali of Arcot obtained British assistance and recovered some of his lost territory.

Haidar bought off the Mahrattas by promise of payment of tribute.

The Pēshwa Mādhava Rao died and was succeeded by his brother Nārayan Rao; but his uncle Raghunātha Rao actually governed for his nephew, and entered on a war against the Subahdār Nizām Ali. This did not last long and peace was made.

The Emperor Shāh Ālam, overawed by the Mahrattas, admitted them into Delhi and granted them two provinces, one of which was Allahabad.

Warren Hastings became Governor of Bengal.]

A.D. 1773. [The Pēshwa Narāyan Rao imprisoned his uncle Raghunātha Rao, but was himself murdered. Raghunatha was then made Pēshwa.

Muhammad Ali of Arcot, with English aid, advanced against Tanjore, which was captured in June. Rāja Tuljāji was made prisoner, but was released after a Treaty had been signed, by which the Rāja consented to allow the English to garrison Tanjore. He also bound himself to protect English interests and gave a grant of 277 villages.]

A.D. 1774. An inscription in Mysore names Chāma Rāja VIII as Rāja, but states that the ' ruler of the earth ' was Haidar Ali Bahādur. (*E.C. v, Bl. 65.*)

[Raghunātha Rao, the new Pēshwa, came to terms with Haidar Ali and gave him three Mahratta districts. The birth of a posthumous son to the late Pēshwa Nārāyan Rao destroyed Raghunātha's claim to be Pēshwa.

The English in Bombay took Thānā and Salsette from the Portuguese.]

A.D. 1775. [The Navāb of Bengal ceded Benares and other large tracts to the English.

Raghunātha Rao of Poona made a Treaty, called the ' Treaty of Surat,' with the English ceding to the Company in Bombay, in return for their support, some large tracts. The Bengal Government disapproved of this Treaty, but it was upheld by the Directors in England.

Beṭṭada Chāma Raja VIII of Mysore died, and Haidar Ali placed on the throne a child, Khāsa Chāma IX.]

An inscription in Salem district of 'Immaḍi Vīra' mentioning him as Raja of Mysore. It is doubtful whether this was a name of Beṭṭada Chāma or of his successor Khāsa Chāma.

(*V.R. ii. Salem, 135.*)

Another shews Chāma Rāja IX on the throne of Mysore, ruling from Seringapatam.

(*E.C. iv. Yl. 4.*)

Tuljājī of the Tanjore Mahratta dynasty built the wall of a temple in the capital.

(*V.R. ii. Tan., 892 ; 516 of 1904.*)

A.D. 1776. [A new Treaty, called the 'Treaty of Purandhar', was made between the Company and the Pēshwa. It superseded the Treaty of Surat and was not so favourable to the English. By it Raghunātha Rao agreed to retire and accept a pension. The Directors in England, however, insisted on the full confirmation of the Treaty of Surat 'under every circumstance'. Raghunātha Rao therefore again took the field, but unsupported by the English.

Lord Pigot, Governor of Madras, insisted on the restoration of Tuljajī, Rāja of Tanjore, who had been conquered by the English and the Navāb of Arcot, Muhammad Ali, in 1773. In doing so, he seriously offended the Navāb.

Haidar Ali overran Cochin and exacted tribute from the Rāja.

Tīpū, his son, devastated the country about Ānegundi and dispossessed its Raja Tirumala or Timmappa, who was now the representative of the dispossessed Fourth Dynasty of the older Vijayanagar Empire.]

A.D. 1777. [Rāma Rāja, or Rājā Rām, of Sātāra, died.

Hector Munro was made Commander-in-Chief in Madras, under the Governor, Sir Horace Rumbold.]

A.D. 1778. [Haidar Ali and the Sātāra Mahrattas fighting against one another near Bellary. Haidar defeated his enemies near Adoni.

War between France and England broke out again in Europe. The news reached Madras in July. Haidar Ali sided with the French. All parties seemed to be in disagreement with one another about the Pēshwa Raghunātha Rao's anomalous position.

In October, the English took Pondicherry and other French places.

In November, Basālat Jang, brother of Nizām Ali, the Subahdār of the Dekhan, ceded Guntūr to the English for a fixed annual payment, promising to dismiss the French.]

A.D. 1779. Nānā Farnavīs, or 'Phaḍnavīs', became Minister to Mādhava Rao II, the Pēshwa in name, aged six years, and took the field to drive out Raghunātha Rao, the ex-Peshwa, who actually governed. He attacked the English in the Konkan who assisted Raghunātha and drove them back.

The last French Settlement, Mahē, was captured by the English. Haidar protested, but in vain. Haidar then, bitterly opposed to the English, obtained the assistance of the Subahdār Nizām Ali and invaded Guntūr to prevent its becoming the property of the Company.]

A.D. 1780. An inscription records the grant of a village in Cuddapah by the Navāb Wālājāh.

(*V.R. i. Cudd., 111.*)

[In the Dekhan, an English force defeated the Mahrattas who attacked them and captured Ahmadābād.

The Supreme Court disapproved of the cession of the Guntūr Sarkar, and ordered its restoration to Basālat Jang.

Near Conjevaram Haidar Ali contrived to interpose a strong force between two British Brigades, and at Puḷḷalūr (Polilore), the English were badly beaten, only sixteen out of eighty-six officers with the troops surviving the action, and the regiments losing heavily. Munro was compelled to retire to Madras, throwing his guns into the lake at Chingleput. Haidar then seized Arcot.

A disastrous famine this year in the southern Telugu districts.]

A.D. 1781. [The English again took the field and under Sir Eyre Coote fought and defeated Haidar Ali. Coote took Chittoor but could not hold it as his force was weak. Haidar was driven away from Wandewash.

At Ahmadābād the English were compelled to retire, the Mahratta army being very large.

War broke out in Europe between the Dutch and the English, and Lord Macartney, Governor of Madras, seized the Dutch Settlements at Sadras and Pulicat. The Dutch settlements of Negapatam and other places submitted to the English.

A Treaty was made between the English and Muhammad Ali of Arcot, whereby he was recognized as hereditary ruler of Arcot and the territories under the Navāb, and in return he assigned the revenues of those districts for five years to the Company.]

An inscription of this year shews that a Muhammadan officer in authority in Kurnool ordered a certain Mallā Reḍḍi to put down dacoity and robbery which were so prevalent in the country, to save the peaceful population from the ravages committed by Haidar's soldiery, and to assist the officers of the 'Honourable Company.' (*V.R. ii, Kurn. 201.*)

A.D. 1782. An inscription records the death of Haidar Ali in this year (*E.C. ii, Sr. 23*). Another mentions Haidar, calling him 'Navāb Haidar Ali'. (*E.C. xi, Mi. 18, 19.*)

[The English defeated Haidar Ali and Tīpū his son, and relieved Vellore. But Tīpū succeeded in defeating a British force, and in capturing Cuddalore. Haidar was now unsupported by the French. He compelled Sir Eyre Coote to retire to Madras.

Haidar Ali died in camp near Chittoor, and was succeeded by Tīpū, now practically King of Mysore.

The English captured Tellicherry from the Mysoreans.

Basālat Jang, brother of Nizām Ali, Subahdār of the Dekhan, died this year.]

A.D. 1783. [Tīpū left Arcot and retired to Bednūr. He was defeated there, and Bednūr and Anantapūr were captured by the English.

But a little later, Tīpū recovered them.

Several of the Madura Pāḷēgārs in Madura and Tinnevelly rose against the English, but they were reduced to subjection, and Karūr and Dinḍigal were occupied by British troops.

Peace was proclaimed between the French and the English in Europe, and Pondicherry was restored to the French and Trinkomalī to the Dutch.

Palghāt and Coimbatore were captured from Tīpū, but were restored under orders from Madras.]

A.D. 1784. [Tīpū besieged Mangalore for a year and compelled the British ı late. Then he and the English came to terms, each party agreeing to surrender its

A.D. 1785. [Tīpū now fought against the Mahrattas.

A Treaty was made between the English and the Company as to the method of settling Muhammad Ali, Navāb of Arcot's debts. Some territory was ceded to the English.]

A grant of villages by Tīpū Sultan in Cuddapah District. *(V.R. i, 364.)*

A.D. 1786. Tīpū Sultān called, in an inscription in E. Mysore, 'Emperor of the Faithful'. *(V.R. x, Kl. 119.)*

[The Mahrattas joined the Subahdār Nizām Ali and made war on Tīpū. The allies captured Bādāmi, then held by the Mysoreans, and Adoni; but did not hold the latter place and Tīpū reoccupied it.]

A.D. 1787. [Tīpū seized Raidrug and Harpanhalli in the Bellary District, part of the territories belonging to the Rāja of Ánegundi, the descendant of the Vijayanagar Emperors. He concluded an Armistice with the Mahrattas, giving up to them Bādāmi, Kiṭṭūr and Nārgunḍ, and agreeing to pay a sum of money.

Amara Simha or Amīr Singh became ruler of Tanjore on Tuljāji's death. He asked the English for support and agreed to pay 45 lakhs of rupees per annum in return for the defence of his country.]

A.D. 1788. [The Guntūr Sarkar was this year finally surrendered to the English Company by the Subahdār Nizām Ali.]

An inscription records a grant of villages in Cuddapah District by Tīpū Sultān. *(V.R. i, Cudd. 390.)*

[A contemporary writer states that wherever they moved (and they were constantly on the move), the Mahratta soldiers were merciless in their treatment of the country-folk, destroying the crops, driving off the cattle and plundering the villages. *(Firishta, Scott's Edit., ii, 295, 331.)*

The Rohillas under Ghulām Khādir seized Delhi and the person of the Mughal Emperor Shāh Ālam II. The Emperor refusing to disclose the whereabouts of his treasures, Ghulām Khādir caused the Emperor's children to be lifted high up and dashed to the ground before their father's eyes. The Emperor was then himself thrown to the ground, sat upon, and his eyes stabbed out with a dagger. The people of Delhi deserted the city in crowds. The Mahrattas arrived on August 16, and also plundered the city. No food was given to those inhabiting the places and two infant princes died of starvation. Between August 21 and 26, eleven ladies of the palace were starved to death, and their bodies were thrown over the walls. On the 27th, four other ladies threw themselves over the walls, and their bodies were stripped by the soldiers. The Mahrattas cut off all supplies from the country. On September 10, Ghulām Khādir set fire to all combustible parts of the citadel, and then marched out to meet the Mahrattas.] *(Firishta, Scott's Edit., ii, 293 ff.)*

A.D. 1789. [A Tripartite Treaty was made this year between the English Company at Madras, the Pēshwa Mādhava Rao II of Poona and the Subahdār Nizām Ali, with the object of crushing Tīpū Sultan of Mysore. All conquered lands were to be divided, and the English were to send into the field a force of 10,000 men.

In Europe, the French Revolution broke out.

There was a prolonged drought in South India lasting for three years. A tenth of the population of the Northern Sarkars died of starvation.]

A.D. 1790. [Tīpū took Travancore, Erode and other places, and laid siege to Trichinopoly, devastating all those districts. The English freed Travancore from Tīpū's troops, and defeated them at Calicut.]

A.D. 1791. An inscription relates that Nizām Ali of Haidarābād, Subahdār of the Dekhan, appointed an agent to manage his affairs in Kurnool District. (*V. R. ii, Kurn. 195.*)

[A Treaty was made between the English and Rāmavarma, Rāja of Cochin—the English to protect the Rāja against Tīpū, the Rāja to pay a certain sum every year.]

The English stormed and took the fort at Bangalore. They fought Tipū nine miles from Seringapatam but were compelled to retire as their allies did not come up to their assistance. On their arrival the allies captured Hōsūr, Rāyakoṭṭa and Nandidrūg, and returned to Bangalore. The English then occupied Krishṇagiri.

Tīpū captured Coimbatore, inducing the garrison to march out on favourable terms. On their doing so, he seized them and sent them in chains to Seringapatam.

A.D. 1792. [Piracy was very rife on the West Coast. Some of their strongholds were captured.

The English captured Shimōga in N.-W. Mysore.

The allies attacked Seringapatam. Tīpū temporized, and a temporary suspension of arms was ordered, to allow for discussion of terms of a treaty. But while the discussion was going on, Tipū's cavalry attacked the English camp. They were beaten off; afterwards the Treaty was duly made. Large tracts were ceded to the English. Tīpū agreed to pay heavy ransom, and to release all prisoners, his two sons joining the English camp as hostages.

The Treaty left Tīpū in possession of Mysore proper. The Bāramhāl country, Dindigal, Malabar and Coorg were given to the English; some country North of the Tungabhadra River and the district of Cuddapah were given to Nizām Ali of Haidarabād; and to the Mahrattas, it was given to extend their boundary to the Tungabhadra.

Tīpū's two sons thereupon arrived in the British camp; and the British army retired to Madras.]

A.D. 1793. [War was again declared in Europe between France and England. The English therefore again seized the French settlements.

The Rāja of Tanjore made a treaty with Lord Cornwallis at Madras promising to pay the expenses of garrisoning his country with British troops.

The English Company's government declined to assist Nizām Ali of Haidarabad to start a war on his own account against the Mahrattas, their treaty engagement only being to help him against his enemies if he were attacked or was in danger. The Nizām however, frightened by the large demands made on him by the Mahrattas, prepared for war.

Tīpū paid his treaty-indemnity and his two sons were restored to him.]

A.D. 1795. Tīpū reigning in Bellary District. Inscription shewing that a mosque was built at Hospet in Hijra 1210. (*680 of 1922.*)

[After a year of manœuvring the armies of Nizām Ali and of the Mahrattas met at Kardā and a pitched battle was fought—1,30,000 Mahrattas against 1,10,000 men from Haidarābād. The Nizām was beaten. He was surrounded in Kardā fort and was forced to capitulate, promising to cede large tracts to the Pēshwa.

Muhammad Ali, Navāb of Arcot, died, and was succeeded by his son Umdat-ul-Umarā.

The District of Tinnevelly was taken over by the English from the Rāja of Tanjore as payment for a garrison sent for his protection.

The Dutch at Cochin surrendered to the English.

At Sātāra the Peshwa Mādhava Rao II, unable to bear the humiliating treatment accorded to him by Nānā Farnavīs, threw himself in despair from a window and was killed.

The Raja of Travancore made a treaty of perpetual peace and amity with the English, promising to pay a subsidy for his protection and for a garrison of the Company's troops to secure the safety of the country.

Khāsa Chāma Rāja of Mysore died. Tīpū despoiled and imprisoned the dead Rāja's family and seized the throne of Mysore under the title ' Tipū Sultān.']

A.D. 1796. [Abbā Sahib, or Sāhūjī II, adopted son of Rājā Rām II, was now Rāja of Sātāra and Bājī Rao II, son of Raghunātha Rao was Pēshwa. But the latter's brother Chimnāji formed a party hostile to him which proclaimed Chimnājī as Pēshwa.]

A.D. 1797. An inscription on a tank-bund near Mysore at Ānandūr constructed at great cost for irrigation purposes, tells us that Tīpū Sultan of Mysore took from the cultivators using the water, three quarters of the produce, leaving them only one quarter for their support. The inscription quotes the Sultan's command—' Whoever cultivates waste land [under this channel ?] will pay to the God-given government *three parts of the produce, the same as other cultivators*, but the fourth part will be remitted in the way of God'—i.e., in charity. His position clearly was that the whole produce belonged to himself as ruler and owner of the entire soil of the country including the waste, but that out of kindness of heart he allowed the ryots a small portion for their maintenance. This was done purely out of charity—' the way of God.' (*E C. iii, My. 54.*)

Nānā Farnavīz, Dewān of Bājī Rao the Pēshwa, while on a visit to the Mahratta Raja Sindia, was seized by his opponents. Poona was in an uproar and much faction fighting took place. Nānā Farnavīz was taken prisoner to Ahmadnagar.

Amara Simha Rāja of Tanjore governed very badly and was deposed, and Rāja Tuljājī's adopted son Sarfōjī was made Rāja in his place.]

A.D. 1798. [Tīpū Sultan intrigued with the French with the object of overthrowing the English and Lord Mornington, the Governor-Gennral resolved on making open war against him, as all other measures had failed. The Subahdār Nizām Ali concurred and declared his intention of disbanding his French soldiers and maintaining six battalions of English-trained sepoys in their place. This declaration had its effect and Tīpū for a time became more friendly to the English, though he was still very arrogant, and did not cease attempting to get French support.

An Irish officer in the Pēshwa's army, W.H. Tone, has left on record his opinion regarding the state of the people in the principal Mahratta State at this time. He warmly praises the character of the mass of the people, but points out that they were made miserable by misgovernment. ' There is not on record an example of any government so little calculated to give protection to the subject as the ...... system of the Mahrattas; an administration formed of rapacity, corruption and inability. To this may be ascribed the accumulated misery of the people,—oppression, poverty and famine.' Every year, the writer tells us, at the time of the Dasara festival armies were collected for some marauding expedition. In the camp the rulers decided whether they should fight an open enemy, or spread over the country to compel the ryots and merchants to pay *chauth* (enforced extra taxation), or simply to proceed against some neighbouring kingdom and destroy it. So that every year masses of soldiery flooded the country and rendered peaceful agriculture impossible. Dr. Sen, in his work on the *Administrative system of the Mahrattas*, records that the Pēshwa Bājī Rao reintroduced the old system of farming out the revenue (which, to his credit Śivājī had abolished). All the sections of the country were sold to the highest bidder, each of whom paid himself out of the pockets of the ryots and used no mercy in doing so (*Ind. Ant. 1924, vol. liii, p. 72*). And this is not all, for, when some individual had purchased the lease of a district, his lease was often summarily cancelled by the authorities owing to someone having subsequently made a higher offer; so the leaseholders were driven to practise extortion unrestrained. If a farmer of revenue failed in his payments he and those who had stood security for him were often thrown into prison and all their property confiscated. Moreover the administration of civil and criminal justice was entrusted to these very farmers of the revenue, and they increased their own gains by fines and unchecked bribery. And lastly, the *Bombay Gazetteer* (*I. Part ii, p. 113*) states 'the complaints of the people were never listened to by those in authority at Poona.']

A.D. 1799. An inscription in Mysore records the death of Tīpū Sultan at Seringapatam.

(*E.C. iii, Sr. 24.*)

[Open war was declared this year against Tīpū of Mysore. In March a body of Mysoreans was defeated on the Coorg frontier. General Harris, in command of an army of 37,000 men, defeated Tīpū at Maḷavalli, east of Seringapatam, on March 27, and took Seringapatam by storm on May 4. During the assault Tīpū was shot, and died. His body was honourably buried. The troops began sacking the city but their depredations were ruthlessly put down by Colonel Arthur Wellesley (afterwards Duke of Wellington) who flogged and hanged his men till order was completely restored and he gained the confidence of the people of the city.]

[Mysore was then, according to treaty, partitioned between Mysore, the Company and the Subahdār Nizām Ali; the Company taking some Southern Districts and the Nizām an equal portion on the North-East. The Nothern part, including parts of Bellary, Harpanhalli and Ānegundi, which had constituted the home-territory of the family of the Vijayanagar kings were offered to the Mahrattas but they declined to accept them. These tracts had belonged to the Ānegundi (Vijayanagar) Rājas for 400 years, and had been seized by Tīpū only 13 years before this partition. They were then divided between the Company and the Nizām, with the Tungabhadra river as boundary,—the Nizām taking the territory north and the Company the district south of the river.]

[A report by Major Macleod made in 1799 fully noted in the *Coimbatore District Manual* (p. 172), throws great light on the oppression of the population there by their own rulers at this time. A list of no less than sixty separate taxes which were at this time in full force and effect is given by him. Corruption was rampant, the richer inhabitants bribing the village officers to gain exemption from payments, and being given priveleges withheld from the poor. Industry was hampered by requisitions. Men were taxed for their market baskets and empty bags, irrespective of the goods carried which had to pay duty. Women squatting by the roadside and selling petty wares, were made to pay rates varying from a star-pagoda (3½ rupees) to 9½ annas. There was a tax on everyone who wore a caste-mark on his forehead, on every article in a shop, on every head of cattle or sheep, on leaves collected from jungle trees. Two years later the Madras Board of Revenue reported that the toll-collectors on roads wrung from travellers double as much as was due to the treasury.

After the treaty-partition of Tīpū's territory—the major part of his country was constituted into the kingdom of Mysore, of which Mummaḍi Krishna Rāja was made Mahārāja, with Pūrṇayya for his minister. A treaty was then made with Mysore.

Rāja Sarfōjī of Tanjore ceded to the English the whole of his territory for the sake of peace and tranquillity, on condition of receiving a sum equivalent to £40,000 and one-fifth of the annual revenue of the State, and having the fort for his residence.]

A.D. 1800. [Nānā Farnavīs, the minister to the Pēshwa, died this year. The whole of the Mahratta State was now in a condition of anarchy and confusion. The Pēshwa, Sindia, Kolhāpūr and other parties were all fighting one another.

The Subahdār of the Dekhan, Nizām Alī, ceded to the English some of the districts that had come into his hands, amongst others, Cuddapah and Kurnool, in return for British protection in all events.]

A.D. 1801. [Umdat-ul-Umara, Navāb of Arcot, died. His son Husain Ali declined office, since it was burdened with so many concessions to the Company. His cousin Azīmu-d-daula therefore became Nāvāb.

Pondicherry was restored to the French under the Treaty of Amiens.]

A.D. 1802. [Anarchy in the Mahratta Provinces. The Mahārājas, Holkar and Sindia, fighting one another. The Pēshwa, Bājī Rao II (who has a very bad reputation for cruelty) in alarm took refuge with the English in Bombay, and, after some wavering, consented to make a treaty. By this he was again placed in power in Poona and was given for his support and defence a subsidiary force of 16 battalions. On his part he ceded, for their maintenance, territory sufficient to yield 26 lakhs of rupees annually.]

A.D. 1803. [The Subahdār Nizām Ali and the English leagued together to try and compel Holkar and other disaffected Mahratta leaders to submit to the Pēshwa. Holkar and Sindia both refused and the latter even demanded the disbandment of the British army. A war therefore ensued, the British and Haidarābād governments trying to support the Pēshwa against his enemies.

Ahmadnagar was occupied in August by General Wellesley. Sindia was defeated by General Lake, who took Aligarh. The Bombay army took Baroda. General Lake went North, was attacked by the French near Delhi and beat them, and then went to Delhi at the invitation of the Emperor Shah Ālam II.

Wellesley with a small force of 5,000 men attacked the hostile Mahratta army at Assaye, near the North-Western frontier of the Nizam's dominions, and, though they numbered nearly 50,000, completely defeated them. He then seized Asīrgarh and Burhānpūr.

Lake took Agra, and, being attacked by a joint body of Mahrattas and French, defeated them at the battle of Laswārī, and they were again defeated at Argaon.

Sindia then submitted.

Orissa, which had fallen into the power of independent Mahratta chiefs, was conquered by an English force.

Nizām Ali, Subahdār of the Dekhan, died in August and was succeeded by his son Mīrza Sikandar Jāh.

War with the French now raging in Europe, the English again took possession of Pondicherry and the other French possessions.]

A.D. 1804. [A special declaration of war was made against Mahārāja Holkar, and an English army captured his capital Indore. Holkar then moved North and attacked Delhi, but he was repulsed by General Lake, and fled to Deeg (Dīg). On that place being attacked, he was forced to capitulate.

Sindia ceded some territory to Haidarābād.]

A.D. 1805. [Peace was made with Holkar and a treaty drawn up.

Sindia was confirmed as Mahārāja at Gwalior.]

A.D. 1806. [The treaty with Holkar was ratified.

Death of the Emperor Shāh Ālam II at Delhi. His son succeeded him under the title of 'Akbar II.'

At Vellore, where Tīpū's family were sheltered in the fort, a number of sepoys of the British army revolted, shot their officers and hoisted Tīpū's flag. Colonel Gilliespie hurried from Arcot, blew open the gates of the Vellore fort and quelled the disturbance. Some of the Mysore princes were sent to Calcutta.]

A.D. 1808. [Abbā Sahib or Sāhujī II, Mahratta Rāja of Sātāra died, and was succeeded by his son Pratāpa Simha.

A rising in Travancore was subdued.]

A.D. 1809. Two inscriptions in a village near Tanjore, of Rāja Sarfōjī.

(*V. R. ii, Tan. 1276, 1277 ; 166, 167 of 1911.*)

A.D. 1811. Mummaḍi Krishna Rāja IV of Mysore reigning. (*E. C. vi, Kp. 48.*)

[He dismissed this year his minister, Pūrṇayya.]

A.D. 1812. [There was much disturbance in the country caused by Pindāri roving bands, men who had formerly been in the service of the Mahrattas.

Pūrṇayya died. Also Rāja Śivājī III of Kolhāpur. The latter was succeeded by his son Sambhājī, or Abbā Sahib. In return for protection he ceded some territory to the English Company.]

A.D. 1814. [The Dutch rights in Cochin were ceded to the Company.]

A.D. 1815. [Attacks by the Pindāris suppressed.]

A.D. 1816. [The Pindāris attacked the Northern Districts, called the 'Northern Sarkars,' and sacked the town of Kimedi in Ganjam District.]

A.D. 1817. [The Pindāris were badly beaten in actions fought near Haidarābād and in Orissa. They were, later in the year, driven out by British troops.

The wanton cruelties of the Pindāris during their raids is almost beyond belief. Every respectable-looking citizen was put to horrid tortures by them in order to extort from him information as to the whereabouts of his supposed wealth. Everything was destroyed and ruined. Houses were pulled down and their contents stolen. Women and children were ravished and murdered in the presence of their husbands and parents. The whole invaded country was reduced to a condition of chaos, from which it had to be rescued after the English had gained the upper hand. Colonel Tod, who was in Rājputana from 1812 to 1823, states that eight months after peace had been made 'three hundred towns and villages (in the neighbourhood of Udaipur) were *simultaneously* reinhabited and the land, which for many years had been a stranger to the plough-share, was broken up.'

A treaty was made between the English and the Mahratta Pēshwa Bājī Rao. He acknowledged himself a feudatory of the Company and ceded to them Ahmadnagar and other Districts. Later, however, he became more hostile and aggressive, owing to so many British troops being engaged against the Pindāri freebooters. Bodies of Mahrattas collected, Bājī Rao burned the Residency at Poona, and the British garrison at Kirki was attacked, but in vain. Bājī Rao then fled. The Mahratta Rājas of Nagpur and Indore rose against the English but were defeated in the open field, the former at Sītābaldi and the latter at Mahīdpur. The Nāgpur territories North of the Narbadā were ceded to the Company.]

A.D. 1818. [The Mahraṭṭas with 20,000 men attacked a small English garrison at Koregāon, which held out against the enemy, the sepoys behaving with great gallantry.

Bāji Rao, finding his position hopeless, surrendered to the English, and Lord Malcolm, with, as some think, misplaced generosity allowed him to retire and live at Bithūr on a handsome pension. His adopted son was Nānā Sahib who fought against the English in 1857. The office of Pēshwa was now, once for all, abolished.

Holkar submitted, and ceded large tracts. The Rāja of Sātāra and the Rāna of Udaipūr also surrendered. Pratāpa Simha of Sātāra was allowed to retain certain of his dominions but ceded a large portion to the Company.]

A.D. 1819. [Appā Sahib of Nagpūr broke the treaty he had made, two months after signing it. He attacked the English again and his fort, Aligarh, where he had taken refuge was stormed and captured. Appā Sahib fled.

Pratāpa Sīmha, Rāja of Sātāra, was restored to power. He agreed that his territory should be held as subordinate to the Company and that the whole administration of it should be vested in an English Resident for three years.

Azīmu-d-daulah, Navāb of Arcot, died. His son Āzam Jāh succeeded him.]

A.D. 1821. [The Mahratta Rāja of Kolhāpur, Abbā Sahib or Sambhājī was murdered; his infant son also 'died'; and his brother Shāhjī or Bāwā Sahib became Rāja in his place.]

A.D. 1822. [Bāwā Sahib began by governing badly and behaved with cruelty to his people.

The Nizām of Haidarābād was presented with an increase of territory by the English in consideration of his aid against the Pindāris.]

A.D. 1823. [By arrangement with the Nizām of Haidarabād the English Company now became possessed of the Northern Sarkars in absolute ownership. These are the modern districts of Ganjam, Vizagapatam, Godavari, Kistna (Krishna) and Guntūr. A large sum of money was paid to him.]

A.D. 1824. [War with Burmah, whose king was threatening the North-East of India. British troops garrisoned Rangoon for the protection of the merchants and made it their war-base.

In a Mahratta rising at Kiṭṭūr the English Government agent Mr. Thackeray was murdered and the Kolhāpur Rāja Bāwā Sahib took the field.]

A.D. 1825. [A new treaty was made with Bāwā Sahib by which he guaranteed peace and tranquillity.]

A.D. 1829. [Thuggism was very prevalent all over India, and strong measures were taken for its suppression.

Sikandar Shāh, Nizām of Haidarābād and Subahdār of the Dekhan, died, and was succeeded by his son Farkhundah Ali Khān Nasiru-d-daulah. His Dewān was Sir Sālār Jang.

In Travancore Rāmavarma became Rāja.]

A.D. 1830. [A serious rising took place among the agricultural population of Mysore, owing to the Rāja's harsh treatment of them and his oppression. It was suppressed by the English. The ryots' grievances were enquired into and redressed.]

A.D. 1831. [The Mysore Rāja Mummaḍi Krishna was deposed on account of his unjust and cruel treatment of his subjects; and an English Commissioner was appointed to secure proper and just rule in that country.]

A.D. 1832. [The Rāja of Coorg, Vīra Rājēndra, was found guilty of monstrous cruelties and many murders, and was formally pronounced debarred from all friendship with the British in India.]

A.D. 1833. [The Rāja of Coorg was solemnly warned by the English Government in Madras that he must change his ways and rule justly, or must take the consequences.]

A.D. 1834. [He refused flatly to be coerced by any outside power, and would rule as he pleased. A force of 6,000 men was then sent to Coorg. The Rāja submitted and was declared deposed, and his territory was made over to British administration.

The agricultural population of Kimedi in Ganjam broke out into open rebellion against their own Rāja, whose oppression had become unbearable. The rising was put down by the English and an enquiry instituted into the evils complained of.]

A.D. 1837. [Death of the Emperor of Delhi, Akbar Shāh II. He was succeeded by his son Muhammad Bahādur Shāh II.]

A.D. 1838. [War declared against the Afghāns, whose Amīr was led astray by Russian influence working for the overthrow of English supremacy in India. The Amir had formed a federation of Russia, Persia and Afghanistan. A mission had been sent to Kabul headed by Capt., afterwards, Sir Alexander Burns, but it failed of effect, and nothing remained but an appeal to arms. A tripartite treaty was made between the Saduzai chief Shāh Shūjah, the Sikh leader Rānjit Singh and the English. The Barukhzai Amir of Kābul was pronounced deposed and Shāh Shūjah declared Amīr in his place. Shāh Shūjah was in fact by birth the rightful Amīr.]

[Death of Bārrā Sahib of Kolhāpur and accession of Śivāji, as Rāja. A British minister was appointed to ensure good government in the State.]

A.D. 1839. [Shāh Shūjah was enthroned as Amīr of Afghanistān. Sir John Keane took Ghazni from the Barukhzais who declined to accept Shāh Sūjah as Amīr.

In the Khaibar Pass the fort of Ali Masjid was captured by English troops.

The Company took over the administration of the State of Cochin.

At Sātāra, Pratāpa Simha was deposed for misgovernment and his brother Shāhji alias Appā Sāhib was made Rāja.]

A.D. 1840. [In Afghanistān the Barukhzai Amīr Dost Muhammad surrendered to Sir William Macnaghten, the British envoy, at Kābul and was sent to Calcutta.]

A.D. 1841. [The Ghilzai and Khaibarī tribes of Afghans rose against the English. Eldred Pottinger was forced to take refuge in Kābul.

Sir Alexander Burns was murdered in Kābul. The British treasury there was plundered. And Akbar Khān, son of Dost Muhammad, with his own hand, killed Sir William Macnaghten.

General Sale cleared the passes and reached Gandamak.]

A.D. 1842. [General Elphinstone surrendered to the Afghans. He made a treaty, agreed to retire, consented to pay a large ransom, and left hostages at Kābul. But on his retreat he was attacked in the Khaibar Pass and his whole force of 4,500 men and 12,000 camp-followers were massacred. Only one man, Dr. Brydon, contrived to escape to Jalālābād which was held by General Sale. Elphinstone himself was seized by Akbar Khān.

The Afghāns at Kandahār were defeated.

Jalālābād was invested by Akbar Khān. Ghazni was furiously attacked by Ghāzis. At Kābul Shāh Shujah was murdered.

The English then succeeded in defeating the Afghans in the Khaibar Pass, and they marched on Kābul, seized the place, enthroned Fath Khān, son of Shāh Shūjah, as Amīr and retired safely to Peshāwar.

Dost Muhammad was released and allowed to return to Kābul.]

A.D. 1843. [The Gwalior Mahrattas under Mahārāja Sindia again began to concentrate their forces, but they were defeated in two battles, and Sindia's government submitted and ceased fighting.

The Rāja of Kolhāpur continuing to misgovern and oppress his people, the entire State was formally taken under British rule. Its forts were dismantled and its army disbanded.]

A.D. 1844. [More trouble at Kolhāpur, the British agent Dājī Krishna Pandit being seized and imprisoned. Troops were sent and order was restored.]

A.D. 1845. [Tranquebar was sold by the Danes to the Company.

The Sikhs raised the army of the Khālsa and invested Firōzpur, defying the English. Sir Hugh Gough, in command of a British force, fought a great battle at Mūdki (Moodkee) and won a victory, but with heavy loss of life.]

A.D. 1846. [The battles of Aliwal and Sobraon gained by the English over the Sikhs completed the defeat of the latter. A treaty of peace was made.

Rāmavarma, Rāja of Travancore, died, and was succeeded by Mārtāṇḍavarma.]

A.D. 1848. [Shāhji, Rāja of Sātāra, died. There being no heir to the throne, the whole State was annexed to the Company's Government.

The Sikhs again broke out into open warfare. Multan was besieged by the English, but the siege had to be raised for a time because of the desertion from the English army of a large force of sepoys. The siege was resumed later in the year.]

A.D. 1849. [Multan was taken by storm. Shēr Singh, commanding the Sikhs, continued to fight, was defeated at the battles of Chillianwallah and Gujarat, and was compelled to submit.

Mahārāja Dhulīp Singh resigned the whole of the Panjāb into the hands of the English in return for protection and a pension.

A slight rising of Māppilas (Moplahs) on the West Coast.]

A.D. 1850. [A mutiny of sepoy troops was suppressed.]

A.D. 1851. [The Nizām of Haidarābād relinquished further territory to the Company in payment of a debt due by him.

War in Burmah, resulting in Pegu being annexed to Britain.]

A.D. 1852. [The Pēshwa, Bājī Rao, died at Bithūr. His son Dunḍhu Panth, *alias* Nānā Sahib, succeeded him nominally, but the Pēshwa's authority had ceased to exist as long ago as 1818. His father's pension, which was considered a personal one, was not continued to the son.]

A.D. 1853. [Berar ceded to the English by the Nizām of Haidarābad in liquidation of his debt.

Ravivarma was installed as Rāja of Cochin.]

A.D. 1855. [In Calicut the Māppilas (Moplahs) subdued and disarmed. Later, however, some fanatics murdered Mr. Conolly.

The Navāb of Arcot, or 'of the Karnāṭaka,' having died childless, his territories were annexed by the English government and a pension was given to his uncle Āzīm Jāh, who was recognized as titular Navāb. His troops were disbanded in the next year.

Śivājī, Rāja of Tanjore, died without heirs. The title now became extinct. The territory had already been ceded to the Company.]

A.D. 1856. [The former Barukhzai Amīr of Kābul, who had submitted to the Company in 1842, seized Kandahar.

Annexation of Oudh.

Tanjore was occupied by British troops.]

A.D. 1857. [Great Mutiny of the sepoys in the north at Bahrāmpur, Meerut and Lucknow The sepoys marched on Delhi, where also the sepoys mutinied and killed many European residents. There were more risings in many places. Nānā Sahib of Bithūr joined the rising, captured 130 English and killed them all. The English army moved up to save Delhi and captured the Ridge. At Cawnpore Nānā Sahib offered refuge in boats to 450 English, and then, opening fire on the boats, killed the men and carried off the women. A horrible massacre then took place, the bodies of the dead being thrown into a well.

Havelock won several victories and Nānā Sahib fled.

The Lucknow Residency was besieged.

In September, Delhi was stormed by the English forces. The Palace was captured. The two sons and a grandson of the Emperor Bahādur Shāh were killed. The English also relieved Cawnpore and were successful at many other places against scattered bodies of mutineers. The Lucknow Residency was relieved on November 9.

At Haidarābād, the Nizām Nāsiru-d-daulah died and was succeeded by his son Afzūlu-d-daulah.]

A.D. 1858. [The English continued to gain many victories over the mutineers.

The Emperor Bahādur Shāh was deposed.

In Central India more fighting. Jhānsi was besieged and taken. Battles with Tāntia Topi, the Maharatta chief, cousin of Nānā Sahib. Gwalior was captured.

A rising in Dhārwār, where the British Political Agent was murdered, was put down.

In this year on November 1, the whole of the East India Company's territories in India was transferred to the Crown.

The Sepoy Mutiny was finally quelled by the end of year.]

A.D. 1859. [A general peace was proclaimed throughout India. In all places, durbars were held and the disaffected Rājas and Chiefs submitted to the rule of Queen Victoria.]

A.D. 1860. [Death of Mārtāṇḍavarmā of Travancore, who was succeeded by his nephew Rāmavarmā.

A treaty was made with the new Nizām Afzūlu-d-daulah, and Raichūr and other districts north of the Tungabhadra were restored to him.]

A.D. 1862. [The State of Kolhāpur was restored, on his attaining majority, to the Rāja Śivāji, who promised to rule under the advice of the British authorities.]

A.D. 1864. [Ravivarma, Rāja of Cochin died. Rāmavarma became Rāja.]

A.D. 1865. [In Mysore the Rāja Mummaḍi Krishna adopted Chāma Rājēndra as his son.]

A.D. 1866. [Death of the Kolhāpur Rāja Śivājī without issue. He adopted as his son his nephew Rājā Rām.]

A.D. 1868. [Chāma Rājēndra became Rāja of Mysore on the death of Mummaḍi Krishna Rāja.

A.D. 1869. [Death of Afzūlu-d-daulah, Nizām of Haidarabād, and succession of his son Mīr Mahbub Ali Khān.]

A.D. 1876. [Queen Victoria proclaimed 'Empress of India.']

GENEALOGICAL TABLES

EARLY NORTH INDIA

SAIŚUNĀGA DYNASTY OF MAGADHA

Śiśunāga

C. 600 B.C.

He was succeeded in turn by *Kākavarṇa*, *Kshēmadharma*, *Kshattraujas* or *Kshatraujit*, and *Bimbisāra*

Bimbisāra

543–500 B.C

alias Śrēṇika, or Śēṇiya.
Md. princesses of the Kōsala and Lichchavi families.
Murdered by his son.

|

Ajātaśatru

C. 500–475 B.C.

Captured Vaiśāli. Fortified Pāṭaliputra

|

Darśaka

or Nāgadaśaka. *C.* 475–450 B.C.

|

Udayin

or Udaya, or Udayibhaddha

C. 450–417 B.C.

He was succeeded by *Nandivardhana* (*C.* 417–375 B.C.), and he by *Mahānandin* (*C.* 375 B.C.).

[*N.B.* Authorities differ as to the dates of the reigns of the kings down to the end of the Nanda dynasty. The dates here given are taken from the *Cambridge History of India*, with which, I note, Dr. L. D. Barnett generally agreed. Vincent Smith placed them all about forty years earlier. There is no dispute as to Chandragupta's initial date, 322-21 B.C.]

NANDA DYNASTY

Mahānandin's illegitimate son *Mahāpadma Nanda* usurped the throne of Magadha about 371 B.C.

He was succeeded by nine kings, all included in two generations. The dynasty was rooted out by the Maurya *Chandragupta* in 322–21 B.C.

MAURYA DYNASTY

Chandragupta was a man of mixed birth, the illegitimate son of a Nanda Prince by a woman of the people. In the troubles following Alexander's invasion he collected troops, fought the Macedonian garrisons and acquired extensive power. Then he turned against Nandas, killed the last king of that line, and finally established his authority over the greater part of Northern India from about 322-21 B.C.

Chandragupta
322/21—296 B.C.
|
Bindusāra
{ 'Amitraghāta.' 296–268 B.C. Extended his rule far to the south. }
|
Aśōka.
268–226 B.C.
He was crowned 264 B.C. (*Hultzsch*)
|
(a son)
|

Daśaratha (ruling Eastern Provinces)	***Samprati*** (ruling Western Provinces)

Several kings of the Maurya dynasty followed the grandsons of ***Aśōka*** but little is known about them. The Empire broke up in 184 B.C. when the Āndhra kings of the Telingana country and others had acquired power. The last Maurya king ***Brihadratha*** was killed in 185 B.C. by his general ***Pushyamitra***, who usurped the throne and founded a new but short-lived dynasty.

SUNGA DYNASTY

Pushyamitra
{ 184—148 B.C. Claims to have defeated the Āndhra king, Yājna-Śrī-Śātakarni in 170 B.C }
|
Agnimitra
148—140 B.C.
|

Sujyēshtha *C.* 140—133 B.C.	***Vasumitra*** *C.* 133—123 B.C.

Five successors are named but their relationships and dates are not definitely established. The last king of the line was ***Dēvabhūmi*** (82—72 B.C.). He was killed, in the carrying out of a plot against him, by his minister ***Vāsudēva***, who founded the Kāṇva dynasty.

KANVA DYNASTY

Vāsudēva
C. 72—63 B.C.
|
Bhūmimitra
{ *C.* 63—49 B.C. The Śakas were now in great force in Upper India }
|
Nārāyaṇa
C. 49—37 B.C.
|
Suśarman
{ *C.* 37—27 B.C. He was killed by an Andhra king. }

The Śakas then swept the dynasty out of existence, and the Kushan dynasty then founded which lasted till about 124 A.D.

KUSHAN DYNASTY

It seems useless at present to attempt to fix dates for the individual kings of this dynasty, as authorities differ widely on the subject; but it is advisable to give some notion to guide readers, and I have noted against some of the kings' names, dates which have received support from some quarters. At the same time it must be noted that Dr. Sten Konow's fixture for Kanishka's accession is about A.D. 125 or later.

Vajheshka

Kanishka
{ Founded a capital city near Peshawar and annexed Kashmir. Fleet's date for his accession is 58 B.C.[1] }

Vaśishka (predeceased his father) — *Huvishka* (?) 38 B.C.—A.D. 3.

After Huvishka the Kushan rule ceased for a time. *See* Fleet (*J.R.A.S*, 1912, p. 1009).

Vasudēva ruled *c.* A.D. 17-41. In his day *Gondophares* was ruling Bactria.

Kozulo-Kadphises, *c.* A.D. 45-85 (Fleet's date for him is A.D. 65). In his time the Yuch-chi hordes overran Afghanistan and Gandhara.

His son *Wima-Kadphises*, *c.* A.D. 85-125. Sent an Embassy to Rome in A.D. 99.

ŚAKA SATRAPS OF MAHĀRĀSHṬRA

A line of Śaka Satraps established themselves as rulers in the country about the Western Ghāts, with capital at or near Nasik. The names of only two are known—*Bhūmaka* and *Nahapāna*. Nahapāna was completely defeated by the Āndhra king Gautamiputra-Vilivāyakura II about A.D. 124, and his kingdom annexed.

THE ŚAKA DYNASTY

These rulers called themselves at first 'Satraps' or 'Kshatrapas'. Afterwards they were further dignified by the title 'Mahākshatrapa'. This line of kings was quite distinct from the Mahārāshṭra Kshatrapas (*Cf.: Bombay Gazetteer I, Part I, Gujarat, p. 20 ff., and p. 54*)

1. *Ghsamoṭika*
2. *Chashṭhana*, *c.* A.D. 125-130 Capital at Ujjain. Recaptured territories conquered by the Āndhra king.
3. *Jayadāman*, A.D. 130-140.
4. *Rudradāman*, *c.* A.D.[2] 140-158. Defeated the Āndhra king, Puḷumāyi II, his son-in-law.

Children of 4:
- 5. *Dāmaghsada* or Dāmajada I, *c.* A.D. 158-168.
- 7. Rudrasimha I, *c.* A.D. 180-197/8.
- Dau. *Dakshamitra* (*Md.* the Āndhra king, Puḷumāyi II.)

Children of 5:
- *Satyadāman.*
  - 9. *Prithvisēna* (?) A.D. 222.
- 6. Jivadāman, A.D. 178, 197/8.

Children of 7:
- 8. *Rudrasēna I*, *c.* A.D. 197/8-222.
  - 12. *Dāmajada II*, A.D. 232.
  - 13. *Viradāman*, A.D. 236
    - 17. *Rudrasēna II*, A.D. 256-272
      - 18. *Viśvasimha*, A.D. 272-278.
      - 19. *Bhartṛidāman*, A.D. 278-294.
        - 20. *Viśvasēna*, A.D. 294-300.
  - 14. *Yaśodāman I*, A.D. 239.
- 10. *Sanghadāman*, A.D. 222-226.
- 11. *Dāmasēna*, A.D. 226-236.
  - 15. *Vijayasēna*, A.D. 238-249.
  - 16. *Dāmajada III*, A.D. 249-256.

After A.D. 300 the old line ceased to exist.

[1] *J.R.A.S.* 1913, pp. 914 f.

[2] This ought to be 130 corresponding to 52 of the Andhau inscription—*Editor.*

21. Rudrasimha II, 'son of Jivadāman.' A.D. 308, 311, 317 (*E.I. xvi. 230*).
22. Yaśodāman II, A.D. 320
23. Dāmasiri, his brother A.D. 320.
24. Rudrasena III, 'son of Rudradāman.' A.D. 348-376.
25. Simhasena, 'sister's son of Rudrasena' III. Ruled as Western Kshatrapa. *c.* A.D. 382.
26. Rudrasena IV 'son of Simhasēna.'
27. Satyasimha, *c* A.D. 388, and his son Rudrasimha III

DYNASTIES OF SOUTH INDIA

ADIGAIMAN CHIEF

Also called 'Adigan', or 'Adiyamān', or 'Adiyan'. Ruled the tract in N. of Salem district and S Mysore with capital at Tagaḍūr, modern Dharmapuri. Very little is known about them.

An early Chera king is said to have conquered the Adiyamān and taken Tagadūr. An Adiyan fought against the Pāṇḍya king Neḍunjaḍaiyan, in alliance with the Pallava and Keraḷa kings—when there were battles at Āyiraveli, Āyirūr, and Pugaliyūr Another Adiyan fought against the Chōla king.

One of the Adigaimāns was named *Eḷini alias Yavanikā*. Another was *Vagan*, or *Rājarāja*, whose son was Viḍugādaḷagiya-Perumāl, *alias Vyāmukta-Śravaṇōjjvala* (*E. R. 1906, §34 ; E. I. VI, 331*). He was subordinate to the Chōla king Kulottunga Chola III (1178—1216), and a contemporary of the Śengēṇi chief Ammaiyappan-Attimallan Sambuvarāya (1171-1210). He was alive in A.D. 1198-1200. He was called 'Lord of Takaṭa' i. e. Tagaḍūr, and is said to have ruled over the three rivers, Pālār, Southern Peṇṇār, and Kāveri. He made compacts with the Śambuvarāya chief and with Karikāla Chola-Aḍaiyūr-Nāḍāḷvān—, that the three chiefs would keep the peace, and not (as was their previous custom) fight against one another (*E. I. VI, 332 ; E. R. 3, 107, 115 of 1900*).

Eḷini or Yavanikā is said to have been of royal Chera birth.

ADIL SHĀHS OF BIJĀPŪR

Āgha Murād or Amurāth II
of Anatolia.
|
1. *Abūl Muzaffar Yusuf Ādil Shāh.*
{ Subordinate to the Bāhmanī sovereign. Defeated Immaḍi Narasimha of Vijayanagar in 1493, and plundered his country. }

(Children, by karni …:)

- 2. *Ismāīl Ādil* independent, 1510–1534.
- Dau: (*Md.* Ahmad Shāh Bāhmanī).
- Dau: (*Md.* Burhān Nizām Shāh of Ahmadnagar).

Children of Ismāīl Ādil:

- 3. *Malū Ādil* 1534–1535, deposed and blinded.
- 4. *Ibrahīm Ād* A.D. 1535–15
- Vasu…
- Dau: (*Md.* Alāu-d-dīn Imād Shāh of Birar).

Children of Ibrahīm Ādil:

- 5. *Ali Ādil I* 1557–1580. Murdered by an eunuch, 11th April, 1580.
- *Tahmasp*

Children of Tahmasp:

- 6. *Ibrahīm Ādil II* 1580–1626.
- *Ismāil.*

Children of Ibrahīm Ādil II:

- 7. *Muhammad Ādil* 1626–1656. Revolt of Sivajī the Mahratta leader.
- Dau: (*Md.* Prince Dānyāl, son of the Mughal Emperor Akbar).

|
8. *Ali Ādil II* 1656–1672. He lost all the Konkan country to the Mahrattas.
|
9. *Sikandar* 1672–1686. An infant at his succession. Aurangzīb seized Bījāpūr, September 12, 1686 and annexed the country.

No. 7. Muhammad Ādil by 1654 had conquered part of S. India as far south as Tanjore. He seized Mysore and adjacent provinces from Ranga VI of Vijayanagar, *c.* 1645.

AHMADNAGAR

Rulers of—, See Nizam Shāhs.

AHMADĀBĀD

Rulers of—, See Barid Shāhs.

ĀLUPA, ĀḶVA, ĀḶUVA PRINCES

A line of rulers from the 7th to the 11th centuries A.D., who had their headquarters at Paṭṭi-Pombuchcha, modern Humcha, in the Nagar Taluk of Shimoga District, Mysore State. Their tract is called in old records the 'Āḷuvakhēḍa 6,000.' It is mentioned as late as the 12th century in an inscription of the time of Hoysala Vishnuvardhana. Dr. Hultzsch states that the name is probably derived from the Dravidian Āḷ 'to rule,' e. g. Kongāḷvas, Changāḷvas, Nāḍāḷvas (*See Mr. Krishna Sastri's remarks in Arch. Ann. Report for 1907-08, p. 238. n. 4*).

Guṇasāgara [1]
Governed Kadamba-manḍala, or Banavāsi province
in or before the reign of Chāḷukya
Vinayāditya A.D. 680—697.
|
Chitravāhana II [2]
A.D. 692.

Chitravāhana I [3]
Time of Rāshṭrakūṭa Gōvinda III.
Seized Udiyavāra in N. Kanara.
Ousted by Raṇasāgara.

Raṇasāgara [3]
Driven out by Svētavāhana.

Svētavāhana [3]

Prithvisāgara. [4]
'Udayāditya', 'Uttama Pāṇḍya.'

Vijayāditya Māramma [4]
'Uttama Pāṇḍya.'

Kavi Āḷupēndra Bhujabala [6]

Kulaśēkhara-Āḷupēndra
A.D. 1205/6

Bankidēva Āḷupēndra
Resided at Mangalore. A.D. 1302/3

Sōyidēva Āḷupēndra
A.D. 1315/16, 1324/25

AMARĀVATI CHIEFS,

See KOṬA CHIEFS

[1] *E. C. VI*, Kp. 38.
[2] *E. I. IX*, 15-24; *E.C. VIII*, Sb. 10.
[3] *E I. IX*, 19f., No. VII.
[4] *I. A. XIX*, 147; *E. C. VI*, Kp, 37.
[5] *E. I. IX*, 19f. Nos. *IV, V*.
[6] *E. R.* 1901, p. 5.

ĀNDHRA KINGS.

Śātavāhana or Śātakarṇi kings. Originally chiefs of a tribe in the neighbourhood of the Vindhya hills. Aśōka's rock-edict XIII. *c.* B.C. 250 mentions them as ruling a country beyond his borders. Khāravela's inscription of 168 B.C. in the Hāthigumpha cave (*I.A. 1920, p. 43*, vol. XLII, 276, 281) says that the Āndhra kingdom lay to the West of Kalinga (See I. *Ramadas's Monograph* in *I.A. April 1923*). The ancient Kalinga kings were Jains. The Āndhras were Buddhists. The latter rose to great power on the decay of Aśoka's Empire about 220 B.C. Pliny (A.D. 77) and the author of the *Periplus* mentions the Āndhra kingdom, which at one time, about the second century B.C., extended almost all across India as far as Nasik. An inscription discovered as Kodavalu near Piṭhāpūr, Godavari district, shews that at least about A.D. 208 the Āndhras were ruling that country. The Amarāvati *Stupa* with its wonderful marble sculptures, the Guntupalle cave-group, and many Buddhist stupas about the Godavari and Kistna tracts were the work of the Āndhras. The relationship of successive kings to one another is not clearly known.

The dates given here are taken from Vincent Smith's 'Early History of India', pp. 183 f., with which generally Dr. Barnett concurs (*Antiquities of India*).[1]

Approx. dates of accessions.

1. *Simuka* (or, variously, Śisuka, Sipraka, Sindhuka) Śātakarṇi. 23 years ... ... B.C. 220
2. *Kanha, or Krishna.* Brother of No. 1, 18 years. His rule extended across India from the West of Kalinga to Nasik ... 197
3. *Yajña-Śri Śātakarṇi*, or Śrīmallakarṇi, or Śāntakarṇa. 10 years. Defeated by Agnimitra of Magadha about 170, B.C (Dr. Barnett holds that the ultimate end was an Āndhra success). 179
4. *Pūrṇōtsanga.* 18 years. The Kalinga king Khāravēla's war in the West, 169. B.C. (*I.A. 1920, p. 43*). ... 169
5. *Śātakarṇi.* 40 years ... 151
6. *Lambodara.* 18 years ... 111
7. *Apīlaka*, or Apilaka, or Ivilaka. 12 years ... 93
8. *Sangha*, or Mēghasvāti. 18 years ... 81
9. *Sātakarṇi*, or Śātasvāti. 18 years ... 63
10. *Skandasvāti*, or Skanda Śātakarṇi. 7 years ... 45
11. *Mrigēndra Śātakarṇi*, or Mahēndra. 3 years ... 38
12. *Kuntala*, or Svātikarṇa. 8 years ... 35
13. *Sata Śātakarṇi*, or Svātikarṇi, or Svātishēna. 1 year ... 27
14. *Pulumāyi* I, or Pulōmāvi, or Paṭumāvi, or Paṭumat. 32 years. One of the three last slew Śuśarman the last king of the Kaṇva dynasty of Magadha. 27 B C. ... 26
15. *Mēgha 'Śātakarni.* 38 years ... A.D. 6
16. Arishṭa 'Śātakarṇi, or Arishṭakarṇi, or Nēmi Krishna or Gaura-Krishna, or Gorakshāsva-Śri. 25 years ... 44
17. *Hāla*, or Hālēya, patron of scholars and poets. 5 years ... 69
18. *Manḍalaka*, or Manṭalaka, or Paṭṭalaka. 5 years ... 74
19. *Purīndrasena*, or Purīshasēna, or Pravilasēna. 5 years ... 79
20. *Sundara Śātakarṇi.* 1 year. Mentioned in the *Periplus*. The Greeks called him 'Sandanes.' He was in possession of Kalyān. The Śaka Satraps seized some of the northern possessions of the Āndhras ... 84
21. *Vilivāyakura* I, or Vāśishṭhīputra, or Chakora, or Rājada Śātakarni. Six months 85

[1] The given dates are not all certain. The *Matsya, Vāyu*, and *Brahma Purāṇas* give lists of the kings, but differ here and there in their statements of lengths of reigns. Vincent Smith has attempted to reconcile them. Between Nos. 4 and 5 the *Matsya Purāṇa* interpolates 'Śrīvasvāni, alias Skandasthambi. No. 15 is omitted by Fergusson and Burgess.

22. *Śivāḷakura*, or Mādharīputra Śakasēna, or Śivasvāti Śātakarṇi. *Md.* Bālaśiri. 28 years ... A.D. 85

23. *Viḷivāyakura II*, or Gautamīputra Śrī Śātakarṇi, 25 years. Drove out from his western dominions the Śakas, Yavanas and Pahlavas. His Śaka enemy, the Kshatrapa Nahāpāṇa was killed about A D. 124, and his kingdom annexed (*I.A. 1918, p. 149.*) But a little later the Āndhras were defeated by the Śaka king Chasṭhana and lost all their territories north of the Narbadda river. Capital, Kolhapur, Ptolemy's 'Hippokoura.' (Dr. Barnett's date for his accession is A.D. 106) ... 113

24. *Puḷumāyi II*, or Vāsishṭhīputra, or Pulōmat, or Puḍumāyi called by Ptolemy 'Siro Polemaios.' 32 years. Married Dakshamitrā, daughter of the Śaka Kshatrapa Rudradāman I. Capital Paiṭhan. Lost to Rudradāman all his western dominions including Kāthiāwār, Kachch, Mālwa, the Konkan, etc., but not Poona or Nasik (Dr. Barnett's date for his accession is A.D. 131). 138

25. *Śivaśrī*, or Vāśishṭhīputra, or Avi-Śātakarni. 7 years. (Dr. Barnett places his accession about A.D. 163. He finds that he was living in A.D 155) 170

26. *Śivaskanda Śatakarṇi*, or Skandasvāti. 7 years. May be the same as Vāśishṭhiputra Chandrasāti who, according to Dr. Barnett, was living in A.D. 165 177

27. *Yajña Srī Gautamīputra.* 29 years. Recovered some lost territory; but Poona and Nasik were held by the Chuṭu-Śātakarṇis, a branch of the old royal family (*see below*) who were apparently tributary to the Śaka kings, and ruled at Baṇavāsi; so that his dominions were mostly confined to the Telugu districts and the eastern Dekhan country 184

28. *Vijaya-Śrī Śātakarṇi.* 6 years 213

29. *Vada-Śrī*, or Chandravijña, or Vāśishṭhīputra Chandra-Śrī, Śātakarṇi. 10 years 219

30. *Puḷumāyi III*, or Pulomāvi or Pulōmarchis. 7 years. The Dynasty came to a complete end about A.D. 236. The reason for its collapse is not well known. About the years A.D. 225 to 250 the Pallava king Bappa established a dynasty which ruled from the Krishna river to Kānchī in the south, while the Kalinga kings held the country to N.-E. 229

CHUṬU SĀTAKARṆIS OR CHUṬU-NĀGAS.[1]

As already mentioned a branch of the Āndhra family established themselves at Banavāśi, Poona and Nasik and became independent about A.D. 200 or later, on the death of Yajña-Sri Gautamīputra, being tributary to the Śaka Satraps. Only two kings' names are known.

Hāritīputra-Vishṇukada
Chūṭukulānanda-Śātakarṇi
c. A.D. 200

Hāritīputra-Śivaskanda
alias Sivaskanda-Nāga, or
Skanda-Nāga Śātavāhana
Ruled at Baṇavāśi before its seizure by the early Kadambas.

ĀRAVĪḌU—FAMILY OF—,
SEE UNDER VIJIYANAGAR KINGS.

[1] Chūṭu = a crest, a cobra's hood, a similar name to 'Nāga.' (Prof. Krishnaswami Aiyangar's '*Culture*,' *p. 139*.)

ARCOT—NAVĀBS OF—,
ANGLICE 'NABOBS OF ARCOT,' OR 'OF THE CARNAṬIC.'

1. *Zulfiqār Ali Khān*

Created Navāb of the Karnāṭaka country by the Emperor Aurangzib. A.D. 1690 or 1692–1703.

2. *Dāūd Khān*

Became friendly with the English. A.D. 1703–1710.

Agībatti Muhammad Khān

- 3. *Saādat-ullah Khān I.* 'Muhammad Saiyyid' created Navāb by the Emperor Bahādur Shāh 1710–1732.
- *Ghulām Ali Khān* Made Jaghīrdār of Vellore by Saādat-ullāh-Khan.
  - 4. *Dost Ali Khān* 1732–1740. Adopted by No. 3. His Dewan was Chanda Sahib, who was disloyal and seized Trichinopoly and Madura 1736, 1738. Killed in battle at Dāmalcheruvu.
    - *Husain* Killed in battle at Dāmalcheruvu.
    - 5. *Safdar Ali* 1740–1742. Sided with the French. Murdered by Ghulām Murtazā Ali.
      - 6. *Saādat-ullāh Khān II.* {'Muhammad Sayyid' 1742–1744 Murdered by a Paṭhān.}
    - Dau. Md. Ghulam Murtazā Ali.
    - Dau. Md. Taqi Sahib of Wandewash.
    - Dau. *Md.* Chanda Sahib, *alias* Husain Dost Khān, who sided always with the French, who proclaimed him Navāb, 1749.
      - *Rājā Sāhib* {Proclaimed Navāb by the French, 1759.}
  - *Baqīr Ali* Governor of Vellore 1732.
    - *Ghulām Murtazā Ali* (*Md.* Dostali's dau.) Governor of Vellore.
      - *Sahib Jadda* (*Zāda*) (Murdered.)
  - *Saādat-Ali*
  - *Akbar Muhammad*

7. *Anwaru-d-dīn Muhammad.*

Appointed Navāb by Nizām ul-Mulkh, Subahdār of the Dekhan. Supported by the English, and opposed by the French who favoured Chanda Sahib. Killed in battle. 1744–1749.

- *Mahfuz Khān* Appointed Governor of Madura.
- 8. *Muhammad Ali.* 1749–1795 'NavābWalajah.' 'The Company's Nabob.'
  - 9. *Umdat-ul-Umarā* 1795–1801.
    - *Ali Hussain* Declined office.
  - *Amīru-l-Umarā*
    - 10. *Azīm-ud-Daulah* 1801–1819, Resigned all power
      - 11. *Azam Jāh.* 1819–1825.
      - 12. *Azīm Jāh Bahādur* 'Prince of Arcot' 1867–1874.
- *Abdul Rahim.*
- *Abdul Wahāb.*
- *Najīb-ullah.*

ĀY KINGS OF MALAINĀḌU

SEE KERALA KINGS.

BĀHMANI DYNASTY

1. *Alāu-d dīn Hasan-Gangū-Bāhmanī.*
August 3, 1347–February 2, 1358. Rose to power under Muhammad Tughlak of Delhi. Made Sultan. Capital Kulbarga.

2. *Muhammad I.* February 2, 1358–April 21, 1375. Attacked Bukka I of Vijayanagar.

Mahmud Khān

Ahmad Khān

3. *Mujahīd* April 21, 1375—April 16, 1378. Assassinated.

Fath Khān

4. Dāūd. April 16–May 21, 1378. Assassinated.

5. Muhammad II (May 21, 1378-1397.)

8. *Firūz* 1397–September 24, 1422.

9. *Ahmad I* September 24, 1422—February 27, 1435.

6. *Ghiyāsu-d-dīn Khan* 1397. Assassinated.

7. *Shamsu-d-dīn* 1397. Deposed and blinded.

Hasan Khān.

Mubārak Khān.

10. *Alāu-d-dīn II* Feb. 27, 1435–1458.

Muhammad or *Mahmūd Khān.*

11. *Humāyūn* 1458-1461.

Hasan Khān

Yahya Khān

12. *Nizām* 1461–1463.

13. *Muhammad III.* 1463–March 21, 1482.
{ 9 years old at accession. His minister was Khwājā Mahmud Gawān, whom he murdered. }

Jamshīd

14. *Mahmūd* March 21, 1482–1518
{ Rebellion of the nobles. The kingdom broke up. }

Two daughters.

15. *Ahmad II*[1] 1518-1521.

16. *Alāu-d-dīn III* 1521–1523 assassinated.

17. *Wali-Ullah* 1523–1525. Poisoned.

18. *Kalīm-Ullah* 1525–1527.

NOTE.—For information see *I. A., 1899*, p. 119f.

[1] The dates and names after 14 Mahmūd are as given by Firishta.

BĀṆA CHIEFS

The Bāṇas were a very ancient family in the Chittoor and N. Arcot Districts. About A.D. 450 the then paramount Pallava king Simhavarman consecrated the first Ganga king for the express purpose of crushing the Bāṇas who had become unruly. The chronology of the Bāṇas is obscure and confusing. For comparison of the pedigrees put forward by different writers see Dr. Hultzsch's paper (*E. I. xvii., p. 3.*).[1] The following seems reasonable.

A. D. 719–20. *Vikramāditya-Bali-Indra*, a vassal of the W. Chāḷukya king Vijayāditya (696–733). (*E. R. 1921, p. 87.*)

A. D. 739. *Vikramāditya* governed the country 'West of the Telugu Road,' as vassal of the Pallava king Nandivarman II (717–779). (*E. R. 1903–04, pp 6, 12 ; S.I.I., iii. 43.*)

1. *Nandivarman*

{ or Jaya-Nandivarman. Ruled the land west of the Āndhra country. }

2. *Vijayāditya I*

3. *Malladēva*

'Jagadēkamalla'

4. *Vikramāditya I*

'Jayamēru,' 'Bāṇavidyādhara.' *Md.* Kundavvai, dau. of the Ganga King Prithivīpati I ; and Mārikanimma. *C.* 872–890.

5. *Vijayāditya II.*

'Vira Chuḷāmaṇi,' 'Prabhumēru.' Ruling in A.D. 898–99, 905–06, 909–10.[2]

6. *Vikramāditya II.*

Heir apparent in A.D. 898.[3]

7. *Vijayāditya II*

'Pugaḻvippavargaṇḍa.'

8. *Vikramāditya III.*

'Vijaya-Bāhu.' 'Dear friend of Krishna Rāja,' *i.e.* the Rāshṭrakūṭa king Krishna III, or Kannara who reigned 937–38 to 965–66.

Notes.—Vikramāditya I's accession date is derived from an inscription which mentions the year 'Vijaya' (A.D. 873–74) as being in the second year of Bāṇavidyādhara. He was ruling the country 'west of the Telugu Road' in the 24th year of Pallava Nripatunga, *c.* 878. Also in the 23rd year of Pallava Nandivarman III, i.e. in 852, when he may have ruled as Yuva-Rāja. About 870 he fought (as Yuva-Rāja) against the Rāshṭrakūṭa king Amōghavarsha I. About 878 he fought against Varaguṇa Pāṇḍya II. About 878 occurred the raid into the Pulināḍu, a Bāṇa tract, by the Noḷamba chief Mahēndra I who captured Koyatūr and burned the town of Permāvi. He was defeated by Vijayāditya II. About the same time was fought the battle of Soremati where the allied Bāṇas and Vaiḍumbas were opposed to the same Mahēndra I and the Ganga-king Rāchamalla. Many *Vīraklas* testify to these events. (*e.g. V. R. i. 175, 196, 243, 255 ; 306, 318 of 1912 ; 542, 571 of 1906 ; etc. ; E. C. x, Sp, 5,6.*)

About A. D. 915 the Bāṇas were completely defeated by Parāntaka Chōla I, and the country given to the Ganga king Prithivīpati II.

For later Bāṇas we have the following.—

A. D. 1088–89. Chikkarasa, vassal of the W. Chāḷukya king. (*566 of 1915.*)
A. D. 1123. Chittarasa, vassal of Vikramāditya VI. (*356 of 1920.*)
A. D. 1275. A Mahābali-Bāṇa was vassal ("Piḷḷai") to Māravarman Kulaśēkhara Pāṇḍya I.
A. D. 1453. Urangāvillidāśan, ruling Madura.
A. D. 1477. Tirumāliruñjōlai. Do.
A. D. 1476. Sundarattōḷ-Uḍaiyār Do.
A. D. 1499. Muttarasā-Tirumalai-Māvalivāṇa, also ruling Madura.
A. D. 1517-18 Mahābali-Bāna Nāyakka in Ramnad District. (*V. R. ii. Ram : 131 ; 113 of 1903.*)

---

[1] See also *E. I. iii.*, 74 ; *S.I.I., iii.*, 92 ; *E. R.* 1907, §. 45.
[2] *E. I.* iv., 224 ; *S.I.I.*, ii., 389. [3] See the Guḍimallam plates.

BAṆAVĀSI,—SEE KADAMBAS OF

BARĪD SHĀHI DYNASTY *of* BĪḌAR, *or* AHMADĀBĀD.

1. *Kasim Barīd I.*
A. D. 1492–1504. Minister to the
Bāhmanī Sultan Mahmūd II.

2. *Amīr Barīd.*
1504–1549. Became independent 1527.

3. *Alī Barīd.*
1549–1562.
Lost most of his possessions to Burhān
Shāh of Aḥmadnagar.

4. *Ibrahīm Barīd.*
1562-1569.
Amīr Barīd ruled from 1609.

5. *Kāsim Barid II*
1569-1572.

6. *Mirza alī Barīd.*
1572–1609. Deposed.

BEDNŪR,—RĀJAS OF. *See* KEḶADI KINGS.

BIJAPŪR,—RULES OF. *See* ĀDIL-SHĀHI,—DYNASTY OF

BURMA—SOME KINGS OF

The following few dates are those of kings of Burma who came into contact with South India and Ceylon in the 11th and 12th centuries. (*Epigr. Burmanica, i, pp. 3,4 : Arch : Surv. of Burma Rep. for 1919-20.*)

Anorata. A. D. 1044-1077. Sent a mission to Ceylon, begging for the Tooth-relic. Counter-mission from Ceylon. Trade by sea brisk between Burma, India, and China. Indians settling for trade in Burma, the Straits, Sumatra, etc.

Sawlu, his son, A. D. 1077–1084.

Kyānzittha, A. D. 1084–1112.

Alaungzittha, or *Sithu*. A. D. 1112–1187. In 1180 Parākrama Bāhu of Ceylon sent a fleet to Burmah.

Narapati,-Sithu. A. D. 1173–1210.

In the 13th Century there was a large South-Indian community at Pāgān.

CEYLON,—KINGS OF

N.B.—In the following list the dates set against the accessions of the kings from No. 1 Vijaya to No. 64 Dhātusēna are in the first column those based on the theory that the Nirvāṇa of Buddha occurred in B.C. 543, and in the second column those based on 483 B. C. as the date of that event.

From No. 65 Kassapa II to 89 Hatthadāta the dates are still doubtful. In default of full information I have repeated the dates given in L. C. Wijesimha Mudaliār's list in his *Māhavamśa* (*1889*). Dr. Hultzsch informs me that he has as yet no suggestion to offer regarding them.

From No. 90 Mānavamma to 135 Sahāsamalla we are on safe ground, the date, A. D. 1200, for the latter being 'absolutely certain' (*Dr. Hultzsch in J. R. A. S. 1913, p. 518*). With this dictum Mr. Wijesimha Mudaliar concurs.

No.			Date of accession: Older computation	Date of accession: Recent computation
1	Vijaya	B.C.	543	483
2	Upatissa I. Regent	,,	505	445
3	Pāndu-Vāsudēva	,,	504	444
4	Abhaya	,,	474	414
	Interregnum	,,	454	394
5	Pāṇḍukābhaya	,,	437	377
6	Mutaśiva	,,	367	307
7	Dēvānāmpiya-Tissa	,,	307	247
8	Uttiya	,,	267	207
9	Mahāśiva	,,	257	197
10	Śūra Tissa	,,	247	187
11	Sōna and Guttika (foreign usurpers)	,,	237	177
12	Asēla	,,	215	155
13	Eḷāra (a Tamil usurper)	,,	205	145
14	Dutṭhagāmaṇi, or Dutugemunu	,,	161	101
15	Saddhā-Tissa	,,	137	77
16	Thullatthana, or Tuluna	,,	119	59
17	Lajji-Tissa, or Ladē-Tissa	,,	119	59
18	Khallāta-Nāga	,,	109	49
19	Vaṭṭagāmaṇi Abhaya, or Valagam-Bāhu	,,	104	44
20	Pulahattha ⎫	,,	103	43
	Bāhiya ⎪	,,	100	40
	Panayamāra ⎬ (Tamil usurpers)	,,	98	38
	Pilayamāra ⎪	,,	91	31
	Dāthiya I ⎭	,,	90	30
21	Vaṭṭagāmani Abhaya, or Valagam-Bāhu (reinstated)	,,	88	28
22	Mahāchūḷa Mahātissa, or Mahaśilu Mahātissa	,,	76	16
23	Chora-Nāga	,,	62	2
24	Tissa, or Kudā Tissa	,,	50	A.D. 9
25	Anulā	,,	47	,, 12
26	Makalan Tissa, or Kālakanni Tissa	,,	42	,, 16 or 17
27	Bhātikābhaya	,,	20	,, 38 or 36
28	Mahādāthiya Mahānāga I, or Mahā Deliyā	A.D.	9	69
29	Āmandagāmaṇi Abhaya	,,	21	81
30	Kanijānu Tissa	,,	30	90
31	Chūlābhaya Tissa, or Kuḍā Abā	,,	33	93
32	Śivali	,,	35	95
	Interregnum of three years			
33	Iḷanāga, or Eḷunā	,,	38	98
34	Chandamukha Śiva, or Sandamuhunu	,,	44	104
35	Yaśalālaka Tissa	,,	52	112
36	Śubha Rājā	,,	60	120
37	Vasabha, or Vahap	,,	66	126
38	Vankanāsika Tissa	,,	110	170
39	Gajabāhu I	,,	113	173[1]
40	Mahāllaka Nāga, or Mahālu Nāga	,,	135	195[2]
41	Bhāṭiya, or Bhāṭika II	,,	141	201
42	Kaniṭṭha Tissa, or Kanitu Tissa	,,	165	225[2]
43	Chūla Nāga, or Sūlu Nāga	,,	193	253[2]
44	Kuddā Nāga	,,	195	255
45	Śiri Nāga I	,,	196	256
46	Vohāraka Tissa	,,	215	275
47	Abhaya Tissa	,,	237	297
48	Śiri Nāga II	,,	245	305
49	Vijaya II, or Vijayindu	,,	247	307
50	Sangha Tissa I	,,	248	308
51	Śiri Sanghabōdhi I, or Daham Śiri Sanghabō	,,	252	312
52	Goṭhābhaya, or Mēghavarṇābhaya	,,	254	314
53	Jeṭṭha Tissa I, or Detu Tis I	,,	267	327
54	Mahāsēna, or Mahāsen	,,	277	337[2]
55	Kitti Śiri Meghavaṇṇa, or Kit-Śiri-Mēvan. (He sent an embassy to Samudragupta)	,,	304	364[2]

[1] Wickremasinghe's dates (*Arch. Sur. of Ceylon I, 216*) slightly differ. For No. 39 he gives the accession date, A.D. 177. Geiger says A.D. 171.

[2] Wickremasinghe's date for No. 40 is A.D. 199 | for No. 54 ... ... A.D. 331
Do. for No. 42 do. 229 | for No. 55 ... ... ,, 358
Do. for No. 43 do. 247 | for No. 64 ... ... ,, 517

No.	—	Date of accession: Older computation	Date of accession: Recent computation
56	Jeṭṭha Tissa II, or Detu Tis II ...	332	392
57	Buddhadāsa, or Bujas	341	401
58	Upatissa II	370	430
59	Mahānāma	412	472
60	Soṭṭhi Sēna	434	494
61	Chattagāhaka	434	494
62	Mitta Sēna	435	495
63	Pāṇḍu (Tamil usurpers) ...	436	496
	Pārinda (Tamil usurpers) ...	441	501
	Khudda Pārinda (Tamil usurpers) ...	444	504
	Tiritara (Tamil usurpers) ...	460	520
	Dāthiya II (Tamil usurpers) ...	460	520
	Pithiya (Tamil usurpers) ...	463	523
64	Dhātusēna, or Dāsenkeliya	463	523[1]
	Dates from this point to No. 90 are doubtful. They are based on 543 B.C. for Buddha's nirvāna. Dr. Hultzsch's date for No. 86 is practically certain.		
65	Kaśśapa I, Kāsyappa, or Sigiri Kasub, or Kasup ... ... ,,	479	
66	Moggalana I, or Mugalan ... ... ,,	497	
67	Kumāra Dhātusēna II, or Kumaradāsa ... ... ,,	515	
68	Kittisēna, or Kirtisēna, or Kitsen .. .. ,,	524	
69	Śiva, or Mēdi Śivu ... ... ,,	524	
70	Upatissa III, or Lēmēni Upatissa ... ... ,,	525	
71	Amba Sāmanēra Śilākāla, or Ambaherana Salamevan ... ... ,,	526	
72	Dāthāppabhuti, or Dāpulu Sen I ...	539	
73	Chūla Moggalāna II, or Sūlu Mugalan ...	540	
74	Kittiśiri Mēghavaṇṇa II, or Kudā Kitsiri Mēvan ...	560	
75	Mahānāga II, or Senevi	561	
76	Aggabōdhi I, or Agrabōdhi, or Agbō, or Akbō ...	564	
77	Aggabōdhi II, or Kudā Akbō	598	
78	Sanghatissa, or Asiggāha Sanghatissa	608	
79	Dalla Moggallāna, or Dala Mugalan, or Lēmēni Bōnā, or Lēmēni Singā ,,	608	
80	Śilāmēghavaṇṇa I, or Asiggāhaka, or Asiggrāhaka Śilamēgha ... ,,	614[2]	670–79[2]
81A	Aggabōdhi III, or Śirisangabodhi II, or Agrabōdhi, or Akbō, or Śirisangabō ... ... ,,	623[2]	
82	Jeṭṭhatissa, or Lēmēni Katusara, or Dētutissa ... ... ,,	623	
81B	Aggabōdhi III (etc., as *above*) recovered the kingdom ... ... ,,	624	
83	Dāthōpatissa I, or Dalapatissa ...	640	
84	Kaśśapa II, or Kāsyappa, or Pēsulu Kasub, or Kasap ... ... ,,	652	
85	Dappula I, or Dāpulu ... ... ,,	661	
86	Haṭṭhadātha I, or Dāthopatissa II, or Lēmēni Dalapatissa ... ... ,,	664	640
87	Aggabōdhi IV, or Śirisanghabōdhi, or Agrabōdhi, or Akbō ... ,,	673	
88	Datta, or Valpiti Datta ... ... ,,	689	
89	Unhanāgara Haṭṭhadātha II, or Hunannaru Riyanaudala[3] killed in battle with No. 90 Mānavamma ... ... ,,	691	667–78
	Dates from this point down to A.D. 1200 are given first according to Wijesimha's computation and secondly according to Dr. Hultzsch, J.R.A.S., 1913, pp. 518 f.	(Wijesimha)	(Hultzsch)
90	Mānavamma. Fled to Kāñchī in reign of No. 86 Dāthopatissa II about A.D. 641, and took refuge with Narasimha Pallava, whom in 642 he aided in his war with the W. Chāḷukya king Pulakēśin II; with Pallava support he twice invaded Ceylon. The first attempt proving unsuccessful he remained with king Narasimha during the reigns of Nos. 86–89. His second expedition was successful. No. 89 was killed, and Mānavamma became King of Ceylon ... ,,	691	668
91	Aggabōdhi V, or Agrabōdhi, or Akbō ... ... ,	726	703
92	Kaśśapa III, or Kaśyapa, or Kasub, or Sūlu Kasubu ... ... ,,	732	709
93	Mahinda I, or Mihindu	738	715
94	Aggabōdhi VI, Śilāmēgha II, or Agrabōdhi, or Akbō Salamēvan ...	741	718
95	Aggabōdhi VII, or Agrabōdhi, or Kudā Akbō, or Dēvēni Kudā Akbō ...	781	758
96	Mahinda II, or Śilāmēgha III, or Salamēvan Mihindu	787	764
97	Dappula II, or Dāpula	807	784

[1] *See* foot-note 2, p. 330.

[2] Wickremasinghe (*Arch. Sur. of Ceylon, I, 217*) fixes the accession of No. 80 in A.D. 670 and his death in 679, when No. 81A Aggabōdhi III came to the throne. His dates for later kings down to No. 134 vary similarly from those entered here.

[3] Dr. Hultzsch (*J.R.A.S., 1913, p. 528*) has conclusively fixed the date of accession of No. 90 as in A.D. 668. Since No. 89 only reigned for six months when he was killed it follows that his accession must have taken place in A.D. 667–68, and that the dates of accessions from No. 65 to 89 require correction.

No.	——		Date of accession	
			Older computation	Recent computation
98	Mahinda III, or Dhammika Śilāmēgha IV, or Dhārmika Śilāmēgha, or Akbō Salamēvan Mihindu	A.D.	812	789
99	Aggabōdhi VIII, or Medi Akbō	,,	816	793
100	Dappula III or Dāpulu, or Kudā Dāpulu	,,	827	804
101	Aggabōdhi IX	,,	843	820
102	Sēna I, or Śilāmēgha Sēna, or Salamēvan Sen, or Śilāmēghavarṇa V ...	,,	846	823
103	Sēna II	,,	866	843
104	Udaya I	,,	901	878
105	Kassapa IV, or Kāśyapa, or Kasup	,,	912	889
106	Kassapa V. Sent an expedition, which proved unsuccessful, to support the Pāṇḍya King of Madura, Rājasimha III, against the Chōla King Parāntaka I	,,	929	906
107	Dappula IV, or Dāpulu	,,	939	916
108	Dappula V, or Kudā Dāpulu. In his reign the Pāṇḍya King of Madura left his crown and the 'necklace of Indra' in Ceylon (*Mahāwamsa liii, vv.* 4–9.)	,,	940	917
109	Udaya II, or Udā	,,	952	929

No.	——		Date of accession	
			Wijesimha	Hultzsch
110	Sēna III	A.D.	955	932
111	Udaya III. In or about A.D. 943 during this king's reign Parāntaka Chōla I invaded Ceylon, and gained possession of the Pāṇḍya royal jewels; but in a subsequent expedition into Chōla territory the Singhalese recovered them	,,	964	941
112	Sēna IV	,,	972	949
113	Mahinda IV	,,	975	952
114	Sēna V	,,	991	968
115	Mahindu V. Some time between A.D. 1001 and 1004 Rājarāja Chōla I invaded Ceylon. In 1013–14 Mahindu was captured by the Chōla army of Rājēndra I and sent to India. This was in Mahindu's 36th year. Rājēndra seized the Pāṇḍya crown jewels and the 'necklace of Indra,' which had been left in Ceylon by the Pāṇḍya king in the reign of Dappula V. Mahindu died after twelve years captivity at the Chōla court.	,,	1001	978
116	Vikrama Bahu, *alias* Kassapa. He had little power	,,	1037	1026
117	Kitti or Kitti. A general. Usurper. Only reigned 8 days	,,	1049	1038
118	Mahālāna Kitti or Kirti. Usurper	,,	1049	1038
119	Vikkama Pāṇḍu, or Vikrama. Usurper. A Pāṇḍya prince. Killed in battle in A.D. 1042 when Rājādhirāja Chōla I invaded Ceylon ...	,,	1052	1041
120	Jagatipāla. Usurper. Perhaps also called 'Vira Salamēgha. The Maṇimangalam inscription of Rājādhirāja Chōla I's 29th year (A.D. 1046) states that the Chōla king slew 'Vira Salāmēgha' and Śri-Vallabha Madanarāja, kings of Ceylon, and Mānābharaṇa, and decapitated Vikrama Bāhu (No. 116) and Vikrama Paṇḍu (No. 119). Chōla records say that Vira Salamēgha had come originally from Ayōdhya and the *Mahāwamsa* calls Jagatipāla 'An Aryan of the race of Rāma.' (*S.I.I. iii. 52*).	,,	1053	1042
121	Parākkama. Usurper. Son of the Pāṇḍya king. He was 'killed by the Chollians' (*Mahāwamsa, ch. lvi.*)	,,	1057	1046
122	Lōka, or Lōkissara. Usurper	,,	1059	1048
123	Vijaya-Bāhu, *alias* Sirisanghabōdhi, or Vijaya Bahu, or Mahalu Vijaya Bāhu. Grandson (?) of No. 115 Mahindu V, or in some way related. Between 1052 and 1055 Rājēndradēva Chōla invaded Ceylon and slew another Vira Salamēgha and another Mānābharaṇa. (*See above under No. 120*). The former was a prince of Kalinga; the latter was 'King of Ceylon.' Vijaya Bāhu in A.D. 1073 drove out the Chōla forces and occupied Anuradhapura (*Epig. Zeilanica, ii. 207*)	,,	1065	1054
124	Jaya Bāhu I. Brother of the last king. Ousted by No. 125. Lived retired	,,	1120	1109
125	Vikkama Bāhu I, or Vikrama—*Md.* Sundara Mahādēvi	,,	1121	1110

No.	—	Date of accession	
		Wijesimha	Hultzsch
126	Gaja Bāhu II, son of No. 125 Vikkama-Bāhu	1142	1131
127	Parakkama Bāhu I, surnamed 'The Great.' He sent a large force under his general Lankāpura to invade the Pāṇḍya country, over the whole of which and in South India generally there was prolonged warfare. The invasion took place, apparently, shortly before A.D. 1167 ,,	1164	1153
128	Vijaya Bāhu II, son of No. 126 Gajabāhu II ,,	1197	1186
129	Mahinda VI. Usurper. Assassinated ,,	1198	1187
130	Kitti Niśśanka, or Kirtti Niśśanka Malla, a Prince of Kalinga ,,	1198	1187
131	Vira Bāhu I ,,	1207	1196
132	Vikkama Bāhu II, or Vikrama— ,,	1207	1196
133	Chōḍa-Ganga ,,	1207	1196
134	Līlāvatī, Widow of No. 127, Parākkama Bāhu I ,,	1208	1197

No.	—		Dates now considered certain
135	Sahāsamalla. His accession, on August 23, 1200 is, according to Dr. Hultzsch the earliest *absolutely certain* date in Singhalese history. (*J.R.A.S.*, *1913*, *p. 518*)	A.D.	1200
136	Kalyāṇavati	,,	1202
137	Dharmāśōka	,,	1203
138	Aṇikanga	,,	1209
	Līlāvatī (No. 134) restored and again deposed	,,	1209
139	Lōkissara, or Lōkēśvara. Usurper	,,	1210
	Līlāvatī (No. 134) again restored and once more deposed	,,	1211
140	Parakkama Pāndu II, or Perakum Pāṇḍi. Usurper	,,	1212
141	Māgha, or Kalinga, Vijaya Bāhu. Usurper	,,	1215
142	Vijaya Bāhu III	,,	1236
143	Parakkama Bāhu III, or Kalikāla Sāhitya Sarvajña Paṇḍita	,,	1240
144	Vijaya Bāhu IV, or Bosat Vijaya Bāhu	,,	1275
145	Bhuvanēka Bāhu I	,,	1277
146	Parakkama Bāhu IV, or Parākrama—In his reign the Tamils invaded Ceylon in great numbers, took away the Tooth-relic of Buddha, and gave it to King Māravarman Kulaśēkhara Pāṇḍya I at Madura	,,	1288
147	Bhuvanēka Bāhu II	,,	1293
148	Parakkama Bāhu V, or Pandita Parākrama	,,	1295
149	Bhuvanēka Bāhu III, or Vanni Bhuvanēka Bāhu	,,	?
150	Jaya Bāhu I	,,	?
151	Bhuvanēka Bāhu IV	,,	1347
152	Parakkama Bāhu VI	,,	1351
153	Vikkama Bāhu III	,,	?
154	Bhuvanēka Bāhu V, or Aḷagakkōnāra, or Alakēśvara. Reigned 20 years	,,	?
155	Vira Bāhu II	,,	?
156	Parakkama Bāhu VII. Reigned 52 years	,,	1410
157	Jaya Bāhu II. Put to death	,,	1462
158	Bhuvanēka Bāhu VI	,,	1464
159	Parakkama Bāhu VIII, or Paṇḍita Parākrama—	,,	1471
160	Parakkama Bāhu IX, or Vira Parākrama	,,	?
161	Vijaya Bāhu V	,,	?
162	Bhuvanēka Bāhu VII	,,	?
163	Vira Vikkama, or—Vikrama	,,	1542
164	Mayādhanu, or Māyādunu	,,	?
165	Rājasīha I, or Rājasimha	,,	?
166	Vimala Dhamma Sūriya I, or Dharma Sūrya, or Daham Sūriya	,,	1592
167	Sēnāratna, or Senerat	,,	1620
168	Rājasīha II, or Rājasimha (Reigned 52 years)	,,	1627
169	Vimala Dhamma Sūriya II (or names as with No. 166)	,,	1679
170	Śiri Vira Parakkama Narinda Sīha, or—Narēndra Simha	,,	1701
171	Śiri Vijaya Rāja Sīha, or Hanguranketa Rāja Simha	,,	1734
172	Kitti Śiri Rāja Sīha, or—Simha	,,	1747
173	Śiri Rājādhirāja Sīha, or—Simha	,,	1780
174	Śiri Vikkama Rāja Sīha. The Singhalese banished him on account of his cruelty and misrule; and the English took possession of the kingdom	,,	1798

EARLY CHĀĻUKYA KINGS

The family belonged to the Mānavya Gōtra and claimed descent from Hārīti. The kings bear the title 'Vallabha' and 'Satyāśraya.' Their capital was at Bādāmi, and they ruled over a large part of the Dekhan.

Jayasimha I
A.D. c 500.

Raṇarāga
'Raṇavikrama' 'Rājasimha'.

1. *Pulakēśin I*
'Raṇavikrama.' Real founder of the dynasty. Seized Bādāmi. Md. Durlabha-dēvī. A. D. c. 550–566.

2. *Kīrttivarmā I.*
'Raṇaparākrama.' Conquered Kadamba Krishṇavarman II of Baṇavāsi. A.D. 566–597.

3. *Maṅgaḷēśa.*
'Raṇavikrānta.' Defeated the Kaṭachchuri King Buddha-Raja, killed Swāmi Rāja. Lost his throne to Pulakēśin II. A D. 597–609 to 10.

Sons of Kīrttivarmā I:

4. *Pulakēśin II.*
'Eṟeyya.' Defeated Harsha of Kanauj, and made large conquests. A.D. 609–10 to 642.

Kubja Vishṇuvardhana.
'Vishama-Siddhi-' 'Makara-dhvaja.' Founded the *Eastern Chāḷukya Dynasty* (*q.v.*)

Jayasimha.
'Dharāśraya.'
— son: *Nāgavardhana.*

Son of Maṅgaḷēśa:

Indravarman.
'Dhruva-rāja.'

The reign of Pulakēśin II was followed, owing to heavy defeats, by an interregnum of thirteen years. The early family was divided; Pulakēśin II's descendants being the 'Western Chāḷukyas'; Kubja Vishṇuvardhana's 'the Eastern Chāḷukyas,' ruling over territory conquered by Pulakēśin II from Kaliṅga, Southern Kosala, Pishṭhāpura (Piṭhāpur — the Godāvari river tract) and from the Pallavas of Kānchi.

WESTERN CHĀĻUKYA DYNASTY.

(Pulakēśin II.)

Children:

Chandrāditya.
Eldest son according to Kielhorn.

Ādityavarma.
Eldest son according to Fleet.

5. *Vikramāditya I*[1]
'Raṇaraśika', 'Rājamalla' 'Anivārita.' Seized Kānchi. Defeated Chōlas, Kēraḷas, and three Pallava kings. A. D. 654–5 to 680.

(?) *Jayasimha*
mentioned, with his descendants, in some questionable records.

Dau. *Amberā.*
(*doubtful*).

6. *Vinayāditya*
'Yuddhamalla.' Warred in Mysore and against Kaḷabhras; and in A.D. 693 against Pallavas. (A.D. 680–696.)

7. *Vijayāditya.*
A.D. 696–733.

Sons:

8. *Vikramāditya II.*
Claims to have conquered Kānchi three times, but to have spared the city. *Md.* Lokamahādēvī, a Haihaya princess. A.D. 733–743 to 44.

Bhīma I.

[1] Pallava inscriptions confirm the fact of their king's war against the W. Chāḷukyas, but state that Pallava Paramēśvara I defeated 'Raṇaraśika' at Peruvaḷa-Nallūr. For the three Pallava kings see *E. I. x, 100* Vikramāditya was close to Trichinopoly on April 25, A. D. 674.

WESTERN CHĀḶUKYA DYNASTY—*contd.*

9. *Kīrtivarmā II.*
'Nripasimha.' Completely crushed by the Rāshṭrakūṭa king, Dantidurga, and deprived of his sovereignty.
A.D. 743-4 to 753.
[*The Rāshṭrakūṭas held the W. Chāḷukya territories till* A.D. 973.]

Kīrtivarmā III.

Tailapa, or Taila I.

Vikramāditya III.

(?) *Bhīma II.*
E. I. xii, 142. Omitted in some inscriptions.

Ayyaṇa I.
Md. Dau. of Rāshṭrakūṭa king Krishṇa II who reigned *c.* 877-913.

Vikramāditya IV.
Md Bonthādēvī, Dau. of the Chēdi king Lakshmana.

10. *Tailapa or Taila II.*
'Ahavamalla' *Md.* Jākabbe, Dau. of Rāshṭrakūṭa king Kakka III. Conquered the Rāshṭrakūṭas and restored the W. Chāḷukya monarchy, also called 'Nūrmaḍi Taila' and 'Trailōkyamalla.'
A.D. 973-997.

11. *Satyāśraya*
'Irivibhujanga,' 'Sattiga' 'Akaḷankacharita', 'Āhavamalla.' Fought against Rājarāja Chōla I.
A. D. 997-1008.

Daśavarman or Yasōvarman. *Md.* Bhāgata.

Children of Satyāśraya:

- Dau. *Md.* Pallava Irivi Noḷamba.
- *Kunda*, or *Kundiga* Ruling Baṇavāsi in 1019, 1028, 1031.

Children of Daśavarman:

- 12. *Vikramāditya V.* 'Tribhuvamalla,' 'Vikramānka A.D. 1008-1014.
- 13. *Ayyaṇa II.* 1014-1015
- Dau. *Akkā-dēvi.* Ruling Kiśukāḍ Province 1010-1054. *Md.* a Kādamba chief of Hāngal.
- 14. *Jayasimha III* 'Jagadēkamalla' Fought with Chōla Rājēndra I. *Md.* Suggalā-dēvi. A.D. 1015-1042.

Children of Jayasimha III:

- 15. *Sōmēsvara I.* Āhavamalla', 'Traillōkyamalla'. Warred against three Chōla kings. *Md.* Ganga princess Mailāḷa and a Pallava princess. Battles of Koppam, Kūḍal-sangamam, etc., Drowned in the Tungabhadra river. A.D. 1042 Mar. 30, 1068.
- Dau. Hanmā Or Āvallā-dēvi. *Md.* Yādava King Bhillama III of Sēuṇa-dēśa.

Children of Sōmēsvara I:

- 16. *Sōmēśvara II.* 'Bhuvanēkamalla' Mar. 30, 1068-1076
- 17. *Vikramaditya VI* 'Tribhuvanamalla' 1076-1126.
- *Jayasimha IV.* 'Aṇṇanasinga'. Governed Noḷambavāḍi and Baṇavāsi provinces.
- *Vishṇuvardhana Vijayāditya.*

Children of Vikramaditya VI:

- *Jayakarṇa.* 'Trailōkyamalla.' Died early.
- 18. *Sōmēśvara III.* 'Bhūlōkamalla.' 1126-1138.
- Dau. Mailāḷa-dēvi. *Md.* Jayakēśin II of the Kādambas of Goa.

WESTERN CHĀḶUKYA DYNASTY—*contd.*

19. *Perma-Jagadēkamalla II.* Suppressed an invasion from the Hoysalas of Mysore. Captured Bēlāpura. 1138–1151.

20. *Tailapa III.* 'Nurmaḍi Taila', 'Trailōkyamalla.' Deprived of his throne by Bijjala Kalachūri 1151–1156. Died 1163.

(?) *Bhūlōkamalla.* Believed to be son of Taila III. Ruled a province in 1160, under the Kalachūri king.

(?) *Jagadēkamalla III.* Believed to be son of Taila III Ruled some tracts under the Kalachūri king. 1163–1184.

Sōmēśvara IV. 'Tribhuvanamalla.' *Md.* Gangamahādēvī. 1184–1200 when dynasty came to end.

NOTES

For chronology of the dynasty see Venkaṭa Subbiah's article, *Ind. Ant.*, 1918, p. 285.

Vikramāditya I. The Nērūr plates (*I. A. vii. 163*) fix his accession as later than September 24, 654. The Talamanchi grant fixes it as earlier than July 13, 655.

Vinayāditya (*E. I. ix, 201*). His accession was in the year following October 10, 680. (*E. C. xi. Dg. 66*).

Kīrtivarmā. His accession was in the year following April 7, 743. See the Kēndūr plates, Poona District. (*E. I. ix. 200*).

Sōmēśvara II's anointment as king was on April 11, 1068 (*E. C. vii. Sk. 136*).

Vikramāditya VI established from A.D. 1076 the Chāḷukya-Vikrama era, dating from the beginning of his reign. He was crowned February 11, 1076. (*I. A., 1919, p. 2*).

Sōmēśvara III's accession was apparently between July 24 and October 5, 1126. (*695 of 1919*).

Tailapa III. His death is mentioned in an inscription at Anumakoṇḍa of January 20, 1163.

Bhūlōkamalla, son(?) of Taila III. (*See Mys. A. A. R., 1923, No. 112*).

Jagadēkamalla III, son(?) of Taila III. (*E. C. xi. Dg. 43 ; Cd. 13*).

Sōmēśvara IV. Earliest known date = November 5, 1184. (*555 of 1915*). Latest = January 17, 1200. (*E. C. xi. Cd. 36.*)

EASTERN CHĀḶUKYA DYNASTY

(See *I. A. xx, 12, 93, 266 ; E. I. v, 118 ; vii. App. 92.*)

1. *Kubja-Vishṇuvardhana I*
Brother of early Chaḷukya king Pulakēśin II
'Vishama-Siddhi,' 'Śrī Biṭṭa.'
A.D. 615-633.

2. *Jayasimha I.* 'Sarvasiddhi.' 633–663.

3. *Indra-Bhaṭṭāraka* 'Simha-Vikrama.' A.D. 663. Reigned 7 days.

4. *Vishṇuvardhana II* 'Rājanandana,' 'Makaradhvaja' 'Vishamasiddhi.' 663–672.

5. *Mangi-Yuvarāja* 'Sarvalōkāśraya.' 'Vijaya-Siddhi.' 672–696.

6. *Jayasimha II* 696–709

8. *Vishṇuvardhana III* 709–746

7. Kokkili. Reigned for 6 months 709.

9. *Vijayāditya I* 'Bhaṭṭāraka,' 'Śaktivarma.' 746–764.

10. *Vishṇuvardhana IV* 'Makaradhvaja.' 764-799.

11. *Vijayāditya II* 'Narēndra-Mrigarāja,' 'Niravadya,' 'Chaḷukyārjuna.' Fought 108 battles in 12½ years against Gangas and Raṭṭas. 799–843.

Nripa-Rudra.

EASTERN CHĀḶUKYA DYNASTY—*contd.*

12. *Kali-Vishṇuvardhana V* 843–844.

13. *Guṇaka-Vijayāditya III* 'Guṇānka,' 'Parachakra-Rāma,' 'Tribhuvanāmkuśa.' 844–888.

Vikramāditya I (Yuva-rāja)

14. *Chāḷukya-Bhīma II* 'Drōhārjuna.' 888–918.

Yuddhamalla I

18. *Tārapa, Tādapa*, or *Tāla I*. Reigned 1 month 925.

15. *Vijayāditya IV* 'Kollābhigaṇḍa,' 'Kaṇṭhika-Beta.' *Md.* Mēlāmbā. Reigned 6 months in A.D. 918.

19. Vikramāditya II Reigned 11 months 926.

21. *Yuddhamalla II* 927–934.

16. *Amma I* 'Vishṇu-vardhana VI,' Rājamahēndra.' 918–925.

22. *Chāḷukya-Bhīma III* 'Gaṇḍamahēndra,' 934–945

Bādapa

Tāla II 'Vishṇuvardhana.'

17. *Bēta Vijayāditya V* 'Kaṇṭhika.' Reigned 15 days, 925.

20. *Bhīma II* Reigned 8 months 926–27.

24. *Dānārṇava* *Md.* Ārya-Mahadēvī 970–973.

23. *Amma II* 'Vijayāditya VI,' 'Rāja-mahēndra.' 945–970.

see pedigree of the Pithāpūr princes of E. Chāḷukyā descent.

(*After an unexplained interval of 27 years.*)

25. *Śaktivarman* 999–1011.

26. *Vimalāditya* 'Mummaḍi-Bhīma,' 'Bhūpa-Mahēndra,' 'Birudanka-Bhīma.' *Md.* Kundavvā, dau. of Rājarāja Chōla I. 1011-1022.

27. *Rājarāja Narēndra I* *Md.* Ammangā-dēvī, dau. of Rājēndra Chōla I. 1022–1063.

Dau. *Md.* a Yādava king.

Vijayādityā VII. Viceroy of Vengi under his nephew Kulōttunga Chola I. 1063–1076.

28. *Rājēndra II* Reigned as Chāḷukya king 1063-1070. United the Chāḷukya and Chōla crowns and reigned as *Kulōttunga Chōla I*, 1070–1118. *Md.* Madurāntakī, dau. of Rājēndradēva Chōla. He was called 'Saptama Vishṇuvardhana,' etc. . . .

Dau. *Kundavvai.*

[*For descendants of Rājēndra II, Kulōttunga Chōla I, see pedigree of Chōḷas.*]

NOTES

4. *Vishṇuvardhana II's* accession was between February 18, and March 13 A.D. 663. (*Kielhorn E. I. vii. App. 93 ; E. R. 1917, App. A. Nos. 14, 15.*)

21. *Yuddhamalla II.* For his sons, see *E. R.* 1921, pp. 90, 91.

23. *Amma Rāja II* was crowned on December 5, 945. (*Masulipalam C. P. grant, V. R. ii, Kistna 3 ; Bm. C. P. grant No. 7.*)

23. and 24. It seems uncertain whether 24 *Dānārṇava* or 23 *Amma II* was the elder son. I follow some other pedigrees, but certainly it would naturally be supposed that Amma II was the elder.

26. *Vimalāditya* was crowned on May 10, 1011 (*Raṇastipūndi grant, E. I. vi, 347*).

27. *Rājarāja Narēndra I* was crowned on August 16, 1022. (*I. A. xix, 129*).

28. Rājēndra II was by blood three-quarters Chōla. He fought his Chōla cousins, and being completely successful, was crowned a second time as Chōla king in 1070. His other *birudas* were 'Karikāla Chōla,' 'Abhaya,' Jayadhara,' 'Virudarāja-Bhayaṁkara.'

PRINCES OF EASTERN CHĀḶUKYA DESCENT—A

(*See E. I v, 32–37 ; 332, 352 of 1896 ; V. R. i. Ganjam, 210, 230*).

26. *Vimalāditya*
1011–1022

27. *Rājarāja Narēndra*
1022–1063
(*relationship not clear*)

Vijayāditya I

Rājarāja
Vassal of the Kalinga king
Vīra Narasimha I
(middle of 13th century)

Vijayāditya II
or Vijayārka, A.D. 1273

Purushōttama
1277–1318

Jagannātha
or 'Viśvanātha', A.D. 1309. Vassal of the Kalinga king Vīra Bhānu II.

PRINCES OF EASTERN CHĀḶUKYA DESCENT—B

These are mentioned in records in the Sarvasiddhi Taluk, Vizagapatam District. Each has the titles 'Vishṇuvardhana Mahārāja' and 'Sarvalōkāśraya'. (*V. R. iii. Vizag. 21–33.*)

Vijayāditya
'of the family of Kulōttunga' Chōla I.
Md. Chandāmbikā. *c.*A.D. 1170.

Mallapa I
Md. Lakshmī. 1175–*c.* 1225.

Upēndra I
Md. Gangāmbā. *c.* 1225.

Mallapa II
Md. Chōḍāmbā. *c.* 1250.
Record of 1266. (*V. R. iii. Vizag. 69*).

Upēndra II
Md. Mallāmbā. 1283–4.

Koppa-Rājanārāyaṇa
Md. Gangāmbā.

Upēndra III
'Rājanārāyaṇa,' *Md.* Bimbāmbā
1355–56.

Channēśa

Upēndra V
Md. Atyamāmbā

Upēndra VI

Nāgēndra

Kumāra Yerrama
1432–3.

Chōḍēndra
1403

Upēndra IV
Md. Lakkāmbikā.

Viśvēśvara
'Rāyagaṇḍagopāla,' 'Dharaṇīvarāha.'
1407.

Nrisimha
Md. Vīrāmbā. 'Dharaṇīvarāha'
Records in 1422–3, 1428–9 ; 1437–8.

NOTE.—The date of accession of Mallapa I, A.D. 1175, is fixed by a record of his 3rd year at Bhimavaram, Godavari District. (*V. R ii. Godav. 45 ; 486 of 1893.*)

CHANGĀḶVA CHIEFS

They ruled at Nañjarāyapaṭṭaṇa, on the Kāvērī river in Coorg, and afterwards at Periyāpaṭṭaṇa, west of Mysore city (*See Rice in E. C. iv, Introd. 16 ; and 'Coorg Inscriptions,' Introd., 13*). They were subordinate to the Hoysala kings.

Nanni-Changāḷva, alias 'Rājēndra-Chōḷa.' *Md.* Padmalādēvī. A.D. 1034, 1037, 1058, 1077.

Mādēvaṇṇa. 1089–90.

Kulōttunga-Chōḷa Changāḷva Udayāditya. 1097, 1114.

Kulōttunga-Chōḷa Mahādēva, alias Pemma-Vīrappa. Inscriptions from 1173 to 1186.

Kulōttunga-Chōḷa Sōmadēva Boppadēva. 1246, 1252.

Mallidēva. 1280.

Harikaradēva. 1296, 1298.

(Unfilled break of about a century. Then ———).

Nāga c. 1425.
|
Ranga c. 1450.
|
Piriyaṇṇa c. 1475.

- *Nañja* or Nañjuṇḍa. 1502–1533.
- *Mahādēva*

(*Relationship unkown*). *Chennayya* 'Kulōttunga-Śrīkaṇṭha. 1544.

- *Vīra Chikka Rāja* 'Kulōttunga-Changāḷva.' 1568.
  - *Vīrappa.* 1612, 1615. (*E. C. iv Hs. 56*).
  - *Krishna Rāja,* 1617. Vīra Rāja 1619–1641.
- *Piriya Rāja* 1532–1591
- *Rudragaṇa* 1600.

In A.D. 1641 Vīra Rāja's capital Piriyāpaṭṭana was seized by the king of Mysore Kaṇṭhīrava Narasa Rāja. After a vain defence Vīra Rāja killed his own wives and children and then was himself killed fighting.

CHĒRA KINGS

They were early kings of Kēraḷa, with capital Vañji on the Periyār river near Cochin, now called Tiru-Karūr. There is a difference of opinion in the matter of dates. My chronology is roughly based on the assumption that the date of Gajabāhu I king of Ceylon, who was a guest of the Chēra king Śenguṭṭuvan, was A.D. 173–195. Burnell gives dates nearly a century earlier. For kings after the last in this table see Table of Kēraḷa kings (below).

Kuḍakkō-Neḍum-Śēral-Ādan I

c. A.D. 125 Fought against Chōla Peru-nar Kiḷḷi. Both kings killed in the same battle, A D.c. 150.

(*Relationship unkown*) *Perum-Śēral Ādan II*

A.D.c. 150 *Md.* dau. of Karikāla-Chōla. Fought against his father-in-law, and was defeated at battle of Veṇṇil. Allied himself with Pāṇḍya Neḍuñjeḷian I. Starved himself to death after his defeat.

- *Śen-guṭṭuvan* A.D.c. 175. 'Imayavaramban.' Fought against 9 Chōla princes (*Kiḷḷis*) at Nērivāyal, near Trichinopoly. Rescued Chōla Neḍumuḍi-Kiḷḷi from his brother, and restored him to throne. Vanquished 'Āryan' princes Kanaka and Vijaya. Gajabāhu I of Ceylon was his guest at Vañji.
- *Iḷangō-vaḍigaḷ* author of the *Silappadikaram*, or 'Epic of the Anklet.'

(*Relationship unkown*) *Śēy or Yānaikkaṭ-Śēy.*

A.D.c. 200. Warred against Chōla Peru-nar-Kiḷḷi II, and Pāṇḍya Neḍunjeḷian II, who captured him at battle of Talai-Ālangānan.

(*Relationship unkown*) *Perum-Śēral Irumborai* or 'Peruñjēral.' c. A.D. 6th cent.

CHŌLA KINGS

One of the most ancient families in South India, known to King Aśōka and mentioned by him, 250 B.C. Vijayālaya, who seized Tanjore, brought them into great prominence in the A.D. 9th century. They are little heard of after A.D. 1350. The early kings ruled from Puhār or Pugār, now identified with Kāvēripaṭṭaṇam on the east coast, which was overwhelmed by a tidal wave in the 2nd century A.D., and later at Tanjore. Uraiyūr near Trichinopoly was one of their principal cities.

Peru-nar-Kiḷḷi I
'Vēr-paha-raḍakkai.' A.D. *c.* 125.
Fought against the Chēra Kudakkō-Neḍumśēral-Ādan I, killed in battle, *c.* 150.

Iḷañ-jēṭ-Śenni
'Uruvuppaharēr Iḷayōn.' Did not reign. An early poem says he was father of Karikāla Chōla.

(?)

Karikāla Chōla
A.D. *c.* 150–180. Fought against the Chēra King Ādan II. Dammed the Kāvērī river. Very celebrated in ancient literature.

Neḍumuḍu Kiḷḷi
c. 180–200. 'Kiḷḷi Vaḷavan,' 'Vaḍivēr Kiḷḷi,' 'Māvaṇ-Kiḷḷi,' civil war. Raided Chēra country up to Vañji. Battle of Nērivāyil. Deposed by his brother. Restored by Chēra Śenguṭṭuvan. Puhār, the capital, destroyed by a storm. Battle of Kāriyāṛu.

(*Illegitimate*)
Toṇḍamān Iḷam-Tirayan A.D. *c.* 200.

Śēṭ-Śenni-Nalam Kiḷḷi
Rebelled against his brother unsuccessfully.

Dau. *Md.* the Chēra King Ādan II.

. . . . (*Relationship unknown*).

Peru-nar-Kiḷḷi II
'Rājasūyamvēṭṭa,' A.D. *c.* 200, or later.
Fought against Chēra king Śēy.

. . . . (*Relationship unknown*).

Śubhadēva
Md. Kamalavati.

Kō chchengaṇ
(?) A.D. 6th cent. Fought against Chēra king Kaṇaikkāl-Irumporai and defeated him at Kaḻumalam.

Nallaḍikōn

. . . . (*Relationship unknown*).

Kōkiḷḷi
Alias 'Śrīpathi'.

. . . . (*Relationship unknown*).

[*Henceforth the Chōla kings bore alternately the titles 'Parakēsari' and 'Rājakēsari' abbreviated here into 'Para' and 'Rāja.'*]

1. *Para. Vijayālaya*
Seized Tanjore. *c.* 846–880.

2. *Rāja. Āditya I*
c. 880–907.

3. *Para. Parāntaka I*
A.D. 907–947. 'Amśumāli,' 'Maduraikoṇḍa,' 'Vīra-Nārāyaṇa,' 'Vīra-Chōḷa,' 'Samgrāma-Rāghava.' *Md.* Kōkkiḻānaḍi.

4. *Rāja. Rājāditya I*
947–949. Killed fighting against Rāshṭrakūṭa king Krishṇa III at Takkōlam
'Kōdaṇḍarāman,' 'Mūvaḍi Chōḷa.'

5. *Para. Gaṇḍarāditya*
Md. Śembiyan-Mahādēvī
949—(?) 965.

6. *Rāja. Ariñjaya*
'Arikula-kēsari.'
(?) 965.

CHŌLA KINGS—*contd.*

9. *Para. Madurāntaka Uttama* (?) 969–985.

7. *Rāja. Parāntaka II* 'Sundara-Chōla,' 'Nityavinōda' 'Ponmāḷigaittunjina.'

8. *Rāja. Āditya II*, or 'Karikāla II.' Ousted by Madurāntaka-Uttama (?) 965–969.

Dau. *Kundavvaiyār Md.* to Vallavaraiyar Vāndyadēva

10. *Rāja. Rājarāja I* 'Mummaḍi-Chōla,' 'Nūrmaḍi-Chōla,' 'Arumoḷi-dēva.' 985–1016.

11. *Para. Rājēndra I* A very powerful king. 'Paṇḍita-Chōḷa,' 'Madurāntaka-Uttama,' 'Muḍikoṇḍa-Chōḷa,' 'Gangaikoṇḍa-Chōḷa,' 'Nigarili-Chōḷa' 1012–1043.

Gangaikonda-Chōla

Dau. *Kundavvai Md.* E. Chāḷukya king Vimalāditya

Dau. *Ammangādēvi Md.* Rājarāja I of the E. Chāḷukyas. Her son was E. Chāḷ. Rājēndra II (*see note below*)

12. *Rāja. Rājādhirāja I* 'Jayamkoṇḍa Chōla.' Reigned jointly with his father 1018–1043; then alone 1043–1052. Killed in battle at Koppam.

13. *Para. Rājēndradēva* 1052–1063

15. *Rāja Vīrarājēndra* 1063–1070 (*see note below*)

Three other sons

14. *Rājamahēndra*

Dau. *Madurāntakī Md.* E. Chāḷ. Rājēndra II

Five other sons

16. *Para. Adhi-Rājēndra* Killed 1070

Gangaikoṇḍa-Chola

Dau. *Md.* Vikramāditya VI of the W. Chāḷukyas

Note.—Rājēndra II of the Eastern Chāḷukyas claimed the throne in right of his mother Ammangā. He was opposed by the male heirs, fought them and defeated them, killing Adhi-Rājēndra. He seized the Chōla throne, united the two crowns, and was crowned as Chōla king on June 28, 1070, under the name of *Kulōttunga-Chōḷa I*, having been already E. Chāḷukya king since 1063.

17. *Rāja. Kulōttunga Chōla I*

Rājarāja 'Chōḍaganga' Viceroy of Vengi 1084–1088 to 9

Rājarāja 'Mummaḍi-Chōla,' Viceroy of Vengi 1076–1078

Vīra Chōḷa Viceroy of Vengi 1078–1084 and 1088–9 to 1092–3

18. Para. Vikrama-Chōḷa 'Akaḷanka,' 'Tyāgasamudra,' Viceroy of Vengi 1092–3 to 1118. King 1118–1133

Three other sons, and a dau. who *md.* Rājarāja of Kalinga

19. *Rāja. Kulōttunga-Chola II* 1133–1146

20. *Para. Rājarāja II* 1146–1163

(*The relationship of the remaining kings has not yet been established.*)

21. *Rāja. Rājadhirāja II.* A.D. 1163–1178.

22. Para. Kulōttunga III. 1178–1216. 'Kōnērinmaikoṇḍān,' 'Vīra-Rājēndra,' 'Tribhuvana-Vīra.'

23. Rāja. Rājarāja III, 1216–1246. 'Arumoḷi.' Taken captive by the powerful noble, Pallava Peruñjinga II (*see end of Pedigree of pallavas*). Liberated by the Hoysala king of Mysore Narasimha II, whose daughter he had married.

24. Para. Rājēndra III, 1246–1267. Probably son of No. 23. Helped to the Chōḷa throne by Hoysala Vīra-Sōmēśvara. But the kingdom broke up and the fragments were seized by local nobles, the Telugu-Chōḍa family who bore the title 'Gaṇḍagōpāla' (*see Pedigree of Telugu-Chōḍas*), the Śambuvaraiyan chiefs of the Śengēṇi family, and others of lesser note. The Chōḷa kingdom was extinct in 1267.

NOTES

For the early Chōḷa kings see the Anbil and Udayēndiram plates (*E.I. viii, App. ii, p. 21; xv, 46; S.I.I., ii, 152, 375;* Krishnaswami Aiyangar's, '*Ancient India*' *p. 90 f.; S.I.I., i, 112; iii, 196. T.A.S. iii. 101; I.A., xviii, 259 f; E.I. xv. 46*). My dates for them are tentative. They depend largely on the assumption that Śenguṭṭuvan Chēra's guest Gajabāhu I of Ceylon came to the throne in A.D. 173. Śenguṭṭuvan was contemporary with Neḍumuḍi-Kiḷḷi.

Parāntaka I began to reign between January 15 and July 25, 907 (*E. I. viii, 261*).

Rājarāja I's reign began between June 25 and July 12, 985.

Rājēndra I's reign began on May 30, 1012 (*341 of 1917*).

Rājādhirāja I began to reign as co-regent with his father between May 10 and November 22, 1018. He was killed at Koppam on May 28, 1052 (*S.I.I. ii, 303*).

Rājēndradeva's reign began May 23, 1052.

Vīra Rājēndra's reign began in the year following March 13, 1063.

Kulōttunga I's reign as Chōḷa king began on June 9, 1070 and ended on June 29, 1118 (*386, 389 of 1893 ; E. I vi, 221 ; vii, 7, n 5 ; S.I.I. iii. 190, 192*).

The order of birth of his sons as given in the above pedigree is taken from the Chellūr and Ṭēki plates. (*S.I.I. i, p. 31f*, corrected by Dr. Hultzsch in *E. I. vi. 335.*)

Rājarāja, second son of Kulōttunga I was 'crowned,' or installed as Viceroy of Vengi on July 27, 1076. (*A. R. 1921–22, p. 116.*)

Vikrama-Chōla's reign began on June 29, 1118.

Kulōttunga II's reign began between May 10 and July 14, 1136.

Rājarāja II's reign began between May 22 and June 26, 1146.

Rājādhirāja II's reign began between March 7 and 30, 1163.

(*Prof. Jacobi in E. I. xi, 123.*)

Kulōttunga III's reign began on July 6, 7 or 8, 1178.

Rājarāja III's reign began on June 27, 28 or 29, 1216.

Rājēndra III's reign began between March 28 and April 20, 1246.

CHŌLA RULERS OF COIMBATORE

See below, *List of Kongu-Choḷa Chiefs*

CHŌḶA-MAHĀRĀJAS OF THE RĒNĀNḌU COUNTRY

A family of early Chōḷa rulers has been brought to light by the contents of the Malepāḍu C.-P. grant Cuddapah District (*E. I. xi, 337f ; V. R. i, Cudd. 435, 455 ; E. R. 1904–5, p. 48*). They ruled part of the Telugu country about the 7th century A.D. The seal on the grant resembles that of the Vishṇukuṇḍin kings, shewing a maned lion with the tail twisted over the back in a loop. V. Venkayya identified the family with the 'Chu-li-ye' spoken of by Hiuen-Thsang A.D. *c.* 639. In his time they resided in the tract S. of Amarāvati on the Krishna river, and bordering on Kurnool. The 'Rēnāṇḍu' was a 'seven-thousand' village tract. The chiefs belonged to the Kāśyapa-gōtra. They claim descent from Karikāla Chōla (A. D. *c. 150–180*).

Nandivarman

- *Simhavishṇu*
- *Sundarānanda*
- *Dhanañjaya* (*see 380 of 1904*)
  - *Mahēndra-Vikrama* 'Mudita-Śilākshara,' 'Navarāma,' 'Lord of Chōla, Pāṇḍya and Kēraḷa countries.'
    - *Guṇamudita*
    - *Puṇya-Kumāra* 'Pōrmukha-Rāma,' 'Purusha-Śārdūla,' 'Mārdava-chitta,' 'Madana-vilāsa.' About A.D. 650 according to V. Venkayya.

Puṇya-Kumāra seems to have ruled over the Cuddapah District and part of Nellore.

Each chief has the title 'Chōḷa-Mahārāja.'

At a later date we hear of two chiefs of apparently the same family.

Vikramāditya-Chōḷa-Mahārāja and his Queen Eḷañ-Chōla (*400 of 1904 ; V. R. i. Cuddapah, 409*) ; and—

Atyana-Chōla-Mahārāja, in A.D. 1124–25 (*V. R. i. Cudd. 348 ; 350 of 1905*).

CHŌLA-MAHĀRĀJAS OF NIḌUGAL

See *Niḍugal Chiefs*, below

COORG—RĀJAS OF

Coorg was ruled in succession by the Kongāḷva and Changāḷva chiefs, of the Mysore plateau about the western ghāts, from about the 11th century A.D. till about A.D. 1641; but they were always subject to the Hoysala kings and after them the sovereigns of Vijayanagar. In A.D. 1687 a Bednūr chief succeeded in getting possession of Coorg, and his family ruled there till in 1834, the last Rāja was deposed by the British owing to his cruelties and excesses.

Vīra Rāja
- *Appāji*
  - 1. *Muddu Rāja* 1681(?)–1687.
    - *Dodda Vīrappa* 1687–1736
      - A son died 1729
        - 3. *Chikka Vīrappa* 1736–1766
    - *Appāji*
      - 4. *Muddu* Ruled jointly with his cousin Muddayya 1766–1770
        - *Appāji*
      - 6. *Linga* 1775–1780
        - 7. *Vīra* or *Dodda Vīra Rājēndra* 1780–1809
          - 8. *Dēvammājī* 1809–1811
        - 9. *Linga* 1811–1820
          - 10. *Vīra* 1820–1834. Deposed by the British for misrule.
        - *Appāji*
        - *M*
      - 4. *Muddaya* Ruled jointly with his cousin Mudd. 1766–1770.
        - 5. *Dēvappa* 1770–1775.

No. 1 *Muddu* made Mercara his capital in 1681. No. 6 *Linga* ousted Dēvappa by the support of Haidar Ali. When he died Haidar took Coorg. In 1782 the people of Coorg rebelled against Haidar, but were subdued by Tipu, who kept Vīra (No. 7) a prisoner. Vīra escaped in 1788, fled to the English for refuge and with their aid regained his throne. No. 10 Vīra is said to have been a 'Monster of Cruelty,' guilty of 'wholesale murders' and one who 'established a reign of terror in the country' (*L. Rice*). Coorg was taken under British protection by the request of the people.

DAṆṆĀYAKANKŌṬṬAI CHIEFS

They came into power with the decay of the Hoysala dynasty in Mysore, after the destruction of the latter's capital, Dorasamudra in A.D. 1310 by Malik Kāfur (*443, 444 of 1906; Arch. Rep., Southern Circle 1920–21, p. 22*).

Perumāḷadēva
'Nīlagiri-Sādhara.' Governed the Padināḷkunāḍ tract in Mysore. Minister to Hoysala Narasimha III who reigned 1254–1291.
- *Mādhava Daṇṇāyaka*
  - *Singaṇa* Semi-independent in 1346.
  - *Kētayya* 'Nīlagiri-Sādhara,' 'Sitaraganḍa.'

DEKHAN—SUBAHDARS OF THE—OR NIZĀMS OF HYDERABAD

1. *Nizām-ul-Mulkh Āsaf Jāh.*
Created Subahdar of the Dekhan by the Mughal Emperor Farrukhsiyar, 1713. Became independent 1724, 1713–1748.

- *Ghāziu-d-dīn Khān.* (Poisoned, 1752).
- 2. *Nāsir Jang.* 1748–1750. Sided with the English. Shot by Navāb of Cuddapah.
- 3. *Salābat Jang.* 1751–1761. Deposed 1761 by Nizām Ali. Murdered 1762.
- 4. *Nizām Ali.* 1761–1803. Allied himself with the English.
  - 5 *Mīrza Sikandar Jāh.* 1803–1829.
    - 6. *Nāsiru-d-daulah. Farkhundah Ali Khan.* 1829–1857. Navāb Sir Sālār Jang was his Minister after 1853.
      - 7. *Afzulu-d-daulah.* 1857–1869. Sir Sālar Jang was his minister
        - 8. *Mīr Mahbūb Ali Khān.* 1869–1912. Sir Sālār Jang died 1883.
- *Bassalat Jang.* Obtained Guntur Circar as his personal estate. Died 1782.
- *A daughter*
  - *Muzaffar Jang.* Proclaimed Subahdar by the French 1750. Killed by the Navāb of Kurnool, 1751.

NOTES. 1. The family name of Nizām-ul-Mulkh was Chin-kuli-Khān Āsaf Jāh. Titles—'Mīr Kamrū-d-dīn Khan', 'Fath, Jang', 'Nizāmu-d-daulah.' He was Wazīr to the Emperor Muhammad Shāh, 1722. He became reconciled to his sovereign in 1736. Waged war against the Mahrattas till peace was made in 1740.

3. Salābat Jang gave Koṇḍavīḍu, Nizāmpaṭam, etc., to the French, but in 1759 ceded those districts to the English.

4. Nizām Ali was allied with the English in their war with Tīpū Sultān.

DELHI—DYNASTIES OF,

Delhi was captured from its Hindu ruler by Sultan Muhammad of Ghor in A.D. 1193. Kutbu-d-dīn Aibak an ennobled slave, was made Sultan of Delhi in 1206.

I. THE SLAVE KINGS

1. *Kutbu-d-din Aibak.* 1206–1210.

- 2. *Aram.* d. 1211. Deposed.
- A Dau. *Md.* 3. *Shamsu-d-dīn Altamsh,* or Altmish or Iyaltimish. 1211-1236.
  - 4. *Ruknu-d-dīn Firoz Shah.* Deposed and Killed, 1236.
    - 7. *Alāu-d-dīn Mas'ūd.* 1245–1246. Deposed.
  - 5. Dau. *Rāziyah.* deposed, 1236–1240.
  - 6. *Muizzu-d-dīn Bahram.* 1240–1242. Killed.
  - 8. *Nasiru-d-dīn Mahmūd* 1246–1266.
  - Dau. *Md.* 9. *Ghiyāsu-d-dīn Balban, Ulugh Khān.* Seized the throne 1266–1286.
    - *Muhammad* Killed, 1281.
    - Dau. *Md. Nasiru-d-dīn Mahmūd.*
    - *Bughra Khān* appointed Governor of Bengal.
      - 10. *Muizzu-d-dīn Kai Qubād.* 1286–1290. Killed.

On Kai Qubād's death the nobles placed on the throne a general Jalālu-d-dīn Khilji, who established the Khilji dynasty.

II. KHILJI DYNASTY

- 1. *Jalālu-d-dīn Firōz Khilji* 1290–1296. Murdered.
  - *Khān-i Khānān.* Murdered.
  - *Arkali Khān.* Murdered.
  - 2. *Ruknu-d-dīn. Ibrahim, Kādir Khān.* Deposed Fled.
- *Ma'sūd*
  - 3. *Alāu-d-dīn. Sikandar* 1296–1316.
    - *Khizr Khān.* Blinded.
    - *Shādī Khān.* Blinded.
    - 4 *Shahābu-d-dīn* Blinded and deposed 1316.
    - 5. *Mubārak Kutbu-d dīn* 1316–1320
  - *Almas Beg*

Mubārak was assassinated in 1320, and, since there were no fitting survivors of the Khilji family, the nobles placed on the throne a general, *Ghāzi Malik*, who assumed the name of *Ghiyāsu-d-dīn Tughlak*.

III. TUGHLAK DYNASTY

- 1. *Ghiyāsu-d-dīn Tughlak.* 1321–1325
  - 2. *Muhammad Tughlak Fakru-d-dīn, Jūna, Ulugh Khān.* 1325–1351.
- *Rajab, Sipāh Sālār.*
  - 3. *Fīrōz Tughlak.* 1351–1388.
    - *Fath Khān.*
      - 4. *Ghiyāsu-d-dīn.* 1388–1389. Deposed and killed.
      - 8. *Nusrat Shāh.* 1395–1398.
    - *Zafar Khān*
      - 5. *Abū Bakr.* 1389–1390. Deposed
    - 6. *Muhammad Shāh.* 1390–1394
      - 7. *Humāyūn Sikandar* 1394
      - 9. *Mahmūd Shāh.* 1394–1413.

In A.D. 1398 Delhi was overwhelmed by the invasion of Taimūr, and the city was sacked. A period of anarchy followed, and then a Saiyid General Khizr Khān who had been governor of Lahore established the short-lived Saiyid dynasty.

IV. SAIYID DYNASTY

- 1. *Khizr Khān* 1414–1421
  - 2. *Mubārak Muizzu-d-dīn.* 1421–1434. Killed.
  - *Farīd Khān.*
    - 3. *Muhammad Shāh.* 1434–1445
      - 4. *Alāu-d-dīn Alim Shāh.* 1445–1451

In 1451 Alāu-d-dīn retired from Delhi, and the throne was seized by Bahlōl Lōdi, a General and Governor of Sirhind.

V. LŌDI DYNASTY

- 1. *Bahlōl Lōdi* 1451–1489
  - 2. *Sikandar Lōdi.* Nizām Khān. 1489–1517.
    - 3. *Ibrahīm Lōdi.* 1517–1526.

In 1526 India was invaded by Bābur from Kābul. At Panipat after a great battle, the Delhi forces were completely defeated and Ibrahīm Lōdi was killed. Bābur seized the throne and established the Mughal dynasty. (*For their pedigree see below.*)

GAJAPATI KINGS, *See* ORISSA KINGS.
GAṆAPATI KINGS, *See* KĀKATĪYA DYNASTY.
EASTERN GANGA KINGS, *See* KALINGA KINGS.

WESTERN GANGA KINGS

An early dynasty ruling originally in Anantapur district and Kolar in Mysore,—Extending later and embracing the whole of Mysore and the Kongu-country of Salem and Coimbatore, when their capital was Talakāḍ (S.-E. of Mysore Town) and their dominions were called the 'Gangavāḍi 96000'.

Their titles were 'Permānaḍi' and 'Konguṇivarman.' Towards the end of the 5th century A. D. Mrigēśavarman, the Kadamba chief of Baṇavāśi is said to have conquered the Gangas. They were subordinate to the Chaḷukyas in the 7th century, but recovered power when the latter were conquered by the Rāshṭrakūṭas in A.D. 753. They were generally subordinate to their great neighbours.

Previous writers, e.g., Fleet, Jouveau-Dubreuil, Rice, etc., differ widely in their estimate of the dates of early kings. I only enter therefore dates that seem fairly proved (*see notes below*). I dispense with traditionary ancestors (see S. Krishnaswami Aiyangar's *Culture, p. 189; E. I xiv, 337; E. C. ix Introd. p. 6 f.; E. I. v. 153; vi, 59.*).

1. *Harivarman, or Ayyavarman.*
Consecrated about A.D. 450 by Simhavarman Pallava to conquer the Bāṇas.

2. *Vishṇugōpa.*
(omitted in some records)

|

3. *Mādhava I.*
or Simhavarman. Installed about 470 by Skandavarman Pallava.

5. *Durvinīta.*
Annexed the territory of his father-in-law the Punnāḍ Rāja in S.-W. Mysore. Battles at Andari, Allattūr, Puruḷarē, Pērnagara.

Prithvīpati
V.R. i. Chittoor 215; 326 of 1912.

|

6. *Mushkara.*

|

7. *Śrīvikrama.*

|

8. *Bhūvikrama.*
or 'Bhimakopa,' or 'Śrīvallabha.'
'Defeated the Pallavas at Viḷanda.'

|

9. *Śivamāra I.*
or 'Nava-kāma' or 'Chāgi.'

|

10. (?) *Erēyanga I.*
(*Sometimes omitted*).

|

11. *Śrīpurusha.*
'Muttarasa.' Said to have killed a Pallava king at Viḷarde. *Md.* Kānchiabbe (*see notes below*).

The dates entered hereafter are mostly taken from those determined by Fleet.

WESTERN GANGA KINGS—*contd.*

12. *Śivamāra II.* (?) *c.* 805–810. 'Saigotta,' 'Vīra Martāṇḍa,' 'Narasimha.' Imprisoned by Rāshṭrakūṭa king Dhruva. Released. Again captured. Reinstated by Govinda III.

13 *Vijayāditya.* 'Raṇavikrama,' 'Nītimārga.' *c.* 810–840. Fought against Eastern Chāḷukyas.

Durgamāra. or *Ereyappa II.*

(?) *Mārasimha I.* 'Lōka Triṇētra.' Yuvarāja in 797.

14. *Prithivīpati I.* *c.* 840–877 to 8. 'Diṇḍika.' Battle at Vaimbalguḷi. Killed in battle against Varaguṇa Pāṇḍya at Tirupurambiyam. Contemp. with Rāshṭrakūṭa Amōghavarsha I and Aparājita Pallava.

Rājamalla I. or Rācha.' 870. Md. Sister of Noḷamba Pallava Chief.

15. *Mārsimha II.* *c.* 878–900.

Dau. *Kundavvai.* *Md.* to Vikramāditya Bāṇa I.

(?) *Ereyappa*, or *Ereyanga (sometimes omitted).*

Dau. *Jayabbe.* *Md.* Noḷamba-Pāllava Chief Poralchōra I.

16. *Prithivīpati II.* 900–940. Vassal of Parāntaka. Chōla I, who conferred on him the title 'Śembiyan-Māvalivāṇarāya,' and gave him the territories of the Bāṇa chiefs.

Vikramāditya or 'Vikkiyaṇṇa.' Killed in a quarrel with the Pallava chief Dhavaḷa. Governed the Pulināḍu country *(332 of 1912).*

Rāchamlla II, or Rājā 'Satyavākya.' Battle of Sāmiya. Driven out by Rāshṭrakūṭa Krishna II. Date *c* 870–907.

Būtuga I. Yuva-Rāja in 870. 'Guṇaduttāranga.' *Md.* Abbalabbe, dau. of Rāshṭrakūṭa Amōghavarsha I. Defeated Noḷamba-Pallava Mahēndra I at Sāmiya.

Ereyappa IV. (*Doubtful*). Said to have been crowned as king by Rāchamalla II. *Md.* a Chāḷukya princess Jākambā. Dates Nov. 25, 904, 913, 934. Died 938.

Narasimha 'Satyavākya.'

Rāchamalla, or Rāja III. 'Kachcheya Ganga.' 'Nītimārga.' *c.* 938. Defeated Noḷamba-Pallava chief Aṇṇiga at Kottamangala. Killed by his brother Būtuga II.

Dau. *Pambāmba.* *Md* Dhora. Died 971 (*E.C vi, Kd.* 1).

17. *Būtuga II.* 'Nanniya-Ganga,' Jayaduttaranga 939–40 to 953. Allied with Rāshṭrakūṭa Krishna III. Killed the Chōla King Rājāditya I at battle of Takkōlam. Murdered his brother. *Md.* Rēvakannimmadi sister of Krishṇa III, and Kallabbarasi.

(*By Rēvakannimmadi.*)

18. *Maruladēva* *Md.* Bijabbe dau. of Rāshṭrakūṭa Krishṇa III *c.* 953–961 (?)

Indra

Dau. *Somidēvī.*

(*By Kallabbarasi*)

19. *Mārasimha III.* 'Satyavākya,' Guttiya-Ganga' (?) 961–974. Conquered and annexed the Noḷambavāḍi province. A Jain by religion. Starved himself to death in 974.

20. *Rāchamalla, or Rāja IV.* 'Satyavākya.' 'Rakkasa-Ganga 974–(?) 1004. His minister Chāmuṇḍa erected the Jain colossus at Śravaṇa-Beḷgoḷa.

(?) *Rakkasa-Ganga Rāchamalla* (See note)

Arumoḷidēva 'Rakkasa-ganga.'

Rāja-Vdiyādhara.

No. 20 *and his two brothers are entered as given by Rice in* 'Mysore and Coorg', *p. 50, but it certainly looks unlikely that two brothers would have had precisely the same name and biruda. The dynasty came to an end by the war which ended with Rājarāja Chōla I's conquest of the Gangas in A.D. 1004. His enemy was called Rāchamalla Nītimārga.*

NOTES.—The dates of 1, Harivarman and 3, Mādhava I seem fairly well-proved.

An inscription of No. 11 Śripurusha (*E. C. vi. Mg., 36*) bears date = April 21 750 (Ś 672), and being in his 25th year makes his accession to have taken place in the year following April 21, 725. Allowing four generations to a century we should have 3 Mādhava I's accession as about A.D. 550; but he is said to have been installed in 470. The chronology is confusing. Jouveau-Dubreuil makes Mādhava I's reign begin in A.D. 540. Fleet made it begin about 460. Jouveau-Dubreuil makes 4 Avinita's reign begin in 565, and his son Durvinita's in 605, an assignment quite reasonable in view of the date for 11 Śrīpurusha's accession—A.D. 725. According to Rice, Durvinīta's accession was in A.D. 483–4. Fleet's date for 11 Śrīpurusha is 765–805, but that seems contradicted by the inscription I have mentioned. Again, if 11 Śrīpurusha's began to reign in 725 his son 12 Śivamāra could hardly have begun to reign in 805, which is Fleet's date for his accession. I cannot explain these difficulties, whose removal must be left for future research.

A.D. 1060, 1074. Inscriptions shew a Nanniya-Ganga-Bhuvanēka-Udayāditya-Vikrama-Ganga ruling N.-W. Mysore as vassal of the Western Chāḷukya king Sōmēṣvara II (*E. C. xi, Dg. 140 ; vii. Sk. 221*).

A.D. 1122, Aug. 14. Date of death of the same (?) Nanniya-Ganga (*E. C. xi, Hk. 68*).

A.D. 1158. Another Nanniya- Ganga mentioned (*E. C. vii, Sk. 18*).

A.D. 1180. Śiyaganga mentioned in an inscription at Kāḷahasti of the third year of Kulottunga Chōla III (*V. R. i. Chittoor, 64*). He is mentioned also at Conjevaram in 1204 (*S. I. I, iii, 122, 207*). He was called 'Śiya. gangan-Amarābharaṇan,' and 'Tiruvēgambam Uḍaiyān.' Other records of his in 1211-12 and 1212/13. He married Àriyā-Piḷḷai. His father's name was Chōḷēndra-Simha, who was 'Lord of Kovaḷālapura' (*589 of 1919 ; S.I.I. iii. 122*). In 1224–5 a grant was made 'for his merit' in which he is called 'Amarābharaṇa-Akaḷanka Śiyaganga, alias Uttama Chōḷa-Ganga.' (*V. R. I. Chittoor 235*).

A.D. 1247–8. In this year Akkarasa-Gangarasa Rajayya was ruling the Cuddapah country (*V. R. I. Cudd. 925*).

A.D. 1397 a Ganga chief mentioned in Cuddapah (*V. R. i. Cudd. 52*).

A long inscription at Humcha (*E. C. viii, Nr. 35*) gives a pedigree of descendants of Būtuga II, which differs from the above, as follows.

17. *Būtuga II.*

18. *Mārulad̄eva.* — 19. *Mārasimha III.* — *Rājamalla.* — *Govindarasa* '*Nītimārgā*' — *Vāsava* *Md.* Kañchalādēvī

Govindarasa '*Satyavākaya*'. — *Arumoḷidēva.* *Md.* Gāvabbarasī

Dau. *Chattalē.* *Md.* a chief of Pallava descent called 'Kāḍuveṭṭi, lord of Kānchī'. She built a Jain *basti* in A.D. 1077.

Dau. *Kañchalā.* *Md.* the Sāntara king Vīradēva, father of Taila II (*c.* 1050.)

Rājavidyādhara.

An inscription in Sorab Taluk, Mysore (*E. C. viii, Sb. 140*) gives another pedigree of descendants of 19 Mārasimha III. Date early in A.D. 1198.

Bittiga, or 17 Būtuga II.
|
19. *Mārasimha*
|
Kīrti

Mārasimha. — Dau. *Suggiyabbe.*

Ekkaladēva. A.D. 1139. — Dau. *Chattalā-dēvī.* *Md.* Daśavarmarasa.

Ereya. or *Ereyanga.* — *Keśava.* — *Nanniya-Ganga.* 'Singadēva' or 'Narasinga' *Md.* Lakshmadēvī (?) 1158. (*See notes above*)
|
Ekkala. Early in A.D. 1198.

GOLKONDA

KUṬB-SHAHI—DYNASTY OF

Kuṭbu-l-Mulkh was governor of Telingāna under Muhammad Bāhmani III. He withdrew from court after his master's murder of Mahmūd Gawān, but remained loyal to the crown till A.D. 1512, or, as some say, 1518, when he proclaimed himself independent. He made Golkonda his capital.

1. *Kuṭbu-l-Mulkh Muhammad.*
Kuli Kutb Shāh I.
A.D. 1512 (or 1518)—1543 murdered.

Children:

- *Kuṭbu-d-dīn.* Blinded by Jamshid.
- 2. *Jamshid.* 1543–1550.
  - *Subhān.* an infant.
- *Haidar* died without issue
- 3. *Ibrahīm.* 1550–1581. Captured and annexed Rājamundry and the East Coast Districts.

Children of Ibrahīm:

- *Abdul Kādir.* Poisoned by his father.
- A son. Died young
- 4. *Muhammad Kuli II.* 1581–1612.
- *Muhammad Amīn.*
  - 5. *Muhammad.* 1612–1635.
    - 6. *Abdullah.* 1635–1672

NOTES 5 Abdullah Kuṭb Shāh was succeeded by Abūl Hasan, whose relationship to Abdullah seems doubtful. In the *Imperial Gazetteer* he is called son-in-law in the pedigree table (II. 390), but in vol. xiii, p. 239 he is 'nephew.' [He was a member of Kuṭb Shahi family and was the third son-in-law of Abdulla. Sarkar's Aurangzeb IV, also article in *Journal of Indian History*, Vol. x, ii.]—*Editor.*

Abūl Hasan, *alias* 'Tānā Shāh' was defeated by Prince Shāh Ālam in 1685; Hyderabād was again looted and Abūl Hasan compelled to submit. In 1687 Golkonda was annexed to Delhi.

GUPTA DYNASTY—THE—

Founded by Chandragupta I, a Hindu chief who married a princess of the Lichchāvi family of Behar and made himself master of Pāṭaliputra, becoming its king about A.D. 308.

1. *Chandragupta I.*
Crowned A.D. 319 or early in 320.
Md. A Lichchāvi princess Kumarādevi.
Reigned till *c.* 336.

2. *Samudragupta*
A.D. 336–380 *Md.* Dattādēvi.
Conquered Orissa 340. Captured Mahēndragiri, Pishṭhāpura and the Kolēr lake. Defeated Vishṇugopa Pallava of Kānchi. Captured Vengi province.

3. *Chandragupta II.*
'Vikramāditya,' 'Deva-gupta.' 360–413
Md. Dhruvādēvī and Kubēra-nāgā.

Children:

- 4. *Kumāra-Gupta I.* 'Mahēndra.' 413–455.
  - *By Devakī*
    - 5. *Skandagupta*[1] 455–468 (?) Hun invasions from the north in his reign, certain dates 456–7, 467–8. (reigned perhaps jointly with)
- *Dau. Prabhāvatī.* *Md.* the Vākāṭaka king Rudra-Sēna II.
  - (By Ānanda-dēvi).
    - *Puragupta* Ruled in the east (?)

[1] The pedigree after 5 Skandagupta is somewhat doubtful. I follow the course proposed by R.C. Mujumdar. (*I. A. 1918, 166*) for dates; and for relationships the fixtures of Radhagovinda Basak (*E. I. xv, 118*).

GUPTA DYNASTY—THE—*contd.*

7. *Kumāragupta II.*
472–477 to 8 More wars with Huns.

8. *Buddhagupta.*
477-8 to 500. The Huns broke up the Gupta kingdom.

(?)

9. *Bhānugupta.*
Dates in 510–11 and 533-4. The king was tributary to the Hun leaders Toramāṇa and Mihirākula.

6. *Narasimhagupta*
'Bālāditya. 468–472.

Kumāragupta III

GUTTA FAMILY

Of Guttavoḷal or Guttal in Dhārwar district. The chiefs claimed descent from the ancient Guptas.

1. *Mahāgutta or Māgutta*

2. Gutta I

3. Malla or Mallidēva.
A.D. *c.* 1115 Subordinate to Gōvinda Rāja who was vassal of the W. Chāḷukya Vikramāditya VI

4. *Vikramāditya I*

5. *Jomma, Jōma,* or *Joyideva* I. 1181. Feudatory of Kalachuri Āhavamalla.

6. *Gutta II*
Md. Padmalā-dēvi.

7. *Vikramāditya II*
'Āhavāditya' Md. Paṭṭamādēvi.
1182–1213.

Dau: Tuḷuvalādēvi
Md. Baḷḷāḷa of a Sāntaḷigē family.

8. *Jōvideva or Jōyidēva II*
1237. Feudatory of the Dēvagiri Yādava king Singhaṇa.

9. *Vikramāditya III.*
Md. Mailāḷadēvi

Gutta III
1262–1265. Feudatory of Dēvagiri-Yādava King Mahādēva.

Hiriyadēva.

Jōyidēva III.

See Fleet in *Bombay Gazetteer* I., pt. I, p. 579, and Kielhorn (*E. I. viii, App, ii., p. 10*). Fleet thinks that Vikramāditya II was practically independent pending the issue of the struggle between the Yādavas of Dēvagiri and the Hoysalas for the possession of the former's southern provinces.

HARSHA'S KINGDOM

Harsha, or Harshavardhana established a short-lived sovereignty, but one in its time powerful, about A.D. 600. Capital Thānasar, near Ambāla.

1. *Prabhākaravardhana*
A.D. *c.* 580–605. Rāja of Thānesar. His mother was a Gupta princess. He became powerful on the break-up of the Gupta kingdom.

2. *Rājyavardhana*
A. D. 605–606. Attacked the Huns. Treacherously killed by Śaśānka, king of Bengal.

3. *Harsha, or Harshavardhana*
Succeeded in A.D. 606. Crowned 612. Died 647. Attacked the Dekhan 620 but was unable to defeat the W. Chāḷukya Pulakēśin II. Attacked Ganjam in 643. Captured Orissa 640.

On Harsha's death his throne was usurped by his minister Arjuna, A.D. 647, but he was defeated and taken prisoner by Chinese and Thibetans. The kingdom then dissolved.

Harsha established the 'Śrīharsha Era' which began on the day of his accession in October 606.

HOYŚALA DYNASTY

Capital Dorasamudra or Haḷebiḍ in Mysore. Rose to great power on the decline of the Western Chāḷukya kingdom. They claimed to belong to the Yādava stock.

1. *Nṛipakāma*
'Rāchamalla-Permānaḍi'
1022—(?) 1040

2. *Vinayāditya.*
'Tribhuvanamalla', 'Biṭṭiga'. *c.* 1040–1100
Md. Kalayabbe. Feudatory of W. Chāḷukya Vikramāditya VI.

Ereyanga
Did not reign. *Md.* Echalādēvī.

3. *Ballāḷa I*
(?) 1100–1106. *Md.* Padmalā, Chavalā and Boppā. Defeated Sāntara Jagaddēva.

4. *Vishṇuvardhana*
C. 1106–1141. 'Biṭṭi', 'Vikrama-Ganga', *Md.* Sāntalā and Lakshmī. 'Bhujabala-Ganga', 'Tribhuvanamalla'. Captured Talakāḍ 1116. Drove Chōḷas out of Mysore.

Udayāditya, Died 1122.

5. *Narasimha I.*
1141–1173. 'Jagadēkamalla'.
Md. Echalā-dēvī.

6. *Ballāḷa II.*
Crowned July 22, 1173. Died (?) 1220. 'Tribhuvanamalla', 'Śanivārasiddhi', 'Giridurgamalla'. Seized Uchchangi, and captured and restored its governor Kāma-dēva. Seized some Kalachuri territories, 1183.

7. *Narasimha II.*
1220—(?) 1234–5 *Md.* Kālalādēvī and Padmalādēvi. Rescued Rājarāja Chōla III from imprisonment by Pallava Perunjinga, and restored him.

8. *Sōmēśvara, or Sōyi-dēva.*
(?) 1234–5 to 1254. Was at Kannanūr in 1228, and made it his residence, *Md.* Bijjalā and Dēvalā (a Chāḷukya princess).

By Bijjalā. — *By Devalā.*

9. *Narasimha III.*
1254–1291. Kingdom divided. He reigned in the north. Drove back the Dēvagiri-Yādavas.

Dau. Ponnambala.

10. *Rāmanātha.*
1255–1295. Reigned in the south. *Md.* Kāmalādēvi, a Ganga princess.

Sons of Narasimha III:

11. *Ballāḷa III.*
Crowned Jan. 31, 1292. Died Sept. 8, 1342. Reunited the kingdom. Dorasamudra sacked by Malik Kafur 1310, and destroyed by Muhammad Tughlak 1327. Killed by Ghiyāsu-d-din Sultan of Madura, 1342.

Sōma

Mallidēva

Sons of Rāmanātha:

Viśvanātha.
1294–5. He was ousted by Ballāḷa III.

Mañjayya-Māgutiar

Sons of Ballāḷa III:

12. *Ballāḷa IV* alias *Virūpaksha* crowned Aug. 11, 1343. He had no real power, and his country fell to the strength of the Vijayanagar kings.

Tipparasa-Bhairava.

NOTES—4. *Vishṇuvardhana* is stated in inscriptions to have (i) conquered the Kēraḷa king and seized the Nilagiri Hills; (ii) defeated Narasimha, Adiyama Jagaddēva (? Sāntara chief); (iii) Defeated Irungōḷa Chōḷa (? of Niḍugal, *q. v.*); (iv) defeated Sāntara Jayakēsin; (v) 'defied' the Western Chaḷukyas.

5. *Narasimha I* was said to be reigning on May 3, 1173 (*E. C. v, Hn. 154*); but another inscription, whose date is not perfect, dates his death as on Jan. 15, 1170 (*E. C. vii, Ci. 36*).

6. *Ballāla II* was alive early in A.D. 1220 (*E. C. ix, Ma. 77*). He seems to have lost much territory N. of the Tungabhadra river to the Dēvagiri-Yādavas.

7. *Narasimha II* reigning in April 1220 and was crowned on the 16th (*E. C. v, Bl. 85 ; vii, Ci, 72 ; v, Cn. 172*).

8. *Sōmēśvara's* accession was in the year following June 15, 1234 (*E. C. vi, Tk. 87*). He was at Kaṇṇanūr on March 15, 1228, when Yuva-Rāja (*E. C. iii, Nj. 36*). A record of Jaṭāvarman Sundara Pāṇḍya (1251–1268) says that he drove Sōmēśvara out of Kaṇṇanūr (*E. I. iii, 7*).

9. *Narasimha III.* There is a record of his of date = Nov. 26, 1254 (*E. C. v, Bl. 125*).

10. *Rāmanātha* is recognized as king, in his portion of the kingdom, in inscriptions which shew his accession to have taken place between June 16 and July 12, 1255 (*E. C. x. Mb. 100 ; Bp. 23*). He recovered possession of Kaṇṇanūr shortly after the beginning of his reign, for an inscription of his at that place bears date = January 24, 1257.

11. *Ballāla III* was crowned on January 31, 1292 (*E. C. vi. Cm. 36*). His death at the hands of Ghiyāsu-d-din took place on September 8, 1342, he being then 80 years of age (*E. C. vi. Kd. 75*). Before his coronation he was reigning for some months (*E. C. vi. Kd. 49 ; ix. Kn. 64*). Ibn Batuta relates his tragic end, how he was put, to death and his skin stuffed with straw and exposed to the public. Two records shew him alive on July 3 and September 5, 1342 (*E. C. ix. Bm. 21 ; Dv. 21*).

12. The coronation of *Virupāksha*, alias *Ballāla IV* is mentioned in *E. C. vi. Cm. 105*.

Tipparasa-Bhairava is mentioned in 738 of 1917.

HYDERĀBAD—NIZAMS OF,

See DEKHAN—SUBAHDARS OF,

IKKĒRI KINGS

See KEḶADI KINGS

KADAMBA DYNASTY OF BAṆAVĀŚI

The dates appended to the names of kings are taken from Jouveau-Dubreuil (' *Ancient History of the Dekhan*' *p. 95f*). They are tentative.

- 1. *Mayūraśarman.* A. D. 340–360. Took Baṇavāśi and Halsi (Palāśikā), and crushed the Chuṭu-Śātakarṇi rulers. (*See* the Table of Āndhra Kings.)
  - 2. *Kangavarman.* 360–385. Much fighting in his reign.
    - 3. *Bhāgīratha.* 385–410.
      - 4. *Raghu.* 410–425.
      - 5. *Kakutsthavarman.* (425–450. One of his daughters *Md.* a Gupta king.)
        - 6. *Śāntivarman.* 450–475.
          - 7. *Mrigēśavarman.* 475 (or 471, *see notes*) —488. ' Vijayaśiva ' *Md.* Kaikeya Prabhāvatī.
          - 8. *Māndhātrivarman.* 488–500.
        - *Krishṇavarman I.* *Md.* the dau. of Kaikeya chief.
          - *Vishṇuvarman I* or *Vishṇudāsa* Killed by Ravivarman.
          - *Dēvavarman* or *Śivānandavarman.* Became an ascetic.

KADAMBA DYNASTY OF BAṆAVĀSI—*contd.*

Ravivarman 500–537. | *Bhānuvarman.* | *Śivaratha* 541/2. | *Simhavarman*

Ravivarman →
10. *Harivarman* 537–550. Lost his country to Chaḷukya Pulakēśin I.

Śivaratha →
11. *Krishṇavarman* 550–565. The country seized by Chaḷukya Kīrttivarman I.
Ajavarman.
Bhōgivarman.
Vishṇuvarman II.

Daughter *Md.* the Ganga king Mādhava II

NOTES.—For 1 *Mayūraśarma*, see the Taḷagunda inscription, (*E. I. viii. 30*). He was a Brahman of the Mānavya Gōtra, and claimed descent from Hāriti, as did the Chaḷukya princes. He attacked the Pallavas of Kānchī and made himself independent at Baṇavāsi.

7. *Mrigēśavarman* may have come to the throne in A.D. 471. For an inscription of his third year bears a date in A.D. 473, given as in the year Pausha, which, in the 12 year cycle = Kīlaka (*I. A., 1878, p. 35*).

10. *Harivarman's* accession may have been in A.D. 538. See the Sangoli plates of A.D. 545 (*E. I. xiv., 166*).

Śivaratha ruled Uchchangi-drūg in Harivarman's fourth year (*I. A. vi, p. 30, the Halsi plates*).

LATER KADAMBAS OF BAṆAVĀSI

A.D. 911. A certain Kalivitta ruled the province under Rāshṭrakuta Krishṇa II. He killed a Kadamba chief named *Ayyavarman* (*E. C. viii, Sb., 88*).

987–8. *Āryavarman*, 'Lord of Baṇavāsi,' ruled part of Bellary District under the W. Chāḷukya king Tailapa II. He was succeeded by Ādityavarman, mentioned in A.D 992–3 (*E. R. 1903–4, p. 8*).

1048–9. *Chāvunda Rāja* ruling under the W. Chāḷukya Sōmēśvara I. Fleet says Chāvunḍa was a Kadamba chief (*I. A., 1875, 179*).

1055–6. *Arikēśari*, 'a descendant of *Mayūraśarman*' governing as vassal of the W. Chāḷukyas.

1064–5, or 1067–8. Toyimadēva, whose mother Akka, a W. Chāḷukya princess, had married a Kadamba chief of Hangal, ruled over the two provinces, Baṇavāsi and Hāngal (*E. I. xvi, 81*),

1074–5. Mention of a Kadamba Lord Śāntivarman on October 7 (*E. I. xvi, 69*).

1187. A *vīrakal* in Sorab Taluk, Mysore, shews a Kadamba chief Konḍema ruling Baṇavāsi under the W. Chāḷukya Sōmēśvara IV (*E. C. viii, Sb. 47*).

KADAMBAS OF HĀNGAL, OR PĀNUNGAL

The pedigree is taken from Fleet's as given in *Bombay Gazetteer I, Pt. II, p. 559*, with some additions.

It begins with thirteen chiefs, each the son of his father and predecessor, who governed Hāngal in succession. Their names are 1. *Mayūravarmā I*; 2. *Krishṇavarmā*; 3. *Nāgavarmā I*; 4. *Vishṇuvarmā*; 5. *Mrigavarmā*; 6. *Satyavarmā*; 7. *Vijayavarmā*; 8. *Jayavarmā I*; 9. *Nāgavarmā II*; 10. *Śāntivarmā I*; 11. *Kīrttivarmā I*; 12. *Ādityavarmā*; 13. *Chattaya*, whose son was—

14. *Jayavarmā II* or Jayasimha. *c.* A.D. 1030.

Māvulidēva | 15. *Tailapa*, or *Taila I. c.* 1050 (*Md.* Chāvunḍalā) | 17. *Śāntivarmā II* or *Śānti*, or *Śāntaya* 1088. *Md.* Pāṇḍya princess Śiriyādēvī. | *Chokidēva* or *Joki.* | *Vikrama*, or *Vikramānka.*

KADAMBAS OF HĀNGAL, OR PĀNUNGAL—*contd.*

15.

16. *Kīrttivarmā II* or Tailana-Singa 1068–1077. Feudatory of W. Chāḷukyas.

17.

18. *Taila II* or Tailapa, or Tailaha. Dates from 1099–1135. *Md.* Bāchalā, a Pāṇḍya princess, and Chāmalā.

19. *Mayūravarma II* 1131. Governing in conjunction with his father, under Sōmēśvara III of the W. Chāḷukyas.

20. *Mallikārjuna* 1132, 1135, 1144.

21. *Tailama* or Māvuli-Taila. Dates from 1147 to 1160.

22. *Kīrttideva III* 1172

23. *Kāmadēva* Dates from 1181 to 1207. *Md.* Kētalā. Feudatory to W. Chāḷukya Sōmēśvara IV

Barmma

Sōma

Malla 1218. (See *notes* below).

NOTES.—For the reign of 13 Chattaya we have dated records in A.D. 972, 973, 1012 (*E. C. viii. Sb. 454, 455, 471*). For 19, Mayūravarman II see *E. C. viii. Sb., 80*. For 21, Tailama, see Mysore Arch. *Rep., 1923, No. 112*, and *E. I xvi, 31f*. A record of A.D. 1202 in Kadūr Taluk, Mysore makes Hoysala Baḷḷāḷa III governing Banavāsi and Hāngal. Malla's accession was between March 3, 1218 and January 7, 1219 (*E. C viii, Sb., 180, 221, 224*).

KADAMBAS OF GOA

See *Bombay Gazetteer I, Pt. II, 564f ; I. A. xi, 273 ; xiv, 289 ; E. I. viii, App. II, 9*. The Kadambas of Goa hold the (vain) title of 'Lords of Banavāsi' (*E. I. vii, 198*).

1. *Gūhalla I* 'Vyāghramārin,' or 'Gūvala.'

2 *Shashṭhadēva I* 'Chaṭṭa,' 'Chaṭṭala,' 'Chaṭṭaya.' A.D. 1007.

3. *Jayakēśin I* 1052. Feudatory of W. Chāḷukya Somēśvara I.

4. *Gūvaladēva II* 1098

5. *Vijayāditya I* 'Vijayārka.' *Md.* Chaṭṭalādēvī.

6. *Jayakēśin II* 1119, 1147. *Md.* Mallāḷā, *dau.* of Vikramāditya VI, W. Chāḷukya king.

7. *Permāḍi-Śivachitta* 1147–1187 to 8. *Md* Kāmalādēvī, *dau.* of Kāma-Bhūpa

(*These two reigned jointly*)

8. *Vijayāditya II* 1147, 1158, 1171. 'Vishṇuchitta' 'Vikramārka,' 'Vāṇibhushaṇa.' *Md.* Lakshmīdēvī.

9. *Jayakēśin III* 1187–1210. 'Vīra-Jaya.' *Md.* Mahādēvī.

10. *Tribhuvanamalla* *Md.* Māṇikyā-dēvī.

11. *Shashṭhadēva II* 1246, 1250, 1257. 'Śivachitta,' 'Chaṭṭaya.'

Dau. md. to Kāmadēva, or Kāvaṇa.

KĀḌAVAS, *see* PALLAVAS

KĀKATĪYA DYNASTY

Capital Warangal, or Anumakoṇḍa. The family grew to power towards the close of A.D. the 11th century. They claimed descent from Karikāla Chōḷa, but such connection remains unproved (*see E. I. iii, 94 ; ix, 164, 256 ; I. A. 1892, p. 197 ; A. R., 1909-10, 130*).

1. *Durjaya*
' Of the family of the Raghus.'

2. *Prōḷa I*

3. *Tribhuvanamalla Bēta*
or ' Betma.' Feudatory of W. Chāḷukya Vikramāditya VI.

4. *Prōla II*
' Prōda,' ' Jagatikēśarin,' 1117–1163. *Md.* Muppaladēvī. Fought the Chāḷukyas.

Sons of 4:

5. *Pratāpa Rūdra I*
1163–1199. *Md.* Padmādēvī Burned the city of Chōdōdaya ' Defeated Yādava Mallugi.

Mahādēva
Md. Bayyāmbikā

(Three other sons)

Children of Mahādēva:

6. *Gaṇapati*
' Chhalamatti-gaṇḍa.' *Md.* Naramā and Pēramā, sisters of his general Jaya. Defeated Yādava Singhaṇa II. 1199-1260.

Dau. Mailalā or *Mēlāmbikā*
Md. Rudra, son of Nātavāḍi chief Buddha.

Daughters of 6:

7. *Rudramma (Dau.)*
Reigned after her father. Given male name, ' Rudra-Mahāraja,' and ' Chalamarti-gaṇḍa.' 1260–1291.

Dau. Gaṇapāmbikā
Md. Amarāvatī chief Kōṭa Bēta.

Daughter of 7:

Dau. Mummaḍāmbā
Md. Mahādēva.

Sons of Mummaḍāmbā:

8. *Pratāpa-Rudra II*
1291–1330. Defeated by Malik Kāfur in 1309, and country looted. In 1316 his general Muppiḍi entered Kānchī and made Mānavīra its Governor. Kingdom overthrown by the Khilji Sultan of Delhi.

Annamdēva
Founder of the Bastar family of Chiefs. (*E. I. ix. 160*)

9. *Krishna*
or ' Vīrabhadra.' Joined Hindu confederation against the Mussalmans in 1344.

10. *Vināyaka*
or ' Nāgdēva.' Brutally murdered by Muhammad Shāh Bahmanī 1364.

NOTES —Two inscriptions say that 7 Rudramma married Vīrabhadrēśvara, a Chāḷukya prince (*94 of 1917 ; 740 of 1920*)

The Paithān C.-P. grant of A.D. 1271 and a record at Bahāl of 1222 of the Yādava king Singhaṇa, both state that the Yādava king Jaitugi ' liberated ' Gaṇapati, apparently from some confinement, and made him Lord of the Āndhra country (*E. I. iii, 110 ; I. A. xiv, 316 ; xxi, 198*).

KALACHŪRI DYNASTY

The family was descended from the earlier Kaṭachchuris of Chēdi (*See Bombay Gazetteer I, Pt. II, 468f; E. I. xii. 30; xv. 315*).

Krishna
Ruling near Nasik
|
Śankaragaṇa
|
Buddha
Reigning about A.D. 607–10. Defeated by Chāḷukya king Mangaḷēśa (*E. I. iv. 294*)

Kannama
'Karṇa,' 'Krishṇa,' 'Lord of Trikaliṅga'
1042 (*E. I. ii. 297*).

Sons of Kannama: *Bijjala I*; *Rāja* or *Rājala*

Sons of Bijjala I: *Ammugi*; *Sankama I*; *Kannara*
Son of Rāja or Rājala: *Jōgama*
|
Permāḍi
or Hemmāḍi. Feudatory of W. Chāḷukya Sōmēśvara III. A.D. 1128.

Children of Permāḍi:

1. *Bijjala II*
'Tribhuvanamalla,' 'Niśśankamalla.' 'Vijjala,'
1156. Abdicated 1167. Crushed the W. Chāḷukya monarchy 1157. Murdered.

Mailugi

Children of Bijjala II:

2. *Sōmēśvara* — 'Sovidēva,' 'Soyi,' 'Rāya-murāri.' 1167–1175
3. *Śankama* — 'Samkhavarṇa,' 'Niśśankamalla' 1175–1180
4. *Āhavamalla* — 'Apratimalla,' 'Rāyanārāyaṇa.' 1178–1183
Singaṇa — Dates 1183, 1184.
Dau. *Siriyādēvī* — *Md.* Chāmuṇḍa II of the Yādavas of Erambarage.

NOTE—Bijjala II assumed royal titles after his overthrow of the W. Chāḷukya kingdom. According to tradition he was murdered by the Lingayat Basava, whose sister he had married. His accession was between September 25 and December 6, 1156 (*E. C. vii. Sk. 102; viii Sb. 131*). He was alive on May 2, 1175 (*ibid. viii. Sa. 66*).

KAḶASA—CHIEFS OF

Kaḷasa is a town in the Muḍigēre Taluk, Kaḍūr District, Mysore. Only a list of rulers can be given, as their relationships are unknown.

In A.D. 1154 *Sāntara Māru* ruled and in 1162. See Sāntara pedigree below.

In 1246, *Jākala-Mahadēvī*, who succeeded Māru-dēva (*E. C. vi. Mg. 65, 66*).

1270, 1277, 1279, 1281. *Kāḷaḷa-mahādēvī* (*ibid., Mg. 71, 67, 72, 73*).

1285. *Rāya-Ballaha* (*ibid., Mg. 69*).

1292, January 31. Kāḷaḷa-mahādēvī's son *Paṇḍya* fought and killed Mārakāla, and was himself attacked by the people of two *Nāḍus* (*E. C. vi. Cm. 36*).

1419. *Bhāyirarasa*, a Lingāyat (*ibid. Mg. 47*).

1431, 1436. *Vīra Pāṇḍya*, son of Bhairava (possibly the last mentioned), who 'belonged to the family of Jinadatta,' ancestor of the Sāntaras of Humcha'. Vīra Pāṇḍya erected the great statue of Gomata at Kārkaḷa in 1432 (*V. R. ii. S. Kanara, 208, 210*).

1457. *Abhinava Pāṇḍya* of Humcha 'of the family of Jinadatta' (*ibid. 215*).

1493. *Bhayirarasa* (*E. C. vi. Mg. 50, 54*).

1516, 1524, 1530. *Immaḍi Bhayirarasa*, son of Bommalā-dēvī and son in-law of Hiriya Bhayirarasa (*ibid. Mg. 41, 62, 47*).

1542. *Vīra Pāṇḍya*, son-in-law of Bhayirarasa (*ibid., Mg. 64*).

1552, 1555. *Bhayirarasa*, son of Bomma-rāja (*ibid., Mg. 40, 60*).

1586. *Immaḍi Bhayirarasa* built a Jain *basti* at Kārkaḷa. In 1588 an inscription calls him 'son of Gummaṭa-dēvī. He is also mentioned in 1598 (*E. I. viii. 122; 62 of 1901; E. C. vi. Kp. 57, 50*).

1593(?) *Pāṇḍyappa*, son of Bhayirarasa; and in 1630 when his brother is mentioned (*68 of 1901; E. I. vii. 110*).

1609. Bhayirarasa, son of Bhayirarasa mentioned (*E. C. vi. Mg. 63*).

KALINGA—KINGS OF—, AND EASTERN GANGAS

Kalinga was attacked by the Maurya king Aṣōka in 256 B.C. when 100,000 of its inhabitants were killed and 150,000 taken captive! Aśōka, repenting of this, afterwards protected the country. Mr. Sankara Aiyar's chronology of early rulers is as follows (*I. A. 1920, 43*). He differs slightly from others.

B.C. 218. *Nanda*, king of Kalinga; a prince of the Chēta dynasty.
B.C 208. *Kētubhadra* succeeded him.
B.C. 194. Birth of *Khāravēla*, son of Jīva-dēva.
B.C. 170. Death of Jīvadēva.
B.C. 169. Khāravēla sent an army to the west. In 167 he subdued the Rāshṭrikas and Bhōjakas. *Md.* a Vajra princess, Dhūsi. In 163 B.C. he stormed Rājagriha.
B C. 159. Khāravēla humbled the Sunga king of Magadha, Pushyamitra. B.C. 157 is the date of Khāravēla's inscription at Hāthigumpha.

The following notes are taken from various sources.

About A.D. 450 *Vāsishṭhīputra Śaktivarman* was king of Kalinga, according to the Rāgōlu C.-P. inscription (*E. I. xii. 2*), and reigned at Piṭhāpūr, N. of the Godavari river.

About A.D. 500-525 the Vishṇukuṇḍin princes seem to have driven the Kalinga king out of his dominions, the conqueror making his residence at Deṇḍalūru, near Ellore (*J. B. B. R. A. S. xvi. 116*).

Sometime between A.D. 500 and 615 we hear of two kings of Kalinga, *Nandaprabhañjana* and *Sāmantavarma* (*I. A. 1884, 48; E. I. xv. 275*).

About A.D. 615 the Kalinga monarchy was crushed by the Chāḷukya prince Kubja-Vishṇuvardhana, who established the Eastern Chāḷukya dynasty.

The Pedigree-table which follows is collated from several sources. It is a table of the dynasty known as the 'Eastern Gangas of Kalinga' (*E. I. iv. 186; I. A. 1889, 161, 170f; J. A. S. B. lxiv. 128f; lxv, 229f., etc*). The chronology is based on the assumption that the seventh king, Kāmārṇava III, established the 'Kalinga-Ganga' era as a family era, whose epoch was the year of his accession, viz. A.D. 877–78. The length of reigns is given as in inscriptions, not as necessarily accurate.

1. *Vīrasimha*

- **2. *Kāmārṇava I*** — **36 years**
- **3. *Dānārṇava*** — **40 years**
  - **4. *Kāmārṇava II*** — **50 years.**
    - **5. *Raṇārṇava*** — **5 years.**
      - **6. *Vajrahasta II*** — **15 years A.D. *c* 863-878**
        - **8. *Guṇārṇava II*** — **or Guṇamahārṇava. 27 years, 897–924**
          - **(?) *Vajrahasta III*[1]**
            - **9. *Jitānkuśa*** — **15 years. 924–939.**
            - ***Gunnama***
              - **10. *Kaligālānkuśa*** — **12 years. 939-951.**
            - **12. *Kāmārṇava IV*** — **25 years. 958–983.**
              - **13. *Vajrahasta IV*** — **'Aṇiyankabhīma.' 35 years 983-1017.**
                - **14. *Kāmārṇava V*** — **Half a year. 1017.**
                - **15. *Gunḍama II*** — **3 years. 1017–1019.**
                - **16. *Madhu-Kāmārṇava VI*** — **19 years. 1019-1038. *Md.* Vinayā, a Vaiḍumba princess.**
                  - **17. *Vajrahasta V*** — **'Guṇārṇava,' 'Anantavarma.' *Md.* Anangā. Crowned April 9, 1038. Reigned till 1070.**
            - ***Vinayāditya*** — **3 years. Perhaps jointly with his brother.**
        - **11. *Gunḍama I*** — **7 years. 951–958.**
      - **7. *Kāmārṇava III*** — **19 years accession, and epoch of the Kalinga-Ganga family era, A.D. 877-78. Died 897.**
- ***Guṇārṇava I***
- ***Mārasimha***
- ***Vajrahasta I***

[1] Vajrahasta III's reign of (so-stated) 44 years is sometimes omitted in inscriptions. The Vizagapatam C.-P. grant (*I. A. 1889, p. 171*) omits him and makes *Jitānkuśa* and his brothers, sons of Guṇārṇava II.

KALINGA,—KINGS OF—, AND EASTERN GANGAS—*contd.*

18. *Dēvēndravarman Rājarāja I*[1]
8 years. Crowned May 20, 1070.
Md. Rājasundarī, *dau.* of Kulottunga Chōla I

19. *Anantavarman Chōḍa-Ganga*
Crowned February 17, 1078. Reigned till 1142 or 1146.

Jayavarman

20. *Madhu-Kāmārṇava VII*
'Kumāra,' 'Anantavarman,' 'Jaṭēśvara.'
1142 or 1146 (?)—1152.

21. *Rāghava*
Md. Chandralēkha (?) 1152—1166 to 7

22. *Anantavarman-Rājarāja II*
1166–7 to 1192.

23. *Aniyanka-Bhīma*
Md. Bāghallā.(?) 1192-1202.

24. *Rājarāja III*
'Guṇa,' or 'Ṣaḍguṇa.' 17 years, (?) 1219-1235.

25. *Ānanga Bhīma*
Md. Kastūrā. 34 years (?) 1219-1253.

26. *Narasimha I*
Md. Sītādevī.(?) 1253-1256.

Dau. Chandrikā
Md. Parmadi, a Haihaya prince.

27. *Vīra Bhānudēva I*
1256-1275. *Md.* Jākallā, a Chāḷukya princess.

28. *Narasimha II*
'Pratāpa Anantavarman.' 1275—1305 to 6

29. *Vīra Bhānu II*
'Vīrādhi-Vīra.' *Md.* Lakshmī.
1305-6 to 1322-3, or 1324-5.

30. *Pedda Narasimha III*
'Gajapati.' 1322-3, or 1324-5 to 1346 or 1350.

31. *Vīra Bhānu III*
Md. Tārā and Hīra. 1346 or 1350-1378.

32. *Narasimha IV*
Md. Pārvatī. 1378, at least, 1397.

33. *Vīra Bhānu IV*

In 1434 Kapilēndra, who had been, so it is said, a herd-boy and who had risen to be minister to Vīra Bhānu IV, seized the throne and established his family as 'Gajapati' kings of Orissa and Kalinga (*see pedigree of Orissa Gajapati kings below*).

NOTES.—*Vinayāditya*. The long Vizagapatam C.-P. grant does not distinctly say that he 'reigned,' but merely that he 'protected the earth' for three years. He may, therefore, have been only a Viceroy (*I. A. 1889, 171*)

The Shikulla plates (*E. I. iv 183*) differ in respect of the relationship of the early kings, and give 35 years to 12. *Kāmārṇava IV*.

17. *Vajrahasta V* is praised for having saved the Kalinga country when threatened by the strength of Kulōttunga-Chōla I during his wars against his Chōla cousins for the Chōla throne (1062-1070). For his coronation date see *E. R. 1918-19, C.-P. 4. E. I. iv. 185*, and connections p. vi.

18. *Dēvēndravarman-Rājarāja I* protected the E. Chāḷukya prince Vijayāditya VII when he vacated his post as Viceroy of Vengi in 1077-8.

19. *Anantavarma-Chōḍaganga* had a very long reign. His 65th, 68th and even his 73rd year are mentioned in inscriptions (*V. R. i. Ganjam, 315, 333, 350 ; 164, 182, 199 of 1896*).

For the kings from Nos. 19 to 32 see *J. A. S B. lxv. 128, 229*.

20. The accession of Madhu-Kāmārṇava VII is by several records in 1146 (*V R. i. Ganjam, 261-263, 329, 355, 420, 421*); but Kielhorn fixed it as in 1142 (*E. I. viii. App. I, 17*).

[1] The Coronation-day of No. 18 is given in *E. R.* 1919, App. A. C. P. No. 4.

28. *Narasimha II's* accession took place between May 22 and September 20, 1275 (*J. A. S. B. lxv. 229; V. R. i. Ganjam, 245; E. I. vi. 260*).

29. *Vīra Bhānu II's* accession is proved by 327 of 1899; *V. R. iii.* Vizagapatam, 155.

30. *Narasimha III's* accession-year is 1322–3 by several records (*V. R. i. Ganjam, 186–188, 197, 221, 222, 233, 236*). But one (*ibid. 178*) makes it 1324–5.

31. *Vīra Bhānu III* accession-year is 1346–7 by *V. R. iii.* Vizagapatam 96, but 1350–1 by *ibid. i* Ganjam 214.

Graham's set of C.-P. grants now in the Madras Museum (*V. R. i. Ganjam 2–6*) require study. As quoted they are somewhat confusing.

KĀṬAMA NĀYAKA FAMILY

see KOḶANU RĀJAHS

KĀYASTHA FAMILY—THE

In Southern India the earliest chief known was *Gāngeya Sāhini*, who was a general of the Kākatīya king, Gaṇapati (A.D. 1199–1260.) The family acquired large territories in Kurnool and in parts of Mysore and Hyderabad. (*See V. R. ii. Kurnool Nos. 260, 261, etc. and note, p. 932*).

1. *Gāngeya-Sāhini*
   'Gaṇḍapeṇḍara,' 'Maṇḍalika-Brahma-Rākshasa.
   A.D. 1255.
   | (*relationship uncertain*)
   2. *Jannigadēva*
   (same titles). A.D. 1259.
   - 3. *Tripurāridēva* 1272–73
   - 4. *Ambadēva* c. 1273–4—at least 1302.

NOTES.—For No 2 see *V. R. i. Cuddapah 824, 850; ii. Guntur 500, 502, 520.*
For No. 3 see V. Rangachari's notes to his *Kurnool 262, (II. p. 932).*

KEḶADI, IKKĒRI or BEDNŪR CHIEFS

Their territory lay in West Mysore and S. Kanara. They ruled the Āraga and Gutti (Chandragutti) tracts above the ghāts and Bārakūr and Mangalūr in S. Kanara. The following table is founded mainly on Rice's List in 'Mysore and Coorg' p. 157, with some changes of dates.

'N'—'Nāyaka.'

1. *Hulibail-Basappa* (a cultivator)
   - 2. *Chauḍappa N:* 1499–1513. Built palace at Ikkēri, 1511.
     - 3. *Sadāśiva N:* 1513–1560. Assisted Sadāśiva of Vijayanagar
       - *Doḍda Sankaṇṇa N: I* lived in retirement.
         - 5. *Rāmarāja N:* 1570–1582
         - 6. *Venkaṭappa N: I* 1582–1629. Became independent 1565 after the destruction of Vijayanagar. Also called 'Venkaṭadri.'
           - *Bhadrappa or Bhairava N: I*
             - 7. *Vīrabhadra N:* 1629–1645. Died without issue.
       - 4. *Chinna Sankaṇṇa N: II* 1560–1570
         - *Siddappa N:*
           - 8 *Śivappa N:* 1645–1660
             - 10. *Bhadrappa N: II* 1661–1663.
             - 11. *Sōmaśēkhara N:* 1663–1671. Many coast-towns sacked by the Mahrattas; murdered. *Md* Chennamāji who ruled 1671–1697.
           - 9. *Venkaṭappa N: II.* 1660–1

KELADI, IKKERI or BEDNŪR CHIEFS—*contd.*

12. ***Basappa** N : I*
1697–1714.

13. *Sōmaśēkhara N : II*
1714–1739

Vīrabhadra N :
Md. Mallāmbikā.

14. *Basappa N : II*
1739–1754. *Md.* Vīrammajī.
Died without issue.

NOTES.—3. Sadāśiva N :. According to Rice his reign ended in 1545, but he is mentioned as alive in 1556 and 1560 (*E. C. i. Sk. 55 ; viii. Tl. 103*).

6. Venkaṭappa was known to the Portuguese as 'Venkapor, king of Canara.'

Chennamājī gave shelter to Śivaji's son Rāma-rāja when he was fleeing from the Mughal troops. She made peace with Mysore, 1694.

Vīrammājī adopted Chenna Basavaṇṇa N :, who reigned 1754–1756 when she had him strangled, and seized the throne for herself. She ruled 1756–1763. In 1763, Haidar Ali captured her capital Bednūr and sacked the city. The Rāṇī and her adopted son Sōmaśēkhara N : III were taken prisoners ; and the State came to an end.

KĒRAḶA KINGS

In this list are included the known kings of the Kēraḷa country proper (the West Coast Districts below the western ghāts) as well as those of the Vēṇāḍ or Travancore country. This cannot well be avoided in the present state of historical knowledge. For very early rulers see the list of CHĒRA kings above, which ends about the A.D. 6th century.

The Nāmakal (Salem District) plates(*E. R. 1906, p. 75*) give the names, excluding mythological ones of five kings, each the son of his predecessor ; viz. *Kōla* (son of Maṇikuṭṭuva); *Ravi I* who married Kouḍā ; *Kaṇṭha I* who married a Pallava princess ; *Ravi II* who married Kannā, a Ganga princess ; and *Kaṇṭha II*.

Ravi II is the same as Sthanu-Ravi, son of Kaṇṭha, a contemporary of Āditya Chōla I (A.D. 880–907) and Varaguṇa Pāndya II (*V. R. i. Coimbatore 107 ; Travancore 89, 90*).

Kaṇṭha II is the same as Kō-Kaṇḍan-Vīra-Nārāyaṇa mentioned in *V. R. i*, Coimbatore 106 ; 147 of 1910.

In A.D. 936 a king named *Vijayarāgava* was reigning (*160 of 1912*).

In 955 *Indu-Kōdaivarman* began to reign (*T. A. S. iii. 161, 171, 176*). He may be the same as *Ravi kōdai* alias *Kō-Kalimukan* (*12, 15 of 1891*). He was living in 972.

In 973–4. *Śrīvallavan-kōdai* is mentioned (*V. R. iii. Travancore 93, T. A. S. iv. pt. I, p. 7*).

In 978 *Bhāskara-Ravi* was ruling for the last mentioned. He himself began to reign in 982. His 58th regnal year is named in *V. R. iii*, Travancore 202 ; *T. A. S. ii*, 31 ; *iii*, 182. He gave a village to Joseph Rabban and a colony of Jews near Cranganore (*E. I. iii. 66.*).

Little is known of rulers from this time till after the death of Kulōttunga Chōla I in 1112 (*I. A. 1895, p. 96*) The following list contains names and dates for five centuries.

Vīra Kēraḷa Tiruvaḍi, or *Kōdai-Kēraḷa* these are only titles of Travancore kings. A.D. 1126–1150 (*I. A. xxiv. 249, 337 ; T. A. S. iv. 17, 18, 21*).

Vīra Ravivarman Tiruvaḍi. May 1161, August 1166.

Udaiya-Mārtāṇḍa I. March 1173, November 1188 (*T. A. S. iv. 26*).

Āditya Rāma, 1189.

Vīra Kēraḷa, or *Vīra Rāma*, alias 'Maṇikaṇṭha Rama.' 1196–1215. *Ravi-Kēraḷa* of A.D. 1216–1237 may be the same (*T. A. S. i. 289 ; iv. 84n*).

Udaya Mārtāṇḍa II, A.D. 1222–23 (*ibid. 296 ; V. R. iii. Travancore, 195*). He may be the same as *Padmanābha-Mārtāṇḍa* and *Udaiya-Mārtāṇḍa* mentioned in records of A.D. 1251–52 (*T. A. S. iv. 88 ; V. R. iii. Travan : 226*).

Ravivarman-Kulaśēkhara Saṃgrāmadhīra was born in A.D. 1266–7. He was son of Jayasiṃha Kēraḷa (*E. I. iv 145*). According to a record of Tiruvadi in S. Arcot (*V. R. i. S. Arcot 295 ; 34 of 1903*) his reign began in the year following December 29, 1309. He married a Pāṇḍya princess Umā. After Malik Kāfur's raid on Southern India in 1311 he seized Madura and afterwards Conjevaram where, being then 46 years old, he was crowned a second time (*see text, s. v. A. D. 1312*). He was driven out of Conjevaram in 1316.

Vīra Rāghava gave the Koṭṭayam plates to the Syrian Christians there, on a day which Kielhorn decided to be March 15, 1320. But this is not certain.

Udaiya Mārtāṇḍa III, alias *Vīra Pāṇḍya*. Accession in year following February 15, 1313 (*T. A. S. iv. 89*).

Ādityavarman-Sarvāṅganātha ruled at Trivandrum, 1374–5 (*T. A. S. i. 171*).

Mārtāṇḍavarman IV, A.D. 1390(?), 1403–1439 (*V. R. iii. Travan : 108 ; T. A. S. i. 299*).

Mārtāṇḍa V. 1480 (*E. I. iv. 203, 204*).

Jayasiṃha II. June 22, 1496 (*T. A. S. ii. 26*).

Veṇṟumāṇkoṇḍa-Bhūtala-Ravivarman IV, 1533, 1537, 1547 (*V. R. iii. Travan : 39, 106, 40–B, 163, 148*).

Ravivarman V, 1595–1607 (*V. R. iii. Trav : 193, 194, 213 ; T. A. S. i. 175*).

ĀY KINGS OF MĀLAINĀḌU (S. TRAVANCORE)

These rulers of the hill-country of S. Travancore may well be included in this section. Only a few names are known.

Ṣaḍaiyan or *Jaṭila* bore a title used by Pāṇḍya kings.

Karunanda, son. Probably contemporary with the Pāṇḍya king Śrīmāra whose reign ended in A.D. 862.

Aḍakkan, his son, or 'Karunandaḍakkan,' or 'Śrīvallabha,' who began to rule June 23, 858.

Vikramāditya-Varaguṇa, his son, gave a grant on December 30, 868 (*see for these rulers T. A S. I. I, 187*).

KOḶANU RĀJAS OF THE GODAVARI RIVER TRACT

These chiefs belonged to a family of Kāṭa, or Koḷani-Kāṭama, Nāyaka. Records of about A.D. 950–1000 give the following.—

- *Chōḷāditya*
  - *Nripa-Kāma* 'Kārmukārjuna,' 'Lord of Koḷanu,' *alias* 'Sarōnātha.'
    - *Gaṇḍa-Nārāyaṇa* *alias* 'Satya-Ballāṭa.'

- ?
  - *a son* *Md.* Nāyamāmbā
  - *Dau:* *Sākāmbā*
    - *Chandana.*

Later Rajas. *Okkeṭṭu-gaṇḍa.* January 2, 1125 (*728 of 1920*).

Koḷani-Kōṭappa-Nāyaka. 1134–5 (*V. R. ii. Kristna, 126*).

Kāṭa, or Koḷani-Kāṭama, Nāyaka. 1143 (*Chellūr plates, V. R. ii. Godavari 48-B ; I. A. xiv. 56 ; E. I. vii. 9*).

Sōmava-Rāja of Koḷanu. His wife gave a grant in 1194–5 (*V. R. ii. Kistna, 211 ; 528 of 1893*).

Kēśava-dēva of Koḷanu. Inscriptions from 1192 to 1218 (*V. R. ii. Kistna 210, 212, 214–216, 230 ; 723 of 1920*).

Yeṛagaya-dēva of Koḷanu. A.D. 1260.

KŌNA OR KŌNAMANḌALA CHIEFS

The chiefs belonged to the Haihaya family, and claimed descent from Kārtavīrya. The Kōnamaṇḍala was the delta country of the Godavari river. The family disappears from history in the 14th century.

- 1. *Mummaḍi-Bhīma* *Md.* Chadvī-dēvī. Received the country from the E. Chāḷukya Rajēndra II, *c.* A.D. 1063.
  - *Venna*
    - 3. *Mummaḍi-Bhīma II* 1128, 1135–6. *Md.* Rājā-dēvī.
      - 4. *Lōka-bhūpālaka* or 'Mahīpāla,' or 'Rajēndra-kōna-Lōka.' 1150.
        - *Manma Chōḍa II.*
    - *Rājēndra Chōḍa* 1128. *Md.* Mallārā.
      - *Bēta*
        - *Sūrya.*
      - *Mallidēva* 1155, 1195.
      - (3 other sons)
  - 2. *Rājaparēndu I.*
    - *Satya I, or Satyāśraya.* 1135–6.
      - *Rājaparēndu II* *Md.* Pārvatī.
        - *Vallabha* *Md.* Āchamāmbā
          - *Manma-Satya II* 1195–1207.
          - *Mahīpālarēndu*
      - 4. *Bhīma III* 1153–4.

NOTES.—*Rājēndra-Chōḍa*, 1128 (*V. R. ii. Godavari 188 ; 283 of 1893*).

4. *Lōkabhūpālaka* and *Bhīma III* ruled jointly (*V. R. ii. Guntur 50 ; 213 of 1897*).

In later years are mentioned three chiefs.

Gaṇapati-dēva, 1292, 1296, who was evidently a vassal of the Kākatīya king. He married a daughter of Vishṇuvardhana-Mahārājā, *alias* Mahādēva (*V. R. ii. Kistna 301, 310 ; 511, 520 of 1893*).

Kōna-Bhīma-Vallabha, A.D. 1318 (*V. R. ii. Kistna 303 ; 513 of 1893*).

Another *Kōna-Bhīma-Vallabha*, 1364–5 (*V. R. ii. Kistna 312 ; 522 of 1893 ; E. I. iv. 83 ; a pedigree is given in 491 of 1893*).

KONḌAPAḌAMAṬI CHIEFS

The family ruled the country west of the strong hill-fortress of Konḍavīḍu—hence their name 'West of the hill.' The first known chief, Buddha or Buddha I, obtained his territory from the Chaḷukya conqueror Kubja-Vishṇuvardhana in the 7th century A.D. Nothing more is known till the early 12th century.

Manda I
'Erramanda.'
|
Buddha II
'Eladāya-Simha,' 'Ganda.'
Md. Gadiyā
|
Manda II
'Manma Manda,' 'Aṇiyanka-Bhīma.'
Contemp. of Velanāṭi chief Rājēndra Chōḍa.
Md. Kunḍāmbikā. Dates A.D. 1130–1139.
|

- *Malla or Malleraja* 1147–8.
  - *Manda III or Manderāja* 1172, 1173.
- *Buddharāja III* 'Eladāya-Simha,' 'Aṇiyanka-Bhīma.' *Md.* Gundāmbhikā. Vassal of Kulōttunga Chōla II. 1143, 1148, 1171.
  - *Chōḍa.*
- *Dau. Ankamma* *Md.* Rājēndra-Chōḍa Gonka of Velanāndu.

NOTE.—For pedigrees see Dr. Hultzsch's article (*E. I. vi. 268f*). For dates and names his list on pp. 273–278.

KONḌAVĪḌU—REḌḌI CHIEFS OF—See REḌḌI CHIEFS

KONGĀḶVA CHIEFS OF W. MYSORE

These chiefs ruled in Coorg and its neighbourhood. South of their country was that of the Changāḷvas. Both were probably off-shoots of the Āḷva or Āḷupa chiefs of S. Kanara (*see Āḷupa pedigree above*). The Kongāḷvas were vassals of the powerful Chōla king Rājēndra I. They were crushed by the Hoyśalas. Only a few names are known.

1. *Badiva Kongāḷva.*
2. *Rājēndra-Chōḷa-Kongālva.* A.D. 1022–1026.
3. *Rājēndra-Kongāḷva-Adaṭarāditya.* A.D. 1066–1100.

No. 2 Rājēndra fought against the early Hoyśala Nripa-Kāma and won a battle at Maṇṇi in 1026 (*E. C. v. Ag. 76*).

KONGU-CHŌLA AND KONGU-PĀNḌYA CHIEFS

They governed parts of Salem and Coimbatore Districts. Only names are known, and relationship, if any existed, cannot be traced. The chiefs may have been Viceroys. The numbers mentioned are those of V. Rangachari's '*Inscriptions*,' I, Coimbatore District.

1. *Vikrama-Chōla Kōnāṭṭān I.* Title 'Parakēśari.' Accession A.D. 1006–7. Ruled till at least 1045–6 (*Nos. 121, 190 ; 154 of 1910 ; 614 of 1905*).
2. *Abhimāna-Rājādhirāja-Chōla,* A.D. 1100 (*Nos. 225, 226, 228, 244 ; 573, 574, 576, 592 of 1905*).
3. *Rājādhirāja Vīra-Chōla.* Accession 1118–9 (*Nos. 245 ; 593 of 1905*).
4. *Kulōttunga-Chōla.* Accession 1149–50 (*Nos. 22, 250 ; 191, 598 of 1905*). Ruled till at least 1162–3.
5. *Vīra-Rājēndra-Chōla.* Accession 1207–8. His 45th year, 1251–2 is mentioned (*Nos. 432, 436 ; 135, 136 of 1909*).
6. *Vikrama-Chōla II.* Accession 1256–7. His 7th year 1263–4 mentioned (*Nos. 207, 230 ; 555, 578 of 1905*).
7. *'Rājakēśari' Vīra-Pāndya.* Accession 1266–7. His 15th year mentioned, 1280–81. Although of Pāṇḍya birth he is given Chōla titles (*Nos. 194, 196, 221 ; 618, 544, 569 of 1905 ; E. R. 1906, p. 79*).
8. *Vikrama Chōla III.* Title 'Parakēśari.' Accession 1274–5 (*No. 186 ; 610 of 1905*).

NOTE.—In *E. R.* 1923, p. 113 the Government Epigraphist notes some other names, but as no dates are available I omit them. On the strength of the inscription 618 of 1922 he gives us a second Kulōttunga Chōla with accession in A.D. 1196–7—the record mentioning Ś. 1125 or A.D. 1203–4 as his 7th year. If this is confirmed he must come between Nos. 4 and 5 of the above list.

KONIDĒNA CHIEFS—See TELUGU-CHŌḌAS

KŌṬA CHIEFS OF AMARĀVATI

The old name of Amarāvati was Dhānyakaṭaka and it was known later as Dharaṇikōṭa. It is celebrated for the great marble-sculptured *Stūpa* of Buddha which was constructed there about the beginning of the Christian era, and whose remains are in the British Museum and the Madras Museum. The Stupa was finally destroyed by a local Rāja in the eighteenth century. The Kōṭa chiefs had the title 'Gaṇḍa-Bhēruṇḍa', and each name has the prefix 'Kōṭa' (*see E. R. 1916, pp. 137, 138*).

1. *Bhīma I*
c. A.D. 1100

2. *Kēta I*
c. 1130

3. *Bhīma II*
Md. Sabbāmbikā, sister of Gonka III of Velanāṇḍu.

Chōḍa, or *Chōḍe*
1182.

Rudra

7. *Bēta*.
Md. Gaṇapāmba, *dau.* of the Kākatīya king Gaṇapati, alive in 1250. Died before 1253.

8. *Gaṇapati*
1258, 1262, 1263.

5. *Kēta II*
Md. Proḷa-dēvī? 1182, 1231.

Bhīma III
Md. Sabbāmbikā.

6. *Kēta III*
or Manma-Kēta. 1234–40.
Md. Bayyalā, *dau.* of Rudra of the Nātavāḍi family.

9. *Bhīma IV*
1265. *Md.* Sōmalādēvī.

NOTES.—*Kēta II* gave a grant on May 1, A.D. 1213 (*79 of 1917*).
For *Gaṇapati's* grant of August 13, 1262 (see *E. R., 103 of 1917*. Also *V. R. ii. Kurnool 311 ; 218 of 1905*).
There is a record of a Kēta-Rudra in A.D. 1275-6 (*V. R. ii. Guntur, 271 ; 152 of 1899*).

KULBARGA—See THE BĀHMANĪ DYNASTY

KUTB SHĀHI DYNASTY—See GOLKONDA

MADURA—MUHAMMADAN GOVERNORS OF

For Madura under Pāṇḍya kings see the list of *Pāṇḍyas* below. In A.D. 1327, after the southern expedition of Muhammad Tughlak, Madura fell into the hands of the Sultan of Delhi. The Muhammadan Governor in 1335 was Jalālu-d-dīn Aḥsan Shāh, who broke away from his allegiance and became independent, beginning to rule in that year as Sultan of Madura. Successive Sultans held the country till in 1371 Kampana II son of Bukka I of Vijayanagar, now very powerful, marched to the south and seized Madura. What follows is not very clear, for coins have been found of Sultan Alāu-d-dīn Sikandar as late as 1378.

1. *Jalālu-d-dīn Āḥsan Shāh.* Independent of Delhi 1335. Murdered in 1340. Ibn Batuta, the chronicler of local events of the time, was his brother-in-law.[1]
2. *Alāu-d-dīn Udauji.* An Emir, unconnected with No. 1 by family. Ruled for one year when he was accidentally killed. 1340–41.
3. *Kutbu-d-dīn Firōz Shah*, brother's son of Jalālu-d-dīn. Killed after a rule of forty days.
4. *Ghiyāsu-d dīn Dhāmagani.* 1340–1 to 1342. A cruel tyrant. He defeated and killed Hoyśala Baḷḷāḷa III.
5. *Nasiru-d-dīn.* 1342—?. Length of rule not known.
6. *Ādil Shāh.* A coin of his, of date 1356 has been found.
7. *Fakru d-dīn Mubārak Shāh.* c. 1359–1368.
8. *Alāu d dīn Sikandar.* c. 1368-1378. But his rule must have been purely nominal.

[1] Ibn Batuta, writing about Ghiyāsu-d-dīn, says that the latter married a daughter of Jalālu-d-din, whose wife (the mother of that daughter) was his (Batuta's) wife's sister. [I am not sure what authority Mr. Sewell follows here. The latest translator of Ibn Batuta, Professor Gibbs, has, 'He (Ghiyathad-Din) was married to the daughter of the late Sultan Jalalu-d-din, and it was her sister that I had married in Delhi.' Ibn Batuta in *Broadway Travellers Series* p. 162. *Editor.*]

BĀṆA GOVERNORS OF MADURA AND OTHERS

These were perhaps Viceroys appointed from Vijayanagar. But little is known about them beyond their names; and the last of them is mentioned at a time when Viśvanātha Nāyaka was certainly the Vijayanagar Viceroy of the place.

A.D. 1404–1451. Joint rule of the Vijayanagar king Dēvarāya II's generals, Lakkanna and Mādanna.
A.D. 1453. Urangāvillidāsan Mahābali-Bāṇa.[1]
A.D. 1477. Tirumāl-Irunjōlāi-Mahābali-Bāṇa.
A.D. 1476. His son. Sundara-Tōḷ-Mahābali-Bāṇa I.
c. A.D. 1499, or earlier. Muttarasa-Tirumalai-Mahābali-Bāṇa.
A.D. 1500. Narasa Nāyaka.
A.D. 1500–1515. Tenna Nāyaka.
A.D. 1515–1519. Narasa Piḷḷai.
A.D. 1519–1524. Timmappa Nāyaka.
A.D. 1524–1526. Kaṭṭiyam Kāmaiya Nāyaka.
A.D. 1526–1530. Chinnappa Nāyaka.
A.D. 1530. Ayyakarai Vaiyappa Nāyaka.
1528–1537. Sundara-Tōḷ-Mahābali Bāṇa II.[2]

N.B.—This list is taken from other sources and I am uncertain as to its accuracy, except in the two instances where reference is given to inscriptions. The last Bāṇa ruler is mentioned as ruling in 1546 (*see text*).

THE NĀYAKA DYNASTY OF MADURA

Nāgama Nāyaka was a trusted officer of Krishṇadēva-Rāya of Vijayanagar (1509–1529), but he became insubordinate. The king allowed Nāgama's son Viśvanātha to quell the disturbances that arose, and, apparently in gratitude for the son's loyalty, did not punish the father. Viśvanatha ruled Madura and the southern dominions till 1564, and became practically independent at Madura. After the destruction of Vijayanagar in 1565 the family's independence was assured, though not always admitted. (See R. Sathyanatha Aiyer's '*History of the Nayaks of Madura*,' with S. Krishnaswami Aiyangar's Introduction.)

1. *Nāgama Nāyaka.*[3]
|
2. *Viśvanātha N: I*
Md. Nāgamā. 1529–1564.
|
3. *Kumāra Krishṇappa N: I*
Md. Lakshmī. 1564–1572.
|
4. *Vīrappa N: I* . . . (*The brothers were joint rulers*) . . . 5. *Viśvanātha N: II.* 1572–1595.
alias 'Krishnappa', or 'Vira Bhūpati.'
Md. Tirumalāmbika. 1572–1595.

Sons of 4:
6. *Lingayya N:* . . . (*Joint rulers*) . . . 7. *Viśvanātha N: III.* 1595–1601. — *Kastūri Rangappa.*
alias 'Kumara-Krishṇappa.' 1595–1601.

Son of 7:
8. *Muttu Krishṇappa N:*
Assumed royal titles, 1601–1609.

Sons of 8:
9. *Muttu Vīrappa N: I* 1609–1623.
10. *Tirumala N:* Threw off all allegiance to the Vijayanagar sovereign. 1623–1659.
Kumāra Muttu N:

Son of 10:
11. *Muttu Vīrappa N: II* 1659.

Sons of 11:
12. *Chokkanātha N: I*
Md. Mangammāḷ. 1659–1682.
13. *Muttu-Linga N:* or 'Muttu Aḷakādri.' Ruled for a few months. 1678.

Son of 12:
14. *Ranga Krishṇa Muttu Vīrappa III*
1682–1689, when he died. Mangammaḷ ruled 1689–1706, when she was put to death.
|
15. *Vijaya-Ranga Chokkanātha N: II*
Md. Mīnākshī. 1706–1732. Died without issue.

NOTES.—This pedigree follows that given in the Kuniyūr plates (*E. I. iii. 239*) in making 8. Muttu-Krishṇappa son of 7. Viśvanātha III.

12. Chokkanātha I. was deposed in 1677 but restored.

The last Nāyaka's widow Mīnākshī carried on the government with great difficulty from 1732 to 1736 when Chanda Sahib seized Madura and Mīnākshī committed suicide.

---

[1] *T.A.S.I.*, p. 46, No. 6; *V. R.* ii. Ramnad, 177, 177a.
[2] 109, 121 of 1903; 585, 587 of 1902.
[3] 'Nāyaka' is abbreviated to '*N:*' in the Table.

MAGADHA—DYNASTIES OF—*above under* 'Early North India' *Table*

MAHRATTA SOVEREIGNS OF SĀTĀRA AND KOLHĀPŪR, AND PESHWAS

1. *Bābājī Bhonsla*
(Headman of three villages near Ellora.)

- 2. *Mālōjī Bhonsla*
  (Jaghirdar of Poona and Supa.)
  - 3. *Shāhjī Bhonsla*
    Born 1594. Died 1664.
    - *Sambhājī*
      Killed in battle.)
    - 4. *Śivājī I*
      'Mahārāja' in 1674. Died 1680.
      - 5. *Sambhājī I*
        1689. Subdued by Aurangzīb and executed, 1689.
        - 8. *Shāhūjī, or Sāhu I*
          1707–1749. Government carried on by a Pēshwa, Bālājī Viśvanātha.
      - 6. *Rāma Rāja, or Rājā Rām*
        1689–1700. *Md.* Tārā-Bāi.
        - 7. *Sivājī II*
          1700–1707. Ousted by Shāhūji. Died 1712.
          - 9. *Rājā Rām II*
            or Rāma-Rāja. Adopted by Shāhūjī. 1749–1777.
            - (*adopted*)
              10. *Abbā Sāhib, or Shāhūjī II*
              1777–1808.
              - 11. *Pratāpa Simha*
                1808–1839. Deposed.
              - *Rāma Rāja.*
              - 12. *Shāhjī or Appā Sāhib*
                1839–1848. Died without issue.
        - *Sambhājī II*
          Seized Kolhapūr and made it a separate kingdom. 1712. (*See below*.)
    - *Venkājī or Ekōjī*
      Seized Tanjore 1674.
    - (*illegitimate*)
      Santājī.
- *Vinājī.*

NOTES.—2. Mālōjī rose to power as a soldier.

3. Shāhji was patronized by the Emperor Shāh Jahān, and received a large *jāghīr* in Mysore from the Bījāpūr Sultan.

8. *Shāhūjī I* seized Sātāra from Śivājī II. His Peshwa gradually acquired all power in the State (*see below*). Kolhāpūr was recognized as a separate State in 1730.

9. *Rāja Rām* was practically kept as a prisoner by the Peshwa.

On the death of 12. Shāhjī, without heirs Ṣātāra was annexed by the British Government in 1849

MAHRATTAS OF KOLHĀPŪR

1. *Sambhājī II*
Second son of Rāma Rāja of Sātara Seized Kolhāpūr, 1712, and became its independent ruler in 1730. Died 1760.

2. *Śivājī III*
Adopted by Sambhājī's widow, Jijī Bai.
1760–1812.

- 3. *Sambhājī*
  or Abbā Sāhib. 1812–1822. Murdered. Left an infant son who at once 'died.'
- 4. *Shahjī*
  or Bāwā Sahib. 1822–1837.
  - 5. *Śivājī IV*
    (*adopted*). 1837–1866.
    - 6. *Rājā Rām*
      (*adopted*). 1866–1870.
      - 7. *Śivājī V*
        (*adopted*). 1870–18
        - 8. *Jaswant*
          or Babā Sahib. (*ado*

THE PESHWAS

- 1. ***Bālājī Viśvanātha***
  The first Peshwa. Created by Shāhūjī of Sātāra, 1714–1720. The office became hereditary.
  - 2. ***Bājī Rāo I***
    1720–1740.
    - 3. ***Balāji Baji Rao***
      1740–1761.
      - 4. ***Vishvas Rao*** *alias* ' Sadāśiva [1] Bhāu '. 1761. (Killed in battle).
      - 5. ***Mādhava Rao I*** 1761 -1772.
      - 6. ***Narrain Rao*** (Murdered. 1773).
        - 8. ***Mādhava Rao II*** 1774–1795.
    - 7. ***Raghunātha Rao, or Rāghōba*** 1773
      - 9. ***Bāji Rao II*** 1795–1818.
        - 10. ***Dundu Panth*** *alias* ' Nāna Sahib.' Fought against English in 1857.
      - ***Amrit Rao.***
      - ***Chimnāji.***

NOTES.—2, ***Bāji Rao I*** invaded the Karnāṭaka country in 1726. He defeated Nizām-ul-Mulkh, Subahdar of the Dekhan, in 1728 ; and obtained several districts from the Mughal Emperor as his own ***Jāghīr***. He levied ***chauth*** in all directions.

3. ***Bālājī Rao*** attacked Haidar Ali at Secunderabad in 1757. Captured Delhi 1760. He was defeated by the Durāṇi Muhammadans at Panipat 1761, when his son Viśvaś Rao was killed.

7. ***Raghunātha Rao*** sided with the English against the French. He murdered his nephew (6) Narrain Rāo.

9. ***Bājī Rao II*** became a feudatory of the English ' Company.'

MAṬLA ' FAMILY.' THE

A family of chiefs in Cuddapah claiming to be descended from the old Chōla kings, and having the title ' Chōla Mahārāja.'

[The numbers referred to in this list are those of V. Rangāchāri's ' *Inscriptions*,' vol. i, Cuddapah District. ' M ' stands for ' Maṭla ;' ' C.–M.' for ' Chōḍa Mahāraja.']

M : Kumāra C.–M. A.D. 1522 (*No. 832*).
M : Pōcha C.–M., and his son Varadayya C.–M. 1542–1570 (*No. 854*).
M : Tirumala 1572. (*No. 845 and V. R. i. Chittoor 168A*).
M : Ananta C.–M. 1600, 1634, 1644 (*Nos. 644, 659A, 675, 402c*).
M : Venkata Rāma, son of Ananta C.–M. 1684, 1688, 1690 (*Nos. 656, 657, 663, 681, 682, 863A, B*).
M : Kumāra Ananta, son of Ananta C.–M. 1697 (*No. 644*).
M : Tiruvēngaḍanātha C.–M. 1707, 1709 (*Nos. 892, 897*).
M : Perumāḷa, son of *Venkaṭa-Krishna C.–M.* 1712 (*No. 705*).
M : Ananta C.–M. 1714–1732 (*Nos. 706, 870–72, 883, 895*).
M : Venkaṭa-Rāma C.–M., son of *Tiruvēngaḍanātha* 1740, 1755–1760. (*Nos. 864, 865, 881, 882, 889, 899*).
M. Kumāra Tiruvēngaḷanātha, son of Venkaṭapati. 1755, 1757, 1765, 1770, 1806 (*Nos. 680, 686, 867, 874, 884, 936*).
M. Venkaṭa-Rāma 1799. (*No. 876*).

MATSYA FAMILY CHIEFS IN ORISSA

These chiefs had at one time some status in Ganjam and Vizagapatam Districts. A long list of ancestors of Arjuna (A.D. 1269) is given in the Dibbida C.–P. grant (*E. I. v. 108*); but as it is not confirmed, all names earlier than that of Arjuna are omitted here (*see E. R. 1900*, § *87*).

Arjuna. April 6, A.D. 1269, (*Dibbida grant*). Also called Narasimhavardhana. *Md.* Lakshmīdēvī.
Mankāditya, alias ' Śrī-Rangavardhana.' *Md.* Śrīdēvī. 1278 (*V. R. iii. Vizagapatam, 143 ; 315 of 1899*).
Annama, alias Gōpālavardhana. 1286, 1292 (*ibid. Vizag : 186, 130 ; 358, 302 of 1899*).
Jayanta, Md. Chimmā-dēvī. July 26, 1292 and 1296 (*ibid. 132 133 ; 304, 305 of 1899*).
Jayantika. Md. Chengamā-dēvī. 1298 (*ibid. 144 ; 316 of 1899*).
Jayanta, alias ' Śrī-Krishṇavardhane.' 1339 (*ibid. 115 ; 287 of 1899*).

---

[1] Sadāsiva Rao Bhau was the son of Chimnāji Appa, brother of Bāji Rao I, and first cousin of Bālaji Baji Rao. He was a different person from Viśvaś Rao, whose guide or governor he was at the time of Panipat.—*Editor*.

MUGHAL EMPIRE OF DELHI

Founded by Bābur of Samarkhand, who invaded the Punjab in A.D. 1524–25, and in 1526 completely defeated at Panipat the army of Ibrahim Lodi of Delhi, killing the Sultan. Bābur seized Delhi and Agra and was proclaimed 'Pādshāh' on April 27, 1526. He was fifth in descent from Taimūr.

1. ***Zahīru-d-dīn Muhammad Bābur***
1526–1530

Children of Bābur:

2. ***Humāyūn*** 1530–1540, and 1555–1556. Was a refugee in Persia 1540–55.

Kamran

Hindal

Mirza Askeri

Children of Humāyūn:

3. ***Akbar*** 'Abūl Fath,' 'Jalālu-d-dīn.' 1556–1606. Proclaimed king of the Dekhan, 1602.

Mirza Muhammad Hakim (Governor of Kabul. Died 1586.)

Children of Akbar:

4. ***Jahāngīr*** 'Abūl-Muzaffar-Nūru-d-dīn-Muhammad,' Prince Salim. 1606–1627.

Murād (Died 1599)

Danyāl *Md.* dau. of Ibrahim Ādil Shāh II of Bijāpūr. Died 1605.

Children of Jahāngīr:

Khusrū Rebelled. Imprisoned. Died 1622.
 — ***Dāwar Baksh*** Put to death by Shāh Jahān, 1628.

Parviz (Died 1625.)

5. ***Shāh Jahān*** 'Shahābu-d-dīn-Ghāzi,' Prince Khurram. 1627–1658 *Md.* Mumtāz Mahāl

Shāhryār (blinded)

Children of Shāh Jahān:

Dārā Shikoh (Beheaded by Aurangzīb 1659.)

Shuja (Murdered 1659)

6. ***Aurangzīb*** or Ālamgīr I. 1658–1707.

Murād (Murdered by Aurangzīb, 1661)

Children of Aurangzīb:

Muhammad Sultān (Poisoned 1676)

7. ***Bahadūr Shāh I, or Shāh Ālam I*** (Muhammad Muazzam) 1707–1712.

Muhammad Āzam (killed, 1707)
 — ***Bedār Bakht*** (killed 1707)

Akbar Rebelled. Defeated Fled to Persia 1704
 — ***Nekusiyar*** (1719)

Kāmbaksh (killed 1709)

Children of Bahadūr Shāh I:

8. ***Jahāndār Shāh*** (1712–1713. Murdered.)

Azīm-us-Shān (killed. 1712)

Rafīu-s-shān (killed. 1712)

Jahān Shāh (killed. 1712.)

Next generation:

12. ***Ālamgīr II*** (1754–1759. Murdered) — son of Jahāndār Shāh

9. ***Farrukhsiyar*** 1713–1719. Deposed and murdered — son of Azīm-us-Shān

Rafīu-d-Darajat Died 1719 — son of Rafīu-s-shān

Rafīu-d-Daula Died 1719 — son of Rafīu-s-shān

Muhammad Ibrahim Reigned one month in 1720. — son of Rafīu-s-shān

10. ***Muhammad Shāh*** 1719–1748. — son of Jahān Shāh

13. ***Shāh Ālam II*** 1759–1806. Blinded. Lived under British protection. — son of Ālamgīr II

11. ***Ahmad Shāh*** 1748–1754 Deposed and blinded. — son of Muhammad Shāh

14. ***Akbar II*** 1806–1837 — son of Shāh Ālam II

15. ***Bahādur Shāh II*** 1837–1857. Deposed. — son of Akbar II

MYSORE—DYNASTY OF—

The genealogy here given of this family is taken, with a few omissions, from that published as probably the most reliable by Mr. S. Krishnaswami Aiyangar in his *Ancient India*, p. 313. It differs somewhat from that given by others (*see his pp. 309–312*) since the sources of information themselves differ in details. The family claimed to be of Yādava descent.

- 1. *Vijaya, or Yādu* 1399–1423
  - 2. *Here Beṭṭada Chāma I* 1423–1458
    - 3. *Timma-Rāja I* 1458–1478
      - 4. *Here, or Ārberal, Chāma II* 1478–1513
        - 5. *Beṭṭada Chāma III* or Chāma-Bhūpati. 1513–1552
          - 6. *Timma-Rāja II* or Appan Timma, 1552–1571
          - *Krishṇa-Rāja I*
          - 7. *Boḷe, or Doḍḍa, Chāma IV* Defeated Tirumala Rāya at Seringapatam, 1571–1576
            - *Beṭṭada Chāma V* 1576–1578
            - 9 *Rājādhirāja* or Rāja-Mahīpati, seized Seringapatam and founded the kingdom of Mysore. 1578–1617.
              - *Narasa Raja* (died before his father)
                - 10. *Chāma VII* 1617–1637 Died without issue.
              - 3 sons Died young
              - 11. *Immaḍi Rāja* 1637–38. Poisoned
              - 12. *Kanṭhīrava Narasa I* 1638–1659
              - *Doḍḍa-Dēva*
                - 14. *Chikkadēva* *Md.* Dēvamāmbā. 1672–1704.
                  - 15. *Kanthīrava Narasa III* *Md.* Chelvājā. 1704–1713.
                    - 16. *Doḍḍa Krishna II* *Md.* Dēvājā 1713–1731
                - *Kanṭhīrava-Narasa II*
              - *Chikka-dēva Rajēndra*
              - 13. *Kempadēva* 1659–1672
              - *Mari-dēva*
            - *Beṭṭada Chāma VI*
            - *Muppindēva* (*Md* Kempamāmbā)
  - *Chāma-rāja*

The direct line came to an end in 1731. The powerful Daḷavāy Dēvarāja placed on the throne a remote connection of the reigning family, *Chāmārja VIII*, who reigned three years, 1731–34, and was deposed by the Daḷavāy. He was replaced by another member of the family, a child, *Immaḍi Krishṇa III*, three years old, who occupied the throne from 1734 to 1761, but never had any real power.[1] In 1761 Haidar Ali seized the Government of Mysore. *Immaḍi Krishṇa III* died in 1766 leaving two sons, *Nanja Rāja*, who was ejected from the palace by Haidar Ali in 1767 and was strangled in 1770, and *Beṭṭada-Chāma-Rāja IX*, who died childless in 1775.

Haidar then placed on the throne a member of another family living at Kārugahalli who became *Khāsa-Chāma-Rāja X*—1775-1795. On his death in 1795 Tipu Sultān ruled till his death at Seringapatam in 1799, when the English crowned Chāma X's son *Mummaḍi Krishṇa IV* (1799–1831). His minister was Pūrṇayya. In 1831 Krishṇa IV was deprived of political power for misrule. In 1881 his adopted son *Chāma Rāja X* was made Mahārāja of Mysore.

NANDYĀLA FAMILY—THE—

See under VIJAYANAGAR

[1] Some inscriptions declare that Immaḍi Krishṇa III was son of Doḍḍa Krishṇa II, and Mr. Krishnaswami Aiyangar's Table referred to enters him and his predecessor Chāma VIII as such; but this contradicts his text (p. 307). *See E. C. III, Tn. 63, IV, Yd. 17*, which makes Immaḍi Krishṇa a member of a branch of the family at Kenchengōḍu.

NĀTAVAḌI, OR NĀTHAVĀḌI CHIEFS

They belonged to a family that ruled part of the country about Bezwada and Amarāvati on the Krishṇa river.

Durga
|
Buddha, or *Budda*[1]
Md. Muppāmbikā (1)
|
Rudra I
Md. Mailalā, or Mēlāmbikā, sister of the Kākatiya king, Gaṇapati
April 12, 1201.[2]
|
- *Rudra II* 1248–49.
- Dau. *Bayyalā*, or *Bayyāmbā*, *Md.* Koṭa-Kēta III of Amarāvati, May 11, 1234.[3]
- *Mahādēva* 1248–49.
- *Mummaḍi-Gaṇapa* 1248–49.

NIḌUGAL FAMILY,—THE

A family of 'Chōla-Mahārājas' in North Mysore, owning a few tracts. They called themselves 'Lords of Oraiyūr,' or Uraiyūr, near Trichinopoly and claimed descent from Karikāla Chōla (*E. C. xii, Pg. 35, 50, 53, 79; Si, 7; Ng., 70*). One of their principal towns was Henjēru, in Śira Taluk, Tumkur District.[4]

1. *Jāla* . . . . .
|
2. *Brahma-Bhōgēndra*
|
3. *Mangi*[5] or *Kali-mangi*
|
4. *Bīchi*, or *Babbe*
|
5. *Gōvinda*
|
6. *Irungōḷa I*
The Hoysala King Vishṇuvardhana claims to have defeated him.[6]
Dates in A.D. 1128, 1139, 1142
|
7. *Mallidēva*
'Jagadēkamalla', 'Priya-bhōga.'
Became independent when the Western Chāḷukya monarchy was destroyed by Bijjala Kalachūri in A.D. 1157. Dates in A.D. 1167, 1169, 1176.[7]
|
8. *Brahma-Nṛipāla*
(or Bammidēva. *Md.* Bāchalādēvī)
|
9. *Irungōḷa II*
or Irungōṇadēva. A Jain by religion
1248, 1277.[8]
|
10. *Vira Bomma*
|
11. *Ganēśa*
1292

[1] *E. I. vi, 158.* [2] *E. I. vi, 159; 279 of 1892.*
[3] She gave a grant for Buddhist worship at the Amarāvati *stupa* (*E. I. vi, 157*). For her three brothers see 318, 320, 321 of 1905.
[4] Henjēru is Hēmāvati in Anantapur District on the western border. See p. 180, *Anantapur Gazetteer* I, 180.—*Editor.*
[5] *Mangi* may be same as 'Mangarasa, Lord of Oraiyūr,' who was residing at Kaneyakallu and was called 'Ghateyanka,' in a W. Chāḷukya record of Vikramāditya VI (1076-1126). (*439 of 1920*)
[6] *V. R. i. Anantapur 31, 122; E. R. 1907, p. 75.* [7] 733 of 1917.
[8] *V. R. i. Anantapur 123; 40 of 1917; E. C. xii, Pg., 35, 50.*

NĪLAGANGARAIYAN—
CHIEFS SO NAMED.

There are a number of inscriptions which mention chiefs who bore this name. The following list ranges from A.D. 1183 to 1306-7. I have not been able to trace their relationships satisfactorily. The Epigraphist to Government, in his Report for 1913 (p. 126), thinks that because the Nīlagangaraiyan who is referred to in an inscription of A.D. 1259 (117 of 1912) is called a *piḷḷaiyār* of the powerful Vijaya-gaṇḍa-gōpāla; therefore he was really a son (*piḷḷai*) of that ruler. But I hardly think this is justified. In A.D. 1193 the then Nīlagangaraiyan is called a *piḷḷaiyār* of Kulōttunga-Chōla III. Rājarāja Śambuvaraiyan is also called in 1257 a *piḷḷaiyār* of Vijayagaṇḍa-gōpāla, and it has been argued that therefore Nīlagangaraiyan was brother to that Śambuvaraiyan. I cannot consider this proved. In the inscription, for instance, 357 of 1922, the Mahābali-Baṇa chief is called a *piḷḷai* of the Pāṇḍya king Māravarman Kulaśekhara I. This was in A.D. 1275.

The inclusion in their name of 'Ganga'-raiyan may perhaps justify the belief that these rulers belonged to the Ganga family stock; while the syllable *Vāṇan* may point to descent from the Bāṇa chiefs.[1] Their records are mostly found in Chingleput district.

Pañchanadivāṇan-Nīlagangaraiyan. A.D. 1183, May 26. Records in 5th year of Kulōttunga Chōla III (*V. R. i. Chingleput 20; II Madras 233, 312; 297 of 1895; 513 of 1913; 297 of 1905*). The same in the 10th year, 1187-8 (*V. R. i. Chin. 683; 318 of 1911*). The same, with the prefixes 'Piḷḷaiyār-Kulōttunga-Chōla-Kaṇṇapan-Nallanāyanār' in the 16th year, A.D. 1193-4 (*V. R. i. Chin. 858; 2 of 1911*). The same in the 33rd year, with the affix 'Chōla-Ganga,' A.D. 1210 (*V. R. i. Chin. 930; 557 of 1912*).

Nīlagangaraiyan. '7th year of Rājarāja Chōla III,' A.D. 1222-3 (*V. R. i. Chin. 854; 187 of 1901*). In the same year 1222, on March 21 an inscription of 'Nīlagangaraiyan-Kaḍakkan-Chōla-Ganga.' (*V. R. i. Chingleput 908; 535 of 1912*). The same in '2nd year of Kō-Peruñjinga.' (?) 1244-5 (*V. R. i. N. Arcot, 460; 505 of 1902*). The same in the 28th year or Rājarāja Chōla III (*V. R. ii. Tanjore, 1071; 437 of 1912*). The same 'in the reign of Vijaya-Gaṇḍa-Gōpāla,' which was A.D. 1250-1291 (*V. R. i. Chin. 870; 14 of 1911*).

Pañchanadivāṇan-Nīlagangaraiyan, with prefix '*piḷḷaiyār*,' in the 10th year of Vijaya-Gaṇḍa-Gōpāla. Date = Sept. 13, 1259 (*V. R. i. Chin. 986; 117 of 1912*). Nīlagangaraiyan is also mentioned, as well as his wife Nangai-Āḻvār,[2] perhaps an Āḷupa princess, in the 27th year of Kō-Peruñjinga,—A.D. 1269-70 (*V. R. i. N. Arcot, 472, 473; 517, 518 of 1902*).

Aruṇagiri-Perumāḷ Nīlagangaraiyan in the 17th year of Jaṭāvarman Sundara Pāṇḍya III. The date = July 30, 1292 (*V. R. i. Chin: 910; 537 of 1912*).

Pañchanadivāṇan-Tiruvēgamban, *alias* Nīlagangan, in the 37th year of Māravarman-Kulaśekhara Pāṇḍya I. The date = July 8, 1304 (*V. R. i. Chin: 928; 555 of 1912*).

'Prince Nīlagangariyar,' in the 39th year of the same king, i.e., in 1306-7 (*V. R. i. Chin. 815; 285 of 1907.*)

NIZAMS OF HYDERABAD

See DEKHAN—SUBAHDARS OF THE

NIZAM SHAHI DYNASTY
OF AHMADNAGAR

Nizāmu-l-Mulkh Bahrī was one of the Emirs of the Bāhmanī kings. He contrived the death of Mahmūd Gawān at the hands of Muhammad Bāhmanī III, which led to the break-up of the kingdom. His son Malik Ahmad revolted, defeated a Bāhmanī army and became independent, establishing himself as head of a new State with capital at Ahmadnagar, in A.D. 1489.

Nizāmu-l-Mulkh Bāhrī
|
1. '*Malik*' *Ahmad Nizām Shāh*
1489-1508.
|

[1] Vāṇan is a Tamil word meaning resident in or being master of. Here it is the name of Śiva in Tiruvaiyār (Trivāḍi) in Tanjore. —*Editor*.

[2] Āḷvār or even Āḻvār, meaning 'My Lady', a term of honorific use.—*Editor*.

NIZAM SHAHI DYNASTY—*contd.*

2. ***Burhān I***
Md. Maryam, *dau.* of Yusuf Ādil Shāh of Bijapūr. 1508—1554

Sons of Burhān I:

- 3. ***Husain*** — Wars against Ādil Shāh, and destruction of Vijayanagar 1554-1565. Died 7 June 1565.
- ***Abdul Khādar*** or ***Abdullah.***
- ***Shāh Ali***

Children of Husain:

- 4. ***Murtazā*** — 1565–1588. Murdered by his son.
  - 5. ***Mirān Husain*** — 1588-1589. Murdered many of his family, and was himself slain
- 7. ***Burhān II*** — Fought against his son and deposed him. 1590–1595
  - 6. ***Ismail*** — 1589–1590 Deposed.
  - 8. ***Ibrahīm*** — Four months in 1595. Killed in battle
    - 9. ***Bahādur*** — 1595–1600. Ahmadnagar captured by Mughal army after gallant defence by Chānd Bibi in 1599. She was murdered and Bahādur thrown into prison.
- *Dau.* Chand Bibi *Md.* Ali Ādil Shah of Bijapur

Son of Shāh Ali:

- 10 ***Murtazā*** — Set up by his minister Malik Ambar, who ruled till 1626. 1600-1631
  - 11. ***Husain*** — 1631–32.

Ahmadnagar was annexed to Delhi in 1635.

NOḶAMBAVĀḌI COUNTRY—RULERS OF

The 'Noḷambavaḍi 32000' province was one of the principal divisions of Central South India in early days. Others were the 'Gangavāḍi 96000', and the 'Baṇavāsi 12000'. Uchchangi-drūg, Henjeru and Chitaldrūg were the principal cities. The dominion of its rulers spread at times over the Bellary, Anantapur, Salem and part of North Arcot Districts, etc., and over the Bangalore and Kolar Districts of Mysore.

For the early period see Mr. H. Krishna Sāstri's article in *E. I. x. 54 f.*

From about A.D. 700 to 1052 the province was governed by a Pallava family, with occasional intrusion of Chāḷukya, Ganga and Chōla viceroys. After the battle of Koppam in 1052 it seems to have remained under Chāḷukya domination, but in 1079 we find a Pāṇḍya chief in possession, and a Pāṇḍya family ruled till about 1178 when the Hoysala king Baḷḷāḷa II seized Uchchangi.

NOḶAMBA-PALLAVAS.

1. ***Mangaḷa***
c. A. D. 700

2. ***Simhapōta*** [1]
or Singapota-Kaḷi, vassal of the Ganga king Śivamāra II.
c. 810

3. ***Chāruponnēra*** [2]
or Kolli-Pallava-Noḷamba, vassal of Rashṭrakūṭa Govinda III (794–813)

---

[1] *E. C. xi. Cl, 8.*

[2] *E. C. viii, Sb, 10*

NOLAMBA-PALLAVAS—*contd.*

4. *Poralchōra* '*Nolamba*' *I*.
Md. Jāyabbe, *dau.* of W. Ganga king Rāchamalla I, his suzerain. Dates in 840, 853 (when he ruled as far as Conjevaram), 870.

5. *Mahēndra I*
Fought against Chōlas. Raided the Pulināḍu country *c*. 877–8, fighting Bāṇa and Vaiḍumba chiefs with the support of the Ganga ruler. Battle of Soremaṭi. Capture of Kōyattūr. Defeated by W. Ganga Butuga I at battle of Samiya. Killed by Ganga Ereyappa IV. *c*. 895.

(?) *Nolipayya, or Irivi-Nolamba I, 898.*

6. *Ayyapadeva Nanniga*
Fought against E. Chāḷukya Bhīma II. Dates in A.D. 897–920.

7. *Anniga, or Aṇṇayya*
Dates in 931, 936. Defeated in 940 by Rāshṭrakūṭa Krishna III.

8. *Dilīpayya*
or Dilīparasa-Irivi-Noḷamba I. Dates from 942 to 966

9. *Nanni Noḷamba*
'Trailōkyamalla' 'Chaladanka-kāra.' 969. Crushed by the Ganga king Mārasimha III.

10. *Poralchōra II*
'Vajjaladēva.' 965

11. *Vīra Mahēndra II*

NOTES.—In A.D. 878 Mahēndra I was in occupation of Tagaḍūr, or Dharmapuri in Salem District (*348 of 1901*).

The Pulināḍu raid cannot have taken place much later than A.D. 878 for several reasons. At that time the Gangas and Pallavas were acting in union. By A.D. 892 they were fighting against one another as enemies. (*E. C. iii, Ng., 139.*)

For No. 8 Dilīpayya and a possible second son Nolipaya, who married Pariyabbarasī and by her had a son Ayyappa see the Epigraphist's remarks on No. 17 of 1917 (*also E. I. xvi, 27*).

Two records at Morigeri in Bellary District both dated on October 28, 1045 (*V. R. i. Bell : 215, 217 ; 441, 443 of 1914*) give the following three generations.

1. *Irivibeḍanga Noḷamba-Ghaṭeyankakāra*
Vassal of W. Chāḷukya, Satyāśraya II (997–1008) whose *dau.* he married.

2. *Jagadēkamalla Noḷamba-Udayāditya*
Dates 1018–1037. Vassal of W. Chāḷukya Jayasimha III. *Md.* Sigādēvī.

3. *Jagadēkamalla-Noḷamba*
'Immaḍi,' or 'Nūrmaḍi.' Vassal of the same king (1015–1042)

4. *Trailōkyamalla-Nanni-Noḷamba*
Installed by W. Chāḷukya king Somēśvara I on April 5, 1044.[1]

NOTES.—For No. 2 dates in A.D. 1018, 1027, 1033 (*V. R. i. Bellary, 279, 42, 16 ; 87 of 1904 ; 199, 208 of 1913*).

For No. 3, in A.D. 1037 (*228 of 1918*).

For No. 4, October 28, 1045, 1048, 1052 (*V. R. i. Bell. 217, 78, 245 ; 443, 523 of 1914 ; 67 of 1904*).

After the battle of Koppam in 1052 the Noḷamba country seems to have remained in possession of the W. Chāḷukyas.

From and after 1079 (*V. R. i. Bell. 278 ; 86 of 1904*) till about 1183 the Noḷambavāḍi province seems to have been governed by a Pāṇḍya family, generally known as 'Pāṇḍyas of Ucchangi' (*see following* Pedigree).

[1] *V. R. i. Bellary, 130 ; 232 of 1913.*

PĀNḌYAS OF UCHCHANGI.

Ruling the Noḷambavāḍi province from about A.D. 1079 to 1183.

The list given by L. Rice (*E. C. xi. Introduction 16*) is here combined with results gained from inscriptions (*ibid. Dg., 5, 6; 296 of 1918 ; E. R. 1918, p. 103*). But it is not free from doubt.

Mangaya, or Ādityadēva.
- *Teja-Raya Pāṇḍya.*
  - *Chēdi, or Chēta-Rāja Pāṇḍya.* (So-called because he subdued the Chēdi king.)
    - *Palanta-Pāṇḍya.* or Palamanda-Palatta.
      - *Irukkavēḷa*, or 'Tribhuvanamalla Pāṇḍya.'
        - *Rāya-Pāṇḍya.* 'Tribhuvanamalla,' *Md.* Sōvaladēvī.
          - *Paṇḍita-Pāṇḍya.*
            - *Tailapa.*
          - *Vīra-Pāṇḍya.* 'Jagadēkamalla,' *Md.* Gangādēvi and Vijayadēvi, 1143, 1162.
          - *Vijaya-Pāṇḍya.* 'Nigaḷankamalla,' *alias* Kāmadvēa, 1163, 1165, 1167, 1183.
            - *Paṇḍita-Pāṇḍya.*
              - *Vijaya-Paṇḍya.*
          - *Palatta-Pāṇḍya.*
  - *Irukkapāla.* (*Md.* a Chōla princess, *c.* A.D. 1098)
    - *Dau. Mahādēvi.* (*Md.* to Hoysala king Ereyanga.)

NOTES.—In A.D. 1079 a Paṇḍya chief, with title 'Nigaḷankamalla,' was Governor (*V. R. i. Bellary, 278 ; 86 of 1904*). Prior to A.D. 1178 the Hoysala king Ballāḷa II seized Uchchangi (*E. C. iv, Ng., 70*) from its ruler Vijaya-Pandya *alias* Kāma-deva, imprisoned him, and afterwards restored him (*E. C. ii, Sr.-Bel : 124 ; v, Bl., 137 ; vi, Tk., 10*). After Kāmadēva's time the Noḷamba province was absorbed into the dominions of the Hoysalas. Vijaya-Paṇḍya, in a record of date = A.D. 1167–8, was called 'Nigaḷankamalla' (*E. C. xi. Dg., 39*).

ORISSA—GAJAPATI KINGS OF

When the Kalinga-Ganga kings of the East coast lost power early in the 15th century, Kapilēndra, said to have been a herd-boy who rose to be minister to the last Kalinga king Bhānu IV, seized his master's throne and established a short-lived dynasty of 'Gajapati' Kings, with capital at Cuttack. His usurpation, according to two inscriptions at Śrīkūrmam (*V. R. i. Ganjam 152, 191*), must have been either in A.D. 1429-30 or 1431-1432. By 1455 he had seized all the country as far South as the Krishna river (*I. A. xx. 390*), for in that year a member of his family gave away a village near Bezwada. Before 1459 he had captured Warangal and Koṇḍavīḍu (*110 of 1902*). He seems to have died in 1464–5 (*V. R. i. Ganjam, 225, 243, 244*).

According to Firishtah's chronology there was a gap between Kapilēndra's death and the actual occupation of the throne by the next member of his family ; for the chronicler, writing of A.D. 1471–2, says that when the King of Orissa died the throne was seized by a slave named Mangaḷa, and on the representation of the late king's cousin 'Ambur Ray' Muhammad Bāhmanī sent an army, defeated Mangaḷa, and placed Ambur Ray on the throne. This matter requires investigation, for which the present work is no place.

At present we have information of two kings 1. Kapilēndra and his son 2. Purushōttama between 1429 and 1496. The relationship between 2 Purushottama and 3 Pratapa Rudra is not known.

- *3. Pratāpa Rudra.* A.D. 1496-1539.
  - *Vīrabhadra.* Captured in 1515 by Krishṇadēva Raya of Vijayanagar.
  - *Kaluyadēva.*
  - *4. Katharuya-dēva* murdered by a minister in 1541.
- *Tirumala-Rāghava* or Tiru. Kānta.

PALLAVA KINGS

The dates given in the following Table, and the relationships of members of the family to one another, are mostly taken from Professor Jouveau-Dubreuil (' *Ancient History of the Deccan,*' *p. 70*) who has made an exhaustive examination of the inscriptions bearing on the subject. The information, however, must not be accepted as entirely free from doubt. For instance while the Professor's date for the accession of No. 13, Simhavarman is A.D. 475, the late Dr. Fleet placed it in the year following August 25, 436 (*J. R. A. S. 1915, pp. 476, 485*).

The first King Bappa seems to have risen to power on the decline of the Āndhra monarchy about A.D. 225. He certainly reigned over their southern dominions from the Krishna river to South of Kāñchī (Conjevaram).

1. *Bappa*
   c. A.D. 225–250
2. *Śiva Skandavarman I*
   ' of Kāñchī.' c. 250–275
3. 275–300. *Md.* Chāru-dēvī
4. *Buddhyankura*
   300–325
5. *Vishṇugōpa I*
   325–350
6. *Skandavarman II*
   350–375
7. *Kumāra-Vishnu I*
   alias ' Kāḷabhartṛ.' 375–400

Sons of No. 7:

- 8. *Buddhavarman II*
  400–425
  - 9. *Kumāra Vishṇu II*
    425–450
- 10. *Skandavarman III*
  or ' Chuṭu-Pallava '
  - 11. ' *Vīravarman*
    or 'Vīrakūrcha'
    - 12. *Vijaya Skandavarman IV*
      alias Skandaśishya 450–475 (Fleet makes reign end in 436).

Sons of No. 12:

- 13. *Simhavarman I*[1]
  475–500. (Fleet makes his accession as in the year following August 25, 436). This king crowned the Ganga Harivarman or Ayyavarman for the purpose of crushing the Bāṇa chiefs, about A.D. 450
  - 14. *Skandavarman V*
    alias ' Chandadanda.' 500–525. (*c.* 460. Fleet). Installed the Ganga Mādhava I about 470 (Fleet).
    - 15. *Nandivarman I*
      525–550
- ' *Yuvamahārāja* ' *Vishṇugopa II*
  or ' Kumāra-Vishṇu.' Did not reign. Recaptured Kāñchī from the Chōlas.
  - *Simhavarman II*
    Did not reign ?
  - *Vishṇugopa III*
    Did not reign ?
    - 16. *Simhavarman II*
      550–575

Sons of No. 16:

- 17. *Simhavishṇu*
  or ' Avanisimha-Pottarāja '
  575–600
  - 18. *Mahēndravarman I*
    600–630
- *Bhīmavarman*
  - *Buddhavarman*

[1] For Fleet's date see *J. R. A. S.* 1915, p. 471 f., especially p. 485.

PALLAVA KINGS—*contd.*

19. *Narasimhavarman I*
630–668. Captured Bādāmi from the W. Chālukyas, 642.

20. *Mahēndravarman II*
668–670

21. *Paramēśvara Pōtavārman I*
670–690. 'Destroyed the city of Ranarasika.' Won battle of Peruvaḷanallūr.

22. *Narasimhavarman II*
690–715

23. *Paramēśvara-Pōtavarman II*
715–717. The line ended with him.

Ādityavarman

Gōvindavarman

Hiraṇyavarman
Md. Rōhiṇī

24. *Nandivarman II*
717–779. Won battles at Maṇṇaikuḍi and Śankaramangal against the Pāṇḍyas. Pāṇḍya records however claim the victory, prior to A.D. 769

Mahēndravarman

25. *Dantivarman*
779–830. Vanquished by Rāshṭrakuṭa Govinda III, to whom he became feudatory, about 804

26. *Nandivarman III*
830–854. *Md.* Śankhā, dau. of Rāshṭrakūṭa Amoghavarsha I

27. *Nṛipatunga*
854-880. The Bāṇa chief Bāṇa-Vidyādhara was his tributary

28. *Aparājita*
880 c.-898 crushed by the Chola King Āditya I, and territory annexed

Vijaya-Kampa

NOTES.—No. 2. *Skandavarman* I granted, about A.D. 257, a village in the 'Sātāhani' province of the Āndhra country, which had been conquered by his father. (*E. I. i, 2.*)

No. 5. *Vishṇugopa* I's viceroy in Vengi Hastivarma was defeated by Samudragupta (vide *the Allahabad pillar inscription*), *c.* A.D. 338. About A.D. 340 Samudragupta conquered and captured Vishṇugōpa himself, and for a time occupied Kāñchī. Then he restored the Pallava king and left Kāñchi. About the same time the Chuṭu-Satavāhana branch of the Āndhra monarchy was brought to an end by the Kadamba chief Mayūraśarma seizing Baṇavāśi. This chief acknowledged Pallava overlordship.

No. 13. *Simhavarman* I. The Pallavas at this time (about A.D. 450 by Fleet's chronology) began to recover the ground they had lost after their defeat by Samudragupta. The Vēlūrpālaiyam plates (*S.I.I. ii. 502*)imply that they had lost Kāñchī some time previous to their date, since that inscription records the recovery of the city by Simhavarman's brother Kumāra-Vishṇu, or Vishṇugōpa (*E. I. xv, 248*). Simhavarman was overlord to the Gangas of the Toṇḍamaṇḍalam and Mysore countries.

Mr. Krishnaswami Aiyangar, and following him, Mr. C. S. Srinivasachari, make (8) Buddhavarman and (9) Kumāra-Vishṇu II respectively son and grandson of a younger brother of (13) Simhavarman I, and Vishṇugopa, whose name was Kumāra-Vishṇu ('*Some Contributions, etc. . .*' p. 155. *History and Institutions of the Pallavas*, p. 9).

No. 18. *Mahēndravarman* was also called by many other names, viz 'Pōtaraiyan' or 'Pōtarāja,' 'Guṇabhara', 'Vichitra-Chitta', 'Pagāppiḍugu', 'Śatrumalla', 'Lalitānkura' 'Avanibhājana', 'Purushōttama', 'Toṇḍaiyan', 'Satyasaṁdha' and 'Matta-Vilāsa.' His country was swept by the Chaḷukyas. He excavated many rock-cut temples.

No. 19. ***Narasimha I*** also called 'Māmalla,' 'Atyantakāma', 'Śrīnidhi' and 'Srībhara', is said to have won the battles of Pariyaḷa, Maṇimangalam, and Śūramāra in his war with the Chaḷukyas (*S. I. I. i, p. 144*). He took the title 'Vātapikoṇḍa' after his capture of Bādāmi. He gave asylum to Mānavamma, King of Ceylon, in his exile from the island.

For the wars of No. 21 Paramēśvara-Pōtavarman I see *E. I. x..100, E. C. x. Kl. 63, xi, Dg, 66.* He was also known as 'Ugradaṇḍa,' 'Īśvara-Pōtarāja' 'Lōkāditya,' 'Atyanta-Kāma', 'Śrīnidhi,' and 'Śrībhara' and 'Raṇajaya.'

No. 22. ***Narasimha II*** was also called 'Rājasimha,' 'Atyanta-Kāma,' 'Śrībhara', 'Raṇajaya', and 'Kālakāla,' He built the Shore temple at Mahābālipuram and the Kailāsanātha temple at Conjevaram.

No. 24. ***Nandivarman II.*** Suffered serious defeats at the hands of the Chāḷukyas, his capital Kāñchī being captured by the enemy; who, however spared the city. Battles of Śankaramangai, Maṇṇaikuḍi, Nelvēli, Pugaliyūr, etc., against the Pāṇḍya king Arikēśari Parāntaka. In some battles, e.g. at Maṇṇaikudi each side claims the victory; and the Pāṇḍya claims a victory over the Pallava at Peṇṇāgāḍam on the Kāvērī river. Nandivarman's 62nd year of reign is mentioned (*V.R. i. N. Arcot, 330 ; 76 of 1889*). He was helped in his war by the chief Perumbiḍugu Muttaraiyan (*E.R. 1907, §22 ; and note below under pedigree of 'Tanjore chiefs of the 8th century'; and E.I. xiii, 134.*). He had other names, viz: 'Nandipōtaraya', 'Pallavamalla,' Śrībhara', 'Kshatriyamalla', etc.

No. 25. ***Dantivarman*** was also known as 'Mārpiḍugu,' 'Dantipotaraya,' and 'Vairamēgha.'

No. 26. ***Nandivarman III*** was called 'Avani-Nārāyaṇa', 'Viḍēlviḍugu', Mānabharaṇa' and 'Teḷḷārṟerinda'.

No. 27. ***Nripatunga.*** For events of the reign see the text, s.v. A.D. 862 to 878 (*E.I. ix. 84 ; Arch. Ann. Report 1903–04, p. 270*). He was known also as 'Vikramavarman', 'Viḍēlviḍugu', and 'Ganga-Pallava'.

28. ***Aparājita.*** According to the Anbil grant (*E.I. xv. 44*) he was killed in war with the allied Pāṇḍya Varaguṇa II and Chōla Āditya I.

The principal inscriptions of the Pallava dynasty are the following. The Vēlūrpālaiyam plates (*E.I. ii, 510*) ; the Uruvupalli plates (*I.A. v, 50*) ; the Mangaḍūr plates (*I.A. v, 154*) ; the Pikira grant (*E.I. viii, 159*) ; the Hire-hadagali plates (*ibid. 143*) ; the Udayēndiram plates (*E.I. iii, 142*) ; the Chendalūr plates (*E.I. viii, 233*) ; the Penukoṇḍa plates (*J.R.A.S., 1915, p. 471*) ; the Ōmgōḍu grants A and B (*E.I. xv, 246*) ; the Kaśakuḍi plates (*S. I. I. ii. 342*), and the Kūram grant (*S. I. I. i. 144*).

PALLAVA PERUṆJIṄGA

A 'Ko-Peruṅjiṅga' always called a Pallava, or Kāḍava chief, became very famous as a rebel against the Chōla king Rājarājā III (A.D. 1916–1246). There were possibly, as has been suggested in *E. R. 1923, p. 96,* two chiefs of the same name, father and son.

Also an ***Ammaiyappan Pallavaraiyan*** is known in A.D. 1175–78 as a feudatory of the Chōla king Rājādhirāja III (*V.R. i. Chittoor 339, 345 ; 468. 474 of 1905.*).

The name of the elder Peruṅjiṅga (if there were two) was Aḷagiya-Śiyan-Avaniyāḷa-Pirandān-Peruṅjiṅga. He appears to have revolted against his sovereign the Chōla king Rājarājā III about A.D. 1221. A battle was fought near Teḷḷāru. The Hoysala king Narasimha II intervened and saved the Chōla throne, and put down the rebellions ; after which Peruṅjiṅga returned to his allegiance. About the same time the Pāṇḍya king Māravarman Sundara Pāṇḍya attacked, and says that he burnt Tanjore and Uraiyūr ; a record at Vriddhāchalam of A.D. 1229 (*136 of 1900*) speaks of Peruṅjiṅga as an officer under Rājārāja Chōla III.

About A.D. 1231 Perunjiṅga (possibly the son, but possibly the same) again revolted, and made prisoner of his suzerain Rājarājā Chōla, carrying him to his own town Śōndamangalam.

(*For details of events see the Text ; and see E.I. vii, 160*)

In A.D. 1243 the second Peruñjinga (if there were two of the name) had himself crowned as a king, between May 9 and 13 in that year, under the title 'Avanyāvaṇōdbhava-Rājasimha'. 'He had great power in his day during the decay of the Chōla kingdom.

PĀṆḌYA KINGS

The origin of the Pāṇḍya kingdom is lost in the mists of time. The kingdom was known to the Greek geographers, and is mentioned in the Edicts of Aśōka (*c.* 250 B.C.). The earliest names known, viz. the first few in the list next following, are derived from the *Śilapadhikāram*, or 'Epic of the Anklet,' and other ancient writings (compare Dr. Barnett's *Antiquities of India*, p. 43). Early dates are tentative. We are on safe ground with the accession of Varaguṇa II in A.D. 862, but as to earlier kings can only say that I have done the best I could with a difficult subject. The dates should be compared with those of the early Chēra and Chōla sovereigns.

1. *Neḍuñjeḻiyan Pāṇḍya I*

'Neḍuñjaḍaiyan', 'Ugra-Paṇḍya', 'Ugra-Peruvaḻudi',[1] *c.* A.D. 150. Contemp. of Chēra king Adan II. Defeated an 'Āryan' army in the Dekhan.

|

2. *Veṟṟi-vēṟ-Śeḻiyan*

c. A.D. 190. 'Ilañjeḻian', as a prince he was viceroy of Korkhai.

|

3. *Neḍuñjeḻiyan II*

c. A.D. 200 Contemp. of Chōla king, Neḍumuḍi-Kiḷḷi. Battle of Talai-Ālangā-nam. Made prisoner the Chēra king Śēy.

. . . . (*Relationship unknown*).

4. *Ugra-Peruvaḻudi*

. . . . (Do.)

5. *Nan-Māran*

. . . . (Do.)

6. *Kaḍungōn*[2]

c. A.D. 575

|

7. *Māravarman*

'Avaniśūḷāmaṇi', *c.* 600.

|

8. *Jayantavarman*

'Śeḻiyan-Śēndān', *c.* 625.

|

9. *Māravarman Arikēśari*

'Asamasaman', 'Neḍumāran', 'Parāṅkuśan', 'Akāḷakālan', 'Alanghya-Vikrama', *c.* 650. Victories at Pāḻi and Śennilam and at Nelvēli. Capture of Chōla city, Uraiyūr.

|

10. *Kō-chchaḍaiyan*

'Saḍaiyan', 'Raṇadhīra', 'Neḍunjaḍaiyan'. *c.* 675. Won battle at Marudūr. Defeated Āy-vēḷ chiefs, and Raṭṭas.

|

11. *Arikēśari-Parāntaka*

'Rājasimha I', 'Māravarman', 'Māranjaḍaiyan', 'Tēr-Maran', 'Neḍumāran', 'Parāṅkuśan', *c.* 700 or later. Battles of Śankaramangai, Kuḷumbūr Neḍuvayal, Maṇṇaikuḍi or Kurichi. *Md.* Sundari.

|

12. *Jaṭila Parāntaka*

'Śrīvara', 'Neḍunjaḍaiyan', 'Tennan-Vānavan'. Donor of the Vēḷvikuḍi grant in 769–70. Defeated Pallavas at Peṇṇāgaḍam, and won other victories.

|

13. *Rājasimha II*

|

14. *Varaguṇa I*

'Jayantavarma' *c.* 825.

|

[1] Perhaps the same as the 'Palyāgasālai' or Palśālai-Mudukuḍmi-Peruvaḻudi' mentioned as having reigned 'a long time' before Kaḍungōn (*T.A.S. iii 101*).

[2] The dates here given of kings from Kaḍungōn to Varaguṇa II are adapted from Professor Jouveau-Dubreil's reckoning (*see also E.R. 1907, p. 62, and 1908, p. 62 ; T.A.S. i. 154 ; I.A. 1908, 193 ; 1922, 211 ; E.I. viii. 318*).

PĀNḌYA KINGS—*contd.*

15. *Śrīmāra*
'Ekavīra', 'Śrīvallabha', 'Parachakra-Kolāhala' 'Pallava-bhanjana', 'Avanipa-Śēkhara.' *c.* 830. Won many victories.

16. *Varaguṇa II*
'Māranjaḍaiyan', came to throne A.D. 862. Victories at Iḍavai and Vēmbil against Chōlas and Gangas. Penetrated to Araiśūr. Was defeated at Tiruppurambiyam, or Śrīpurambiyam, by the Gangas, whose king Prithivīpati I was killed, 877–8(?).

17. *Parāntaka Vīra-Nārāyaṇa*
'Saḍaiyan', 'Jaṭila-Neḍunjaḍaiyan'. Destroyed Peṇṇāgaḍam. *Md.* a Bāṇa Princess.

18. *Rājasimha III*
'Mandara-Gaurava', 'Māravarman'. 'Abhimānamēru', 'Rājaśikhāmaṇi', completely defeated by Parāntaka Chōla I between 907 and 916.

The list of Pāṇḍya princes which follows is gathered from inscriptions. Relationships are generally not traceable. Probably these princes ruled States separated from one another but formerly belonging to the old joint kingdom, which was occasionally re-formed as a whole and then again became disjointed (*see Kielhorn's Lists E. I. vii. 10 ; viii. 8, App. ii, p. 24 ; ix, 226*).

The titles 'Ponnin-Perumāḷ', 'Korkai-vēndan' are common to all the members of the Pāndya family.

A.D. 965. *Vīra Pāṇḍya*, who took the head of the Chōla, fought against the Chōla Āditya II, and was called 'Chōlāntaka.' (*Suchīndram Rock-Inscription, T. A. S. iii, Pt. I, 67*). About the same period several records of a '*Śaḍaiya-Māran*.'

Period 985–1012. *Amarabhujanga-Panḍya* a contemporary of Rājarāja Chōla I.

Period 1012–1042. Chōla princes were made Viceroys of their king in the Pāṇḍya country, under the title, 'Chōla-Pāṇḍya,' (*see e. g. V. R. ii, Madura, 10, 11 ; 64, 65 of 1905 and others*).

Prior to 1046. *Mānābharaṇan* alias *Vīrā Pāṇḍya*. Decapitated by Rājādhirāja Chōla I.

1041. *Vikrama Pāṇḍya* usurped the throne of Ceylon. He was killed in battle in 1042 when Rājādhiraja Chōla I raided the island.

1046–1048. *Parākrama Pāṇḍya* usurped the throne of Ceylon and reigned two years (*Māhāwamśa, ch. lvi*).

c. 1060. 'Vira Pāṇḍya, son of Vikrama', mentioned in an inscription at Chidambaram. He was defeated by the Chāḷukya Chōla king Rājēndra II—Kulottunga-Chōla I, and the government of Madura was made over to the Chōla prince Gangaikoṇḍa Chōla, renamed '*Sundara-Chōla-Pāṇḍya*'.

1065–67. *Vīrakēśarin*, son of Srīvallabha Pāṇḍya, was killed by being trampled to death by an elephant by order of Vīra-Rājēndra Chōla.

1080–1084. *Sundara Pāṇḍya*, a contemporary of *Jaṭāvarman* Srīvallabha who fought against Kulōttunga-Chōla I.

c. 1090–1133. *Parāntaka Pāṇḍya* supported Kulōttunga-Chōla I and Vikrama in some of their wars. He claims to have taken Viḷiñam, to have destroyed ships at Kāndalūr, to have subjugated southern Kalinga, and to have captured Kuḷam (the Colair Lake near Ellore) from 'Telugu-Vīman,' i.e., the Telugu chief Bhīma (*T. A. S i. 19. See Text s. v. A. D. 1090, etc*).

1132. *Māravarman-Śrīvallabha-Pāṇḍya I.* Accession in year following February 1, 1132. Inscription of hi 37th year (*426 of 1916*) i.e., 1168–9 at Ambāsamudram, Tinnevelly District.

1160–1. (Another) *Māravarman-Śrīvallabha-Pāṇḍya* II. Accession in this year. He had a son *Kulaśēkhara*, one of his feudatories was the Kēraḷa ruler Vīra-Ravivarma (*101 of 1908*).

1167–1171. *Kulaśēkhara-Pāṇḍya*, probably the prince just mentioned, murdered *Parākrama-Pāṇḍya*, who ruled at Madura, and seized the throne. There followed the War of Pāṇḍya succession, and the invasion of the Pāṇḍya country by the Singhalese under general Lankāpura (*see Text s. v., A. D. 1067*). (*Prof. Krishnaswami Aiyangar believes that the war began in 1171–2.*) Parākrama's son *Vīra-Panḍya* was placed on the throne by Lankāpura, and Kulaśēkhara fled and shortly afterwards died. He was succeeded by *Vikrama-Pāṇḍya*, who was supported by the Chōla king (*1 of 1899 ; E.R. 1899, § 38*).

1190. Between May 30 and July 8, accession of *Jatāvarman-Kulaśēkhara* 1, alias ' Rājagambhīra '. He lived till at least 1217 (*E.I. viii., App. ii, 24 ; ix, 226 ; 337 of 1916 ; V. R. ii. Ramnad, 170 ; E.I. viii, 274 ; E. R. 1900, p. 6*).

1216. Between June 25 and September 3 accession of *Māravarman Sundara-Pāṇḍya I*, ' Kōnērinmaikoṇḍān '. He reigned till at least 1235. ' Performed the anointment of heroes at Muḍikoṇḍa-Sōḷapuram ' (*E.I. vi, 301, etc.*). A record of A.D. 1222-3 says that he burnt Tanjore and Uraiyūr ' (*E.I. viii, App. ii, 24*).

1238. Between July 13 and August 12, accession of *Māravarman Sundara Pāndya II* (*E.I. viii. App. ii, 24*). His 13th year fell in 1250 (*572 of 1916*). His last known date is in 1251 (*E.I. vi. 301*) on January 18. He claims to have taken Śrīrangam from Hoysala Sōmēśvara. This perhaps refers to the latter's occupation of Kaṇṇanūr, near Srīrangam.

1249. According to Mr. L.D. Swamikannu Pillai a Pāṇḍyā king reigned at this time whose name was *Māravarman-Vikrama-Pāndya*, bearing the title ' Bhuvanēka-Vīra '.

1251. Between April 20 and 28, accession of *Jaṭāvarman-Sundara-Pāṇḍya I*, with title ' Kōdaṇḍa-Raman '. He lived till his 23rd year in 1273 (*V. R. i. S. Arcot 556-558 ; 198 of 1906 ; E.I. iii, 7 ; viii, App. ii, 25*). Before 1255 he had conquered Malabar, marched through Pudukoṭṭai, defeated the Hoysala general and taken possession of Kaṇṇanūr (*E.R. 1900, p. 6*). He attached the powerful chief Perunjinga at Śēndamangalam, took that place and restored it. He was anointed at Chidambaram ; and is said to have covered the temple at Śrīrangam with gold after his solemn coronation there (*E.I. xi, 266 ; vi. 221 ; V.R. i, Chingleput, 133, 167, 168 ; S. Arcot, 798.*). He defeated the Bāṇa chief of N. Arcot, and drove back the forces of the Kākatīya king towards the north. He was crowned a second time at Nellore.

1253. Between April 30 and July 13, accession of *Jaṭāvarman- Vīra-Pāṇḍya*, who ruled till at least 1269 (*67, 73 of 1911 ; 34 of 1920 ; E.I. vii, 10 ; viii, App. ii, 25 ; E.I. xi 226 ; x. 139*).

1262. In the year following July 30. Accession of *Māravarman-Vīra-Pāṇḍya* (*V. R. i., S Arcot, 178 ; 386 of 1913.*).

1268. Between June 10 and 20, accession of *Māravarman-Kulaśēkhara I.* (*E.I. viii App. ii, 25*), who ruled till at least March 1308 (*see text s.v. A.D. 1308*). He partitioned his country into separate governorships, which eventually led to each governor trying to become independent. (*For events of the reign see text s.v. 1310, etc.*) According to Wassaf, Kulaśēkhara was assassinated in 1309–10 (*416, 417, 460 of 1916*).

1270. Between January 15 and March 1, accession of Māra-varman Sundara Pāndya, according to Mr. Swamikannu Pillai's dates (*342-344 of 1911 ; E.R. 1922, p. 92*).

1276. Between August 10 and 25, 1276—or, according to Mr. L.D. Swamikannu Pillai, between February 28 and March 14, 1277 (*E.R. 1916, p. 97.*)—accession of *Jaṭāvarman-Sundara Pāndya II*, ' Kodaṇḍa Rāma ' (*E.I. viii. App. ii, 25 ; E.I. xi, 259 ; V.R. i., Chingleput, 979 ; 110 of 1912 ; 305 of 1921 ; 418 of 1909 ; 432 of 1913 ; 529, 570 of 1920*). He took away the Tooth-relic from Ceylon and gave it to Kulaśēkhara I in Madura (*Mahāwaṁśa, ch. xc.*). Wassaf records the death of this ruler in 1293, earlier than December 2.

1283. Between January 12 and August 29, accession of *Māravarman-Vikrama Pāṇḍya*, as determined by Mr. Swamikannu Pillai. The date however seems a little uncertain (*compare V.R. i. S. Arcot, 222, 343, 439, 440, 813, 844 ; 135 of 1902 ; 53, 54 of 1905 ; 78, 79 of 1903 ; 410 of 1909 ; 116 of 1900*). He lived till at least 1291. He was called ' Rājākkaḷ-nāyan '. One record in S. Arcot shews him ruling there in 1288 in his 6th year, while in the same place another inscription shews Jaṭāvarman Sundara Pāṇḍya II ruling there in his 13th year. These difficulties await solution by future students. He is said to have defeated Vijaya-Gaṇḍagōpāla (*V.R. i. Chingleput 473, 480 ; S. Arcot, 157 ; 410, 418 of 1909*).

1291. Between April 20, 1291 and April 3, 1292, accession of *Jaṭāvarman Śrīvallabha*, as determined by Mr. Swamikannu Pillai (*E. R. 1918, p. 155*).

1293. In the year following February 8, accession of *Jaṭāvarman-Sundara-Pāṇḍya III*, also determined by the same.

1296–17. Between December 17, 1926 and April 29, 1927, accession of *Jaṭāvarman-Vīra-Panḍya*, illegitimate son of Mārav. Kulaśēkhara I. He was driven out by Malik Kāfur in 1311. Ravivarman III of Kēraḷa also claims to have driven him out (*E. R. 1900, p. 6*).

1303. Between March 31, and May 16 (*E. R. 1916, p. 97*), provisionally fixed by Mr. Swamikannu Pillai as the period of accession of *Jaṭāvarman-Sundara-Pāṇḍya*, legitimate son and heir of Kulaśēkhara I. The son murdered the father, and fled to Delhi when defeated in 1310 (*E. R. 1921, p. 100*). A record of his 11th year is dated January 26, 1314.

1314. Between March 6 and 29, accession of *Māravarman-Kulaśēkhara II* (*E. I. viii. App. ii, p. 25 ; E R 1921, 100*). His last known date is 1325.

1315. Between April 15 and August 10, accession of *Jaṭāvarman-Parākrama-Pāṇḍya*, who ruled for at least eight years (*E. I. ix, 228; xi. 264 ; V. R. iii. Tinnevelly 259 ; 487 of 1909 ; 17 of 1894 ; I. A. 1913, p. 229*).

1333–4. *Māravarman-Vīra-Pāṇḍya* II. Two inscriptions make his accession in the year following December 6, 1334 (*494, 495 of 1921*). One makes it in the year following October 19, 1333 (*277 of 1910 ; see E. R. 1922, p. 92*).

1335. Between April 30, and July 30, accession of *Māravarman-Parākrama-Pāṇḍya*, who lived till at least 1352. In this year the Muhammadan Viceroy of Madura under Muhammad Tughlak, Jalālu-d-din Ásan declared himself independent Sultan of Madura. He had ruled Madura since about 1330 (*V. R. i, N. Arcot, 420; 78, 509, 525 of 1918*).

1357–8. Between February 5, 1357, and January 9, 1358, accession of Jaṭāvarman-Parākrama-Pāṇḍya (*E. I. vii. 12 ; xi. 228 ; 408 of 1917 ; 159 of 1911 ; E. R. 1922, p. 93*).

In 1384 mention of a Parākrama-Pāṇḍya in Tinnevelly District, whose rule began in this year and who ruled till at least 1415 (*V. R. iii, Tinn. 337; 203 of 1895*).

1396–7. Accession of a *Kulaśēkhara-Pāṇḍya II* with prefix '*Jaṭāvarman*' (*E. R. 1918, p. 158 ; 528 of 1911 ; T. A. S. i. 45, No. 2*). Apparently the same Kulaśēkhara had the prefix 'Māravarman' in 270 of 1908.

1401. Between January 13, and July 27, accession of *Jaṭāvarman-Vikrama-Pāṇḍya*, alias Kōnērinmaikoṇḍān' who ruled for at least 21 years (*E. I. ix, 228 ; viii, App. ii, 25 ; xi, 265 ; V. R. i, Chingleput 378 ; 232 of 1910*).

1422. Between November 8 and December 6, (?) accession of *Jaṭilavarman-Arikēsari-Parākrama-Pāṇḍya*, also called 'Mānābharaṇan', 'Mānakavacha' 'Kumāra Parākrama', and perhaps 'Vīra-Pāṇḍya'. He was born under the constellation Mrigaśira. Died 1463 or 1464. Fought with the King of Kēraḷa (*T. A. S. i, 45 No. 3 ; E. R. 1906, p. 72 ; 1910, p. 100 ; 1905, p. 56 ; 518, 533, 547 of 1917 ; E. R. 1918, p. 158 ; 172, 178, 199 of 1895*). (*See pedigree below.*)

1430. Between November 9 and 28, accession of *Kulaśēkhara-Śrīvallabha-Pāṇḍya*, also called 'Aḷagan-Perumaḷ', and 'Kumāra-Kulaśēkhara.' He lived till at least A.D. 1473–4 (*T. A. S. i, 45 ; 198 of 1895 ; 278 of 1908 ; 476, 544, 649 of 1917*). He was 'born in the Uttara Nakshatra.'

1443. Between March 13 and July 28, accession of *Māravarman-Vīra-Pāṇḍya* III ('*M*' *of Kielhorn's list*). His 14th year is mentioned. He lived in the reign of Dēva-Raya II of Vijayanagar. From at least 1404 Madura was governed by viceroys from Vijayanagar, Bāṇa chiefs and others (*see the Madura list above*).

1453-1455. Accession of *Jaṭilavarman-Parākrama-Pāṇḍya* alias 'Srīvallabha'. He was born under the constellation Ārdrā (Tamil, 'Tiruvādirāi'). He was alive in 1458.

1468. Between February 6 and October 13, accession of *Jaṭilavarman-Parākrama-Pāṇḍya*, alias 'Aḷagan-Perumāl', 'Kōnērinmai-Koṇḍān,' 'Vīra Pāṇḍya', 'Ponnin-Perumāl'. Born under the constellation Sravishṭhā or Dhanishṭhā (Tamil 'Aviṭṭam'). Lived till at least 1507 (*T.S.A. i, 46, No. 12 ; E R. 1918, p. 159*).

1480. Between January 12 and August 1. Accession of *Parākrama-Kulaśēkhara-Pāṇḍya*, who was born in Krittikā' (or Kārttikai). Lived till at least 1500 (*T.S.A. i, 46, No. 7 ; 618 of 1917*).

The pedigree of these few Pāṇḍyas is probably as follows :—

? Kulaśēkhara
acc = 1396

- *Arikēśari-Parākrama* (Accession in 1422. 'Born in Mrigaśira').
- *A daughter*
  - *Parākrama-Śrīvallabha* (Accession in 1453–55. 'Born in Ārdrā'.)
  - *Parākrama-Aḷagan-Perumāḷ* (Accession in 1468. 'Born in Aviṭṭam', or Dhaṇishṭha).
- *Kulaśēkhara-Śrīvallabha* (Accession in 1430. 'Born in Uttaranakshatra')
  - *Parakrama-Kulaśēkhara* Accession in 1480. 'Born in Krittikā'.

1485-6. Accession of ***Parākrama-Pāṇḍya***, whose second year was 1486-7 (*V.R. ii, Ramnad, 178—D*).

1490-1. Accession of another ***Parākrama-Pāṇḍya***, whose second year was 1491-2 (*V. R. iii, Tinnevelly, 304—D*).

1531-2. Accession of ***Māravarman-Sundara-Pāṇḍya III, alias*** 'Kōnērinmai-Koṇḍān'. He lived till at least 1555 (*V.R. iii, Tinnevelly, 405 ; 2 of 1916*).

Between October 4 and November 1, 1535, accession of Abhirāma Parākrama, also called ***Jaṭilavarman-Śrīvallabha***, and 'Kōnērinmai-Koṇḍān', and 'Iranda-Kālam-Eḍutta' ('he who brought back the old time'). He was son of Āhavarāma. Lived in the reign of king Achyuta of Vijayanagar, who, after defeating the 'Tirūvaḍi', or king of Travancore, established Abhirāma-Śrīvallabha in Madura. He was reigning on October 4, 1545 (*577, 666 of 1917, etc ; E.I. ix, 226, 'P'*).

1543. July 20. Accession of ***Jaṭilavarman-Kulaśēkhara III*** (*450, 545 of 1917*). Elder son of Abhirāma-Parākrama. 'Born in Aśvati' (Aśvinī). Also called 'Parākrama', and 'Perumāḷ'. He lived till at least 1560 (*466, 525, 531, 532, 536, 540 of 1917*).

1550. Between June 14 and 27. Accession of ***Śalivāṭipati***, the younger son of Abhirāma-Parākrama (*387, 403, 481, 511, 543 of 1917*). Also called 'Tirunelvēli-Perumaḷ-Kulaśēkhara,' 'Vīravenbāmālai,' 'Ponnan-Paṇḍya', etc. He was crowned in 1552 (*V.R. iii, Tinnevelly, 362, 302*).

1563. Between June 1 and 13, accession of ***Jaṭilavarman-Ativīrarāma-Śrīvallabha***, son of Śalivaṭipati *alias* 'Śivalavēl', 'Śivaladēva' 'Aḻagan-Perumāḷ'. He was 'born in Punarvasu. His 42nd year 1604-5 is mentioned in an inscription at Kuttalam (*V.R. iii, Travancore, 142 ; 482, 501 of 1917 ; T.A.S. i, 49, Nos. 22, 26 ; V.R. iii, Tinnevelly, 278—R ; ii, Ramnad, 168—B*).

1572-3. Inscriptions of the second year of a prince (?) ***Kulaśēkhara-Parākrama-Aḻagan Śokkanār*** (*482 of 1909 ; E.R. 1918, p. 162*).

1574. Mention of ***Kūn-Pāṇḍya*** (*E.R. 1904-5, p. 57*).

1586-7. Accession of ***Abhirāma-Varatungarāma***, alias Vīra-Pāndya, also called 'Aḻagan-Perumaḷ-Ativīrarāma'. A grant by him on October 9, 1590 (*605 of 1917 ; V.R. ii, Madura, 80, A, B*).

1593. ***Abhirāma-Ativīrarāma-Pāṇḍya*** mentioned (*E.R. 1912, § 40*).

For the following pedigree see *T. A. S. i.* 44.

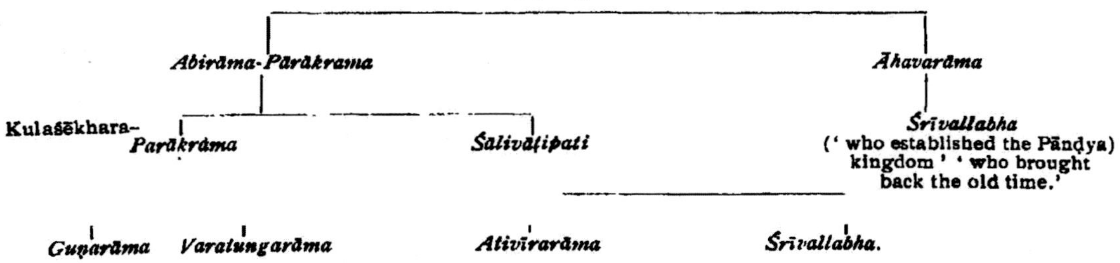

In A.D. 1614-17, a Pāṇḍya prince ***Perumāḷ-Śivala-Māran-Varaguṇarāma*** is mentioned, who was also called 'Kulaśēkara-Sōmāśiyār-Dīkshitar.' He carried out a religious (Yāga) ceremony at Tenkāśi. He may be identical with Srīvallabha, son of Śālivātipati (*V. R. iii, Tinnevelly, 393—A ; Travancore, 127 ; T.A.S. i. 147; 268 of 1908*).

In 1754-5 a descendant of the Pāṇḍya Kings Kulaśēkharā Dikshitar Śivala-Varaguṇa is mentioned in an inscription, which states that like the earlier Śrīvāllabha he 'brought back the old time,' his title being 'Irandakālām-eḍutta' (*T.A.S. i.* 149).

NOTES.—The author of the *Periplus* (1st century A.D.) gives the name 'Paralia' to the country about Quilon and Cape Comorin. This probably represents the river 'Pahruḷi' (modern Tālaiyāru) mentioned in early Tamil epics.

Rāshtrakūṭas No. 10. Kōchchaḍaiyan's alleged defeat of the Raṭṭas (*i.e.* Chālukyas) probably refers to an event of the year A. D. 674 when the Chāḷukya king Vikramāditya I penetrated southwards as far as Trichinopoly and was encamped at Uragapuram.

PĀṆḌYAS OF UCHCHANGI

See NOḶAMBAVĀḌI COUNTRY—RULERS OF

PESHWAS OF SĀTĀRA

See MAHRATTAS

PIṬHĀPURAM PRINCES OF EASTERN CHĀḶUKYA DESCENT

See Pedigree of Eastern Chāḷukyas above.

When King ***Kaṇṭhika-Bēta Vijāyāditya V*** of the Eastern Chāḷukyas was ousted by Tādapa in A.D. 925, he established himself as ruler of the small territory of Piṭhāpuram, an ancient province to the north of the lower Godavari river.

Kaṇṭhika-Bēta Vijayaditya V.
(of the Eastern Chāḷukyas, A.D. 925)

1. *Satyāśraya*
('Uttama Chāḷukya.' *Md.* Gauri, a Ganga princess.)

2. *Vijayāditya II* (*Md.* Vijayā-dēvi)	*Vimalāditya*	*Vikramāditya*	*Vishṇu Vardhana I*	*Mallapa I*	*Kāma I*	*Rājamārtāṇḍa*

Sons of 2. *Vijayāditya II* and others:

3. *Vishṇuvardhana II* — Living in 1145. Became chief in A.D. 1125–6.

4. *Mallapa II* — *Md.* a Haihaya princess Chandalādēvi.

Sāmidēva.

Son of 4. *Mallapa II*:

5. *Vijayāditya III* — Crowned January 11, 1158. *Md.* Gangā *dau.* of 'the lord of the Āradavāda' and Lakshmī.

(*By Gangā*)
6. *Mallapa III.*
Gonaga' or 'Vishṇuvardhana III.'
Dates 1174–5, June 16, 1202.
7. *Udayachandra.*

(*By Lakshmī*)
Narēndra
(Gave a grant in 1176.)

NOTES.—As to the relationship between Bēta Vijayāditya V and Satyāśraya I note that Fleet accepted the latter as son of the former; but must point out that such a fixture allows only five generations between A. D. 925 and 1202. It seems more probable that Satyāśraya lived about 150 years later than his E. Chāḷukya ancestor.

The date of 6 Mallapa's accession is doubtful. Two inscriptions at Bhīmāvaram make its date 1174–5, while the Śarpāvaram pillar inscription fixes it as in 1193–4. Dr. Hultzsch, (*E. I. iv. 230*) finds it impossible to reconcile the statements. It may be that, as in other cases of which we have clear information, the son was made joint ruler with his father some years before the latter's death.

For 6 'Gonaga' see *V. R. ii, Godavari 103 ; 198 of 1893.*

QUTB SHĀHI DYNASTY OF GOLKONDA

See GOLKONDA, KUTB SHAHI DYNASTY.

RAJAHMUNDRY—REḌḌI CHIEFS OF

See REḌḌI CHIEFS

RĀSHṬRAKŪṬA DYNASTY—THE—

See Fleet in *Bombay Gazetteer* Pt. ii, 386 and *E. I. iii. 55 ;* R. G. Bhandarkar '*Early History of the Dekhan*' p. 55, n. 2, and 57 ; *E. C. ii, App. B.*

1. *Dantivarmā I.*
2. *Indra I.*
3. *Govinda I.*

QUTB SHÂHI DYNASTY OF GOLKONDA—*contd.*

4. *Karka, or Kakka I.*

5. *Indra II* (*Md.* a Chāḷukya princess)

7. *Krishṇa I* 'Akālavarsha,' 'Subhatunga,' 'Kalivallabha,' 'Prithvivallabha.' A.D. 768, 772. Constructed the Kailāsa rock-cut temple at Ellora.

Nanna (*See E. I. ix. 194 ; xi. 276*)

6. *Dantidurga* 'Vairamēgha,' 'Khaḍgāvalōka,' 'Sāhasatunga.' Conqured the W. Chāḷukyas. Died childless. A.D. 748, 753, 754.

8. *Gōvinda II* 779–783. Dethroned by Dhruva (*See notes below*)

9. *Dhruva* 783 (*See notes below*)

Śamkaragaṇa 793.

Kamba 'Sthamba,' 'Raṇāvalōka' Seems to have lived privately. Record in 802.

10. *Govinda III* 783–(?)814. Conquered Kēraḷa, Gujarat, etc. *Md.* Gāmuṇḍabbe.

Indra III Made sovereign of Gujarat by his brother Govinda before 812 and became first of a dynasty in Gujarat.

11. *Amōghavarsha I* or 'Śarva.' (?) 814–877. War with the E. Chāḷukyas

12. *Krishṇa II* 877–913. *Md. dau.* of Kōkalla Chēdi or Kalachuri king.

Dau : *Śankhā* *Md.* the Pallava king Nandivarman III.

13. *Jagatunga* *Md.* Lakshmi, a Kalachuri princess.

Dau. *md.* the W. Chāḷukya king Ayyana II.

14. *Indra III.* 913–(?) 922. *Md.* Vijāmbā, a Kalachuri princess.

17. *Baddiga, or Amōghavarsha* III. 933–937. *Md.* Kundakā, a Kalachuri princess.

15. *Amōghavarasha II.* Ruled 1 year, and deposed by his brother, 922.

16. *Gōvinda IV* (?) 922–933

Dau. *Rēvakā* *Md.* W. Ganga king Būtuga II.

18. *Krishna III* 937–8 to 965–6

19. *Khoṭṭiga* 965–6 to 972–3

Nirūpama.

a son.

Indra IV (died March 20–982).

20. Kakkala or Karka II., or Amōghavarsha IV. 972–3.

Notes.—6. *Dantidurga* completely crushed the W. Chāḷukya family, so that the Western territories of the latter were ruled by the Rāshṭrakūṭas for two centuries. He gave a grant in 753 (*I. A. 1882, p. 108*). He was in occupation of Kāñchi some time after 754 (*I. A.*, 1906, p. 332).

7. *Krishna* I was encamped at the W. Ganga capital Maṇṇai, near Bangalore in A. D. 768 (*E. I. xiii, 275.*). Grants by him in 770 and 772 (*E. I. vi, 171 ; xiv, 123*).

8. *Gōvinda II* has the names 'Vallabha', 'Prabhūtavarsha', 'Pratāpāvaloka', 'Vikramāvalōka.'

9. *Dhruva* was also called 'Nirupama', 'Dhārāvarsha', 'Kalivallabha', 'Srivallabha.' He was also called 'Dhora' or 'Dora.' He defeated and imprisoned the W. Ganga king Śivamāra II.

10. *Gōvinda III.* (For his elder brother Kambha see *E.C. ix. Nl. 61*, of which the date is November 13, 802). Govinda had the titles 'Jagattunga', 'Jagadrudra', 'Prabhūtavarsha', 'Vallabha-Narēndra.' There was heavy fighting in his reign. He was contemporary with and fought against the E. Chaḷukya king Vijayāditya II alias 'Narēndra-Mṛigarāja' whose inscriptions say that he fought 108 battles in 12½ years against the Gangas and Raṭṭas, or Rashṭrakūṭas. Gōvinda says he defeated the E. Chāḷukyas (*E. I. vii, 26*). He released from imprisonment the W. Ganga king Sivamāra II, and again captured and imprisoned him. For his queen Gāmuṇḍabbe see *E. C. ix, Nl. 61.*

11. *Amoghavarsha I* or *Śarva* was also called 'Durlabha,' 'Śrīvallabha,' 'Shaṇḍa,' 'Nripatunga,' 'Atiśaya-Dhavala,' 'Vīranārāyaṇa,' 'Lakshmī-Vallabhēndra,' and 'Lord of Laṭṭalūru' (*E. I. xiii, 176*).

12. *Krishna II* was also called 'Kannara,' 'Akālavarsha,' and 'Subhatunga.' Before A. D 888 he suffered heavy reverses at the hands of the Eastern Chāḷukya King Guṇaka-Vijayāditya (*E. I. vii. 26 see text s. v. May 10, 930 A.D.*).

13. *Jagatunga* was also known as 'Jagadrudra' (*E. I. iv, 283 ; v. 193*).

14. *Indra III* was also called 'Nityavarsha-Narēndra' (*271* of 1918 gives a date in his reign).

16. *Gōvinda IV* was known as 'Suvarṇavarsha,' 'Nṛipatunga,' 'Vallabha-Narēndra,' 'Prabhūtavarsha,' 'Raṭṭa-kandarpa,' 'Sāhasāṅkha,' and 'Goggiga.' He seems to have had a very bad reputation for cruelty.

18. *Krishna III* was also called 'Kannara', 'Akālavarsha,' 'Kachchiyum-Tañjaiyum-koṇḍa' ('capturer of Conjevaram and Tanjore') and 'Irivikannara.' For his exploits see the text.

19. *Khoṭṭiga*, alias 'Nityavarsha,' was defeated by Harsha, king of Malwa in 971. His accession was between March 24, 965 and February 17, 966.

20. *Kakkala* was also called 'Vallabha-Narēndra.' He was overthrown by the Western Chāḷukya king Tailapa II, who married Kakkala's daughter Jākabbe, or Jakkalā-dēvī. With him the dynasty came to an end.

For Indra IV's date of death see *E. C. ii, 57* at Srāvaṇa-Beḷgoḷa, the date of which is quite sound.

RAṬṬA CHIEFS OF SAUNDATTI

(See *Bombay Gazetteer, i., Pt. i, 550 ; I. A. xix, 248 ; E. I. viii, App. ii, 7*).
The family claimed descent from Rāshṭrakūṭa Krishna III.

1. *Nanna*
   [1] 'Kanthēyabharada,' 'Nannapaya.'
   - 2. *Kārtavīrya I or Katta I* — Feudatory of W. Chāḷukya Tailapa I. A.D. 980.
     - 3. *Dāvari*, or *Dāyima*
       - 5. *Eṛaga* 1040
         - 7. *Sēna I* or Kālasēna. *Md.* Mailaladēvī
           - 8. *Kannakaira II*, or *Kanna II, c 1069–1087.*
           - 9. *Kārtavīrya, or Katta II* (*Md.* Bhāgalā-dēvī, *c.* 1069–1087)
             - 10. *Sēna II* (or Kalasēna. *Md.* Lakshmī-dēvī, *c.* 1087–1121.)
               - 11. *Kārtavīrya, or Kattama III* (*Md.* Padmalā-dēvī, 1143, 1145)
                 - 12. *Lakshmidēva I* or Lakshmīdhara. *Md.* Chandalā-dēvī, or Chandrikā. (?) 1209.
                   - 13. *Kārtavīrya IV* *Md.* Echalā-dēvī and Mādēvī 1199, 1208, 1218.
                     - 15. *Lakshmidēva II* 1228, 1229.
                   - 14. *Mallikhārjuna* (Yuvarāja. 1204 1208.)
     - 4. *Kannakaira I*, or *Kanna I*
       - 6. *Anka.* 1048

[1] This name I do not find mentioned in any of the authorities quoted and in one or two others where the matter is under discussion.—*Editor*.

REḌḌI CHIEFS OF KONḌAVĪḌU AND RAJAHMUNDRY

REḌḌIS OF KONḌAVĪḌU

These chiefs are said to belong to the Panṭakula family. Their original seat was Addanki in Nellore District, and their tract was called the Punginādu, or Pākanāḍu. The founder of the family was Donti-Allāda-Reḍḍi, who acquired a fortune (*E. I. iii. 286 ; iv. 321 ; viii. 13 ; xi. 313 ; 162 of 1899 ; B. and V. C. iii. 1022, 1462, etc. . .*).

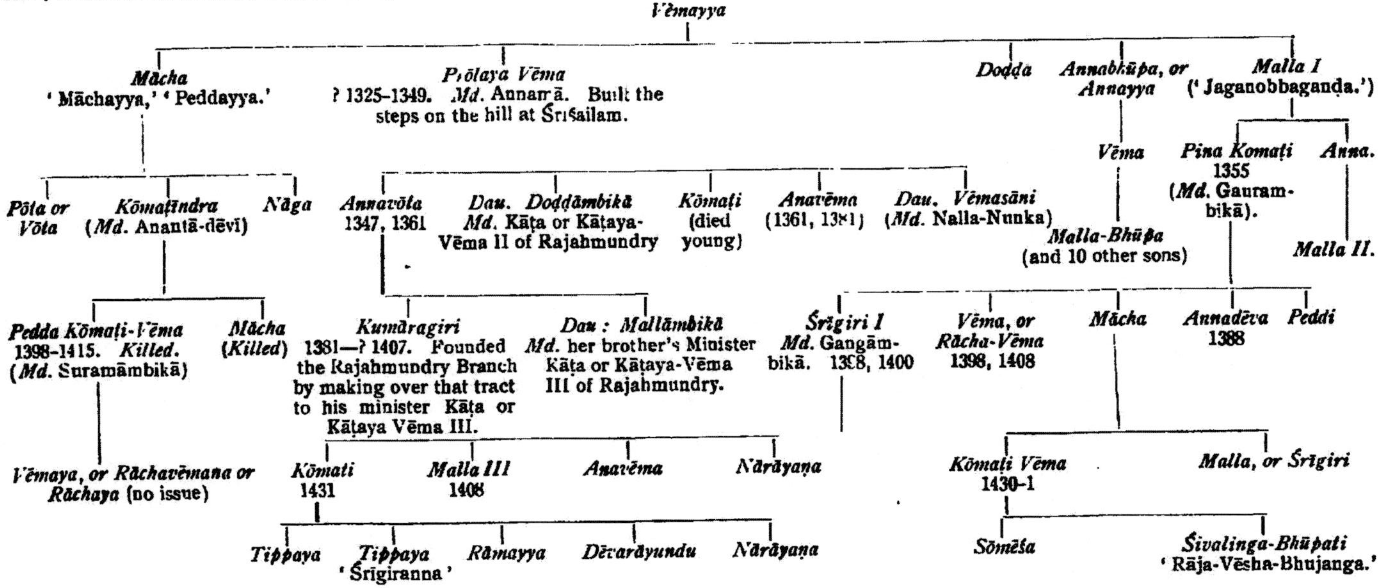

NOTES.—Annamā, the wife of *Prōlaya-Vēma* (1325—), was daughter of Doḍḍa. Her nephew was *Nalla-Nunka*, or Nūkabhūpāla, who married Prōlaya-Vēma's daughter Vēmasāni. Prōlaya-Vēma also built the steps up the hill at Ahōbilam. He was called ' Pallava-Trinētra ' and ' Jaganobbaganḍa.' He fought against the Khilji Muhammadans of Delhi during their invasion ; and seized the Amarāvati tract from the officers of the Kākatiya king.

For Malla I and his son and grandson see *V. R. i, Cuddapah 880 ; 433 of 1911.* Malla I commanded the army.

Annavēma, son of Prōlaya-Vēma was also called ' Vasantarāya,' ' Pallava-Trinētra,' ' Kshurikāsahaya.'

Vēmasāni, wife of Nalla-Nunka, had by him a daughter Hēmāmbikā who married King Dēvarāya I of Vijayanagar.

For *Pina Komaṭi* son of Malla I see *B. and V. C. ii, 549.* For *Pedda Kōmaṭi*, son of Komaṭīndra, see *V. R. ii, Guntur 803 ; 162 of 1891.*

For *Kumāragiri* and the division of the Kingdom see *V. R. ii, Gōdāvari 17 ; E. I. iv, 318 ; E. R. 1900, p. 25.*

The Reḍḍi dynasty of Konḍavīḍu was overthrown by Ahmad I Bāhmani about A.D. 1427.

For Śrīgiri's descendants see *B. and V. C. i. 495 ; ii. 502, 507, 549.*

REḌḌI CHIEFS OF RAJAHMUNDRY—BRANCH A

Kāṭa, or Kāṭama I

Māra

Kāṭa, or Kāṭaya II
Md. Doḍḍāmbikā, *dau.* of Prōlaya-Vēma of Konḍaviḍu

Kāṭaya-Vēma III
Md. Mallāmbikā, *dau.* of Anna-Vōta of Konḍaviḍu, to whom he was minister and was given the Rajahmundry Province
c 1385–1423.

Kumāragiri
1414–1416.

REḌḌI CHIEFS OF RAJAHMUNDRY—BRANCH B

The pedigree follows the Konduküru plates of Allaya Doḍḍa and others. (*E.I. v. 53 ; xiii, 237*)

Perumāḍi Reḍḍi
Headman of Duvvūr village, *Md.* Annamā.

Allaya — *Pedda-Kōṭa* — *Anna-Prōla* — *Doḍḍa, or Doḍḍaya I* (' Panṭakula-Rāja. *Md.* Annamā) — *Pinna-Kōṭa*

Prōla, or Anna-Vṛōla (or Anna-Vōta. 1416, 1422) — *Kōṭaya* — Allāda- or Alla, or Allaya. *Md.* Vēmāmbikā *dau.* of Bhīma of the Chōda family. 1416, 1422, 1431.

Vēma, or Allaya-Vēma Ruled jointy with Vīrabhadra 1433, 1434, 1437. — *Vīrabhadra, or* Vīra. *Md.* Anitalli *dau.* of Vēma 1422 — *Doḍḍa, or Allaya Doḍḍa, II* (Dates January 14, 1431 ; June 7, 1434) — *Anna*

NOTES.—Doḍḍa I's son *Allāda* defeated Alp Khān. Made an alliance with the Gajapatis. Another account makes his wife Vēmāmbikā grand daughter of king Anavēma, probably of Konḍaviḍu. (*E.I. v. 53 f*)

For *Vēma or Allaya-Vēma* (1433, etc. . .) see *E.I. xiii. 238. Virabhadra's* wife Anitalli was ' daughter of the elder Kāṭaya's son Vēma ' (*ibid*).

Doḍḍa II was also called ' Karpūra-Vasantarāya', Samgrāma-Bhīma ', and ' Jagannobbaganḍa.'

RĒNĀNḌU TRACT—CHIEFS OF THE

See above under 'CHŌḶA-MAHĀRĀJAS.'

ŚAKA DYNASTY OF KSHATRAPAS, OR SATRAPS

See above under 'Early North India' Table.

ŚĀḶUVA FAMILY CHIEFS

Their distinctive family titles were 'Kaṭhāri-Sāḷuva', 'Mēdinimīsaragaṇḍa' and 'Dharaṇīvarāha.' See J. Rāmayya's article on the Dēvulapalli plates (*E. I. vii. 74*). For Pedigree see *A. R. 1908–9, p. 168.*

- *Vanki-dēva*
  - *Gunḍa* I (*Md.* Kamalā. Lived at Kalyāṇapura.)
    - *Gunḍa* II, or *Bomma*
    - *Mādirāja*
    - *Gautayya* I
    - *Vīrahōtala*
    - *Sāvitri-mangi*
    - *Śāḷuv Mangu* 1362. Assisted Kampana II of Vijayanagar in his Southern Campaign.
      - *Gautaya* II
        - *Gunda* III *Md.* Mallāmbikā
      - *Narasimha*[1] 1354
        - *Śāḷuva*
          - *Tirumallayya* or Timma, 1450, 1455, 1463.
          - *Narasimha-Rāya* Minister and General to Virūpāksha III king of Vijayanagar, whose throne he usurped 1485–6. Died 1492.
            - (*A son*) Killed according to Nuniz, 'by a page.'
            - *Immaḍi-Narasimha* or *Tammaya*, or *Tamma-dēva*, king of Vijayanagar, 1492–3 to 1505. Assassinated. His Minister Narasa usurped the throne.
              - (?) *Dēvappa* or *Dēpanna*
        - *Boppa*
          - *Parvatayya* or *Parvata-Rāya* February 22, 1468.
            - *Tirumalayya* or *Timma-Rāja*
            - *Tippa* or Tripurāntaka
      - (*Four other sons*)
        - *Tippa* *Md.* Sister of king Dēva-raya II of Vijayanagar. 1441–2
          - *Gopa-Rāja* 1430–1
          - *Tippa* 1442

NOTES. Pedigrees of the family are given in *V.R. ii, Nellore 606, 620; B. and V.C. iii, 1184, 1203; and in E.I. vii. 76.*

[1] *V.R. i, Anantapur, 49 ; 92 of 1912.*

An inscription at Simhāchalam in Vizagapatam District gives the following names, saying that Śambu-rāya came from Kannaḍa-dēśa (*293 of 1899*); (*V. R. ii, Guntur, 128*).

Śāḷuva Vibhala
|
'*Pedda*' *Śāmbu, or Sāmparāya*
1426
|

Bhūpa Gōvinda alias Telungarāya 1428–9

Vibhala
|
Dau : Tippalādēvī
Md. Raja Jagatāba-singa
1438
|
Timma-Rāja.

A *Śāḷuva Malla* lived in A.D. 1441–2 (*V. R. i, Cuddappah*, 659).

A *Śāḷuva Yerra Kampa* lived in 1405–6 (*ibid.*, 662).

For *Parvatayya's* place in the pedigree see *V. R. ii, Kurnool 469*.

Śāḷuva Pedda Mallapa 'son of Yaṟam (? Yeṟra) Kampa' is mentioned, August 25, 1485 (*V. R. ii, Kuṟnool 462 ; 26 of 1915*).

The principal minister of Krishṇadēva Rāya of Vijayanagar, throughout his reign Śāluva Timma, *alias* Appājī. Śāḷuva Gōvinda was also prominent during the reign.[1]

In 1589 Sāḷuva Narasimha, 'Singa-bhūpāla', who was related to Bāhubalēndra, was ruling some tracts— Rajahmundry, and part of Kalinga.

The Rajas of Karvēṭinagar in Chittoor District belonged to the Śāḷuva family. In 1622–3 Tirumala, 'son of Śrīranga Raja and grandson of Kaṭhāri-Śāḷuva-Mahārāja,' was chief of that tract (*V. R. i, Chittoor, 267, 268; 376,[1] 377 of 1911*).

ŚAMBUVARĀYA CHIEFS OF THE ŚENGĒṆI FAMILY

Their province was mainly in the present North Arcot and Chingleput Districts. In the times of the Vijayanagar empire it was known as the 'Paḍaiviḍu-Rājya', drawing its name from Paḍaiviḍu near Pōḷūr.

The names only can be given, as the relationships are not yet sufficiently established. To save space 'Śambuvarāya' is shortened to 'Samb.'

A.D. 1163–4. *Rājanārāyaṇa Śamb.* in 18th year of Rājarāja Chōla II, (1146–1163), (*V.R. i, Chingleput, 479 ; 244 of 1901*).

1167–8. *Edirili-Chōla-Śamb.* in the 5th year of Rājādhirājā Chōla II (1163–1178), to whom he was feudatory. He is said to have obtained the departure from South-India of the Singhalese armies under general Lankāpura, which invaded the country in his day, by his intervention with a holy priest of Śiva who by earnest prayer and fasting secured the Deity's favour. Edirili had a son *Pallava-rāya* (*V. R. i, Chingleput, 248, 345; 20 of 1899 ; 474 of 1905*).

1171–(?)1210. A number of records of this period contain names which possibly owing to the recurrence of the name 'Attimallan,' refer to one chief. These are as follows :—

Ammaiyappan-Pāṇḍi alias Rājarāja Śamb., A.D. 1175–6 the 13th year of Rājādhirāja Chola II, which was his own 5th year. Hence his accession was in 1171–2 (*V. R. i, S. Arcot, 373 ; 222 of 1904*).

Ammaiyappan-Gandarśūriyan-Śamb., 1179–80. In the second year of Kulōttunga Chōla III, 1178–1216, (*V. R. i, N. Arcot, 997 ; 190 of 1904.*)

Minḍān-Attimallan-Śamb. 1185–6. In the 8th year of the same king (*V. R. i, N. Arcot, 341 ; 301 of 1897*).

Minḍān-Attimallan-Vikrama-Chōla-Śamb., 1189–90. In the same king's 12th year (*V. R. i, N. Arcot, 26 ; 405 of 1905*).

Ammaiyappan-Rājarāja Śamb., 1190–1. In the same king's 13th year (*V. R. i, S. Arcot 374 ; 223 of 1904*). In this record two chiefs bind themselves to be faithful to the Śengēṇi chief.

Ammaiyappan-Attimallan-Vikrama-Chōla-Śamb., 1197–8. In the same king's 20th year. Agreements between rival chiefs. This chief was also called 'Kaṇṇuḍai-Perumāḷ' (*S. I. I. iii. 208*) in 1204–5, in the King's 27th year (*V. R. i. N. Arcot, 414, 422 ; 107, 115 of 1900*). He had a son—as next noted.

[1] The Sāḷuva Brothers Timma and Govinda were Brahmans, and could have had no connections with these families. Sāḷuva in these cases must be regarded as a mere title that it actually was in its origin—*Editor*.

1212–13. ***Aḻagiya-Chōla-Edirili-Chōla Śamb.***, alias 'Chōla-Piḷḷai'. Record in the 35th year of the same king (*V. R. ii. Salem, 28; 435 of 1913*). Son of the next above.

He was also called 'Vīrasāni-Ammaiyappan.' Two records of his are dated in the 22nd and 28th years of Rājarāja Chōla III, i.e. in 1237–8 and 1243–4. Another is dated in the 3rd year of Vijaya-Gaṇḍagōpāla, the Telugu-Chōḍa ruler, i.e. in 1252–3, and here he is called 'Aḻagiya-Pallava' (*V. R. i, N. Arcot, 554, 559, 333; S.I.I. i, Nos. 59, 60, 63*).

1235–6. ***Attimallan-Śambukula-Perumāḷ-Rājagambhīra-Śamb.*** This was his 12th year, so his accession took place in 1224–5 (*S.I.I. i. Nos. 102, 105*).

1257–8. ***Rājarāja Śamb.*** in the 8th year of Vijaya-Gaṇḍagōpāla. Here the chief is called a 'Piḷḷaiyār', or vassal, of his lord (*V. R. i. N. Arcot, 230, 231; 302, 303 of 1912; S.I.I. i. 87 to 136; iii. 121, 123, 136, 208*). He was also called 'Rājagambhīra.'

c. 1314–5. ***Vīra-Champaṇāyan***, 'alias Samb.' in the 12th year of Jaṭāvarman-Sundara-Pāṇḍya, whose accession was in 1303. Also, apparently, called 'Vīra-Chōla-Samb' (*V. R. i, N. Arcot 290; 97 of 1900*).

1322. Accession, between May 11 and June 20, of 'Sakalalōka-Chakravarti' ***Veṅṟumāṇkoṇḍa-Samb.*** There are records of his 14th year, 1335–6, in which the Muhammadan invasions of the country are mentioned; and of his 18th year, of date June 30, 1339. (*V. R. i, N. Arcot, 548; 24 of 1897; 42, 48 of 1921; E. I. xi. 251; E. R. 1903, p. 16; V. R. i, S. Arcot, 1048; 434 of 1903*).

1337–8, ***Rājanārāyaṇa-Samb.***, alias 'Mallinātha,' or 'Tirumallinādan' (in Tamil), or 'Jīyadēva'. Several records make his accession in 1337–8, though the fixture clashes with the last date of the chief last-mentioned. It may be that that chief retired into private life before his death. Rājanārāyaṇa's 20th year is mentioned, i.e., *1356–7* (*30 of 1890; 49, 302 of 1921; 48, 49 of 1922; V. R. i, S. Arcot, 799; 396 of 1909*).

The Śambuvarāya chiefs were conquered by prince Kampaṇa II, son of Bukka I of Vijayanagar during his southern campaign about 1351, (*E. I. xv. 8*).

N.B.—The Rājarāja-Samb. of A.D. 1257 sometimes has prefixed to his name the title also borne by his lord Vijaya-Gaṇḍagōpāla, viz., 'Avaniyāḷa-pirandān', or 'Āḷappirandān'. This, and the fact of his being called '*piḷḷaiyār*', has led the Government Epigraphist to the opinion that he really was a son of Vijaya-Gaṇḍagōpāla. I doubt. See my remarks appended to the list of Nīlagangaraiyan chiefs given above.

SĀNTARA CHIEFS
OF PAṬṬIPOMBUCHCHA—MODERN HUMCHA.

Humcha is in the Shimōga District of N.-W. Mysore, near the Western Ghāts. The family is said to have originated in the north. Its members were Jains by religion. For their pedigree see *E. C. viii, Nagar, 35.* Mythical and traditional ancestors are omitted here.

1. *Vikrama.*
'Kandukāchārya', 'Dānavinōda.'
Formed the 'Sāntaḷigē 1000' into a principality. *c.* A.D. 800.
|
2. *Chāgi.*
(*Md.* an Āḷuva princess, *dau.* of Raṇanjaya).
c. 825.
|
3. *Vīra I*
(*Md.* Jākalā-dēvī, *c.* 850).
|
Kannara. — 4. *Kāvadēva.* (*Md.* Chandalā-dēvī. *c.* 875.)
|
5. *Tyāgi.*
(*Md.* Nāgalā-*c.* 900).
|
6. *Nanni.*
(*Md.* Siriyā, *c.* 925).
|

SĀNTARA CHIEFS OF PATTIPOMBUCHCHA.— MODERN HUMCHA—*contd.*

7. *Rāya.*
(*Md.* Akkā, *c.* 950).

8. *Chikka Vira.*
(*Md.* Bijjalā, *c.* 975).

9. *Ammana.*
(*Md.* Hōchalā, *c.* 1000)

- *Dau. Biralā, or Birabbarasi*
  Md. an Āḷuva chief, Bankidēva.
- 10. *Taila, or Tailapa I*
  Md. Mānkabbarasi, an Āḷuva princess and Kaleyabbarasi, a Ganga princess. *c.* 1025.
  - 11. *Vira II.*
    or Bira, or Biruga, *c.* 1050.
    Date in 1062. *See note below.*
    - 12. *Taila, or Tailapa II.*
      1077
      - *Dau. Pampādēvi.*
      - 13. *Śrivallabha.*
        'Vikrama-Sāntara,'
        1096.
        - 15. *Taila IV, or Tailapa.*
          1115-6, 1162.
    - *Goggiga*
      or 'Nanni-Sāntara'
      or 'Gōvindara.'
    - *Odduga*
      or 'Vikrama-Sāntara.'
      Md. a Pāndya princess, Chandalā.
      - 14, *Taila III.*
        'Tailuga,' 'Tailaha'
        Md. Akkā-dēvi
        1089, 1096.
        - 16. *Kāmadēva.*
          Md. a Pāṇḍya princess, Bijjalā.
          - 17. *Jagadēva.*
            Defeated by Hoyśala Vishnuvardhana. 1160.
          - *Singidēva.*
          - *Dau. Aḷiyā-dēvi.*
            Md. Honneya, or Honna-Ponna, a Ganga chief, by whom—
            - *Jayakēsi.*
              1140.
            - *Sānteyadēva.*
              1189.
        - *Simha.*
        - *Ammana.*
      - *Govinda.*
        'Rāya-Sāntara,'
        1096.
    - *Barmmadēva II*
      or Bamma II.
      - *Boppuga.*
  - *Singidēva.*
  - *Barmmadēva I.*
    or Bamma.

NOTES.—*Tailapa I.* His wife Mankabbā was sister of the Āḷuva chief Bankidēva, who married Tailapa I's sister Biralā.

Vira II. He is said, in *E. C. viii, Nr. 47* the date of which is *1062-3*, 'to have freed his State from those who had no right to it'. This probably refers to the occupation in 1042 of the Sāntaḷigē 1000 by the Chaḷukya princes Bijjarasa and Gonarāja (*E. C. viii, Sa. 109, bis*). Vira II's wife Bijjalā was daughter of the Noḷamba ruler Narasimha, who governed Uchchangi in 1054. He also (*E. C. viii, Nr. 35*) had a wife Kanchalā-dēvi who was the mother of his four sons. She and her sister Chattalā are noted above in the pedigree of the Western Gangas (*q. v.*) Another record (*ibid , Nr. 37*) states that the mother of the four sons was Chattalā daughter of 'Rakkasa-Ganga, lord of Kānchi,' which may have been a title of Arumoḷidēva, husband of Gāvabbarasi, who, according to *E. C. viii, Tl. 192*, were the parents of Chattalā and Kanchalā. Chattalā was the wife of the Kāḍuveṭṭi chief of Kānchi, and Rice expressed the opinion that when she became a widow she claimed her sister's four sons as her own. These different statements are confusing at present. The puzzle awaits solution. (See note 1 on p. *86* above.—*Editor.*)

Tailapa II was also called 'Bhujabala Sāntara' (*E. C. viii, Nr. 35*).

For *Goggiga* see *E. C. vii, Sk. 53*.

For *Śrīvallabha* and his sister Pampādēvi see *E. C. viii, Nr. 37*.

For *Taila IV* son of Śrīvallabha see *Mys. A.A.R. 1923, p. 75, and p. 117*. The date of the latter inscription is A.D. 1115–6. That of the former is 1162. These dates are rather far apart, but are not impossible. It may turn out that there was later a father and son of the same names.

Jagadēva. Before his defeat by the Hoysala king he had, as a feudatory of the Western Chāḷukya king, attacked the Kākatīya king Prōla II's capital Anumakoṇḍa or Warangal, but had been driven back. He fought against the Kadambas is 1160 (*Mys. A. A. R. 1923, p. 113*).

Jayakēśi raided the Hāngal country in 1140 (*E. C. vi, Cm. 122*).

ŚENGEṆI FAMILY

See ŚAMBUVARĀYA CHIEFS

SĒTUPATI RULERS OF RĀMNĀD

They belonged to an ancient Marava family, who were hereditary guardians of the Isthmus of Ramnād, and who were re-estabished during the rule in Madura of Muttukrishnappa (A.D. 1602–1609) in the person of Śaḍayakan-Uḍaiyān-Sētupati I. The Nāyakas of Madura were their overlords.

1. *Śaḍayakan-Sētupati-Kātta I* (1604–1621. Fortified Ramnad)
   - 2. *Kūttan Sētupati-Kātta* 1621–1635
     - 3. *Śaḍayakan II* or Daḷavāy Sētupati, 1635–45 was deposed and reinstated 1640, and was murdered by Tambi. He adopted Raghunātha Tēvan
     - (*illegitimate*) *Tambi* (Revolted. Died 1646.)
     - *Dau. Gangāyi-Nātchiyār*
       - 4. *Raghunātha-Tēvan I* 1645–1670.
       - *Tanakka-Tēvan* (*died young*)
       - *Nārāyaṇa-Tēvan*
         - 5. *Sūrya-Tēvan* 1670. Put to death by the Daḷavāy of Madura after 6 months' rule.
           - (*illegitimate*) 6. *Raghunātha-Tēvan II* 'Kiḷavan'. 1673 (after 3 years of anarchy)—1710. Became independent of Madura 1702.
             - 7. *Vijaya Raghunātha-Tevan.* 1710–1720.
             - (*illegitimate*) *Bhavāni-Śankara Tēvan*. Seized throne 1724. Deposed 1729.
           - *Tāṇḍa-Tēvan I* (*illegitimate*)
             - *Tāṇḍa-Tēvan II* (*Md.* Kuḷandai-Nātchiyār) 1720–1724, was opposed all his time by Bhavāni-Śankara, and by him was killed.

Bhavāni-Śankara was deposed in 1729. He was succeeded by Kūtta-Tēvan II, who was brother of Kuḷandai-Nātchiyār and who was also called 'Kumāra-Muttu-Vijaya-Raghunātha'. He ruled till 1752.

SEUṆA DYNASTY

See YĀDAVAS OF DĒVAGIRI

ŚILĀHĀRA DYNASTIES

They did not largely come in contact with the ruling families of the South, and it is not necessary here to insert all their pedigrees.

(A) For the Śilāhāra family of the Northern Konkan for a century and a half down to the reign of Anantadēva or Anantapāla in 1094, see *Bombay Gazetteer I, Part III, 539*; and Kielhorn's List in *E.I. viii, App. ii, p. 11.*

After Anantapāla we have a few names and dates, but the relationships cannot be traced.

Haripāla, A.D. 1149, 1154. *Mallikhārjuna*, 1156, 1160. *Aparājita*, 1185, 1187 and 1198. *Kēshi-dēva*, 1203, 1238. *Sōmēśvara*, 1259.

(B) For the Śilāhāras of the Southern Konkan from about A.D. 775 to 1008, see *Bombay Gazetteer i, Part iii 537*; and Kielhorn's List in *E.I. viii, App. ii, p. 11.*

(C) The Śilāhāras of Kolhāpūr and Beḷgaum.

1. *Jatiga I*
2. *Nāyimma* or '*Nāyivarman*'
3. *Chandra-rāja*
4. *Jatiga II*

Sons of Jatiga II:

- 5. *Gonka* or Gōkala, or Gonkala
  - 6. *Mārashimha* 1058
    - 7. *Gūvala II*
    - *Gangadēva*
    - *Bhōja I*
    - *Baḷḷāḷa*
    - 8. *Gandarāditya* 1110, 1118, 1135
      - 9. *Vijayārka, or* Vijayāditya, 1143 1150, 1153.
        - 10. *Bhōja II* or 'Vira-Bhōja' 1178–1207. Defeated by king Singhaṇa II of the Dēvagiri-Yādavas)
- *Gūvala* or Gūhala
- *Kīrti-rāja*
- *Chandrāditya*

For information see *Bombay Gazetteer* I, Pt. iii, 537; and Kielhorn's List. (*E.I. viii, App. ii, p. 11*).

SINDA FAMILIES

A. SINDAS OF SINDAVĀḌI

The Sindavāḍi country embraced parts of N. Mysore, Bellary, Dhārwār and Bijāpūr. It is mentioned in an inscription in A. D. 750 (*E. C. vi, Mg. 36*). The chiefs were always vassals to more powerful families. The Sinda capital was at first at Hallavūr on the Tungabhadra river, and later at Beḷagutti in Honāḷi Taluk N.-W. Mysore (See *E. C. vii, Introd. p. 35.*)

Niḍudōḷ Sinda ruled at some early date. Then the pedigree is as follows.

Piriya Chattarasa I (*Md.* Dōrabarasi, or Lōkabarasi.)

Jōgarasa

Chattarasa II A. D. 1117.

(*Relationship not known.*)

- *Mācha*
- *Mallidēva*
  - '*Rāyarasa* (*See note below*)
- [. . . .] *harasa* (*See note below.*)

SINDA FAMILIES—A. SINDAS OF SINDAVĀḌI—*contd.*

Īśvaradēva I
(or Īśvara-bhūpati. 1166, 1180.)

Pindyadēva

Malla, or Mallidēva
Attacked by Hoyśalas in 1196-7
1187, 1195, 1204

Īśvaradēva II
1215, 1222.

Dau. *Sovala*

Dau. *Kālale*

Kēśavadēva
1232.

Bīradēva or Harabīra.
1244-1247.

Rāya

Vijaya

NOTES. That Īśvaradeva I was son of [. . . .] harasa is stated in *E. C. vii, Hl. 50.* Rice (*ibid. vi, Introd. 35*) makes him son of Mallidēva's son Rāyarasa.

Records at Kurugōḍ, Bellary District (*V. R. i. Bell. 106, 108; 56, 58 of 1904*), mention *Sinda Rāchamalla* as feudatory of the Kalachūri king in, apparently, A. D. 1175 and 1177. But the details of the dates are unsatisfactory. Two others (*V. R. i. Bell. 87, 128; 211, 206 of 1913*), of dates 1141 and 1147 mention *Rāchamalla* and his elder brother *Bhīma*, but with no clue as to relationship.

Another Kurugōḍ record (*E. I. xiv, 265*), edited by Dr. Barnett, gives the following pedigree—to which I have ventured to add the prince Bhīma mentioned above. There is, here again, no clue as to relationship to the main line

(?)

Bhīma

'*Piriya*' *Rāchamalla I*
(*Md.* Sōvaladēvī; 1141, 1147)

Irungōḷa
(*Md.* Baladēvī and Echaladēvī)

Rāchamalla II
also called 'Gōvinda of the Sindas'
1173, 1181.

Sōma

SINDAS OF EṚAMBAṚAGE

Eṛambaṛage = Yelburga in H. H. The Nizam's Dominions (*See Bombay Gazetteer I, Pt. III, p. 573; E.I. viii, App. II, 10; xiv, 268; xv, 109; I A. 1876, p. 174*).

(?)

1. *Āchugi I,*
or Ācha vassal of
W. Chāḷukyas

Nāka

Singa I
or *Simha*

Dāsa
or *Dāna*

Dāma
or *Dāva*

Chāvuṇḍa I
or *Chauṇḍa*

Chāva

Bamma

Singa II
Āchugi II
or Ācha, or Āchama. *Md.*
Mādēvī, 1122.

Permāḍi I
or Pemma. 'Jagadēkamalla.'
Claims to have defeated the Kadambas
of Goa and Hoyśala Vishṇuvardhana,
1104, 1144.

Chāvuṇḍa II
Md. Śiriyādēvī, *dau.* of the Kalachūri king Bijjala II, and Dēmalādēvī.

Āchugi III
(or Āchidēva, 1163)

Permāḍi II
(or Pemmaḍi, 1163)

Bijjala
(or Vijjala, 1169)

Vikrama
or Vikkaya, or Vikramāditya
1169, 1180.

The family was crushed by the triumph of the Hoyśalas in the latter part of the 12th century A.D.
Vikrama governed the Kiśukāḍ tract (*E I. xv. 109. Inscription at Sudi.*).

TAGAḌŪR—CHIEFS—

See under Adigaman chiefs above.

TANJORE—RULERS OF

A. A FAMILY OF CHIEFS IN THE 8TH TO THE 11TH CENTURIES A.D.

These chiefs seem to have been vassals to the Pallava kings and to have ruled over parts of Tanjore and Pudukotta.

Perumbiḍugu—Muttaraiyan I
alias *Kuvāvanmāran*
|
Iḷangōvaḍivar-aiyan
alias *Māran-Paramēśvaran.*
|
Perumbiḍugu-Muttaraiyan II
alias *Śuvāvan-Māran* or *Neḍumāran*
A.D. 717 and later.

The last chief was known by many other titles—amongst others 'Lord of Tanjore.' He fought many battles (twelve are mentioned in inscriptions) against the Pāndyas, the people of Kōnāḍu etc . . . He went to Conjevaram to receive the newly-installed Pallava king, who was almost certainly Nāndivarman II (A.D. 717–779). He had been a vassal of the Pallava Paramēśvara-Pōtavarman II (*See the Anbil plates, E.I. xv, p. 49, n-1 and E.I. xiii, 134*).

Viḍēlviḍugu-Viḷuppēraḍi-Araiśan, alias *Sāttān-Māran*, who was a contemporary of Pallava Nandivarman II and was son of queen 'Perumbiḍugu-Perundēvi,' was very probably a son of Perumbiḍugu-Muttaraiyan II (*E. I. xiii, 137 f*).

Mārpiḍugu was a contemporary of Pallava Dantivarman (779-830).

Viḍēlviḍugu, contemp. of Pallava Nṛipatunga (854–888).

Śāttān-Paḷiyili was his son.

Śatrubhayankara-Muttaraiyan was a contemporary of Śaḍaiyamāran Pāndya. Date doubtful as more than one Pāṇḍya king was so called.

Vijayālaya-Muttaraiyan was the name of an officer serving under Kulōttunga Chōla I (1070–1118).

B. THE NAYAKKA DYNASTY OF TANJORE

Timma
Md. Vayyamāmba. (*E. I. xii 340*)
|
1. *Śevvappa Nāyaka*
Made governor of Tanjore by Achyuta Raya
of Vijayanagar, who married his wife's
sister. Independent after 1565.
1549–1572.
|
2. *Achyutappa Nāyaka*
1572–1614.
|
3. *Raghunātha Nāyaka*
(*Md.* a Pandya princess. 1614–1640.)
|
4. *Vijayarāghava*
Deprived of his throne by Chokkanātha
Nāyaka. 1640–1674.
|
5 *Śengamala Dās*
His throne seized by Ekōjī, *alias* Venkājī, brother
of the Mahratta Śivājī, 1674.

C. THE MAHRATTA DYNASTY OF TANJORE

A branch of the Mahratta family of Satara (see Mahrattas above) descended from Śivājī's brother Venkāji. In 1674 by order of the Sultan of Bijapur, Venkaji, then a general, went to Tanjore and placed Śengamala, or Chengamala, Dās on the throne, driving out Aḷagiri Nayaka who had been made governor by Chokkanātha of Madura. Shortly afterwards Venkāji usurped the throne.

Shāhjī Bhonsla.

- *Śivājī*
- 1. *Ekōjī*, or *Venkājī* 1674–1685, confirmed in his post by Śivājī in 1678.
  - 2. *Shāhjī* (1685–1711. No issue.)
  - 3. *Sarfōjī*, or *Sarabhōjī* (1711–1727. No issue.)
  - 4. *Tukājī* (1727–1735)
    - 5. *Bāvājī*, or *Bābā Sahib.* 1735–1738. His widow ruled for 2 years.
    - 6. *Sāhujī*, or *Saiyājī*. 1738–1741, and 1749–1765
      - 8. *Tuljājī* 1765–1787
        - ... (*adopted*) 10. *Sarfōjī* 1797–1824.
          - 11. *Śivājī* 1824–1855.
    - *Anna Sahib* (died early)
    - *Nānā Sahib* (died early)
    - (*illegitimate*) 7. *Pratāpa-Simha*, or *Partab Singh*. 1741–1749.
      - 9. *Amara*, or *Amir*, *Simha* 1787–1797.
- *Santājī*

NOTES (1) *Venkājī* was ruling on April 5, 1685 (*540 of 1918*). (6) *Sāhujī* was, soon after his accession, driven out by faction feuds; and his brother Pratāpa-Simha seized the throne and ruled from 1739 to 1749, when the English restored Sāhuji.

(9) *Amara Simha* was deposed for mis-government, and pensioned, in 1798, Śarfōji's adoption being declared valid. Śarfōji ceded Tanjore to the English, receiving the fort as his residence and an estate for his support.

(11) *Śivājī* died without issue in 1855, and the line became extinct.

TELUGU-CHŌḌA CHIEFS

The following Table is tentative, information regarding some of the relationships being as yet somewhat confusing.

The family ruled a portion of the present Nellore District and the Kāḷahasti tract in Chittoor. Some records say that they were of Pallava origin. Others call them descendants of the Chāḷukyas and call them by the title 'Śaśikula-Chaḷukki.' Some claim that their ancestor was Karikāla Chola. Certainly most of them were called by the family name 'Chōḍa' (the Telugu form of 'Chōla'). One of their ancient cities was Pottapi, which is the old name of Kāḷahasti, whence they derive their titles 'Pottapi-Chōla' and 'Tirukāḷatti.' One of their characteristic titles was 'Gaṇḍa-Gōpāla.'

For much information see Mr. S. Krishnaswami Aiyangar's *South India and her Muhammadan Invaders* pp. 59f.

I identify the oft-mentioned 'Nalla Siddha' with Betta II, son of Ērasiddha. A record at Kāvali in Nellore district (*V. R. ii, Nell. 441 ; B, and V. C. ii. 735, No. 39*) of date A.D. 1207–8, makes Nalla Siddha, elder brother of Tammu Siddha I, and it says that though Nalla was anointed, his younger brother Tammu was 'by his favour' ruling the kingdom. That is to say Nalla retired into private life leaving his brother to rule. An inscription at Tiruvālangaḍu (*E. I. vii, 120*) confirms this. It says (v. 19) that 'the middle brother, king Betta, being given to the practice of austerities, conferred the government on his younger brother Tammusiddhi' Thus Betta II was the same as Nalla,[1] which is merely a nickname, 'black'. In A.D. 1205 the eldest brother Manma Siddha I was dead. Again an inscription at Nandalūr in Cuddapah District (*V.R. i, Cudd. 792; 578 of 1907*) informs us that Nallasiddharasa was son of Ērammasiddha. It is necessary to mention these matters because some writers make Nalla Siddha an uncle of Tammu Siddha I.

[1] See Editor's note p. 130 above.

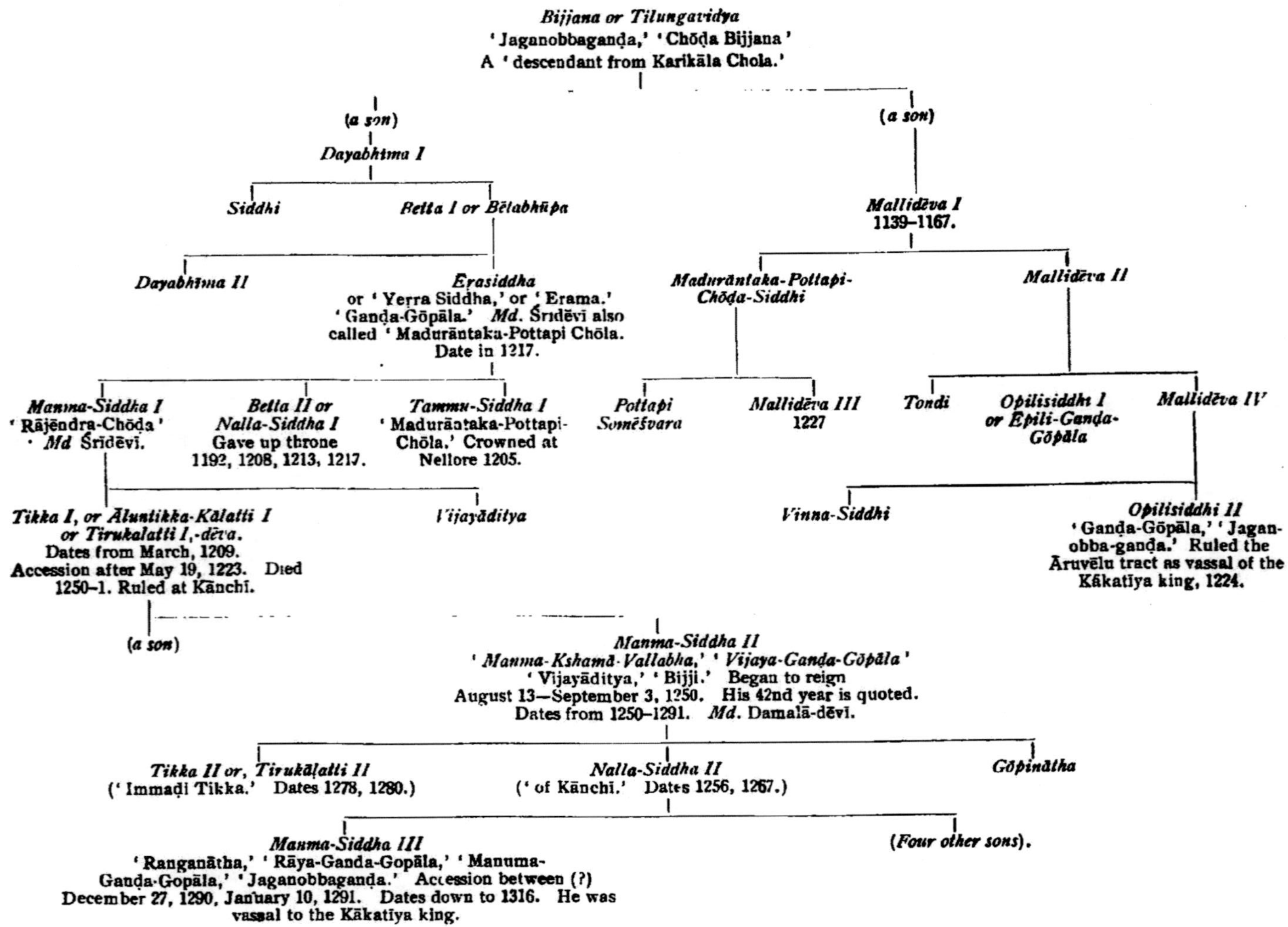

NOTE.—For information see *E. R. 1900, p. 18 ; I. A. 1909, p. 92 ; 1914, p. 12 ; E. I. vii, 74 ; Note E. C. xi, Cd. 29.*

KŌNIDĒNA, OR KŌṬYADONA, BRANCH, which ruled at Pottapi (Kaḷahasti)

Daśavarman
|
ḍa Ballaya Chōḍa

Kāma
Md. Śrīyādēvī. Date 1137.
His wife lived till 1163.
|
Tribhuvanamalla Pottapi-Chōḍa
{ *Md.* Mābaḷā-dēvī. Dates from 1137–1153. }
|
Nanni-Chōḍa
'Kannara Chōḍa,' or 'Śrī Chōḍa.'
1148, 1151.

TRAVANCORE—RULERS OF

See KERALA KINGS

VAIḌUMBA CHIEFS

These rulers at one time governed parts of Arcot, Cuddapah, Nellore and the country south of the Krishna river—the 'Rēnāṇḍu 7,000' village tract. They were a Telugu family claiming descent from the early Western Gangas. In the 9th century A.D. they fought against the then ruling Gangas.

Irigaya-Vaiḍumba lived in the 9th century (*V.R. i, Chittoor, 148, 162 ; 439 of 1914 ; 295 of 1905*).

Gaṇḍa-Trinētra, who may be the same as *Manuja-Trinētra* (298 of 1905), in alliance with the Bāṇa chief fought and defeated at the battle of Sorematī the allies Mahēndra I of the Noḷamba-Pallavas and the Western Ganga king Rāchamalla II about the year A.D. 878 (*V.R. i. Chittoor, 167, 168, 170 ; 295, 296 of 1905 ; 533 of 1906 ; E.R. 1907, pp. 78-79*).

In the next century three generations are known—

Śandaiyan-Tiruvayan I
('Vikramāditya.' *Md.* Śuttira, A.D. 931, 958.)
|

Śandaiyan-Tiruvayan II alias Śrīkaṇṭha. 962.	*Śaṃkara-dēva*	*Chandraśēkhara.*
	Sōmanātha 1014	

Śandaiyan I was conquered about A.D. 915 by Parāntaka Chōla I. He acknowledged as his overlord at one time the Noḷamba-Pallava chief Irivi-Nulipaya II who was also called Dilīpayya, and ruled from 942 to 966, or perhaps Irivi I—Nolipayya). (*E.C. x. Bp, 4.*)

The Chōla king Ariñjaya, *c.* 965, married a Vaiḍumba princess.

One of the Sandaiyans is mentioned in records of 21st, 24th, and 25th years of the Rashṭrakūṭa king Krishna III,—probably the son, as he is called '*Śrīkanṭha,*' A.D. 958, 960, 961 (*E. I. v, 142 ; E.R. 1905, p 57 ; V.R. i, S. Arcot 668, 567; 267 of 1902 ; 743 of 1905*). *Śrīkanṭha* was chief between at least 960-1 and 968 (*16 of 1905 ; S.I.I iii, pp. 53, 107*).

A Vaiḍumba Rāja with title '*Bhuvana Trinētra*' was crowned in 972/3 (*V.R. i, Cuddapah, 583 ; 325 of 1905*).

An inscription of 992-3 mentions the Vaiḍumba chief '*Vishṇudēva,* alias *Durai-araiśan*'.

In A.D. 1004-5 lived a Vaiḍumba chief *Tukkarai,* who had a son *Nannama* and ruled over the Ingallūr-nāḍu (*V. R. i, N. Arcot, 362 ; 14 of 1890*).

Vaiḍumba *Sōmanātha, son of Śamkara,* lived in 1014-15 (*V. R. i. N. Arcot, 336 ; 92 of 1889*).

Vaiḍumba *Rājēndra-Chola Mummaḍi* in A.D. 1251-2, the second year of Vijaya-Gaṇḍa-Gōpāla of the Telugu-Choḍas (*V. R. ii, Nellore 633 ; B. and V. C. 1314*).

See also *V. R. i, Anantapur, 122, bis : 86 of 1913* and note the Government Epigraphist's remarks in *E. R. 1923, pp. 98-101.*

VĀKĀṬAKA RĀJAS

These chiefs at one time owned extensive tracts in the Dekhan and penetrated southwards into the Kuntaladēśa. They occupied parts of Bellary and Mysore (*J. R. A. S. 1914, p. 322 ; I. A. 1920, p. 174 ; E. I. ix, 268 ; xvii, 12*). The dates given are those of the late Dr. Vincent Smith and others.

Vindhyaśakti, c. A.D. 275–300

Pravarasēna, c. 300-330.

Gautamīputra (*Did not reign*)

Rudraēsna I, c. 330–340.

Prithvisēna I, c. 340–390
'Conquered the lord of Kuntala' (*Ajanta inscription*)

Rudrasēna II, c. 390–395.
Md. Prabhāvatī, dau. of Chandragupta II,
who reigned 380–413.

Divākarasēna

Pravarasēna II, c. 395–420

(*son*). c. 420-445

Dēvasena, alias *Prithvīsēna II*
c. 445–465

Harisēna, c. 465–500.

NOTE.—Mr. V. S. Sukthankar in *E. I. xvii*, 12, argues that the dates given are too early and that the reign of Prithvisēna I was as late as A.D. 7th century. But this could not be so if the pedigree is accurate and if Rudrasena II married the daughter of Chandragupta II. (For further information see S. K. Aiyangar's Vākāṭāka Supplement *Jour. Ind. Hist.*, vol. vi.—*Editor.*)

VELANĀNḌU CHIEFS.

The Velanāṇḍu country proper, otherwise called the 'Shaṭsahasra' tract of 6,000 villages, was the Telugu country south of the Krishna river. To its north, between the Krishna and Godavari lay the Vengi country, otherwise known as the 'Gudravāra' or 'Guddavāḍi'-Vishaya a portion of which, about the Godavari delta was called the 'Konamaṇḍala.' North of the Godavari, also containing another division, called Guddavāḍi, was the Prōlunāḍu, with capital at Piṭhāpuram. The Velanāṇḍu capital was Isandōl.

The whole territory was ruled by the Āndhra kings till about A.D. 225, when the Pallavas of Kānchi seized the Velanāṇḍu tract. They lost it to the eastern Chaḷukyas about A.D. 615 and from them it passed to the Chōlas under Kulōttunga Chōla I in 1070.

The following pedigree is taken from Mr. H. Krishna Sāstri's Table (*E. R. 1917, p. 119*), with some dates added as gathered from published inscriptions (*See also E. R. 1921, pp. 110, 111*). The Table is tentative as records sometimes appear to differ.

1. *Malla I*, 'Piduvarāditya.'

2. *Erṟiya I.*

VELANĀNḌU CHIEFS—*contd.*

3. *Malla II*
Subject to E. Chāḷukya, Chāḷukya-Bhīma II.
Md. Kollapāmbā.

4. *Erriya II*
Founder of the family.
Md. Kattāmba.

Kōrapa

Malla III

5. *Kudiyavarman*
Was given the two provinces of Gudravāra by Vimaladitya of the E. Chāḷukyas. (1011–1022).

Ganḍa I

Panḍa I

Nanna
General of Rājarāja I of the E. Chaḷukyas
Md. Gunḍāmbikā

Kāpana.

Vedura I

Ganḍa II

Vedura II
Minister of Vīra-Chōla
Viceroy of Vengi.
Was given the Vengi country by the Chōla king.

6. *Gonka I*
Was given the Velanānḍu province by Kulōttunga-Chōla I. *Md.* Sabbāmbikā 1077–(?) 1108.

7. *Rājēndra-Choḍa I*
Md. Gundāmbikā. Dates from 1115 to 1130

8. *Gonka II.*
Md. Sabbāmbikā. Was called 'Kulōttunga-Chōda-Gonka' Dates from 1132 to 1160.

9. *Rājēndra Chōda II*
General of Rājarāja Chōḷa II *Md.* Akkāmbikā. Dates from 1163 to 1180.

10. *Gonka III.*
alias 'Kulōttunga-Manma Gonka'
Md. Jeyāmbikā

11. *Prithvīśvara*
1786–87

Malla IV

Panḍa II

NOTES.—For pedigree, etc., see Dr. Hultzsch's article on the Piṭhāpuram inscription (*E I. iv, 35*).

There are some 13th century dates for chiefs of the line, e.g. *Kulōttunga-Rājēndra-Chōḍa-Gonka.* A.D. 1237–38, and 1239–40 and 1254–55 (*V.R. ii, Godavari, 317, 342 ; 411, 436 of 1893 ; Guntur 854 ; 160 of 1899*). And the same name in A.D. 1270–1. (*V.R. ii, Godavari, 341 ; 435 of 1893*).

Before 1112 (when Kulōttunga-Chōla I died) *Rājēndra-Chōḍa I* had the Vengi province conferred on him by that king, after the king had adopted him as his son.

Gonka II is said to have ruled the whole Telugu country from Kāḷahasti to the Mahēndra mountain in Ganjam. His wife Sabbāmbikā was daughter of the 'Giripaśchima,' or 'West of the hill' chief. (*See 'Kondapaḍmati' chiefs pedigree—Table above*).

VELLORE CHIEFS

See the Viḷāpāka grant (N. Arcot) of A.D. 1601 (*E.I. iv, 269*).

Vīrappa-Nāyaka
(of the Anukūla gotra)

Bomma-Nāyaka
or Śinna Bomma. Patron of Appayadīkshita. Dates in 1549 and 1566

Lingama-Nāyaka
Subordinate to Venkaṭapati I, king of Vijayanagar. Date in 1601.

VĒNĀḌ KINGS

See KĒRAḶA KINGS.

VIJAYANAGAR—DYNASTIES OF

A. The first—Sangama—Dynasty

I have omitted, to save space, one or two names noted in Mr. S. Krishnaswami Aiyangar's pedigrees ('*Sources of Vijayanagar History*,' *pp. xi, xiv*), as not being of historic importance. I concur with T. A. Gopinātha Rao (*E. I. xv, p. 8, f*) in believing that Bukka III, Vijaya, had only one son whose name was Dēva-Rāya and not two sons each named Dēva-Rāya. But the question still requires study before a clear answer can be given. From the Satyamangalam, Sajjalūr and Śrīśailam plates (*E. I. iii, 37 ; E. C. iii, Ml. 121 ; E. I. xv, 8*) we learn that there was an elder son Dēva Rāya and a younger son Prātapa-Dēva-Rāya, and that Virūpāksha was son of the latter. The Madras Museum plates (*E. I. viii, 306*) and the Satyamangalam plates state—the former that 'Śrigirīndra' was governing the Marakatanagara on November 3, A.D. 1424-5—the latter that in the same year on June 26 the same place was being governed by 'Pratāpa-Dēva-Rāya.' This would imply that Śrīgirīndra and Pratāpa-Dēva-Rāya were one and the same person. And adding this information to what has been said above we should have to assume that Virupāksha was son of Śrigirīndra. However I dare not take upon myself to correct Mr S. Krishnaswami Aiyangar's pedigree. Kampana II's son Jommana is clearly mentioned in A.D. 1375 in *E.C. x, Ct, 94*. The order of birth of the sons of Bukka I is given as in '*Sources* . . . ' p. xi, though it differs from Gopinātha Rao's pedigree. Inscriptions differ on the point. Sangama is said (*E.C. v, Hn, 36*) to have been of the Yādava stock, an assertion often made of Hoysala rulers.

Sangama I
(*Md.* Kāmākshi)

- 1. *Harihara I* 1336—(?) 1355
- *Kampana I* ('Governor of East and West')
  - *Sāvana I* (Dates 1351-1364)
  - *Sangama II* (Dates 1348-1361.)
- 2. *Bukka I* (*Md.* Jommā and Gauri 1355-1377.)
  - 3. *Harihara II* *Md.* Mallā and Pampā 1377-1404
    - 4. *Bukka* II *Md.* Tippāmbā 1404-1406
      - *Bhūpati Udaiyār* (Dates 1386, 1409, 1422) *alias* (?) Ōbaladēva.
    - *Virūpāksha* II or Virupanna. Disputed succession
    - 5. *Dēva Rāya* Md Hēmāmbikā and Mallayavve 1406-1422.
      - *Mallapa* or *Mallana* (1412, 1421.)
      - 6. *Vijaya, alias Bukka III* or Vijaya-Bhūpati. Reigned a few months, 1422. *Md.* Nārāyaṇi
        - Harimā *Dau. Md.* Śāḷuva-Tippa.
        - 7. *Dēva Rāya II* 'Abhinava,' 'Praudha-Pratāpa,' 'Gajabēnṭekāra' *Md.* Siddalā and Ponnalā. 1422-1446
          - 8. *Mallikārjuna* 'Praudha-pratāpa,' 'Immaḍi,' 'Vijaya.' 1446-1465
          - 9. *Virūpāksha III* Crowned November 8, 1465. Was driven out by Śāḷuva Narasimha, who usurped throne between July 29, 1485 and November 1, 1485
            - *Praudhadēva.*
        - *Śrīgirīndra* or 'Parvata-Rāya' or 'Pratāpa-dēva-Rāya.' Killed 1442-43
      - *Harihara III*
      - *Rāmchandra* Ruled at Udayagiri, 1407, 1416
    - *Chikka Rāya*
    - *Jommana* (1375.)
  - *Kampana II* Did not reign.
  - *Virupanna*, or *Virūpāksha I* (Dates 1354 to 1378)
  - *Bhāskara Bhavadūra* Ruled at Udayagiri
  - Mallinātha (1362)
    - *Chennappa* or *Channappa* (1397.)
  - (and others) ?
- *Mārappa*
  - *Sāvana* II
- *Muddapa*

B. THE SECOND—ŚAḶUVA—DYNASTY

1. *Śāḷuva Narasiṁha* I (usurper)
1485-6—1492-3

A son
Killed by a page named 'Timmarasa'
(*so Nuniz*)

2. *Immaḍi-Narasiṁha*
or 'Tamma,' or 'Tammaya'
(*Dharma-rāya*) assassinated 1505.
Throne usurped by the Tuḷuva
Minister Narasa-Nāyaka, 1505.

C. THE THIRD—TUḶUVA—DYNASTY.

Timma
(*Md.* Dēvakī)

Īśvara
alias Kshitipālaka. *Md.* Bukkamā
and Dēvakī.

1. *Narasa Nāyaka*
Usurped the throne of Vijayānagar,
and died shortly afterwards.
Md. Tippāji, Nāgalā, and
Ōbāmbikā, 1505.

(*by Tippāji*)
2. *Vīra Narasiṁha*
Bhujabala-Rāya.' 1506–1509.

(*by Nāgalā*)
3. *Krishnadēva Rāya*
1509–1529. Crowned
January 23, 1510. Died between
October 27, and December 28,
1529

Tirumala
died young)

Dau. Tirumalāmbā
Md. Aḷiya-Rāma-Rāya
of the Āraviḍu family

Dau. Vengalā
Md. Tirumalā of the Āraviḍu
family, brother of Rāma-Rāya

(*by Ōbāmbikā*)
4. *Achyuta*
1529–1542

5. *Venkaṭādri*
(Killed 1542.)

Ranga
Md. Timmāmbā.

6. Sadāśiva
1542-(?)1570. The city
of Vijayanagar completely
destroyed in 1565 by the
Dekhani Muhammadans.

D. I. THE FOURTH-ĀRAVĪḌU-DYNASTY, IMPERIAL BRANCH.

Sadāśiva of Vijayanagar had little power, the kingdom being administered by his minister Aḷiya Rāma of the Āravīḍu family and his brothe Tirumala, Sadaśiva's cousins by marriage. The date of Sadaśiva's death is not exactly known. Aḷiya Rāma was killed at Talikōta fighting the Muham madan invaders. Tirumala became king after Sadāśiva's death.

- *Tāta-Pinnama*
  - *Sōmidēva*
    - *Rāghavadēva*
      - *Pinnama* 'Lord of Araviḍu.'
        - *Bukka* Minister to Śāḷuva Narasimha who usurped the throne of Vijayanagar in 1485-6.
          - *Singa Rāja* of Nandyāl (*see D. II, below*)
          - *Rāma-Rāja* *Md.* Lakkāmbikā.
            - *Timma* (*see D. II, below*)
            - *Pedda Konḍa* (*see D. II, below*)
            - *Śrīranga* (*Md.* Tirumalāmbā. Died 1570-71)
              - *Kōna*
              - *Timma*
              - *Aḷiya-Rāma* Minister to King Sadāsiva killed at Talikōta, 1565
                - *Krishna*
                - *Pedda Timma*
                - *Konḍa*
                  - *Rāma*
                - *Chinna Timma*
                - *Śrīranga*
                  - 6. *Pedda Venkaṭa II* *Md.* Bangārā. 1630–1642
                  - *Chinna or Pinna Venkaṭa.*
                    - *Tirumala*
                    - *Venkaṭa*
                    - 7. *Śrīranga III* Adopted by Gōpāla 1642–1670
                      - 8. *Venkaṭa III* (Dates 1678, 1690)
                        - 9. *Śrīranga* 1692
                          - 10. *Venkaṭa IV* (1706, 1716)
                      - (*a son*)
              - 1. *Tirumala* Seized throne of Vijayanagar about 1570. Died 1578. *Md.* Vengalā and others.
                - *Raghunātha*
                - 2. *Śrīranga I* *Md.* Tirumalā and Krishnā. 1578–1586
                - *Rāma I.*
                  - *Tirumala*
                  - 4. *Śrīranga II* Murdered with all his family, except one son who was rescued, (?) 1614
                    - 5. *Rāma II* (1614–1630)
                - 3. *Venkaṭapati I* Died at Chandragiri. 1586–1614
              - *Venkaṭādri*
                - *Rāma*
                - *Śrīranga*
                  - *Venkaṭa*
                  - *Gōpāla* adopted Śrīranga I son of Chinna Venkaṭa
              - (*Four daughters*)

D. II. THE ĀRAVĪḌU FAMILY—COLLATERAL BRANCH.

This branch had no members that occupied the throne of Vijayanagar, but they were powerful Rājas in Nandyal and the neighbourhood.

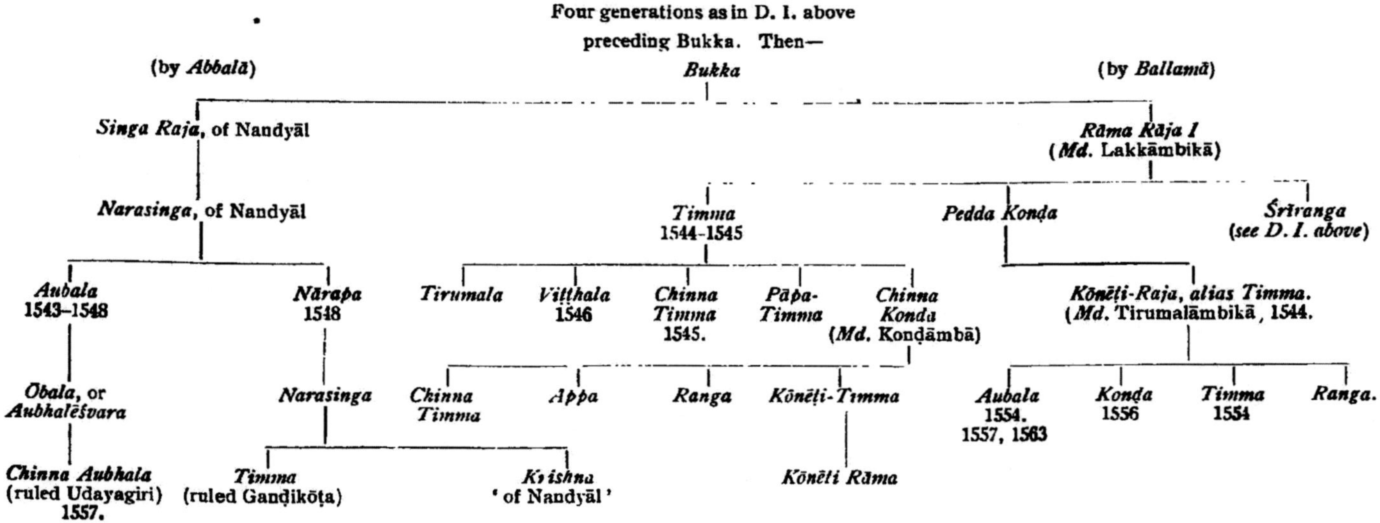

NOTES.—(A) (1) *Harihara I* was crowned on April 18, 1336 (*V. R. ii. Nellore, 189; B. and V. C i. 109*). He was alive on August 18, 1346 (*E. C. x. Mr. 61*). (2) *Bukka I* is believed to have died on or about February 24, 1377 (*E. C. iv. Yd. 46*), when (3) *Harihara II* succeeded. Harihara II died August 16, 1404 (*E. C. viii. Tl. 129*). His minister was Irugapa, son of Baicha who had been minister to his predecessors. Kampana II's death in 1374 has been assumed on the strength of *S I.I.* i, p. 103; but the date given in the record is not satisfactory in detail. (4) *Bukka II's* succession was disputed. He was recognized as king in an inscription of October 19, 1374 (*E. C. vi. Kp. 25*); but one dated November 29 or 30 of that year makes *Virūpāksha I* sovereign (*ibid. viii. Tl. 196*); while another (according to T. A. Gopinātha Rao, whose reference seems erroneous) shews that he had regained the throne before July 27, 1405. (5) *Dēva Rāya I* was crowned on November 5, 1406 (*E. C. v. Hn. 133*). He died before August 3, 1422 (*E. C. iv. Gu. 24*). For *Jommana*, son of *Kampana II* see *E. C. xi*, Ct. 94, whose date is 1375. *Chennappa*, son of *Mallinātha* was Governor of Adoni, which he lost to the Musalmans. Regaining possession of it he presented it to *Harihara II* (*E. C. xii. Kg. 43*). (6) *Bukka III*, '*Vijaya*,' was king on August 17, 1422 (*E C. ix. An. 79 ; vii. Sk. 93*). (7) *Dēva Rāya II's* earliest record is February 25, 1423 (*ibid. viii. Sb. 565*). For a note on events of his reign, his attempted assassination, etc. see T. A. Gopinātha Rao's note (*E. I. xv. 8f. etc. . .*). He died on May 24, 1446 (*I. A. xxv. 346*). For date of *Śaluva Narasimha's* usurpation of the throne see *J. R. A. S*, 1915, p 385. (9) *Virūpāksha III's* son *Praudhadēva* is mentioned in an inscription of 1486-7 (*593 of 1902*).

B. *Immadi Narasimha* was on the throne on January 27, 1493 (*E. C. vi. Mg. 54, 56 ; V. R. i. Cuddapah, 618*).

C. (1) *Narasa Nāyaka's* usurpation and death both occurred between February 28 and August 14, 1505 (*J. R. A. S. 1915, p. 385f*). (2) *Vīra Narasimha* was reigning on August 14, 1505 (*E. C. x. Gd. 77*). He died between May 4 and July 26, 1509, on which latter day (3) *Krishnadēva Rāya* was on the throne (*703 of 1919*). *Krishnadēva Rāya* died between July 28 and December 28, 1529 (*V. R. ii. Nellore 113: B. and V. C. 361 ; E. I. xiv. 311*). His son *Tirumala* died at the age of 6 years about A D. 1525 (*115-117, 122 of 1918*). (4) *Achyuta* lived till at least May 29, 1542 (*E. C. vi. Kd, 158*). (6) *Sadāśiva* was on the throne on June 27, 1542 (*I. A., 1881, p. 63*). It seems therefore that (5) Venkaṭādri's accession and death both occurred between those two dates, which would lead to the supposition that he was killed. The disastrous battle of Talikōta was fought on January 25, 1565 (*Note E. I. i. 361f; E. C. viii. Nr. 64; x. Gd. 77*).

D. I. *Sōmideva* is renowned for having 'taken seven hill-forts in one day' (*E. C. xii. Tm. 1*). *Rāma-Rāja I, son of Bukka of Nandyāl,* captured Adoni, and fought against an enemy who had 70,000 horse in his army (*E I. xvi. 299*).

Śrīranga, the father of Aliya Rāma and his brothers, died on some day in the year following March 28, 1570 (the first anniversary of his death was in Ś. 1493).

(1) *Tirumala* was recognized as king of Vijayanagar and was given full imperial titles in inscriptions of 1569 (April 30) and 1571 (*E. C. xii, Mi. 10 ; viii, Sb. 55*). The earlier one may give him honorific titles, but the latter says he was 'on the throne'. His reign ended between March 8, and November 9, 1578 (*E. C. x. Mr., 41, 57*).

(3) *Venkaṭapati I* was on the throne early in 1586 (*V. R. ii. Kurnool, 585 ; 71 of 1915*). For his death and the tragedy which followed it in the murder of (4) *Śrīranga* II and his family see the full account given by the contemporary writer Barradas in December, 1616, ('*A Forgotten Empire,' p. 222 f*). That (5) *Rāma II* reigned as late as 1630 is shewn by two inscriptions (*E. C. x, 164,*)[1]. (7) Srīranga III was reigning on March 10, 1643 (*E. C. iv. Yd., 5*). He lived till 1670 (*E. C. xii, Pg., 46*).

D II. In the Kurnool and Cuddapah districts are a good number of records of the Āraviḍu family of Nandyāl.

VISHṆUKUNḌIN KINGS

The family became powerful at Denḍalūr and Vengi in the country between the Godavari and Krishna rivers after the fall of the Sālankāyanas and the crushing out of the Āndhra monarchy. The pedigree and dates (which, up to No. 8, Mādhava III are tentative) are taken from Mr. K. V. Lakshman Rao's paper (*Journal of Department of Letters, Univ. of Calcutta, xi, 31*).

1. *Mādhava I*
c. A. D. 357–382
|
2. *Dēvavarma*
c. 382–407
|
3. *Mādhava II*
c 407–444
|
4. *Vikramēndra I*
c. 444–469
|
5. *Indrabhaṭṭāraka*
c. 469–496
|
6. *Vikramēndra II*
c. 496–521
|
7. *Gōvinda*
c 521–546
|
8. *Mādhava III*, 'Janāśraya'
546–(?)610
|
9. *Manchanna-Bhaṭṭāraka*
(?610)–?

NOTES.—(3) *Mādhava II* reigned for at least 37 years (*C. P, No. 12 of 1919–20*) and is given that period in the table, but he may have reigned longer. He married a Vākāṭaka princess. (5) *Indrabhaṭṭāraka* reigned at least 27 years (*E. I xii, 133*) and is given that length of reign, but, similarly he may have reigned longer. He defeated a confederation of rulers headed by a king of Kalinga, and became master of the Vizagapatam district. 8. *Mādhava III's* date is fixed by an inscription of his 48th year which shews his accession to have taken place in the year following February 10, A. D. 546 (*for reference see heading.*) This record, which comes from Polamūru in the Godavari district, states that Mādhava III crossed the Godavari and marched northwards to conquer Kalinga. He was contemporary with the Chaḷukya kings Mangaḷīśa, Kubja-Vishṇuvardhana and Pulakeśin II, and was defeated by them about A. D. 610, losing his kingdom.

---

[1] These two records, both of the same year and in the same village, are interesting incidentally as shewing that people used indiscriminately the expired or current Śaka year. Both belong to the year 'Pramōda' but one names the expired and the other the current Śaka year.

YĀDAVA KINGS OF DĒVAGIRI

The early Yādavas are also called 'Yādavas of Sēuna-dēśa', and date from about the middle of the eighth century A. D., but they do not come in contact with Southern India, so far as our knowledge goes, till the time of Bhillama, son of Mallugi, who obtained the sovereignty of Kalyāṇa, founded the city of Dēvagiri and defied the Hoysala king, the Yādava Baḷḷāḷa II. Bhillama was crowned at Dēvagiri about 1187. Fierce war followed, ending in the defeat of Bhillama's minister Jaitrasimha at Lakkuṇḍi, by which victory the Hoysala dynasty became rulers of the Kuntala-dēśa (*I. A. ii. 300 ; See Bombay Gazetteer I, Pt. II, pp. 231 f ; R. G. Bhandarkar. 'Early History of the Dekkan,' pp. 75 f*).

Mallugi
|
1. *Bhillama*
(1187-1191)
|
2. *Jaitrapāla I*
or Jaitugi. 1191—1210-11
|
3. *Singhaṇa*
1210-11—1246-7
|
Jaitrapāla II
or Jaitugi. Did not reign
|

4. *Krishna*
or Kanhara or Kandhara
1246-7—1259-60
|
Rāmachandra
or Rāmadēva. 1271-1309

5. *Mahādeva*
1259-60—1271
|
Amana

(children of Rāmachandra:)

Śaṁkara
Lost his kingdom to the
Sultan of Delhi
1309-1312

A daughter
Md. Harapāla, who was flayed
alive by Mubārak Khilji in 1318

NOTES.—For the wars of (2) *Jaitrapāla I* see *E. I.* v. 28.

(3) *Singhaṇa's* defeat of Hoysala Baḷḷāḷa II is testified to by an inscription of Singhaṇa's at Gadag in Dhārwār of date A. D. 1213-14 (*I. A. ii. 297*). Singhaṇa was ruling in Shimōga district Mysore in 1218, 1237 and 1241 (*E. C. viii, 250, 256, 387*). One record says that his general Bichana erected a triumphal column on the bank of the Kāvēri river (*J. B. B. R. A. S. xv, 386 ; xii, 43*). The date of this is 1238-9. Bichana was Singhaṇa's viceroy in the south.

(5) *Mahādēva* lost his possessions in Mysore. They were recovered by the Hoysala king Narasimha III. The celebrated author Hēmādri was minister to both Mahādēva and Rāmachandra.

Rāmachandra made an attempt to conquer the Telugu country but was driven back by Kākatīya Pratāpa Rudra. In 1294 he was attacked by the Musalman army commanded by Alāu-d-din Khilji, nephew of the Sultan of Delhi, and Dēvagiri was invested. Alāu-d-din retired on receipt of an immense ransom. Later, when Rāmachandra failed to pay tribute in 1307, Malik Kāfur was sent to compel his obedience, and Rāmachandra was captured and sent as a prisoner to Delhi, but was released after a time. He died in 1309.

Śaṁkara also refused to pay tribute and Malik Kāfur was again sent to reduce him to obedience. Śaṁkara was killed in 1312.

INDEX

E

H

I

K

S

T

U

V